Polybius and his Legacy

Trends in Classics – Supplementary Volumes

Edited by
Franco Montanari and Antonios Rengakos

Associate Editors
Evangelos Karakasis · Fausto Montana · Lara Pagani
Serena Perrone · Evina Sistakou · Christos Tsagalis

Scientific Committee
Alberto Bernabé · Margarethe Billerbeck
Claude Calame · Jonas Grethlein · Philip R. Hardie
Stephen J. Harrison · Richard Hunter · Christina Kraus
Giuseppe Mastromarco · Gregory Nagy
Theodore D. Papanghelis · Giusto Picone
Tim Whitmarsh · Bernhard Zimmermann

Volume 60

Polybius and his Legacy

Edited by
Nikos Miltsios and Melina Tamiolaki

DE GRUYTER

ISBN 978-3-11-068528-2
e-ISBN (PDF) 978-3-11-058484-4
e-ISBN (EPUB) 978-3-11-058479-0
ISSN 1868-4785

Library of Congress Cataloging-in-Publication Data
A CIP catalog record for this book has been applied for at the Library of Congress.

Bibliographic information published by the Deutsche Nationalbibliothek
The Deutsche Nationalbibliothek lists this publication in the Deutsche Nationalbibliografie;
detailed bibliographic data are available on the Internet at http://dnb.dnb.de.

© 2019 Walter de Gruyter GmbH, Berlin/Boston
This volume is text- and page-identical with the hardback published in 2018.
Editorial Office: Alessia Ferreccio and Katerina Zianna
Logo: Christopher Schneider, Laufen
Printing and binding: CPI books GmbH, Leck
♾ Printed on acid-free paper
Printed in Germany

www.degruyter.com

Preface

This volume brings together 21 papers on Polybius, which were first presented at a conference on "Polybius and his Legacy: Tradition, Historical Representation, Reception", held at the Aristotle University of Thessaloniki from 27 to 29 May, 2016, to mark the 10th anniversary of the *Trends in Classics* conference series.

We would like to thank all invited speakers, chairs and participants who made this conference an intellectually stimulating event, as well as the graduate and undergraduate students whose collaboration contributed to its success.

A special debt of gratitude is owed to our co-organizer Professor Antonios Rengakos for helping us run a rewarding and enjoyable conference.

We are deeply grateful to our donors, the Stavros Niarchos Foundation and the Aristotle University Research Committee, for their confidence and generosity without which the conference would never have passed the planning stages. The Museum of Byzantine Culture of Thessaloniki and its director Agathoniki Tsilipakou hosted the event and provided much-needed practical assistance during the three days of the conference. Special thanks are owed to the Foundation for Education and European Culture (IPEP, Athens) for the financial support of our research over the last two years.

Last but (obviously) not least, we would like to express our appreciation to Professors Franco Montanari and Antonios Rengakos, General Editors of *Trends in Classics*, for the publication of the proceedings in the *Trends in Classics Supplementary Volumes* series.

Nikos Miltsios
Melina Tamiolaki

Contents

Introduction —— 1

Part I: **Key Themes and Ideas**

Erich S. Gruen
Polybius and Ethnicity —— 13

Craige Champion
Polybian Barbarology, Flute-Playing in Arcadia, and Fisticuffs at Rome —— 35

Cinzia Bearzot
Polybius and the Tyrants of Syracuse —— 43

Felix K. Maier
Past and Present as *paradoxon theōrēma* **in Polybius** —— 55

Bruce Gibson
Praise in Polybius —— 75

Lisa I. Hau
Being, Seeming and Performing in Polybius —— 103

Part II: **Narrative and Structure**

Roberto Nicolai
τὰ καιριώτατα καὶ πραγματικώτατα. A Survey on the Speeches in Polybius —— 117

Nicolas Wiater
Documents and Narrative: Reading the Roman-Carthaginian Treaties in Polybius' *Histories* —— 131

Kyle Khellaf
Incomplete and Disconnected: Polybius, Digression, and its Historiographical Afterlife —— 167

Christopher Baron
The Historian's Craft: Narrative Strategies and Historical Method in Polybius and Livy —— 203

Part III: Intertextual Relationships

Maria Seretaki and Melina Tamiolaki
Polybius and Xenophon: Hannibal and Cyrus the Great as Model Leaders —— 225

Evangelos Alexiou
Τόπος ἐγκωμιαστικός (Polybius 10.21.8): The Encomium of Philopoemen and its Isocratic Background —— 241

Antonis Tsakmakis
Polybius and Biography ——257

Giovanni Parmeggiani
Polybius and the Legacy of Fourth-Century Historiography——277

Carlo Scardino
Polybius and Fifth-Century Historiography: Continuity and Diversity in the Presentation of Historical Deeds —— 299

Part IV: Reception

Nikos Miltsios
Polybius and Arrian: The Cases of Philip V and Alexander the Great —— 325

Brian McGing
Appian, The Third Punic War and Polybius —— 341

Dennis Pausch
Lost in Reception? Polybius' Paradoxical Impact on Writing History in Republican Rome —— 357

Thomas Biggs
Odysseus, Rome, and the First Punic War in Polybius' *Histories* —— 381

Evangelos Karakasis
Silius Italicus and Polybius: *Quellenforschung* and Silian Poetics —— 341

Luke Pitcher
Polybius and Oscar Wilde: *Pragmatike Historia* in Nineteenth-Century Oxford —— 417

List of Contributors —— 445
General Index —— 451

Introduction

Like Thucydides before him, Polybius anticipated that his work would capture the attention of future generations. "Who", he asks in the preface to his first book (1.1.5), "is so worthless or indolent as not to wish to know by what means and under what system of polity the Romans in less than fifty-three years have succeeded in subjecting nearly the whole inhabited world to their sole government—a thing unique in history? Or who again is there so passionately devoted to other spectacles or studies as to regard anything as of greater moment than the acquisition of this knowledge?" (Transl. W.R. Paton). The reception of the *Histories* has not belied this expectation. Despite its fragmentary state, Polybius' account of Rome's rise to world power has attracted readers through the ages and his treatment of the mixed constitution in the sixth book has earned him wide recognition among theorists of government. Scholarly research into the *Histories* has carried throughout the twentieth century, especially during its second half, when several new monographs and around 200 articles emerged,[1] while in recent years there has been a remarkable renewal of interest in this important work.

Although scholars continue to address old questions about Polybius, such as the purpose behind his numerous methodological and critical remarks, his political ideas, and his controversial attitude toward Roman imperialism, it is clear that they are also turning their attention to aspects of his history that have been inadequately dealt with in the past or have even gone largely unnoticed. Polybius' history is increasingly treated not just as a source of valuable information on the impressive expansion of Roman rule in the Mediterranean world, but also as a complex and nuanced narrative with its own interests and purposes. Taken together, more recent approaches to Polybius constitute a systematic attempt to identify the internal mechanisms of the Polybian text and to unveil the literary workings and the compositional strategies that went into shaping it.

This significant change of direction in Polybian scholarship is reflected in a series of recent studies that have deepened our understanding of the complexity and richness of Polybius' work. Several monographs, such as those of Eckstein, Champion, McGing, Baronowski, Maier, and Miltsios, have helped us realize that Polybius is a more sophisticated and subtle historian than has generally been acknowledged.[2] Moreover, within the last few years important edited volumes

---

1 According to Walbank 2002, 2. For a systematic discussion of scholarship on Polybius before 2000, see *ibid*. 1–27.
2 Eckstein 1995, Champion 2004, McGing 2010, Baronowski 2011, Maier 2012, Miltsios 2013.

have been published which, in either posing new questions or reformulating old ones, also attest to the ardent scholarly interest currently directed toward Polybius, as well as to the variety of hermeneutical issues raised by his work.[3]

This volume brings together contributions representative of the various interpretive approaches to Polybian studies. A number of papers explore Polybius' political ideas or central themes in his history (Gruen, Champion, Bearzot, Maier, Gibson, Hau). Others are preoccupied with specific formal structures of Polybius' narrative (Nicolai, Wiater) or investigate intertextual relationships (Seretaki and Tamiolaki, Alexiou, Tsakmakis, Parmeggiani, Scardino). In addition, as the title of the volume suggests, particular emphasis has been placed on Polybius' reception in subsequent literature. Since (apart from Livy's use of the *Histories*, which has been thoroughly discussed[4]) most studies of Polybius' reception focus on the modern world, especially in relation to the theory of mixed government,[5] finding out more about Polybius' impact on ancient Greek and Roman authors remains a major desideratum.[6] This collection contains papers that examine Polybius' reception in Greek and Roman historiography (Khellaf, Baron, Miltsios, McGing, Pausch), in Roman poetry (Biggs, Karakasis), and in the early modern era (Pitcher).

In greater detail, the four main sections of this volume on Polybius and his Legacy address the following topics.

The first main section concentrates on discussing Polybius' cultural and political ideas as well as significant recurrent themes in his work. Erich Gruen explores Polybius' attitude toward non-Greeks, toward *xenoi*, *barbaroi*, aliens and adversaries, toward the nations and cultures that stood outside the Hellenic world. He raises the question of whether Polybius' estimate of the "other" represents a judgement on ethnicity. The investigation examines numerous passages on Gauls, Carthaginians, Egyptians, and even Romans. It argues that the differences and distinctions on which the historian focuses were social, moral, and

---

[3] Schepens and Bollansée 2005, deriving from a 2001 Leuven conference; Smith and Yarrow 2012, from the 2008 Oxford conference in memory of Peter Derow; Grieb and Koehn 2013, from a 2010 Hamburg conference; Gibson and Harrison 2013, from a 2007 Liverpool conference commemorating the fiftieth anniversary of the publication of the first volume of Walbank's *Historical Commentary on Polybius*.

[4] See e.g. Luce 1977, 196–221, Tränkle 1977.

[5] For a useful overview of Polybius' reception and influence from classical antiquity to the modern world including relevant bibliography, see McGing 2010, 203–22.

[6] Although the contributions in the above-mentioned published collection of Schepens and Bollansée 2005 investigate issues of intertextuality, they deal exclusively with Polybius' generic predecessors.

behavioral, rather than racial or ethnic. Craige Champion examines the military parades of L. Aemilius Paullus, Antiochus IV Epiphanes, and L. Anicius Gallus as public expressions of the cultural politics of Greek and Roman interactions in the second century BCE. He focuses especially on Polybius' narrative strategy and political messages in representing Anicius Gallus' display at Rome in 167 BCE. Cinzia Bearzot then turns her attention to Polybius' references to the history of the West and particularly the Syracusan tyranny. She argues that Polybius looks to the phenomenon of the Syracusan tyranny with a certain interest, evaluating its representatives on the basis of their qualities of government, which he often considers remarkable, and that this behavior of the historian is in part independent from issues of historiographical polemic and quite probably associated with perspectives of Achaean and Roman origin.

The next three papers deal with central themes of Polybius' historical thought. Felix Maier analyzes the phrase *paradoxon theorema*, which is used right at the beginning of the Polybian work to describe history. He explains why this striking antagonism ("something logical, which is paradoxical") appears so prominently in the *Histories*, why, in Polybius' view, it perfectly characterizes history, and what consequences this contradictory term had for Polybius' purpose of writing history, that is: learning from the past. Polybius is noted for his polemic, but rather less attention has been paid to his praise. Bruce Gibson examines the role of praise within Polybius' narrative on the level of content, but also considers how Polybius theorizes praise given by himself and by other historians, especially in terms of its protreptic qualities and broader similarities with Aristotelian epideictic. Gibson then discusses examples of evaluative praise in the *Histories*, before considering the role of Polybius himself as a provider of praise and blame. Lisa Hau examines the use of *dokein*, "to seem" (or "to have a reputation for", "to be known for"), and *doxa*, "opinion"/"reputation", in Polybius in order to investigate the role played by the traditional dichotomy between *ergon* and *logos* ("action" and "speech", or "reality" and "pretence") in his *Histories*. The paper falls into two parts: first, the relationship between reputation and reality in the Polybian text is explored through a close reading of the long digression in Book 31 on the training of Scipio Aemilianus for political life; secondly, the perspective is widened to encompass the use of *dokein* and *doxa* more broadly in the rest of the *Histories*, partly in the light of Davidson's theory of the gaze in Polybius.[7] It is concluded that perceptions of actions or characteristics are often more important than the actions or characteristics themselves in the *Histories* and that decisions are often made on the basis of perceptions rather than reality. This

---

7 Davidson 1991.

means that Polybius is not writing a history where great men themselves make historical events happen, but rather a history where other people's perception of men as great make historical events happen.

The second main section investigates various aspects of Polybius' narrative. Roberto Nicolai examines the function of Polybius' speeches, avoiding the false question of their truthfulness and focusing on the battle exhortations. The speeches are analyzed in the frame of the scene, which can be considered a type-scene—adopting the method applied by Arend to Homer[8]—and as pieces of rhetoric. This kind of analysis can help us understand the hierarchy of the functions of the speeches in connection with the different historical situations and to discover the dynamics of success and failure of the speeches, apparently through Polybius' eyes.

Nicolas Wiater offers the first narratological analysis of Polybius' digression on the Roman-Carthaginian treaties in Book 3 of the *Histories* within their narrative context. From the beginning in chapter 6, he argues, Polybius construes the question of the causes and *kriegsschuld* as an unresolved dilemma, a controversy that had its beginning among historical actors in the past and has since continued in historical and political discourse long after the end of the war. His text thus creates a "blank space", the need for the definitive investigation of and solution to this controversy which should have been resolved decades ago. And when these unresolved issues reach their most critical point in the past, in the confrontation between Romans and Carthaginians in Carthage in 218, Polybius "steps in" with his digression and provides exactly the kind of clear vision of the existing treaties and their implications which the reader needs for a full understanding of the events—one which the historical agents lacked. As regards the form of the digression on the treaties, its peculiar structure of *verbatim* citations alternating with analytical commentary, historical information and Polybius' final conclusion on the *kriegsschuld*, it is suggested, mirrors the political discourse of Graeco-Roman interstate arbitration as it was memorialized on inscriptions. By prompting his recipients to read his discussion in the key of Graeco-Roman interstate arbitration, Polybius supports his claim that his discussion of the treaties is not only about understanding the past but also about shaping politics in the present and future. In the digression on the Roman-Carthaginian treaties, Polybius' two roles as historian and "man of action" (ἀνὴρ πραγματικός), history-writing and politics, coincide.

In the following two papers narrative analysis is combined with insights from reception. Kyle Khellaf explores the central role Polybius played in shaping the

---

[8] Arend 1933.

historiographical tradition of the digression. Although the literary practice can already be traced from Archaic poetry down through the fragmentary historians of the fourth century BCE, it was ultimately Polybius who defined excursus as a fundamental element of historiography and first delineated rules for its usage as part of the proper "interweaving" of events (symplokē). These demarcations were subsequently re-examined by Roman annalistic historians and Graeco-Roman rhetoricians who found reason to either reaffirm or revise them in light of new developments in the historiographical genre. Christopher Baron attempts a comparison between our two major sources for the outbreak of the Second Punic War, Polybius Book 3 and Livy Book 21. Livy's later books clearly show that he had read Polybius, and recent scholarship (especially by David Levene[9]) has demonstrated that Livy used Polybius as a source and intertext in Book 21. If so, the opening chapters of those books provide an excellent opportunity to illuminate and compare the two historians' methods—their choices concerning selection of material, arrangement, commentary, tone, portrayal of character and scenes etc. The analysis first focuses on Polybius' text and one of the most notorious difficulties with his account of the outbreak of the Second Punic War, the role of the Ebro River Treaty. It is argued that the solution to this apparent problem is to consider 3.6-33 as a narrative and argumentative arc, crafted by the historian, in which he introduces the second-century Roman claims about the causes of the war only to undermine them, gradually bringing the reader to see their weaknesses. There follows the comparison of this unit in Polybius with the corresponding section of Livy (21.1–19), in order to reveal some of the effects Livy produces by his selection and arrangement of the material. At the same time, it is also demonstrated that Polybius' account is just as consciously crafted by its author.

The third main section deals with Polybius' intertextual relationship with previous writers both within and without the historiographical tradition. Maria Seretaki and Melina Tamiolaki explore the relationship between Polybius and Xenophon. They propose a comparison between the third book of Polybius' *Histories* and Xenophon's *Cyropaedia* with regards to the presentation of two model leaders, Hannibal and Cyrus respectively. Through a detailed examination of several linguistic parallels and common themes, they advance the hypothesis that a possible source of influence for Polybius' representation of Hannibal could have been Cyrus the Great, the hero of Xenophon's *Cyropaedia*. Evangelos Alexiou compares Polybius' remarks on his encomiastic biography of the Achaean statesman and general Philopoemen, which he wrote in three books, with recurring motifs and conventions in encomiastic texts, such as Isocrates' *De bigis, Busiris*,

---

[9] Levene 2010.

Encomium of Helen and above all his *Evagoras*. The last holds a prominent position in the encomiastic literature, both because it is claimed to be the first prose encomium of a historical person, and because it contains several theoretical remarks on the techniques and role of encomiastic oratory. Alexiou concludes that Polybius' description of the characteristics of his laudatory biography bears strong and evident marks of the influence of Isocrates' encomiastic works, as it adopts not only their rhetorical terminology and strategies but also their educational aims and didactic functions.

Antonis Tsakmakis studies the use of biographical methods of representation in the *Histories*. He first provides a definition of biography as a genre based on cognitive poetics. On the basis of this definition and the cognitive semantics of the Greek term βίος Tsakmakis proposes two criteria for the characterization of a text as biographical: the enactment of the schema of biography and the approach of life as a single phenomenon which can be understood, observed and characterized as a coherent whole. The analysis of key passages from Polybius' work shows an affinity between his theory of world history and his historiographical praxis and biographical writing.

The next two papers issue warnings against taking Polybius' debt to Herodotus and Thucydides for granted. Giovanni Parmeggiani argues that Polybius' views on history and historical methodology were mainly influenced by post-Thucydidean historians (Ephorus and Theopompus especially) through examining some of Polybius' crucial statements on the aims of history writing, on methodology of research, and on aetiology. Those very instances where Polybius seems to recall Thucydides, it is suggested, are due to the mediation of fourth-century historians, confirming that the modern view that Greek historiography suffered a decline after Thucydides must be rejected. Carlo Scardino claims that despite recent attempts to identify points of contact between Herodotus and Thucydides on the one hand and Polybius on the other, no direct influence of Herodotus or Thucydides on Polybius' work can be ascertained (as a model or an intertext). It is rather doubtful that either was used by Polybius as a source. Similarities with Herodotus and Thucydides can be put down to Polybius writing in the same genre. A brief survey of Polybius' third book shows how the historian developed his own style within the genre of historiography. Some of his historiographical techniques find parallels in Herodotus and Thucydides (as well as in later historians such as Ephorus or Timaeus), while others reveal Polybius' innovative contribution. His πραγματικὴ ἱστορία represents, therefore, a new way of writing history compared with the contemporary trend of "rhetorical" (or "tragic") historiography. The need to establish a new paradigm further suggests that Herodotus and Thucydides were no longer considered influential figures in the second century BCE.

The final main section is entirely devoted to Polybius' reception. Nikos Miltsios offers a comparison between Philip V's portrayal in Books 4 and 5 of Polybius' *Histories* and that of Alexander the Great in Books 3 and 4 of Arrian's *Anabasis*, attempting to identify whether the striking similarities in content and form between the two accounts are due to common sources or to Arrian's reception of Polybius. Brian McGing investigates Polybius' influence on Arrian's younger contemporary Appian. By a close examination of the narrative of the preliminaries to the Third Punic War (*Lib.* 67.301–94.447) he suggests that Appian's hostile interpretation of Rome's behavior owes much to Polybius' attitude toward Rome's treatment of Carthage.

Dennis Pausch explores Polybius' impact on Roman historiography. After Polybius' involuntary stay in Rome as an exile in the middle of the second century BCE Roman historians are influenced by his promotion of a more serious, more "scientific" way to reconstruct the past. Yet, precisely at the same time, authors of historiographical works in Rome also commit themselves to a more literary, a more entertaining and reader-friendly way of writing history. The idea at the heart of this contribution, therefore, is that Polybius with his detailed and emphatic description of the dos and don'ts in writing history properly not only had the effect which he intended on his Roman contemporaries, but also had the paradoxical impact of opening their eyes to other recently evolved ways of representing the past. Both directions of Polybius' influence on Roman historical writing are nicely illustrated in Livy's *ab urbe condita*, a work whose relationship with the *Histories* has often been discussed.[10] Pausch, however, takes a step back and looks at the Roman historians from the middle of the second to the middle of the first century BCE. Despite the circumstance that most of the surviving fragments are too short to provide insight into their narrative technique, some observations are possible, most notably regarding the individual historian's choice of a particular subgenre (namely universal history or historical monograph), the relation between reasons and emotions in the explanation of events and the use of speeches as a tool of the didactic function of historical writing.

The next two papers examine Polybius' reception in Roman poetry. Thomas Biggs shows how the relationships crafted in early Latin literature between Homeric worlds and Rome's first naval experiences during the First Punic War could be evoked for a Roman reader by marked features of Book 1's depiction of the conflict. Polybius' narration of traumatic maritime loss (1.37) prompts the

---

10 See above, n. 4.

transition to a mode that processed such experience through Odyssean myth (1.39). The introduction of Odysseus will have recalled a character with a deep local legacy for Roman audiences, particularly one whose narrative defined Latin literature of the First Punic War era (Livius Andronicus' *Odusia* and even Naevius' *Bellum Punicum*). Whether or not Polybius knew of Odysseus' place in Rome's cultural innovations of the late third century, when he depicts Roman history using Odyssean language or imagery, a separate Roman semantics is potentially activated. Ultimately, Polybius' use of Odysseus is shown to activate the Greek historiographical tradition going back to Hecataeus and Herodotus while simultaneously tapping into unique Roman contexts. Evangelos Karakasis investigates the way deviations from Livy, Silius Italicus' main historiographical source, towards Polybian material may illuminate Silian Poetics and contextualize the Silian narrative within a Flavian literary milieu and cultural ideology. By examining the way Silius' assimilation of Polybian information is combined with intertexts from Vergil, Propertius, Seneca, Lucan and Statius, the article aims at shedding light on the importance of *Quellenforschung* used as a means for elucidating Silius' composite and sophisticated tools for producing meaning.

The volume closes with a paper discussing Polybius' reception in the early modern period. In his 1879 essay "Historical Criticism Among the Ancients", a still-neglected early chapter in the study of ancient historiography, Oscar Wilde accords an important role to Polybius. Luke Pitcher argues that Polybius' importance for Wilde lies in Polybius' explicitness about the methodology of history, his usefulness structurally as a Greek writing about Rome, and the analogies which Wilde draws between Polybius and himself. The article also resituates Wilde's essay in its own historical context, showing that its responsiveness to academic work on Roman History in the 1870s has been much underrated, and identifies some previously undetected classical sources for the essay.

As the foregoing overview shows, by addressing a wide range of questions, this volume seeks to stimulate conversation about a variety of topics relevant to Polybius. The large number of papers by scholars with different backgrounds, interests and approaches illustrates the broad spectrum of contexts in which Polybius' *Histories* can be read. It is hoped that the collection will help promote understanding of and further research into this great work of classical literature.

Bibliography

Arend, W. (1933), *Die typische Szenen bei Homer*, Berlin.
Baronowski, D.W. (2011), *Polybius and Roman Imperialism*, London.
Champion, C.B. (2004), *Cultural Politics in Polybius's* Histories, Berkeley.
Davidson, J. (1991), "The Gaze in Polybius' *Histories*", in: *JRS* 81, 10–24.

Eckstein, A.M. (1995), *Moral Vision in the Histories of Polybius*, Berkeley.
Gibson, B./T. Harrison (eds.) (2013), *Polybius and his World. Essays in Memory of F.W. Walbank*, Oxford.
Grieb, V./C. Koehn (eds.) (2014), *Polybios und seine Historien*, Stuttgart.
Levene, D.S. (2010), *Livy on the Hannibalic War*, Oxford/New York.
Luce, T.J. (1977), *Livy. The Composition of his History*, Princeton.
Maier, F. (2012), *"Überall mit dem Unerwarteten rechnen". Die Kontingenz historischer Prozesse bei Polybios*, Munich.
McGing, B.C. (2010), *Polybius' Histories*, Oxford.
Miltsios, N. (2013), *The Shaping of Narrative in Polybius*, Berlin/Boston.
Schepens, G./J. Bollansée (eds.) (2005), *The Shadow of Polybius: Intertextuality as a Research Tool in Greek Historiography*, Leuven.
Smith, C./L.M. Yarrow (eds.) (2012), *Imperialism, Cultural Politics, and Polybius*, Oxford.
Tränkle, H. (1977), *Livius und Polybius*, Basel/Stuttgart.
Walbank, F.W. (2002), *Polybius, Rome, and the Hellenistic World*, Cambridge.

Part I: **Key Themes and Ideas**

Erich S. Gruen
Polybius and Ethnicity

Polybius was not one to disguise his likes and dislikes. He held little back. The historian showed firmness and passion in expressing his assessment of individuals, groups, and nations. His admiration for men like Aratus, Philopoemen, or Scipio Aemilianus is plain, as is his distaste, on various grounds, for such persons as Timaeus, Callicrates, or Prusias II. The gallery of heroes and villains was long. And he had sharp opinions to express about peoples as well. His own Achaeans stood foremost among those with positive evaluations, the Romans largely so, at least in much of his work, whereas the Aetolians, Cretans, and Alexandrians fared far less well. Polybius' opinions were usually clear and unequivocal.

One would expect similar clarity in the historian's evaluation of the "other", of the nations and cultures that stood outside the world of the Greeks and the Romans, whose characteristics, behavior, and customs kept them distinct from the civilizations of which Polybius was a part and with which he felt most comfortable. How did he appraise the *xenoi*, the *barbaroi*, the aliens, indeed the adversaries of those with whom he identified? The subject has never received systematic investigation. It is, of course, easy to cite a range of hostile and censorious remarks. But a more fundamental issue needs to be addressed. Did Polybius' estimate of the "other" represent a judgment on ethnicity? Is there a racial element in the expressed attitudes? Was the inferiority of the "other" inherited and inescapable?

1 "Barbarians"

Let us look first at Polybius' view of "barbarians". He was not particularly fond of them. He shared a common Hellenic sense of superiority over those who did not speak Greek or did not enjoy the benefits of Greek history, culture, and traditions. How profound was this antipathy? Did Polybius reckon barbarians as substandard by nature, a case of racial distinction that subjected them to irremediable disdain?

The term *barbaros* or forms thereof occur with some regularity in Polybius' historical work. As normally construed, of course, it has a negative ring, a pejorative tone. The historian, and indeed Greeks in general, hardly reckoned it as a desirable designation. It need not follow, however, that the phraseology signified a deep prejudice, let alone a sense that a "barbarian" possessed character failings derived from inherent ethnic liabilities.

A closer look at the passages in which Polybius employs the word or its cognates delivers a somewhat different impression.[1] The vast majority of its occurrences, more than 70%, carry with them no condemnatory assertion or implication. The designation appears generally as a label to mean little more than non-Greek. In certain passages that meaning is explicit; everyone is either a Greek or a barbarian.[2] And any language other than Greek would be barbarous by definition. The Roman intellectual A. Postumius composed a history in Greek, apologizing in his preface for any "barbarisms" he might have inadvertently committed—a point that Polybius mercilessly mocked.[3] Other passages pin the label on individual nations or tribes. Polybius' narrative of the Mamertini, Campanian mercenaries who had seized the town of Messana, and their compatriots who occupied Rhegium, paving the way for the First Punic War, designates them on several occasions as *barbaroi*. They were an unsavory lot, to be sure, but the term itself is a neutral one, equivalent in the context simply to "mercenary".[4] Polybius applies the designation frequently to the Gauls, whether those who allied with or who fought against Hannibal, those who threatened Italy from across the Alps, or those who migrated to Anatolia and clashed with Greek communities and principalities.[5] But it serves as a mode of identification, not as a description of character traits.[6] *Barbaros* has this same connotation for a wide range of peoples who appear in Polybius' work: Persians,[7] the inhabitants of Anatolia,[8] Spanish tribes,[9] those bordering on Macedon,[10] Thracians and Galatians around the Pontic Sea,[11] peoples near Mt. Zagrus,[12] tribes in the upper satrapies resisting Antiochus III,[13]

---

[1] See the convenient collection of testimony by Champion 2004, 245–53, with a summary discussion at 241–44. See also Eckstein 1995, 119–25.
[2] Plb. 5.33.5–6, 8.9.6; cf. 8.19.9.
[3] Plb. 39.1.7–8.
[4] Plb. 1.9.3–4, 1.9.7–8, 1.11.7, 3.43.1–2.
[5] Plb. 2.35.6, 3.42.4, 3.43.1–2, 3.43.5, 3.43.9, 3.43.10, 3.43.12, 3.49.2, 3.50.2, 3.50.5, 3.50.9, 3.51.1, 3.51.3, 3.52.3, 3.52.7, 3.53.2–3, 3.53.4, 3.53.6, 3.60.10, 5.111.7, 9.30.3, 9.35.1, 9.35.3, 10.37.5.
[6] Plb. 2.15.8: Ταυρίσκοι καὶ Ἄγωνες καὶ πλείω γένη βαρβάρων ἕτερα.
[7] Plb. 9.34.2–3, 9.39.4–5, 38.2.4.
[8] Plb. 3.6.10–11,
[9] Plb. 3.14.6, 3.14.8, 11.32.5, 35.5.1.
[10] Plb. 4.29.1–2, 7.11.5, 9.35.2–4, 23.8.3–4, 23.10.5; cf. frag. 168, B–W.
[11] Plb. 4.38.7, 4.38.10, 4.45.7–8.
[12] Plb. 5.44.7.
[13] Plb. 5.55.1, 5.55.4.

those in Media and Hyrcania,[14] those near Elymais,[15] Italian tribes,[16] and Carthaginian mercenaries.[17] Reference to barbarians turns up also in the context of larger geographic areas, especially those at great distance, at the outskirts of the known world.[18] In all of these passages which comprise by far the bulk of instances in which the term "barbarian" appears, Polybius passes no moral judgment on ethnic attributes. The people so designated, on the whole, do not live in cities or enjoy a settled existence, are warlike and fierce, and sometimes engage in harsh and cruel behavior. But Polybius does not tie those actions to natural tendencies determined by descent. He can occasionally even show admiration for the boldness and courage of barbarians.[19]

Do Romans also fall into the category of "barbarian"? Polybius' attitude toward Rome was a complex and shifting one, a problematic mixture of admiration and disappointment. This is not the place for a discussion of that tangled topic.[20] But were they barbarians? Romans do receive the label "barbarian" on a few and select occasions. But the circumstances of those occasions deserve notice. They do not come in Polybius' own voice. He puts a notorious speech into the mouth of the Aetolian leader Agelaos at Naupactus in 217 BCE, urging Philip V of Macedon and the Greeks to put an end to their squabbles, lest all of Hellas fall victim to the "cloud from the west". Agelaos urged his countrymen to shed their differences and unite together to drive back the invasion of "the barbarians," thereby saving themselves and their cities.[21] The Aetolian made reference to the war between Rome and Carthage, warning that whoever emerged victorious from that contest would turn attention to the east and extend their power over it.[22] Fear of falling under the authority of either of the *barbaroi* motivated the intervention of Agelaos. He specifies no anticipated barbarities, just concern about subordination to a non-Greek power.[23]

---

14 Plb. 10.27.3–4, 10.29.3–4, 10.30.2–3, 10.30.7, 10.30.9, 10.31.2–3, 10.31.11–13, 10.48.8.
15 Plb. 31.9.2.
16 Plb. 2.39.7, 10.1.2–3, 33.8.3, 34.10.13–14
17 Plb. 15.1.4–5.
18 Plb. 3.37.11, 3.58.8, 23.13.2.
19 Plb. 3.43.8, 33.10.6.
20 See the extensive treatment by Champion 2004, especially 47–57, 105–22, 193–203, with bibliography. Cf. also Erskine 2000, 165–82, Thornton 2010, 45–76.
21 Plb. 5.104.1: δύναιντο τὰς τῶν βαρβάρων ἐφόδους ἀποτριβόμενοι συσσῴζειν σφᾶς αὐτοὺς καὶ τὰς πόλεις.
22 Plb. 5.104.3. The cloud metaphor at 5.104.10.
23 Cf. Plb. 10.25.1–5.

The point becomes sharper in a subsequent speech delivered by an Acarnanian spokesman a few years later in the narrative of Polybius. The speaker denounces Aetolia for its alliance with Rome, a partnership with barbarians instead of men of their own race, partners who seek only to enslave them.[24] Then a third speech, evidently by a Rhodian and set in 207, reiterates the charge, brands the Romans once more as barbarians, warns about the enslavement of Hellas, and here explicitly contrasts Greek behavior with that of Roman conquerors who would subject their victims to wanton outrage and violence.[25]

The condemnation is harsh. But is it Polybius' own? We can avoid here the controversial and much discussed question of whether the speeches are authentic or fabricated, or possess a genuine core much embellished and manipulated.[26] On any reckoning what we possess are Polybius' compositions. How faithful they were to the originals remains a matter of guesswork. Like any ancient historian worth his salt, Polybius would put the most persuasive rhetoric and the most appropriate arguments for the speakers' purposes into their mouths. Representing Romans as foreigners who seek to subjugate Hellas and terrorize its people would suit the circumstances. One can make no legitimate inferences from these texts with regard to Polybius' own attitude.

More telling is the fact that Polybius nowhere calls Romans "barbarians" in his own voice. He does say that Hiero of Syracuse allied himself to the Carthaginians in order to drive the "barbarians" who occupied Messana out of Sicily. But this evidently refers to the Mamertini, rather than to the Romans. Even if both are meant, Polybius ascribes this mode of thinking to Hiero and takes no responsibility for it.[27] There is a comparable ambiguity in his reference to the practice of sacrificing a horse prior to battle, which he ascribes to Romans and "nearly all barbarians".[28] It is by no means obvious that Romans are included in the latter company. The only other depiction of Romans as barbarians comes in a report by messengers to Philip V—once again not in the historian's own voice.[29] It can hardly be a coincidence that Romans receive that direct designation nowhere in Polybius' long history. Whether out of prudence or sincerity, the historian avoided applying it to the Romans.

---

24 Plb. 9.37.4–10, esp. 5–6, 9.38.5.
25 Plb. 11.5.2, 11.5.6–7.
26 See e.g. Pédech 1964, 259–76, 295–302, Lehmann 1967, 135–49, Morkholm 1967, 240–53, *id.* 1974, 127–32, Deininger 1971, 23–37, *id.* 1974, 103–08, Walbank 1985, 254–59, Champion 1997, 111–28, *id.* 2000, 433–37, Baronowski 2011, 149–51.
27 Plb. 1.11.7.
28 Plb. 12.4b.2.
29 Plb. 18.22.8.

The more fundamental issue remains. Did Polybius ascribe to the "barbarian" qualities or characteristics that adhered to his very being and defined his identity? A number of passages, at least on the surface, might appear to justify that conclusion. Polybius certainly had no brief to make for the *barbaroi*, and he shared the Hellenic penchant for disdaining the non-Greek. How deeply did this run? Did it constitute a bias against the "other"? Certain key passages deserve a close look. As always, context plays a vital role.

The most general statement comes in connection with the aftermath of the First Punic War. The brutal contest between Carthaginians and their own disaffected mercenary troops prompted a sweeping judgment by Polybius: the circumstances taught us what and how far the difference is between those with confused and barbarous practices and those raised with education, laws, and civilized customs.[30] The reach and scope of that claim, however, may not be quite as broad as it seems. It was provoked by the unusually ferocious "truceless war", and it had special association with mercenary soldiers who did indeed have "confused and barbarous practices", in view of their shifting lives and absence of settled loyalties. That need not extend to all *barbaroi*.

Relatively few comments by Polybius suggest character flaws that might typecast barbarians in general. He castigates the Epirotes for hiring Gallic mercenaries to protect their chief city only to have them betray it to their enemies. Polybius sneers that no people should entrust their fortunes to a garrison stronger than themselves, especially if it consists of barbarians.[31] That is an indirect swipe at Gallic untrustworthiness, which Polybius notes with some frequency. But it is the only instance in which he ostensibly extends the slur more broadly—and even here, the *barbaroi* may refer simply to the Gauls. A more troubling statement appears in Polybius' narrative of a Spanish leader wavering between support for Rome or Carthage and deciding ultimately to betray the Carthaginians by turning over hostages to the Romans, for their prospects seemed to him the brighter ones. Polybius describes the decision as based on a "Spanish and barbaric reasoning".[32] The meaning here is not that "barbaric reasoning" leads to treachery but that the prominent Iberian made his calculation on pragmatic rather than moral grounds. Making decisions on pragmatic grounds would hardly be confined to *barbaroi* alone, and could not be a defining feature.

---

30 Plb. 1.65.7: τί διαφέρει καὶ κατὰ πόσον ἤθη σύμμικτα καὶ βάρβαρα τῶν ἐν παιδείαις καὶ νόμοις καὶ πολιτικοῖς ἔθεσιν ἐκτεθραμμένων.
31 Plb. 2.7.12: ἄλλως τε καὶ βαρβάρων.
32 Plb. 3.98.3–4: συλλογισμὸν Ἰβηρικὸν καὶ βαρβαρικόν.

Ruthlessness in war also characterizes "barbarians". In the context of clashes between Thracians and Byzantium, Polybius asks "what could be more dreadful than war with neighbors who are also barbarians?". Does this signify a special brand of barbarian warfare? Not very likely. Polybius proceeds to elaborate on this by pointing to the devastation of crops by barbarians.[33] Such behavior was certainly not limited to non-Greeks. When Polybius describes a battle between Roman cavalry and that of Iberians and Celts as "truly barbarian", he refers to dismounting and hand-to-hand fighting.[34] The reference is to tactics, not to character. Polybius notes the savagery of barbarians, but speaks here specifically of the tribes on Hannibal's contemplated route from Spain to Italy, rather than to a universal barbarous trait.[35]

Only very rarely does Polybius insert a comment that might have broader application to "barbarian" character or deportment. Three of them can be identified. But they do not get us very far. First, the ruler of Bactria, in Polybius' narrative, seeks to deflect Antiochus III from an invasion of his land by warning that this would only bring hordes of nomads into the region who would wholly "barbarize" it (ἐκβαρβαρωθήσεσθαι).[36] Just what that means is quite unclear. It is worth noting, however, that the word does not reappear in Polybius' text. It can hardly serve as a touchstone for the historian's understanding of the concept. Second, in recording the arrival of envoys from Spanish tribes in Rome for an audience with the *praetor urbanus*, Polybius notes that, although they were *barbaroi*, they delivered lengthy speeches and delineated the cause of their countrymen in great detail.[37] This ought not to be taken as a snide comment about barbarian inadequacy. The envoys took on a tough task and discharged it, while having to do so in a language that was not their own. If anything, that is a positive assessment. One last passage could be construed as portraying negative traits that attach to barbarians in general. Polybius, in his bitter denunciation of the Achaean leaders who had led his land into a calamitous war with Rome, asserts that one would not easily find such stupidity and lack of judgment among *barbaroi*.[38] In this appraisal, barbarians appear to be a benchmark for the height of folly. The portrayal, however, is far from a recurrent theme in Polybius, and one can hardly cite

---

[33] Plb. 4.45.5–8.
[34] Plb. 3.115.2–3.
[35] Plb. 9.24.4–5.
[36] Plb. 11.34.5–6.
[37] Plb. 35.2.6: οἱ δὲ καίπερ ὄντες βάρβαροι.
[38] Plb. 38.18.7–8: τοιαύτης δὲ τῆς ἀνοίας καὶ τῆς ἀκρισίας συμβαινούσης περὶ πάντας οἵαν οὐδ' ἂν ἐν βαρβάροις εὕροι τις ῥᾳδίως.

it as exemplary. Only those Achaeans for whom he had the fiercest contempt managed to prompt him to such indignation.[39]

In short, the frequent use of the term *barbaros* in Polybius ought not to be misconstrued. The large majority of cases are inoffensive, without condemnatory implications, merely neutral designations of non-Greeks. And the Romans, with whom Polybius lived and was closely aligned, escaped even that designation. Polybian statements that suggest the ascription of inherent characteristics when applying the term are remarkably few. And even they have limited pertinence and lack sweeping significance. In designating people as barbarians, the historian was not driven by ethnic considerations.

2 Gauls

Apart from the wide connotation that "barbarian" carried, Polybius had much to say about individual foreign peoples who were enemies of Greeks or Romans or both. The comments, as might be expected, are normally negative. But did they possess a racial dimension that set such people forever outside the realm of Greco-Roman society?

The Gauls or Celts can serve as a valuable case in point. They play a role of some significance in Polybius' text. As fearsome foes of both Greece and Rome at critical points, they certainly drew the historian's attention. Gauls notoriously had swooped down upon Delphi in 279 BCE, intent upon destroying the sacred shrine, repelled only by a coalition of Greek states headed by the Aetolians—and, as tradition had it, by emergence of the god Apollo himself who supplied thunder, lightning bolts, a snow storm and a rock slide to scatter the invaders.[40] The event had terrified the Greek world. An equally traumatic experience had afflicted early Roman history and reverberated in subsequent centuries. The Celts had descended from the Po Valley upon Rome itself in 390 BCE, routed a Roman army, and sacked the city, a catastrophe burned in searing fashion into Roman memory.[41] That was just the start. After being turned back at Delphi, Gallic tribes

---

[39] Another figure for whom Polybius had great contempt is Prusias II of Bithynia. He describes the king's excessively luxurious habits as "the barbarian life-style of Sardanapallos" (36.15.5–6). Little can be made of that pejorative outburst. The "barbarians" of whom Polybius regularly speaks in his history could hardly afford extravagant life-styles.
[40] See esp. Pausanias, 1.4.4, 22.12–23.14, Justin, 24.6.6–8.15.
[41] Fullest testimony in Livy, 5.33–44.

migrated to Anatolia where they swiftly gained the reputation of menacing fighters and enemies of Hellenic civilization. That image was sedulously fostered by the Attalids of Pergamum who portrayed themselves as champions of Hellenism through monuments and inscriptions, an image enhanced by representing the Celts as brutal barbarians bent on destruction.[42] Further, the Romans engaged in repeated battles with Gallic peoples in northern Italy from the mid-fourth through the second century BCE.[43] That was well within the lifetime of Polybius.

When the Achaean historian took up his pen hostilities were still fresh in mind and some were yet to come. It is hardly surprising that Polybius had unflattering things to say about the Gauls.[44] He had reason to delineate their animosity and their failings, either to embolden his Roman readers or to reassure them. Celts had a general reputation for greed and untrustworthiness, a reputation the historian played upon and exploited.[45] In his presentation, Celts did not hesitate to appropriate the property of neighbors or allies.[46] Avariciousness became a hallmark.[47] They were susceptible to drunken excesses.[48] Polybius more than once charges them with ἀθεσία: they were fickle and unreliable.[49] They were also prone to unreasoning passion, governed in their actions more by fervor than by calm calculation.[50] He makes reference to their arrogance, their violence, and their lawlessness.[51] On the battlefield, they could produce a spirited opening thrust, but lacked the ability to sustain it.[52] Polybius hammers at the unattractive qualities of Celtic behavior. No wonder that scholars have interpreted Polybius' assessment of the Gauls as a representation of the quintessential "other".[53]

It is well to remember, however, that almost all of the comments come in the context of warfare. And the Gauls regularly enter the picture as enemies of Rome and fierce foes on the battlefield. Concentration on the negative should hardly cause surprise. Yet Polybius does not indulge exclusively in disparagement. He

---

42 See Schalles 1985, Gruen 2000, 17–31, with references. Polybius, 18.41.7, takes note of Attalus I's exploitation of his victory over Gauls to burnish his image.
43 See the valuable survey by Dyson 1985, 17–86.
44 Berger 1992, 105–26, id. 1995, 517–25.
45 On the Gallic reputation generally, see Williams 2001, 18–69.
46 Plb. 2.7.5–6, 2.19.3–4.
47 Plb. 2.17.3–4, 2.22.2–3, 3.78.5.
48 Plb. 2.19.4.
49 Plb. 2.32.8, 3.49.2, 3.70.4, 3.78.2.
50 Plb. 2.21.2, 2.35.3.
51 Plb. 3.3.5, 18.37.9, 21.41.2–3.
52 Plb. 2.33.2–3, 2.35.6; cf. 3.43.12.
53 See especially the extensive study by Foulon 2000, 319-54, id. 2001, 35–64. Cf. also Berger 1992, 105–26.

sketches those qualities that made Gauls worthy adversaries for Rome. They had impressive size and attractive appearance.[54] Some at least had a reputation for courage.[55] In battle they exhibited boldness, even desperate boldness—which could strike terror into their adversaries.[56] Those Gauls who had migrated to Anatolia gained repute as the toughest and most warlike people in Asia.[57] Polybius praised the good order of their military formation.[58] More revealing still is the historian's account of the renewal of hostilities between Gauls and Romans in 232 BCE after a long hiatus. He ascribes the origin of the conflict squarely to Roman aggression. Expansion and expropriation of land by Romans in Picenum had resulted in expulsion of the Senones, and the Boii feared (with some justice) that they were next. The latter now seized the opportunity to initiate warfare on perfectly reasonable grounds: they were convinced that Roman action presaged no mere conflict for supremacy but the implementation of genocide.[59] Gallic enmity toward Rome is thus far from irrational.[60] Polybius plainly does not represent Gauls merely as raving savages. They fought for their homelands against the greater power determined to eradicate them.

The picture is a more complex and nuanced one than is often understood. Gauls possessed admirable as well as disreputable qualities, a point that Polybius does not suppress or disguise. But his portrayal goes beyond a balancing act between depictions of worthy and unworthy traits. Polybius avoids reducing the Celts to the stereotyped and cardboard image of a people whose character and behavior derive from genetic deficiency. The various tribes who dwelled in and around the Po Valley, according to the historian, led simple lives, dwelling in villages, with minimal possessions, lacking knowledge of intellectual matters or the crafts, and absorbed with agriculture and warfare.[61] That description, while hardly flattering, contains no pejorative overtones.[62] The Gauls had limited means and limited needs. The circumstances of geography and history determined the way of life, not inborn character. In speaking of the Gallic penchant for excessive drinking followed by seizure of neighbors' property and a falling out among themselves over spoils, Polybius ascribes it to customary behavior rather

---

54 Plb. 2.15.7.
55 Plb. 2.15.7, 3.34.2, 5.111.2.
56 Plb. 2.18.1–2, 2.35.2.
57 Plb. 18.41.7.
58 Plb. 2.29.5.
59 Plb. 2.21.7–9.
60 Cf. Plb. 3.34.2, 3.78.5.
61 Plb. 2.17.9–12.
62 See Gruen 2011, 142–43. *Contra* Williams 2001, 79–88.

than to ethnic deficiency.⁶³ Nor does his reference to Gallic passion, θυμός, constitute an ethnic brand. Romans too could yield to it.⁶⁴

Does Polybius anywhere suggest that Gallic characteristics have an innate or genetic basis? Take their supposed greediness. Far from an inherent trait, it appears in Polybius as a rumor: φήμη.⁶⁵ The historian does make reference to Γαλατικὴ ἀθεσία ("Gallic fickleness"), which, on the face of it, could be interpreted as a national characteristic.⁶⁶ But the context suggests something quite different. Polybius refers here to the untrustworthiness of Gallic allies enlisted by Romans against other Gauls, an understandable concern about their allegiance—not allusion to an innate tendency.⁶⁷ Elsewhere and similarly, when Polybius calls attention to the ἀθεσία of the Celts and the unlikelihood of their keeping faith, he has a particular context in mind: Gallic mercenaries in the service of Carthage whose loyalty could not be relied upon if they were forced to endure an extended period of inactivity and idleness.⁶⁸ Paradoxically, Polybius also has Hannibal suspect the reliability of Gauls in his army on the opposite grounds of their softness and resistance to labor—without noticing any inconsistency.⁶⁹ Are the Gauls impatient for action or resistant to it? Either way the passages have reference to Gallic mercenaries in the hire of others. The special circumstances of mercenary service, where loyalty is always a troublesome issue, do not translate into reflections of national character.⁷⁰

The Achaean historian refrains from portraying the Celts as a people of unchanging disposition or of a nature fixed by genetic inheritance. An interesting passage warrants notice in this connection. Polybius reports that after the wars of the early third century, the Gauls kept the peace for forty-five years. A whole generation and more whose memories had been seared by the distress and afflictions of war preferred to keep it at arm's length. Matters changed only when a new generation had grown up, one inexperienced in the sufferings and dangers of battle. The young men, hot-headed and spirited, began to dismantle the accords and stirred up conflict once again with the Romans before falling out among themselves and engaging in internal strife that led eventually to Roman

---

63 Plb. 2.19.3–4: τοῦτο δὲ σύνηθες.
64 Plb. 2.19.10. For Gallic θυμός, see Plb. 2.21.2, 2.35.2–3.
65 Plb. 2.7.5–6.
66 Plb. 2.32.8. So Berger 1995, 521–22.
67 Plb. 2.32.1–10.
68 Plb. 3.70.4, cf. 3.78.2.
69 Plb. 3.79.4–7.
70 For Polybius on mercenaries, see Eckstein 1995, 125–29, Gibson 2013, 165–72.

aggrandizement.⁷¹ Polybius' narrative here negates the idea of an inflexible Gallic militancy bent on perpetual conflict, whether for material gain or out of heedless passion.⁷² A change in the generations accounts for the dramatic new situation that shattered a lengthy peace. The Gauls were not trapped in a locked ethnicity.

3 Carthaginians

Polybius' history had good reason to engage with the Phoenicians, or rather with their direct descendants the Carthaginians. His narrative of Roman imperial expansion covered three major clashes with Carthage, the most formidable of Rome's antagonists, the so-called Punic Wars. One might anticipate a less than favorable verdict on that Phoenician power who almost halted Rome's overseas expansion when it was still in its infancy. Yet Polybius paints no simple or one-sided picture. Phoenicians had long had a somewhat mixed reputation among Greek writers. They were admired as merchantmen, shippers, and wide-ranging colonists. But those achievements could lend themselves to the more questionable impressions of greed, chicanery, and the deviousness of overseas traders.⁷³ Polybius was not immune from some of the negative stereotypes. He claims that Carthaginians saw no shame in grubbing after profit.⁷⁴ And he records assertions regarding numerous acts of injustice committed by Carthaginians.⁷⁵

Polybius, however, hardly engages in Punic character assassination. It is noteworthy, for example, that he provides no echo of the hostile slogan that later surfaced among Roman writers, the supposed *Punica fides* (Carthaginian perfidy). On the contrary. In narrating the mutual charges of treaty violations that Romans and Carthaginians slung at one another in the preliminaries to the Second Punic War, the historian is rather more than even-handed. He puts into Hannibal's mouth the bold assertion that Carthaginians would not overlook the treaty

---

71 Plb. 2.21.1–9.
72 Polybius' phrase at 2.21.3, ὃ φύσιν ἔχει γίνεσθαι, indicates the natural change that comes with a generational shift, and says nothing about Gallic nature.
73 Cf. Diod. 5.35.4, Ps. Arist. *De Mir. Ausc.* 135; see Mazza 1988, 548–67, Capomacchia 1991, 267–69; other references in Gruen 2011, 116–22.
74 Plb. 6.56.1; cf. 9.11.2, 9.25.4.
75 Plb. 10.37.8–10.

infractions committed by Romans because it was his nation's practice not to neglect those who were victims of injustice.⁷⁶ And Polybius in his own voice pronounces unequivocally upon the real perpetrators of the war. The most important cause of the conflict, he maintains, was the Roman seizure of Sardinia and the tribute that was unjustly imposed. Carthage, in short, had good reason to go to war.⁷⁷ Perfidy was on the other side. Polybius' account presupposes that Carthaginians, far from earning the epithet of inveterate treaty-breakers, untrustworthy and even treacherous by nature, made a point of justifying their position precisely in terms of adherence to agreements, a matter of national pride. In Hannibal's mouth this was, of course, a rhetorical piece, something that a spokesman for the cause might have been expected to say. But in addition to his own concurring view, the fact that Polybius assigns the position to Hannibal, Rome's fiercest foe, carries real significance. For Polybius, Carthaginians evidently did not labor under the ethnic stereotype of faithlessness.

Does Polybius anywhere ascribe to the Phoenicians/Carthaginians traits that derive from national character? Two passages might point in that direction. The historian, in describing Hannibal's method of protecting himself against possible assassins among his Gallic allies, notes that he possessed a number of wigs of different colors which he put on or took off at different intervals to disguise his identity. And Polybius designates this deception as a "Phoenician stratagem" (Φοινικικῷ στρατηγήματι).⁷⁸ Does this indicate a natural Phoenician inclination to deceitfulness?⁷⁹ Not necessarily. Polybius refrains from negative judgment on this maneuver; it was merely a clever scheme to frustrate would-be murderers. Since the artifice worked, one might even see it as an affirmative assessment. At worst, it alludes to Phoenician reputation for craftiness, a notion that attached to sailing traders, merchants, and overseas settlers, not an attribute adhering solely to that nation.⁸⁰ The second passage constitutes the one clear reference to innate qualities belonging to Phoenicians and drawing the historian's censure. In commenting on the Phoenicians' tendency to fight among themselves, he refers to

---

76 Plb. 3.15.5–7: οὓς οὐ περιόψεσθαι παρεσπονδημένους. πάτριον γὰρ εἶναι Καρχηδονίοις τὸ μηδένα τῶν ἀδικουμένων περιορᾶν.
77 Plb. 3.10.3–5, 3.15.10, 3.30.4. Cf. Gruen 2011, 123–25.
78 Plb. 3.78.1. Cf. Plato's reference to the "noble lie" as "something Phoenician"; *Rep.* 3.414B–C. Posidonius claims that stories about an oracle and expeditions from Tyre to the Pillars of Herakles are a "Phoenician lie"; Strabo, 3.5.5. That need not signify a proverbial expression about Phoenician falsehood, and may be no more than an indication of the source for this disinformation.
79 It is taken as such by Walbank 1957, 412, and Franko 1994, 158.
80 Cf. Homer, *Od.* 13.271, 15.415.

their inherent greed and love of rule.[81] But greed and ruling ambitions are hardly characteristics exclusive to Phoenicians. Polybius evidently conveyed some long-standing Hellenic impressions of dubious Phoenician qualities.

He did not, however, allow them to dominate his assessment of Carthaginians generally.[82] The Achaean historian, in fact, expands on Aristotle in his admiring evaluation of the Carthaginian constitution. As is well known, Polybius devotes Book 6 of his history to a discussion of Rome's constitutional structure which he adjudges as superior to all others. But he reckons the Carthaginian system as providing a worthy comparison. Its institutions too provide a blend of monarchic, aristocratic, and democratic elements, a well conceived and admirable organization.[83] In Polybius' eyes, to be sure, Rome has the edge, for Carthage has passed its peak and Rome was just reaching its pinnacle.[84] Carthage nonetheless represented the principal criterion by which to measure Roman success.

When appropriate Polybius could pay generous tribute to Carthaginian qualities. After Carthage's defeat at Drepana which effectively concluded the First Punic War, he offers a notably laudatory appraisal of the nation's character. Despite unanticipated defeat, he says, the Carthaginians in their determination and love of honor were even now ready to fight on, yielding only to the force of rational calculation.[85] Polybius refrains from branding the nation with clichés about intrinsic deficiencies.

---

[81] Plb. 9.11.1–2: πρὸς αὐτοὺς ἐστασίαζον, ἀεὶ παρατριβόμενοι διὰ τὴν ἔμφυτον Φοίνιξι πλεονεξίαν καὶ φιλαρχίαν. Other references to greed, though not necessarily as an inborn character, in Plb. 6.56.1, 9.25.4.
[82] Polybius does describe the war fought by Carthaginians against their mercenary soldiers in North Africa, after defeat at Roman hands in the First Punic War, as one that exceeded all prior conflicts in cruelty and violation of law; 1.88.5–6. But the Carthaginians are not singled out as villains. The ferocity owed at least as much to the actions and policies of the mercenaries; Plb. 1.80–81, 1.86.
[83] Plb. 6.43.1, 6.47.9, 6.51.1–2. For Aristotle on Carthage, see Aristotle, *Pol.* 1272b, 1273a–b.
[84] Plb. 6.51–52, 6.56.1–5.
[85] Plb. 1.62.1: ταῖς μὲν ὁρμαῖς καὶ ταῖς φιλοτιμίαις ἀκμὴν ἕτοιμοι πολεμεῖν ἦσαν, τοῖς δὲ λογισμοῖς ἐξηπόρουν. Polybius proceeds to praise to the skies the sagacity and prudence of the Carthaginian general Hamilcar who had used every possible means to keep his nation's chances alive, but yielded gracefully when rational hope was lost and concluded a peace treaty; 1.62.3–7.

4 Egyptians

By contrast, the Egyptians seem to have no saving graces—at least on the face of it. Polybius was deeply affected by the murderous scenes in Alexandria that followed the death of Ptolemy IV in 204, leading to the assumption of power by ministers of the crown and mob riots against those who had seized control. The historian supplies vivid scenes of stabbings, mutilation, torture, the plucking out of eyes, and even vicious biting by relentless crowds. And he employs this as exhibit of the dire cruelty produced by the anger of those who dwell in Egypt.[86] Polybius made a personal visit to Alexandria some time after 145 BCE, and left with a decidedly unfavorable impression. He discerned three different groups in the city: native Egyptians, mercenaries, and the *genos* of the Alexandrians. With regard to the indigenous population in particular, on the usual interpretation, he labeled them as volatile and resistant to civil control.[87] Other incidental comments also deliver negative judgments. In praising the Ptolemaic general in Cyprus, Polybius notes that he was in no way like an Egyptian but rather sensible and competent.[88] And in his generally laudatory obituary of Ptolemy VI Philometor, Polybius includes the comment that when things went well, Ptolemy's spirit slackened a little and there was a certain Egyptian sluggishness and dissoluteness about him.[89]

Are we then to infer that for Polybius Egyptians were by nature cruel, angry, and vicious, volatile and not subject to control, but also sluggish and dissolute? Those characteristics do not easily cohere with one another. And one might raise the question of whether they represent off-hand comments inspired by certain events, circumstances, or individuals rather than profound judgments about Egyptian character.

A somewhat different picture appears elsewhere in Polybius' text. A famous passage speaks of the aftermath of the battle of Raphia in 217, a major victory for the Ptolemaic forces against Antiochus III. Ptolemy had recruited and armed a substantial number of Egyptians prior to this battle. As a consequence, the tri-

---

[86] Plb. 15.33.10: δεινὴ γάρ τις ἡ περὶ τοὺς θυμοὺς ὠμότης γίνεται τῶν κατὰ τὴν Αἴγυπτον ἀνθρώπων.
[87] Plb. 34.14.2: τό τε Αἰγύπτιον καὶ ἐπιχώριον φῦλον, ὀξὺ καὶ [οὐ] πολιτικόν.
[88] Plb. 27.13.1: οὐδαμῶς Αἰγυπτιακὸς γέγονεν, ἀλλὰ νουνεχὴς καὶ πρακτικός.
[89] Plb. 29.7.7: καί τις οἷον ἀσωτία καὶ ῥαθυμία περὶ αὐτὸν Αἰγυπτιακὴ συνέβαινεν. The exiled Spartan king Cleomenes, after a time in Alexandria, expressed dismay at the circumstances in Egypt; Plb. 5.35.10. But his complaints focused on the king and the status of the kingdom, not on the Egyptians.

umph emboldened the native Egyptians, who took great pride in the accomplishment, were no longer eager to fall in line behind the ruler, sought a new leader, and felt ready to rely on themselves—a feat that they accomplished not long thereafter.[90] That would certainly not accord with a portrait of dissoluteness or indolence.

Polybius' depiction of the three groups of people whom he identified in Alexandria requires further scrutiny. He distinguished native Egyptians, mercenaries, and Alexandrians. On the current interpretation, he has hardly a kind word for any of the three, and he felt disgust at the condition of the city. He found the mercenaries oppressive and uneducated, and the Alexandrians not thoroughly attuned to civic society but better than the mercenaries because, though a mixed society, they were Greek by origin and retained customs common to all Greeks.[91] Indigenous Egyptians, however, he describes as ὀξὺ καὶ πολιτικόν. The words have caused bafflement. They would appear to have positive resonance: "keen and civic-minded". Yet scholars find it hard to believe that Polybius would have put Egyptians in a favorable light, especially as the other groups are treated with some disdain. Hence πολιτικόν has been emended to ἀπολιτικόν or to οὐ πολιτικόν and the epithets translated as "volatile and resistant to civil control".[92] But a positive evaluation of Egyptians is not unthinkable. The keenness of the Egyptians reappears in Polybius' account of the determined opposition to the regime in 204. And that opposition could also count as civic-mindedness, since Polybius certainly regarded the regime as illegitimate and loathsome. In view of the uncertainty, the passage cannot be used to establish Egyptian ethnic deficiency in Polybius' eyes.

The viciousness and barbarity displayed in Alexandria in 204 constitute a more serious charge, especially if they are ascribed to an Egyptian nature. But are they? Polybius attributes the anger and cruelty to "the men who dwell in Egypt".[93] The events themselves took place in Alexandria, with its notoriously mixed population, consisting of Greeks, Jews, and a host of mercenaries from a range of nations, in addition to Egyptians. Who were the perpetrators of the savagery? Polybius' account is unspecific. Leadership against the group that held power after the death of Ptolemy IV was taken by Macedonian soldiers in Alexandria, not by

---

90 Plb. 5.107.1–3.
91 Plb. 34.14.1–8.
92 Plb. 34.14.2. See Fraser 1972, 145, n. 184, Walbank 1979, 629, *id.* 2002, 60. Erskine 2013, 347, is more circumspect.
93 Plb. 15.33.10: τῶν κατὰ τὴν Αἴγυπτον ἀνθρώπων.

Egyptians.[94] They were then joined by soldiers from garrisons in Upper Egypt, plainly Greeks and Macedonians.[95] Widespread hostility against those in power expressed itself by "the people", "the populace", "the many".[96] They consisted of men of all nationalities, soldiers and civilians.[97] There is no good reason to confine this outburst to native Egyptians—and none at all to presume that Polybius laid that charge solely or primarily to them.[98] His criticisms of Egyptians stood apart from the strictures of racial shortcomings.

5 Ethnos

Did Polybius think in racial or ethnic terms at all when classifying people? Were they identified as descent groups defined in terms of bloodlines? The historian's terminology might offer a clue, and needs to be explored. He frequently employs the words *ethnos* or *genos* with regard to human groups or collectives. That might initially suggest racial implications. The contexts and usages of those terms, however, require closer scrutiny.

Polybius uses the word *ethnos* or *ethne* on numerous occasions, over one hundred times. Did it have racial implications? Very far from it. The most substantial proportion of instances, about 40%, is political, rather than ethnic, in character. *Ethnos* is the most common designation for "league", a collective polity, or what has most commonly been called a "federal state"—by contrast with *polis*.[99] Polybius regularly employs the term, indeed the vast majority of such instances, to designate his own native state, the *ethnos* of the Achaeans: τὸ τῶν Ἀχαιῶν ἔθνος.[100] In fact, he can shorten the phrase simply to *ethnos*, where the context makes it obvious that the Achaeans are meant.[101] But the word applies also to other collective polities, such as the Aetolian League or the Boeotian

---

94 Plb. 15.26.1–8.
95 Plb. 15.26.10–11.
96 Plb. 15.27.1, 15.27.3, 15.28.8, 15.29.3, 15.30.4, 15.30.9, 15.32.4, 15.32.11, 15.33.5.
97 Plb. 15.29.4: πάντα τὰ γένη συμπεφωνήκει καὶ τὰ στρατιωτικὰ καὶ τὰ πολιτικά. Cf. 15.30.4.
98 The assertion by Fraser, 1972, 82, that "it cannot be doubted that he means the native Egyptians" is unjustified. For similar skepticism, see Erskine 2013, 351.
99 On the hazards of using the phrase "federal state", see now Mackil 2013, 4–8.
100 Plb. 2.6.1, 2.12.4, 2.37.7, 2.40.5–6, 2.43.7, 2.43.10, 4.1.4, 4.17.7, 9.34.6, 9.38.9, 16.35.1, 22.3.5, 22.7.1, 23.9.1, 23.18.2, 24.1.6, 24.6.1, 24.10.10, 24.13.4, 30.13.8.
101 Plb. 2.45.1, 2.45.4, 2.45.6, 2.51.2, 4.60.6, 22.7.9, 23.16.6, 23.16.12, 23.17.9, 28.13.13, 30.32.3, 38.9.6, 38.9.8.

League.¹⁰² The meaning is unambiguous in each case. It refers to a collective entity, operating as a union of communities, engaged usually in political, diplomatic, or military activities. In his fullest description of the *ethnos* of the Achaeans, Polybius puts it in terms of a political union, a constitutional structure, a sharing of laws, weights, measures, and coinage, and joint eligibility for magistracies, council positions, and judicial offices, all political institutions.¹⁰³ None of this bears any relation to ethnicity.

Ethnos comes into play with some frequency as carrying a generic signification, without precision, designating nothing more than a "people" or a "nation," and lacking further specification as to what bound them together. Polybius can employ *ethnos*, for example, for the Numidians, the Arcadians, the Laconians, the Achaeans, the Masylioi, the Aetolians, the Acarnanians, the Boeotians, indeed even the Gauls and the Jews.¹⁰⁴ The historian further utilizes the word *ethnos* to denote peoples normally understood as "tribes", within larger national units. That would hold for peoples like the Ardiaeans and the Dassaretae of Illyria, the Gallic Insubres, Boii, Senones, and others, the Spanish Olcades, Carpedani, Balearics, Vaccaei, and others, the tribes of Media, those settled along the Euxine, the tribes of Macedonia and of Thrace, those of Libya, and a variety of Italian peoples like the Brutii, Lucanians, and Samnites.¹⁰⁵ The dwellers beyond the Pillars of Herakles are lumped together simply as "barbarian *ethne*."¹⁰⁶ Quite apart from nations, peoples, and tribes, the term could be stretched to designate those identified by their city.¹⁰⁷ Polybius employs the loose usage more broadly still in reference to "western nations" as a whole, plainly separating *ethnos* altogether from any sense of ethnic bonds.¹⁰⁸ Indeed the word could attach with even looser connotation to "the most illustrious and noble *ethne* of the world".¹⁰⁹ It can connote territory rather than group identity.¹¹⁰ And Polybius often employs it in unspecific and almost formulaic fashion as a category parallel to cities, kings,

---

102 Plb. 2.12.5, 9.29.4, 9.38.9, 20.3.1, 20.5.2, 21.4.5, 21.33.1, 27.2.10.
103 Plb. 2.37.7–10; cf. 2.38.5–9.
104 Plb. 1.31.2, 2.38.3, 2.41.3, 2.49.6, 2.58.5, 4.32.3, 4.76.1, 5.1.1, 7.14c, 8.12.7, 15.23.8, 16.32.3, 16.39.1, 18.13.8, 18.41.7, 21.29.12, 22.4.14, 22.9.4, 38.10.8, 38.10.12.
105 Plb. 2.12.2, 2.17.4, 2.17.8, 2.22.1, 3.13.5, 3.14.2, 3.33.10-11, 3.35.2, 5.44.4, 5.44.8, 7.11.5, 8.14b.1, 10.1.2, 12.3.4, 13.10.9, 16.40.4, 33.10.12, 34.9.13, 34.11.7.
106 Plb. 3.37.11.
107 The Nucerians: Plb. 3.91.4.
108 Plb. 1.2.6: τῶν προσεσπερίων ἐθνῶν; 18.28.2.
109 Plb. 2.37.5.
110 Plb. 3.56.3, 23.13.2.

places (*topoi*) or some combination thereof, without indication of what determines its composition.[111] Elsewhere, however, he can utilize it even as equivalent to *polis*.[112] The diverse usages set the term apart from any particular or consistent meaning—let alone an ethnic one.

The instances in which *ethnos* appears in a context that might suggest national characteristics associated with a people are extremely rare. Four of them deserve a look. First, the *ethnos* of the Arcadians, Polybius reports, has a reputation among Greeks for virtue. He ascribes this to Arcadians as a whole. But he goes on to elaborate on this quality as exemplified by Arcadian customs and manner of life, particularly their reverence for the gods, that generate their hospitality and love of humankind.[113] Polybius plainly points to Arcadian practices and life style, not inborn traits.

Second, the historian represents Philip V as expressing his favor and good will to the *ethnos* of the Achaeans.[114] But he articulates no particular grounds on which he based this professed affection, whether racial or otherwise. Polybius reiterates the comment a few lines later according Philip an increased enthusiasm for the *ethnos* of the Achaeans, without giving a reason.[115] The whole context, however, is one of gaining advantage through alliance in wartime. Nothing suggests any love for Achaean character.

Third, an ethnic connotation does indeed surface in Philip's comments during negotiations with the Roman commander Flamininus, seeking to discredit the claims of the Aetolians. In the king's view, most Aetolians are not even Greek. Nor is the *ethnos* of the Agraae, Apodotae, and Amphilochians.[116] But not much can be made of that. What exactly are the criteria to distinguish "most" Aetolians from the rest in terms of their Greekness? The king is making a strained rhetorical point, without offering any substance. And the sentiment is set in the mouth of Philip, not Polybius' own.

One final instance requires brief comment. Polybius, in his representation of various Greek opinions on the Roman decision to destroy Carthage, has one

---

111 This usage can be found in Polybius' report of the treaty between Hannibal and Philip V of Macedon; 7.9.5–9, 7.9.16: χωρὶς βασιλέων καὶ πόλεων καὶ ἐθνῶν, and frequently elsewhere; 5.90.5, 9.1.4, 12.25e.5, 12.28.a.4, 18.1.4, 18.47.5, 21.17.12, 21.25.7, 21.43.24–25.
112 The Greek Locrians, he says, do not have one *polis* but two *ethne*; Plb. 12.10.3. He is not distinguishing here between types of states.
113 Plb. 4.20.1 οὐ μόνον διὰ τὴν ἐν τοῖς ἤθεσι καὶ βίοις φιλοξενίαν καὶ φιλανθρωπίαν, μάλιστα δὲ διὰ τὴν εἰς τὸ θεῖον εὐσέβειαν.
114 Plb. 4.72.6.
115 Plb. 4.73.2.
116 Plb. 18.5.8–9: αὐτῶν γὰρ Αἰτωλῶν οὐκ εἰσιν Ἕλληνες οἱ πλείους.

group claim that the Roman *ethnos* generally took pride in conducting warfare simply and honorably, refraining from night attacks and ambushes, but, in the decision on Carthage, they resorted to deceit and fraud.[117] Again there is little to be extracted from this. Polybius does not speak in his own voice, and the assessment is only one of four divergent ones. It hardly suggests that the historian himself endorses the view of an innate Roman character that has here been abandoned. In short, the harvest of passages in which an ethnic overtone is even hinted at is meager indeed. And none of them so much as intimates that Polybius embraced the notion.

6 Genos

If one investigates Polybian usage of the term *genos*, the results are much the same. Ethnicity is not at issue. Of the more than one hundred appearances of the word in Polybius' corpus, nearly half have the bland meaning of "type", "kind", "form", or "sort". So, for example, Polybius uses it right at the outset of his work when asking "what sort of constitution" the Romans employed in conquering the known world, a phrase he then repeated on three other occasions.[118] It serves elsewhere also to signify a "kind of stratagem", "every kind of wine", "every type of wood, earth, and stone", "every form of decrees and proclamations", "a type of reader", "other kinds of animals", "a form of camp", "another mode of walking", "every type of ambush, counter-ambush, and attack", "this sort of fraud", "this form of justification", even "this kind of murderers, robbers, and burglars".[119] Numerous other examples of a similar sort can be found in Polybius' text.[120] The principal work of *genos* is to signal a category.

The versatility of the word, however, lends itself to other meanings as well. Like *ethnos*, though far less frequently, it could carry the general notion of "people" or "nation" without indication of how they might define their collective identity.[121] This usage occurs predominantly in the context of mercenary soldiers hired

---

117 Plb. 36.9.9–10.
118 Plb. 1.1.5: τίνι γένει πολιτείας; 6.2.3, 8.2.3, 39.8.7; cf. 6.3.5, 6.4.6, 6.57.2–3.
119 Plb. 4.38.5, 4.41.9, 5.71.9, 5.106.8, 6.5.8, 6.27.1, 6.40.10, 7.15.1, 9.1.2, 9.1.5, 18.40.2, 30.4.15, 39.8.7.
120 Plb. 1.58.4, 2.16.14, 3.18.9, 3.71.4, 5.53.9, 5.98.1, 5.98.11, 8.4.3, 10.15.1, 10.43.1, 11.1a.2–3, 11.1a.5, 12.4.10, 12.4d.1, 12.12.7, 12.25.5, 12.25a.3, 12.25b.4, 12.25c.2, 18.15.13, 18.17.4, 18.31.2, 20.9.8, 29.8.3, 29.8.5, 31.10.7, 31.18.5.
121 As in the case of the Bithynians; Plb. 36.15.3.

by Carthaginians or by Ptolemies, consisting of multiple *gene* and mustered or paid *kata gene*.[122] The imprecision of the term can be illustrated by the fact that Polybius once employed it in the same context with *ethnos*, a confusing combination in which the distinction between them, if there be any, is altogether obscure: "the most warlike *gene* of the western *ethne* of Europe".[123] On the face of it here, *genos* looks like a subdivision of *ethnos*. But there is nothing whatever in the rest of Polybius' history to suggest such a conclusion. This junction, unique in Polybius, indicates overlapping and fuzziness rather than distinctiveness or exactitude.

In addition to designating a nation or people, *genos*, in a handful of instances, refers to smaller units, essentially tribal units. Polybius uses it to refer to tribes in north Africa, in Gaul, and in Media.[124]

The phrase τὸ γένος, combined with reference to a geographical location, occurs on several occasions, and simply signifies "by birth". That is clear in its usage, as in "Aetolian by birth", "a Seleucian by birth", "a Cretan by birth", "a Megalopolitan by birth", "a Tarentine by birth", or "an Acarnanian by birth".[125] On one occasion only does this usage go beyond a geographical denotation: Polybius makes a solitary reference to a "Celt by birth".[126] One can hardly extrapolate from a single instance.

In a few cases Polybius uses *to genos* to indicate family genealogy. The majority of examples refer to royal lineage.[127] Others apply to aristocratic Roman houses.[128] In one case the historian speaks generally of inheritance within the family (*genos*).[129] In such passages the term certainly designates a bloodline.[130] But that context is irrelevant for the collective identity of a people.

The pliability of *genos* is everywhere evident. It could designate a military unit, a political group or class, or a segment of a city's population.[131] It turns up

---

122 Plb. 1.67.2, 1.67.4, 1.69.1, 1.69.3, 1.69.7, 1.70.2, 1.80.8, 5.64.1, 15.29.4.
123 Plb. 1.2.6: τῆς Εὐρώπης τὰ μαχιμώτατα γένη τῶν προσεσπερίων ἐθνῶν. Paton, in the Loeb edition, does not translate both γένη and ἐθνῶν: "the most warlike nations of western Europe".
124 Plb. 1.77.4, 2.15.8, 2.17.5, 2.223.2, 4.46.4, 5.4.7.
125 Plb. 5.40.1, 5.58.3, 5.61.4, 5.68.4, 8.15.1, 10.22.2, 13.4.4, 15.31.7.
126 Plb. 2.36.1: τινος Κελτοῦ τὸ γένος.
127 Plb. 1.8.3, 2.41.5, 4.1.5, 4.33.6, 4.35.11, 4.35.13, 4.81.1, 6.7.6.
128 Plb. 6.53.2, 31.28.2, 39.1.2.
129 Plb. 20.6.5.
130 Cf. also Plb. 7.10.2, with regard to an eminent Messenian: οὐδενὸς ἦν δεύτερος Μεσσηνίων πλούτῳ καὶ γένει.
131 Military unit: Plb. 6.24.1, 6.34.8; political group: 23.12.6; segment of a city: 34.14.2, 34.14.4.

once with the meaning of "genre", and, surprisingly, twice as designating gender.[132] Polybius can even use it for the whole of humankind: τὸ τῶν ἀνθρώπων γένος.[133]

Does race ever surface as an undertone in the usage of *genos*? There may be a sidelong glance in that direction by Polybius when he mentions "a certain Celt τὸ γένος", or a *genos* of men in Coele-Syria who adapted their political allegiances to circumstances, or the Locrian settlers in Italy whose sympathies were guided more by their *genos* than by choice.[134] But these rare, brief, and undeveloped allusions do not affect the larger picture. The diversity of usages for *genos*, as for *ethnos*, stands out most markedly. That predominant feature foils any attempt to reduce the term to a uniform signification.

In sum, the largest bulk by far of the occurrences of *genos* can be rendered as "type" or "category". It appears periodically with reference to a nation or a tribe, with the meaning of "by birth" or "family", and in an array of other denotations that add up to no pattern and should not have one imposed upon it. Virtually nowhere in the Polybian corpus does the term carry any racial baggage or suggest that the historian thought along the lines of genealogy as defining ethnic identity.

7 Conclusion

Polybius may have had little love for the foreigner. He was certainly no starry-eyed universalist or an advocate for the erasing of distinctions and the blending of humankind. The "barbarian" was set apart. The foes of Greece and Rome stood outside the sphere that Polybius found congenial and sympathetic. The enemy might be wicked and the barbarian uncouth. But the differences lay in society, morality, and mores. The historian drew no racial or ethnic lines.

Bibliography

Baronowski, D.W. (2011), *Polybius and Roman Imperialism*, London.
Berger, P. (1992), "Le portrait des Celtes dans les histoires de Polybe", in: *AncSoc* 23, 105–126.
—— (1995), "La xénophobie de Polybe," in: *REA* 97, 517–525.
Capomacchia, A.M.G. (1991), "L'Avidità dei Fenici", in: *Atti del II Congr. Int. di Studi Fenici e Punici*, Rome, 2167–269.

---

132 Genre: Plb. 15.36.3: τῷ τῆς ἱστορίας γένει. Gender: 10.18.6, 31.26.10: τοῦ τῶν γυναικῶν.
133 Plb. 6.5.5, 6.6.4, 18.15.15–16.
134 Celt: Plb. 2.36.1 (see above); Coele-Syria: 5.86.7–9; Locrians: 12.6b.4.

Champion, C.B. (1997), "The Nature of Authoritative Evidence in Polybius and the Speech of Agelaus at Naupactus", in: *TAPhA* 127, 111–128.
—— (2000), "Romans as Barbaroi. Three Polybian Speeches and the Politics of Cultural Indeterminacy", in: *CPh* 95, 425–444.
—— (2004), *Cultural Politics in Polybius's Histories*, Berkeley.
Deininger, J. (1971), *Der politische Widerstand gegen Rom in Griechenland, 217–86 v. Chr.*, Berlin.
—— (1973), "Bemerkungen zur Historizität der Rede des Agelaus, 217 v. Chr. (Polyb. 5.104)", in: *Chiron* 3, 103–108.
Dyson, S.L. (1985), *The Creation of the Roman Frontier*, Princeton.
Eckstein, A.M. (1995), *Moral Vision in the Histories of Polybius*, Berkeley.
Erskine, A. (2000), "Polybios and Barbarian Rome", in: *MedAnt* 3, 165–182.
—— (2013), "The View from the Old World: Contemporary Perspectives on Hellenistic Culture", in: E. Stavrianopoulou (ed.), *Shifting Social Imaginaries in the Hellenistic Period*, Leiden, 339–363.
Foulon, E. (2000), "Polybe et les Celtes, I", in: *LEC* 68, 319–354.
—— (2001), "Polybe et Les Celtes, II", in: *LEC* 69, 35–64.
Franko, G. (1994), "The Use of *Poenus* and *Carthaginiensis* in Early Latin Literature," in: *CPh* 89, 153–158.
Fraser, P.M. (1972), *Ptolemaic Alexandria*, Vol. 2, Oxford.
Gibson, B. (2013), "Polybius and Xenophon: The Mercenary War", in: B. Gibson /T. Harrison (eds.), *Polybius and his World: Essays in Memory of F. W. Walbank*, Oxford, 159–179.
Gruen, E.S. (2000), "Culture as Policy: The Attalids of Pergamon", in: N.T. de Grummond/ B.S. Ridgway (eds.), *From Pergamon to Sperlonga: Sculpture and Context*, Berkeley, 17–31.
—— (2011), *Rethinking the Other in Antiquity*, Princeton.
Lehmann, G.A. (1967), *Untersuchungen zur historischen Glaubwürdigkeit des Polybios*, Münster.
Mackil, E. (2013), *Creating a Common Polity: Religion, Economy, and Politics in the Making of the Greek Koinon*, Berkeley.
Mazza, F. (1988), "The Phoenicians as Seen by the Ancient World", in: S. Moscati (ed.), *The Phoenicians*, New York, 548–567.
Morkholm, O. (1967), "The Speech of Agelaus at Naupactus, 217 B.C.", in: *ClMed* 28, 240–253.
—— (1974), "The Speech of Agelaus Again", in: *Chiron* 4, 127–132.
Pédech, P. (1964), *La méthode historique de Polybe*, Paris.
Schalles, H.-J. (1985), *Untersuchungen zur Kulturpolitik der pergamenischen Herrscher im dritten Jahrhundert vor Christus*, Tübingen.
Thornton, J. (2010), "Barbari, Romani, e Greci. Versatilità di un motivo polemico nelle *Storie* di Polibio", in: E. Migliaro/L. Troiani/G. Zecchini (eds.), *Società indigene e cultura Greco-romano*, Rome, 45–76.
Walbank, F.W. (1957), *A Historical Commentary on Polybius*, Vol. I, Oxford.
—— (1979), *A Historical Commentary on Polybius*, Vol. III, Oxford.
—— (1985), "Speeches in Greek Historians", in: F.W. Walbank (ed.), *Selected Papers: Studies in Greek and Roman History and Historiography*, Cambridge, 242–261.
—— (2002), "Egypt in Polybius", in: F.W. Walbank (ed.), *Polybius, Rome, and the Hellenistic World*, Cambridge, 53–69.
Williams, J.H.C. (2001), *Beyond the Rubicon: Romans and Gauls in Republican Italy*, Oxford.

Craige Champion
Polybian Barbarology, Flute-Playing in Arcadia, and Fisticuffs at Rome

Twelve years ago, the University of California Press published a book titled, *Cultural Politics in Polybius's Histories*. In that book I tried to show how Polybius employs Greek/barbarian polarities as a politico-cultural strategy, and in particular I wanted to explore how the historian represents Romans in these terms. I strove to keep Polybius' reading public—the educated political elites both in Greece and at Rome—at the forefront of my exposition. I made a case for a narrative strategy that oscillates between a "cultural politics of assimilation" of Romans to the Hellenic cultural commune, for the most part aimed at the Roman senatorial aristocracy as reading public, and a "cultural politics of alienation" that distances the Romans from Hellenism, even suggesting that the Romans occupy a position closer to the negative pole of a Greek/barbarian continuum, maintaining that we may best understand this aspect of Polybius' narration by remembering his Greek readership, many of whom would have appreciated and condoned an independent, and at times seemingly defiant, authorial stance vis-à-vis Rome. Together the "cultural politics of assimilation" and the "cultural politics of alienation" constitute a "cultural politics of indeterminacy," which can allow the Romans to inhabit a liminal zone, and to be both honorary Greeks, as it were, and barbarians. This narrative tension makes great sense when we attend to the historical juncture and political circumstances in which Polybius composed his history. And it is important that we remember always to place Polybius and his history in their immediate political and cultural contexts, as a large part of the cultural wars of this period concerned the appropriate Roman response to Greek culture.

At the time I was somewhat concerned, I can now confess in retrospect, that my designations "cultural politics of assimilation," "cultural politics of alienation," and "cultural politics of indeterminacy" bordered on jargon, but in the end they still seemed to me to capture what I was driving at neatly and concisely, and so I kept them. Fortunately, my fears were unfounded, the book was well-received, and as I look back on it now I am happy to say that there is very little I would change were I writing the book today. That being said, however, in this paper I take up a passage in the history that supports my reading of Polybius' cultural politics, but one that I neglected to discuss in the book.[1] This episode is

---

[1] Plb. 30.22.1–12, from Ath. 14.615; cf. Liv. 45.43.1.

the strange case of the triumphal celebrations at Rome of the praetorian commander L. Anicius Gallus in February of 166 BCE. But in studying this incident Polybius' general cultural representations can take us only so far; we must also pay attention to more immediate political factors for a fuller understanding.

My focus here, then, will be on L. Anicius Gallus' celebrations in Rome in 166. In order to place these events within the context of Polybius' cultural politics, I begin by considering Greek intellectuals' causal explanations for observable differences among collective peoples and examining Polybius' own ideas on these matters. I shall then discuss a famous passage in the history on the ameliorative effects of musical education in Arcadia (4.21). Against this background I shall offer a reading of Anicius Gallus' musical competition as an astounding example of Polybius' cultural politics. Finally, I shall situate this incident within the context of other public spectacles earlier in the year.

1 Ancient Greek Causal Explanations for Collective Group Characteristics

Ancient Greek thinkers devised three basic explanations for collective group characteristics, whether we are to think of these groups in political, cultural, or ethnic terms. The first is quite simple and not very satisfying as a causal explanation; collective physical and behavioral idiosyncrasies are the result of *phusis*, or "nature". This is not really a causal explanation at all, and it amounts to saying that it is simply the way things are. We find some examples of this in Polybius, as when he writes that Italian soldiers are superior to those of the Carthaginians "by nature"; or that Bolis, as a Cretan, was wily "by nature" (in both cases using the instrumental dative *phusei*).[2]

An elaboration of the *phusis* account posited causal geographical and climatic factors, with two notable illustrations in Book 7 of Aristotle's *Politics* and in the Hippocratic treatise *Airs, Waters, Places*. The famous passage in Aristotle is worth quoting in full, as it shows how rationalizing accounts for collective group characteristics almost always had some political dimensions, even to the point of conceptually undergirding imperial projects.

> The *ethnē* (nations) living in cold places and those in Europe are full of spirit (θυμοῦ), but lacking in some measure in intelligence (διανοίας) and skill (τέχνης), so that they live in a

---

[2] Plb. 6.52, 8.16, with Champion 2004, 77–78, for further examples.

free manner, but they do not have any political organization or the ability to rule over others. Those living in Asia are on the other hand intelligent and accomplished in practical matters (τεχνικὰ τὴν ψυχήν), but they lack spirit (ἄθυμα), so that they are always in subjection and even slavery. But the people of Hellas participate in both characters, just as they occupy the middle position geographically, for the Greeks are both spirited and intelligent; and consequently they continue to be free, they have excellent political institutions, and if they retain their unity, they are capable of ruling the world.[3]

In this line of reasoning, then, geographical and climatic conditions have profound influences on both physical and behavioral collective group characteristics. It is possible that Polybius had a great deal to say about the subject in a separate work on geography.[4]

The final causal explanation for collective group characteristics stresses institutional organizations. We might think that the inception of this notion stretches back at least to the Homeric poems, as the brutish Cyclops in Book 9 of the *Odyssey* is a being who knows nothing about formal institutional foundations of society for the maintenance of law and order; and much later for Aristotle the *politeia* (as constitution) was the life-blood of the *polis*.[5] It is clear at any rate that for Polybius the institutional foundations of society are far and away the most important determinant in the formation of a people's collective character. The historian, of course, interrupts his historical narrative with Book 6 in order to give a detailed account of the Roman constitution; and he explicitly states in that book that laws and customs set the tone for men's private lives and for the collective ethical character of the *polis*.[6]

A famous passage in the *Histories* nicely illustrates just how powerful the formal institutional structures of the *polis* are for Polybius in molding collective characteristics, and it also serves as a segue to our consideration of his treatment of the triumphal celebrations of L. Anicius Gallus. In Book 4 Polybius describes how the Arcadians combatted the brutalizing effects of their cold and forbidding climate. These harshest of atmospheric conditions would have rendered the Arcadians more beasts than men, had it not been for the central role of musical education in Arcadian *poleis*. The Cynaethaeans neglected to institutionalize musical education and regular festivals and sacrifices with musical accompaniment, and as a result they became utter savages. Polybius concludes his digression in

---

[3] Arist. *Pol.* 7.1327b23–33; cf. [Hp.] *Aër.* 16, cf. 24.
[4] Plb. 34.1.7–13, with discussion and references at Champion 2004, 80 and n. 39.
[5] Hom. *Od.* 9.112, Arist. *Pol.* 1295a40–b1, esp. 1295a25.
[6] Plb. 6.47.1–5.

the educative function of flute-playing in Arcadia by explicitly stating that only *paideia* can save human beings from their primordial, beastly nature.[7]

2 The Triumphal Celebrations of L. Anicius Gallus (February 166 BCE)

In February of 166 BCE, L. Anicius Gallus celebrated his victory over the Illyrian king Genthius with a triumph at Rome.[8] Genthius was paraded through the streets of Rome as a prisoner of war on the day of the Quirinalia festival.[9] A musical spectacle formed part of the festivities in the Circus Maximus.[10] Polybius was an eyewitness, and we learn something of his reaction from Athenaeus. Polybius' account of the event, recorded in his Book 30, apparently went something like this.

> Lucius Anicius [Gallus], who had been a Roman praetor, defeated the Illyrians and brought home their king Genthius with his children as captives. While holding the games to celebrate his victory, he did something quite laughable (παντὸς γέλωτος ἄξια πράγματα). He had sent for the most famous performers from Greece, and constructed a huge stage in the circus, onto which he first brought all the flute players together: Theodorus the Boeotian, Theopompus, Hermippus, and Lysimachus, who were very well known. He placed these men on the stage and ordered them all to play together with the chorus, but when they began to perform the music with the appropriate movements, he said they were not playing well, and told them to be more competitive (ἀγωνίζεσθαι μᾶλλον ἐκέλευσεν). They were uncertain of what to do, but one of the lictors suggested that they turn and advance against each other as in battle. The flautists quickly understood, and with a gait suited to their own license, they created great confusion, turning the central choristers toward those on the ends, and blowing their flutes in meaningless discord as they led the two sides against each other. At the same time, the choristers came upon the stage together and charged their opponents before turning to retreat. And when one of them girt up his clothes and turned on the spur of the moment, raising his hands like a boxer against the flautist who was approaching him, there was great clapping and cheering from the spectators. While they continued to fight the battle, two dancers were brought into the orchestra to the sound of music, and four boxers mounted upon the stage with buglers and trumpeters. The effect of all these

---

7 Plb. 4.21.1–3 and 11–12.
8 For Gallus' campaign against Genthius, see Liv. 44.30–32, 45.26, App. *Illyr.* 9.
9 For the triumph, see Liv. 45.43, Vell. Pat. 1.9.5, App. *Illyr.* 9, and for the date, *Inscrip. It.* 13. *Fasti et elogia* I, ed. A. Degrassi, Rome 1947, 80–81.
10 Plb. 30.22 (*agōnes epinikioi*); cf. D.H. *Rom. Ant.* 2.34.3.

men contending together was indescribable. And if I tried to describe the tragic actors, I would seem to be jesting.[11]

How are we to make sense of this bizarre episode? Scholars have offered various interpretations. Perhaps the incident was spontaneous, with no real planning behind the way it unfolded. Maybe it was the large, raucous crowd and its enthusiastic cheering and goading that influenced the course of events. Was L. Anicius Gallus simply a cultural boor, appealing to his own base instincts and the violent impulses of rowdy onlookers? Alternatively, we may think that Anicius carefully arranged the whole affair as a disparagement of Greek cultural pretensions and an assertion of Roman superiority. Much like the famous interchange between C. Popillius Laenas and the Seleucid monarch Antiochos IV Epiphanes at Eleusis, Anicius' political theater would have dramatically underscored the fact that the Greeks and their culture were now to be subservient to Roman wishes.[12]

In the end, the impetus for the events seemingly spiraling out of control must be left open, but we can be fairly certain that Anicius' stage performances, and the general tenor of his triumphal celebrations, were responses to the earlier public spectacles of L. Aemilius Paullus, which preceded them. Livy's narrative suggests Paullus' extravaganza was without precedent in terms of its magnificence and splendor, writing that:

> Paullus celebrated with great pomp at Amphipolis a festival which had long been in preparation, he had sent announcements for it to the kings and cities of Asia, himself giving notice to the leading men of the Greek cities. For a crowd of all sorts of professionals in the entertaining arts came from all over, as well as athletes and famous horses; and delegations with sacrifices, and whatever else is usually done at the great festive games of Greece for gods and men. All of this was carried out so as to arouse admiration not only for the lavishness but also for the skill at putting on shows, at which the Romans then were still quite unskilled.

According to Livy, then, Paullus had celebrated his crushing victory over King Perseus of Macedon at Pydna with sumptuous, Hellenistic-style festivities at Amphipolis in the spring of 167, replete with a troupe of "Artists of Dionysos" (*technitai Dionysiakoi*) and famous athletes and performers from all over Greece.[13] After the celebrations, Paullus broke camp and left Amphipolis, making his way to Epirus and reaching Passaron on the fifteenth day. Livy adds that he was not far

---

11 Plb. 30.22.1–12.
12 For various interpretations of the event, see Crowther 1983, 270, Ferrary 1988, 565–66, Gruen 1992, 215–218, Goldberg 1995, 38–39.
13 Liv. 45.32.1–11; cf. Plut. *Aem.* 28.

from the camp of the praetorian commander Anicius, and he sent him dispatches, so that there would be no disturbances during his predatory activities in Epirus.[14]

Livy juxtaposes Paullus' and Anicius' spectacles, indicating that the comparison was in people's minds at the time.

> Haerente adhuc non in animis modo, sed paene in oculis memoria Macedonici triumphi L. Anicius Quirinalibus triumphavit de rege Gentio Illyriisque. Similia omnia magis visa hominibus quam paria; minor ipse imperator, et nobilitate Anicius cum Aemilio et iure imperii praetor cum consule conlatus; non Gentius Perseo, non Illyrii Macedonibus, non spolia spoliis, non pecunia pecuniae, non dona donis comparari poterant. Itaque sicut praefulgebat huic triumphus recens, ita apparebat ipsum per se intuentibus nequaquam esse contemnendum.

> While recollections of the Macedonian triumph remained not only in people's minds, but almost before their eyes, Lucius Anicius celebrated his triumph over King Genthius and the Illyrians on the festival of Quirinus. Men saw in each detail a resemblance, but no equality. The general himself was lesser both in public esteem, as an Anicius compared with an Aemilius, and in rank, a praetor rather than a consul (*nobilitate Anicius cum Aemilio et iure imperii praetor cum consule conlatus*). Genthius could not be compared to Perseus, nor could the Illyrians be compared to the Macedonians, nor were the spoils or money or gifts to the soldiers of the same magnitude as Paullus'. But yet it was clear that Anicius' triumph was not to be scorned (*ita apparebat ipsum per se intuentibus nequaquam esse contemnendum*).

Livy notes that in Anicius' case, the *triumphator* was of lower birth and rank, the conquered opponent was relatively insignificant, and the spoils of war and largesse issuing from it were mean by comparison.[15] As Jonathan Edmondson has reminded us, "[P]ublic spectacles formed part of the increasing cultural interaction between Rome and the Greek East in the mid-second century BCE ... such spectacles involved some element of competitive engagement with the memorable spectacles of the recent past".[16]

Turning from the historical event to historiographical considerations, we can read the fiasco of Anicius and his brawling musicians in terms of Polybius' cultural politics. And here we might invoke Polybius' famous statement in Book 4 on the ameliorating effects of musical education in Arcadia (4.21). Read together, the passage on flute-playing in Arcadia and the episode of Anicius' musical pugilists would seem to constitute an example of a "cultural politics of alienation." The message would be something like this for an elite Greek reader with a well-

---

14 Liv. 45.34.1–2.
15 Liv. 45.43.2.
16 Edmondson 2000, 77.

tuned ear: flute-playing may well have worked for the Arcadians, but among Romans, incorrigible barbarians that they are, it is to be expected that a musical performance could easily degenerate into a scene of violence and brutality.

But we need not stop there. A complementary reading may yield a more satisfying reconstruction, and it is more rooted in the immediate political circumstances, both of this particular passage in question and Polybius' representation of the Romans in general. And in the terms in which I have tried to understand Polybius' politico-cultural strategy, it falls under the rubric of a "cultural politics of assimilation," but not of the Romans to Hellenism, but rather to a general force which exerts itself upon all human beings. This is the theme of degeneration and decline.

L. Anicius Gallus' triumphal celebrations were in some sense responses to the spectacular displays of L. Aemilius Paullus. Regardless of what Anicius' exact motivations were and to what degree he did or did not control their outcome, it is safe to conclude that his public political theater was in competitive rivalry with Paullus' spectacles. With a singular focus on Anicius and his theatrical staging at Rome, we can see an indictment of Roman barbarity in respect to cultural refinement and edification; or Hellenism, in short. But in juxtaposition with the grander and more culturally conciliatory public exhibitions of L. Aemilius Paullus, in historiographical terms we enter another long arc in Polybius' narrative pattern: the theme of contemporary decline from the pristine virtues of a bygone day.[17] We can profitably view Polybius' castigation of Anicius through this lens. Paullus, like Philopoemen, like Paullus' own natural son, Scipio Aemilianus, stands out in Polybius' representations as a throwback to the virtues of a better and less corrupted time, a man who could tastefully and successfully employ Greek cultural forms. His would-be rival Anicius, on the other hand, like many of his contemporaries, both Greek and Roman, represented a contemporaneous degeneration from a rapidly disappearing standard of culture, education, and morality.

Bibliography

Champion, C.B. (2004), *Cultural Politics in Polybius's Histories*, Berkeley.
Crowther, N.B. (1983), "Greek Games in Republican Rome", in: *AC* 52, 268–73.
Edmondson, J. (2000), "The Cultural Politics of Public Spectacle in Rome and the Greek East, 167–166 BCE", in: B. Bergmann/C. Kondoleon (eds.), *The Art of Ancient Spectacle*, New Haven/London, 77–95.

---

[17] See Champion 2004, 144–69.

Ferrary, J.-L. (1988), *Philhellénisme et impérialisme: Aspects idéologiques de la conquête romaine du monde hellénistique*, Rome.
Goldberg, S.M. (1995), *Epic in Republican Rome*, New York.
Gruen, E.S. (1992), *Culture and National Identity in Republican Rome*, Ithaca.

Cinzia Bearzot
Polybius and the Tyrants of Syracuse

Scholars who have dealt in a specific way with Polybius' interest in past history, like Frank W. Walbank and Giuseppe Zecchini,[1] have made only brief observations on the modest references to the Greek West in the *Histories*. These scholars stressed, on the one side, Polybius' minimal interest in the history of the West, and, on the other, the insertion of Polybian references into the western historical context almost exclusively in the framework of the historiographical polemic with Timaeus. While I think that in general these remarks are sound, in my opinion a survey of Polybius' behaviour towards the Syracusan tyranny could enable us to correct them partially and to better approach this issue. Therefore, my contribution aims to argue:

a) first, that Polybius looks to the phenomenon of the Syracusan tyranny with a certain interest, evaluating its representatives on the basis of their government qualities, often considered remarkable;

b) secondly, that the historian's attitude is in part independent from issues of historiographical polemic and that quite probably it is affected by judgment perspectives of Achaean and Roman origin.

As a matter of fact, only the *basileis* Hiero II and Hieronymus fit in the chronological framework embraced by Polybius' *Histories*. Only occasional references are reserved for previous Syracusan tyrants, for the most part originating from the polemic against Timaeus. For the most part, but not exclusively: and indeed, the occurrences which make exceptions are the most interesting for us.

1

First of all, it is advisable to discuss the problem of terminology. Polybius uses in relation to Syracusan tyrants the whole set of terminology referring to absolute power analytically studied by Edmond Lévy:[2] *dunastes*, *turannos* and *basileus*. As

---

[1] Walbank 1990, 28, Walbank 2002 (= 1993), 189–90, Zecchini 2007, 217 and 221. In an earlier contribution Lehmann 1989–1990, while denying that Polybius' interests are almost exclusively focused on fourth century history, does not refer to his interests in western history.
[2] Lévy 1996.

highlighted by Frank W. Walbank, the choice seems to be influenced "by value-judgments as well as legal forms".[3]

Dunastes, dunasteia, with their strong territorial significance,[4] seem to be the preferred terms to define the Syracusan tyranny. In a well-known passage (12.25k) Polybius inserts Hermocrates, Timoleon and Pyrrhus in a positive series of "dynasts of Sicily" dating back to the Deinomenid Gelo: ὅτι τῶν δεδυναστευκότων ἐν Σικελίᾳ μετὰ Γέλωνα τὸν ἀρχαῖον πραγματικωτάτους ἄνδρας παρειλήφαμεν Ἑρμοκράτην, Τιμολέοντα, Πύρρον τὸν Ἠπειρώτην, οἷς ἥκιστ' ἂν δέοι περιάπτειν μειρακιώδεις καὶ διατριβικοὺς λόγους[5] (Of those who were in power in Sicily after the elder Gelo, we have always accepted as a fact that the most capable rulers were Hermocrates, Timoleon, and Pyrrhus of Epirus, and these are the last to whom one should attribute childish and idle speeches).[6]

Dionysius I's tyranny is often called *dunasteia*, according to a model dating back to contemporary historiography (Philistus):[7] see 2.39.7 (ὑπὸ δὲ τῆς Διονυσίου Συρακοσίου δυναστείας), 12.4a (Διονύσιος ὁ πρεσβύτερος παρελάμβανε τὴν ἀρχὴν ἐτῶν εἴκοσι τριῶν ὑπάρχων, δυναστεῦσαι δὲ τετταράκοντα καὶ δύο). The term "tyrant" is on the contrary used in 12.24.3 (ἐπὶ τοῦ Διονυσίου τοῦ τυράννου). A similar ambivalence can be observed concerning Agathocles: see 8.10.12 (κατ' Ἀγαθοκλέους τοῦ Σικελίας δυνάστου); but in the same passage he is also called *turannos* (κατ' ἐχθροῦ καὶ πονηροῦ καὶ τυράννου), as he is in 9.23.2 (Ἀγαθοκλέα τὸν Σικελίας τύραννον/τὴν κατασκευὴν τῆς δυναστείας).

In 15.35, it is worth noticing that Dionysius I and Agathocles are characterized, first of all, simply as "Siceliots" (§1: τῷ δ' Ἀγαθοκλεῖ καὶ Διονυσίῳ τοῖς Σικελιώταις; §6: τοὺς περὶ Ἀγαθοκλέα καὶ Διονύσιον τοὺς Σικελιώτας), even if in the same context they later receive characterization as "tyrants of Syracuse" (τύραννοι Συρακουσῶν) and "kings of the whole Sicily and masters of some parts of Italy" (βασιλεῖς ἁπάσης Σικελίας νομισθέντες καί τινων καὶ τῆς Ἰταλίας μερῶν κυριεύσαντες).

The reign of Hiero II, *basileus* of the Syracusans (1.8.3: τὸν μετὰ ταῦτα βασιλεύσαντα τῶν Συρακοσίων; 1.16.10: ὁ δὲ βασιλεὺς Ἱέρων ... ἀδεῶς ἐβασίλευε τῶν Συρακοσίων τὸν μετὰ ταῦτα χρόνον; 7.8.2: βασιλεὺς τῶν Συρακοσίων) is often called *dunasteia*, exercised on Sicily or on Syracuse (1.83.3: πρὸς τὴν ἐν Σικελίᾳ δυναστείαν; 3.2.7: τὴν κατάλυσιν τῆς Ἱέρωνος τοῦ Συρακοσίου δυναστείας; 7.4.5:

---

3 Walbank 2002 (= 1995), 216–17.
4 Bearzot 2003, 35ff.
5 Bearzot 2006.
6 The translation of Polybius' passages is from Paton 1968–1975.
7 Sartori 1993 (= 1966); about Philistus, see Bearzot 2002.

κατὰ τὴν Ἱέρωνος τοῦ πάππου δυναστείαν; 7.8.5: ἀποθέσθαι τὴν δυναστείαν ἐκωλύθη).

Hieronymus' reign, who is also characterized as *basileus* (7.2.1: κατὰ Ἱερωνύμου τοῦ βασιλέως Συρακοσίων), is more generically called *arche*, overseeing all the Siceliots, in 7.4.5 (τὴν ἁπάντων Σικελιωτῶν ἀρχήν); despite Polybius' reservations on Hieronymus' person, the possibility of a comparison with tyrannical experiences such as those of Phalaris and Apollodorus is expressly denied (7.7.2).[8]

2

In Polybius, as it commonly happens in the Greek sources, cruelty, impiety, and contempt for law appear as typical features of the tyrant;[9] they do not seem, however, to be considered typical of the Syracusan tyranny.

Plb. 7.7, about Hieronymus' fall, is a very useful passage in that its negative characterizations contribute to shaping the character of the typical tyrant. Polybius denies that Hieronymus, for whom he has no special sympathy, could be considered, as someone claims, even fiercer than tyrants like Phalaris of Akragas and Apollodorus of Cassandria (ὥστε μήτε Φάλαριν μήτ' Ἀπολλόδωρον μήτ' ἄλλον μηδένα γεγονέναι τύραννον ἐκείνου πικρότερον). Some historians[10] describe dramatically "the cruelty of his character and the impiety of his actions" (τὴν ὠμότητα τῶν τρόπων καὶ τὴν ἀσέβειαν τῶν πράξεων); but as Hieronymus had seized the power when he was still very young and had survived only very briefly, "in this space of time ... it is hardly probable that there was any excess of unlawful violence or any extraordinary impiety" (κατὰ δὲ τὸν χρόνον τοῦτον ... ὑπερβολὴν δὲ γεγονέναι παρανομίας καὶ παρηλλαγμένην ἀσέβειαν οὐκ εἰκός); and even admitting that "his character was exceedingly capricious and violent" (εἰκαῖον αὐτὸν γεγονέναι καὶ παράνομον φατέον), he cannot be compared in any way with tyrants like Phalaris and Apollodorus.

The passage lists some negative features, typically tyrannical: cruelty (*omotes*), impiety (*asebeia*), contempt for law (*paranomia*), and ferocity (*pikrotes*). Two more passages can be juxtaposed to this, referring to Agathocles and to Dionysius I respectively, while both are connected with Polybius' criticism

---

[8] About the assumption that the tyrants of Syracuse bore in any case the title of kings, see Oost 1976.
[9] Lévy 1996, 45ff.
[10] According to Walbank 1967, 39, Bato of Sinope or historians of Hannibal.

of Timaeus: in these passages the concepts of *poneria* and unrestrained luxury occur.

In Plb. 8.10.12 Agathocles is characterized as "a bad man and a tyrant" (πονηροῦ καὶ τυράννου), so as even to justify Timaeus' *pikria* against him; Agathocles' *poneria*, however, is not explained and it stands in contrast to the different evaluation, far more positive, offered elsewhere about the dynast (see 12.15 and 15.35).[11] We will come back to this discrepancy: for the moment it suffices to say that inconsistency in Agathocles' character emerges in Plb. 9.23.1–2, where, in different phases of his life, *omotes* and *praotes* and, not by chance, also the characterizations as *turannos* and *dunastes*, are combined.

The remark, in Plb. 12.24.3, about the luxury of the tyrant Dionysius I, belongs to Timaeus: according to the Sicilian historian, "he revealed his effeminate tastes by his interest in bed-hangings and the constant study he devoted to varieties and peculiarities of different woven work". Polybius' intent is not so much to blame Dionysius for *truphe*[12] as to challenge Timaeus' statements, according to which the interest of the historians on certain issues reveals their own personal tendencies. However, it is interesting that excessive luxury is a feature associated with the definition of "tyrant".

It can be concluded that the negative features typical of the tyrants are not generally used for the masters of Syracuse. It is only for Agathocles that there seems to emerge in Polybius a partially negative evaluation, mentioning *omotes* (at least for a phase of his career) and *poneria*. The complex of the Syracusan tyrannical experience does not seem, on the contrary, worthy of a negative framing: this is revealed both by the wide use of the terminology of the *dunasteia*, which has a substantially legitimating character,[13] and by the recognition of positive qualities, personal and on the level of bureaucratic administration, in its main exponents.[14]

---

[11] Walbank 1967, 86: "In allowing invective against Agathocles because Timaeus was writing *kat'echthrou*, P. may seem to be relaxing his demand for impartiality; but Agathocles is also *poneros kai tyrannos* and this justifies the historian's full indulgence of hostility".
[12] *Truphe* contradicted by part of the tradition, as noted by Walbank 1967, 380.
[13] Bearzot 2003, 30ff.
[14] For the qualities required to sovereigns, see the discussion by Dreyer 2013.

3

For some personalities, like Dionysius I, Agathocles, and Hiero II, we find in Polybius an explicit acknowledgment of significant personal and leadership qualities.

Certainly positive is the memory of Gelo, inserted within a series of dynasts of Sicily who enjoy good reputation and recalled, on the basis of a version of the events offered by Timaeus, with regards to the request for help by the Greeks at the time of Salamis (12.26b).[15]

Six references occur with regards to Dionysius I, all expressing a certain admiration, if we make an exception for the one regarding the luxury with which Dionysius liked to surround himself (Plb. 12.24.3). Referring to his power, the characterization as *dunasteia* is prevailing; an epochal character is acknowledged to its enterprises, for the history of the western Greeks as well as for the establishment of synchronisms (see *infra*); he is mentioned, together with Agathocles, among the rulers who earned a good reputation (τῶν ἐν πράγμασιν ἐπ' ὀνόματος γεγονότων) and deserved to be considered by Scipio Africanus "the greatest statesmen combining courage and wisdom" (πραγματικωτάτους ἄνδρας γεγονέναι καὶ σὺν νῷ τολμηροτάτους: 15.35, see below). The tradition favourable to the dynast, dating back to Philistus, prevails here, against Timaeus' hostile one.

There is only one reference to Dionysius II: it is neutral and refers to the problem of the kind of ship on which he fled to Corinth (12.4a.2).[16]

In Agathocles' case, his *praotes* is acknowledged, at least in the phase following his seizure of power (9.23.2);[17] the evaluation of πραγματικώτατος ἀνήρ ... καὶ σὺν νῷ τολμηρότατος connects him to Dionysius I. In Plb. 12.15 Polybius defends Agathocles against Timaeus' unfounded attacks, since his own account gives evidence about the qualities which Agathocles had (ὅτι γὰρ ἐκ φύσεως ἀνάγκη μεγάλα προτερήματα γεγονέναι περὶ τὸν Ἀγαθοκλέα, τοῦτο δῆλόν ἐστιν ἐξ αὐτῶν ὧν ὁ Τίμαιος ἀποφαίνεται).[18] His brilliant career, starting from quite modest origins, demonstrates as a matter of fact that "Agathocles must have had something great and wonderful in him, and must have been qualified for the conduct of affairs by peculiar mental force and power" (μέγα τι γεγονέναι χρῆμα καὶ

---

15 See Walbank 1967, 404, Vattuone 1983–1984, Vattuone 1991, 159ff.
16 Walbank 1967, 324–25.
17 On the tradition of Agathocles' *praotes* in the latest phase of his career and on its reliability, see Walbank 1967, 151–52.
18 See D.S. 21.17.1–3.

θαυμάσιον τὸν Ἀγαθοκλέα καὶ *πολλὰς ἐσχηκέναι ῥοπὰς καὶ δυνάμεις πρὸς τὸν πραγματικὸν τρόπον*).

Finally, Hiero II's personality is notable for the typical virtues of the good ruler: he, since his youth, "because of his royal descent was qualified to be a ruler and statesman" (1.8.3: πρὸς δέ τι γένος εὐφυῆ *βασιλικῆς καὶ πραγματικῆς οἰκονομίας*); later, after gaining power, "he administered affairs with such mildness and magnanimity that the Syracusans ... unanimously accepted him as general" (1.8.4: οὕτως ἐχρήσατο *πρᾴως καὶ μεγαλοψύχως* τοῖς πράγμασιν, ὥστε τοὺς Συρακοσίους ... τότε πάντας ὁμοθυμαδὸν εὐδοκῆσαι στρατηγὸν αὐτῶν ὑπάρχειν Ἱέρωνα).[19] Afterwards "king Hiero ... ruled over Syracuse in security, treating the Greeks in such a way as to win from them crowns and other honours" (1.16.10–11: ὁ δὲ βασιλεὺς Ἱέρων ... ἀδεῶς ἐβασίλευε τῶν Συρακοσίων τὸν μετὰ ταῦτα χρόνον, *φιλοστεφανῶν καὶ φιλοδοξῶν εἰς τοὺς Ἕλληνας*); he is to be considered "the most illustrious of princes and the one who reaped longest the fruits of his own wisdom in particular cases and in general history" (ἐπιφανέστατος γὰρ δὴ πάντων οὗτος δοκεῖ καὶ πλεῖστον χρόνον ἀπολελαυκέναι *τῆς ἰδίας εὐβουλίας* ἔν τε τοῖς κατὰ μέρος καὶ τοῖς καθόλου πράγμασιν). This eulogy of Hiero is traced back to Fabius Pictor by Walbank due to the emphasis on his pro-Roman policy, while it is seen as purely Polybian by others.[20] The eulogy is centered on the qualities of *praotes, megalopsuchia, euboulia, basilike kai pragmatike oikonomia* which contribute to shaping the image of the good ruler.[21]

A second eulogy of Hiero can be found in Plb. 7.8. Here it is stated that he obtained the reign thanks only to his own qualities, without inheriting from others wealth, reputation, or other advantages due to *tuche*. Moreover, he became king of the Syracusans without killing, banishing or harming anyone of his fellow citizens; and "during a reign of fifty-four years he kept his country at peace and his own power undisturbed by plots, and he kept clear of that envy which is wont to wait on superiority. Actually on several occasions when he wished to lay down his authority, he was prevented from doing so by the common action of the citizens. And having conferred great benefits on the Greeks, and studied to win their high opinion, he left behind him a great personal reputation and a legacy of universal goodwill towards the Syracusans" (ἔτη γὰρ πεντήκοντα καὶ τέτταρα

---

[19] In the digression in 1.8.2–10.1, which deals with the rise of Hiero II, Walbank 1957, 53ff., recognizes the traces of a western source identified by him with Timaeus. See De Sensi 1977, 19–21 and 197ff. Thornton 2001, 590–91, underlines that Polybius does not merely re-propose Timaeus' judgement, but adheres personally to it, because it corresponds to his political reflection.
[20] Walbank 1967, 69. However, see Eckstein 1985, 269–70, and Thornton 2001, 591 and 599, who stress the coherence with Polybius' political reflection on the exercise of power.
[21] See Walbank 2002 = 1995, 218.

βασιλεύσας διετήρησε μὲν τῇ πατρίδι τὴν εἰρήνην, διεφύλαξε δ' αὑτῷ τὴν ἀρχὴν ἀνεπιβούλευτον, διέφυγε δὲ τὸν ταῖς ὑπεροχαῖς παρεπόμενον φθόνον· ὅς γε πολλάκις ἐπιβαλόμενος ἀποθέσθαι τὴν δυναστείαν ἐκωλύθη κατὰ κοινὸν ὑπὸ τῶν πολιτῶν. εὐεργετικώτατος δὲ καὶ φιλοδοξότατος γενόμενος εἰς τοὺς Ἕλληνας μεγάλην μὲν αὑτῷ δόξαν, οὐ μικρὰν δὲ Συρακοσίοις εὔνοιαν παρὰ πᾶσιν ἀπέλιπε). Concepts like δόξα and εὔνοια and adjectives like εὐεργετικώτατος and φιλοδοξότατος occur in this passage, completing the image of the sovereign endowed with great personal qualities, beloved and popular, able to secure peace and safety in the city.[22]

Overall, therefore, the explicit acknowledgment of personal and leadership qualities of personalities like Dionysius I, Agathocles, and Hiero II emerges quite often; in general, these are qualities expressing energy, effectiveness in action, moderation in exercising power, capability to garner consent and to secure peace and government stability. The wish to correct the evaluation of previous historians, although not always considered adequate, may generate some contradictions, as in the case of Agathocles. For he is, on the one side, considered *poneros*, so as to partially justify Polybius' criticism of Timaeus (9.23), while, on the other hand, important personal qualities are attributed to him (12.15 and 15.35), so that Timaeus' hostile account proves contradictory and unjustified.

Finally we should consider personalities who, though not negative, are at least ambiguous, like Timoleon: according to Polybius, he had been too much exalted by Timaeus in relation to the real value of his deeds (12.23.6–7). The same goes for Hieronymus, a modest personality but too much criticized by an ungenerous historiography which compares him, without good reason, to the worst tyrants of history (7.7.1–5).

4

Two more passages deserve close attention: although historiographical polemic is absent in them, they display a significant interest in the great Syracusan dynasts.

The first one refers to the famous synchronism between the Gallic catastrophe and some events of the Greek history (1.6.1–2)—among the events which are mentioned is the siege of Rhegium by Dionysius I, a consequence of the battle of

---

[22] Thornton 2002, 441.

the Elleporus and of the defeat suffered by the forces of the Italiotes: Ἔτος μὲν οὖν ἐνειστήκει μετὰ μὲν τὴν ἐν Αἰγὸς ποταμοῖς ναυμαχίαν ἐννεα καὶ δέκατον, πρὸ δὲ τῆς ἐν Λεύκτροις μάχης ἑκκαιδέκατον, ἐν ᾧ Λακεδαιμόνιοι μὲν τὴν ἐπ' Ἀνταλκίδου λεγομένην εἰρήνην πρὸς βασιλέα τῶν Περσῶν ἐκύρωσαν καὶ πρεσβύτερος Διονύσιος *τῇ περὶ τὸν Ἐλλέπορον ποταμὸν μάχῃ νενικηκὼς τοὺς κατὰ τὴν Ἰταλίαν Ἕλληνας ἐπολιόρκει Ῥήγιον*, Γαλάται δὲ κατὰ κράτος ἑλόντες αὐτὴν τὴν Ῥώμην κατεῖχον πλὴν τοῦ Καπετωλίου (It was, therefore, the nineteenth year after the battle of Aegospotami and the sixteenth before that of Leuctra, the year in which the Spartans ratified the peace known as that of Antalcidas with the King of Persia, that in which also Dionysius the Elder, after defeating the Italiot Greeks in the battle at the river Elleporus, was besieging Rhegium, and that in which the Gauls, after taking Rome itself by assault, occupied the whole of that city except the Capitol). It is true that the chronology of Dionysius I is interesting for Polybius, as shown by the fact that he challenges Ephorus with regards to the data provided about the duration of Dionysius' tyranny (12.4a.3–6);[23] but the epochal character given to these vicissitudes of the history of the West, juxtaposed to the battles of Aegospotami and Leuctra and to the peace of Antalcidas, is amazing in any case in an author who in general does not show particular interest in this geo-historical sector.

What is the reason of such an appreciation? It can be assumed that Polybius takes the information from Timaeus, who probably established a synchronism between the Gallic catastrophe and the siege of Rhegium (D.S. 14.113.1).[24] Frank W. Walbank also notes in his commentary that the example of the crossing of the Strait by a great power could be linked to the narration of the First Punic War.[25] But there is, in my opinion, something more that can help us in understanding Polybius' choice: there is a passage, in the *excursus* on the Achaen League, which mentions the will of the Achaean colonial cities, starting from Croton, Sybaris and Caulonia, to create a league around the sanctuary of Zeus Homarios, and to prepare a venue for their common meetings (2.39.6–7).[26] These cities adopted the Achaeans' *nomoi* and intended to design their *politeia* accordingly, but they were prevented from doing so by external circumstances: Polybius clarifies that "it was only indeed the tyranny of Dionysius I of Syracuse and their subjection to the

---

23 Walbank 1967, 325–26.
24 Pédech 1964, 442, Meister 1967, 99, does not express his view on the synchronism; however, he considers the immediately preceding account on the capture of Rhegium as "reinster Timaios" (D.S. 14.106–108 and 111–112).
25 Walbank 1957, 46–48.
26 See Thornton 2001, 662, with reference to various studies by Domenico Musti.

barbarian tribes around them which defeated this purpose and forced them to abandon these institutions, much against their will" (ὑπὸ δὲ τῆς Διονυσίου Συρακοσίου δυναστείας, ἔτι δὲ τῆς τῶν περιοικούντων βαρβάρων ἐπικρατείας ἐμποδισθέντες οὐχ ἑκουσίως ἀλλὰ κατ' ἀνάγκην αὐτῶν ἀπέστησαν).

Polybius recounts here the difficulties encountered by Dionysius I in the development of the Achaean colonies in Italy: in fact, the victory of the Elleporus against the Italiot League and the seizure of Rhegium had an epochal significance for the history of the Achaean colonies, because they put an end to the influence of Croton and significantly weakened the alliance.[27] We can conclude that the insertion of the battle of the Elleporus and of the siege of Rhegium in the synchronism with the Gallic catastrophe seems to have been guided, beyond the chronological value of the indication, by the importance of these events for the history of the Achaean colonies: it was a history in which Polybius was interested independent of his historiographical polemic against Timaeus and the other historians of the Greek West. It is therefore the interference with the Achaean colonial history which leads Polybius to consider with interest the tyranny of Dionysius I—who with the battle of the Elleporus and the seizure of Rhegium achieved the height of his power[28]—as well as events of that western history for which he does not seem generally to give specific attention.[29]

The second passage is the judgement of Scipio Africanus on Dionysius I and Agathocles, already partially considered with regards to the qualities of the Syracusan dynasts (15.35). Polybius has just finished recounting the vicissitudes of Agathocles, favourite of Ptolemy IV, and wonders about the necessity to devote much space to the fate of such individuals. "It is otherwise" he adds "with the Sicilian Agathocles and Dionysius and certain other rulers of renown" (τῷ δ' Ἀγαθοκλεῖ καὶ Διονυσίῳ τοῖς Σικελιώταις καί τισιν ἑτέροις τῶν ἐν πράγμασιν ἐπ' ὀνόματος γεγονότων). Moving from obscure origins, both of them became tyrants of Syracuse, kings of the whole Sicily and masters of some parts of Italy (καὶ τὸ μὲν πρῶτον ἐγενήθησαν ἀμφότεροι κατὰ τοὺς ἰδίους καιροὺς τύραννοι Συρακουσῶν …, μετὰ δὲ ταῦτα βασιλεῖς ἁπάσης Σικελίας νομισθέντες καί τινων καὶ

---

27 Walbank 1957, 126, Stroheker 1958, 113ff. On the Western Achaeans, see the papers collected in Greco 2002, Musti 2005, 248ff., Braccesi/Raviola 2008, 152ff.
28 Stroheker 1958, 118–19.
29 With regards to Timaeus' reliability, Polybius recounts (12.10.8–9) that he mentions that the father of his informer on Locri, Echecrates, participated in an embassy to Dionysius (probably Dionysius I). Such an embassy, according to Walbank 1967, 346–47, is connected "with Dionysius' attempt to win over the south Italian cities where there was a Pythagorean opposition".

τῆς Ἰταλίας μερῶν κυριεύσαντες);³⁰ Agathocles tried also to conquer Africa.³¹ For this reason they gained the appreciation of Publius Scipio Africanus: when he was asked to say which men he considered "the greatest statesmen combining courage and wisdom" (πραγματικωτάτους ἄνδρας γεγονέναι καὶ σὺν νῷ τολμηροτάτους), he answered that these were the Sicilian Agathocles and Dionysius. It is to the careers of such men, Polybius concludes, that it is necessary to draw the attention of readers, dwelling on the vicissitudes of fortune and on the uncertainty of the human life and taking lessons therefrom.

This opinion on Dionysius I and Agathocles is perfectly in line with the positive evaluation of their personalities as it emerges elsewhere in Polybius: he stresses the reputation (*onoma*) acquired by the two dynasts in the government activity (*pragmata*) and their main qualities, their pragmatic effectiveness in politics (expressed by the adjective *pragmatikos*) and their daring (expressed by the adjective *tolmeros*). With regards to the latter characteristic, the combination of boldness with *nous* is important: as Paul Pédech notes, rational intelligence plays a primary role in coordinating and exploiting the other qualities of the politician.³² Now, in this case too, the interest in the Syracusan dynasts does not seem to have anything to do with the historiographical polemic against Timaeus. The perspective from which Polybius looks at these characters is rather that of the authoritative opinion of Scipio Africanus, known to him through his relations with the Scipios: Frank W. Walbank assumes that Scipio Africanus seemed to have seen in Dionysius and Agathocles, first of all, the anti-Carthaginian generals,³³ but it must be considered that the Roman political world, as it is well known, saw in Syracuse an interesting precedent of a territorial state able to establish relationships in an articulated way with the various internal components, and therefore a possible model for Rome itself.³⁴ For this reason, the Romans, and as a consequence Polybius, considered with interest the experiences of absolute power which had followed one another in the government of Syracuse.³⁵

---

30 Walbank 1967, 495.
31 See 1.82.8.
32 Pédech 1964, 210–16.
33 Walbank 1967, 495; see Consolo Langher 2000, 333ff., in particular 334–35.
34 Musti 1989, 564ff., 566, Musti 2003, Musti 2004.
35 According to Sanders 1987, 85, Scipio's appreciation for Dionysius I shows his knowledge of Philistus.

5 Conclusions

The analysis developed could have shown, first of all, that Polybius has a certain interest in Greek West which is independent from the historiographical polemic against Timaeus. He considers that the Syracusan tyranny, from Gelo to Hiero II, is represented by rulers of a great value both on a personal and on a political level, displaying qualities such as *praotes, megalopsuchia, euboulia, basilike kai pragmatike oikonomia, euergesia, philodoxia, tolme*. Such tyrannies entailed experiences of absolute power in any case positive; this is congruent with the concept of *basileia*, the good monarchy based on *gnome* and *logismos*, theorised by Polybius in the sixth book (see 6.4–7, particularly 6.4.2, 6.6.12, 6.7.3). Influenced probably by the opinion of the Scipionic circle, he seemed to consider Syracuse a model of territorial state anticipating Rome, with an autocratic leadership, worthy of a certain attention.

Some vicissitudes referring to the Dionysian tyranny, like the conflict with the Italiotes, attract, on the contrary, Polybius' attention for the epochal character that they assume in the history of the western Achaean colonies, preventing them from developing a political system which conforms to that of the Achaeans of the motherland. This perspective is certainly not the one of the western historians, but rather that of those who were interested in the history of the Achaeans as an *ethnos*. Once more, Polybius' interest in the history of the past can be understood mainly in the light of a double perspective: on the one side, a Peloponnesian perspective, on the other, a Roman one.[36]

Bibliography

Bearzot, C. (2002), "Filisto di Siracusa", in: R. Vattuone (ed.), *Storici greci d'Occidente*, Bologna, 91–136.

— — (2003), "Il concetto di *dynasteia* e lo stato ellenistico", in: C. Bearzot/F. Landucci/G. Zecchini (eds.), *Gli stati territoriali nel mondo antico*, Milan, 21–44.

— — (2006), "Ermocrate δεδυναστευκὼς ἐν Σικελίᾳ in Timeo F 22", in: P. Amann/M. Pedrazzi/H. Taeuber (eds.), *Italo–Tusco–Romana. Festschrift Foresti*, Vienna, 23–30.

— — (2010), "Le potenze egemoniche greche nel quadro della storia universale", in: U. Roberto/L. Mecella (eds.), *Dalla storiografia ellenistica alla storiografia tardoantica: aspetti, problemi, prospettive*, Soveria Mannelli, 11–24.

---

[36] See the conclusions of Zecchini 2007, 213: "egli era interessato al passato, peraltro assai nebuloso, della sua patria ... e al passato di Roma". For the Peloponnesian perspective, see Bearzot 2010, 18ff.; for the Roman one, in particular on the problem of absolute power, see Walbank 2002 = 1995, 220ff.

Braccesi, L./F. Raviola (2008), *La Magna Grecia*, Bologna.
Consolo Langher, S.N. (2000), *Agatocle. Da capoparte a monarca fondatore di un regno tra Cartagine e i diadochi*, Messina.
De Sensi, G. (1977), *Gerone II. Un monarca ellenistico in Sicilia*, Palermo.
Dreyer, B. (2013), "Polybios und die hellenistischen Monarchien", in: V. Grieb/C. Koehn (eds.), *Polybios und seine Historien*, Stuttgart, 233–249.
Eckstein, A.M. (1985), "Polybius, Syracuse and the Politics of Accomodation", *GRBS* 26, 265–282.
Greco, E. (ed.) (2002), *Gli Achei e l'identità etnica degli Achei in Occidente*, Paestum/Athens.
Lehmann, G.A. (1989–1990), "The 'Ancient' Greek History in Polybios' Historiae: Tendencies and Political Objectives", in: *SCI* 10, 66–77.
Lévy, E. (1996), "La tyrannie et son vocabulaire chez Polybe", in: *Ktema* 21, 43–54.
Meister, K. (1967), *Die sizilische Geschichte bei Diodor von den Anfängen zum Tod des Agathokles. Quellenuntersuchungen zu Buch IV-XXI*, Munich.
Musti, D. (1989), *Storia greca*, Rome/Bari.
—— (2003), "Prefazione", in: S. Mazzarino (ed.), *Introduzione alle guerre puniche*, Milan, 10–30.
—— (2004), "La *meghiste dynasteia* di Dioniso I e la centralità geo-politica della Sicilia: struttura e immagine", in: *Sicilia Antiqua* 1, 35–39.
—— (2005), *Magna Grecia. Il quadro storico*, Rome/Bari.
Oost, S.I. (1976), "The Tyrant Kings of Syracuse", in: *CPh* 71, 224–236.
Paton, W.R. (ed.) (1968–1975), *Polybius. The Histories*, 6 vols., Cambridge, Mass./London.
Pédech, P. (1964), *La méthode historique de Polybe*, Paris.
Sanders, L.J. (1987), *Dionysius I of Syracuse and Greek Tyranny*, London/New York/Sydney.
Sartori, F. (1993 = 1966), "Sulla dynasteia di Dionisio il Vecchio nell'opera diodorea", in: *Dall'Italia all'Italia*, I, Padova, 169–233 (= *CS* 5, 3–61).
Stroheker, K.-F. (1958), *Dionysios I. Gestalt und Geschichte des Tyrannen von Syrakus*, Wiesbaden.
Thornton, J. (ed.) (2001), *Polibio. Storie*, I, Milano.
—— (ed.) (2002), *Polibio. Storie*, IV, Milano.
Vattuone, R. (1983–1984), "Timeo F94. Gelone tra Erodoto e Polibio", in: *RSA* 13–14, 200–211.
—— (1991), *Sapienza d'Occidente. Il pensiero storico di Timeo di Tauromenio*, Bologna.
Walbank, F.W. (1957), *A Historical Commentary on Polybius*, I, Oxford.
—— (1967), *A Historical Commentary on Polybius*, II, Oxford.
—— (1990), "Polybios' Sicht der Vergangenheit", in: *Gymnasium* 97, 15–30.
—— (2002 = 1993), "Polybius and the Past", in: id. (ed.), *Polybius, Rome and the Hellenistic World: Essays and Reflections*, Cambridge, 178–192 (= in: H.D. Jocelyn (ed.), *Tria Lustra. Essays and Notes Presented to John Pinsent*, Liverpool, 15–23).
—— (2002 = 1995), "The One and the Many", in: id. (ed.), *Polybius, Rome and the Hellenistic World: Essays and Reflections*, Cambridge, 212–230 (= in: I. Malkin/Z.V. Rubinsohn (eds.), *Leader and Masses in the Roman World. Studies in Honor of Zvi Yavetz*, Leiden, 201–222).
Zecchini, G. (2007), "Polibio e la storia non contemporanea", in: P. Desideri/S. Roda/A.M. Biraschi (eds.), *Costruzione e uso del passato storico nella cultura antica*, Alessandria, 213–223.

Felix K. Maier
Past and Present as *paradoxon theōrēma* in Polybius

Writers, poets and philosophers have tried to describe history with short formulas, many of them resorting to contradictory or overly sophisticated phrases to grasp the complex nature of history. One such distillation of history, attributed to Mark Twain, reads "History doesn't repeat itself, but it does rhyme". The suggestion is that history does not recur the same way over and over again, but that there can be patterns which seem to connect events to what has occurred in the past.

Right at the beginning of his work, Polybius—after framing the didactic purpose of his *Historiai*—comes up with an often overlooked but fascinating, and apparently contradictory, characterization of history:[1]

> How striking (παράδοξον) and grand is the spectacle (θεώρημα) presented by the period with which I purpose to deal, will be most clearly apparent if we set beside and compare with the Roman dominion the most famous empires of the past, those which have formed the chief theme of historians.

Polybius calls the past a *paradoxon theōrēma*. W.R. Paton translated this formula as "striking spectacle" and certainly makes a valid point in noting that Polybius wants to convince his readers that his topic surpasses events described by other historians.[2] But Polybius' words are far more complex, and indeed more profound, than we are led to think at first glance. If we take both *paradoxon* and *theōrēma* in their literal sense, we are suddenly confronted with a challenging—since both parts seem to form an inherent contradiction—yet all the more fascinating description of history: *theōrēma* is not only related to vision or sight,[3] but especially in Hellenistic times denotes a theory, or even a system;[4] we come

---
[1] Plb. 1.1.2: ὡς δ' ἔστι παράδοξον καὶ μέγα τὸ περὶ τὴν ἡμετέραν ὑπόθεσιν θεώρημα γένοιτ' ἂν οὕτως μάλιστ' ἐμφανές, εἰ τὰς ἐλλογιμωτάτας τῶν προγεγενημένων δυναστειῶν, περὶ ἃς οἱ συγγραφεῖς τοὺς πλείστους διατέθεινται λόγους, παραβάλοιμεν καὶ συγκρίναιμεν πρὸς τὴν Ῥωμαίων ὑπεροχήν (English translation by W.R. Paton; unless stated otherwise, all translations of Polybius in this article are those of Paton).
[2] For the agonistic character of historians' introductions, see Marincola 1997.
[3] In its original sense, *theōrēma* is connected to *theōria* and denotes a spectacle, Pl. *Lg.* 953a and Dem 18.68.
[4] Arist. *Metaph.* 1083b18, *Top.* 104b1. In a purely mathematical sense as a "theorem", Archim. *Sph. Cyl.* 1. Prooem.

across this meaning in Polybius many times with *theōrēma/theōrēmata* denoting, as Walbank has rightly put it, "the sciences" or "scientific principles".[5]

Para doxan/paradoxos/paradoxōs in Polybius can mean "extraordinary" or "incredible", emphasizing the exceptional character of what is being described. But quite often we can grasp its meaning better if we take it literally: "contrary to expectation", as it is most commonly understood in contexts in which something happens completely against expectations based on prior experience.[6]

Viewed in this context, *paradoxon theōrēma* turns out to be an intriguing formula, forming an explosive pair which immediately prompts the reader to think. It could be understood as "something logical, which is paradoxical", or "a coherent system with an unexpected structure". But even if this apparent antagonism is not immediately comprehensible, it nevertheless catches our attention right away, and the reader realizes that there is more to it than any translation might be able to express. At the very least, *paradoxon theōrēma* seems to illustrate a complex phenomenon of history.

In this chapter I would like to begin with this striking phrase, explaining why this apparent semantic antagonism appears so prominently in Polybius' text. That is, I would like to explain why—in his view—it perfectly characterizes history. Lastly, I would like to explore what consequences this contradictory compound term had for Polybius' purpose of writing history: learning from the past.

1

The first question which I need to deal with when addressing the aforementioned issues is: Why was history for Polybius a *paradoxon*? To what extent did he regard historical events as "unexpected", as "contrary to expectation"? These questions seem to be answered by the fact that there are many passages which suggest that Polybius did not at all consider the rise of the Roman Empire to be an unforeseen

---

[5] E.g. in 10.47.2, where Polybius discusses the different devices for fire-signaling, *theōrēma* refers to the applied system of either signaling words or contexts. See also Plb. 9.14.4 ("principle"), Walbank 1967, 140.

[6] Examples in Mauersberger 1998, 60–62 and in Frazier 2002. A close analysis of *paradoxos* shows that the secondary meaning "exceptional", "extraordinary" can be applied to fewer passages than its most immediate and literal meaning "against all expectation", since Polybius uses *paradoxos* particularly in those instances where he wants to contrast "reality" with "expectation", see 1.6.8, 1.25.3, 1.49.7, 1.75.3, 1.82.3, 1.87.1, 3.43.12, 3.61.9, 8.14.10, 10.8.5, 14.6.8, 20.11.9; see further Maier 2012, 253–54.

process.⁷ His digression on the *anacyclōsis* seems to prove this assumption.⁸ And there are many other cases in which Polybius apparently emphasizes the repetition of expected patterns in history.⁹ In these examples, history seems to be a *theōrēma*. But we find many other instances in which Polybius makes clear that history in general and the rise of Rome in particular was an unexpected, paradoxical process which could have turned out differently and which was not necessarily determined by the will of *Tykhē*.¹⁰ This idea is evident in Polybius' manifold narrative strategies which underline the contingency of history; he builds up suspense, not just for aesthetic reasons, but to illustrate the openness of history.¹¹ Perhaps one of the most important pieces of evidence suggesting that Polybius was convinced of the indeterministic and open structure of history are his frequent counterfactual thought experiments. When presenting alternative scenarios to the reader, Polybius shows that history could have followed a different path, equally plausible, and that Roman rule was but *one* possibility.¹² And there are other narrative devices with which Polybius emphasizes the paradoxical character of history.¹³

I would to like draw attention to another narrative strategy of which Polybius frequently makes use to show that history is a *paradoxon*. This strategy is particularly interesting, as—in my view—it is directly linked to a contemporary histori-

---

7 Particularly in Plb. 1.63.9 or 18.28.2–4.
8 Plb. 6.4.6–6.4.12. Henderson 2001, 38: "The world he was born into became the preparatory background within his story, as he looked back from the perspective of the final superpower's HQ, and reviewed his obsolete Achaean vista with the unimaginable hindsight of a post Macedonian teleology". Walbank 2002, 193: "But in the case of Rome's rise to power he seems, exceptionally, to have invested the process with a teleological character" and some years before in Walbank 1972, 64: "Polybius has confused what has happened with what was destined to happen and so invests the rise of Rome to world domination with a teleological character".
9 Plb. 1.61.2, 1.67.6, 2.19.3–4, 8.24.1.
10 Hau 2011, Maier 2012, 210–47.
11 Miltsios 2009 analyzed the account on the capture of Achaius in Book 8 and convincingly showed that Polybius almost causes the reader to take as an actual occurrence what did not happen.
12 Maier 2013. Olson, Roese, and Deibert 1996, 297 emphasize that the use of counterfactual scenarios indicates that an author considered the "real outcome" as more unlikely than what could have happened: "In naturally occurring counterfactual thoughts, perceivers typically mutate exceptional or unexpected antecedents to be more routine or expected (and then contemplate whether the outcome would have been different if things had been more normal)".
13 For further analysis on narrative evidence which proves Polybius' conviction of indeterministic history, see Maier 2012, 73–208.

cal phenomenon, indicating that Polybius' idea of history as a *paradoxon* resulted from the influence of a historical process: the interaction of formerly disconnected political spheres.

The confluence of several historical events in the third and second centuries BCE made Polybius come to the conclusion that these times were characterized by the *symplokē*—the entanglement of political space due to the Roman expansion.[14] Different arenas and spaces suddenly collided, as the byproducts of initially local conflicts became global. The Second Punic War affected not only the Romans and the Carthaginians, but also the Greek East. And the following expansion of the Roman Empire quickly connected formerly separate political spaces. We get a clear picture of this process in the foreword to Book 3. Here, Polybius presents the most important protagonists to follow. I would like to quote the passage almost in its entirety (emphases added), as its peculiarity is noteworthy:

> First I shall indicate the causes of the above war between Rome and Carthage, known as the Hannibalic war, and tell how the Carthaginians invaded Italy, broke up the dominion of Rome, and cast the Romans into great fear for their safety and even for their native soil, while great was their own hope, such as they had never dared to entertain, of capturing Rome itself.
>
> Next I shall attempt to describe how at the same period Philip of Macedon, after finishing his war with the Aetolians and settling the affairs of Greece, conceived the project of an alliance with Carthage; how Antiochus and Ptolemy Philopator first quarrelled and at length went to war with each other for the possession of Coele-Syria, and how the Rhodians and Prusias, declaring war on the Byzantines, compelled them to stop levying toll on ships bound for the Euxine ... Simultaneously in a digression I shall narrate how the dominion of Hiero of Syracuse fell and after this I shall deal with the troubles in Egypt, and tell how, on the death of Ptolemy, Antiochus and Philip, conspiring to partition the dominions of his son, a helpless infant, began to be guilty of acts of unjust aggression, Philip laying hands on the islands of the Aegean, and on Caria and Samos, while Antiochus seized on Coele-Syria and Phoenicia. Next, after summing up the doings of the Romans and Carthaginians in Spain, Africa, and Sicily I shall shift the scene of my story definitely, as the scene of action shifted, to Greece and its neighborhood. I shall describe the sea-battles in which Attalus and the Rhodians met Philip, and after this deal with the war between the Romans and Philip, its course, its reason, and its result. Following on this I shall make mention of the angry spirit of the Aetolians yielding to which they invited Antiochus over, and thus set ablaze the war from Asia against the Achaeans and Romans. After narrating the causes of this war, and how Antiochus crossed to Europe, I shall describe in the first place how he fled from Greece; secondly how on his defeat after this he abandoned all Asia up to the

---

14 Surprisingly, Polybius' concept of the *symplokē* has not yet been analyzed by modern scholarship with regard to his idea of history, but has always been discussed in the context of methodological discussions, see Ziegler 1952, 1515–1519, Pédech 1964, 496, Walbank 1975, Mohm 1977, 68–91, Roveri 1982, 56–59.

Taurus; and thirdly, how the Romans, suppressing the insolence of the Galatian Gauls, established their undisputed supremacy in Asia and freed its inhabitants on this side of the Taurus from the fear of barbarians and the lawless violence of these Gauls. Next I shall bring before the reader's eyes the misfortune that befell the Aetolians and Cephallenians, and then make mention of the war of Eumenes with Prusias and the Gauls and of that between Ariarathes and Pharnaces. Subsequently, after some notice of the unification and pacification of the Peloponnese and of the growth of the Rhodian State, I shall bring the whole narrative of events to a conclusion, narrating finally the expedition of Antiochus Epiphanes against Egypt, the war with Perseus, and the abolition of the Macedonian monarchy. All the above events will enable us to perceive how the Romans dealt with each contingency and thus subjected the whole world to their rule.[15]

---

15 Plb. 3.2-3: ὑποδείξαντες γὰρ τὰς αἰτίας, δι' ἃς ὁ προδεδηλωμένος συνέστη Καρχηδονίοις καὶ Ῥωμαίοις πόλεμος, ὁ προσαγορευθεὶς Ἀννιβιακός, ἐροῦμεν ὡς εἰς Ἰταλίαν ἐμβαλόντες Καρχηδόνιοι καὶ καταλύσαντες τὴν Ῥωμαίων δυναστείαν εἰς μέγαν μὲν φόβον ἐκείνους ἤγαγον περὶ σφῶν καὶ τοῦ τῆς πατρίδος ἐδάφους, μεγάλας δ' ἔσχον αὐτοὶ καὶ παραδόξους ἐλπίδας, ὡς καὶ τῆς Ῥώμης αὐτῆς ἐξ ἐφόδου κρατήσοντες. ἑξῆς δὲ τούτοις πειρασόμεθα διασαφεῖν ὡς κατὰ τοὺς αὐτοὺς καιροὺς Φίλιππος μὲν ὁ Μακεδὼν τοὺς αὐτοὺς καιροὺς Φίλιππος μὲν ὁ Μακεδὼν διαπολεμήσας Αἰτωλοῖς καὶ μετὰ ταῦτα συστησάμενος τὰ κατὰ τοὺς Ἕλληνας ἐπεβάλετο κοινωνεῖν Καρχηδονίοις τῶν αὐτῶν ἐλπίδων, Ἀντίοχος δὲ καὶ Πτολεμαῖος ὁ Φιλοπάτωρ ἠμφισβήτουν, τέλος δ' ἐπολέμησαν ὑπὲρ Κοίλης Συρίας πρὸς ἀλλήλους, Ῥόδιοι δὲ καὶ Προυσίας ἀναλαβόντες πρὸς Βυζαντίους πόλεμον ἠνάγκασαν αὐτοὺς ἀποστῆναι τοῦ παραγωγιάζειν τοὺς πλέοντας εἰς τὸν Πόντον ... ἅμα δὲ τούτοις κατὰ παρέκβασιν δηλώσομεν τὴν κατάλυσιν τῆς Ἰέρωνος τοῦ Συρακοσίου δυναστείας. οἷς ἐπισυνάψομεν τὰς περὶ τὴν Αἴγυπτον ταραχὰς καὶ τίνα τρόπον Πτολεμαίου τοῦ βασιλέως μεταλλάξαντος τὸν βίον συμφρονήσαντες Ἀντίοχος καὶ Φίλιππος ἐπὶ διαιρέσει τῆς τοῦ καταλελειμμένου παιδὸς ἀρχῆς ἤρξαντο κακοπραγμονεῖν καὶ τὰς χεῖρας ἐπιβάλλειν Φίλιππος μὲν τοῖς κατ' Αἴγαιον καὶ Καρίαν καὶ Σάμον, Ἀντίοχος δὲ τοῖς κατὰ Κοίλην Συρίαν καὶ Φοινίκην. μετὰ δὲ ταῦτα συγκεφαλαιωσάμενοι τὰς ἐν Ἰβηρίᾳ καὶ Λιβύῃ καὶ Σικελίᾳ πράξεις Ῥωμαίων καὶ Καρχηδονίων μεταβιβάσομεν τὴν διήγησιν ὁλοσχερῶς εἰς τοὺς κατὰ τὴν Ἑλλάδα τόπους ἅμα ταῖς τῶν πραγμάτων μεταβολαῖς. ἐξηγησάμενοι δὲ τὰς Ἀττάλου καὶ Ῥοδίων ναυμαχίας πρὸς Φίλιππον, ἔτι δὲ τὸν Ῥωμαίων καὶ Φιλίππου πόλεμον, ὡς ἐπράχθη καὶ διὰ τίνων καὶ τί τὸ τέλος ἔσχεν, τούτῳ συνάπτοντες τὸ συνεχὲς μνησθησόμεθα τῆς Αἰτωλῶν ὀργῆς, καθ' ἣν Ἀντίοχον ἐπισπασάμενοι τὸν ἀπὸ τῆς Ἀσίας Ἀχαιοῖς καὶ Ῥωμαίοις ἐξέκαυσαν πόλεμον. οὗ δηλώσαντες τὰς αἰτίας καὶ τὴν Ἀντιόχου διάβασιν εἰς τὴν Εὐρώπην διασαφήσομεν πρῶτον μὲν τίνα τρόπον ἐκ τῆς Ἑλλάδος ἔφυγεν, δεύτερον δὲ πῶς ἡττηθεὶς τῆς ἐπὶ τάδε τοῦ Ταύρου πάσης ἐξεχώρησε, τὸ δὲ τρίτον τίνα τρόπον Ῥωμαῖοι καταλύσαντες τὴν Γαλατῶν ὕβριν ἀδήριτον μὲν σφίσι παρεσκεύασαν τὴν τῆς Ἀσίας ἀρχήν, ἀπέλυσαν δὲ τοὺς ἐπὶ τάδε τοῦ Ταύρου κατοικοῦντας βαρβαρικῶν φόβων καὶ τῆς Γαλατῶν παρανομίας. μετὰ δὲ ταῦτα θέντες ὑπὸ τὴν ὄψιν τὰς Αἰτωλῶν καὶ Κεφαλλήνων ἀτυχίας ἐπιβαλοῦμεν τοὺς Εὐμένει συστάντας πρός τε Προυσίαν καὶ Γαλάτας πολέμους, ὁμοίως δὲ καὶ τὸν μετ' Ἀριαράθου πρὸς Φαρνάκην. οἷς ἑξῆς ἐπιμνησθέντες τῆς παρὰ Πελοποννησίων ὁμονοίας καὶ καταστάσεως, ἔτι δὲ τῆς αὐξήσεως τοῦ Ῥοδίων πολιτεύματος, συγκεφαλαιωσόμεθα τὴν ὅλην διήγησιν ἅμα καὶ τὰς πράξεις, ἐπὶ πᾶσιν ἐξηγησάμενοι τὴν Ἀντιόχου στρατείαν εἰς Αἴγυπτον τοῦ κληθέντος Ἐπιφανοῦς καὶ τὸν Περσικὸν

The orchestration of this passage is striking: Polybius sketches different processes which impressively illustrate the historical development. Firstly, several military engagements of the Romans in various regions are emphasized: their campaigns against Carthage in Spain, Africa and Sicily, against Philip in Greece and against Antiochus and the Galatian Gauls. Philip's wars against the Aetolians in Greece, his alliance with Carthage, his attempt to lay hands on the islands of the Aegean, Caria and Samos, his clash in sea battles with Attalus and the Rhodians and, finally, his encounter with the Romans. Secondly, apart from these two main agents, there are plenty of others (Antiochus, Ptolemy, the Aetolians), who have their own designs. The enumeration of all these divergent different plans and schemes brings the reader to realize that collisions are inevitable. Widely separated areas suddenly become linked by the agenda of the individual political agents involved in this power game.

As Polybius does not present a time-frame while listing all occurrences, the reader gets the impression that all these incidents occurred in a timeless continuum. Thus, the parallel character of history is emphasized, although many of them came about sequentially.[16] By overplaying the parallel character of these events, however, Polybius aims at providing his readership with a clear picture of the *symplokē* and the consequences resulting therefrom. But what does the *symplokē* imply, and what are its narrative effects?

For Polybius, due to the *symplokē* the *dramatis personae* of history get significantly extended, and the entropy of history—as I like to call it—increases. The term "entropy" is perfectly suited to describe the idea of the *symplokē* in Polybius. Moreover, it enables us to recognize the consequences which—in Polybius' view—result from the *symplokē*. When applied to Polybius' idea of history, namely *symplokē*, the concept of entropy can illuminate further implications of Polybius' perception of the historical process in the third and second centuries BCE. In general, entropy serves as a quantitative measure for disorder in a thermodynamic system. If there are only two or three moving particles in a closed, fixed volume, one can more or less foresee what is going to happen, where possible collisions of the particles might occur. But if there are more particles, moving

---

πόλεμον καὶ τὴν κατάλυσιν τῆς ἐν Μακεδονίᾳ βασιλείας. δι' ὧν ἅμα θεωρηθήσεται πῶς ἕκαστα χειρίσαντες Ῥωμαῖοι πᾶσαν ἐποιήσαντο τὴν οἰκουμένην ὑπήκοον αὑτοῖς.

16 Polybius' allusions to the problem of a "simultaneous" narrative of events, which happened at the same time, point out that the historian faces a new challenge which is due to the entanglement of historical occurrences taking place at different regions but being inextricably linked together. Concerning this problem, which becomes more and more important in Hellenistic historiography, see Maier 2016.

with more energy, the entropy is increased, triggering a higher degree of randomness and disorder. The movement and the sequences of the particles can no longer be predicted.[17] Even though existing conditions (like volume, energy, pressure and temperature) are known, the results of the movements cannot be anticipated.

Applied to history, the correlation between agents and particles is congruent. If there are only a small number of agents, e.g. two parties fighting each other, the movements of each faction are fairly comprehensible. But if the number of agents in history is significantly higher and the "energy"—that is the level of interaction between agents due to the entanglement of formerly unlinked spaces—increases, the whole process becomes unpredictable and leads to accidental occurrences.[18]

Therefore, it is *symplokē* which in Polybius' view made history unforeseeable, because the merging of political events in Africa, Italy and Asia increased historical entropy. Within the *Historiai* we come across many instances in which the Greek historian makes us realize that the increased entropy of history led to complex constellations, making the whole system unpredictable. Polybius applies subtle narrative techniques to make us aware of the coincidental character of history and reality. One of the best examples is Book 5. Therein, the narrative focuses on the struggle for power over Seleucia between Ptolemy IV and Antiochus III during the Fourth Syrian War (219–217 BCE). But Polybius does not narrow his account to mere military matters; instead, he goes far afield, describing plenty of domestic political affairs which preceded the final battle of Raphia and which influenced the course of events. The net of agents becomes more and more dense, their interaction closer and closer. Thus, the entropy of the historical process is increased.

When analyzing the end of the episode, the account of the battle of Raphia, both Ptolemy and Antiochus again appear as the "Great Men" (Carlyle) of history, commanding their troops and trying to outplay their respective opponents. The detailed description of their battle lines and their designs evokes the impression that it was a conflict between two men, not between two armies.[19] However, going back to the prelude of the battle, the reader is confronted with a completely different picture. Polybius first characterizes Ptolemy as "inattentive"

---

17 Sasse 1979, 14–15.
18 I am completely aware of the fact that the scientific term entropy does not fully match the historical constellation I sketched out, but my aim is to establish a term which concisely covers a complex matter.
19 Plb. 5.82.1–13. See also 5.85.8 and 5.86.1.

(ἀνεπίστατον) and "careless" (ὀλίγωρον), as he did not show himself vigilant in regard to affairs inside and outside of Egypt.[20] In the following chapters, the reader realizes why Polybius criticized the Egyptian king: Ptolemy believed that he could control everything, that he had every factor which could influence his life in mind; but he did not take into consideration the increased historical entropy—both inside and outside of Egypt.

Polybius next presents an elaborate narrative, introducing again and again new protagonists with new plans and new courses of action and freely switching between various narrative subjects. These consistent changes of perspective make it clear to the reader that Ptolemy was careless indeed, as he did not take into account this increased entropy, believing he could predict or control the movements of just a few "particles". First, Ptolemy's power is affected by the Spartan king Cleomenes, who was granted asylum in Egypt at that time.[21] Cleomenes suddenly wished to return to Sparta, for three reasons, all of which completely were out of Ptolemy's control, but which had a massive influence on his affairs: King Antigonus died, the Achaeans were busy with war, and the Spartans became allied to the Aetolians against the Achaeans and the Macedonians.[22] These combined incidents, which lead to a unique situation and come into being far from Egypt without any opportunity for Ptolemy to influence or control them, are the most important factors in Cleomenes' decision to return to Sparta and his attempt to seize the throne. This, however, provokes conflicting interests, as Ptolemy fears a mighty Cleomenes in Sparta and attempts to prevent it by any means. Interestingly, Polybius does not describe the following acts from Ptolemy's point of view, but from the perspective of Sosibius, the king's top adviser, who was in charge of all government affairs at that time.[23] Sosibius, however, has no plan for how to remove Cleomenes. He takes council with some other advisers, but they

---

20 Plb. 5.34.3–4.
21 Plb. 2.69.11 and 3.35.1. As Polybius points out that Ptolemy's predecessors were far more able to exercise control over Syria, Coile-Syria and Cyprus, we get a brief glimpse both into what might have happened to Ptolemy (but did not) and which factors were to occur autonomously without any influence by Ptolemy.
22 Plb. 5.35.2: οἱ δὲ κατὰ τὴν Ἑλλάδα καιροὶ μόνον οὐκ ἐπ' ὀνόματος ἐκάλουν τὸν Κλεομένην, μετηλλαχότος μὲν Ἀντιγόνου, πολεμουμένων δὲ τῶν Ἀχαιῶν, κοινωνούντων δὲ τῶν Λακεδαιμονίων Αἰτωλοῖς τῆς πρὸς Ἀχαιοὺς καὶ Μακεδόνας ἀπεχθείας κατὰ τὴν ἐξ ἀρχῆς ἐπιβολὴν καὶ πρόθεσιν τὴν Κλεομένους ("Circumstances in Greece almost called aloud for Cleomenes, Antigonus being dead, the Achaeans being engaged in war, and the Spartans now, as Cleomenes had from the first planned and purposed, sharing the hatred of the Aetolians for the Achaeans and Macedonians").
23 Plb. 5.35.7–5.36.7.

are unable to conceive a plan either to get rid of Cleomenes or to keep him in Egypt against his will.²⁴ But all of a sudden Sosibius'—and Ptolemy's—troubles evaporate: Polybius tells us that "an incident" (συνέργημα) occurred which saved the situation for the Egyptians. By chance, Sosibius meets the Messenian Nicagoras who, he discovers, is a fierce enemy of Cleomenes.²⁵ Polybius then goes on to explain in detail how this favorable constellation came about: Nicagoras has been involved in a peace treaty between Archidamus and Cleomenes, which in the end had been broken off by Cleomenes. Nicagoras still feels humiliated by Cleomenes' betrayal of confidence. When he happens to run into Cleomenes at the harbor of Alexandria, he turns to Sosibius and helps him to plot Cleomenes' death.²⁶

With Cleomenes dead, Ptolemy can launch the military campaign against Antiochus. Both leaders clash at Raphia, but now the reader is well aware that this final encounter was just *one* of many possible paths which history could have taken. A close analysis of Polybius' narration yields numerous points of interest. Firstly, Polybius' narrative strategy of introducing a great number of agents shows that Ptolemy's victory, which is the actual result of the whole episode spanning from the Cleomenes affair to Raphia, should not be ascribed to the king's efforts, but rather should be considered the result of several interferences initiated by various protagonists.²⁷ Secondly, how closely Ptolemy's reign teetered on the brink of disaster is highlighted by Polybius' elaborate technique of interlacing different levels of narration into one another. After the exposition, the narrative switches to the second level "Sosibius", on which all lines of action continue independently from Ptolemy's range of influence. Subsequently, the narrative reaches a third level, that of "Nicagoras", which similarly ties a couple of events together which are causally connected with Egypt but also characterized

---

24 Plb. 5.35.7–13.
25 Plb. 5.37.1–7. It is striking how Nicagoras is introduced: Νικαγόρας τις ἦν Μεσσήνιος, which certainly alludes to Xen. *Anab.* 3.1.4 with the famous phrase ἦν δέ τις ἐν τῇ στρατιᾷ Ξενοφῶν Ἀθηναῖος, where likewise emerges an accidental constellation including someone hitherto unknown appearing on the stage of history and significantly influencing the line of events. The suddenness is marked by the Greek indefinite pronoun *tis*, which, being an enclitic, has an inferior grammatical value and therefore perfectly portrays the coming "out of nowhere".
26 Plb. 5.37.7–5.39.5.
27 Therefore, Ptolemy's final success at Raphia stands in sharp contrast to his manners and his behavior displayed before and during the battle against Antiochus. By his subtle narrative technique, Polybius succeeds in conveying the idea that the Egyptian king's achievement of keeping his power intact was less the result of praiseworthy leadership ability (which Ptolemy did, however, demonstrate at Raphia and which Polybius was bound to emphasize), but in fact more due to accidental events whose interplay eventually secured his reign.

by an autonomous momentum which is far removed from Ptolemy's realm. In between these different levels of historical operation, the actions of many key players intersect and affect one another, thereby leading to accidental occurrences which directly or indirectly influence Ptolemy's situation.[28] If we look at the interplay of all these narrative levels, we immediately realize that the more protagonists are involved in the action, the larger the spectrum of options which history could have followed. In other words: the higher the historical entropy, the less predictable the interaction of the players involved.

We come across these effects of higher entropy in history due to the *symplokē* in other passages.[29] Polybius wants his readers to know that history for contemporaries is not predictable and, for the people looking at it retrospectively, a *paradoxon*—meaning that it does not happen according to what might have been expected, and that it is highly contingent.

2

These examples demonstrate that Polybius perceived history as a process in which the interaction of his protagonists leads to multiple actions of multiple agents, affecting each other and therefore triggering unexpected events, triggering *paradoxa*. But this idea of history does not mean that we can neither understand the causes of past or present events nor grasp the functional interaction of decisive factors. Polybius is convinced that we are able to recognize how a historical process or event came about. This is where *theōrēma* comes in. However, Polybius' thinking is quite complex, and in order to comprehend its pattern, I would like to introduce another metaphor, this time from biology and philosophy: emergence.

"Emergence" refers to a structure in which phenomena on the micro-level can be explained, whereas their interaction cannot, let alone be predicted.[30] The

---

[28] Consequently, Polybius does not mention Ptolemy in the text after the introduction and the final episode at Raphia, thus emphasizing that things were completely out of his reach.
[29] E.g. in Polybius' account on the so-called mercenary war, micro-factors, like the slaves Spendios and Mathios, spark off a riot, which has serious consequences for the Carthaginians' reaction to the war lost to the Romans, for their strategy of the years to come and also on the Romans' behavior against the defeated enemy.
[30] The classical definition is from Broad 1925, 61: "Put in abstract terms the emergent theory asserts that there are certain wholes, composed (say) of constituents A, B, and C in a relation R

concept of emergence can help one understand to what extent Polybius perceives history as an understandable yet simultaneously incomprehensible process, as a *paradoxon theōrēma*. In Book 3 Polybius relates the conflict between Hannibal and the Carpesians. At the end of the episode, he summarizes that the Carthaginians won "against all expectations and predictably" (παραδόξως καὶ κατὰ λόγον).[31]

So what does this mean? We can understand Polybius' seemingly contradictory conclusion if we have a look at the different layers of his account: At the beginning of the story, Polybius informs his readers that the Carpesians were the strongest tribe in the region and that they—from an impartial point of view—should have beaten their enemy.[32] But then Polybius explains how Hannibal made an accurate and excellent plan; he virtually allows us to look over the Carthaginian general's shoulder, sharing his thoughts and strategy. After that, Polybius describes the battle, making clear that every part of the plan Hannibal had set up was playing out. From that angle, we suddenly understand the originally rather cryptic phrase *paradoxōs kai kata logon*: Hannibal won, and this victory may be attributed, to a certain degree, to his careful and magnificent planning skills. But his triumph still remains a *paradoxon*, since despite the brilliant strategy of the Carthaginian general many other things could have happened. Polybius wants us to realize that a crucial defeat was as probable as a stunning victory. It was a *paradoxon theōrēma*.[33]

---

to each other; that all wholes composed of constituents of the same kind as A, B, and C in relations of the same kind as R have certain characteristic properties; that A, B, and C are capable of occurring in other kinds of complex where the relation is not the same kind as R; and that the characteristic properties of the whole R(A,B,C) cannot, even in theory, be deduced from the most complete knowledge of the properties of A, B, and C in isolation or in other wholes which are not of the form R(A,B,C)". The term Emergence was coined by the English philosopher George Henry Lewes in the nineteenth century, but its principle goes back to Aristotle *Metaph.* 1041b10: "Now since that which is composed of something in such a way that the whole is a unity; not as an aggregate is a unity, but as a syllable is—the syllable is not the letters, nor is BA the same as B and A; nor is flesh fire and earth; because after dissolution the compounds, e.g. flesh or the syllable, no longer exist; but the letters exist, and so do fire and earth. Therefore the syllable is some particular thing; not merely the letters, vowel and consonant, but something else besides. And flesh is not merely fire and earth, or hot and cold, but something else besides".

31 Plb. 3.14.5.
32 Plb. 3.14.2–3.
33 *paradoxōs kai kata logon* could also refer to the different perspectives of the protagonists involved: For the Carpesians, Hannibal's victory was a *paradoxon*, whereas for the Carthaginian general his success happened *kata logon*.

Another example: When narrating the battle at Eknomos (256 BCE), Polybius elaborates on the tactics of both sides, dwelling extensively on the battle array of both the Carthaginians and the Romans.[34] Then, during his report of the battle action, Polybius describes every move, emphasizing the equal strength of both parties.[35] In the end, the historian comes to the final phase of the battle. Here the reader comes across an interesting explanation for its result: Polybius says that— as is apparently usually the case—the battle was decided exactly where it began. But without referring to any cause, without mentioning any decisive factor, Polybius merely concludes that Hamilcar's ships were conquered and Hannibal's fleet surrounded. This final remark forms a stunning contrast to Polybius' previous, highly detailed and meticulous description of every precondition and action of the battle. Considering Polybius' usually thorough, accurate and comprehensive analysis of historical events, one might wonder whether Polybius fails here at being a good historian, as his account disappoints any reader interested in a coherent and plausible explanation for why the Romans actually won. But such criticism would be inadequate. Polybius wants us to comprehend the emergent character of history. He shows us that we can trace all strategies, actions and moves; but the final outcome of the battle is not predictable or deducible from all the preconditions that have been taken into account. History is not the result of an equation; we cannot sum up all the parts and then calculate the outcome. History is therefore not a *theōrēma*, but a *paradoxon theōrēma*.

There are other examples which could be referenced when talking about emergence. And they can be combined with what has been said about Polybius' entropy of history. In Book 1 Polybius informs his readers about the numerous conflicts between Romans and Carthaginians around Mount Eryx. In this context, he justifies his way of reporting the events, stating that it would be impossible to report every move both sides made at that time: "The causes or the modes of their daily ambuscades, counter-ambuscades, attempts, and assaults were so numerous that no writer could properly describe them, while at the same time the narrative would be most tedious as well as unprofitable to the reader".[36] Polybius' words— "that no writer could properly describe them"—are striking. Paton translates ἐξαριθμούμενος with "describe", but it would be rather something like "to

---

34 Plb. 1.26.1–1.27.6.
35 Plb. 1.28.4: "However, in each case things fell out as one would expect, when the forces engaged are so equally matched".
36 Plb. 1.57.3: τὰς μὲν γὰρ αἰτίας ἢ τοὺς τρόπους, δι' ὧν ἂν' ἑκάστην ἡμέραν ἐποιοῦντο κατ' ἀλλήλων ἐνέδρας, ἀντενέδρας, ἐπιθέσεις, προσβολάς, οὔτ' ἂν ὁ γράφων ἐξαριθμούμενος ἐφίκοιτο, τοῖς τ' ἀκούουσιν ἀπέραντος ἅμα δ' ἀνωφελὴς ἂν ἐκ τῆς ἀναγνώσεως γίνοιτο χρεία.

count out", as it refers to Polybius' admission of not being able to spot all moves carried out by the two opponents. For Polybius, past events cannot be put into equations adequate to calculate a final outcome.

3

The concepts of entropy and emergence help one to understand Polybius' approach *to* and his complex idea *of* history: He perceives history as something which is explainable, yet at the same time contrary to expectation; it constitutes something akin to an inconsistent system or an incomprehensible theorem. In this section, I would like to shed light on why the particular idea of history as a *paradoxon theōrēma* has something to do with Polybius' intention of writing the *Historiai*.

When looking into Polybius' strategies for describing history as a *paradoxon*, there is one issue that arises: With history as *paradoxon*, he runs the risk of undermining the main objective of his historiography—teaching his readers to learn from history. How could his readers draw lessons from history if they were told that there is nothing predictable or foreseeable within it? What should encourage military readers when they realize that even great generals such as Hannibal, who had ingeniously planned his campaigns and military operations, were doomed to come out on the short end?

The starting point for the following considerations is text passage 9.12. Here, Polybius addresses the question of how his readers, seeking military advice, could succeed in the future by using lessons learned from the past. We come across a statement which perfectly represents Polybius' lesson for his readers:[37]

> And it is no less easy to be convinced by facts that in those actions [*sc.* acting in war] depending on the choice of opportunity failure is far more frequent than success.

By examining the past ("to be convinced by facts"), we must conclude that "failure is far more frequent than success". In this instance, it seems as if the *paradoxon* would not allow for guaranteed success. But immediately afterwards it becomes clear that this depressing perspective does not stand for a type of

---

[37] Plb. 9.12.3: ὅτι γε μὴν αὐτῶν τῶν ἐν καιρῷ πάλιν ἐνεργουμένων πλείω γίνεται τὰ διαμαρτανόμενα τῶν κατορθουμένων, οὐδὲ τοῦτο γνῶναι χαλεπὸν ἐκ τῶν συμβαινόντων.

normative Nihilism or a farewell to human capability. In the same passage, Polybius points out that it is possible—not guaranteed, but possible—to be successful:[38]

> The accidents attendant on military projects require much circumspection, but success is in every case possible if the steps we take to carry out our plan are soundly reasoned out.

Thus, if we use our senses, acting rationally and prudently (σὺν νῷ τις πράττῃ), there is a chance (ἔστι δὲ δυνατόν) that we can be successful. Learning from history is also helpful. Therefore, from time to time, Polybius provides some clues and hints about recurring patterns, which can be applied to situations in the future.[39] But success is not guaranteed, due to the contingent character of reality. Thus, if we make no preparations at all, we are doomed to failure. But if we draw up a decent plan, if we try to take into account as much as possible and—most importantly—if we are aware of the limits of our planning, if we accept that reality cannot be calculated completely, then we will have a great chance of being successful.

This didactic goal can also be deduced from Polybius' description of historical events and his comments on the protagonists' actions: In Book 8, when describing the death of Tib. Sempronius Gracchus, who was ambushed and killed by his enemies in 212, Polybius does not blame the Roman general. Although his death was, technically speaking, a defeat, Polybius points out that Sempronius had made no mistake, as he had acted rationally and *kata logon*.[40] But due to certain circumstances which could not have been foreseen this defeat could not be

---

[38] Plb. 9.12.1: πολλὴν μὲν ἐπισκέψεως χρείαν ἔχει τὰ συμβαίνοντα περὶ τὰς πολεμικὰς ἐπιβολάς· ἔστι δὲ δυνατὸν ἐν ἑκάστοις αὐτῶν εὐστοχεῖν, ἐὰν σὺν νῷ τις πράττῃ τὸ προτεθέν. Later on, Polybius also says that "a single trivial error is sufficient to cause failure in a design, but correctness in every detail barely enough for success", Plb. 9.12.9–10.
[39] E.g. in Plb. 2.19.3–4 Polybius says that the Transalpine Gauls, after having made booty in Roman territory around 300 BCE, fell out with each other over the division of the spoils and succeeded in destroying the greater part of their own forces and of the booty itself. Polybius comments that "this is quite a common event among the Gauls, when they have appropriated their neighbor's property" (εἰς δὲ τὴν οἰκείαν ἀφικόμενοι καὶ στασιάσαντες περὶ τὴν τῶν εἰλημμένων πλεονεξίαν τῆς τε λείας καὶ τῆς αὑτῶν δυνάμεως τὸ πλεῖστον μέρος διέφθειραν. τοῦτο δὲ σύνηθές ἐστι Γαλάταις πράττειν, ἐπειδὰν σφετερίσωνταί τι τῶν πέλας). By using ἐπειδάν with the subjunctive, Polybius frames his statement as iterative behavior, which can be used to make calculations when similar situations may occur. Further examples in Maier 2012, 33–36. However, these examples should not be treated as if Polybius considered history and reality to be determined. He makes clear quite often that these "rules of thumb" do not always work.
[40] Plb. 8.36.1: ὅτι Τιβέριος ὁ Ῥωμαίων στρατηγὸς λόχῳ ἐνεδρευθεὶς καὶ γενναίως ὑποστὰς σὺν τοῖς περὶ αὐτὸν τὸν βίον κατέστρεψεν. περὶ δὲ τῶν τοιούτων περιπετειῶν, πότερα χρὴ τοῖς

avoided. Another example is the fate of Epaminondas. In Polybius' view, the Theban general had considered everything when capturing Sparta in 362. However, he was denied complete success by the Athenian troops when returning to Mantineia—a clash that he could not have foreseen at all. Here, the entropy of history triggered an accidental, indeed unexpected occurrence. In a dramatic phrase, Polybius makes the influence of *Tykhē* responsible, as if this coincidence were beyond human comprehension.[41]

Thus, Polybius' reader is presented the following conclusion: Even if one conceives rational plans, subtle strategies and attempts to have in mind all aspects and potential outcomes, success is still not guaranteed. Every one of us lives in a contingent environment, in which we can influence things to a certain extent, but never fully. But there is no need to surrender to contingency. Polybius makes clear that we have to take into account two things: Firstly, despite realities outside of our control, we nonetheless are compelled to act, to shape our fate by ourselves inasmuch as we can. Secondly, if we adjust our plans and purposes by way of a rational method, we significantly increase our chances for success.

This kind of advice was certainly influenced by contemporary thinking. We find a similar paradigm in Menander's comedies. In these, *Tykhē* is presented as the omnipotent figure in control of everything, whose designs are not known to anybody and who seems to influence events according to her will.[42] On the other hand there are the plans, ideas and wishes of the protagonists. As Gregor Vogt-Spira has convincingly shown, both spheres constantly interact: the will of fate and the will of the protagonists intersect. But despite *Tykhē*'s power, the protagonists can yet hope to succeed—under one condition. For example, in the *Dyskolos*, Sostratus achieves his goal—getting married to Cnemon's daughter—by the influence of *Tykhē*. But, and Menander keeps pointing to it throughout the whole text, equally important and essential was Sostratus' willingness, his cunning plans and strategies while pursuing his aim. If he had not shown such commitment, all other incidents—like Cnemon's fall into the fountain—would not have contributed in any way to the ultimately (for him) happy ending.[43]

Polybius' idea of learning from history might also have been shaped by his own biography. Arthur Eckstein, in a groundbreaking book on Polybius in 1995,

---

πάσχουσιν ἐπιτιμᾶν ἢ συγγνώμην ἔχειν, καθόλου μὲν οὐκ ἀσφαλὲς ἀποφήνασθαι διὰ τὸ καὶ πλείους τὰ κατὰ λόγον πάντα πράξαντας, ὅμως ὑποχειρίους γεγονέναι τοῖς ἑτοίμως τὰ παρ' ἀνθρώποις ὡρισμένα δίκαια παραβαίνουσιν. See also for the same evaluation Plb. 2.7.1–3.
41 Plb. 9.8.13.
42 Men. frg. 372 K.–A.: τύχη κυβερνᾶι πάντα, see also Men. *Asp.* 146–148, frg. 860 K.-A., frg. 682 K.-A.
43 Vogt-Spira 1992, 69.

emphasized that Polybius was hugely influenced by men like Lycortas or Philopoemen. Although Rome more and more took over control of Greece, and despite the complex political situation, these men did not leave everything to the Romans' will, but pursued an active policy, taking charge of their own fates.[44] Since Polybius had been brought up in this context, he wrote appraisals for men who failed in history, but who attempted to be successful by active commitment.[45] These statements "serve his audience as an inspiration to attempt achievement of noble deeds".[46] Eckstein therefore coined the term "nobility of action", referring to the potential audience of Polybius' texts: the Greek aristocrats who are encouraged by Polybius to act, to shape fate with their own hands.[47]

Besides the "duty to act" (Eckstein), Polybius' lesson for the reader is interesting with regard to other approaches. Polybius' idea of history as a *paradoxon theōrēma* also means that he does not want to provide a handbook for how to achieve success in every situation with detailed advice for any or all potential occurrences and situations. Instead, he chooses a different way, giving his readers more general advice on how to deal with unexpected incidents and what idea one should have of the relation between one's plan and reality. If we look at one of Polybius' colleagues, not as historiographer but rather as military writer, we find some remarkably different views and concepts. Aeneas Tacticus, who wrote a treatise on issues in military science and therefore touched upon similar topics, adopted a completely different approach. He presented clear and precise instructions for his readers. Aeneas was very focused on providing as many hints, tips and tricks as possible in order to prepare the reader to deal with the unexpected. He tried to provide a prescription or a solution for every scenario imaginable. With such an approach to potential situations, he was confident he could equip his clients with an adequate guide which would guarantee success in all the challenges they were to face in the future.[48]

---

[44] Marincola 1997, 25: "When Polybius wrote, the states of Greece were only coming to know their Roman master, and there was still a role for political men to play, even under Roman hegemony, as Polybius' own later career made plain".
[45] One of the most prominent ones is the obituary on Hasdrubal who, besides his rational planning and enterprising spirit, represented another of Polybius' main virtues: He accepted his fate with dignity, cf. Plb. 11.2.3 (γενναίως τὰς περιπετείας καὶ τὰς ἐλαττώσεις διετέλει φέρων) and Plb. 1.1.2 (τοῦ δύνασθαι τὰς τῆς τύχης μεταβολὰς γενναίως ὑποφέρειν).
[46] Eckstein 1995, 273 with reference to Plb. 23.14.12. "Mortals may be helpless before circumstances ... but that does not relieve Polybius' aristocratic audience of the duty to act".
[47] Several honorary decrees also testify that political men were judged by their deeds, e.g. I. Sestos 1, 38–41, I. Priene 107.
[48] Whitehead 1990, 17–21.

Polybius, who also wanted to give military advice to his readers, took another path. He refrained from presenting specific suggestions and detailing how to cope with a particular situation; instead, he chose to provide a general guide. But it is not only this formal feature which differs. It is also his concept of a contingent reality which stands out. One text passage perfectly illustrates this idea: In Book 10 Polybius discusses methods of signaling messages by fire in war. He considers the use of fire-signaling as one of the most efficient ways to communicate over long distances. Before presenting his own opinion about the best device, Polybius refers to Aeneas Tacticus and his proposal for sending messages by fire-signaling. Aeneas suggested arranging specific messages like "Cavalry has arrived", "Heavy infantry", "Light-armed infantry", "Infantry and cavalry", "Ships", which then could be relayed by the respective signal. But Polybius immediately points out a precarious flaw in this method, saying that it only refers to the most evident and ordinary events that occur in war. Reality cannot be squeezed into a couple of fire-borne phrases. Therefore, it is both indefinite and deficient:[49]

> For it is evident that it is neither possible to foresee all contingencies, or even if one did to write them all on the rod. So that when circumstances produce some unexpected event, it is evident that it cannot be conveyed by this plan.

Polybius criticizes that Aeneas takes reality as a *theōrēma*, as something which can be systemized, disregarding the option of the unexpected, of the *paradoxon*. Polybius wanted his readers to realize that they cannot control everything, even if they take all measures to make their plans as coherent as possible. The contingency of reality will prevent most human purposes or intentions from reaching fruition, an opinion which certainly was influenced by Polybius' idea of the past. Therefore, Polybius did not give a "list of solutions", as he described Aeneas' approach,[50] but instead wanted his readers to learn from his presentation of the past that they should plan as much as possible, but that they should factor in the unforeseeable and incalculable. In another text passage, when reporting the defeat of the Medionians against the Aetolians, he frames the purpose of his book as a

---

49 Plb. 10.45.2: δῆλον γὰρ [ἔσται] ὡς οὔτε προϊδέσθαι τὰ μέλλοντα πάντα δυνατὸν οὔτε προϊδόμενον εἰς τὴν βακτηρίαν γράψαι· λοιπὸν ὁπόταν ἐκ τῶν καιρῶν ἀνυπονόητά τινα συμβαίνῃ, φανερὸν ὡς οὐ δύναται δηλοῦσθαι κατὰ ταύτην τὴν ἐπίνοιαν.
50 Plb. 10.44.1: Αἰνείας δὲ βουληθεὶς διορθώσασθαι τὴν τοιαύτην ἀπορίαν, ὁ τὰ περὶ τῶν Στρατηγικῶν ὑπομνήματα συντεταγμένος, βραχὺ μέν τι προεβίβασε, τοῦ γε μὴν δέοντος ἀκμὴν πάμπολυ τὸ κατὰ τὴν ἐπίνοιαν ἀπελείφθη ("Aeneas, the author of the work on strategy, wishing to find a remedy for the difficulty, advanced matters a little, but his device still fell far short of our requirements, as can be seen from this description of it").

lesson to mankind never to discuss the future as if it were the present, or to have any confident hope about things that may still turn out quite otherwise. We are but men, and should in every matter assign its share to the unexpected, this being especially true of war.[51]

One final point: Again, Polybius' emphasis of the unexpected, of the *paradoxon*, does not turn out to be a nihilistic notion of human capacity. Instead, he encourages his readers to exploit this uncertainty, the contingency of reality. For this lesson, he provides famous examples: During the First Punic War, he says, the Romans did not abandon the war, although they had suffered terrible losses due to storms and other catastrophes. They persevered, since they knew that they would be offered new opportunities, if they kept planning prudently and acting wisely:[52]

> Yet so determined were the Romans to bring the whole struggle to a successful issue, that, notwithstanding this reverse, they left undone nothing that was in their power, and prepared to continue the campaign.

Their awareness of "contingency"[53] made the Romans keep rethinking their situation and trying to fight the Carthaginians in further sea battles. History proved they were right. There are many other passages, which serve as examples for the reader to illustrate the potential of contingency.[54] Thus, Polybius wants to show us that uncertainty and contingency should not be construed as disadvantages or obstacles; rather, they should be exploited since they offer us the chance to achieve something hitherto considered impossible.

4

To conclude: The starting point of my considerations was Polybius' description of history as a *paradoxon theōrēma*. In the following chapters, I showed that this

---

51 Plb. 2.4.5: Αἰτωλοὶ δὲ τῇ παραδόξῳ χρησάμενοι συμφορᾷ πάντας ἐδίδαξαν μηδέποτε βουλεύεσθαι περὶ τοῦ μέλλοντος ὡς ἤδη γεγονότος, μηδὲ προκατελπίζειν βεβαιουμένους ὑπὲρ ὧν ἀκμὴν ἐνδεχόμενόν ἐστιν ἄλλως γενέσθαι, νέμειν δὲ μερίδα τῷ παραδόξῳ πανταχῇ μὲν ἀνθρώπους ὄντας, μάλιστα δ' ἐν τοῖς πολεμικοῖς.
52 Plb. 1.52.4: οὐ μὴν οἵ γε Ῥωμαῖοι, καίπερ τοιούτων συμβεβηκότων, διὰ τὴν ὑπὲρ τῶν ὅλων φιλοτιμίαν οὐδὲν ἀπέλειπον τῶν ἐνδεχομένων, ἀλλ' εἴχοντο τῶν ἑξῆς πραγμάτων.
53 The term ἐνδεχόμενον is here certainly related to Aristotle's conception of contingency, see Arist. *APr.* 32a18–20 and 32b4–13, *Int.* 19a7-22, Maier 2012, 99–102.
54 Philipp's conquest of Psophis, a city considered impregnable, Plb. 4.70; similarly, the capture of Sardis by Antiochos in 214, Plb. 7.15, see Maier 2012, 286–88.

contradictory but often overlooked phrase serves as a perfect characterization of how Polybius perceived history: As a process which cannot be systemized, either from the retrospective or from the present, since too many factors interact due to *symplokē*. On the other hand, the study of history does reveal some general patterns which, however, never play out exactly the same as they once did.

By applying the concepts of entropy and emergence to Polybius' idea of history, I have attempted to demonstrate that it is precisely the apparently contradictory character of *paradoxon theōrēma*, with which Polybius is able to grasp the nature of history on various levels: from the perspective of the protagonists involved, from the retrospective of historians reconstructing the past, and from the viewpoint of political and military leaders keen on learning from history for their present and the future. And although Polybius' idea of the past is a complex and challenging concept, its bipolar structure forces the reader to look at history from different angles and to think about history as a phenomenon which invariably escapes all attempts to systemize its nature or to fully understand all its mechanisms.

Despite the proud tone in the first chapters of his *Historiai* in which Polybius claims to provide an exact report on how the Romans became masters of the world, there is an ever-present subtext reminding the reader that the historian can only give an approximate explanation for past events, which is a *paradoxon*. However, according to Polybius, the historian is obliged to strive for the best explanation of why history happened the way it happened; the same applies to the political and military leader, who has to plan and to calculate as well as possible. This is where *theōrēma* comes in. But ultimately he must accept that he will not be able to foresee everything, even if he thinks that he has learned from history. History does not repeat itself, it merely rhymes.

Bibliography

Broad, C.D. (1925), *The mind and its place in nature*, London.
Frazier, F. (2002), "L'inattendu et l'extraordinaire. Les emplois de ‹paradoxos› dans les Histoires de Polybe", in: *Ktema* 27, 79–86.
Hau, L.I. (2011), "Tyche in Polybios. Narrative Answers to a Philosophical Question", in: *Histos* 5, 183–207.
Henderson, J. (2001), "From Megalopolis to Cosmopolis. Polybius, or there back again", in: S. Goldhill (ed.), *Being Greek under Rome. Cultural Identity, the Second Sophistic and the Development of Empire*, Cambridge, 29–49.
Maier, F. (2012), *"Überall mit dem Unerwarteten rechnen". Die Kontingenz historischer Prozesse bei Polybios*, Munich.
—— (2013), "How to Avoid Being a Backward-Looking Prophet—Counterfactuals in Polybius", in: A. Powell (ed.), *Hindsight in Greek and Roman History*, Oxford, 149–170.

—— (2016), "Chronotopos. Erzählung, Zeit und Raum im Hellenismus", in: *Klio* 98, 467–496.
Marincola, J. (1997), *Authority and Tradition in Ancient Historiography*, Cambridge.
Mauersberger, A. (1998), *Polybius-Lexikon*, Bd. 2/1, Berlin.
Miltsios, N. (2009), "The perils of expectations. Perceptions, suspense and surprise in Polybius' *Histories*", in: J. Grethlein/A. Rengakos (eds.), *Narratology and interpretation. The Content of Narrative Form in Ancient Literature*, Berlin, 481–506.
Mohm, S. (1977), *Untersuchungen zu den historiographischen Anschauungen des Polybios*, Saarbrücken.
Olson, J.M./N.J. Roese/R.J. Deibert (1996), "Psychological biases in counterfactual thought experiments", in: P.E. Tetlok/A. Belkin (eds.), *Counterfactual Thought Experiments in World Politics. Logical, Methodological, and Psychological perspectives*, Princeton, 296–300.
Pédech, P. (1964), *La méthode historique de Polybe*, Paris.
Roveri, A. (1982), "Tyche bei Polybios", in: K. Stiewe/N. Holzberg (eds.), *Wege der Forschung. Polybios*, Darmstadt, 297–326.
Sasse, J. (1979), *Entropie und Wahrscheinlichkeit. Untersuchungen zum Konzept einer elementaren Einführung des Entropiebegriffs auf mikrophysikalischer Basis*, Osnabrück.
Vogt-Spira, G. (1992), *Dramaturgie des Zufalls. Tyche und Handeln in der Komödie Menanders*, Munich.
Walbank, F.W. (1967), *A Historical Commentary on Polybius*, Vol. 2, Oxford.
—— (1972), *Polybius*, Berkeley.
—— (1975), "Symploke. Its role in Polybius' *Histories*", in: *YClS* 24, 197–212.
—— (2002), *Polybius, Rome, and the Hellenistic World*, Cambridge.
Whitehead, D. (1990), *Aeneas the Tactician*, Oxford.
Ziegler, K. (1952), "Polybios", in: *RE* 21.2, 1440–1578.

Bruce Gibson
Praise in Polybius[1]

Polybius has regularly been cast as a polemical historian, in the light of passages such as his trenchant criticisms of Timaeus in Book 12.[2] This chapter will instead turn the focus in the other direction, in order to examine praise in Polybius' work. The first section will examine the representation of praise within Polybius' narrative. The second and third sections will then consider Polybius' theorizing of praise and flattery, and his use of the terminology of epideictic. The last two sections will then examine evaluative praise conferred by Polybius in his text, and will suggest that the epideictic element of Polybius' writing has an ethical element as well, which can also be linked to Polybius' own role as a bestower of praise or blame.[3]

1 The representation of praise within Polybius' narrative

This section of this chapter will examine how praise is depicted within Polybius' narrative. To begin at the simplest level, we find a number of occasions where a speech act of praise is recorded by Polybius.[4] Thus, at 1.45.4, we hear of how Himilco, a Carthaginian commander, gave a speech and thereafter praised his men as he dismissed them. Similarly, at 1.49.11, another Carthaginian commander, Adherbal, responds to his men's call to lead them to the fight, and is recorded as praising them. On both these occasions ἐπαινέσας, the aorist participle of ἐπαινέω, is used as a simple report of a speech act, where a general praises

---
[1] I am indebted to Andrew Laird for his comments on a draft of this chapter.
[2] See e.g. Walbank 1962 and Meister 1975, a book-length study of historical criticism in Polybius, Miltsios 2013, 125–32. On Polybius and Timaeus in Book 12, see Baron 2009; 2013, 58–88; on Timaeus' own use of polemic and its context, see Baron 2013, 113–37.
[3] All translations of Polybius are taken from the second edition of Paton's Loeb translation with revisions by F.W. Walbank, C. Habicht (and the addition of the fragments edited and translated by S.D. Olson), 6 Vols. (Cambridge, Mass., 2010–2012), except where otherwise indicated.
[4] On oratory within Polybius' work, see Wooten 1974, Thornton 2013a. Thornton 2013b suggests a reading of the *Histories* as a "diplomatic speech"; see further Rubinstein 2013, especially 174–76, for the significance of oral performance in the context of Hellenistic diplomacy, and the possibility that performance of diplomatic speeches was "epideictic icing on a cake of real negotiations that had already taken place backstage" (174).

his troops.⁵ This can also occur in slightly less military settings, such as at 8.24.8, where Hannibal praises the Tarentines Philemenus and Nicon after their secret interview with him.⁶

There are also examples of praise from outside military life. At 21.41.6, the Roman commander Cn. Manlius praises embassies that he has received from Greek communities in Asia. Another diplomatic context for such praise, though a much bleaker one, occurs in Book 36, when the Roman consul praises the envoys from Carthage for coming to ask how they might conclude a settlement with the Romans (36.6.5).⁷ A more detailed example of praise is found at 22.3.8–9, when an envoy from Ptolemy V is being entertained by Philopoemen on behalf of the Achaean League; Polybius then gives the content in indirect discourse of the envoy's praise of his king's prowess in hunting and horsemanship.⁸

These are all straightforward examples of speech acts of praise within the narrative, occurring in military and in non-military contexts. Polybius, however, uses more complex examples to demonstrate the prestige of praise and its enhancing qualities. The celebrated discussion of the Roman funeral oration and of the *imagines* of ancestors in 6.53–4 shows the social power of praise,⁹ with Polybius describing how the orator praises the qualities and accomplishments of the deceased (6.53.2). The speech has the effect of moving the whole populace (6.53.3), not just those who were involved in the dead man's achievements: the loss is truly a public one. After describing the Roman custom of carrying *imagines*, Polybius then explains that the funeral oration is not just about the dead man, but also about the lives and great deeds of those whose images are carried in the funeral procession (6.54.1). The funeral not only ensures the survival of the fame of those commemorated in the speech, but also provides an incentive to the young who are stirred to seek glory for themselves in the future (6.54.3). Praise in this case is not merely something formulaic, but something which can shape future behaviour. Another example occurs in Polybius' discussion of the young Scipio Aemilianus at 31.29.8–12. Here Polybius observes that whereas Scipio's contemporaries sought to win praise by their activities in prosecutions in the law courts (31.29.10), Scipio was able to win a splendid reputation for bravery (τὴν ἐπ' ἀνδρείᾳ δόξαν πάνδημον, 31.29.11) without recourse to such activities. Again,

---

5 Another example is the praise given by Hannibal to his troops at 3.34.9.
6 See also Hannibal's motivation of his troops at 3.13.8 and 3.17.10 with Miltsios 2013, 68.
7 On the identity of this consul, see Walbank 1979, 658 *ad loc.*
8 On this passage, see further Farrington 2011, 327.
9 On the *pompa funebris*, see Flower 1996, 91–127; on the funeral oration, see Flower 1996, 128–58. It should be noted that Polybius himself not infrequently presents death notices of characters in his narrative: see further Pomeroy 1986.

hope of praise and glory can be the spur to action, with both Scipio's contemporaries and Scipio himself embarking on their different routes to win such fame in Rome.[10]

The motivational power of praise in Polybius can be envisaged as affecting a whole nation: thus, at 21.22, when the Rhodians are seeking to restrict Eumenes' territorial gains in the aftermath of the war with Antiochus III, their embassy argues that the Romans have a chance to think instead of the freedom of the Greeks of Asia. The Rhodians then suggest to the Romans that their aims are of a higher character than those of ordinary men, since the normal rewards of war, territory, cities and the like, are superfluous for the Romans in view of the fact that the gods have already granted them world power (21.23.4). Instead, the Rhodians say that the focus of the Romans should be on praise: "obviously praise and glory among men, things difficult enough to acquire and still more difficult to keep when you have them", δῆλον ὡς ἐπαίνου καὶ δόξης παρ' ἀνθρώποις, ἃ καὶ κτήσασθαι μέν ἐστι (δυσχερές), δυσχερέστερον δὲ κτησαμένους διαφυλάξαι (21.23.6). The Rhodians go on (21.23.8–9) to refer to the tribute which Rome was able to impose on Carthage, but then point out that truly praiseworthy qualities (τὸ δὲ καλὸν καὶ πρὸς ἔπαινον καὶ τιμήν, 21.23.9) are in fact only for the gods and for those closest to them. In this fascinating discussion of how the desire for praise can be seen as a political motivation, it is striking that the message itself is cast in the form of praise, with the implicit comparison between the Romans and the gods. Not for nothing does Polybius tell us immediately afterwards of how the speech of the Rhodians went down well with the senate (21.23.13); in the general proposals for the settlement of Asia that ensue (21.24), the Rhodians are rewarded by being assigned territory in Lycia and Caria.

While praise in Polybius can have good effects, it can also have less attractive consequences. Vainglory is one possibility, as a couple of brief examples can illustrate. At 16.21.12 Tlepolemus, who Polybius notes is over-fond of fame (16.21.2) is affected by hearing praise of himself, and by other manifestations of approval such as toasts and inscriptions, so that he starts to behave with excessive conceit and give ever larger gifts to foreigners and to the soldiers. Likewise, Hermeias' disreputable self-praise (φορτικῶς μὲν αὐτὸν ἐγκωμιάζων) combined with his false accusations of Epigenes at 5.49.4 leads to a situation in which he displeases Antiochus III.[11]

Praise can also be given falsely, as when Machatas, trying to win over the Spartans to an alliance with the Aetolians, is described as ἀλόγως δὲ καὶ ψευδῶς

---

10 On Polybius' praise of Scipio Aemilianus in this passage, see McGing 2010, 163–64.
11 On this passage, see further Marincola 1997, 191 with n. 81, Farrington 2011, 337.

ἐγκωμιάζων τοὺς Αἰτωλούς (4.34.7). In this case, we may suppose, the praise may be factually erroneous, hence Polybius' use of the adverb ψευδῶς here, but Polybius is also willing to hint at the possibilities of insincere praise within his work. A notable example is the behaviour of Apelles at 4.87.1–4, who turns his attention against Taurion, in order to have him removed from oversight of Peloponnesian affairs. To accomplish this goal, Apelles' method is to praise Taurion repeatedly, and to say that he was a fit person to be assigned to the king's own protection, which causes Polybius to comment on the way in which this use of praise rather than censure to cause harm to one's enemies is a new feature (καινὸς γὰρ δή τις οὗτος εὕρηται τρόπος διαβολῆς τὸ μὴ ψέγοντας ἀλλ' ἐπαινοῦντας λυμαίνεσθαι τοὺς πέλας, 4.87.3), and one that is particularly appropriate to those who are in royal courts (4.87.4).[12] Another example occurs at 22.19, where Polybius refers to the dispute that Philopoemen had with a fellow Achaean, Archon, and expresses his disapproval at the use of praise in order to achieve harm, a passage which will be considered in more detail later in the last section.

We may turn now from false praise to flattery (κολακεία), which is certainly a possibility which Polybius is aware of; even within the more abstract contents of Book 6, where Polybius notes the dangers of the people being led astray as a result of flattery offered to it by office-holders (6.57.7). But Polybius is also willing to provide practical evidence as well for the dangers of flattery. Thus in 8.22, an enigmatic fragment dealing with the fall of Cavarus, the last Celtic king of Tylis in Thrace (on his kingdom, see 4.46), Polybius is said to have reported that the flatterer Sostratus played a part in his downfall (Πολύβιος ... ἐν ὀγδόῃ ἱστοριῶν, Καύαρος, φησίν, ὁ Γαλάτης, ὢν τἄλλα ἀνὴρ ἀγαθός, ὑπὸ Σωστράτου τοῦ κόλακος διεστρέφετο, 8.22.3). κολακεία also emerges in terms of behaviour of participants in Polybius' narrative towards the Romans. A noted example is the speech of the Achaean Callicrates to the senate in 180 BCE (24.9). Polybius, who has a very dim view of this particular Achaean statesman,[13] notes that, after Calllicrates' recommendation to the Romans only to further the advantage of those who would do their bidding, the senate was well-off in flatterers, but poorly supplied with friends (ἐξ ὧν αὐτῇ συνέβη κατὰ βραχύ, τοῦ χρόνου προβαίνοντος, κολάκων μὲν

---

[12] This concept of praise as a weapon that could be deployed by enemies appears in later texts, such as Tacitus' *Agricola*, where Tacitus comments on the way in which Agricola was harmed through the presence with the emperor of Domitian of "the worst kind of enemy, those who offer praise" (*pessimum inimicorum genus, laudantes*, Tac. *Ag.* 41.1; see further Woodman 2014, 294–95 *ad loc.*). Compare also *PanLat* 3(11).4.5–7 for Julian's enemies finding a way to harm him by praising him to Constantius II.

[13] On the embassy of Callicrates in 180 BCE and its context, see Derow 1970 (= Derow 2014, 169–79); Gruen 1984, 496–501; Eckstein 1995, 204-06, Champion 2004, 155–56, 225–26.

εὐπορεῖν, φίλων δὲ σπανίζειν ἀληθινῶν, 24.10.5).[14] Another moment of a similar but even more spectacular character occurs at 30.18.5, when the Bithynian king Prusias enters the senate and addresses its members as saving gods ("Χαίρετε, θεοὶ σωτῆρες"), prompting Polybius to comment on the extraordinary degree of effeminacy, womanish conduct and flattery which the king's debased conduct reflected (ὑπερβολὴν οὐ καταλιπὼν ἀνανδρίας, ἅμα δὲ καὶ γυναικισμοῦ καὶ κολακείας οὐδενὶ τῶν ἐπιγινομένων).

2 Flattery and the historian

We may now move from considering examples of praise within Polybius' narrative to examining how praise fits into Polybius' historical method. As we have seen, in terms of the contents of the narrative, praise is surprisingly present in Polybius' narrative, being found in military situations, in diplomacy and in politics. As we have seen, Polybius is well aware of the motivational power of praise both for individuals, and for broader groups, even for the Romans as a whole, as we find in the speech of the Rhodians at 21.23 discussed above, or indeed in the Roman funeral oration in 6.53–4.

Flattery is not just an issue for those living in Polybius' world. It is also a problem for those writing about the world, for historians. Polybius, indeed, is not the only historian keen to point out the flattery of competitors within his own work. Thus Polybius at 12.12b.2 reports that Timaeus blamed Callisthenes for being a flatterer towards Alexander, and endorsed Alexander's punishment of Callisthenes.[15] The passage continues with Polybius reporting that Timaeus praised Demosthenes and others for not seeking to confer divine honours on Alexander (12.12b.3).[16] Even though the wider context of this passage in Book 12 is Polybius' hostility to Timaeus, Callisthenes' excessive praise of Alexander illustrates the damage that can be caused to a historian's reputation by allegations of flattery.

---

14 Compare also 28.4.9, where Pantaleon criticizes Lyciscus in the Aetolian assembly for his flattery towards the Romans.
15 See further Walbank 1967, 353 *ad loc.*; Prandi 2005, 77–79, Baron 2013, 61.
16 See further Baron 2013, 123.

In 8.8, Polybius discusses the devastation caused by Philip V in Messenia in 213 BCE,[17] and contrasts his own treatment of these events with the way other historians had chosen either to ignore, or to praise such actions (8.8.3–7):[18]

> προήχθην δὲ καὶ νῦν καὶ διὰ τῆς προτέρας βύβλου σαφέστερον ἐξηγήσασθαι περὶ τούτων οὐ μόνον διὰ τὰς πρότερον ἡμῖν εἰρημένας αἰτίας, ἀλλὰ καὶ διὰ τὸ τῶν συγγραφέων τοὺς μὲν ὅλως παραλελοιπέναι τὰ κατὰ τοὺς Μεσσηνίους, τοὺς δὲ καθόλου διὰ τὴν πρὸς τοὺς μονάρχους εὔνοιαν ἢ τἀναντία φόβον οὐχ οἷον ἐν ἁμαρτίᾳ γεγονέναι τὴν εἰς τοὺς Μεσσηνίους ἀσέβειαν Φιλίππου καὶ παρανομίαν, ἀλλὰ τοὐναντίον ἐν ἐπαίνῳ καὶ κατορθώματι τὰ πεπραγμένα διασαφεῖν ἡμῖν. οὐ μόνον δὲ περὶ Μεσσηνίους τοῦτο πεποιηκότας ἰδεῖν ἔστι τοὺς γράφοντας τοῦ Φιλίππου τὰς πράξεις, ἀλλὰ καὶ περὶ τῶν ἄλλων παραπλησίως. ἐξ ὧν ἱστορίας μὲν οὐδαμῶς ἔχειν αὐτοῖς συμβαίνει διάθεσιν τὰς συντάξεις, ἐγκωμίου δὲ μᾶλλον. ἐγὼ δ' οὔτε λοιδορεῖν ψευδῶς φημι δεῖν τοὺς μονάρχους οὔτ' ἐγκωμιάζειν, ὃ πολλοῖς ἤδη συμβέβηκε, τὸν ἀκόλουθον δὲ τοῖς προγεγραμμένοις ἀεὶ καὶ τὸν πρέποντα ταῖς ἑκάστων προαιρέσεσι λόγον ἐφαρμόζειν.

What induced me to give a more explicit account of these matters in this and the previous book, was, in addition to the reasons I above stated, the fact that while some authors have left the occurrences in Messenia unnoticed others, owing either to their regard for the kings or their fear of them, have explained to us unreservedly, that not only did the outrages committed by Philip against the Messenians in defiance of divine or human law deserve no censure, but that on the contrary all his acts were to be regarded as praiseworthy achievements. It is not only with regard to the Messenians that we find the historians of Philip's life to be thus biased but in other cases, the result being that their works much more resemble panegyrics than histories. My own opinion is that we should neither revile nor extol kings falsely, as has so often been done, but always give an account of them consistent with our previous statements and in accord with the character of each.

In this passage, we can see an implicit contrast (8.8.6) between the work of Polybius on the one hand, characterized as ἱστορία and associated with balanced enquiry into the actions of kings who feature in his narrative, and panegyric (ἐγκώμιον) which he associates with those unnamed historians who have not troubled themselves with the more controversial actions of Philip V, or who have simply praised all his actions.[19]

This passage then leads immediately into a more focused attack on κολακεία directed against Theopompus, whom Polybius blames for his highly inflated praise of Philip II of Macedon at the opening of his work. At 8.9.1–4 Polybius

---

17 For the date, see Walbank 1967, 78.
18 For the wider context of Philip V's actions in Messenia within Polybius' treatment of the king, see now Nicholson 2015, 110–31.
19 See further on this passage Miltsios 2013, 129; Nicholson 2015, 122–23.

makes the point that Theopompus first tells us that never had Europe produced such a figure as Philip, before then going on to relate his various vices:

> Μάλιστα δ' ἄν τις ἐπιτιμήσειε περὶ τοῦτο τὸ μέρος Θεοπόμπῳ, ὅς γ' ἐν ἀρχῇ τῆς Φιλίππου συντάξεως δι' αὐτὸ μάλιστα παρορμηθῆναι φήσας πρὸς τὴν ἐπιβολὴν τῆς πραγματείας διὰ τὸ μηδέποτε τὴν Εὐρώπην ἐνηνοχέναι τοιοῦτον ἄνδρα παράπαν οἷον τὸν Ἀμύντου Φίλιππον, μετὰ ταῦτα παρὰ πόδας, ἔν τε τῷ προοιμίῳ καὶ παρ' ὅλην δὲ τὴν ἱστορίαν, ἀκρατέστατον μὲν αὐτὸν ἀποδείκνυσι πρὸς γυναῖκας, ὥστε καὶ τὸν ἴδιον οἶκον ἐσφαλκέναι τὸ καθ' αὑτὸν διὰ τὴν πρὸς τοῦτο τὸ μέρος ὁρμὴν καὶ προστασίαν, ἀδικώτατον δὲ καὶ κακοπραγμονέστατον περὶ τὰς τῶν φίλων καὶ συμμάχων κατασκευάς, πλείστας δὲ πόλεις ἐξηνδραποδισμένον καὶ πεπραξικοπηκότα μετὰ δόλου καὶ βίας, ἐκπαθῆ δὲ γεγονότα καὶ πρὸς τὰς ἀκρατοποσίας, ὥστε καὶ μεθ' ἡμέραν πλεονάκις μεθύοντα καταφανῆ γενέσθαι τοῖς φίλοις.

In this respect Theopompus is one of the writers who is most to blame. At the outset of his history of Philip, son of Amyntas, he states that what chiefly induced him to undertake this work was that Europe had never produced such a man before as this Philip; and yet immediately afterward in his preface and throughout the book he shows him to have been first so incontinent about women, that as far as in him lay he ruined his own home by his passionate and ostentatious addiction to this kind of thing; next a most wicked and mischievous man in his schemes for forming friendships and alliances; thirdly, one who had enslaved and betrayed a large number of cities by force or fraud; and lastly, one so addicted to strong drink that he was frequently seen by his friends manifestly drunk in broad daylight.

After a lengthy discussion pointing out the failings of Theopompus' analysis of Philip's ways, Polybius then returns to the issue directly at 8.11.1–2, saying that Theopompus is either to be considered to be a flatterer and a liar, or simply a fool:

> προθέμενος γὰρ ὡς περὶ βασιλέως εὐφυεστάτου πρὸς ἀρετὴν γεγονότος οὐκ ἔστι τῶν αἰσχρῶν καὶ δεινῶν ὃ παραλέλοιπε. λοιπὸν ἢ περὶ τὴν ἀρχὴν καὶ προέκθεσιν τῆς πραγματείας ἀνάγκη ψεύστην καὶ κόλακα φαίνεσθαι τὸν ἱστοριογράφον, ἢ περὶ τὰς κατὰ μέρος ἀποφάσεις ἀνόητον καὶ μειρακιώδη τελείως, εἰ διὰ τῆς ἀλόγου καὶ ἐπικλήτου λοιδορίας ὑπέλαβε πιστότερος μὲν αὐτὸς φανήσεσθαι, παραδοχῆς δὲ μᾶλλον ἀξιωθήσεσθαι τὰς ἐγκωμιαστικὰς ἀποφάσεις αὐτοῦ περὶ Φιλίππου.

For after announcing that he was going to write about a king richly endowed by nature with every quality that makes for virtue, he charges him with everything that is shameful and atrocious. So that either this author must be a liar and a flatterer in the prefatory remarks at the outset of his history, or he is entirely foolish and childish in his assertions about particulars, imagining that by senseless and far-fetched abuse he will insure his own credit and gain acceptance for his laudatory estimate of Philip.

Michael Flower has rightly argued that Polybius chooses to misrepresent Theopompus by emphasizing the encomiastic element of his work as a way of pointing to a contradictory approach to Philip II.[20] It is important, however, to note how Polybius once again identifies flattery as a trap into which a historian can fall.

As a target, Theopompus is an interesting choice for Polybius. A writer of many panegyrics and also deliberative speeches (Dion. Hal. *Ad Gnaeum Pompeium* 6.1 = *BNJ* 115 T 20a.1),[21] he is also noted for the evaluative parts of his writing. Dionysius has the following to say about him (*Ad Gnaeum Pompeium* 6.7–8 = *BNJ* 115 T 20a.7–8):

> τελευταῖόν ἐστι τῶν ἔργων αὐτοῦ καὶ χαρακτηρικώτατον, ὃ παρ' οὐδενὶ τῶν ἄλλων συγγραφέων οὕτως ἀκριβῶς ἐξείργασται καὶ δυνατῶς οὔτε τῶν πρεσβυτέρων οὔτε τῶν νεωτέρων. τί δὲ τοῦτό ἐστι; τὸ καθ' ἑκάστην πρᾶξιν μὴ μόνον τὰ φανερὰ τοῖς πολλοῖς ὁρᾶν καὶ λέγειν, ἀλλ' ἐξετάζειν καὶ τὰς ἀφανεῖς αἰτίας τῶν πράξεων καὶ τῶν πραξάντων αὐτὰς καὶ τὰ πάθη τῆς ψυχῆς, ἃ μὴ ῥᾴδια τοῖς πολλοῖς εἰδέναι, καὶ πάντα ἐκκαλύπτειν τὰ μυστήρια τῆς τε δοκούσης ἀρετῆς καὶ τῆς ἀγνοουμένης κακίας. καί μοι δοκεῖ πως ὁ μυθευόμενος ἐν Ἅιδου τῶν ψυχῶν <τῶν> ἀπολυθεισῶν τοῦ σώματος ἐξετασμὸς ἐπὶ τῶν ἐκεῖ δικαστῶν <οὐχ> οὕτως ἀκριβὴς εἶναι ὡς ὁ διὰ τῆς Θεοπόμπου γραφῆς γιγνόμενος. διὸ καὶ βάσκανος ἔδοξεν εἶναι, προσλαμβάνων τοῖς ἀναγκαίοις τινὰ ὀνειδισμοῖς κατὰ τῶν ἐνδόξων προσώπων οὐκ ἀναγκαῖα πράγματα, ὅμοιόν τι ποιῶν τοῖς ἰατροῖς, οἳ τέμνουσι καὶ καίουσι τὰ διεφθαρμένα τοῦ σώματος ἕως βάθους τὰ καυτήρια καὶ τὰς τομὰς φέροντες, οὐδὲν τῶν ὑγιαινόντων καὶ κατὰ φύσιν ἐχόντων στοχαζόμενοι. τοιοῦτος μὲν δή τις ὁ πραγματικὸς Θεοπόμπου χαρακτήρ.

> The final and most characteristic (element) of his work is something neither any earlier nor more recent historians have achieved with such precision. What is this? Not only (is he able) to see and record the actions that are clear to many, but he also explains the unseen reasons for events, for the actors, and their internal motivations, which are not very easy for many to know, and (he) uncovers the mysteries of seeming virtue and unrecognized vice. I also think that the mythical examination of souls released from the body by the judges there in Hades is not as exacting as the one in Theopompos's writing. For this reason he has been thought a slanderer, because he added certain unnecessary details to the necessary reproaches of famous persons [T 25a to T 25b], acting in a way similar to physicians who cut away and cauterize corrupted parts of the body, bringing the cauteries and cuttings to the depths, but not aiming for any of the healthy and sound (parts). Such then is the character of Theopompos in action (Transl. *BNJ*).

The reference in this passage to "looking at the mysteries of seeming virtue and unrecognized vice" would seem to point to an evaluative element in Theopom-

---

[20] Flower 1994, 98–104; on Polybius and Thepompus, see also Bearzot 2005, Vattuone 2014, 19–27.

[21] For a list of Theopompus' works, see *BNJ* 115 T 48. On the letter to Pompeius and its relation to Dionysius' *De imitatione*, see Weaire 2002.

pus' work. This points us more broadly to the issue of historians passing judgements, whether favourable or otherwise, on the topics about which they are writing.

3 The language of epideictic

Polybius' negative observation, discussed above, that other historians who wrote works about Philip V's notorious activities in Messenia were really composers of panegyrics rather than of histories (8.8.6), presents a contrast between Polybius' own work and other historians who are guilty of writing empty panegyric. Polybian historiography, which provides sober judgement, thus appears to be contrasted with less responsible writing which simply draws on the techniques of unqualified praise. This section of the chapter, however, will approach the question of praise and blame in Polybius and examine his usage of the terminology of epideictic.

We can begin with a passage where Polybius discusses the importance of praise and blame for historians. When discussing the historians Philinus and Fabius Pictor as historians and their partiality in relation to the participants in the First Punic War, Polybius admits that it is the task of the historian to be able to assign praise and blame accordingly (1.14.4–9):[22]

> ἐν μὲν οὖν τῷ λοιπῷ βίῳ τὴν τοιαύτην ἐπιείκειαν ἴσως οὐκ ἄν τις ἐκβάλλοι· καὶ γὰρ φιλόφιλον εἶναι δεῖ τὸν ἀγαθὸν ἄνδρα καὶ φιλόπατριν καὶ συμμισεῖν τοῖς φίλοις τοὺς ἐχθροὺς καὶ συναγαπᾶν τοὺς φίλους· ὅταν δὲ τὸ τῆς ἱστορίας ἦθος ἀναλαμβάνῃ τις, ἐπιλαθέσθαι χρὴ πάντων τῶν τοιούτων καὶ πολλάκις μὲν εὐλογεῖν καὶ κοσμεῖν τοῖς μεγίστοις ἐπαίνοις τοὺς ἐχθρούς, ὅταν αἱ πράξεις ἀπαιτῶσι τοῦτο, πολλάκις δ' ἐλέγχειν καὶ ψέγειν ἐπονειδίστως τοὺς ἀναγκαιοτάτους, ὅταν αἱ τῶν ἐπιτηδευμάτων ἁμαρτίαι τοῦθ' ὑποδεικνύωσιν. ὥσπερ γὰρ ζῴου τῶν ὄψεων ἀφαιρεθεισῶν ἀχρειοῦται τὸ ὅλον, οὕτως ἐξ ἱστορίας ἀναιρεθείσης τῆς ἀληθείας τὸ καταλειπόμενον αὐτῆς ἀνωφελὲς γίνεται διήγημα. διόπερ οὔτε τῶν φίλων κατηγορεῖν οὔτε τοὺς ἐχθροὺς ἐπαινεῖν ὀκνητέον, οὔτε δὲ τοὺς αὐτοὺς ψέγειν, ποτὲ δ' ἐγκωμιάζειν εὐλαβητέον, ἐπειδὴ τοὺς ἐν πράγμασιν ἀναστρεφομένους οὔτ' εὐστοχεῖν αἰεὶ δυνατὸν οὔθ' ἁμαρτάνειν συνεχῶς εἰκός. ἀποστάντας οὖν τῶν πραττόντων αὐτοῖς τοῖς πραττομένοις ἐφαρμοστέον τὰς πρεπούσας ἀποφάσεις καὶ διαλήψεις ἐν τοῖς ὑπομνήμασιν.

> In other relations of life we should not perhaps exclude all such favoritism; for a good man should love his friends and his country, he should share the hatreds and attachments of his friends; but he who assumes the character of a historian must ignore everything of the sort,

---

[22] On Polybius, Philinus and Fabius, see further e.g. Ambaglio 2005, McGing 2010, 32, 68–69. On this passage, see also Miltsios 2013, 129.

and often, if their actions demand this, speak good of his enemies and honor them with the highest praises while criticizing and even reproaching roundly his closest friends, should the errors of their conduct impose this duty on him. For just as a living creature which has lost its eyesight is wholly incapacitated, so if History is stripped of her truth all that is left is but an idle tale. We should therefore not shrink from accusing our friends or praising our enemies; nor need we be shy of sometimes praising and sometimes blaming the same people, since it is neither possible that men in the actual business of life should always be in the right, nor is it probable that they should be always mistaken. We must therefore disregard the actors in our narrative and apply to the actions such statements and such judgments as they deserve.

This passage is fundamental to an understanding of Polybius' approach to his subjects. But, even though there has been much interest in Polybius as a polemicist, the elements of praise in his work are a significant feature too: Polybius' method has more in common with epideictic practice than it has perhaps been credited for. This is not an attempt to revive the notion of "rhetorical" historiography, where the older tendency to label historians such as Ephorus or Theopompus as "rhetorical" (often in a pejorative sense), in part because of their links with Isocrates, has been strongly challenged in relation to Hellenistic historiography.[23] Instead a better way to approach the issue of rhetoric in Polybius is offered in an important recent article by Scott Farrington, who has argued that Polybius' use of rhetorical techniques is in fact a key aspect of his method, and part of the process of persuading the audience of the reliability of his work.[24]

There has, however, been a strong tendency amongst Polybian scholars to draw a contrast between Polybius' method and more rhetorical approaches in relation to praise and blame. Thus Pédech in his seminal study charted a firm distinction between the apodeictic method of historical writing and more laudatory modes of operation, as the following illustrative brief quotations from a longer passage of analysis illustrate: "L'histoire ainsi conçue s'oppose au genre laudatif … L'histoire exclut la déformation laudative que est légitime dans la

---

[23] See e.g. Marincola 2001, 111–12, who gives a sense of the history of such approaches, Parmegianni 2014, 2–4, Vattuone 2014, Marincola 2014. On Ephorus and Polybius, see Chávez Reino 2005, Parmeggiani 2011, 40–50.
[24] Farrington 2015; see e.g. some of his concluding remarks (62): "I have argued that Polybius demands that rhetoric is central to historiography. In fact, the historian's duty to persuade instructively helps define the genre and distinguish it from other literary forms. The historian behaves as a juryman when he examines the evidence, witnesses, and written accounts and chooses which source material to accept. Furthermore, the historian behaves as an orator or advocate when he strives to persuade the reader that his account is true".

rhétorique".²⁵ And it is true that there are elements of Polybius' work which might seem to point us away from seeing his work in an epideictic context. A famous instance, discussed by Pédech, is the testimony for his otherwise lost biography of Philopoemen, where Polybius establishes a strong contrast between his approach to the Achaean statesman in his history and in a separate biography of Philopoemen which he had also written (10.21.5–8):²⁶

> εἰ μὲν οὖν μὴ κατ' ἰδίαν ἐπεποιήμεθα τὴν περὶ αὐτοῦ σύνταξιν, ἐν ᾗ διεσαφοῦμεν καὶ τίς ἦν καὶ τίνων καὶ τίσιν ἀγωγαῖς ἐχρήσατο νέος ὤν, ἀναγκαῖον ἦν ὑπὲρ ἑκάστου τῶν προειρημένων φέρειν ἀπολογισμόν· ἐπεὶ δὲ πρότερον ἐν τρισὶ βυβλίοις ἐκτὸς ταύτης τῆς συντάξεως τὸν ὑπὲρ αὐτοῦ πεποιήμεθα λόγον, τήν τε παιδικὴν ἀγωγὴν διασαφοῦντες καὶ τὰς ἐπιφανεστάτας πράξεις, δῆλον ὡς ἐν τῇ νῦν ἐξηγήσει πρέπον ἂν εἴη τῆς μὲν νεωτερικῆς ἀγωγῆς καὶ τῶν νεωτερικῶν ζήλων κατὰ μέρος ἀφελεῖν, τοῖς δὲ κατὰ τὴν ἀκμὴν αὐτοῦ κεφαλαιωδῶς ἐκεῖ δεδηλωμένοις ἔργοις προσθεῖναι καὶ κατὰ μέρος, ἵνα τὸ πρέπον ἑκατέρᾳ τῶν συντάξεων τηρῶμεν. ὥσπερ γὰρ ἐκεῖνος ὁ τόπος, ὑπάρχων ἐγκωμιαστικός, ἀπῄτει τὸν κεφαλαιώδη καὶ μετ' αὐξήσεως τῶν πράξεων ἀπολογισμόν, οὕτως ὁ τῆς ἱστορίας, κοινὸς ὢν ἐπαίνου καὶ ψόγου, ζητεῖ τὸν ἀληθῆ καὶ τὸν μετ' ἀποδείξεως καὶ τῶν ἑκάστοις παρεπομένων συλλογισμῶν.

> Now had I not dealt with Philopoemen in a special work in which I explain who he and his family were, and the nature of his training when young, I should be compelled to give an account of all these matters here. Since, however, I have formerly in three books, which do not form part of the present work, treated of him, stating what was his training as a boy and enumerating his most famous actions, it is evident that in the present narrative my proper course is to omit details concerning his early training and the ambitions of his youth, but to add detail to the summary account I there gave of the achievements of his riper years, in order that the proper character of each work may be preserved. For just as the former work, being in the form of an encomium, demanded a summary and somewhat exaggerated account of his achievements, so the present history, which distributes praise and blame impartially, demands a strictly true account and one which states the ground on which either praise or blame is based.

The opposition that is established here between the encomiastic approach (ἐγκωμιαστικός, 10.21.8) of biography and the approach of history is a powerful one; Scott Farrington has usefully argued that the crucial distinction here is between encomium's concern with amplification (μετ' αὐξήσεως) and history's concern with demonstration (μετ' ἀποδείξεως).²⁷ In the case of Philopoemen, we can

---

25 Pédech 1964, 45–46. On the apodeictic (demonstrative) aspect of Polybius' work, see e.g. Walbank 1972, 57 and n. 153, Sacks 1981, 171–87, Champion 2004, 137, Farrington 2015, 46–48.
26 On this passage, see e.g. Pédech 1964, 45, Farrington 2011, 325–27. See also the contribution of Alexiou in the present volume.
27 Farrington 2011, 329–339.

indeed note that Polybius is willing to criticize him elsewhere in the narrative, as we have seen above at 22.19, when Philopoemen uses praise, ironically, as a weapon against Archon, a passage we will examine in more detail in the final section of the chapter.[28] Nevertheless, the pairing of praise and blame in this passage recalls the classic division of epideictic oratory into praise and blame, illustrated, to give only a couple of examples, in the *Rhetorica ad Alexandrum* at 1425b36ff., where encomiastic oratory and vituperative oratory are considered to be opposites, or at Aristotle's *Rhetoric* 1358b, where epideictic oratory is simply described as consisting of praise or blame: ἐπιδεικτικοῦ δὲ τὸ μὲν ἔπαινος τὸ δὲ ψόγος (1358b12–13),[29] the very same pair of nouns which we find Polybius using at the end of the passage from 10.21 cited above.[30]

It is worthwhile to examine the usage of the word ἐπιδεικτικός in Polybius (the noun ἐπίδειξις does not occur). I shall start with the latest example in Polybius' text, 38.4.1. In the previous chapter, Polybius has explained how Greece's calamities at the time of the Achaean War against Rome were essentially self-inflicted. Polybius ends 38.3 blaming both the people and their leaders for the catastrophe (38.3.13). In 38.4, Polybius then comments on his own writing (38.4.1–2):

Ὑπὲρ ὧν οὐ δεήσει θαυμάζειν ἐὰν παρεκβαίνοντες τὸ τῆς ἱστορικῆς διηγήσεως ἦθος ἐπιδεικτικωτέραν καὶ φιλοτιμοτέραν φαινώμεθα ποιούμενοι περὶ αὐτῶν τὴν ἀπαγγελίαν. καίτοι τινὲς ἴσως ἐπιτιμήσουσιν ἡμῖν ὡς φιλαπεχθῶς ποιουμένοις τὴν γραφήν, οἷς καθῆκον ἦν μάλιστα πάντων περιστέλλειν τὰς τῶν Ἑλλήνων ἁμαρτίας.

It should not surprise anyone if abandoning here the style proper to historical narrative I express myself in a more declamatory and ambitious [ἐπιδεικτικωτέραν καὶ φιλοτιμοτέραν] manner. Some, however, may reproach me for writing with undue animosity, it being rather my first duty to throw a veil over the offenses of the Greeks.

---

28 Cf. Farrington 2011, 338.
29 On Aristotle's concept of epideictic, see e.g. Pratt 2012. Carey 2007 and Pernot 2015 offer broader treatments of epideictic.
30 Though Walbank 1972, 32 and n. 3 suggests that connections between Polybius and Aristotle (whom Polybius does name in several passages noted by Walbank) are superficial, there has been more recent scholarship which has been more sympathetic to drawing out deeper links between the two authors: see Williams 2007 and Hartog 2010, 37–39, who both suggest connections between Polybius and the *Poetics*. Note, however, that Marincola 2013, esp. 85–86 and 90 cautions usefully against placing too much emphasis on possible specific links between Polybius treatment of Phylarchus in Book 2 and Aristotle's *Poetics*; see also n. 40 below. On Aristotle and historical method, see also Bertelli 2014.

Paton's translation of ἐπιδεικτικωτέραν as "more declamatory" is in keeping with a broader tendency to avoid translating the word in Polybius in a way which points to the category of epideictic rhetoric. Nevertheless, as is indicated by Polybius' comments about those who have criticized him for undue harshness towards the Greeks, this is a passage about blame, so there is a case for interpreting the adjective here as a glance at the language of epideictic discourse.

The adjective ἐπιδεικτικός also appears at 16.18.2, where Polybius is writing about the Rhodian historian Zeno,[31] and characterizes his writing in similar terms:

> ἐξηγούμενος γὰρ ὁ προειρημένος συγγραφεὺς τήν τε Γάζης πολιορκίαν καὶ τὴν γενομένην παράταξιν Ἀντιόχου πρὸς Σκόπαν ἐν Κοίλῃ Συρίᾳ περὶ τὸ Πάνιον, περὶ μὲν τὴν τῆς λέξεως κατασκευὴν δῆλός ἐστιν ἐπὶ τοσοῦτον ἐσπουδακὼς ὡς ὑπερβολὴν τερατείας μὴ καταλιπεῖν τοῖς τὰς ἐπιδεικτικὰς καὶ πρὸς ἔκπληξιν τῶν πολλῶν συντάξεις ποιουμένοις, τῶν γε μὴν πραγμάτων ἐπὶ τοσοῦτον ὠλιγώρηκεν ὥστε πάλιν ἀνυπέρβλητον εἶναι τὴν εὐχέρειαν καὶ τὴν ἀπειρίαν τοῦ συγγραφέως.

> I will attempt to make my meaning clear by the following instance. The above-mentioned author in narrating the siege of Gaza and the engagement between Antiochus and Scopas at the Panium in Coele-Syria has evidently taken so much pains about his style that the extravagance of his language is not excelled by any of those declamatory works written to produce a sensation among the vulgar [μὴ καταλιπεῖν τοῖς τὰς ἐπιδεικτικὰς καὶ πρὸς ἔκπληξιν τῶν πολλῶν συντάξεις ποιουμένοις]. He has, however, paid so little attention to facts that his recklessness and lack of experience are again unsurpassed.

Here, and the context is less clear, so that we cannot be sure whether the issue of praise or blame is at stake, Polybius regards Zeno as more "epideictic", again translated in the Loeb as "declamatory".[32]

The last set of examples are found in a famous passage in Book 12, where Polybius discusses the preface to Timaeus' sixth book[33] on the difference between history and what Paton calls "declamatory writing". Here quotation at greater length is necessary (12.28.8–12.28a2, 6):

> κατὰ γὰρ τὸ προοίμιον τῆς ἕκτης βύβλου φησί τινας ὑπολαμβάνειν διότι τινὸς μείζονος δεῖται φύσεως καὶ φιλοπονίας καὶ παρασκευῆς τὸ τῶν ἐπιδεικτικῶν λόγων γένος ἢ τὸ τῆς ἱστορίας· ταύτας δὲ τὰς δόξας πρότερον μὲν Ἐφόρῳ φησὶ προσπεσεῖν, οὐ δυνηθέντος δ' ἱκανῶς ἐκείνου πρὸς τοὺς ταῦτα λέγοντας ἀπαντῆσαι, πειρᾶται συγκρίνειν αὐτὸς ἐκ

---

31 For Zeno of Rhodes, see *BNJ* 523 and Wiemer 2013.
32 On this passage, see Chávez Reino 2005, 32–35, and Parmeggiani 2011, 126, who notes the association of epideictic writing with τερατεία and ἔκπληξις.
33 On the possible context of Timaeus' sixth book, see Baron 2013, 31.

παραβολῆς τὴν ἱστορίαν τοῖς ἐπιδεικτικοῖς λόγοις, πρᾶγμα ποιῶν πάντων ἀτοπώτατον, πρῶτον μὲν τὸ καταψεύσασθαι τοῦ συγγραφέως. ὁ γὰρ Ἔφορος παρ' ὅλην τὴν πραγματείαν θαυμάσιος ὢν καὶ κατὰ τὴν φράσιν καὶ κατὰ τὸν χειρισμὸν καὶ κατὰ τὴν ἐπίνοιαν τῶν λημμάτων, δεινότατός ἐστιν ἐν ταῖς παρεκβάσεσι καὶ ταῖς ἀφ' αὑτοῦ γνωμολογίαις, καὶ συλλήβδην ὅταν που τὸν ἐπιμετροῦντα λόγον διατίθηται· κατὰ δέ τινα συντυχίαν εὐχαριστότατα καὶ πιθανώτατα περὶ τῆς συγκρίσεως εἴρηκε τῆς τῶν ἱστοριογράφων καὶ λογογράφων. ὁ δ' ἵνα μὴ δόξῃ κατακολουθεῖν Ἐφόρῳ, πρὸς τῷ κατεψεῦσθαι 'κείνου καὶ τῶν λοιπῶν <ἅμα> κατέγν<ωκε· τὰ γὰρ παρ'> ἄλλων δεόντως κεχειρισμένα μακρῶς καὶ ἀσαφῶς καὶ τρόπῳ παντὶ χεῖρον ἐξηγούμενος οὐδένα τῶν ζώντων ὑπέλαβε τοῦτο παρατηρήσειν. οὐ μὴν ἀλλὰ βουλόμενος αὔξειν τὴν ἱστορίαν πρῶτον μὲν τηλικαύτην εἶναί φησι διαφορὰν τῆς ἱστορίας πρὸς τοὺς ἐπιδεικτικοὺς λόγους, ἡλίκην ἔχει τὰ κατ' ἀλήθειαν ᾠκοδομημένα καὶ κατεσκευασμένα τῶν ἐν ταῖς σκηνογραφίαις φαινομένων τόπων καὶ διαθέσεων· δεύτερον αὐτὸ τὸ συναθροῖσαί φησι τὴν παρασκευὴν τὴν πρὸς τὴν ἱστορίαν μεῖζον ἔργον εἶναι τῆς ὅλης πραγματείας τῆς περὶ τοὺς ἐπιδεικτικοὺς λόγους ... (12.28a.6) ἐγὼ μὲν γὰρ οὐκ οἴομαι τηλικαύτην διαφορὰν ἔχειν τὰ κατ' ἀλήθειαν οἰκοδομήματα τῶν ἐν ταῖς σκηνογραφίαις τόπων, οὐδὲ τὴν ἱστορίαν τῶν ἐπιδεικτικῶν λόγων, ἡλίκην ἐπὶ πασῶν τῶν συντάξεων τὴν ἐξ αὐτουργίας καὶ τὴν ἐξ αὐτοπαθείας ἀπόφασιν τῶν ἐξ ἀκοῆς καὶ διηγήματος γραφομένων·

For in the preface to his sixth book he says that some suppose that greater talent, more industry, and more previous training are required for declamatory than for historical writing [διότι τινὸς μείζονος δεῖται φύσεως καὶ φιλοπονίας καὶ παρασκευῆς τὸ τῶν ἐπιδεικτικῶν λόγων γένος ἢ τὸ τῆς ἱστορίας]. Such opinions, he says, formerly incurred Ephorus' disapproval, but as that writer could give no satisfactory answer to those who held them, he himself attempts to institute a comparison between history and declamatory writing [τοῖς ἐπιδεικτικοῖς λόγοις], a most surprising thing to do, firstly in that his statement about Ephorus is false. For Ephorus, while throughout his whole work he is admirable in his phraseology, method, and the originality of his thought, is most eloquent in his digressions and in the expression of his personal judgment, whenever, in fact, he allows himself to enlarge on any subject, and it so happens that his remarks on the difference between historians and speechwriters [λογογράφων] are peculiarly charming and convincing. But Timaeus, in order not to seem to be copying Ephorus, besides making a false statement about him has at the same time condemned all other historians. For dealing with matters, treated by others correctly, at inordinate length, in a confused manner, and in every respect worse, he thinks that not a living soul will notice this.

Actually in order to glorify history he says that the difference between it and declamatory writing [διαφορὰν τῆς ἱστορίας πρὸς τοὺς ἐπιδεικτικοὺς λόγους] is as great as that between real buildings or furniture and the views and compositions we see in scene paintings. In the second place he says that the mere collection of the material required for a history is a more serious task than the complete course of study of the art of declamatory speaking [τοὺς ἐπιδεικτικοὺς λόγους] ... (12.28a6) In my opinion the difference between real buildings and scene paintings or between history and declamatory speechmaking [τῶν ἐπιδεικτικῶν λόγων] is not so great as is, in the case of all works, the difference between an account founded on participation, active or passive, in the occurrences and one composed from report and the narratives of others.

As can be seen here, Polybius in this passage engages with the issue of the difference between historical writing and ἐπιδεικτικοὶ λόγοι. In dealing with this phrase, translators cover a range of words: Paton's Loeb translation refers to "declamatory writing" or "declamatory speaking", Shuckburgh's translation here refers to "rhetorical composition(s)".[34] *Brill's New Jacoby* has different translations for this word: its Timaeus (*BNJ* 566 F 7) follows Paton in employing "declamatory writing" or "speaking", but its Ephorus (*BNJ* 70 F 111) translates ἐπιδεικτικοὶ λόγοι in 12.28.8 simply as "oratory".[35] The picture then is a complex one—but what we can see is that translators have avoided using translations of ἐπιδεικτικοὶ λόγοι that reflect the definition of epideictic which is offered in Aristotle's *Rhetoric*, namely praise or blame. This reluctance to evoke epideictic in translations of the phrase is all the more striking since the words ἐπιδεικτικοὶ λόγοι in fact appears in Aristotle's *Rhetoric*, at 1359a29, as the second of Aristotle's three categories of rhetoric.[36]

4 Evaluative praise conferred by Polybius

We now turn to consideration of examples of praise offered by Polybius himself in the text. To begin with, the very opening of the work begins with thematization of praise, as Polybius explains that praise of history is not in fact necessary owing to its having been provided on so many occasions by other writers (1.1.1).[37] Though Polybius declares that he does not need to add to the sum of existing praise for history, he nevertheless endorses the point that has repeatedly been made in its favour by previous writers, its usefulness. As well as conveying the notion that history is a topic worthy of praise, there is a second strand to Polybius' opening emphasis on praise, since the opening chapters also include a passage where Polybius notes the exceptional achievement of Tyche (Fortune) in bringing together events towards a single destiny (τὸ κάλλιστον ἅμα κὠφελιμώτατον

---

[34] Shuckburgh 1889, ii.114–115.
[35] Parmeggiani 2011, 124–39 provides an indispensable discussion of this fragment of Ephorus, though the focus of his discussion of the word ἐπιδεικτικός is on considerations of style: "Il *logos epideiktikos* andava in cerca del preziosismo stilistico assoluto; il *logos historikos* andava in cerca di *aletheia*" (139).
[36] Note that the ordering of the three categories of rhetoric at *Rhet.* 1358b7–8 has epideictic coming third after deliberative and forensic speeches. On Aristotle's tripartite division of rhetoric, see e.g. Pernot 1993, 28–30, Brunschwig 1994, 90–91, Garver 2009.
[37] For praise of historians, cf. e.g. Isocrates 12.1 and see Miltsios 2013, 7–8.

ἐπιτήδευμα τῆς τύχης, 1.4.4), a destiny which of course is the rise of Rome to power in the Mediterranean, the subject of Polybius' own work.[38] And, in the same way, after completing his account of the outbreak of the First Punic War and the Roman crossing to Sicily in 1.12, and his summary of the main events to follow in 1.13, Polybius turns to the question of praise or blame for the historian in 1.14, as we have seen above, where censure of the partisan spirit of Philinus and Fabius Pictor in their coverage of the First Punic War is then followed by an emphatic statement of the historian's proper role in assigning judicious praise or blame to the participants in his narrative.

These kinds of evaluative judgements can be found elsewhere in Polybius. Thus, at 3.4.7, the continuation of his history is seen in terms of whether one might wish to praise or alternatively to blame the Romans for their actions after the downfall of the Macedonian kingdom.[39] Similarly, in 2.61.6, in the context of his discussion of Phylarchus and the fall of Mantinea, Polybius observes that Phylarchus' treatment of Cleomenes' capture of Megalopolis omits the noble refusal of the Megalopolitans to abandon their Achaean allies, even when this refusal is to their own detriment: "So far he makes everything quite clear to us, but he deprives us of what should follow and what is the special virtue of history, I mean praise and honourable mention of conduct noteworthy for its excellence", τὸ δ' ἀκόλουθον καὶ τὸ τῆς ἱστορίας ἴδιον ἀφεῖλε, τὸν ἔπαινον καὶ τὴν ἐπ' ἀγαθῷ μνήμην τῶν ἀξιολόγων προαιρέσεων.[40] For Polybius, history is not just associated with commemoration (μνήμη), but also with praise (ἔπαινος).

Such historical praise (or its being withheld) is not only applicable to recent history. In Book 4, Polybius comments, in the context of a Messenian decision to avoid going to war, that one should not necessarily avoid war at any cost, and then observes that no one praises the Thebans for their behaviour in the Persian Wars, or Pindar for encouraging them to remain on the sidelines (4.31.5–6). By contrast, Polybius singles out the behaviour of the Rhodians in the aftermath of the earthquake of the early 220s BCE[41] as being worthy of praise and emulation (ἐπαίνου γάρ εἰσιν ἄξιοι καὶ ζήλου, 5.90.5), again pointing to the way in which

---

[38] On the συμπλοκή, the interweaving of events, in Polybius, see e.g. Walbank 1975, Quinn 2013.
[39] On this passage and the wider context of Polybius' continuation of his history, see e.g. McGing 2010, 164–66, Gibson 2013, 164–65, Gruen 2013, 258–59, Miltsios 2013, 144.
[40] On Polybius' discussion of Phylarchus in 2.56–63 and the vexed question of "tragic history", see now McGing 2010, 71–74 and Marincola 2013, who has argued that Polybius' censure of the "tragic" should be seen not as an attack on the emotional aspect, but as a critique of Phylarchus' attitude to the truth. See also Miltsios 2013, 125–26, Thornton 2013c.
[41] On the dating of the earthquake, likely to be around 227 BCE, see Walbank 1957, 616 on Plb. 5.88–90, Ashton 1986, 14 n. 35.

positive judgements can be formed in relation to the conduct of historical agents; similarly the Roman practice of allowing individuals to go into exile (6.14.7) is said to be worthy of praise and commemoration, with the same words ἔπαινος and μνήμη as we saw above with the conduct of the people of Megalopolis.

The role of judgement is, however, key to the application of praise (or blame) by Polybius: as we have already seen, the discussion of Philip V and his behaviour in Messenia in Book 8 is concerned with the failings of other historians in preferring more panegyrical treatments instead of providing a properly balanced approach to Philip's reign. This need for balance is also evident in Polybius' comments on the way in which Timaeus has been one-sided in only focusing on criticism of Agathocles (12.15); again Polybius draws attention to the way in which history is expected not just to apportion blame, but praise as well (12.15.9): ὑπὲρ ὧν δεῖ τὸν συγγραφέα μὴ μόνον τὰ πρὸς διαβολὴν κυροῦντα καὶ κατηγορίαν ἐξηγεῖσθαι τοῖς ἐπιγινομένοις, ἀλλὰ καὶ τὰ πρὸς ἔπαινον ἥκοντα περὶ τὸν ἄνδρα· τοῦτο γὰρ ἴδιόν ἐστι τῆς ἱστορίας, "Regarding all this a historian should lay before posterity not only such matters as tend to confirm slanderous accusations, but also what redounds to the credit of his prince; for such is the proper function of history".[42] Polybius shows his own adherence to this precept in 16.28, where he explains that though he would not intend to praise the whole character of Philip V, he is willing to praise his energy and vigour against Attalus and the Rhodians.[43] And at 30.7.4, Polybius is able to praise the allies of Perseus for their fortitude in adversity.

The linking of praise and commemoration also produces a significant qualification to Polybius' use of praise at 9.9. Here Polybius notes that both sides deserve praise for their actions relating to the siege of Capua by the Romans and Hannibal's attempt to relieve it, but then explains why he is offering praise (9.9.9–10):

ταῦτα μὲν οὖν οὐχ οὕτως τοῦ Ῥωμαίων ἢ Καρχηδονίων ἐγκωμίου χάριν εἴρηταί μοι— τούτους μὲν γὰρ ἤδη πολλάκις ἐπεσημηνάμην—τὸ δὲ πλεῖον τῶν ἡγουμένων παρ' ἀμφοτέροις καὶ τῶν μετὰ ταῦτα μελλόντων χειρίζειν παρ' ἑκάστοις τὰς κοινὰς πράξεις, ἵνα τῶν μὲν ἀναμιμνησκόμενοι, τὰ δ' ὑπὸ τὴν ὄψιν λαμβάνοντες ζηλωταὶ γίνωνται παράβολον ἔχειν τι καὶ κινδυνῶδες, τοὐναντίον ἀσφαλῆ μὲν τὴν τόλμαν, θαυμασίαν δὲ τὴν ἐπίνοιαν,

---

42 Slightly different is Polybius' concession at 8.10.12 that Timaeus' trenchant take on Agathocles might be seen as justified, though the context here is Polybius' censure of Theopompus (see above). On Timaeus and Agathocles, see Baron 2013, 18–21, 61–62.
43 On Polybius' praise of Philip V, see e.g. Dreyer 2013, 207, McGing 2013, 192, Nicholson 2015, 256 and 262.

ἀείμνηστον δὲ καὶ καλὴν ἔχει τὴν προαίρεσιν καὶ κατορθωθέντα καὶ διαψευσθέντα παραπλησίως, ἐὰν μόνον σὺν νῷ γένηται τὰ πραττόμενα.

It is not for the purpose of extolling the Romans or the Carthaginians that I have offered these remarks—I have often had occasion to bestow praise on both peoples—but rather for the sake of the leaders of both these states, and of all, in each and every state, who shall be charged with the conduct of public affairs, so that by recalling or picturing to themselves these events they are moved to emulation, and not shrink from undertaking designs, which may seem indeed to be fraught with risk and peril, but on the contrary are courageous without being hazardous, are admirable in their conception, and their excellence, whether the result be success or failure alike, will deserve to live in men's memories for ever, always provided that all that is done is the result of sound reasoning.

This passage points to the way in which praise for Polybius is not only part of what the historian does, but also something which is a pointer to the historian's readers. With Polybius, the epideictic modes (in the Aristotelian sense) of praise and blame are a crucial part of the historian's tools, and vital as a means of guiding others in their future conduct.[44] This is something which finds a counterpart in rhetorical theory, for instance, at Aristotle, *Rhetoric* 1367b37–1368a9 where Aristotle talks of how what one might wish to suggest to an audience (deliberative) is effectively the counterpart of what one might wish to praise (epideictic), but simply with a change of phrasing: ὥστε ὅταν ἐπαινεῖν βούλῃ, ὅρα τί ἂν ὑπόθοιο· καὶ ὅταν ὑποθέσθαι, ὅρα τί ἂν ἐπαινέσειας, "Accordingly, if you desire to praise, look what you would suggest; if you desire to suggest, look what you would praise" (*Rhet.* 1368a7–8).[45] Polybius' conception of how praise from the historian might work as a guide for future conduct in 9.9 finds its analogy in the way Polybius shows Romans learning from hearing praise of the deceased at a Roman elite funeral (6.54.1–3). While Polybius' own use of the word ἐπιδεικτικός in his work has remained enigmatic, at least in terms of how translators have approached it, I hope to have shown that there is scope for giving more consideration to the way in which praise and blame, the key concerns of the epideictic orator, are also a vital aspect of Polybius' text, for all his protestations of how what he is doing is something removed from "epideictic".

---

[44] On the protreptic aspect of Polybius, see Farrington 2011, 334, 338–39.
[45] On this passage, see e.g. Labarrière 1994, 241, Collins 2015, 23–24. For the view that Aristotelian epideictic can be seen in terms of the role of the orator as teacher, see Hauser 1999; see also Braund 1998 on the protreptic function of panegyric in late antiquity.

A further striking example of Polybian praise relates to Scipio Africanus (10.2.4–7):[46]

ὅτι δ' ἔστιν ὑγιὲς τὸ νυνὶ λεγόμενον ὑφ' ἡμῶν δῆλον ἔσται διὰ τῆς ἡμετέρας ἐξηγήσεως τοῖς ἐπισημαίνεσθαι δυναμένοις τὰ κάλλιστα καὶ παραβολώτατα τῶν ἐκείνῳ πεπραγμένων. οἱ μὲν οὖν ἄλλοι πάντες αὐτὸν ἐπιτυχῆ τινα καὶ τὸ πλεῖον αἰεὶ παραλόγως καὶ ταὐτομάτῳ κατορθοῦντα τὰς ἐπιβολὰς παρεισάγουσι, νομίζοντες ὡς ἂν εἰ θειοτέρους εἶναι καὶ θαυμαστοτέρους τοὺς τοιούτους ἄνδρας τῶν κατὰ λόγον ἐν ἑκάστοις πραττόντων, ἀγνοοῦντες ὅτι τὸ μὲν ἐπαινετόν, τὸ δὲ μακαριστὸν εἶναι συμβαίνει τῶν προειρημένων, καὶ τὸ μὲν κοινόν ἐστι καὶ τοῖς τυχοῦσι, τὸ δ' ἐπαινετὸν μόνον ἴδιον ὑπάρχει τῶν εὐλογίστων καὶ φρένας ἐχόντων ἀνδρῶν, οὓς καὶ θειοτάτους εἶναι καὶ προσφιλεστάτους τοῖς θεοῖς νομιστέον.

That what I myself state here is sound will be evident to all who by means of my narrative are able to appreciate the most glorious and hazardous of his exploits. As for all other writers, they represent him as a man favored by fortune, who always owed the most part of his success to the unexpected and to mere chance, such men being, in their opinion, more divine and more worthy of admiration than those who always act by calculation. They are not aware that one of the two things deserves praise and the other only congratulation, the latter being common to ordinary men, whereas what is praiseworthy belongs alone to men of sound judgment and mental ability, whom we should consider to be the most divine and most beloved by the gods.

In this passage, Polybius explains that Scipio is to be praised not for his good fortune, or even for his actual achievements, but for his actual character: the focus of praise is on the temperament which is what makes success possible (τὸ δ' ἐπαινετὸν μόνον ἴδιον ὑπάρχει τῶν εὐλογίστων καὶ φρένας ἐχόντων ἀνδρῶν, whereas what is praiseworthy belongs alone to men of sound judgment and mental

---

46 On the wider context of Polybius' praise of Scipio at the outset in Book 10 (and its anticipation of Polybius' praise of Scipio in Book 14 later on the Second Punic War in his operations against Syphax and Hasdrubal), see Miltsios 2013, 109–11.

ability"),⁴⁷ which is what brings men closest to the gods.⁴⁸ This distinction between external contingencies such as a good fortune, and underlying character which is worthy of praise, has a counterpart in rhetorical (and ethical) theory. Compare Aristotle's *Rhetoric* 1367b28–36:

> ἔστιν δ' ἔπαινος λόγος ἐμφανίζων μέγεθος ἀρετῆς. δεῖ οὖν τὰς πράξεις ἐπιδεικνύναι ὡς τοιαῦται. τὸ δ' ἐγκώμιον τῶν ἔργων ἐστίν (τὰ δὲ κύκλῳ εἰς πίστιν, οἷον εὐγένεια καὶ παιδεία· εἰκὸς γὰρ ἐξ ἀγαθῶν ἀγαθοὺς καὶ τὸν οὕτω τραφέντα τοιοῦτον εἶναι), διὸ καὶ ἐγκωμιάζομεν πράξαντας. τὰ δ' ἔργα σημεῖα τῆς ἕξεώς ἐστιν, ἐπεὶ ἐπαινοῖμεν ἂν καὶ μὴ πεπραγότα, εἰ πιστεύοιμεν εἶναι τοιοῦτον. μακαρισμὸς δὲ καὶ εὐδαιμονισμὸς αὐτοῖς μὲν ταὐτά, τούτοις δ' οὐ ταὐτά, ἀλλ' ὥσπερ ἡ εὐδαιμονία τὴν ἀρετήν, καὶ ὁ εὐδαιμονισμὸς περιέχει ταῦτα.

> Now praise is language that sets forth greatness of virtue; hence it is necessary to show that a man's actions are virtuous. But encomium deals with achievements—all attendant circumstances, such as noble birth and education, merely conduce to persuasion; for it is probable that virtuous parents will have virtuous offspring and that a man will turn out as he has been brought up. Hence we pronounce an encomium upon those who have achieved something. Achievements, in fact, are signs of moral habit; for we should praise even a man who had not achieved anything, if we felt confident that he was likely to do so. Blessing and felicitation are identical with each other, but are not the same as praise and encomium, which, as virtue is contained in happiness, are contained in felicitation (Transl. J.H. Freese).

Here, Aristotle qualifies the proper field for praise as being concerned with character. It also has a counterpart in Aristotelian ethics, where praise can be assigned according to disposition (and therefore possibility, as at *EN* 1103a8–10 ἐπαινοῦμεν δὲ καὶ τὸν σοφὸν κατὰ τὴν ἕξιν· τῶν ἕξεων δὲ τὰς ἐπαινετὰς ἀρετὰς

---

47 For the idea that appropriate praise goes beyond mere congratulation for successes enjoyed, cf. 18.28.4–5, where Polybius contrasts proper praise of Roman success on the battlefield which is founded on cogent explanation from mere celebration of the good fortune of victory: χρήσιμον καὶ καλὸν ἂν εἴη τὸ τὴν διαφορὰν ἐρευνῆσαι, καὶ παρὰ τί συμβαίνει Ῥωμαίους ἐπικρατεῖν καὶ τὸ πρωτεῖον ἐκφέρεσθαι τῶν κατὰ πόλεμον ἀγώνων, ἵνα μὴ τύχην λέγοντες μόνον μακαρίζωμεν τοὺς κρατοῦντας ἀλόγως, καθάπερ οἱ μάταιοι τῶν ἀνθρώπων, ἀλλ' εἰδότες τὰς ἀληθεῖς αἰτίας ἐπαινῶμεν καὶ θαυμάζωμεν κατὰ λόγον τοὺς ἡγουμένους ("it will prove useful and beneficial to inquire into the difference, and into the reason why on the battle-field the Romans have always had the upper hand and carried off the palm, so that we may not, like foolish men, talk simply of chance and felicitate the victors without giving any reason for it, but may, knowing the true causes of their success, give them a reasoned tribute of praise and admiration"). See further McGing 2010, 196–97.
48 For this language of associating the highest praise with a connection to the gods, cf. the Rhodians' comments to the Romans (see above) at 21.23.9, where praise and honour belong to the gods and those closest to them.

λέγομεν).⁴⁹ As can be seen, Polybius' treatment of Scipio in 10.2 is predicated on a very similar understanding of true praise being something associated not with external circumstances, but with the underlying character of the individual.

5 Conclusion

Praise is a regular feature within Polybius' narrative. It is, moreover, a key feature of Roman society, in that the funeral orations honouring distinguished Romans are highlighted as a decisive influence on the next generation of Romans (6.53–4); praise is thus represented as protreptic. Praise is also a significant aspect of Polybius' own historical method. The attaching of praise or blame to individuals and their actions is a fundamental concern for the historian (1.14.4–9). In part, this is a function of the historian being able to weigh up the evidence and form a balanced judgement. But there is also a protreptic element here too: narrative of praiseworthy deeds encourages the audience to seek to do the same, as with Polybius' explanation for why he has praised the conduct of the both the Romans and the Carthaginians at Capua (9.9.9–10).

Thus history is not just something which provides lessons about the endurance of the vicissitudes of fortune, a key theme that Polybius highlights at the outset of his work (1.1.2). It also affords the audience the opportunity to model their future conduct in emulation of those who are praised. As Polybius comments on the behaviour of the Megalopolitans who refused to join Cleomenes even when it was to their advantage to do so (2.61.11): οὗ τί κάλλιον ἔργον ἢ γέγονεν ἢ γένοιτ' ἄν ἐπὶ τί δ' ἄν; μᾶλλον συγγραφεὺς ἐπιστῆσαι τοὺς ἀκούοντας; διὰ τίνος δ' ἔργου μᾶλλον ἂν παρορμῆσαι πρὸς φυλακὴν πίστεως καὶ πρὸς ἀληθινῶν πραγμάτων καὶ βεβαίων κοινωνίαν, "What more noble conduct has there ever been or could there be? To what could an author with more advantage call the attention of his readers, and how could he better stimulate them to loyalty to their engagements and to thus share in an honorable and firmly established state?" Polybius similarly explains that he has provided anecdotes about Philopoemen, Hannibal

---

49 On the gap in language used by Aristotle in the *Rhetoric*, where virtue is concerned with δύναμις, "capacity", and in the *Nichomachean Ethics*, where it is concerned with ἕξις, a "state" or "condition", see Allard-Nelson 2001, who argues that it is possible to reconcile the two positions. On the philosophical problem posed by Aristotelian ethics in terms of whether successful actions (which may be contingent on external conditions or circumstances) are required for virtue, and Stoic responses to this, see Irwin 1990.

and Scipio Africanus in order to preserve their fame, but also encourage others to emulate them (23.14.12).⁵⁰

One further Polybian passage which offers reflections on the importance of praise, which has been briefly mentioned above, is Polybius' story of Philopoemen's false praise of Archon (22.19):

> Ὅτι Φιλοποίμην πρὸς Ἄρχωνα τὸν στρατηγὸν λόγοις τισὶ διεφέρετο. ὁ μὲν οὖν Φιλοποίμην εὐδοκήσας ἐκ τοῦ καιροῦ τοῖς λεγομένοις καὶ μεταγνοὺς ἐπῄνει τὸν Ἄρχωνα φιλοφρόνως, ὡς ἐντρεχῶς καὶ πανούργως τῷ καιρῷ κεχρημένον. ἔμοιγε μήν, φησὶν ὁ Πολύβιος, οὔτε τότε παρόντι τὸ ῥηθὲν εὐηρέστησεν, ὥστ' ἐπαινοῦντά τινα κακῶς ἅμα ποιεῖν, οὔτε μετὰ ταῦτα τῆς ἡλικίας προβαινούσης· πολὺ γὰρ δή τι μοι δοκεῖ κεχωρίσθαι κατὰ τὴν αἵρεσιν ὁ πραγματικὸς ἀνὴρ τοῦ κακοπράγμονος καὶ παραπλησίαν ἔχειν διαφορὰν τῷ κακεντρεχεῖ πρὸς τὸν ἐντρεχῆ· ἃ μὲν γάρ ἐστι κ<άλλ>ιστα τῶν ὄντων ὡς ἔπος εἰπεῖν, ἃ δὲ τοὐναντίον· ἀλλὰ διὰ τὴν νῦν ἐπιπολάζουσαν ἀκρισίαν βραχείας ἔχοντα κοινότητας τὰ προειρημένα τῆς αὐτῆς ἐπισημασίας καὶ ζήλου τυγχάνει παρὰ τοῖς ἀνθρώποις.

> Philopoemen had a verbal dispute with Archon the strategus. Suddenly agreeing with what he said, he changed his attitude and praised Archon warmly for having acted under the circumstances in an adroit and smart manner. But I myself, who happened to be present, neither approved at the time of what he said, lauding a man and at the same time doing him injury, nor do I think so now when I am of riper age. For in my opinion there is a wide difference in the character of a forceful man and an unscrupulous one, almost as great as that between an adroit and a mischievous one. The one quality may be said to be the best in the world and the other just the opposite. But owing to our prevalent lack of judgment, the two, having some points in common, meet with equal approbation and admiration.

Here Polybius describes how Philopoemen, who was in dispute with Archon, used praise as a means of doing his opponent harm, which, as Walbank has argued, can reasonably be understood as ironic praise.⁵¹ Polybius' criticism of Philopoemen here thus confirms his earlier statement at 10.21 about providing even-handed praise and blame in his account of Philopoemen in his history, in spite of having written a separate encomium of the Achaean statesman. But we can also note the emphasis on Polybius himself here, who reports his own indignation in

---

50 On Polybius' treatment of these three figures in 23.12–14, see Pomeroy 1986, 414–16.
51 The translation cited here from the second edition of the Loeb follows the interpretation of this passage provided by Walbank 1979, 210 on Plb. 22.19.1. The original Loeb edition (Paton 1926, 387) translates the key sentence of the passage as "At the time his verbal rejoinders were applauded, but afterwards he regretted them and praised Archon warmly for having acted under the circumstances in an adroit and smart manner", but Walbank argues decisively for an ironic interpretation in his commentary.

response to this false praise both at the time, when he was present, and subsequently at the time of writing.⁵² An anecdote about false praise thus becomes a moment of a different kind of epideictic on the part of Polybius, in assigning blame to Philopoemen for this behaviour, but it also provides reflections on the instability of praise, which can not only be falsely conferred, as we find in the narrative about Philopoemen and Archon, but it can also be wrongly applied, as a result of failures of judgement. This incident of false praise within the narrative thus opens a rich and multi-layered perspective on the wider themes of praise and blame within the work as whole, and the need for historians (and their audiences) to apply sound judgement. The story also serves as an interesting moment of self-praise, since in making a judgement of blame against Philopoemen, Polybius reminds his readers of the qualities that he brings to his history of sound judgement and accuracy of reporting, underlined by the focus on his being present at the original moment when Philopoemen gave his speech.⁵³

In Polybius, as in Aristotle, epideictic can have a moral dimension, and praise needs to be seen as just as important as blame in Polybius' writing. The first book of his *Histories* highlights different areas of praise, by mentioning first the well-worn topic of praise of history (1.1.1), which Polybius does not need to add to, the achievement of Fortune in bringing together events towards the goal of Roman dominance (1.4), and the importance of the need for historians to apply praise and blame (1.14). The work's ending, too, presents examples of praise, which turn the focus towards Polybius himself. Thus our fragments of Book 39 relate: how Polybius was able to save the statues and decrees honouring Philopoemen from being destroyed (39.3), looking back at Polybius' own encomium of Philopoemen but also at his judicious reporting of him in the *Histories*; the role that he took in settling the affairs of Greece after the Achaean War and the honours that he received from the cities of Greece (39.5);⁵⁴ and a summary (39.8), where Polybius confirms the accomplishment of his entire historical work, an achievement which will probably have been underlined further by the likely summary character of the lost Book 40.⁵⁵ It is very striking that earlier honours for

---

52 On Polybius' use of the first and of the third person in his work, see Marincola 1997, 188–92; on Polybius as a character in his work, see Miltsios 2013, 132–40.
53 On self-praise, see further Marincola 1997, 175–82, Pernot 1998.
54 The reference to honours received by Polybius in life and in death in 39.5.4 points to the involvement of a posthumous editor, but this does not necessarily mean that the whole of the chapter is from a posthumous edition, as noted by Walbank 1979, 735 on 39.5.4-6; see also McGing 2010, 146–47.
55 On 39.8, see Miltsios 2013, 117–18. On Book 40, see Walbank 1979, 743–44.

Philopoemen are called into question, but are then saved through the good offices of Polybius, but all in a context which appears to have emphasized the broader achievements of Polybius himself, who now surpasses Philopoemen in terms of the benefits conferred on his fellow Achaeans.

Pausanias' account of honours for Polybius in Megalopolis (Paus. 8.30.8–9) provides an appropriate close to this chapter:

> Μεγαλοπολίταις δὲ ἐπὶ τῆς ἀγορᾶς ἐστιν ὄπισθεν τοῦ περιβόλου τοῦ ἀνειμένου τῷ Λυκαίῳ Διὶ ἀνὴρ ἐπειργασμένος ἐπὶ στήλῃ, Πολύβιος Λυκόρτα· γέγραπται δὲ καὶ ἐλεγεῖα ἐπ' αὐτῷ λέγοντα ὡς ἐπὶ γῆν καὶ θάλασσαν πᾶσαν πλανηθείη, καὶ ὅτι σύμμαχος γένοιτο Ῥωμαίων καὶ παύσειεν αὐτοὺς ὀργῆς τῆς ἐς τὸ Ἑλληνικόν. συνέγραψε δὲ ὁ Πολύβιος οὗτος καὶ ἄλλα ἔργα Ῥωμαίων καὶ ὡς Καρχηδονίοις κατέστησαν ἐς πόλεμον, αἰτία τε ἥτις ἐγένετο αὐτοῦ καὶ ὡς ὀψὲ οὐκ ἄνευ κινδύνων μεγάλων Ῥωμαῖοι Σκιπίωνι * * * ὅν τινα Καρχηδονιακὸν ὀνομάζουσι τέλος τε ἐπιθέντα τῷ πολέμῳ καὶ τὴν Καρχηδόνα καταβαλόντα ἐς ἔδαφος. ὅσα μὲν δὴ Πολυβίῳ παραινοῦντι ὁ Ῥωμαῖος ἐπείθετο, ἐς ὀρθὸν ἐχώρησεν αὐτῷ· ἃ δὲ οὐκ ἠκροᾶτο διδάσκοντος, γενέσθαι οἱ λέγουσιν ἁμαρτήματα. Ἑλλήνων δὲ ὁπόσαι πόλεις ἐς τὸ Ἀχαϊκὸν συνετέλουν, παρὰ Ῥωμαίων εὕραντο αὗται Πολύβιόν σφισι πολιτείας τε καταστήσασθαι καὶ νόμους θεῖναι. τῆς δ' εἰκόνος τοῦ Πολυβίου τὸ βουλευτήριόν ἐστιν ἐν ἀριστερᾷ.

> In the marketplace of that city, behind the enclosure sacred to Lycaean Zeus, is the figure of a man carved in relief on a slab, Polybius, the son of Lycortas. Elegiac verses are inscribed upon it saying that he roamed over every land and every sea, and that he became the ally of the Romans and stayed their wrath against the Greek nation. This Polybius wrote also a history of the Romans, including how they went to war with Carthage, what the cause of the war was, and how at last, not before great dangers had been run, Scipio ... whom they name Carthaginian, because he put an end to the war and razed Carthage to the ground. Whenever the Romans obeyed the advice of Polybius, things went well with them, but they say that whenever they would not listen to his instructions they made mistakes. All the Greek cities that were members of the Achaean League got permission from the Romans that Polybius should draw up constitutions for them and frame laws. On the left of the portrait-statue of Polybius is the Council Chamber (Transl. W.H.S Jones).

As Brian McGing has noted, the reference to Polybius' travels over land and sea evokes Polybius' own interest in Homer's Odysseus.[56] This passage is, moreover, remarkable for its shifts in syntax from indirect to direct discourse, with the account of the inscription in elegiac verse, that records praise of Polybius using the constructions of indirect speech (λέγοντα ὡς ἐπὶ γῆν καὶ θάλασσαν πᾶσαν πλανηθείη, καὶ ὅτι σύμμαχος γένοιτο Ῥωμαίων καὶ παύσειεν αὐτοὺς ὀργῆς τῆς ἐς τὸ Ἑλληνικόν), being followed by the content of Polybius' work presented in di-

---

[56] McGing 2010, 129–30. On the honours paid to Polybius in the Peloponnese (including the still extant honorific portrait from Kleitor), see also Ma 2013, 279–84.

rect speech (with συνέγραψε δὲ ὁ Πολύβιος splendidly echoing the opening of Thucydides 1.1), and then the report of what is said about Polybius as a giver of advice to the Romans, and then the final narrative of honours paid to Polybius across the Achaean League: the effect is to blur the boundaries between the inscription and Pausanias' own report of Polybius here, but all in a laudatory context which also fits with the beginning and ending and close of Polybius' *Histories*. The passage also strikingly places a focus on praise, which I hope to have shown is a key feature of Polybius' work, especially as the ability to confer praise (and blame) that relies on sound judgement is itself something praiseworthy. Polybius' praise and blame of others also reflects well on himself.

Bibliography

Allard-Nelson, S.K. (2001), "Virtue in Aristotle's *Rhetoric*: A Metaphysical and Ethical Capacity", in: *Ph&Rh* 34, 245–59.

Ambaglio, D. (2005), "Fabio e Filino: Polibio sulli storici della prima guerra punica", in: G. Schepens/J. Bollansée (eds.), *The Shadow of Polybius: Intertextuality as a Research Tool in Greek Historiography, Proceedings of the International Colloquium Leuven, 21–22 September 2001*, Leuven, 205–22.

Ashton, R.H.J. (1986), "Rhodian Bronze Coinage and the Earthquake of 229–226 BC", in: *NC* 146, 1–17.

Baron, C.A. (2009), "The Use and Abuse of Historians: Polybios' Book XII and Our Evidence for Timaios", in: *AncSoc* 39, 1–34.

—— (2013), *Timaeus of Tauromenium and Hellenistic Historiography*, Cambridge.

Bearzot, C. (2005), "Polibio e Teopompo: osservazioni di metodo e guidizio morale", in: G. Schepens/J. Bollansée (eds.), *The Shadow of Polybius: Intertextuality as a Research Tool in Greek Historiography, Proceedings of the International Colloquium Leuven, 21–22 September 2001*, Leuven, 55–71.

Bertelli, L. (2014), "Aristotle and History", in: G. Parmeggiani (ed.), *Between Thucydides and Polybius: The Golden Age of Greek Historiography*, Cambridge, Mass., 289–303.

Braund, S. (1998), "Praise and Protreptic in Early Imperial Panegyric", in: M. Whitby (ed.), *The Propaganda of Power: The Role of Panegyric in Late Antiquity*, Leiden, 53–76.

Brunschwig, J. (1994), "Rhétorique et dialectique: *Rhétorique* et *Topiques*", in: D.J. Furley/A. Nehamas (eds.), *Aristotle's Rhetoric: Philosophical Essays*, Princeton, NJ, 57–96.

Carey, C. (2007), "Epideictic Oratory", in: I. Worthington (ed.), *A Companion to Greek Rhetoric*, Malden, Mass., 236–52.

Chávez Reino, A.L. (2005), "Los claroscuros del Éforo de Polibio", in: G. Schepens/ J. Bollansée (eds.), *The Shadow of Polybius: Intertextuality as a Research Tool in Greek Historiography, Proceedings of the International Colloquium Leuven, 21–22 September 2001*, Leuven, 19–54.

Collins, J.H. (2015), *Exhortations to Philosophy: The Protreptics of Plato, Isocrates, and Aristotle*, Oxford.

Derow, P.S. (1970), "Polybios and the Embassy of Kallikrates", in: *Essays Presented to C.M. Bowra*, Oxford, 12–23.

—— (2014), *Rome, Polybius and the East*, Oxford.
Dreyer, B. (2013), "Frank Walbank's *Philippos Tragoidoumenos*: Polybius' Account of Philips' Last Years", in: B. Gibson/T. Harrison (eds.), *Polybius and his World: Essays in Memory of Frank Walbank*, Oxford, 201–11.
Eckstein, A.M. (1995), *Moral Vision in the Histories of Polybius*, Berkeley.
Farrington, S.T. (2011), "Action and Reason: Polybius on the Gap between Encomium and History", in: *CPh* 106, 324–42.
—— (2015), "A Likely Story: Rhetoric and the Determination of Truth in Polybius' *Histories*", in: *Histos* 9, 29–66.
Flower, H.I. (1996), *Ancestor Masks and Aristocratic Power in Roman Culture*, Oxford.
Flower, M.A. (1994), *Theopompus of Chios. History and Rhetoric in the Fourth Century B.C.*, Oxford.
Garver, E. (2009), "Aristotle on the Kinds of Rhetoric", in: *Rhetorica* 27, 1–18.
Gibson, B. (2013), "Polybius and Xenophon: The Mercenary War", in: B. Gibson/T. Harrison (eds.), *Polybius and his World: Essays in Memory of Frank Walbank*, Oxford, 159–79.
Gruen, E. (1984), *The Hellenistic World and the Coming of Rome*, Berkeley.
—— (2013), "Polybius and Josephus on Rome", in: B. Gibson/T. Harrison (eds.), *Polybius and his World: Essays in Memory of Frank Walbank*, Oxford, 255–65.
Hartog, F. (2010), "Polybius and the First Universal History", in: P. Liddel/A. Fear (eds.), *Historiae Mundi: Studies in Universal History*, London, 30–40.
Hauser, G. (1999), "Aristotle on epideictic: The formation of public morality", in: *RSQ* 29, 5–23.
Irwin, T.H. (1990), "Virtue, praise and success: Stoic responses to Aristotle", in: *Monist* 73, 59–79.
Labarrière, J.-L. (2001), "L'orateur politique face à ses contraintes", in: D.J. Furley /A. Nehamas (eds.), *Aristotle's Rhetoric: Philosophical Essays*, Princeton, NJ, 231–53.
Ma, J. (2013), *Statues and Cities: Honorific Portraits and Civic Identity in the Hellenistic World*, Oxford.
Marincola, J. (1997), *Authority and Tradition in Ancient Historiography*, Cambridge.
—— (2001), *Greek Historians. Greece & Rome*, New Surveys in the Classics 31, Oxford.
—— (2013), "Polybius, Phylarchus and Tragic History: A Reconsideration", in: B. Gibson/T. Harrison (eds.), *Polybius and his World: Essays in Memory of Frank Walbank*, Oxford, 73–90.
—— (2014), "Rethinking Isocrates and Historiography", in: G. Parmeggiani (ed.), *Between Thucydides and Polybius: The Golden Age of Greek Historiography*, Cambridge, Mass., 39–61.
McGing, B.C. (2010), *Polybius' Histories*, Oxford.
—— (2013), "Youthfulness in Polybius: The Case of Philip V of Macedon", in: B. Gibson/T. Harrison (eds.), *Polybius and his World: Essays in Memory of Frank Walbank*, Oxford, 181–99.
Meister, K. (1975), *Historische Kritik bei Polybios*, Wiesbaden.
Miltsios, N. (2013), *The Shaping of Narrative in Polybius*, Berlin.
Nicholson, E. (2015), "A Reassessment of Philip V. of Macedon in Polybios' *Histories*", PhD diss., Newcastle.
Parmeggiani, G. (2011), *Eforo di Cuma. Studi di storiografia greca*, Bologna.
—— (2014), "Introduction", in: G. Parmeggiani (ed.), *Between Thucydides and Polybius: The Golden Age of Greek Historiography*, Cambridge, Mass., 1–6.
Paton, W.R. (1926), *Polybius: The Histories Vol. 5*, Cambridge, Mass.
Pédech, P. (1964), *La méthode historique de Polybe*, Paris.
Pernot, L. (1993), *La rhétorique de l'éloge dans le monde gréco-romain*, 2 vols., Paris.

—— (1998), "*Periautologia*. Problèmes et méthodes de l'éloge de soi-même dans la tradition éthique et rhétorique gréco-romaine", in: *REG* 111, 101–124.
—— (2015), *Epideictic Rhetoric: Questioning the Stakes of Ancient Praise*, Austin, TX.
Pomeroy, A.J. (1986), "Death Notices in Polybius", in: *Phoenix* 40, 407–23.
Prandi, L. (2005), "Polibio e Callistene: una polemica non personale?", in: G. Schepens/J. Bollansée (eds.), *The Shadow of Polybius: Intertextuality as a Research Tool in Greek Historiography, Proceedings of the International Colloquium Leuven, 21–22 September 2001*, Leuven, 73–87.
Pratt, J. (2012), "The Epideictic Agon and Aristotle's Elusive Third Genre", in: *AJPh* 133, 177–208.
Quinn, J.C. (2013), "Imagining the Imperial Mediterranean", in: B. Gibson/T. Harrison (eds.), *Polybius and his World: Essays in Memory of Frank Walbank*, Oxford, 337–52.
Rubinstein, L. (2013), "Spoken Words, Written Submissions, and Diplomatic Conventions: The Importance and Impact of Oral Performance in Hellenistic Inter-polis Relations", in: C. Kremmydas/K. Tempest (eds.), *Hellenistic Oratory. Continuity and Change*, Oxford, 165–99.
Sacks, K. (1981), *Polybius on the Writing of History*, Berkeley/Los Angeles.
Shuckburgh, E.S. (1889), *The Histories of Polybius*, 2 vols., London.
Thornton, J. (2013a), "Oratory in Polybius' *Histories*", in: C. Kremmydas/K. Tempest (eds.), *Hellenistic Oratory. Continuity and Change*, Oxford, 21–42.
—— (2013b), "Polybius in Context: The Political Dimension of the *Histories*", in: B. Gibson/T. Harrison (eds.), *Polybius and his World: Essays in Memory of Frank Walbank*, Oxford, 213–29.
—— (2013c), "Tragedia e retorica nella polemica sulla presa di Mantinea", in: M. Mari/J. Thornton (eds.), *Parole in movimento: Linguaggio politico, lessico storiografico nel mondo ellenistico. Atti di convegno internazionale, Roma, 21–23 febbraio 2011*, Studi Hellenistici 73, 353–74.
Vattuone, R. (2014), "Looking for the Invisible: Theopompus and the Roots of Historiography", in: G. Parmeggiani (ed.), *Between Thucydides and Polybius: The Golden Age of Greek Historiography*, Cambridge, Mass., 7–37.
Walbank, F.W. (1957), *A Historical Commentary on Polybius*, Vol. 1, Oxford.
—— (1962), "Polemic in Polybius", in: *JRS* 52, 1–12.
—— (1967), *A Historical Commentary on Polybius*, Vol. 2, Oxford.
—— (1972), *Polybius*, Sather Classical Lectures 42, Berkeley/Los Angeles.
—— (1975), "*Symploke*: Its Role in Polybius' Histories", in: *YClS* 24, 197–212.
—— (1979), *A Historical Commentary on Polybius*, Vol. 3, Oxford.
Weaire, G. (2002), "The Relationship between Dionysius of Halicarnassus' 'De imitatione' and 'Epistula ad Pompeium'", in: *CPh* 97, 351–9.
Wiemer, H.-U. (2013), "Zeno of Rhodes and the Rhodian View of the Past", in: B. Gibson/T. Harrison (eds.), *Polybius and his World: Essays in Memory of Frank Walbank*, Oxford, 279–306.
Williams, M.F. (2007), "Polybius' Histories and Aristotle's Poetics", in: *AHB* 21, 1–64.
Woodman, A.J. (2014), *Tacitus: Agricola*, Cambridge.
Wooten, C. (1974), "The Speeches in Polybius: An Insight into the Nature of Hellenistic Oratory", in: *AJPh* 95, 235–51.

Lisa I. Hau
Being, Seeming and Performing in Polybius

The contrast between *einai* and *dokein*—what is real, and what only seems to be real—is ubiquitous in Classical Greek literature. In Classical Greek historiography (especially Thucydides) this often corresponds to a contrast between *ergon* and *logos*: action and speech, or reality and pretence. If one comes to Polybius with these dichotomies in mind, some passages read rather oddly, especially his long digression in Book 31 on the training of Scipio Aemilianus for political life. This paper proposes to examine the use of *dokein*, to seem (or to have a reputation for, to be known for)[1] and *doxa*, opinion/reputation, in Polybius in order to investigate the role played by this traditional dichotomy in his *Histories*. The paper falls in two parts: first, the relationship between reputation and reality in the *Histories* will be explored through a close reading of the Scipio Aemilianus digression; then, we shall broaden the perspective to the rest of the *Histories* and investigate the use of *dokein* and *doxa*, partly in the light of Davidson's theory of the gaze in Polybius. At the end, this will lead to some conclusions about Polybius' view of historical causation, and the possibility of knowing reality.

1 The reputation of Scipio Aemilianus (Plb. 31.23–30)

This long digression[2] on how Scipio Aemilianus with Polybius' help trained himself for political greatness is central for understanding the relationship between being and seeming in Polybius. Several scholars have argued that the passage shows that it was more important for Polybius that Scipio gained a reputation for being a good man than that he actually was, or became, good.[3] This fits into a pervasive interpretation of Polybius as a pragmatic, even cynical, author, for whom the end justifies the means.[4] I have recently demonstrated at length that

---
[1] E.g. Plb. 1.16.11, 1.56.3, 3.19.13, 4.47.1.
[2] By calling these chapters a "digression" I am only implying that they constitute a temporal pause in the linear narrative, not that they are extraneous to Polybius' project. Polybius' long digressions are always central to his larger project, the best example being Book 6 on the Roman constitution.
[3] E.g. Astin 1967, 31–34, Walbank 1979 *ad* Plb. 31.23–31, esp. *ad* 31.28.10–11 and 31.29.9. *Contra* Eckstein 1995, 149.
[4] See e.g. Aymard 1940, Walbank 1965, 1972, 58 and *passim*, 1977, Ferrary 1988, 265–348, Green 1990, 269–85.

this view of Polybius is far too simplistic, and that his *Histories* are meant to be didactic both on a practical and a moral level;[5] but that raises the question of the role of Scipio's reputation, which manifestly figures prominently in the digression. Let us examine the passage from the beginning.

We begin with the introduction to the narrative of Scipio's training:

> Now that the progress of my narrative and the time period call our special attention to this family, I wish in order to satisfy the reader's curiosity to execute a promise I made in the previous book and left unfulfilled. For I promised to explain why and how the fame/good reputation (δόξα) of Scipio advanced to such a height and became brilliant faster than normally happens, and also how it came to pass that the friendship and intimacy between him and Polybius grew to such an extent that not only did the fame (φήμην) of it spread as far as Italy and Greece, but their preference for each other's company also became known to those further afield (Plb. 31.23.1–3, transl. modified from Paton).

It is striking that Polybius gives as his purpose for this digression not to explain Scipio's character or ancestry, as one might expect, but rather to explain his fame or reputation, and its fast and wide dissemination. Similarly, with regard to the friendship between himself and Scipio the focus is on its widespread fame, but here there is a direct link with reality: when Polybius says that he wants to explain "how it came to pass that the friendship and intimacy between Scipio and Polybius grew to such an extent that ...", it is clear that the fame of the friendship was a direct result of its intensity and not of any publicity strategy.[6] Such a causal link is not spelled out between reality and Scipio's personal fame, and it would at this stage be possible to imagine that Polybius was going to outline the acquisition of an undeserved reputation, perhaps one which exceeded Scipio's actual achievements. However, in the following chapters we shall see that Scipio's reputation does, in fact, have a solid basis in reality.

Continuing Polybius' narrative of Scipio, the next few lines tell how Scipio and his brother first become acquainted with Polybius, and then we get the detailed scene with dialogue in which Scipio asks Polybius to become his friend (31.23.8–12). Here Scipio complains that Polybius seems to prefer his brother to him and says that he has "a reputation for being (or seems to everyone to be) quiet and without initiative, with none of the energetic character of a Roman" (δοκῶ γὰρ εἶναι πᾶσιν ἡσύχιός τις καὶ νωθρός, ὡς ἀκούω, καὶ πολὺ κεχωρισμένος τῆς Ῥωμαϊκῆς αἱρέσεως καὶ πράξεως) and not living up to his family name. We note that it is his reputation that is hurting Scipio, not his own perception of what his

---

[5] Hau 2016. See also Eckstein 1995.
[6] For the historical reality of the friendship, see most recently Erskine 2012 and Sommer 2013.

own character is really like. Polybius-as-a-character responds by praising Scipio for this sentiment, saying that it proves that, in reality, he is high-minded (δῆλος γὰρ εἶ διὰ τούτων μέγα φρονῶν). This makes Scipio very happy, and he implores Polybius to be his friend and mentor, saying that he would then "seem to himself to be" (δόξω … ἐμαυτῷ) worthy of his family and ancestors (31.24.9–10). The fact that Scipio uses the same verb, δοκεῖν, to express his self-perception as he does to express his reputation in the eyes of his peers is our first hint that δοκεῖν does not just describe outward semblance, but can denote something deeper as well although, of course, a person's self-perception does not necessarily match reality.

The passage detailing the beginning of the friendship between Scipio and Polybius ends with a statement that introduces a level of reality into all the talk about appearances (31.25.1). Here, the narrator says that Scipio and Polybius from that point onwards "kept giving each other trials/evidence of themselves in actual action (ἐπ' αὐτῶν τῶν πραγμάτων πεῖραν αὐτῶν διδόντες ἀλλήλοις) and by that means became as close as close relatives". The expression "actual action", αὐτῶν τῶν πραγμάτων, is partly an antithesis to the warm words spoken by Scipio and Polybius, to emphasise that their later actions lived up to those words, that their *erga* matched their *logoi*; but it is also a contrast to all the talk of semblance and reputation, to show that they did *in reality* become both good men and close friends.

We then get to the actual beginning of Scipio's training (31.25.2). This is introduced by the statement that "The first impulse and ambition for what is good that came upon him (πρώτη δέ τις ἐνέπεσεν ὁρμὴ καὶ ζῆλος τῶν καλῶν) was the impulse and ambition to acquire a reputation (δόξαν) for moderation (σωφροσύνῃ) and to exceed in this respect his peers in age". In the next line, this *doxa* is called a "fine prize" (μέγας … στέφανος) by the narrator. Here we get an indication of an intrinsic relationship between reputation and reality: it is Scipio's real and existing "impulse and ambition for *ta kala*" that leads him to want a reputation for moderation. We are surely meant to understand that this "impulse and ambition" lead him to want to actually learn moderation and actually be moderate, but that he also wants to be rewarded for this moderation by a reputation for it. It is worth remembering that *ta kala* means not just the morally good, but also the glorious: both the moral behaviour and its worldly reward.

The following chapter describes the general decadence of Roman youth at the time, and then how Scipio "combatted all his desires" (πάσαις ταῖς ἐπιθυμίαις ἀντιταξάμενος) and made his life "coordinated and harmonious" (ὁμολογούμενον καὶ σύμφωνον) in all respects and so "made universal (πάνδημον) his reputation for an orderly lifestyle and for moderation" (τὴν ἐπ' εὐταξίᾳ καὶ σωφροσύνῃ δόξαν, 31.25.9). Again, it is clear that Scipio actually became moderate and in reality did live a well-ordered life, but the emphasis is on the reputation, or fame, he gained from it.

In the next chapter, Scipio sets out to "distinguish himself from others" (διενεγκεῖν τῶν ἄλλων) in generosity. This obviously means that he wants to actually be more generous than other people, but the methods he chooses are conspicuous because they are meant to enhance his reputation, and Polybius is careful every time to report the reactions of the intended audience: the women who witness Scipio's mother's new wealth are "shocked", and so are his brothers-in-law when they receive the full sum of their dowries three years early. The verbs used to express shock here are verbs normally used of panicked soldiers: ἐκπλήττεσθαι (31.26.8), καταπεπληγμένοι (31.27.16). When Scipio gives his part of an inheritance to his brother, this becomes "widely talked about" (περιβοήτου) and provides "obviously visible evidence" (δεῖγμα ... ἐμφανέστερον) of his character (31.28.4), again emphasising the visible, public—one might almost say performative—aspect of the generous act.

The whole thing ends with a conclusion that emphasises Scipio's reputation, and—most distasteful to modern readers—the relatively low cost at which he gained it:

> ταῦτα μὲν οὖν προκατεσκευασμένος ἐκ τῆς πρώτης ἡλικίας Πόπλιος Σκιπίων προῆλθε πρὸς τὸ φιλοδοξεῖν σωφροσύνῃ καὶ καλοκἀγαθίᾳ. εἰς ἣν ἴσως ἑξήκοντα τάλαντα δαπανήσας, τοσαῦτα γὰρ ἦν προειμένος τῶν ἰδίων, ὁμολογουμένην ἔσχε τὴν ἐπὶ καλοκἀγαθίᾳ φήμην, οὐχ οὕτω τῷ πλήθει τῶν χρημάτων τὸ προκείμενον κατεργασάμενος ὡς τῷ καιρῷ τῆς δόσεως καὶ τῷ χειρισμῷ τῆς χάριτος. τὴν δὲ σωφροσύνην περιεποιήσατο δαπανήσας μὲν οὐδέν, πολλῶν δὲ καὶ ποικίλων ἡδονῶν ἀποσχόμενος προσεκέρδανε τὴν σωματικὴν ὑγίειαν καὶ τὴν εὐεξίαν, ἥτις αὐτῷ παρ' ὅλον τὸν βίον παρεπομένη πολλὰς ἡδονὰς καὶ καλὰς ἀμοιβὰς ἀπέδωκεν ἀνθ' ὧν πρότερον ἀπέσχετο τῶν προχείρων ἡδονῶν.

Having thus from his earliest years laid the foundations of it, Publius Scipio advanced in his pursuit of this reputation (φιλοδοξεῖν) for temperance and nobility of character. By the expenditure of perhaps sixty talents—for that was what he had bestowed from his own property—his reputation (φήμην) for the second of these virtues was firmly established, and he did not attain his purpose so much by the largeness of the sums he gave as by the seasonableness of the gift and the gracious manner in which he conferred it. His temperance cost him nothing, but by abstaining from many and varied pleasures he gained in addition that bodily health and vigour which he enjoyed for the whole of his life, and which by the many pleasures of which it was the cause amply rewarded him for his former abstention from immediate pleasures (Plb. 31.28.10–13, transl. modified from Paton).

Three things are clear from this passage. Firstly, this is the conclusion that fulfills Polybius' promise in the introduction to the digression to explain how Scipio's reputation could grow so fast and to such a height. Secondly, Polybius sees nothing odious in deliberately and strategically building up a reputation for virtue. Thirdly, however, while gaining this reputation, Scipio did, in reality, act with great generosity, just as he did become moderate and, indeed, benefitted from this moderate lifestyle for the rest of his life. It may be relevant here to remind ourselves of Aristotle's theory that virtue is created by habitual practice:[7] Scipio made himself generous and moderate for the rest of his life by practising these virtues in his youth, and this practice also gained him a solid and very useful reputation for these virtues.

With this conclusion it sounds as if the digression on Scipio is over, but Polybius adds a chapter on how Scipio trained and proved his courage, not in the law-courts like his peers, but in hunting:

> ὁ δ' ἁπλῶς οὐδένα λυπῶν ἐξεφέρετο τὴν ἐπ' ἀνδρείᾳ δόξαν πάνδημον, ἔργῳ πρὸς λόγον ἁμιλλώμενος. τοιγαροῦν ὀλίγῳ χρόνῳ τοσοῦτον παρέδραμε τοὺς καθ' αὑτὸν ὅσον οὐδείς πω μνημονεύεται Ῥωμαίων, καίπερ τὴν ἐναντίαν ὁδὸν πορευθεὶς ἐν φιλοδοξίᾳ τοῖς ἄλλοις ἅπασι πρὸς τὰ Ῥωμαίων ἔθη καὶ νόμιμα.
>
> Scipio, on the other hand, without harming anyone, gained his universal reputation (δόξαν) for courage, competing in deed against their words. So that in a short space of time he had outstripped his contemporaries more than any other Roman, although the path he pursued to gain glory (ἐν φιλοδοξίᾳ) was quite the opposite of that followed by all others in accordance with Roman usage and custom (Plb. 31.29.11–12, transl. modified from Paton).

Polybius is driving his own pro-hunting agenda here, and setting up hunting as the real and worthy *ergon* to oppose the artificial and useless *logoi* that take place in the law-courts. Interestingly for our purposes, *doxa* is placed outside of this *ergon-logos* dichotomy. Whereas deeds are presented as better, more honest, and more real than words, reputation is presented, not as further empty words as one might think, but as a true reflection of reality, *i.e.* on the side of *erga* rather than *logoi*.

After this passage on Scipio's courage, the digression is rounded off by an overall conclusion:

> I have spoken at such length of the practice (αἱρέσεως) of Scipio from his earliest years, partly because I thought such a history (ἱστορίαν) would be agreeable (ἡδεῖαν) to the old and beneficial (ὠφέλιμον) for the young, but chiefly in order to secure credence for all I

---

[7] Arist. *EN* 1103a30.

shall have to tell of him in the books which follow, so that readers may neither hesitate to accept as true anything in his subsequent life that seems astonishing nor depriving the man himself of the credit of his meritorious achievements put them down to chance from ignorance of the true cause of each. There were some few exceptions which we may assign to good luck and chance. After having narrated these events up to this point in a digression, I shall return again to the point where I left my regular narrative (Plb. 31.30, transl. modified from Paton).

Here Polybius describes the digression as being not about Scipio's reputation, but about his αἵρεσις, his "practice", or perhaps "training for virtue", if Polybius is using it like the Aristotelian προαίρεσις. He then declares explicitly that the digression has been included partly for the sake of moral didacticism and partly to underpin the subsequent narrative of Scipio, which might otherwise be hard to believe. These two purposes would obviously not be served if the digression had been solely about Scipio's reputation, even less if it had been about how he acquired an undeserved reputation for virtue. They can only be fulfilled by a digression explaining how Scipio trained his innate qualities to come out to their fullest so that he became a man capable of doing the great deeds he would go on to do (explaining Polybius' subsequent narrative), and, by extension, how the reader can train to become a good man and so be rewarded with a positive reputation (didacticism).

On the basis of this reading of the digression on Scipio Aemilianus' practice of and reputation for virtue, two conclusions can be drawn. Firstly, that pursuing a good reputation deliberately is not considered a bad thing—on the contrary, Scipio becomes good by striving for a reputation for excellence. *Doxa* and *dokein* are used not to denote a false impression, but to put emphasis on the perception of Scipio's actions, by himself and by others. Secondly, that Polybius considers it natural that a person wants to be rewarded for his good actions, and that his natural and expected reward is a good reputation, which we might then assume will lead to practical advantages further down the road.

In a large number of passages throughout the *Histories* this situation pertains: reputations are accurate reflections of reality, and the way that characters are perceived is often given more weight than the reality of their deeds or personalities. Thus, the Achaean League deals justly with everyone and so has a universal reputation for trustworthiness and nobility (πίστιν καὶ καλοκἀγαθίαν, 2.39.9–10), and Hiero II is a great benefactor to the Greeks and eager for a good reputation, which wins him honours while alive and an immortal reputation after his death (7.8.6). In a great comparative passage, Antigonus Doson and Philip II are said to have been rewarded with "immortal honour and glory" (ἀθανάτου τέτευχε τιμῆς καὶ δόξης, 5.9.9) because of their restrained treatment of those they had defeated, whereas Philip V treats conquered territory in the opposite way and so acquires the opposite reputation (5.10.11). Later on, Polybius' criticism of Philip V's taking of Cius is phrased as Philip "confirming his reputation" for cruelty and impiety (ἔμελλε κυρώσειν τὴν περὶ αὑτοῦ διαδεδομένην φήμην ὑπὲρ τῆς εἰς τοὺς φίλους ὠμότητος, ἐξ ἀμφοῖν δὲ δικαίως καὶ κληρονομήσειν παρὰ πᾶσι τοῖς Ἕλλησι τὴν ἐπ' ἀσεβείᾳ δόξαν, 15.22.3). As with the digression on Scipio's training the focus here is on the perception of Philip's actions more than on the actions themselves, and the end of the passage expresses the result: because of Philip's renewed reputation for/proof of his cruelty and impiety, the Rhodians begin to consider him their enemy (15.22.5–23.10).

In other words, in much of the *Histories* a man's reputation is considered a true reflection of reality, which makes a good reputation the natural reward of a good man and a bad reputation the equally natural punishment of a bad man. In Polybius' eyes this is perhaps how the world works, but it is also a didactic tool. Throughout the *Histories* Polybius is explicit about his didactic purpose, which is both practical and moral.[8] One of his major moral lessons is—as I have shown in detail elsewhere—that being good pays.[9] This may seem odious to readers steeped in a Christian tradition where good deeds are supposed to be done for their own sake (or that of a promised afterlife), but in an ancient Greek perspective it makes perfect sense for a reader to ask: why would I want to be good when it often pays better to be bad? Indeed, this question is repeatedly asked by Socrates' interlocutors in Plato.[10]

2 Perceptions and Performativity

Moral didacticism aside, what is most striking in Polybius' digression on Scipio's training for virtue is the fact that the focus throughout so much of it remains on the reputational results rather than on the moral results of Scipio's actions. It often seems that the perception of Scipio held by his fellow-Romans is more important than his actual character. Likewise, in the other passages on characters' reputations mentioned above, the impressions their actions make on other people are foregrounded at the expense of a detailed description of those actions. This state of affairs corresponds rather neatly to the model advanced by

---

8 E.g. 1.1, 1.35, 3.4, 10.21. See Hau 2016.
9 Hau 2016.
10 Most famously by Thrasymachus in *Rep.* 1.

J. Davidson more than twenty years ago in an article that has not gained the influence it deserves.[11] Davidson argues that perceptions are of central importance in the military narrative of the *Histories*, and that Polybius shows military commanders repeatedly putting on a show for each other and the civilian population in order to demonstrate overwhelming superiority and thus achieve their twin goals of galvanizing the courage of their own side and terrifying their opponents. Davidson distinguishes three levels in Polybius' narrative: at the bottom there is the action-level where things happen; one step up there is the perception-level where these actions are perceived in different ways by different characters; and at the very top there is the result-level where these perceptions—rather than the actions themselves—motivate characters to do things and so cause events to happen (Davidson calls this the pathological level). It is the perception-level that is given most space and attention in Polybius' narrative.

Applied to the Scipio digression, at the action-level there are Scipio's actions of moderation, generosity, and courage; at the perception-level these shock and impress his fellow-Romans (interestingly, the words used to express their shock are the same words Davidson identifies as expressing the reaction to the deliberate shows of force of military commanders)[12] and create his reputation. Then, at the result-level, this reputation means that he is appointed to command in Spain at a time when he would otherwise have been thought too young for such responsibility (Plb. 35.4).[13] For Scipio, and for history, it is this last fact that is the salient point, and it is the direct result of Scipio's reputation rather than of his character. Similarly, in the passage comparing Philip V unfavourably to Antigonus Doson and Philip II, the focus is overwhelmingly on the perception level where Philip's actions are perceived as cruel and impious by the other Greeks, and based on this perception the result of the Rhodians' enmity ensues.

Throughout the *Histories*, numerous political decisions are made on the basis of men's reputation. These passages are most often focalised through the decision-makers, e.g. the Senate or the Assembly at Rhodes, rather than through the character who holds the reputation. Most often the reputation matches what the narrator has said about the character (action-level), but that is less important than the influence his reputation has on the process of decision-making (perception-level) and the results of the decision eventually made (result-level). For instance, in the lead-up to the Battle of Cannae, we are told that:

---

[11] Davidson 1991.
[12] Davidson 1991, 19.
[13] Walbank 1979 *ad loc.* doubts that Scipio was actually that young, but acknowledges that the phrasing here is meant to complete the picture painted in 31.23–30.

It happened that everyone looked to Aemilius and placed their hopes especially in him because of the high moral quality of his life generally (τὴν ἐκ τοῦ λοιποῦ βίου καλοκαγαθίαν) and because he seemed (δοκεῖν) to have handled the Illyrian War a short time earlier both bravely and advantageously (ἀνδρωδῶς ἅμα καὶ συμφερόντως) (Plb. 3.107.8, my translation).

This description matches Polybius' narrative of the Illyrian War and echoes his short narrative of Aemilius' homecoming and triumph, where he also stressed the perceptions of his achievements among his fellow-Romans (ἐδόκει γὰρ οὐ μόνον ἐπιδεξίως, ἔτι δὲ μᾶλλον ἀνδρωδῶς κεχρῆσθαι τοῖς πράγμασιν, 3.19.3). However, the reader already knows—and Polybius' intended readers will surely have known—that Aemilius is going to suffer a disastrous defeat at Cannae. So in this case, despite the fact that the reputation of a character accurately reflects his character and conduct, and that the decision-makers' perception of the past and present is consequently correct, that is no guarantee for success in the future. A similar passage is 1.73.3 where the Carthaginians appoint Hanno "because he seemed (δοκεῖν) to have" handled an earlier crisis well, but in fact the appointment turns out to be disaster.[14] Both Aemilius and Hanno are shown by Polybius' narrative to deserve their reputation, and it is not hard to imagine that they had both been conscious of their countrymen's eyes on them when they were conducting war on their behalf and so had made some of their decisions with this gaze (to use Davidson's expression) and their own reputation in mind. But in these decision-making passages that is not important. What matters is that the intended audience of the performances that have led to their reputations, namely Aemilius' and Hanno's elite country-men, use these reputations as a basis for decision-making. We see how, realistically, political decisions are made on the basis not of reality, but of perceived reality. The fact that neither appointment goes well adds a bitter taste to the passages: even based on the most reliable information, human decsion-making is always fallible, and unexpected events must be expected.[15]

In this focus on the uncertainty of the outcome of decisions made on the basis of reputations/perceptions of character, these passages are closely related to a number of passages in the *Histories* where people make decisions on the basis of perceptions of their surroundings, also expressed by *dokein*. Sometimes this perception rests on the interpretation of sources, such as spies or messengers. For instance, in 2.27.4, a Roman consul takes hope because it seems (δοκεῖν) on the

---

[14] Another similar example is 3.98 where the high reputation (*doxa*) of the Iberian Abilyx is stressed just before he betrays the Carthaginian hostages to the Romans.
[15] See Maier 2012. For Polybius on *tykhe*, see Hau 2011 with bibliography.

basis of his scouts' reports that the enemy is caught between two Roman armies. This turns out indeed to be the case, and the Romans win a resounding victory. But such a direct correlation between perception and reality is not always the case: in 3.103.1–2, an exaggerated report of Minucius' victories in the field makes it seem (δοκεῖν) to the Romans that their previous lack of succes was due to Fabius Cunctator's lack of initiative. The reader knows from Polybius' narrative that Fabius has been avoiding battle with good reason and so knows that the Romans are being deceived. But this deception is not integral to the meaning of *dokein* in Polybius, it is understood only from the context.[16]

In these passages, *dokein* is used to express the perception of the focaliser or focalisers, on which they base their decision-making. *Dokein* is entirely subjective; it does not tell the reader anything about reality, only about the perception. The same is true in passages that deal with moral perceptions which influence decision making. Thus, in 1.11.1, it seems to (ἐδόκει) the Roman Senate that the unreasonableness of sending help to the treacherous Mamertines is of equal weight to (ἰσορροπεῖν) the advantage that might accrue from it, but we are not told what the narrator thinks. Similarly, in 3.20.7, before the outbreak of the Second Punic War, of the two alternatives offered by the Romans to the Carthaginians one seems to (ἐδόκει) the Carthaginians to entail disgrace and harm while the other seems to lead to great dangers. Again we are not told what the narrator thinks; the emphasis, as with Roman decision-making about the Mamertines, is on the decision-makers' perception of the situation and the way it influences their decision, *i.e.* on the perception-level and the result-level rather than on the basic action-level.

We can go further. In numerous passages, δοκεῖ or δοκεῖ μοι is used to express Polybius' interpretation or evaluation of his sources. Sometimes it is an interpretation of the motives behind an action as in 4.5.5–6 where the narrator qualifies the motives of Cleomenes by a ὥς γ᾽ ἐμοὶ δοκεῖ. At other times it is an evaluation of an action, either in intellectual terms ("in this situation Hasdrubal seems (δοκεῖ) to have done a clever and intelligent deed", 3.116.7) or in moral ones ("[this] seems to me the very height of villainy" [ἐμοὶ μὲν δοκεῖ τῆς πάσης γέμειν κακοπραγμοσύνης], 4.27.2). These expressions lend credibility to Polybius as historian becasue they give the reader the impression that he has questioned and evaluated his sources.

In the light of our reading of the numerous passages in the *Histories* that use *dokein* to signal the importance of the perception-level over the action-level it is

---

[16] Occasionally it is used of a character who pretends (3.15.12, 3.68.9—to themselves, 3.92.6, 4.19.10).

impossible not to think that Polybius is deliberately signalling the subjectivity of such perceptions. He is warning the reader to be aware that the historian's perception is fallible too and that the reader, with his or her greater hindsight, must draw their own conclusions.

3 Conclusion

The dichotomy of being vs seeming is not very important to Polybius. The important thing is what influences decision-making and causes events to happen, and Polybius knows that this is the perceptions people hold rather than reality itself. As a view of historical causation this is rather sophisticated: in recognising that it is often not people's actual character that lead to epoch-making decisions, but rather what other people perceive their characters, or the general situation, or the morality of the situation to be, Polybius is not writing great-man history; he is writing fallible-human-perception history.

Bibliography

Astin, A.E. (1967), *Scipio Aemilianus*, Oxford.
Aymard, A. (1940), "Le fragment de Polybe 'sur les traîtres' (xviii, 13–15)", in: *REA* 42, 9–19.
Davidson, J. (1991), "The Gaze in Polybius' *Histories*", in: *JRS* 81, 10–24.
Eckstein, A.M. (1995), *Moral Vision in the Histories of Polybius*, Berkeley.
Erskine, A. (2012), "Polybius Among the Romans: Life in the Cyclops' Cave", in: C. Smith/L.M. Yarrow (eds.), *Imperialism, Cultural Politics, and Polybius*, Oxford, 17–32.
Ferrary, J.-L. (1988), *Philhellénisme et Impérialisme. Aspects idéologiques de la conquête Romaine du monde hellénistique, de la seconde guerre de Macédoine à la guerre contre Mithridate*, Rome.
Green, P. (1990), *From Alexander to Actium: The Historical Evolution of the Hellenistic Age*, Berkeley/Los Angeles.
Hau, L.I. (2011), "*Tyche* in Polybios: Narrative Answers to a Philosophical Question", in: *Histos* 5, 183–207.
—— (2016), *Moral History from Herodotus to Diodorus Siculus*, Edinburgh.
Maier, F. (2012), "*Überall mit dem Unerwarteten rechnen*". *Die Kontingenz historischer Prozesse bei Polybios*, Munich.
Paton, W.R. (1922–1928), *Polybius. The Histories*, 6 vols., Loeb Classical Library, Cambridge, Mass.
Sommer, M. (2013), "Scipio Aemilianus, Polybius, and the Quest for Friendship in Second-Century Rome", in: B. Gibson/T. Harrison (eds.), *Polybius and his World: Essays in Memory of F.W. Walbank*, Oxford, 307–318.
Walbank, F.W. (1965), "Political Morality and the Friends of Scipio", in: *JRS* 55, 1–16.
—— (1972), *Polybius*, Berkeley/Los Angeles/London.
—— (1979), *A Historical Commentary on Polybius* III, Oxford.

Part II: **Narrative and Structure**

Roberto Nicolai
τὰ καιριώτατα καὶ πραγματικώτατα.
A Survey on the Speeches in Polybius

1 Preliminary remarks

My interest in Polybius' speeches began about 20 years ago, when Greek historians were the object of research mainly by other historians, who thought of themselves as colleagues of Thucydides and Polybius.[1] I cannot analyze in detail how and how far the situation has changed, but the change has been considerable. When in 1992 I published my book on historiography in ancient education, I was criticized by some Italian scholars for considering ancient historiography as a literary genre. In the last 25 years, books on historiography with a literary focus or combining historical and literary analysis have become no less numerous than the old-fashioned purely historical studies on Thucydides or Polybius. In December 2002 I presented a paper at Columbia University (New York) on Polybius' speeches: I will briefly recount some of my conclusions as a point of departure for further consideration.[2]

On that occasion, I observed that some scholars have tried to find Polybius' sources in order to assess his reliability in reporting speeches.[3] A source is evidence against the historian's invention and exculpates him from charges such as anachronism, unlikelihood and so on. According to a common opinion, the speeches by Claeneas and Lyciscus in 9.28–39 are "based on a genuine record, perhaps by way of a literary source".[4] Polybius also knew that literary sources could be unreliable.[5] Why does he criticize Timaeus, while accepting conventional speeches as actually delivered?[6] Polybius does not refuse rhetoric, but only

---

[1] Despite Loraux 1980. On the difference between modern and ancient historians as far as the speeches are concerned, see Baron 2013, 170.
[2] See, in more detail, Nicolai 2006.
[3] According to Walbank 1965 = 1985, 258f., if we leave out Hannibal, Mago and some Roman generals, Polybius' speakers are Greeks and the historian had good sources for their speeches. See also Pédech 1964, 259–76.
[4] So Walbank 1967, 163.
[5] According to Musti 1974, 194.
[6] Pausch 2010, 46f.

its improper use,[7] and he is capable of writing a speech. We cannot exclude that Polybius himself could have invented the speeches. Moreover, we do not have the sources of Polybius' speeches, some of which are based on oral traditions.[8]

Ancient historians usually avoided including speeches which the orator himself had published in some way.[9] In Book 30 Polybius informs us that Astymedes, a Rhodian politician, had published a speech. The historian sums up the speech and lingers on criticism of the main argument. The speech has failed in its intended effect and Polybius has to reveal the reasons for its failure, according to his own principles (12.25b.1). If this rule is valid, Polybius can report only unpublished speeches in detail.

Another test of reliability consists in repetitions of metaphors, sentences and ideas found in two speeches or in speech and historical account. Walbank examines only a few passages in this regard, and in his opinion there is no evidence of invention.[10] However, we should remember 29.12.10, where style and content both belong to the historian. When we find the same idea in speeches and narratives, we can be confident that that consideration belongs to the historian. The importance of the battle of Zama for the world empire is stressed by Polybius (15.9.2) and then by Scipio (15.10.2), but this idea may be anachronistic or a kind of *post eventum* prophecy.

The most controversial way to assess reliability is content. The content of Agelaus' speech can be used to demonstrate both Polybian invention (Mørkholm 1974) and the contrary (Deininger 1973). Vollmer (1990) and Champion (1997) have shown that the stress on the interconnection (συμπλοκή) is Polybian:[11] the actual speech would have had limited aims; the Polybian one is a kind of prophecy. The intervention of Polybius can be demonstrated by the coherent political analysis throughout the four speeches of Agelaus, Thrasycrates, Claeneas and Lyciscus.

Another way to gauge reliability is to analyze speeches from the audience's point of view. John Marincola remarks about the couple of speeches before Ticinus: "to be sure, the speakers say what we would expect them to". And concludes: "In any case, there is no reason to think that Polybius considered the speeches to be other than historical, or that his version was not the substance of

---

7 See Guelfucci 2005.
8 See Champion 1997, 114f.
9 Brock 1995.
10 Walbank 1965 = 1985, 254–56.
11 See Walbank 1957, 269f.

the speeches there".[12] Nevertheless, no ancient historian would provide clues to his inventions of his own accord. Both the preliminary evaluation of the appropriateness of the speeches and full correspondence with the audience's expectation can be clues themselves. In his important book on *Literary Texts and the Greek Historian*, Christopher Pelling says: "if there were no clear reason why the sources should misrepresent, if (particularly) a statement even *harmed* their argument, we should be more likely to believe it".[13] As far as the reliability of the speeches is concerned, I think we should reverse the argument: if there were no clear reasons why the historian could and should report what was actually said, we should be more likely to consider speeches as his own inventions or as inventions of his sources.

To sum up, I tried briefly to suggest the reasons why Polybius includes speeches in his work, sometimes with heavy interventions of his own in composition or else by relying on historiographical sources of at least uncertain reliability. These tenets of Polybius' speeches are most intelligible when viewed against Thucydides:

1. Interest in single *gentes* or personalities (Scipiones, Philopoemen, Hannibal, Philip V). Thucydides is less interested in this, since he often refers to anonymous speakers, to groups (ambassadors) and so on. The only great personalities in Thucydides are Pericles and Brasidas and, with minor stress, Alcibiades and Nicias.

2. Dramatic presentation, especially in private conversations. This kind of approach is hardly present in Thucydides.

3. Compositional structure (speeches in Book 3: the great battles in Italy). This feature is absent in Thucydides, who offers annalistic units and not books in the editorial sense.

4. Ideology and aetiology. These features are fully Thucydidean. In my Columbia talk I tried to show what seems to me to be the great difference between Thucydides and Polybius considering the practice of speeches: Thucydides uses speeches in order to reveal deep strata of human feelings and political motivations; Polybius, on the contrary, is much more concerned with specific events and the circumstances of whatever moment he is currently talking about.[14]

Polybius' interventions cannot be calculated in detail. This is particularly evident in speeches by generals before battles, though such speeches do correspond to what is fitting (πρέπον) in a given circumstance. I think that some very

---

12 Marincola 2001, 131.
13 Pelling 2000, 252.
14 See Marincola 2001, 132f.

effective and peculiar formulations probably came from actual speeches. I am quite sure that Polybius thought himself the most reliable historian, according to his own statements, not because he had complete evidence or because he was able to reconstruct speeches accurately, but because he had political and military experience. Concerning practice, Polybius is a good historian: his weak point is theory, which, in the case of speeches, he derives from Thucydides[15] (another weak theory is the constitution theory in Book 6). Speeches are a test that allows us to understand what was truth for him: literary and rhetorical analysis can reveal important signs for the understanding of Polybius' views. We have to correct our ideas about the reliability of an historian and in particular of an ancient historian: neither Thucydides nor Polybius can be isolated from their cultural context and they cannot be thought of as modern historians inspired by the idea of history as a science. Some modern scholars have asserted Thucydides' and Polybius' reliability even in speeches, in order to provide a last line of defense against what is perceived as an overemphasis upon rhetorical ideas on historiography. But rhetorical history—and ancient historiography is always rhetorical—is not rhetoric only, and rhetoric is not an actual danger. In this perspective reliability is not the main problem. In my opinion an actual danger for modern historians is, for example, the rhetoric of numbers and statistics. Tacitus offers us the formula *sine ira ac studio*, thus stressing the importance of the attitudes of the historian. Polybius' criticism of Timaeus, who just relied on books and evidence but had no political and military experience, suggests that Polybius attributed the greatest importance to this sort of expertise and to the resulting authority.[16]

2 The battle exhortation as a type-scene and as a piece of rhetoric

In recent years interest in Polybius' speeches has grown, regarding both theory and practice.[17] In order to evaluate the theoretical propositions of Polybius as far

---

15 See Nicolai 1999.
16 See Marincola 1997.
17 About the theory, see Nicolai 1999, Pausch 2010, Wiater 2014 with further bibliography; about the practice Champion 1997, Champion 2000, Usher 2009, Wiater 2010, Baronowski 2011, especially 149–51. About the importance of political debate in Polybius' times, as it is reflected in the *Histories*, see Thornton 2013.

as the speeches are concerned, I have chosen to investigate the battle exhortations.[18] Only in a few cases could Polybius have been a witness to the moment of the battle, and he would have mainly used other witnesses and previous historiographical works as the basis for his history. Moreover, these speeches have become an object of study due to the modern debate about battle exhortations in antiquity and their frequently topical content.

Every speech, in epic poetry and historiography, is situated in a context, made up of circumstances, presentation of the speaker and of the audience, reaction of the audience and effects of the speech and so on. All this may be described as a type-scene, according to the analysis of epic poetry by Walter Arend.[19] The content of the speech is one of the elements of the scene, and one should find out the main arguments in order to compare different scenes and speeches. What distinguishes one speech from another is context: the enemies are more numerous, the troops are tired and not so confident, the battle field is unfavorable or, on the other hand, the situation seems favorable, but this may be a danger because the troops are too confident. Every kind of situation requires different lines of argumentation.

First it is useful to study the passage in which Polybius criticizes Timoleon's speech in Timaeus (Plb. 12.26a):

τί δὲ πάλιν ὅταν ὁ Τιμολέων ἐν τῇ αὐτῇ βύβλῳ παρακαλῶν τοὺς Ἕλληνας πρὸς τὸν ἐπὶ τοὺς Καρχηδονίους κίνδυνον, καὶ μόνον οὐκ ἤδη μελλόντων συνάγειν εἰς τὰς χεῖρας τοῖς ἐχθροῖς πολλαπλασίοις οὖσι, πρῶτον μὲν ἀξιοῖ μὴ βλέπειν αὐτοὺς πρὸς τὸ πλῆθος τῶν ὑπεναντίων, ἀλλὰ πρὸς τὴν ἀνανδρίαν; καὶ γὰρ τῆς Λιβύης ἁπάσης συνεχῶς οἰκουμένης καὶ πληθυούσης ἀνθρώπων, ὅμως ἐν ταῖς παροιμίαις, ὅταν περὶ ἐρημίας ἔμφασιν βουλώμεθα ποιῆσαι, λέγειν ἡμᾶς "ἐρημότερα τῆς Λιβύης", οὐκ ἐπὶ τὴν ἐρημίαν φέροντας τὸν λόγον, ἀλλ' ἐπὶ τὴν ἀνανδρίαν τῶν κατοικούντων. καθόλου δέ, φησί, τίς ἂν φοβηθείη τοὺς ἄνδρας, οἵτινες τῆς φύσεως τοῦτο τοῖς ἀνθρώποις δεδωκυίας ἴδιον παρὰ τὰ λοιπὰ τῶν ζῴων, λέγω δὲ τὰς χεῖρας, ταύτας παρ' ὅλον τὸν βίον ἐντὸς τῶν χιτωνίσκων ἔχοντες ἀπράκτους περιφέρουσι; τὸ δὲ μέγιστον ὅτι καὶ ὑπὸ τοῖς χιτωνίσκοις, φησί, περιζώματα φοροῦσιν, ἵνα μηδ' ὅταν ἀποθάνωσιν ἐν ταῖς μάχαις φανεροὶ γένωνται τοῖς ὑπεναντίοις...

Again, in the same book, Timoleon is exhorting the Greeks to engage the Carthaginians; and when they are on the very point of coming to close quarters with the enemy, who are many times superior to them in number, Timaeus represents him as saying, "Do not look to

---

[18] About the battle exhortation in ancient historiography, see Luschnat 1942, Leimbach 1985, Hansen 1993, Kendrick Pritchett 1994, Clark 1995, Ehrhardt 1995, Hornblower 1996, 82, Hansen 2001, Kendrick Pritchett 2002, Iglesias Zoido 2007, Anson 2010, Bruno Sunseri 2010, Pausch 2010.
[19] Arend 1933, Edwards 1992, 303 (battle speeches) and 316–19 (speeches and deliberation), Carmona 2014.

the numbers of the foe, but to their cowardice. For though Libya is fully settled and abounds in inhabitants, yet when we wish to express complete desolation we say 'more desolate than Libya', not meaning to refer to its emptiness, but to the poor spirit of its inhabitants. And after all, who would be afraid of men who, when nature gives hands as the distinctive feature of man among all living creatures, carry them about all their life inside their tunics idle? And more than all, who wear shirts under their inner tunics, that they may not even when they fall in battle show their nakedness to their enemies?..." (Transl. E.S. Shuckburgh).

The text is not complete, but we are able to spot the main targets of Polybius' criticism.[20] First of all, the speech is not suitable in the circumstances, when the battle was about to begin. Second, the arguments: the number of enemies is a traditional topic of battle exhortation, but the elaboration is presented by Polybius as ridiculous. The complicated interpretation of a saying, the ethnographic information about the hands under the cloak and the underwear of the Lybians are absurd as contents of such a speech. We do not have Polybius' commentary on these points, but we can guess that he criticizes the unlikelihood of the arguments at the moment of the battle and their ineffectiveness.[21] In Diod. 16.79.2 the same speech is briefly summed up: Timoleon' arguments concern the cowardice of the Carthaginians and the wealth of Gelon. Plutarch (*quaest. conv.* 676d) lingers only on the story about the parsley, which we find in Diodorus as well.

The exhortations before the battle of Raphia (217 BCE) in Plb. 5.83 provide a good example of the problems arising from battle speeches.[22] Here we do not have direct speeches, but only a short sketch of the arguments used by Ptolemy IV and Antiochus III: according to Polybius the two kings used the same arguments to urge the troops. The scene is an *epipolesis* (i.e. a typical scene of battle exhortation), with kings and officers riding through the troops. Both kings exhort the troops, but are also assisted by friends, technically speaking, and officers. They ride through the troops and employ only two incentives: the ancestors' glory and the great benefits they could have after victory. I do not know whether Polybius

---

[20] On the problems arising from Polybius' testimony about Timaeus, see Baron 2009 and Baron 2013, 170–201; on Timoleon's speech, see Baron 2013, 194–97.
[21] Baron 2013, 196: it is likely that, according to Polybius, "Timoleon, or any general going into battle against great odds, would not speak in such a way"; see also 197: "Ironically, then, *ta deonta* in the context of generals addressing their troops leads Polybius to include speeches which could not have been delivered in that form—as at Ticinus and Zama—while we may suspect that Timaeus' speech for Timoleon reflects the particularities of the historical character".
[22] These speeches are two of the five Greek generals' speeches about which, see Wooten 1974, 243 (5.83, 11.9, 15.28, 38.12).

had good sources for the battle of Raphia, but, as Polybius says, these were recently appointed kings, and therefore the arguments at their disposal were limited in number. Even without witnesses, Polybius had to use only this set of arguments. The debate about speeches often has the consequence that the scene is neglected: the ranked armies, the kings and officers riding through the lines, the interpreters at work.

The speeches before the great battles of the Second Punic War are consistent with the importance of the war and the generals. Both speeches before the battle of Ticinus, in Polybius' opinion, fit the situation (3.62.1 κατὰ δὲ τὸν καιρὸν τοῦτον ἤδη συνεγγίζοντες ἀλλήλοις Ἀννίβας καὶ Πόπλιος ἐπεβάλοντο παρακαλεῖν τὰς ἑαυτῶν δυνάμεις, ἑκάτερος προθέμενος τὰ πρέποντα τοῖς παροῦσι καιροῖς). The speech of Hannibal (3.62f.) is only a part of a theatrical scene well prepared by the general. The royal garments given to the fighters are evidence for the theatrical character of the scene (καθίσας οὖν τούτους εἰς τὸ μέσον προέθηκε πανοπλίας Γαλατικάς, οἴαις εἰώθασιν οἱ βασιλεῖς αὐτῶν, ὅταν μονομαχεῖν μέλλωσιν, κατακοσμεῖσθαι). The fight between two prisoners is shown to the army in order to demonstrate that it is better to die than to fall into the enemies' hands. The traditional argument that there is no alternative to either winning or dying gains new life through the scene the soldiers have seen. The whole scene is carefully built up and ends with the positive reaction of the army.

The scene Hannibal showed to the troops is described by Polybius in a way which recalls poetry, and especially tragedy. Compare Gorgias, *Helen* 9:

> τὴν ποίησιν ἅπασαν καὶ νομίζω καὶ ὀνομάζω λόγον ἔχοντα μέτρον· ἧς τοὺς ἀκούοντας εἰσῆλθε καὶ φρίκη περίφοβος καὶ ἔλεος πολύδακρυς καὶ πόθος φιλοπενθής, <u>ἐπ' ἀλλοτρίων τε πραγμάτων καὶ σωμάτων εὐτυχίαις καὶ δυσπραγίαις</u> ἴδιόν τι πάθημα διὰ τῶν λόγων ἔπαθεν ἡ ψυχή.

> I both deem and define all poetry as speech with meter. Fearful shuddering and tearful pity and grievous longing come upon its hearers, and at the actions and physical sufferings of others in good fortunes and in evil fortunes, through the agency of words, the soul is wont to experience a suffering of its own (Transl. G. Kennedy).

For tragedy as spectacle we may also look at Gorgias fr. 23 D.-K. The emotional dynamic of tragedy is connected by Polybius with the paradigmatic function of historiography, as defined by Thucydides (1.22.4): ὅσοι δὲ βουλήσονται τῶν τε γενομένων τὸ σαφὲς σκοπεῖν καὶ τῶν μελλόντων ποτὲ αὖθις κατὰ τὸ ἀνθρώπινον τοιούτων καὶ <u>παραπλησίων</u> ἔσεσθαι, ὠφέλιμα κρίνειν αὐτὰ ἀρκούντως ἕξει. Compare Polybius εἰς <u>παραπλήσιον</u> γὰρ αὐτοὺς ἀγῶνα καὶ καιρὸν and <u>παραπλήσια</u> τοῖς νῦν ἆθλα. Hannibal stages a tragedy in order to show the soldiers the situation clearly: the stress on the vision (ἐναργῶς θεασάμενοι)[23] deserves to be underlined. Hannibal is in some way an *alter ego* of the historian: the general has to educate his soldiers, the historian his audience. The tool is the paradigm: it is explained, as in tragedy, by the general and understood by the troops (τῶν δὲ πολλῶν ἀποδεχομένων τό τε παράδειγμα καὶ τοὺς λόγους), and narrated by the historian. The speech becomes a kind of *mise en abyme*, which enables the historian to give depth to his narrative, creating a mirroring effect between narrative and speeches.[24]

The speech, in *oratio obliqua*, is rhetorically accurate and effective: the metaphor of games is stressed by the *polyptoton* (παραπλήσιον ... παραπλήσια) and by the personification of τύχη; the *topos* of the three alternatives is highlighted by the *polysyndeton* (γὰρ ἢ νικᾶν ἢ θνῄσκειν ἢ τοῖς ἐχθροῖς ὑποχειρίους γενέσθαι ζῶντας) and by the climax with *cola* of increasing extension. The explication of the alternatives evokes the metaphor of games, whose prizes are compared to the benefits of victory. The structure οὐχ ... ἀλλά is amplifying and prepares the hyperbolic μακαριωτάτους. Another *polyptoton* (παντὸς ... πάσης) stresses the outcomes of defeat, if one chooses to save his life. The *tricolon* with *asyndeton* is joined to the *anaphora* of μνημονεύων, variated by εἰδώς. The end of the speech is in ring composition with the beginning. Hannibal compares the psychological situation of his army with that of the Romans, whose forces are weakened by the possibility of returning home. The speech was effective, as Polybius states, and it is a good example of the Polybian practice of displaying the most suitable and effective speeches: οὔτε τοῖς ἱστοριογράφοις ἐμμελετᾶν τοῖς ἀκούουσιν οὐδ' ἐναποδείκνυσθαι τὴν αὑτῶν δύναμιν, ἀλλὰ τὰ κατ' ἀλήθειαν ῥηθέντα καθ' ὅσον οἷόν τε πολυπραγμονήσαντας διασαφεῖν, καὶ τούτων τὰ καιριώτατα καὶ πραγματικώτατα (36.1.7).

The speech of Publius Scipio (3.64) is not framed by a scene. The topic statements about the glory of Rome and the ancestors' victories are passed by and the speech begins in *oratio obliqua* by expressing a concern about the enemy's knowledge. Publius expresses confidence about the victory: this is a weak point in his speech because confidence must derive from argumentations and paradigms. The alleged weakness of the Carthaginians is supported by the *tricolon* with *asyndeton* and reinforced by *figura etymologica* and *anaphora* (πολλάκις ... πολλούς) and by the climax from defeat to slavery. The *oractio recta* begins with a rhetorical question recalling the theme of the enemy's knowledge. The previous

---

[23] About ἐναργῶς and related terms, see Mauersberger 2003, 797.
[24] See Nicolai 2011 about Thucydides' speeches.

contact with the Carthaginians and their decision to cross the Alps should be another piece of evidence of their weakness, leading to the long march through the Alps and the loss of soldiers and horses. Saying that it should be enough to stay in front of the enemy is another weak point of the speech. This statement is in *oratio obliqua*. The final address, insisting on the general's personality and decisions, has no connection with the body of the speech, and the positive reaction of the audience may be considered as an approval of Publius and his words, but without the effectiveness of Hannibal's speech. The result of the battle was in some way already "written" in the speeches of Hannibal and Publius. Of course, the historian knows the events and is able to compose *post eventum* prophecies or better to prepare the audience, revealing causes and motivations.

Walbank's commentary is concise, but, as usual, very useful and clever: "In both authors [sc. Polybius and Livy] the speeches are based on commonplaces about the strength of forces and the chances of battle … Since Scipio did not expect a major battle at this stage, his speech is clearly unhistorical, and included partly to balance Hannibal's, partly to inflate Scipio into a figure comparable with his opponent … This treatment may go back to P.'s source, perhaps Fabius".[25] About the duel of the prisoners, Walbank observes: "The story, probably apocryphal, interests P. for the moral Hannibal drew from it".[26]

The speeches held before Cannae (3.108.2–109.13) are the most extensive of Polybius' generals' speeches. Lucius Aemilius' speech begins in *oratio obliqua* and then turns to *oratio recta*. Polybius states that Lucius Aemilius' speech is appropriate to the situation and that he spoke ἐξ αὐτοπαθείας. The core argument is the difference between the previous battles and the one coming up: the presence of both consuls, the good preparation of the troops, and the enemy's knowledge. The rhetoric is based on figures of *amplificatio*: οὐ μόνον …, ἀλλὰ καί twice; *tricolon* with *asyndeton* (τοὺς καθοπλισμούς, τὰς τάξεις, τὰ πλήθη τῶν πολεμίων); *figura etymologica* (ἐναντίως … ἐναντίον); *climax* (καὶ γὰρ ἄτοπον, μᾶλλον δ' ὡς εἰπεῖν ἀδύνατον); *polysyndeton* (οὐχ ὑπὲρ ἑτέρων ἀλλ' ὑπὲρ σφῶν αὐτῶν καὶ πατρίδος καὶ γυναικῶν καὶ τέκνων ὁ κίνδυνος συνέστηκεν); rhetorical question (τίς γὰρ οὐκ ἂν βούλοιτο κτλ.); *polyptoton* (πᾶσαν γὰρ τὴν αὐτῆς προθυμίαν καὶ δύναμιν εἰς ὑμᾶς ἀπήρεισται, καὶ πάσας τὰς ἐλπίδας). The frequent use of second-person plural pronouns is another common device to increase the connection between the orator and the audience. The whole speech appears full of commonplaces, as Walbank notes.[27] Concerning the composition of the speech,

---

25 Walbank 1957, 397. See also Baron 2013, 172 and n. 12.
26 Walbank 1957, *ibidem*.
27 Walbank 1957, 442.

which may come from Polybius' sources, there is a little clue of probable Polybian *inventio*: the distinction between αἴτια and πρόφασις. The general acts like the historian, using the same categories and the same terms, as happens in Brasidas' speech in Thuc. 4.126.[28]

Hannibal's situation is quite different: his troops have been defeated in minor skirmishes and need exhortation. This speech also begins in *oratio obliqua* and turns to *oratio recta*. Hannibal begins by showing the troops the battlefield, which is suitable for cavalry. In this way Hannibal aims to gain attention through ἐνάργεια (vividness). Short *cola* are more vigorous and incisive than long periods. The argument based on the uselessness of exhortation, which is exploited by both Aemilius and Hannibal, is reinforced by the series of Carthaginian victories and the rhetorical question (ποῖος ἂν ἔτι λόγος κτλ.), including the *topos* λόγος vs ἔργα, which comes back at the end of the speech.

Walbank lingers on the sources of the speeches: "it is unlikely that they go back to a genuine record ... They may well come from Fabius".[29] I am not interested in finding out the sources or in evaluating the reliability of Polybius' report; I would only stress that they are different as they are introduced and rhetorically exploited. Aemilius' speech cannot be criticized, but it is not as effective as Hannibal's.

The situation of the two armies before Zama is completely different to that of the previous battles. Both speeches (15.10f.) begin with *oratio obliqua* and turn to *oratio recta*. The topical argument about the consequences of victory and defeat is developed by both Publius and Hannibal. Publius lingers on the alternative between victory and death, as Hannibal did before Ticinus; Hannibal remembers the previous victories. Both scenes are of the *epipolesis* type; Hannibal commands the officers to exhort the mercenary troops, but the argument is not so strong: he suggests trusting him and the troops he brings from Italy. Publius' idea of the universal empire may be anachronistic.[30] From these speeches, too, one may foresee the result of the battle.

Another *epipolesis* type speech is pronounced by Flamininus before Cynoscephalae (18.23.1–6). The rhetoric is not as complicated: rhetorical questions with *anaphora*. Walbank comments: "commonplaces, like Hannibal's at Zama

---

28 See Nicolai 2001.
29 Walbank 1957, 442. See also Baron 2013, 172 and n. 12.
30 See Walbank 1967, 456: "Whether Scipio used this expression is uncertain, for the speech here recorded (whatever its source) contains little but commonplaces ...; and there may be some anachronism. After Magnesia the phrase itself becomes a commonplace (cf. xxi. 16.8 (Syrian envoys), 23.4 (Rhodian envoys))".

(xv. 11.7–9). But references to former victories are an obvious theme for such an occasion and were probably made by Flamininus, whatever P.'s source here".[31]

3 Reliability vs. function

Recently Brian McGing wrote that Polybius' battle speeches are "outright invention"; he was criticized by Mary Frances Williams, who stressed the role of sources such as Sosilus and Silenus, Greek historians who accompanied Hannibal.[32] The question of reliability is a wrongly posed question:[33] the point should not be sources, mostly lost, but the *function* of the speeches within the work and the way of interpreting them.[34]

The debate between Hansen and Kendrick Pritchett (and other scholars) about pre-battle exhortations has been taken up by Anson,[35] but the approach is misplaced again: asking if it was possible to speak to a large number of soldiers drawn up on the battlefield, one has to face every battle and every speech, analyzing the number of the soldiers and of the lines, the nature of the battlefield, the composition of the troops, the presence of horses, elephants, camels and so on. The only possible answer is that the generals would have chosen different ways of addressing the troops according to the situation. The point is not whether ancient generals exhorted the troops or not: they surely did so. The point is why and how the historians composed these speeches. The question is not a military or historical one, but a literary one. Since Homer, generals had to address the troops and their speeches were not the few words of exhortation every general would have pronounced: their speeches should be as solemn and important as the battle. I do not rule out the possibility that generals could have pronounced extended speeches. I limit myself to saying that this is not the point.

As is clear from the speeches before the battle of Ticinus, Polybius had a strong interest in moral paradigms: the duel of the prisoners and Hannibal's subsequent speech, probably found in his sources, hold an important place in Polybius' account of the battle. The main function is a moral one, but there is a rhetorical function as well: Hannibal's speech is more effective, since it is connected

---

31 Walbank 1967, 581.
32 McGing 2010b, xxx-xxxi; *id.* 2010a, 86–91; Williams 2011, 22.
33 For a similar view about Agelaus' speech, see Champion 1997, 112–17 and 126.
34 On the function of the speeches within ancient historical works from the point of view of the reader-response, see Pausch 2010.
35 See *supra* n. 17.

with the scene of the duel; Publius' speech is weaker, based on commonplaces and on the figure of the general.

To sum up, the general has to exhort his troops, in real life as well in historiography.[36] The historian, following other historians or inventing, has to present speeches before the most important battles. The epic heritage of historiography compels the historian to respect at least the basic rules of narrative: one of these is the presence of spoken words in order to prepare the narration, to display motivations and so on. Before decisive battles, speeches also have the function of amplifying the events, bringing on stage the generals, presented as epic heroes. This results in conventional speeches, based on a limited group of commonplaces, inside typical scenes including: the situation that requires an exhortation, the general riding through the lines and/or speaking at a war council, the reaction of the troops. What is the difference between these speeches? The most effective speeches (τὰ καιριώτατα καὶ πραγματικώτατα) are strongly connected with the situation, sometimes through gestures and actions (Hannibal before Ticinus and Cannae). In these cases, the reader is able to guess in advance who will win and who will be defeated. Therefore the function of speeches within the historical narrative is to offer paradigms, continuing a tradition of paradigms and respecting the corresponding literary conventions.

Bibliography

Anson, E. (2010), "The General's Pre-Battle Exhortation in Graeco-Roman Warfare", in: G&R 57, 304–318.
Arend, W. (1933), Die typische Szenen bei Homer, Berlin.
Baron, C. (2009), "The Use and Abuse of Historians: Polybios' Book 12 and Our Evidence for Timaios", in: AncSoc 39, 1–34.
Baron, C.A. (2013), Timaeus of Tauromenium and Hellenistic Historiography, Cambridge.
Baronowski, D.W. (2011), Polybius and Roman Imperialism, London.
Brock, R. (1995), "Versions, 'Inversions' and Evasions: Classical Historiography and the 'Published' Speech", in: Papers of the Leeds International Latin Seminar 8, Leeds, 209–224.
Bruno Sunseri, G. (2010), "Le arringhe dei generali alle truppe fra retorica e realtà", in: ὅρμος– Ricerche di Storia Antica, n.s. 2, 5–16.
Champion, C. (1997), "The Nature of Authoritative Evidence in Polybius and Agelaus' Speech at Naupactus", in: TAPhA 127, 111–128.
—— (2000), "Three Polybian Speeches and the Politics of Cultural Indeterminacy", in: CPh 95, No. 4, 425–444.
Carmona, D. (2014), La escena típica de la "epipólesis". De la épica a la historiografía, Rome.
Clark, M. (1995), "Did Thucydides Invent the Battle Exhortation?", Historia 44, 375–376.

---

36 See Bruno Sunseri 2015.

Deininger, J. (1973), "Bemerkungen zur Historizität der Rede des Agelaos 217 v. Chr. (Polyb. 5, 104)", in: *Chiron* 3, 103–108.
Edwards, M.W. (1992), "Homer and Oral Tradition: The Type-Scene", in: *Oral Tradition* 7/2, 284–330.
Ehrhardt, C. (1995), "Speeches before Battle", in: *Historia* 44, 120–121.
Guelfucci, M.-R. (2005), "La vérité, la rhétorique et l'histoire : les formes de la persuasion chez Polybe", in: *CEA* 42, 237–253.
Hansen, M.H. (1993), "The Battle Exhortations in Ancient Historiography. Fact or Fiction?", in: *Historia* 42, 161–180.
—— (2001), "The Little Grey Horse. Henry V's Speech at Agincourt and the Battle Exhortation in Ancient Historiography", in: *C&M* 52, 95–116.
Hornblower, S. (1996), *A Commentary on Thucydides*, II, Oxford.
Kendrick Pritchett, W. (1994), "The General's Exhortations in Greek Warfare", in: *id., Essays in Greek History*, Amsterdam, 97–109.
—— (2002), *Ancient Greek Battle Speeches and a Palfrey*, Amsterdam.
Iglesias Zoido, J.C. (2007), "The Battle Exhortation in Ancient Rhetoric", in: *Rhetorica* 25, 141–158.
Leimbach, R. (1985), *Militärische Musterrhetorik. Eine Untersuchung zu den Feldherrnreden des Thukydides*, Stuttgart.
Loraux, N. (1980), "Thucydide n'est pas un collègue", in: *QS* 12, 55–81.
Luschnat, O. (1942), *Die Feldherrnreden im Geschichtswerk des Thukydides*, Philologus, Suppl. 34.2.
Marincola, J. (1997), *Authority and Tradition in Ancient Historiography*, Cambridge.
—— (2001), *Greek Historians*, Greece & Rome, New Surveys in the Classics, 31, Cambridge.
Mauersberger, A. (2003), *Polybios-Lexikon*, I (δ-ζ), 2. verbesserte Auflage von C. F. Collatz, M. Gützlaf, und H. Helms, Berlin.
McGing, B. (2010a), *Polybius' Histories*, Oxford.
—— (2010b), *Introduction*, in: Waterfield (2010), VII-XXXV.
Mørkholm, O. (1974), "The Speech of Agelaus again", in: *Chiron* 4, 127–132.
Musti, D. (1974), *Società antica. Antologia di storici greci*, Rome/Bari.
Nicolai, R. (1999), "Polibio interprete di Tucidide: la teoria dei discorsi", in: *SRCG* 2, 281–301.
—— (2001), "Il generale, lo storico e i barbari: a proposito del discorso di Brasida in Thuc. IV 126", in: G. Arrighetti/M. Tulli (eds.), *Letteratura e riflessione sulla letteratura nella cultura classica*, Atti del Convegno di Pisa, 7–9 giugno 1999, Pisa 145–155.
—— (2006), "Polibio e la memoria della parola: i discorsi diretti", in: R. Uglione (ed.), *Scrivere la storia nel mondo antico*, Atti del Convegno Nazionale di Studi, Torino 3–4 maggio 2004, Alessandria, 75–107.
—— (2011), "*Logos Didaskalos*: Direct Speech as a Critical Tool in Thucydides", in: G. Rechenauer/V. Pothou (eds.), *Thucydides—A Violent Teacher*, Goettingen, 159–169.
Pausch, D. (2010), "'Und seine Worte waren ungefähr die folgenden: ...'. Reden in der antiken Geschichtsschreibung zwischen Verwendung und Problematisierung", in: U. Tischer/A. Binternagel (eds.), *Fremde Rede—Eigene Rede. Zitieren und verwandte Strategien in antiker Prosa*, Frankfurt, 35–57.
Pédech, P. (1964), *La méthode historique de Polybe*, Paris.
Pelling, C. (2000), *Literary Texts and the Greek Historian*, London/New York.
Thornton, J. (2013), "Oratory in Polybius' *Histories*", in: C. Kremmydas/K. Tempest (eds.), *Hellenistic Oratory. Continuity and Change*, Oxford, 21–42.

Usher, S. (2009), "Oratio Recta and Oratio Obliqua in Polybius", in: *Greek, Roman, and Byzantine Studies* 49, 487–514.
Vollmer, D. (1990), Symploke. *Das Übergreifen der römischen Expansion auf den griechischen Osten (Untersuchungen zur römischen Außenpolitik am Ende des 3. Jhs. v. Chr.)*, Hermes, Einzelschriften, 54, Stuttgart.
Walbank, F.W. (1957), *A Historical Commentary on Polybius*, Vol. 1, Oxford.
—— (1965 = 1985), "Speeches in Greek Historians", Third J.L. Myres Memorial Lecture, Oxford = id. (ed.), *Selected Papers. Studies in Greek and Roman History and Historiography*, Cambridge, 242–261.
—— (1967), *A Historical Commentary on Polybius*, Vol. 2, Oxford.
Waterfield, R. (2010), *Polybius. The Histories*, Introduction and notes by B. McGing, Oxford.
Wiater, N. (2010), "Speeches and Historical Narrative in Polybius' Histories. Approaching Speeches in Polybius", in: D. Pausch (ed.), *Stimmen der Geschichte. Funktionen von Reden in der antiken Historiographie*, Berlin/New York, 67–107.
—— (2014), "Polybius on Speeches in Timaeus: Syntax and Structure in *Histories* 12.25A", in: *CQ* 64. 1, 121–135.
Williams, M.F. (2011), "Review of Waterfield 2010", in: *AHB Online Reviews* 1, 20–24.
Wooten, C. (1973), "The Ambassador's Speech: A Particularly Hellenistic Genre of Oratory", in: *The Quarterly Journal of Speech* 59/2, 209–212.
—— (1974), "The Speeches in Polybius: An Insight into the Nature of Hellenistic Oratory", in: *AJPh* 95/3, 235–251.

Nicolas Wiater
Documents and Narrative: Reading the Roman-Carthaginian Treaties in Polybius' *Histories**

At 3.21.8, Polybius suddenly interrupts his lively narrative of the encounter between Romans and Carthaginians in 218 BCE just short of the famous declaration of war by the leader of the Roman embassy,[1] and presents his readers with a lengthy survey of all Roman-Carthaginian treaties which, at his time, still survived in inscriptional form (3.22–28). The purpose of this "digression" (παρέκβασις, 33.1) is to resolve the controversial question of the legal responsibility for the Hannibalic War (28.5), or, more precisely, to resolve the question of whether any treaties were broken by either Romans or Carthaginians before the war and, if so, whether any of these treaty violations constituted a cause of the war and could, therefore, help determine the question of *kriegsschuld*.[2] The documents listed by Polybius are subdivided into two groups: Polybius begins with three treaties "before the First Roman-Carthaginian War" (22, 24.1–13 and 25.1–5), the second treaty being an updated renewal of the first and the third constituting an addendum to the second. He then records the oaths sworn after the first and the second and third treaties, respectively (25.6–9), and refutes the historian Philinus' claims about different agreements between Rome and Carthage (26). This is followed by two treaties "after the war", the Lutatius Treaty (27.1–6), including the addendum concerning Sardinia and the additional reparations to be

---

* I would like to thank Nikos Miltsios for inviting me to contribute to the conference on which this volume is based and for his patience with the submission of my chapter. I am also grateful to the audience at the conference for their questions and suggestions, especially Stephanie Craven and Bruce Gibson.

1 Q. Fabius, according to Liv. 21.18.3; Polybius simply speaks of ὁ πρεσβύτατος.

2 See esp. 28.5: διευκρινῆσαι καὶ σκέψασθαι περὶ τοῦ κατ' Ἀννίβαν πολέμου ποτέροις αὐτῶν τὴν αἰτίαν ἀναθετέον; 30.3: ἀδίκως ἐξενηνοχέναι τὸν πόλεμον; 30.4: εὐλόγως πεπολεμηκέναι τὸν κατ' Ἀννίβαν πόλεμον τοὺς Καρχηδονίους· καιρῷ γὰρ πεισθέντες ἠμύνοντο σὺν καιρῷ τοὺς βλάψαντας. These passages, as well as the contents of Polybius' entire discussion, clearly show that Polybius, *pace* Derow 1979, 13, does, in fact, seek "to answer questions about war-guilt". The question was bound up with the question of the causes and is, in fact, inherent in the very term αἰτία which, from the beginning of Polybius' discussion at 3.6, oscillates between "cause" and "responsibility"; cf. below, n. 19.

https://doi.org/10.1515/9783110584844-009

paid by the Carthaginians (27.7–8), and the Ebro Treaty (27.9–10).[3] Each of the treaties is first cited *verbatim* (τοιαίδε τινές, 22.4)[4] and then followed by a commentary in which Polybius gives his interpretation of the meaning and implications of the clauses (23, 24.14–16, 28).

After his survey of the treaties, Polybius does not, however, return to the main narrative, the encounter between Romans and Carthaginians in 218. Instead, he presents the reader with the views of his Roman contemporaries, in the

---

[3] Polybius dates the first treaty to the first year of the Roman *respublica*, which corresponds to our modern date 507; this date or, at any rate, a date in the early years of the *respublica*, is now widely accepted (Polybius' date: e.g. Walbank 1957, 338, Scardigli 1991, 27–28, Cornell 1995, 214; a date in the late sixth/early fifth century: e.g. Huss 1985, 91, Marotta 1996, 74, Oakley 1998, 256, Welwei 2001, 77). Polybius does not date the second treaty, but it is now generally identified with the treaty of 348 mentioned by Liv. 7.27.2 (cf. Diod. Sic. 16.69.1); the decisive discussions are Toynbee 1965, 534–39, and Werner 1963, 360. Attempts to return to Mommsen's dating of the first two treaties (348 and 306, respectively) e.g. by Bringmann 2001, remain isolated and unconvincing. The third treaty is dated by Polybius to "the time of Pyrrhus' crossing", sc. into Italy (κατὰ τὴν Πύρρου διάβασιν, 25.1; the phrase πρὸ τοῦ συστήσασθαι τοὺς Καρχηδονίους τὸν περὶ Σικελίας πόλεμον, which is sometimes taken to refer to the war of the Carthaginians against the Greek cities in eastern Sicily 280–278 (cf. StV 466, p. 105, for references), must be construed with τελευταίας, which otherwise makes no sense, and therefore taken to refer to the First Punic War; it has no relevance to the date of the treaty). This is compatible with the more precise date of Liv. per. 13, which mentions a *cum Carthaginiensibus quarto foedus renovatum* after the battle of Ausculum 279, when, according to Just. 18.2.1 (cf. Val. Max. 3.7.10), Mago arrived with a fleet of 220 ships in Ostia and offered the Romans Carthaginian support. This date is accepted by the majority of scholars today; see the references cited in StV 466, p. 106; further, Huss 1985, 211, Scardigli 1991, 188. The date of the Lutatius Treaty, 241, is not disputed; Polybius (2.13.6) connects the conclusion of the Ebro Treaty with the Romans' fear of a Gallic invasion which suggests a date somewhere between 228 and 225 (Rich 1996, 23, Eckstein 2012, 221); most scholars favor autumn 226 or spring 225 (Huss 1985, 277; 226: e.g. Walbank 1957, 168, Scardigli 1991, 268; 225: e.g. Hoyos 1998, 157, Erdkamp 2009, 504–05, 508–09). The scholarly controversy about the so-called "Philinus Treaty" need not concern us here (see StV 438, Scardigli 1991, 129–62, Serrati 2006, Eckstein 2010, the best discussion). For present purposes, all that matters is that Polybius regarded the treaty as unhistorical and that his refutation of Philinus is an integral part of his commented survey of the treaties.

[4] Some scholars have taken this phrase to imply that Polybius has altered or abridged the text of the treaty or even that he merely paraphrases it (e.g. Walbank-Paton-Habicht: "more or less", Oakley 1998, 253; Serrati 2006, 116, even claims, wrongly, that Polybius "does say that he is not quoting the full text (3.22.3–4)"). But τοιόσδε (with or without τις) is used already by Thucydides without any noticeable difference to τόδε and τάδε; see Classen-Steup on τοιόνδε τι, 2.75.6. In Polybius, τοιοῦτός τις is merely formulaic ("presque automatiquement", de Foucault 1972, 222), without any implications whatsoever regarding the reliability and precision of what follows; cf. 3.1.11, 18.9, 97.8, 4.18.1.

mid-second century, on the legal aspects of the Hannibalic War, a belated answer, as it were, to the legal arguments put forward by the Carthaginians almost sixty years earlier.[5] This, in turn, is followed by Polybius' own assessment of his Roman contemporaries' arguments (29.7–10) and his own conclusions regarding the question of *kriegsschuld*, which, at the same time, concludes Polybius' detailed exploration of the causes, beginnings and legal implications of the Hannibalic War which had begun in chapter 6.[6] Polybius' conclusions on the question, which he presents at 30.3–4, are complex and can only be summarized briefly here. From the Roman point of view, Polybius explains, Hannibal's violation of the Lutatius treaty, the attack on Saguntum, caused the war; according to the Romans, the Carthaginians are, therefore, guilty both on account of breaching, first, the Lutatius Treaty and then, second, the Ebro Treaty.[7] Polybius, by constrast, offers an alternative interpretation. He acknowledges that the Carthaginians breached these two treaties, but to him neither of these treaty violations *caused* the war: for Polybius, the fact that the Carthaginians are guilty of these treaty violations, one of which even prompted the Roman declaration of war, does not automatically mean that they "began the war unjustly" (ἀδίκως ἐξενηνοχέναι τὸν πόλεμον, 30.3). In his view, by contrast, it was the *Romans'* violation of Carthaginian rights when they annexed Sardinia in 238 that was the principal cause of

---

5 3.29.1: τὰ μὲν οὖν ὑπὸ Καρχηδονίων τότε ῥηθέντα δεδηλώκαμεν, τὰ δ' ὑπὸ Ῥωμαίων λεγόμενα νῦν ἐροῦμεν· οἷς τότε μὲν οὐκ ἐχρήσαντο ... λέγεται δὲ πολλάκις καὶ ὑπὸ πολλῶν παρ' αὐτοῖς; the contrast between τότε μὲν οὐκ ἐχρήσαντο and the present tense λέγεται (mistranslated by Paton-Walbank-Habicht as "has been given") demonstrates clearly that 29.2–6 summarizes a contemporary, lively debate in Rome at Polybius' time. Note also the polyptoton, alliteration and assonance (πολλάκις ... ὑπὸ πολλῶν παρ' ... πρῶτον) designed to evoke the image of a lively discussion.

6 Cf. esp. 30.3 with 6.1–2, 8.1, 28.5.

7 Polybius clearly does not assume, as many modern scholars have, that the outbreak of the war between the two peoples after the attack on Saguntum invalidated all other treaties: even after the breach of the Lutatius treaty and the declaration of war, the Carthaginians were still, at least according to Polybius, bound by the Ebro treaty. There is also no need to assume that Polybius here wrongly locates Saguntum north of the Ebro (thus e.g. Walbank 1957, 358, with the older literature, Huss 1985, 288 n. 26, Scardigli 1991, 278–79; for the correct interpretation, see Rich 1996, 11, Hoyos 1998, 165. Cf. Chris Baron's contribution to this volume). Polybius is not saying that the Carthaginians broke the Ebro Treaty *by* attacking Saguntum. He is explaining how different interpretations of the causes of the Hannibalic war affect the question of whether the Carthaginians are to blame for the war (ἀδίκως ἐξενηνοχέναι τὸν πόλεμον Καρχηδονίους). The Carthaginians did breach two treaties, the Lutatius Treaty by attacking Saguntum and (subsequently!) the Ebro Treaty by crossing that river in arms, but in Polybius' view their war against the Romans is "unjust" (ἀδίκως) only if either one of these treaty violations did, in fact, *cause* the war which, according to him, they did not.

the Hannibalic War (3.10.1–5).[8] From the Carthaginian perspective, the war was, therefore, a delayed, but well-timed and "justifiable" (εὐλόγως) "defense" against the Romans' unjust act of aggression 20 years earlier (ἠμύνοντο ... τοὺς βλάψαντας).[9] Polybius thus might not go as far as attributing the *kriegsschuld* to the Romans explicitly, but he does, at the very least, cast considerable doubt on the validity of the Romans' simple and clear-cut view according to which the *kriegsschuld* lay unambiguously with the Carthaginians while their own war was unambiguously a *bellum iustum*.[10]

Polybius then considers the general political importance of inquiries such as the one he has just conducted (3.31–32)—understanding causes, that is, the motivations of historical agents, is essential to successful political and military action in real life outside history inasmuch as the latter presupposes a precise understanding of the motives, aims and purposes (προαίρεσις, 31.7) of the people we are dealing with which, in turn, requires precise knowledge of their *past* actions (31.6–9)—before he finally returns, after a total number of 21 chapters covering the key stages of the relationship between Rome and Carthage across no fewer than four centuries, to his account of the Roman embassy to Carthage in 218 and the Roman declaration of war (33.1–4).

In stark contrast to the treaties themselves, which can without much exaggeration be regarded as one of the most thoroughly studied and most controversially debated topics in ancient history,[11] the peculiar and original design of Polybius' narrative has received hardly any attention from scholars. The only explicit such statement in recent scholarship that I have been able to find is Dexter Hoyos' description of the narrative structure of 3.6–33.4 as "irritating" and of the conclusion of Polybius' account of the Roman declaration of war in 218 as a "[c]lumsy or careless follow-up after" the long digression on the treaties.[12] Often,

---

8 For a more detailed exposition of Polybius' theory of the causes of the war see the following section. On the rights of the Carthaginians violated by the Romans in 238 in particular, see n. 22.
9 30.4, cited above, n. 2. On εὐλόγως "justifiable" see PL s.v. εὔλογος 3a ("mit gutem Grunde; mit Recht").
10 I am currently preparing a more detailed discussion of this chapter and Polybius' position on the *kriegsschuld*.
11 On the treaties Walbank's commentary and the discussion in StV remain fundamental. Scardigli 1991 provides an encyclopedic treatment of the scholarly debate about the treaties based on a comprehensive review of the scholarship published until the early 1990s. Important more recent discussions include Ameling 1993, 130–34, 140–54, Cornell 1995, 210–14, Marotta 1996, Oakley 1998, 252–62, Hoyos 1998, 150–73 (the most balanced discussion of the Ebro Treaty), Bringmann 2001, Welwei 2001, Nörr 2003, Espada Rodriguez 2013, all with further literature. Cf. above, n. 3.
12 Hoyos 1998, 244, 255.

the very fact that Polybius presents his discussion of the treaties as a "digression" has prompted scholars (e.g. Walbank 1957, 336, 356) to assume that Polybius must have added the information on the treaties later (and hastily?) shortly before the publication of this part of his work ("just before 150", Walbank 1957, 356), after the documents had unexpectedly appeared during the political debate that preceded the outbreak of the Third Punic War.[13]

The purpose of this chapter is to provide the first in-depth analysis of the structure and function of Polybius' digression on the Roman-Carthaginian treaties in the wider context of Polybius' argument and narrative; as such, this chapter is also an attempt to offer an alternative, narratological (in a broad sense) approach to *verbatim* citations of documents in Polybius' *Histories*. The first section examines the integration of the treaties in their narrative context. I will argue that the digression on the treaties is neither "irritating" nor "clumsy" or "careless", as Hoyos believed, nor a late addition to a previously coherent text, as Walbank and others assumed, but part of a carefully designed narrative structure: Polybius deliberately chose the narrative device of the "digression" (παρέκβασις) for his discussion of the treaties and he deliberately placed this digression in the middle of his account of the Roman embassy at Carthage.

Moreover, Polybius, I will argue, has prepared the introduction of the digression since the very beginning of his discussion of the causes of the Hannibalic War and the related question of the *kriegsschuld*: from the very beginning, Polybius' text construes these questions as an unresolved dilemma, a controversy that started among the historical actors in the past itself and has since continued in historical discourse long after the end of the war. His text thus creates a "blank space", as it were, the need for the final and definitive systematic investigation of and solution to this controversy which should have been resolved decades ago. And it is when these unresolved issues reach their most critical point in the past, in the confrontation between Romans and Carthaginians in Carthage in 218, that Polybius "steps in" with his digression and provides the reader with exactly the

---

13 Similarly, Laqueur regarded the digression on the treaties as part of a third edition of the *Histories*, which, he believed, Polybius created in the 150s (1913, 266). In Laqueur's view, the digression constituted a "stylistic blunder" ("Stillosigkeit") and thus testified to a new phase of Polybius' intellectual development ("geistige Entwicklung") that eschewed formal rhetorical composition in favor of rational analysis ("... daß nicht mehr ein nach formalen Gesichtspunkten arbeitender Historiker schaffend ist ... bezeugen den Wunsch nach Sachlichkeit", 271). For a more differentiated view, see de Sanctis 1967, 204. For a good and concise discussion of the question, with further bibliographical references, see Scardigli 1991, 25–26. Scardigli rejects the hypothesis of a late addition on the grounds that there is no reason to assume that the treaties and the discussion of *kriegsschuld* became prominent in Rome only as late as the 150s.

kind of clear vision of the existing treaties and their implications that they need and which the historical agents lacked.

The second section will then focus on the design of the digression itself. Its peculiar structure, which combines *verbatim* citations of documents with historical-analytical commentary and, on that basis, a final judgment on the legal status of the claims of the parties involved, I will argue, mirrors the political discourse of Graeco-Roman interstate arbitration as it was memorialized on inscriptions.[14] I will then suggest some ways in which this intertextual, or interdiscursive, dialogue between Polybius' text and this kind of Graeco-Roman political discourse as well as its medium, the inscriptions, can contribute to our understanding of Polybius' discussion of the causes of the Hannibalic War and the *kriegsschuld*. By prompting his recipients to read his discussion in the key of Graeco-Roman interstate arbitration, Polybius, I will suggest, seeks to support his claim, made at 3.21.9–10, that his discussion of the treaties is about more than just providing reliable knowledge about the past: its purpose is also to shape the political and public debate in contemporary Rome. In Polybius' digression on the Roman-Carthaginian treaties, his two roles as historian and "man of action" (ἀνὴρ πραγματικός), history-writing and politics, coincide: Polybius makes politics by writing history. At the same time, the association with the epigraphic medium of such arbitrations allows Polybius to set up his own, literary work, as a *monumentum* not only to the debate about the causes and *kriegsschuld* itself but also and most importantly to his own, decisive contribution to it: the *Histories* confers the same permanence and visibility on Polybius' political *and* historical contribution that inscriptions confer to successful political settlements in the world outside the text.

1 Interacting Voices: The Roman-Carthaginian Treaties in Context

A literary and narratological reading of Polybius' "digression" on the treaties, as I propose to undertake it in this chapter, might well start with the observation that Polybius' characterisation of his discussion as a "digression" does by no means imply that it was a late addition. By ancient standards, such interruptions of the "flow" (the ancients would say, "the path", cf. Quint. 4.3.14: *cum ... a recto*

---

[14] I should like to thank Stephanie Craven very much for prompting me to explore the potential relationship between Polybius' digression on the treaties and Greek interstate arbitration.

itinere declinet oratio) of the narrative were by no means a sign of negligence, clumsy organisation or lack of competence. The παρέκβασις was, on the contrary, a firmly established and universally acknowledged feature of rhetorical theory and practice.[15] Such digressions could even be introduced rather abruptly as long as the author marked the return to his narrative, the so-called ἄφοδος, with sufficient clarity by inserting phrases such as *longius evectus sum, sed redeo ad propositum* (Quint. 9.3.87).[16]

It is worth noting that Polybius, when returning to his account of the Roman embassy at Carthage at 33.1, does precisely that and mentions the technical term παρέκβασις to boot: "the Roman envoys—for this is where I embarked on this digression (τὴν γὰρ παρέκβασιν ἐντεῦθεν ἐποιησάμεθα)—after listenting to the Carthaginians' statement …".[17] Furthermore, the digression itself is integrated into its context by the immediate relevance of its contents to the issues raised by Polybius' narrative. This point is worth stressing because a close integration of a digression with its context was by no means regarded as a requirement in rhetorical theory (Quint. 4.3.12–13, 16): Polybius goes beyond what was strictly necessary for a "digression" to be regarded as sufficiently motivated and integrated by ancient standards. Rather than betraying any signs of clumsy composition or hasty insertion, Polybius' discussion of the Roman-Carthaginian treaties is a textbook example of a well-established narrative and rhetorical technique.[18] In terms of the basic formal design of Polybius' digression there is, therefore, no reason to doubt that Polybius always intended to insert the παρέκβασις into his narrative precisely where he did. Modern criticism of Polybius' "clumsy" and "irritating" narrative design and his lack of a sense for style, by contrast, are anachronistic.

This impression is confirmed further by a closer look at the very point of his narrative where Polybius inserts the digression. As mentioned above, the digression on the treaties cuts through the middle of Polybius' account of the Roman

---

15 Cf. the definition in Quint. 4.3.14: παρέκβασις est, ut mea quidem fert opinio, alicuius rei, sed ad utilitatem causae pertinentis, extra ordinem excurrens tractatio. See Lausberg 2008, 187–88, with further references.
16 Abrupt beginnings: Quint. 4.3.13, on Cicero's virtutum Cn. Pompei commemoratio in the (now lost) speech pro C. Cornelio: in quam ille divinus orator, veluti nomine ipso ducis cursus dicendi teneretur, abrupto quem incohaverat sermone devertit actutum.
17 Translations are based on Walbank and Habicht's revised edition of Paton's Loeb, frequently adapted.
18 This makes it seem all the more curious that Laqueur (above, n. 13) regarded the digression as a "stylistic blunder" and a sign that Polybius no longer cared about formal, rhetorical composition. On the fundamental influence of rhetoric on Polybius' historical method, see now Farrington 2015.

embassy to Carthage in 218. More precisely, Polybius inserts his discussion of the treaties and their legal implications immediately after the discussion of the legal aspects of the controversy between Romans and Carthaginians (δικαιολογίαν, 21.3; on this crucial term see further below) which, in turn, forms the basis for the assessment of whether the war which the Romans are about to declare is just or unjust.

In fact, the Carthaginians' legal argument is designed to prove that the Romans do *not* have sufficient legal grounds for a declaration of war and that any such war would, by implication, not qualify as "just": the Ebro Treaty, the Carthaginians hold, is invalid because it had not been ratified by the Carthaginian people (21.1), and Hannibal's conquest of Saguntum did not violate the Lutatius Treaty, which guaranteed the safety of the Roman allies from Carthaginian attacks and vice versa (the so-called *asphaleia* clause, 27.3), because at the time of the conclusion of the treaty in 241, Saguntum was not a Roman ally (21.3–5). The Roman envoys' reply to these detailed arguments could hardly be less satisfactory: instead of refuting the Carthaginians' claims, they "refused ... any debate about the legal issues (δικαιολογεῖσθαι)" and simply repeated their ultimatum to surrender Hannibal or face another war (21.6–8). It is at this point that Polybius steps in with his digression and, in so doing, provides precisely the kind of solid legal argument which the Roman ambassadors failed to present (21.8–9): "On this occasion the question [*i.e.* the legal issues] was dealt with in more or less general terms, but to me it seems necessary not to leave it unscrutinized...".

In order to appreciate the full significance of Polybius' decision to insert his digression half-way through the confrontation between Romans and Carthaginians in 218, it is important to read this confrontation within the larger context of Polybius' narrative of the development of the diplomatic relationship between Romans and Carthaginians during the years prior to the Hannibalic War. Polybius, I will argue, construes this development as a series of disagreements and miscommunications about the very treaties that eventually became the focus of the argument between Romans and Carthaginians in 218 and remained a contentious issue in the historical literature beyond the end of the Hannibalic War well into Polybius' own time. Polybius' narrative creates a polyphonous space which confronts the reader with the conflicting perspectives on the significance of these treaties of the historical agents, historical writers from Greece and Rome, Polybius' Roman contemporaries and Polybius himself. And just at the point when the controversy between the historical agents reaches its climax, during the confrontation between Romans and Carthaginians in 218, Polybius' digression offers his reader a privileged perspective that allows him to transcend the confusion among historical agents and previous historical writers alike. Thanks to Polybius' digression, his reader can thus follow his narrative of the Roman declaration of war at 3.33.1–4 and the "hot" phase of the Hannibalic War which begins with it, from the superior perspective of the exact knowledge of which treaties existed between the two peoples; what their significance was; which of these treaties were broken, and whether or not these treaty violations had a bearing on the outbreak of the Hannibalic War. The reader will know exactly, that is, "to which of the two parties we should attribute the responsibility (αἰτίαν) for the Hannibalic War" (28.5).[19]

From the beginning, Polybius presents the question of the causes of the Hannibalic War, and the question of *kriegsschuld* that is bound up with it, as a matter of controversy. Polybius introduces the subject immediately after the preface to Book 3. At 6.1–2, Polybius summarizes and contests the view of anonymous "Hannibal historians" that the "causes" (αἰτίας, 6.1) of the Hannibalic War were, first, "the siege of Saguntum by the Carthaginians" and, second, the Carthaginians' "crossing, contrary to the treaty (παρὰ τὰς συνθήκας, 6.2; the Ebro Treaty), the river whose native name is the Iber [the Ebro]". Polybius criticizes these historians for confusing causes and beginnings and takes their—in his view erroneous—explanation of the war as an opportunity to introduce his own concept of historical causation which is centred on the psychology, as it were, of the historical agents. Causes, as Polybius defines them, are "what is leading up to decisions and judgments, that is to say our notions of things, our state of mind, our reasoning about these, and everything through which we reach decisions" (6.7).[20] From the beginning, then, Polybius develops his own position on the question by way of an engagement with his historical predecessors and their points of view: Polybius enacts his discussion of the subject as part of a controversy, carried out in and through his text, with other historical writers.

---

[19] Paton-Walbank-Habicht's translation, "to which of the two states which should attribute *the cause* of the Hannibalic war" (emphasis added), distorts the sense of the passage. The *causes* of the war have already been clearly identified by Polybius as the wrath of Hamilcar, the Roman annexation of Sardinia and the Carthaginian successes in Spain (see further below). Chapters 29–30 are about the consequences of this identification of the causes, namely who is responsible for the war and, consequently, which of the two parties waged the war "unjustly" (ἀδίκως; cf. 30.3). However, inasmuch as the "cause" of the war is bound up with the question of treaty violations and, thus, "(legal) blame", the term here clearly oscillates between both meanings. "Responsibility" therefore seems to be the most appropriate translation. Cf. also Xen. *Ath.* 2.17, l. 12: καὶ ἂν μέν τι κακὸν ἀναβαίνῃ ἀπὸ ὧν ὁ δῆμος ἐβούλευσεν, αἰτιᾶται ὁ δῆμος ὡς ὀλίγοι ἄνθρωποι αὐτῷ ἀντιπράττοντες διέφθειραν, ἐὰν δέ τι ἀγαθόν σφίσιν αὐτοῖς τὴν αἰτίαν ἀνατιθέασι. Cf. above, n. 2.
[20] On this passage, especially on the Thucydidean echoes, see Wiater 2017, 660–62, with further literature.

Polybius takes this controversy to the next stage at 8.1, moving from the anonymous "Hannibal historians" to Fabius Pictor:

> Fabius the Roman historian says that besides the violation of the rights (ἀδίκημα) of the Saguntines, another cause of the war was Hasdrubal's ambition and love of power (πλεονεξίαν καὶ φιλαρχίαν).

Just as Polybius had taken the "Hannibal historians'" theory of the causes as an opportunity to introduce his own, general concept of causation, he responds to Fabius Pictor's theory with his own theory of what, precisely, caused the Hannibalic War. In the present case, however, Polybius' involvement with his Roman predecessor goes beyond a simple rejection of the latter's theory. Rather, Polybius' own theory to a significant extent draws on and re-works Fabius Pictor's. With Fabius Pictor, and in accordance with his own psychological theory of causation (see above), Polybius regards Hannibal's psychology as a decisive factor. But unlike Fabius Pictor, Polybius regards Hannibal's father, Hamilcar, as the crucial influence. And from him, not Hasdrubal, Hannibal inherited not some general "ambition and love of power", as Fabius Pictor had claimed, but his implacable wrath and hatred of the Romans specifically. Hamilcar's hatred of the Romans, and with it the notion of the "wrath of the Barcids", thus becomes Polybius' "first cause" of the war (10.6–9, 11.1–12.4).[21]

Furthermore, and most importantly, Polybius rejects any explanation of the war that defines treaty violations as such as causes: neither Hannibal's attack on Saguntum, which breached the Lutatius Treaty (ἀδίκημα), nor, as the "Hannibal historians" had claimed, his crossing of the Ebro were "causes" of the war, even though they might have provoked the Roman declaration of war; these violations, as pointed out above, Polybius regards merely as "beginnings". Causes are what prompted these. To be sure, Polybius does accept Fabius Pictor's (and the "Hannibal historians'") general point that the search for the causes of the Hannibalic War involves treaty violations. But he rejects any explanatory model that conceives of treaty violations and wars in the simple terms of causes and effects. Polybius develops an entirely different approach to the role of treaties as causes: in accordance with his psychological concept of historical causes (see above), he accepts treaty violations as causes only inasmuch as they had a significant *psychological* impact on the historical agents that prompted them to begin the war.

---

[21] Derow 1979, 9, rightly notes that "First, second and third" in Polybius' theory of the causes "serve to indicate chronological order". On the "hot emotions" which according to Polybius lay "at the heart of the Hannibalic War", see Eckstein 1989, 5–8.

Neither Hannibal's violation of the Lutatius nor his breach of the Ebro Treaty fulfilled this criterion. Led by his concept of causality, Polybius, by contrast, identified an entirely different treaty violation as a cause of the war, a treaty violation which had occurred about 20 years prior to the outbreak of the war and, moreover, been committed by the Romans (3.10.1–3):

> When, on the suppression of this disturbance [the mercenary war] by the Carthaginians, the Romans announced their intention of making war on Carthage, the Carthaginians at first were ready to negotiate on all points (εἰς πᾶν συγκατέβαινον), thinking that they would prevail on legal grounds (τοῖς δικαίοις) … but as the Romans would not accept any negotiations, the Carthaginians yielded to the circumstances (εἴξαντες τῇ περιστάσει). Though deeply aggrieved (βαρυνόμενοι), there was nothing they could do about it: they re-ceded from Sardinia and con-ceded to pay further twelve hundred talents in addition to the sum previously agreed, in order not to be forced to accept war at that time. This, then, we must take to be the second and most important (μεγίστην) cause of the subsequent war; for Hamilcar, with the anger (ὀργή) felt by all his compatriots about this situation added to his own resentment (τοῖς ἰδίοις θυμοῖς) … at once threw all his efforts into the conquest of Spain, with the object of using the resources thus obtained for the war against Rome.

To the treaty violations by Hannibal, which were at the centre of the theory of the causes of the war proposed by the "Hannibal historians" and the Romans (Fabius Pictor), Polybius opposes the violation of Carthaginian rights committed by the Romans in 238,[22] because this violation humiliated the Carthaginians and, thus, caused them to align their collective anger with Hamilcar's personal hatred of the Romans. This explains why Polybius regards the annexation of Sardinia as the "most important" (μεγίστην) cause of the war: it is only because of the Romans' unlawful actions, their violation of the Carthaginians' δίκαια, that Hamilcar's private desire for vendetta became a collective desire for vendetta and that the Barcids' pursuit of their private vendetta could lead to a new, full-blown war between

---

[22] Sardinia had been recognized as Carthaginian sphere of influence in two earlier treaties with the Romans (507 BCE: 22.4–13; 348 BCE: 24.3–13); despite claims of later authors (cf. Cassius Dio frg. 43.22 with Plb. 1.31.4–6 on the Treaty of Regulus, 256/5 BCE, StV 483) nothing suggests that this had ever been contested prior to 238 BCE. On the contrary, the Lutatius Treaty had left the Carthaginian sphere of influence untouched apart from Sicily and the Lipari and Aegadian Islands and stipulated explicitly that Romans and Carthaginians were not to interfere in the area controlled by the other (ἐπαρχία) (27.2–6; cf. 1.63.3); nothing substantiates the claim of later authors (e.g. Livy) that the surrender of Sardinia had been stipulated by the treaty; Sardinia remained an acknowledged part of the Carthaginian ἐπαρχία after the first war. The date (238) is that given by Zonaras and is used here for the sake of convenience. It was contested already in antiquity; see Walbank 1957, 149–50 for discussion, Carey 1996.

the two peoples.²³ When the Carthaginians' successful military operations in Spain then boost their confidence in their power and ability (10.6)—Polybius' third cause (note, again, the focus on the psychological impact of the military events)—war is all but inevitable. At the end of chapter 10, the reader is thus left with the impression of the debate about the causes of the Hannibalic War as a highly contested topic in historical discourse: Polybius' own solution included, he is confronted with no less than three different theories one of which, moreover, was proposed by the Roman senator and eye witness Fabius Pictor (9.1–5, discussed below). Polybius' text enacts the analysis of the causes as a field of multiple competing perspectives. Instead of simply presenting the reader with his own view, he develops his own theory as part of a struggle for superiority in a long-lasting and "international" controversy.²⁴

This controversy at the level of the historical narrator has its counterpart at the level of Polybius' narrative of the past, among the historical agents. The conflict over the annexation of Sardinia marks the beginning of a pattern that will define the relationship between Romans and Carthaginians up to and including the Roman declaration of war in 218: from the end of the First Punic War onwards, the historical agents continuously fail to establish any kind of meaningful communication, let alone mutual agreement, about their respective legal rights and obligations as defined by the various existing treaties, particularly the two treaties that will eventually become the focus of the controversy about the *kriegsschuld* (3.10.1–3):

> When, on the suppression of this disturbance [the mercenary war] by the Carthaginians, the Romans announced their intention of making war on Carthage, *the Carthaginians at first were ready to negotiate on all points, thinking that they would prevail on legal grounds* (τοῖς δικαίοις) ... *but as the Romans would not accept any negotiations*, the Carthaginians yielded to the circumstances (εἴξαντες τῇ περιστάσει).²⁵

The Romans' categorical refusal of any discussion about the legal basis of their actions anticipates the Romans' similar behavior in Polybius' account of the confrontation between Romans and Carthaginians in 218 later in Book 3 (21.6–8), discussed above, when the Romans will once more refuse to consider the Carthaginians' legal arguments (δικαιολογία). But this is not all. The miscommunication

---

23 Walbank's (1957, 313) comment: "This is the greatest cause ..., since it contributed most towards Hamilcar's will to war", misses Polybius' point.
24 Cf. below, n. 74, on Polybius' "argumentative posture" (Farrington) as part of his attempt to establish credibility.
25 On the rights (τοῖς δικαίοις) violated by the Roman annexation of Sardinia see above, n. 22.

about the "legal rights" in 238 also anticipates a heated encounter between Hannibal and Roman envoys in Iberia in 220, which, in turn, serves as a precursor to the large-scale confrontation between Romans and Carthaginians in Carthage two years later. In 220, when Hannibal is evidently preparing the siege of Saguntum, Roman envoys warn him not to attack Saguntum or break the Ebro Treaty (3.15.5).[26] Hannibal responds with a violent and irrational outburst. He levels wild accusations against the Romans of having themselves violated treaty obligations towards the Saguntines when the town called them in as arbitrators in a *stasis* and arrogates for himself the role of the avenger of the Saguntines in a manifestly paradoxical attempt to justify his plans to attack the town (15.7).[27] Polybius' portrayal of Hannibal as irrational is deliberate: the reader is meant to see that Hannibal's accusations are unfounded, even outright absurd, and recognize them as a sign of the famous "wrath of the Barcids", Polybius' "first" cause of the war.

Most significant for the present discussion is Polybius' subsequent auctorial comment, in which he criticizes Hannibal for this irrational (πλήρης ἀλογίας, 15.9) behavior and unfounded allegations. Hannibal, according to Polybius, wasted a precious opportunity to confront the Romans with the real reason of his attack on Saguntum, namely the *Romans*' violation of Carthaginian rights when they annexed Sardinia in 238 (15.9–11), that is, Polybius' own second and "most important" cause: "by keeping silent as to the real cause and by inventing a non-existing one about Saguntum, he [Hannibal] gave the idea that he was entering on the war (κατάρχειν τοῦ πολέμου) not only unsupported by reason (ἀλόγως) but without justice on his side (ἀδίκως)".

The debate about *kriegsschuld* among Polybius and his historical predecessors is thus prefigured in the controversy about the same issues among the historical agents: since the confrontation between the Romans and Hannibal in 220 at the latest, the debate about *kriegsschuld* was part of the development of the historical events themselves. But Polybius' readers will also realize that this debate had, in fact, its roots further back in the past, in the Roman violation of the Carthaginians' rights and their refusal to discuss their actions, in 238. Polybius' narrative thus draws a clear line of political escalation and an escalation of failed

---

26 *Pace* Walbank 1957, 171–72, this passage does not imply that Polybius, "fogged by the confused discussions" in his own time (Walbank 1957, 321; cf. Huss 1985, 288), assumed any sort of link between the Ebro Treaty and Saguntum, as it was construed by later historians (e.g. Liv. 21.2.7), let alone that Polybius assumed that Saguntum lay north of the Ebro (thus e.g. App. *Hisp.* 7); cf. above, n. 7. On the contrary, as already Gelzer 1933, 158 n.1 (cf. Eucken 1968, 39), saw correctly, the very fact that the Romans are issuing separate warnings about attacking Saguntum and crossing the Ebro, demonstrates that the latter was unrelated to the former.
27 For an excellent discussion of this episode, see Eckstein 1989.

communications about δίκαια between Romans and Carthaginians from the Roman annexation of Sardinia via the encounter between the Romans and Hannibal in 220 and the confrontation between Romans and Carthaginians in 218, the climax of the crisis which results in the "official" outbreak of the war, directly to the controversy about these same issues among the historical writers that is carried out in Polybius' text.

The defining characteristic of this process of escalation among the historical agents is the refusal of rational analysis and discussion. This is particularly evident in Polybius' account of the confrontation between Hannibal and the Romans in 220: ἀλογία and (perception of) ἀδικία are interrelated (15.11, cited above).[28] Rational analysis, by contrast, is the distinctive characteristic of the historical narrator and Polybius himself in particular. Hannibal's failure to confront the Romans with the "real" reason for his behavior, the Roman annexation of Sardinia, thus also points to the fundamental problem that underlies the development of the historical events: the historical agents do not apply the same rational analysis to their own situation as historical narrators such as Polybius apply to the analysis of the past. That Hannibal should have done exactly that—and wasted a precious opportunity to align historical action with historical analysis—is clear from Polybius' statement that Hannibal, had he remained rational and calm, would have identified the same event, the annexation of Sardinia, as the "real" cause of his behavior and, thus, the principal cause of the impending war, as Polybius himself.[29] For a brief moment, the level of the historical agents and the level of the historical narrator could, and should, have merged and the course of events been influenced by rational analysis, rather than uncontrollable emotions.[30]

---

[28] On ἀλογία and its (negative) implications in Polybius, see Eckstein 1989, 9–12.

[29] Polybius thus, of course, also authorizes his own interpretation of the causes by attributing them, if only implicitly, to one of the historical agents.

[30] Such an alignment of rational analysis and political action is precisely what Polybius' *Histories* as a "handbook for statesmen" (Eckstein 1989, 14) is designed to bring about in Polybius' readers: for successful political and military action, they need to apply the same kind of analysis to their present situation that is characteristic of Polybius' approach to the past. See esp. 12.25b.3 with Wiater 2017a, 207 and n. 30, 3.31–32 (above); on the *Histories* being designed to shape history beyond the end of Polybius' narrative, see Wiater 2016. On the ἀνήρ πραγματικός, the "man of action", as Polybius' envisaged reader whom his narrative is supposed to provide with the "political formation" that he requires for successful action, see e.g. 1.35.9, 3.31.3–13, 3.59.39.2.5, 9.9.9–10, 11.18a.1–3. The fundamental precondition for history being useful to military and political leaders is that the historian himself is, or has been, such a "man of action", see esp. 12.28.2–5; cf. 12.25k.8. See e.g. Meissner 1986, Wiater 2010, 99–104, and cf. Eckstein 1995, 284, on Polybius conceiving of his work as itself an "action" designed to bring about change, but Eckstein unnecessarily limits this change to "ethical conduct" (of political leaders). Against this

The final result of the course of events, to be sure, would most likely have remained unaltered: the wrath of the Barcids and the Carthaginians' collective resentment of the Romans had advanced too far to be stopped.[31] But at least one of the greatest and most important wars in history would not have been waged under false pretenses but on the basis of a mutual understanding of the motives of the historical agents, including the role of treaty violations. The past events themselves could have offered all the answers, and the confusion about the causes of and legal responsibility for the war among the historical agents as well as later generations of historical writers could have been avoided.

As it is, the "near miss" of the alignment of historical-rational analysis with the actions and behavior of the historical agents only underlines even further how badly such a rational analysis of causes, treaties and *kriegsschuld* is needed. Polybius' text creates a multi-perspective, polyphonous network of different views, opinions and debates about Roman-Carthaginian treaties and their validity and significance which cuts across the levels of historical narrator and historical agents. He construes the debate about the causes and legal implications of the outbreak of the war as an unresolved dilemma, an open question which neither the historical agents nor his historical predecessors have been, and are, able to resolve on the basis of the information available to them. By designing the pre-history of the Hannibalic War as a series of failures of the historical agents to communicate about the treaties, Polybius' narrative, one could say, creates a "blank space" in history,[32] an event that could and should have happened, but did not: rational communication about the treaties is conspicuous by its absence.

This "blank space" remains unnoticed by the historical agents themselves, who are too strongly involved in their own motives, emotions and intentions to take such a distanced view of their own situation.[33] It is noticed and experienced, by contrast, by Polybius' *readers* whom alone the carefully designed architecture of Polybius' narrative enables to achieve the necessary distance, a sort-of "bird's-

---

background, Hannibal in the above episode, as Eckstein (1989, 2) rightly notes, serves as "a model of the 'bad' Polybian statesman".

[31] The reader might be prompted to consider, however, whether and how history might have changed if the Romans had been open to discussion about the Carthaginian δίκαια in 238.

[32] I borrow the concept of "blank spaces in history" ("historische Leerstellen") from Jaeger 2002, 250–53.

[33] On Hannibal failing to confront the Romans with the real reason for his behavior because of his anger and emotions, see above, pp. 143–144, Eckstein 1989, 11–15. On the Romans' failure to discuss δίκαια in Carthage in 218 due to *their* anger (θυμόν) about the fall of Saguntum, see 29.1.

eye view" on the events,[34] to perceive the patterns of attitudes and behaviors over several decades that underlie, inform and, to an extent, govern the course of events. The "blank space" in (Polybius' narrative of) the past thus translates into the readers' perception of a long-unresolved dilemma and open question that should have been addressed a long time ago and remains unanswered even at their own time.

This sense of dissatisfaction with this unresolved dilemma builds up over the entirety of 3.6–30.2 and reaches its climax precisely in the Romans' reply to the Carthaginians in 218, in the passage cited above (21.6–8).[35] Even a casual reader will notice that in this confrontation between Romans and Carthaginians, the Carthaginians appear to be in a much stronger position. They, at least, present a clear argument for which treaties are (or, indeed, are not) relevant on the basis of the text of the existing documents and the historical circumstances of their conclusion. The Romans, by comparison, play an at best questionable role in these proceedings: on the one hand, they admit that there are, indeed, "disputed points" (ἀμφισβητούμενα, 21.6), on the other, they simply maintain that these are now irrelevant because Hannibal has already captured Saguntum. This is an embarrassingly weak position given that the main argument of the Carthaginians is, in fact, that nothing in the existing legal agreements between the two peoples forbade Hannibal to attack the Iberian town in the first place and that, consequently, the violation (παρεσπονδημένης, 21.7) cited by the Romans as the principal justification for their threat to declare war never even happened.

Such a refusal to discuss legal issues on the part of the Romans is particularly problematic because questions of the violations of rights of Roman allies constituted such a crucial element of the Roman concept of the "just war".[36] And even though it is doubtful whether the concept of the *bellum iustum ac pium* (Cic. *Resp.* 2.31) already existed at Polybius' time in the same elaborate form as we know it primarily from Cicero's writings,[37] the fact that Fabius Pictor identified Hannibal's ἀδίκημα against Saguntum specifically as one of the two causes of the war strongly suggests that the Romans were conceiving of causes of wars in terms of legal causes already in the late third century.[38] When Polybius' Romans refuse

---

[34] Enabling such a "bird's-eye perspective" of the past (Polybius uses the term *synopsis*) is a crucial element of Polybius' historical method; see 1.4.1, Zangara 2007, esp. 40–50, Wiater 2017a, 204 with n. 5; cf. below, n. 61.
[35] See above, p. 138.
[36] Cf. esp. Cic. Resp. 3.35: noster autem populus sociis defendendis terrarum iam omnium potitus est.
[37] See Loreto 2001; Botermann 2002.
[38] See Harris 1979, 171–72, Ager 2009, 20–21, Clavadetscher-Thürlemann 1985.

any discussion of the legal foundations of their declaration of war, they cast serious and unnecessary doubt on the war's status as *iustum* and, thus, the very legitimacy of their declaration of war. And while their success with this kind of behavior in 238 might explain why the Romans in 218 thought that this strategy would once again be effective by intimidating the Carthaginians and forcing them to accept their demands, their brusque and arrogant treatment of the Carthaginians will have the opposite effect on Polybius' readers: to them, the Romans' bland refusal to discuss the crucial legal questions makes the lack of a competent, objective and balanced analysis of these issues all the more evident. It is precisely by having the Romans leave the Carthaginians' arguments unanswered that Polybius increases the readers' awareness of the "blank space", the open question that so urgently needs to be addressed and resolved, a question, moreover, that should have been addressed and resolved almost 70 years earlier.

It is at this point of the narrative that Polybius' digression does exactly that: he presents his reader with a comprehensive overview of the existing treaties, including the *verbatim* citation of the documents and a commentary on those aspects of the treaties that pertain directly to the controversy. This much-needed "common ground" (ὁμολογουμένη θεωρία in the quotation below) fills in, retrospectively, the "blank space" in the historical events, the absence of any meaningful communication about the treaties and their significance at the level of the events, and resolves at the same time the on-going controversy between the different theories of the causes proposed by the "Hannibal historians", Fabius Pictor and Polybius himself.[39] The digression will thus finally provide answers to the questions which Polybius' narrative has prompted since chapter 6: who is right, the Romans or the Carthaginians? Did any treaty violations occur? Were any of these relevant to the outbreak of the Hannibalic war and, if so, which ones? Finally, who committed the treaty violations that led, directly or indirectly, to the outbreak of the war; with whom, that is, does the *kriegsschuld* lie? Polybius' digression will end the past and present confusion about these questions and the polyphony, as it were, of multiple and often mutually exclusive perspectives. Thanks to the ὁμολογουμένη θεωρία which the digression will establish, at the crucial moment of the Romans' dramatic declaration of war (33.1–4), the final and

---

[39] Insofar as the digression represents an interruption on the part of the narrator of the actions of the historical characters it falls under the category of the "ordinary and innocent" narrative metalepses that "play on the double temporality of the story and the narrating … *as if the narrating were contemporaneous with the story* and had to *fill up the latter's dead spaces*" (Genette 1972 [1980], 235, emphases added).

most decisive expression of the Romans' claim that their war is justified, Polybius' readers—in stark contrast to the historical agents—will have an advanced understanding of whether the Romans' legal claims are correct and the Hannibalic War truly was "just" and, indeed, of the complexities and difficulties inherent in this question.[40]

But Polybius' digression is not simply meant to be relevant to his readers' understanding of the past. It will also finally establish the kind of alignment of political action and historical-rational analysis in *present and future* which Hannibal had the chance to bring about in the past, but failed (21.9–10, note especially μηθ' ... συμπλανώμενοι ταῖς ἀγνοίαις καὶ φιλοτιμίαις τῶν συγγραφέων):[41]

> [In contrast to the Roman ambassadors in 218] I think it necessary not to leave this aspect [the Carthaginians' legal arguments] unexamined, so that neither those whose duty and interest it is to be accurately informed about this (σαφῶς εἰδέναι τὴν ἐν τούτοις ἀκρίβειαν) may deviate from the truth (τῆς ἀληθείας) in critical debates (ἐν τοῖς ἀναγκαιοτάτοις διαβουλίοις), nor students, led astray by the ignorance or partisanship of historians (συμπλανώμενοι ταῖς ἀγνοίαις καὶ φιλοτιμίαις τῶν συγγραφέων), acquire mistaken notions on the subject, but that there may be some generally recognized understanding (τις ὁμολογουμένη θεωρία) of the legal agreements between Romans and Carthaginians up to our own time.

This passage has convincingly been seen as a reference to the political discussions in Rome in the period preceding the third and final Roman-Carthaginian War.[42] Polybius' discussion of the treaties is thus meant to be more than just a source of reliable information about the past; its purpose is to influence contemporary politics.[43] As such, the resulting ὁμολογουμένη θεωρία will enable the Romans to avoid the continuation of the pattern that characterized the events that preceded the previous war and, in particular, another embarrassing failure properly to evaluate their legal position such as it had occurred before in Carthage in 218.

And just as Polybius' text is designed to prepare and justify the digression on the treaties by creating the need for exactly this kind of comprehensive analysis,

---

40 See above, pp. 133–35.
41 See the discussion of 15.9–11 above, p. 144.
42 Mommsen 1859, 322; cf. Walbank 1957, 336. Differently, Scardigli 1991, 26, who wants to link the digression with the final phase of the controversy between Carthage, Rome and Massinissa about the possession of the Lesser Syrtis and the *emporia*.
43 Cf. Walbank 1957, 337. I will argue in the next section that this claim is supported by the particular design of the digression which mirrors characteristics of the form and language of the discourse of Graeco-Roman international diplomacy.

it also presents the reader with "proof" of the successful influence of the digression on the contemporary public debate in Rome. Polybius' claim of the political relevance of his digression is borne out by his account of how the Romans of his own time finally reply—with a delay of almost 70 years—to the Carthaginians' legal arguments of 218 (29.1–6):

> I have already stated what the Carthaginians alleged, and will now give the reply of the Romans—a reply indeed which they did not make at the time owing to their indignation at the loss of Saguntum, but it is being given on many occasions and by many different people at Rome (λέγεται δὲ πολλάκις καὶ ὑπὸ πολλῶν παρ' αὐτοῖς). In the first place they contend that the treaty with Hasdrubal should not be ignored, as the Carthaginians had the audacity to say; for there was no conditioning clause at the end as in the treaty made by Lutatius: *"This treaty shall be valid if the Roman people also agree to it"* ("κυρίας εἶναι ταύτας, ἐὰν καὶ τῷ δήμῳ δόξῃ τῶν Ῥωμαίων"), but Hasdrubal acting with full authority made the agreement in which it said that *"The Carthaginians shall not cross the Ebro in arms"* ("τὸν Ἴβηρα ποταμὸν μὴ διαβαίνειν ἐπὶ πολέμῳ Καρχηδονίους"). Again, in the treaty about Sicily there was, as the Carthaginians admit, the clause: *"The allies of either party are to be secure from attack by the other"* ("ὑπάρχειν τοῖς ἀμφοτέρων συμμάχοις τὴν παρ' ἑκατέρων ἀσφάλειαν"), and this does not mean *"those who were allies at that time"*, as the Carthaginians interpreted it; for in that case there would have been a further clause to the effect either that neither party should enter into other alliances than their existing ones or that those subsequently received into alliance should not be admitted to the benefits of the treaty. But since neither of these clauses was appended, it is evident that each party undertook that all allies of the other, both those then existing and those subsequently admitted to alliance, should be secure from attack.

In form and contents, this passage interacts both with Polybius' account of the Roman embassy to Carthage that preceded the digression and the digression itself. Polybius' Roman contemporaries' informed answer, based on actual knowledge of the text of the treaties as evidenced by the *verbatim* citations of relevant passages, stands in stark contrast to the failure of the Roman ambassadors in 218 to counter the Carthaginians' δικαιολογία and justify the Romans' declaration of war on the basis of a thorough knowledge of the documents in question and their implications. This thorough knowledge, the sequence of Polybius' text implies, Polybius' Roman contemporaries have gained from the immediately preceding παρέκβασις which provides the very *verbatim* citations of the treaties on which the Romans can now draw in their reply to the Carthaginians (see the passages in italics in the above quotation): in form and contents, the Romans' answer to the Carthaginians, as Polybius presents it, is informed by Polybius' digression. It is thanks to the information he provided that the Romans are finally able to formulate an effective and convincing reply to the question left open by their envoys in 218 and thus redress the balance between their own and the Carthaginians' standing in the controversy.[44]

Moreover, in chapter 29 rational analysis and political action, which in the narrative before the digression were assigned to the separate levels of historical events, on the one hand, and Polybius' auctorial comments, on the other, have merged to represent real-life political action no longer dominated by irrational emotions, as had been the case with Hannibal in 220 and the Romans in 218 (note "a reply indeed which they did not make at the time owing to their indignation at the loss of Saguntum" in the above quotation), but informed by the kind of rational and systematic analysis that had previously been the domain of the historical narrator alone: thanks to Polybius' narrative, the two levels of historical-critical analysis and political action have merged in (his image of) the contemporary public debate in Rome.[45] Chapter 29, one could say, puts the historical-analytical approach to the questions of the causes of the Hannibalic War and the *kriegsschuld* that is represented in Polybius' digression into real-life political practice.

The discussion in this section has demonstrated, I hope, that the narrative design of Polybius' discussion of the causes of the Hannibalic War and the *kriegsschuld* and the place of his digression on the treaties within this larger context are neither "clumsy" nor "careless" or "irritating": the παρέκβασις is integrated into the discussion exactly where the course of Polybius' argument requires it—after the Romans' failure to counter the Carthaginians' arguments and before their declaration of war, the proper assessment of which depends on exactly the kind of information provided by the digression. It is embedded into the narrative through proper transitions both at its beginning and, above all, its end (chapter 29), and Polybius has prepared its introduction from the very beginning of his discussion in chapter 6 by creating a "blank space" in his narrative of the historical events and the reader's experience of these events. By filling this "blank space" the digression transforms the coexistence of conflicting multiple perspectives on the issues in question into one ὁμολογουμένη θεωρία in Polybius'

---

[44] Whether the debate in contemporary Rome, which this passage undoubtedly seeks (or purports) to represent, was actually influenced by the results of Polybius' narrative is impossible to determine. My point here is that Polybius, by inserting his account of that contemporary debate at this point in his narrative, invites the reader to establish a direct connection between Polybius' inquiries and that debate.

[45] Cf. above, p. 144. That does not mean, of course, that Polybius unconditionally accepts the Roman view of the *kriegsschuld* that results from this analysis, as, indeed, he does not; see above, pp. 133–34.

present in which the perspectives of the historical agents and the kind of methodical-analytical approach that is characteristic of the historical narrator are reconciled in the systematic and methodical analysis of the facts (πράγματα) that have been made available, for the first time (26.2), in Polybius' παρέκβασις.

The following section will now turn to the digression itself, with its peculiar mixture of historical information, *verbatim* citation of documents and analytical commentary. I will argue that this particular structure mirrors the political discourse of interstate arbitration in the Graeco-Roman world as it has been preserved on inscriptions, and explore the function and implications of this interdiscursive dialogue between the *Histories* and the discourse of interstate arbitration in the context of Polybius' discussion of the causes of the Hannibalic War.

2 Arbitration and Monumentality: The Narrative Function of the Digression on the Roman-Carthaginian Treaties

By Polybius' time, drawing on and citing documents as such was not a novelty: Hellenistic historians, as Jacoby put it, were "more generous ... with quotations of records, poems and documents" than their predecessors.[46] Craterus of Macedon, for example, had compiled at least eight books of decrees at the beginning of the third century (*FGrHist* = *BNJ* 342) which seem to have contained "a sort of narrative" connecting the individual documents, "or rather excursuses or notes in which he discussed" each of them.[47] And Polemon of Ilium (*FHG* 3, 108–148), "in the early second century, included in his works accounts of the various Greek states, with particular attention to buildings and monuments ...: he was such an enthusiast for collecting and citing inscriptions that he was referred to as *stelokopas*, a glutton for *stelai* (Ath. 6.234d)".[48] The fragmentary state of late classical and Hellenistic historiography renders it impossible to know how exactly these authors integrated inscriptions into their accounts and how frequently they did

---

[46] Jacoby on *FGrHist* 342 (the quote at 96). Helpful overview in Rhodes 2007; on Polybius specifically, see Pédech 1964, 377–89. Biraschi-Desideri-Roda-Zecchini 2003 contains individual studies of the use of documents in ancient historians, including Polybius; cf. further Marincola 1997, 101–05, for brief, but important remarks on the evidentiary value attributed to documents by ancient historians.
[47] Jacoby *ibid.*
[48] Rhodes 2007, 64.

so. However, if the use of documents in compilatory works such as Diodorus' *Bibliotheke* can give us even the slightest idea of the practice of his Hellenistic predecessors, it would appear that even authors such as Hieronymus of Cardia (*FGrHist* 154), who drew extensively on documents in his *History of the Diadochi*, did not

> simply reproduc[e] documents, since instances of copies set out in full ... were exceptional. And even in the directly quoted pieces he confined himself to those items which were relevant to the immediate context.[49]

We might, therefore, surmise with all due caution that the close succession of a substantial number of long, *verbatim* quotations separated from each other solely by the historian's interpretive commentary, which constitutes Polybius' digression on the Roman-Carthaginian treaties, might have been seen as exceptional by Polybius' readers even against the background of the standard practice of the use of documents in contemporary historical writing. The peculiar design of the digression certainly sets it apart not only from its immediate narrative context: there is nothing quite like it in the entirety of what remains of Polybius' *Histories* either.

It is this very narrative design, together with the, as shown above, deliberately chosen position of the digression in Polybius' narrative, I suggest, that contain the key to its understanding. Both structure and vocabulary, I will argue now, link Polybius' digression and their immediate narrative context with the realities of international diplomacy and interstate arbitration in the Graeco-Roman world: the digression evokes an extra-textual political and diplomatic context with which Polybius and many of his (Greek as well as Roman) readers had, no doubt, first-hand experience and which was present in everyday life through numerous inscriptions which transformed these oral negotiations into permanently available historical events.

Let us begin by considering the following excerpt from an inscription recording the settlement brokered by Magnesian arbitrators, who had been appointed by the Romans, in a land dispute between the two Cretan cities of Hierapytna and Itanos.[50] The fascinating historical questions raised by the inscription cannot be

---

[49] Rosen 1967, 42; cf. Hornblower 1981, 131–37.
[50] IC III,iv 9, Ager 1996, 431–46, Chaniotis 1996, 183–85, 303–10, both with further literature. The arbitration described here occurred under the Roman consul C. Laelius Sapiens, who is named in the inscription (l. 87), and therefore belongs into the year 140 BCE. The essentials of the historical background are as follows: Hierapytna had defeated Praisos and adopted its land, which bordered the territory of Itanos. Itanos promptly disputed Hierapytna's ownership of this

discussed in the present context; my interest here is in the narrative design of the inscription, which combines historical information (an overview of the main stages of the land dispute up to and including the nomination of the Magnesians as arbitrators, 37–54) with *verbatim* citation of documents, political and legal analysis of these documents and, on this basis, a final judgment on the status of the claims of the parties involved. The part containing the legal analysis and subsequent judgment is the one that is most relevant to the present argument. It details the legal case (δικαιολογίας, 54) presented by both parties along with *verbatim* citations of a variety of documents and evidence, including letters, treaties and works of historians, on which the arbitrators' final decision is based (54–140). The following excerpt offers a good impression of the style and design of this part of the inscription (54–67):

> On the basis of the legal evidence presented by each side (ἐκ τῆς ὑφ' ἑκατέρων γενηθείσης δικαιολογίας) we find that the land that has been brought into dispute is held in possession by the Itanians ... and has been the Itanians' from the beginning, as also the boundary descriptions (περιορισμοί) informed (ἐμήνυον) us that were shown to us ([οἱ ἐπιδειχ]θέντες) by both parties: the one made with their former neighbors, the Dragmians, containing the following (περιέχων οὕτως): "The boundaries of their territory shall be thes[e: where the river Sedamnos flows,] up to Karymai, and beyond to the ridge of the mountain and all around the ridge of the mountain, straight up to D[orthanna to the] pit/reservoir and up to the road and beyond that up to the Mollos";[51] and furthermore the one made between the Itanians and Praisians, as written underneath (ὑπογέγραπται): "Itanians and Praisians decreed to make peace for all times on the basis of the territory which each of them now holds, the boundaries of which are the following: [list of the landmarks]". And again the boundary description made between Hierapytnians and Praisians, stating in writing as follows: [*verbatim* citation of the document].

---

newly-won land and war broke out between the two. This war was subsequently stopped by Roman legates under Servius Sulpicius Galba in 141, who re-established the boundaries of the two cities' respective territories from before the war (IC III,iv 10, 55–58 = Ager 1996, 434 = Sherk 14, p. 81). Itanos, unhappy with this outcome, appealed to the senate who appointed Magnesia as arbitrator. Other documents show that the agreement reached in that year did not last: the Magnesians were called upon to arbitrate again three decades later, in 112, by L. Calpurnius Piso Caesonius and delivered their final judgment in the matter in either that year or the year after. For further details see Sherk 1969, 83–84, Ager 1996, 442–46, Chaniotis 1996, 309–10.

51 The translation of this and the following treaties cited in the inscription follows Chaniotis 1996, 183, 304. The first περιορισμός appears to belong to the early third, the second one to the 60s of the second century BCE; the *terminus ante quem* of the third document is 145 BCE (Chaniotis 1996, 185, 305–06, 307). Not much is known about the places named in these agreements; see the discussion in Chaniotis 1996, 184–85, 304–05; these details are not relevant to the purpose of this chapter.

The very design of this protocol—the combination of historical narrative, *verbatim* citation of documents and legal-political analysis by a third party—shows some striking similarities with the design of Polybius' chapters on the Roman-Carthaginian treaties.

This similarity is not limited to the macro-structure, as it were, of the texts but also extends to the form of individual legal arguments ascribed by Polybius to the Carthaginians and applied by the Magnesian arbitrators as documented on the inscription. For example, the Carthaginians attempt to extrapolate the intention of the Lutatius Treaty from its exact wording (21.3–5):[52]

> they emphasized and insisted on the last treaty ..., in which they said there was *no written provision* (ἔγγραφον οὐδέν) regarding Iberia, but it was *expressly set down* (ῥητῶς κατατετάχθαι) that the allies of each power should be secure from attack by the other. They pointed out that at that time the Saguntines were not the allies of Rome, and to prove their point they several times *read aloud the terms of the treaty* (παρεγίνωσκον ... πλεονάκις τὰς συνθήκας).

This procedure is remarkably similar to the argument made by the Magnesian arbitrators who cite the exact wording of the ruling of Serv. Sulpicius regarding the boundaries of the land of the Hierapytnians and Itanians, respectively,[53] in order to refute the Hierapytnians' claim that part of the disputed land was "holy land" (ἱερὰ χώρα) and, therefore, belonged to the temple of Zeus Dictaeus, which happened to be controlled by the Hierapytnians:[54]

> about a "holy land" they [the Romans under Servius Sulpicius] *did not write anything* (οὐκ ἔγραψαν οὐδέν), even though the Hierapytnians had *expressly* (ῥητῶς) petitioned the Senate regarding "holy land" ... they only seem to have *made mention* (μνείαν πεποιημένοι) of "land", *writing* (γράψαντες): "they shall have it and possess it and cultivate it" ..., even though the Romans, when dealing with quarrels about holy land, *expressly write that* (γραφόντων ῥητῶς), as is the case also in the decisions of theirs which have been made available to us by others.[55]

The similarities in both the macro- and micro-structure of the passages are further reinforced by similarities in the vocabulary employed in Polybius' narrative and

---

[52] The procedure itself recalls one of the strategies of juridical rhetoric, the question of whether the letter of a given law or the law-giver's intention is decisive (κατὰ ῥητὸν καὶ κατὰ ὑπεξαίρεσιν, *scriptum et voluntas*), one of Hermagoras of Temnus' four *status legales*; see Woerther 2012, lxix, Martin 1974, 44–48.
[53] See above, n. 50.
[54] Cf. Chaniotis 1996, 310.
[55] IC III,iv 9, l. 76–79, 82–84 (= Ager 1996, 439).

the protocol of the Magnesians' settlement alike. To begin with, both the inscription, as mentioned above, and Polybius use the term δικαιολογία to refer to the legal arguments presented by the conflicting parties.[56] Polybius, it is true, uses the term only with reference to the legal case made by the Carthaginians in 218. However, his digression on the treaties, as I argued in the previous section, "intervenes" in the debate between Romans and Carthaginians where the Roman envoys should have present *their* legal case (δικαιολογία), but failed to do so. Moreover, in its form and contents, the alternation of *verbatim* citation of relevant documentary evidence and legal argument based on that evidence, the digression mirrors exactly the Carthaginians' δικαιολογία as well as the answer to this δικαιολογία which Polybius attributes to his Roman contemporaries (3.29).[57] Polybius' readers would, therefore, have had no difficulty to see Polybius' digression, too, as a δικαιολογία, even though Polybius does not explicitly characterize it as such. In form and contents, the digression thus mirrors not only the chapters that immediately precede and follow it in Polybius' narrative but also the discourse of interstate arbitration *outside* that narrative.

In addition to the technical term δικαιολογία, there is significant overlap of the vocabulary used in the inscription with the conceptual vocabulary and methods of historical research more generally.[58] The very use of documents as a sort of historical "witnesses" belongs here, as does the stress on autopsy. Both are, in fact, interrelated in our inscription: the Magnesian arbitrators emphasize that the Roman legates, on whose statements their own judgement partly relies,[59] had personally inspected the disputed territory (ἑωρακότες, 74–75, 75–76), while they, the arbitrators, had personally inspected the *documents* describing the land in question (διὰ τῶν ἐπιδεικνυμένων ἡμῖν χωρογραφιῶν εὐσύνοπτον ἦν, 71) as well as the Roman decree (φανερὸν δὲ τοῦτο ἐγίνετο καὶ ἐκ τοῦ δόγματος ... τοῦ γραφέντος, 73–74; note also σαφῶς, 68).[60] Autopsy and the notion of the "clear

---

[56] See above, pp. 138, 153.
[57] See above, pp. 149–50.
[58] This close interrelation of the vocabulary of historical method and international arbitration is not limited to our inscription. See Curty 1989 on IPri 37 (= 162 McCabe), esp. 31–35. Curty notes some striking similarities between the historical method of Polybius (or, one should rather say, the kind of historical inquiry represented by Polybius' *Histories*) and the reasoning of the Rhodian arbitrators in the settlement of a land dispute between Samos and Priene. Chaniotis 1989 remains fundamental on the interrelation of inscriptions and history/historiography.
[59] Above, p. 154.
[60] This kind of "indirect" autopsy, that is, the inspection of documents based on autopsy, is somewhat unusual in this kind of inscription; since boundary arbitrations required "not only

vision" of the past (*sapheneia*) that results from careful historical research are both key elements of ancient historical method in general and Polybius' historical method in particular.⁶¹ Moreover, like the Magnesian arbitrators, Polybius emphasizes his personal knowledge (and at the very least implies personal inspection) of the bronze copies of the Roman-Carthaginian treaties (3.26.1–2).

Another significant area of overlap is the language of "demonstration" (ἀπόδειξις) and "proof/evidence" (τεκμήριον).⁶² Both terms have been closely associated with historical inquiry and narrative since Herodotus, but they do, once again, assume particular prominence in Polybius, who links both notions in his concept of ἀποδεικτικὴ ἱστορία, defining documents as a particularly important category of the "evidence" that qualify a historical work as "demonstrative"/*apodeictic*.⁶³ This connection between historical discourse and the discourse of diplomacy/arbitration is at its closest when the "demonstrations of historians" are themselves cited as evidence as part of the legal argument, thus integrating the two spheres of historical inquiry and δικαιολογία.⁶⁴

These elements of structure, form of argument and vocabulary strongly suggest, I submit, that Polybius' discussion of the Roman-Carthaginian treaties in the context of the dispute about the causes of the Second Roman-Carthaginian

---

legal, but also topographic, decisions", arbitrators usually visited the contested land personally. See Ager 1996, 13–14 (the quote at 13), 445 with n. 9.

61 On autopsy in Polybius specifically, see 12.25e.1; in ancient historiography in general, Marincola 1997, 63–86; on *synopsis* and visuality in ancient historical writing generally, Zangara 2007, 21–54, 175–206 (on *synopsis* and *eusynopton*); in Polybius specifically, see 1.4.1, 14.1a.1, Zangara ibid., 40–54, Wiater 2017a, esp. 203–09; cf. above, n. 34. *Sapheneia*: Hdt. 1.21.1, 2.44.1, Thuc. 1.1.3, 22.4, 2.60.6, 3.12.2, 4.126.6, Plb. 1.12.9, 64.2, 3.21.9 (τὸ σαφῶς εἰδέναι τὴν ... ἀκρίβειαν), 36.2, PL s.v. σαφής III.

62 .... ἀποδεικνύντες ἄνωθεν τὰ διαμφισβητούμενα Ἰτα[νίων] γεγονότ[α, l. 91; [.... τῶ]ν Ἱεραπυτνίων ἐξωμολογημένας εἶχεν τὰς *ἀποδείξε[ις*, 95; [ἰσχυρ]ίζεσθαι τὰς ἀποδείξεις ἐπιστολαῖς βασιλικαῖς, 98; [... π]ροειρημένων *ἀποδείξεων* ἰσχυροτέραν *πίστιν*, 132; τὸ δὲ πάντων μέγιστον καὶ ἰσχυρότατον τεκμήριον, 84.

63 ἀπόδειξις: Hdt. 1.praef., 2.101, Thuc. 1.97.2; τεκμήριον: Hdt. 2.58, 7.238.2, Thuc. 1.20.1, 2.39.2. On Polybius' ἀποδεικτικὴ ἱστορία (2.37.3), see Pédech 1964, 43–53, esp. 51–52, on the interrelation of ἀποδεικτικὴ ἱστορία and "proofs". PL s.vv. ἀπόδειξις, τεκμήριον and πίστις III2 for references. Pédech also provides a brief but useful overview of the development of *apodeixis* and rightly stresses the close links of the term with philosophy and rhetoric; cf. Farrington 2015, 46–47; Sacks 1981, 171–78.

64 [ποιη]τῶν καὶ ἰστοριαγράφων ἀποδείξεις, ἃς καὶ αὐτοὶ ἡμ[ῖ]ν π[......]εσ[- -] [.....]τους δικαιολογίᾳ, ll. 93–94. The "testimony" of historians plays an even more prominent role in IPri 37 (= 162 McCabe), where the inscription records the judges' evaluation of the credibility of different historical accounts regarding the possession of disputed land (ll. 107–124 McCabe); see Curty 1989 for discussion.

war is designed to evoke (the inscriptional protocols of) arbitration processes in the Graeco-Roman world.⁶⁵ Contents, vocabulary and structure of Polybius' text invite the recipient to read his account of the Carthaginians' δικαιολογία in 218, the digression, the Roman response to the Carthaginians' δικαιολογία and Polybius' final judgment, as a kind of protocol of a large-scale arbitration in a dispute that spanned several decades (not unlike the dispute between Hierapytna and Itanos) and involved Romans, Carthaginians and Greeks including Polybius, the "arbitrator", himself.⁶⁶ Such cross-fertilization between historical literature and inscriptions was facilitated by the close interrelation of historical discourse and inscriptions in ancient communities in general, which is so amply documented in Chaniotis' study on *Historie und Historiker in den griechischen Inschriften*.⁶⁷ Literary historical narratives such as Polybius' *Histories* and inscriptions represented different but interrelated, and often complementary, ways of engaging with the past within the larger framework of ancient historical discourse and cultural memory, rather than separate types of discourse altogether.⁶⁸ In the remainder of this chapter, I will draw out some of the implications of this intertextual/interdiscursive relationship between Polybius' text and the discourse of Greek interstate arbitration itself as well as its epigraphic medium.

In his discussion of the relationship between historiography and inscriptions in Thucydides John Moles observes that "Thucydides images his *History* as being (among other things) an *inscription*", a "literary monument",⁶⁹ and convincingly

---

65 Cf. above n. 58.
66 Farrington 2015, 40–46, likens the historian's role to that of a dikast in that "historians must survey (συνθεωρεῖν, 3.32.5), interpret (συγκρίνειν, 3.32.5), perform examinations (δοκιμασία, 3.34.5), and decide which sources to follow and what their import is" (45).
67 Chaniotis 1988; a broader approach is taken by Osborne 2011, who argues that "all inscriptions are pieces of historical writing" (120), the main difference between epigraphic texts and literary histories being the degree of selectivity: "While the writers of literary histories have, and are expected to have, many histories to tell, epigraphic texts are in almost all cases single-dimensional ... inscriptions tell on a much more strictly 'need-to-know' basis" (119). On inscriptions as part of the historical culture and collective memory in Rome, see Cooley 2011.
68 See Cato FRH 5 F (= Gell. 3.7.19), Fest. s.v. *monimentum*, p. 123L., with the discussion in Wiseman 1986 [1994], 39 n. 13. Cf. Purcell 2003, 16, on "the genre of literary historiography" as "only a rather small and stylized part of the whole universe of historical thinking". On cross-fertilization between epigraphy and literary historiography, see Moles 1999; Koehn 2013 examines possible influence of the language of inscription on the language and style of Polybius.
69 Moles 1999, 32–33. Moles also considers Polybius, but his focus is rather more narrowly on Polybius' engagement with Thucydides' concept of history as inscription in one particular passage, 3.31.12–32.10. My interest here is in how Moles' observations on inscriptions and Thucydides' *History* can provide a useful starting point for an analysis of the interaction between Polybius' *History* and inscriptions independently of Polybius' engagement with Thucydides.

links this association of Thucydides' literary work with inscriptions to central elements of Thucydides' historical method, namely authority, truth, durability and visibility:

> An inscription stands for authority (it is written in a durable medium; it permits no rivals), truth (purported at any rate) and permanence (in contrast to any "competition piece for present hearing"), and its "open-access" quality ("for anyone who wishes to look") underlines the fact that Thucydides' "possession" is "free" to all who want it.[70]

These same factors, I would argue, are crucial also to Polybius' dialogue with the discourse of Greek diplomacy and its epigraphic representation. To begin with, the association with the political discourse of international arbitration lends support to Polybius' claim, made explicitly at 21.9–10, that the purpose of his discussion is to shape the public political debate in contemporary Rome.[71] By appropriating the form and language of inscriptions protocolling real-life political disputes and their solution, Polybius makes his analysis and subsequent judgment appear authoritative, "official" and inherently political; structure and form reinforce the purported political importance of the contents. This effect is strengthened further by the fact that historical works, as mentioned above,[72] played a prominent role as "testimony" in processes of arbitration: historical narratives were regularly consulted and cited in such negotiations and influenced the judgment of the arbitrators; the information provided by historians thus shaped real-life politics and had a concrete and tangible impact on the lives of the communities involved. By casting his discussion in the form of the discourse of international arbitration, Polybius thus also avails himself of the generally acknowledged importance of historical narratives in politics and diplomacy in the Graeco-Roman world.

Polybius' attempt to endow his work with political authority by way of the association with Graeco-Roman diplomatic discourse is particularly important because Polybius himself lacked any such authority in Roman political discourse. This lack of political authority needed to be addressed forcefully not the least because one of the main voices in the controversy about the causes of the Hannibalic War and the *kriegsschuld* with which Polybius had to compete and which he, quite literally, sought to overwrite,[73] was the voice of Fabius Pictor. As Polybius says at 3.9.1–5, what made Fabius' interpretation of the causes and *kriegs-*

---

70 Moles 1999, 42.
71 See above, p. 148.
72 See above, p. 156.
73 Cf. above, p. 140.

schuld appear so credible (πίστις) was not its quality but the fact that its author was both a Roman senator and an eye-witness to the events he was describing: readers paid attention to the man (τὴν ἐπιγραφήν; τὸν λέγοντα), not to the facts he narrated (τὰ πράγματα; τὰ λεγόμενα). If Polybius wanted to become the dominant and, in fact, only voice (ὁμολογουμένη θεωρία, 21.10) in that controversy, he needed to attempt to build up an authority that could at least match the prestige of his Roman competitor.

Even if we assume that Polybius' close connections with the Scipiones set him apart from other foreigners at Rome at the time, Polybius remained a Greek exile who had no official standing in Rome: any influence he could hope to exert on contemporary Roman political discourse depended entirely on the credibility and persuasiveness of his narrative and his voice as a historical narrator. This credibility and authority result, on the one hand, from the methodological aspects of his work, especially the demonstration of his comprehensive knowledge of the entire debate in both the international, as it were, historical literature and the discussions in contemporary Rome; his ability critically to evaluate the historical information, as demonstrated by his polemical engagement with the "Hannibal historians" as well as Fabius Pictor; his research in the Roman archives and resulting access to exclusive material as evidenced by the *verbatim* citation of the treaties; and his expertise in historical analysis as shown by his detailed discussion of the principles of historical causation, the development of a novel approach to historical causes, and the numerous analytical passages throughout the discussion.[74]

But Polybius goes further than that. He supplements this "epistemic" authority, which is based on the demonstration of his skills and expertise as a historian,[75] with the association of his historical inquiry with political discourse *outside* the genre of literary history:[76] his voice is not simply that of the highly skilled

---

[74] On these means of establishing historical authority, cf. Marincola 1997, 12–19, 95–117, 218–24, 283–85; cf. Farrington 2015, 40–51, on the historian's credibility depending on "his ability to effectively judge the quality of his sources" (48, with reference to Polybius) and Polybius' "argumentative posture": "Polybius does not simply place his narrative before the reader and expect the factual truth of it, or his claim of factual truth, to satisfy the reader's scepticism ... he stresses that he places before the reader a credible case".

[75] On "epistemic authority", see de George 1985, 22; cf. Marincola 1997, 235. Wiater 2017b, esp. 231–36.

[76] On literary authority resulting not only from the self-presentation of the author but more generally from the "specific design of [a] text', see Wiater 2017b (on Dionysius of Halicarnassus; the quote at 234); on creating authority *within* a text at least partly through association with discourses *external* to this specific text, see *ibid.*, 237 n. 23.

historian but also echoes that of respected, officially appointed arbitrators who have been given the task of determining the truth value of competing claims in an international controversy and broker a solution of that controversy on the basis of their findings. While the reference to his superior knowledge of the requirements of proper historical research emphasizes Polybius' competence as a historical narrator, the association with interstate arbitration emphasizes Polybius' experience as a political and military leader, an ἀνὴρ πραγματικός, which he brings to the difficult question of the causes of the Hannibalic War and the *kriegsschuld*.[77] The voice of Polybius the historian merges with the voice of Polybius the seasoned politician, and the analytical discussion and narrative of Polybius the historian is at the same time the medium through which Polybius the man of action shapes contemporary political debate: Polybius makes politics *by* writing history.

To the *pistis* of authors such as Fabius Pictor, inasmuch as it is based on their social status, Polybius opposes an auctorial voice based on the combined authority of his demonstrated competence as a historical narrator and of his role as "historical arbitrator" that is enacted through the form and language of his discussion. Fabius' status as an "eye witness", on the other hand, Polybius counters with an account that makes the reader himself "see" the πράγματα and, thus, provides him with the only reliable foundation for their own judgment: Fabius might have seen the historical events but the "documentary design"[78] of Polybius' narrative purports to offer the reader an unfiltered view of the events and, through the *verbatim* citations, all the relevant documents themselves whose authenticity is guaranteed by Polybius' autopsy of the documents in situ. The specific design of Polybius' discussion of the treaties which is authenticated by its appropriation of the form and language of international diplomatic discourse just as its contents is authenticated by Polybius' expertise and his autopsy, enables the reader to "see the facts themselves" (πρὸς τὰ πράγματα βλέπειν/ἐπὶ τὰ λεγόμενα συνεπιστήσαντες/ἐξ αὐτῶν τῶν πραγμάτων) without having their view blocked by the author (τὸν λέγοντα, 3.9.3–5, discussed above).

The discussion of the dialogue between Polybius' text and the discourse of interstate arbitration has added a further dimension to Polybius' claim that his

---

77 Cf. above, n. 30.
78 By "documentary" I mean the specific way in which inscriptions create and preserve a visible and durable record of a past event and the immediate access ("snap shot") to the recorded event which they purport to offer. Inscriptions are not, however, as Alison Cooley (2012, 220–28, esp. 221–22) warns us, "objective documents" that offer an unfiltered view of the past, as they have sometimes been seen by modern scholars. Inscriptions were set up in order to create and memorialize a specific image of the past, not "document" the past for its own sake.

investigation of the causes of the Hannibalic War and the *kriegsschuld* is of political significance and, thus, I hope, offered novel insight into the ways in which Polybius thinks of his *historical* narrative as political beyond its didactic purpose of educating present and future statesmen (ἄνδρες πραγματικοί). It also connects the political dimension of Polybius' narrative to his battle, as it were, with his historical predecessors, especially Fabius Pictor, and, thus, with one important element of the "polyphony" which is, I have suggested, characteristic and, indeed, constitutive of Polybius' discussion of the causes and the *kriegsschuld* as a whole.

One could, indeed, go so far—and with this suggestion I shall conclude this chapter—as to argue that this "polyphony" itself becomes a subject of Polybius' narrative. The protocols of interstate arbitrations such as the one discussed above purport to memorialize and, thus, monumentalize a crucial event in the past; they provide a "snap shot", as it were, of the decisive moment that brought about the solution of an often long-standing conflict. In the process, however, they also memorialize the conflict itself, which is manifest in the polyphony of the inscription: the competing claims of the parties involved, the documents and other "witnesses" that are cited in support of these claims and the evaluation of the arbitrators which aims to channel the polyphony of the controversy into a universally accepted agreement.

The preceding discussion has shown that Polybius' discussion of the causes of the Hannibalic War echoes this process from polyphony to one, universally agreed-upon view, the ὁμολογουμένη θεωρία (21.10) brought about by his narrative. And just as the inscriptional protocols of the arbitration processes "record" the controversy along with the solution, Polybius' narrative gives permanence to or, rather, creates a picture of the controversy itself. It constitutes the contemporary debate, as it emerges from his discussion, as a historical event that remains permanently visible in and through his text, just as the controversies between different city states remain permanently visible and accessible through the inscriptional protocols. The polyphony of Polybius' narrative, to put it differently, "documents" the polyphony that characterized the debate about the causes of the Hannibalic War and the *kriegsschuld* in second-century Rome.[79] This "documentation" includes, of course, Polybius' own contribution to the controversy.

---

[79] Cf. Jaeger 2002, 253–54, commenting on Natalie Zemon Davis' *The Return of Martin Guerre*, which provides the reader with access to the past by presenting different perspectives of French peasants alongside each other, thus enabling the reader "to understand the perception of the events as it influenced the historical agents, the villagers, by re-experiencing it for themselves [an sich selbst nachzuvollziehen]".

Polybius' narrative can thus be seen as a medium to memorialize his own (as he presents it) pivotal role in the process: Polybius' discussion of the causes of the war and the question of *kriegsschuld* in his historical narrative is an instrument of political change as much as it is a *monumentum* to this change as it was brokered by Polybius the historian and "man of action" alike.[80]

Bibliography

Ager, S.L. (1996), *Interstate Arbitration in the Greek World, 337–90 B.C.*, Berkeley.
── (2009), "Roman Perspectives on Greek Diplomacy", in: C. Eilers (ed.), *Diplomats and Diplomacy in the Roman World*, Leiden, 15–43.
Ameling, W. (1993), *Karthago. Studien zu Militär, Staat und Gesellschaft*, Munich.
Botermann, H. (2002), "Gallia pacata—perpetua pax. Die Eroberung Galliens und der 'gerechte Krieg'", in: J. Spielvogel (ed.), *Res Publica Reperta. Zur Verfassung und Gesellschaft der römischen Republik und des frühen Prinzipats*, Stuttgart, 279–296.
Bringmann, K. (2001), "Überlegungen zur Datierung und zum historischen Hintergrund der beiden ersten römisch-karthagischen Verträge", in: K. Geus/K. Zimmermann (eds.), *Punica—Libyca—Ptolemaica. Festschrift für Werner Huß, zum 65. Geburtstag dargebracht von Schülern, Freunden und Kollegen*, StudPhoen. 16, Leuven, 111–120.
Carey, W.L. (1996), "*Nullus videtur dolo facere*: The Roman Seizure of Sardinia in 237 B.C.", in: *CPh* 91, 203–222.
Chaniotis, A. (1988), *Historie und Historiker in den griechischen Inschriften: epigraphische Beiträge zur griechischen Historiographie*, Wiesbaden.
── (1996), *Die Verträge zwischen kretischen Poleis in der hellenistischen Zeit*, Stuttgart.
Clavadetscher-Thürlemann, S. (1985), *ΠΟΛΕΜΟΣ ΔΙΚΑΙΟΣ und Bellum Iustum. Versuch einer Ideengeschichte*, Zurich.
Cooley, A.E. (2011), "History and Inscriptions, Rome", in: A. Feldherr/G. Hardy (eds.), *The Oxford History of Historical Writing*, Vol. 1: *Beginnings to AD 600*, Oxford, 244–264.
── (2012), *The Cambridge Manual of Latin Epigraphy*, Cambridge.
Cornell, T.J. (1995), *The Beginnings of Rome. Italy and Rome from the Bronze Age to the Punic Wars (c. 1000-264 BC)*, London.
Curty, O. (1989), "L'historiographie hellénistique et l'inscription n° 37 des *Inschriften von Priene*", in: M. Piérart/O. Curty (eds.), *Historia testis. Mélanges d'épigraphie, d'histoire ancienne et de philologie offerts à Tadeusz Zawadzki*, Fribourg, 21–35.
de Foucault, J.-A. (1972), *Recherches sur la langue et le style de Polybe*, Paris.
de George, R.T. (1985), *The Nature and Limits of Authority*, Lawrence, KS.
de Sanctis, G. (1967), *Storia dei Romani*, Vol. 3.1, 2nd edn, Florence.
Derow, P. (1979), "Polybius, Rome, and the East", in: *JRS* 69, 1–15.

---

[80] Cf. Wiseman 1986 [1994], 39 on the works of "Fabius, Cincius and their senatorial successors" as "*monumenta litterarum* designed, like other *monumenta*, to preserve *res gestae* from oblivion"; on the interrelation between concepts of writing history and monuments more generally, with particular reference to Herodotus and Thucydides, see Immerwahr 1960, Moles 1999.

Eckstein, A.M. (1989), "Hannibal at New Carthage: Polybius 3.15 and the Power of Irrationality", in: *CPh* 84, 1–15.
—— (1995), *Moral Vision in the Histories of Polybius*, Berkeley.
—— (2010), "Polybius, 'The Treaty of Philinus', and Roman Accusations against Carthage", in: *CQ* 60, 406–426.
—— (2012), "Polybius, the Gallic Crisis, and the Ebro Treaty", in: *CPh* 107, 206–229.
Erdkamp, P. (2009), "Polybius, the Ebro Treaty, and the Gallic Invasion of 225 BCE", in: *CPh* 104, 495–510.
Espada Rodriguez, J. (2013), *Los dos primeros tratados romano-cartagineses: análisis historiográfico y contexto historico*, Barcelona.
Eucken, H.C. (1968), *Probleme der Vorgeschichte des zweiten punischen Krieges*, PhD diss., Freiburg i.Br.
Farrington, S. (2015), "A Likely Story: Rhetoric and the Determination of Truth in Polybius' *Histories*", in: *Histos* 9, 29–66.
FRH T.J. Cornell (ed.), *The Fragments of the Roman Historians*, 3 vols., Oxford 2013.
Gelzer, M. (1933), "Römische Politik bei Fabius Pictor", in: *Hermes* 68, 129–166.
Genette, G. (1972), *Narrative Discourse. An Essay in Method*, transl. by J.E. Lewin, Foreword by J. Culler, Ithaca, NY 1980.
Harris, W.V. (1979), *War and Imperialism in Republican Rome, 327–70 B.C.*, Oxford.
Hornblower, J. (1981), *Hieronymus of Cardia*, Oxford.
Hoyos, B.D. (1998), *Unplanned Wars. The Origins of the First and Second Punic Wars*, Berlin.
Huss, W. (1985), *Geschichte der Karthager*, Munich.
Immerwahr, H.R. (1960), "History as a Monument in Herodotus and Thucydides", in: *AJPh* 81, 261–290.
Jaeger, S. (2002), "Erzähltheorie und Geschichtswissenschaft", in: V. Nünnung/A. Nünning (eds.), *Erzähltheorie transgenerisch, intermedial, interdisziplinär*, Trier, 237–263.
Koehn, C. (2013), "Polybios und die Inschriften: zum Sprachgebrauch des Historikers", in: V. Grieb/C. Koehn (eds.), *Polybios und seine Historien*, Stuttgart, 159–181.
Laqueur, R. (1913), *Polybius*, Leipzig.
Lausberg, H. (2008), *Handbuch der literarischen Rhetorik. Eine Grundlegung der Literaturwissenschaft*, 4th edn, Stuttgart.
Loreto, L. (2001), *Il bellum iustum e i suoi equivoci. Cicerone ed una componente della rappresentazione Romana del Völkerrecht antico*, Naples.
Marincola, J. (1997), *Authority and Tradition in Ancient Historiography*, Cambridge.
Marotta, V. (1996), "Tutela dello scambio e commerci mediterranei in età arcaica e repubblicana", in: *Ostraka* 5, 63–138.
Martin, J. (1974), *Antike Rhetorik. Technik und Methode*, Munich.
Meissner, B. (1986), "ΠΡΑΓΜΑΤΙΚΗ ΙΣΤΟΡΙΑ: Polybius über den Zweck pragmatischer Geschichtsschreibung", in: *Saeculum* 37, 313–351.
Moles, J. (1999), "ΑΝΑΘΗΜΑ ΚΑΙ ΚΤΗΜΑ: The Inscriptional Inheritance of Ancient Historiography", in: *Histos* 3, 27–69.
Mommsen, T. (1859), *Die römische Chronologie bis auf Caesar*, 2nd edn, Berlin.
Nörr, D. (2003), "*Fides Punica—fides Romana*. Bemerkungen zur *demosia pistis* im ersten karthagisch-römischen Vertrag und zur Rechtsstellung des Fremden in der Antike", in: L. Garofalo (ed.), *Il ruolo della buona fede oggettiva nell'esperienza giuridica storica e contemporanea*, Vol. 2, Padua, 497–541.
Oakley, S.P. (1998), *A Commentary on Livy Books VI–X*, Vol. 2, Oxford.

Osborne, R. (2011), "Greek Inscriptions as Historical Writing", in: A. Feldherr/G. Hardy (eds.), *The Oxford History of Historical Writing 1: Beginnings to AD 600*, Oxford, 97–121.

Pédech, P. (1964), *La méthode historique de Polybe*, Paris.

PL *Polybios-Lexikon*, bearbeitet von A. Mauersberger, C.-F. Collartz/ M. Gützlaf/ H. Helms, Berlin 1956–2004.

Purcell, N. (2003), "Becoming Historical. The Roman Case", in: D. Braund/C. Gill (eds.), *Myth, History and Culture in Republican Rome. Studies in Honour of T.P. Wiseman*, Exeter, 12–40.

Rhodes, P.J. (2007), "Documents and the Greek Historians", in: J. Marincola (ed.), *A Companion to Greek and Roman Historiography*, Vol. 1, Malden, MA, 56–66.

Rich, J. (1996), "The Origins of the Second Punic War", in: T.J. Cornell/B. Rankov/P. Sabin (eds.), *The Second Punic War. A Reappraisal*, London, 1–37.

Rosen, K. (1967), "Political Documents in Hieronymus of Cardia (323–302 B.C.)", in: *AC* 10, 41–94.

Sacks, K. (1981), *Polybius on the Writing of History*, Berkeley, CA.

Scardigli, B. (1991), *I Trattati Romano-Cartaginesi. Introduzione, edizione critica, traduzione, commento e indici*, Pisa.

Serrati, J. (2006), "Neptune's Altars: The Treaties between Rome and Carthage (509–226 B.C.)", in: *CQ* 56, 113–134.

StV H. Bengtson/R. Werner (eds.) (1975), *Die Staatsverträge des Altertums*, Vol. 2: *Die Verträge der griechisch-römischen Welt von 700 bis 338 v. Chr.*, Munich. Schmitt, H.H. (ed.) (1969), *Die Staatsverträge des Altertums*, Vol. 3: *Die Verträge der griechisch-römischen Welt von 338 bis 200 v. Chr.*, Munich (cited by no.).

Toynbee, A.J. (1965), *Hannibal's Legacy. The Hannibalic War's Effects on Roman Life*, Vol. 1, London.

Walbank, F.W. (1957), *A Historical Commentary on Polybius*, Vol. 1, Oxford.

Welwei, K.W. (2001), "Piraterie und Sklavenhandel in der frühen römischen Republik", in: H. Bellen/H. Heinen (eds.), *Fünfzig Jahre Forschungen zur antiken Sklaverei an der Mainzer Akademie 1950-2000. Miscellanea zum Jubiläum*, Stuttgart, 73–81.

Werner, R. (1963), *Der Beginn der römischen Republik. Historisch-chronologische Untersuchungen über die Anfangszeit der libera res publica*, Munich.

Wiater, N. (2010), "Speeches and Historical Narrative in Polybius' *Histories*", in: D. Pausch (ed.), *Stimmen der Geschichte. Funktionen von Reden in der antiken Historiographie*, Berlin, 67–107.

— — (2016), "Shifting Endings, Ambiguity and Deferred Closure in Polybius' *Histories*", in: A. Lianeri (ed.), *Knowing Future Time in and through Greek Historiography*, Berlin, 243–265.

— — (2017), "Polybius and Sallust", in: R. Balot/S. Forsdyke/E. Foster (eds.), *The Oxford Handbook of Thucydides*, Oxford, 659–676.

— — (2017a), "The Aesthetics of Truth: Narrative and Historical Hermeneutics in Polybius' *Histories*", in: L. Hau/I. Ruffell (eds.), *Truth and History in the Ancient World. Pluralising the Past*, London, 202–225.

— — (2017b), "Expertise, 'Character' and the 'Authority Effect' in the *Early Roman History* of Dionysius of Halicarnassus", in: J. König/G. Woolf (eds.), *Authority and Expertise in Ancient Scientific Culture*, Cambridge, 231–259.

Wiseman, P. (1986), "Monuments and the Roman Annalists", cited after the reprint in: T.P. Wiseman, *Historiography and Imagination. Eight Essays on Roman Culture*, Exeter 1994, 37–48.

Woerther, F. (2012), *Hermagoras, Fragments et Témoignages*, Paris.

Kyle Khellaf
Incomplete and Disconnected: Polybius, Digression, and its Historiographical Afterlife

> Second consequence: the notion of discontinuity assumes a major role in the historical disciplines. For history in its classical form, the discontinuous was both the given and the unthinkable: the raw material of history, which presented itself in the form of dispersed events—decisions, accidents, initiatives, discoveries; the material, which, through analysis, had to be rearranged, reduced, effaced in order to reveal the continuity of events. Discontinuity was the stigma of temporal dislocation that it was the historian's task to remove from history. It has now become one of the basic elements of historical analysis ... The notion of discontinuity is a paradoxical one: because it is both an instrument and an object of research; because it divides up the field of which it is the effect; because it enables the historian to individualize different domains but can be established only by comparing those domains. And because, in the final analysis, perhaps, it is not simply a concept present in the discourse of the historian, but something that the historian secretly supposes to be present: on what basis, in fact, could he speak without this discontinuity that offers him history—and his own history—as an object?
>
> Michel Foucault,
> *The Archaeology of Knowledge*, 8–9

Early in his genealogical account of the utterance (*énoncé*) as the basic constitutive element of human epistemology, Michel Foucault makes a striking claim regarding the role of discontinuity in early modern historical thought.[1] He claims that the discontinuous was both the raw material (*le donné*) which presented itself to the historian and the unimaginable consequence (*l'impensable*) of disparate events (*des événements dispersés*); the very substance of history, which required narration by the historian to trace out a linearity of affairs. Foucault goes on to claim that, traditionally, "the historian's task was to remove" this discontinuity "from history", even though this dislocation was the very thing which offered the historian the object of his inquiry (*cette rupture qui lui offre comme objet l'histoire—et sa propre histoire*).

When Foucault spoke of "history in its classical form" (*l'histoire dans sa forme classique*), he was not referring to the classical world per se, but rather to

---

[1] I wish to thank Ann Hanson, Christina S. Kraus, and Jeffrey Rusten for reading earlier versions of this paper, as well as the editors for their invitation to contribute and their wonderful *xenia* in Thessaloniki. Any remaining errors or omissions are entirely my own.

early modern Europe after the Renaissance.² Moreover, apart from the classical world's frustration with Foucault's own readings of antiquity,³ he appears to have gotten many things right regarding historical discontinuity: historians—not the least so Polybius—regularly strive to organize their various domains of inquiry (geographical and spatial separation; temporal discontinuity; political difference) in order to construct coherent narratives that unite some of these dislocations, and to create a history from otherwise inherent discontinuities. Foucault's only oversight, I would suggest, was viewing the digressive form of historical analysis as a recent phenomenon based on postmodern criticism.

If anything, our ancient sources amply demonstrate that historical disunity, as well as its role in shaping historiographical investigations, originated well over two millennia earlier. From the Homeric catalogues and embedded battle genealogies to the innately expansive model of Herodotean inquiry (*historiē*), thematic and narratological unity was merely a secondary consequence of *poēsis* ("literary production") and *sungraphē* ("prose narrative composition" and "organization"—literally, a "writing together"). Moreover, digression continued in Greek historiography from the fifth century BCE into the Hellenistic Era, as is clear from the significant extant portions of Thucydides' *History of the Peloponnesian War*, and later testimonia on fragmentary historians such as Ephorus of Cyme and Theopompus of Chios, many of these recorded by Polybius himself.⁴

However, the recognition of the digression as a fundamental historiographical tradition—and one that was openly discussed by historians and rhetoricians alike—did not emerge until a slightly later date. In this paper, I argue that this development can be situated precisely in the *Histories* of Polybius; that it was only as a result of Polybius' legacy—specifically, the subsequent recognition of his innovations to digressive narratology and the need to create an "interweaving" of events (*symplokē*) from distinct corners of the Mediterranean—that a consensus around this historical convention finally emerged; and that its afterlife, in both the imperial Roman annalists and the Roman rhetoricians who commented on the historiographical tradition, shows a pervasive Polybian influence. Indeed, if Roman antiquarianism is any guide, it was Polybius who provoked one of the

---

2 See, for example, Foucault 1970, 136–79 and Foucault 1972, 157–65.
3 Larmour, Miller, and Platter 1998, 4: "What may be most important, however, is the success Foucault has had as a catalyst. The reaction to and debate over *The History of Sexuality* is ongoing and rich".
4 Thucydides' digressions have been explicated in detail by Pothou 2009. For the moralizing tendency of digressions in classical and hellenistic historiography—and a useful schema of the motivations for such discursions—see Hau 2016, 9–11. For an analysis of the digression in Herodotus, Thucydides, and Xenophon, see Spada 2008.

most significant shifts in the genre's narratology, discursive self-awareness, and understanding of how best to situate the paratextual past.

1 Early Historical Discursiveness: Homer, Herodotus, and Thucydides

Historical digression certainly did not begin with Polybius. In fact, we can readily discern as early as Homer's *Iliad* a tendency to situate historiographic modes of discourse in narrative discontinuities: in catalogues, such as the Catalogue of Ships and Trojan heroes (*Il.* 2.484–760 and 2.816–877) and the Catalogue of the Myrmidon leaders (*Il.* 16.168–97), both of which make extensive usage of geography, genealogy, accounts set in the plupast, and counterfactual histories, all within a constellation of Panhellenic origins;[5] in the genealogies of lesser heroes (or *kleine Kämpfer*) embedded in battle sequences,[6] which Charles Rowan Beye has also labeled as catalogues, and which contain many of the same historiographic tendencies; and in the ekphrastic histories begun from material objects, such as armor and helmets, which Jonas Grethlein has recently analyzed on such terms.[7]

Narrative discursiveness also began as what seems like a natural reflex in Herodotus' *Histories*. It was likely a response to Ionian intellectual models, which led our inquirer to create a generic sponge that would lead many subsequent readers to label Herodotus' work as digressive, even if he himself only viewed this

---

[5] Beye 1964, 346: "In the Catalogue each item provides the same facts, that is, the names of towns, the names of leaders, and the number of ships. The order in which these facts are presented is variable, but every item contains each of these facts". See also Sammons 2010, 136, n. 3, who labels these various "elaborations" as being "sometimes genealogical ... sometimes pertaining to the leader's special qualities ... sometimes the leader's personal history". That these details are historical in nature can be corroborated by the fact that they were subsequently viewed as evidence by Thucydides for his claims about the comparative greatness of his own subject matter (1.10), by the second century BCE historian Apollodorus of Athens, and by the geographers Strabo and Pausanias.
[6] The term originates from the title of a 1954 dissertation by Strasburger, *Die kleinen Kämpfer der Ilias*.
[7] For a recent study, see Grethlein 2008. My list of categories does not include the speeches, such as those of Nestor (1.254–84), Antenor (3.205–24), Glaucus and Diomedes (6.119–236), and Phoenix (9.434–605), which offer extensive backstories to pre-Iliadic events. An excellent start has been made on this topic by Austin 1966, who treats such speeches that open the narrative to earlier time periods as narratological digressions.

as the expected outcome of an expansive "inquiry" (*historiē*).⁸ History, as we know, was the name Herodotus gave his "display of inquiry" (or the ἱστορίης ἀπόδεξις, praef.),⁹ which for him entailed extensive exploration based upon the presumption that great accomplishments were displayed by both Greeks and barbarians, that human fortunes were mutable, and that change was inevitably wrought upon all civilizations, great cities and small towns alike.¹⁰ As Katherine Clarke explains, "This provided the basis for the structuring of his work. Because history brings to the fore one region after another, Herodotus' readers move around accordingly".¹¹ If Herodotean history is unreservedly mobile, then the digression becomes a natural consequence of viewing the past on peripatetic terms.¹²

By contrast, Thucydides avows from the outset to compose a history focused specifically on the Peloponnesian War: "Thucydides the Athenian has written into historical narrative *the Peloponnesian War*"—Θουκυδίδης Ἀθηναῖος ξυνέγραψε τὸν πόλεμον τῶν Πελοποννησίων καὶ Ἀθηναίων, 1.1.1).¹³ Thus, even though Thucydides' narrative is geographically synoptic and presents a broad imperial setting, the history nonetheless tries to limit its scope of inquiry. Indeed, Thucydides' view that the Peloponnesian War is the singular event most worthy of a historical account (ἐλπίσας μέγαν τε ἔσεσθαι καὶ ἀξιολογώτατον τῶν προγεγενημένων, 1.1.1) has an impact on how both the historian *constructs* and the reader *construes* narratives that seem either temporally or geographically to move away from this topical focus. Unlike Herodotus, who from the outset allows

---

8 For a detailed study of Herodotus' Ionian epistemology, see Thomas 2000.
9 All translations of Greek and Latin texts are my own.
10 The verbs Herodotus employs in his preface emphasize this mobility and sense of historical becoming, and often include verbs of motion for his own historical inquiry. A recent detailed analysis is given by Wood 2016, 14–23. For an earlier exploration of the way in which Herodotus creates a path (*hodos*) of discourse, see Lang 1984, 4. Cf. Jacoby 1909, who considers the Herodotean *logoi* as acts of *periēgeisthai* emerging out of the historian's usage of the earlier generic model of the *Periodos Gēs*, 89.
11 Clarke 1999a, 15–16.
12 De Jong 2002, 255–58, gives an extensive summary of the debate surrounding the question of the Herodotean digression and its long history.
13 Marincola 2001, 65–66: "Thucydides defined his topic narrowly: he 'wrote up (ξυνέγραψε) the war of the Athenians and Peloponnesians, how they fought with each other'. He chose a single conflict that lasted many decades, but unlike Herodotus he did not use the conflict as a starting-point for wide-reaching investigations". For a different perspective, see Greenwood 2006, 11–12, 43, 47–48.

himself the freedom to wander wherever his "inquiry" (*historiē*) takes him, Thucydides straightway limits the scope of his history in response to his predecessor.[14]

We see this again quite clearly when Thucydides labels his extensive *Pentekontaetia* backstory (1.89–117) as a digression that he feels the need to justify in light of his overall historical endeavor:[15]

ἡγούμενοι δὲ αὐτονόμων τὸ πρῶτον τῶν ξυμμάχων καὶ ἀπὸ κοινῶν ξυνόδων βουλευόντων τοσάδε ἐπῆλθον πολέμῳ τε καὶ διαχειρίσει πραγμάτων μεταξὺ τοῦδε τοῦ πολέμου καὶ τοῦ Μηδικοῦ, ἃ ἐγένετο πρός τε τὸν βάρβαρον αὐτοῖς καὶ πρὸς τοὺς σφετέρους ξυμμάχους νεωτερίζοντας καὶ Πελοποννησίων τοὺς αἰεὶ προστυγχάνοντας ἐν ἑκάστῳ. ἔγραψα δὲ αὐτὰ καὶ τὴν ἐκβολὴν τοῦ λόγου ἐποιησάμην διὰ τόδε, ὅτι τοῖς πρὸ ἐμοῦ ἅπασιν ἐκλιπὲς τοῦτο ἦν τὸ χωρίον καὶ ἢ τὰ πρὸ τῶν Μηδικῶν Ἑλληνικὰ ξυνετίθεσαν ἢ αὐτὰ τὰ Μηδικά: τούτων δὲ ὅσπερ καὶ ἥψατο ἐν τῇ Ἀττικῇ ξυγγραφῇ Ἑλλάνικος, βραχέως τε καὶ τοῖς χρόνοις οὐκ ἀκριβῶς ἐπεμνήσθη. ἅμα δὲ καὶ τῆς ἀρχῆς ἀπόδειξιν ἔχει τῆς τῶν Ἀθηναίων ἐν οἵῳ τρόπῳ κατέστη.

As leaders of initially autonomous allies who made policy that originated from common assemblies, they accomplished so many things in both war and administration of affairs during the period of time which came between this war and the Persian War, which matters came to pass for them in their dealings with the barbarian, with their rebellious allies, and with whichever of the Peloponnesian states they happened to encounter on any given occasion. Yet I have recorded these matters and have made an excursus from my main narrative for the following reason, because this space of time was omitted by all those before me who narrated in writing either Hellenic affairs before the Persian Wars or the Persian Wars themselves. Granted, a certain one among them, Hellanicus, touched upon these affairs in his Attic History, yet his recollections were of few words and inaccurate with respect to chronology. Furthermore, it contains an elucidation of the Athenian Empire, specifically in what manner it came into being (Thuc. 1.97).

Thucydides' statements are extremely illuminating for how we ought to understand the development of the digression in subsequent historical writing, especially that of Polybius. First, Thucydides gives his narratological act of digression an explicit title. The use of a nominal term ἐκβολή for a narrative action or function, literally a "throwing out from" (ἐκ + βάλλω) the main storyline (τοῦ λόγου),

---

14 Pothou 2009, 119–20: "In Herodotus, as a result of his insertion of diverse narrative elements—especially his long ethnographic digressions—we cannot possibly consider his primary subject matter in terms of uniformity. In this respect, the narrative structure in the work of Thucydides is characterized by singularity and unity, whereas in the work of Herodotus it displays a certain plurality and multiplicity" (my translation).
15 The *Pentekontaetia* refers to the so-called "fifty-year" period that began with the end of the Persian War (479 BCE) and concluded with the outset of the Archidamian War (431 BCE).

has almost no prior instantiation, and represents the only such semantic intervention for the entirety of the work.[16] The sense of the digression as a movement outside of, rather than as an insertion, may not be an entirely novel way of conceiving of the digression (given at least one statement in Herodotus of returning to the main narrative from which one departed), yet it is different from the previous "insertion" label (πρός + τίθημι, or παρά + ἐν + τίθημι) which had been given to the digression twice by Thucydides' predecessor (προσθήκη, Hdt. 4.30.1 and παρενθήκη, Hdt. 7.171).[17] In fact, many terms employed by Polybius for narrative digressions consist of similar formulations: compound forms of βαίνω, such as παρέκβασις ("a going aside from"—3.2.7, 12.28.10, 38.6.1) and μεταβαίνω ("pass from one subject to another"—38.5.2, 38.6.1); of ῥίπτω, such as ἀπορρίπτω ("throw away, cast out"—8.11.3); and of λείπω, such as ἀπολείπω ("leave" or "depart from"—38.5.2, 38.6.6). Moreover, the shared spatial language for narrative disjunction is also evident in Thucydides' usage of the term (χωρίον) for a historical period that had been omitted by his predecessors as a rationale for his digression,[18] as well as Polybius' emphasis on the need for narrative "interweaving" (*symplokē*) amidst the widening world of Hellenistic Mediterranean imperialism.

A closer look at the passage confirms the extent to which Thucydides was keenly aware of his "constructive" narrative process when he made use of this digression. On the one hand, he sees this as the form which his writing has taken: whereas the phrase ἔγραψα δὲ αὐτὰ refers to the historian textualizing (ἔγραψα) his content (αὐτὰ)—much like the very first statement in his work (Θουκυδίδης Ἀθηναῖος ξυνέγραψε τὸν πόλεμον, 1.1.1)—the accompanying phrase καὶ τὴν ἐκβολὴν τοῦ λόγου ἐποιησάμην διὰ τόδε provides his reader with the narrative form this subject matter has taken (τὴν ἐκβολὴν τοῦ λόγου),[19] as well as a first

---

[16] Greenwood 2006, 62: "Although there are other digressions in Thucydides' text, this is the only passage where he uses an explicit term for the digression". Cf. Spada 2008, 59. Rhodes 2014, 246, noting its pivotal role, rightly labels this phrase as a "second introduction" to the *Pentekontaetia* narrative, just as Rood 1998, 229, refers to it as "the 'second preface'". Before Thucydides, this specific verbal noun had remained limited to literal acts of jettisoning (*i.e.* ballots into an urn at Aesch. *Eu.* 748), or to acts of political expulsion and banishment (Aesch. *Supp.* 421).
[17] For a discussion of these terms as justification for using the term digression or *Exkurs* for a Herodotean diegetic shift, see de Jong 2002, 255.
[18] Greenwood 2006, 47–48, noting this quality, offers an excellent analysis of this passage in light of Herodotean precedent.
[19] Jeffrey Rusten has brought to my attention the fact the Thucydides regularly uses *logos* to refer to an "argument" (cf. LSJ VI 3—"discussion, debate, deliberation", citing Thuc. 1.140). Such an overdetermined usage of the word in this context would make a great deal of sense, given that, from a narratological perspective, several crucial "debates" and "deliberations" leading up to the outbreak of the war quite literally surround the *Pentekontaetia* digression (the Corinthian

person verb of physical construction and literary *poēsis* (ἐποιησάμην) that seems to reflect the topics found within the *Pentekontaetia* narrative which our historian is composing—*building* the long walls, *constructing* ships for a navy, *assembling* the foundations of an empire.[20] In many respects, these prefigure the central concern that drives Polybian historiography—the conquest of the Mediterranean and its various powers by Rome.[21]

This brings us to a second novelty in the Thucydidean digression: the need for an explanation. Whereas Herodotus envisions his *Histories* as mirroring his expansive "inquiry" (*historiē*) in both narrative form and the motivations for such discursiveness (often little more than a *thauma megiston*)[22]—and explicitly declares within his Scythian ethnography, "For, as you know, my narrative has been seeking out supplements from the start" (προσθήκας γὰρ δή μοι ὁ λόγος ἐξ ἀρχῆς ἐδίζητο, 4.30.1)—Thucydides, by contrast, and perhaps as the result of his

---

and Athenian debate followed by the speech of Archidamus at 1.67–87 immediately precede it; the speech of the Corinthians to their allies at 1.119–25 immediately follows it). In many respects, this separation of the digression (*ekbolē*), which is aimed at rooting out the true causes (*prophaseis*) of the war, from the various allegations and pretexts put forward in these debates (*logoi*) found within the main narrative (*logos*), might be read as a digressive reformulation of the famous *logos/ergon* dichotomy in Thucydides, discussed extensively by Parry 1981 and Price 2001. Nonetheless, we ought to note a similar usage of the expression by Arrian to mark the conclusion of the ethnographic section of his *Indica* (ταῦτα δὲ ἐκβολή μοι ἔστω τοῦ λόγου, 17.7), as well as LSJ V ("continuous statement, narrative"), which lists Thuc. 1.97 as an example under this subheading.

20 See Rood 1998, 230–31, who explains the belated justification for the excursus and Athenian hegemony as emerging only after the necessary preconditions have been met, in particular the construction of the long walls as a guarantee against Spartan political interference. See also Stadter 1993, 45: "Again, as at 93.2, details of the construction of the walls reinforce the account. In both cases the circumstantial account of construction serves as a rhetorical *auxesis* of the achievement".

21 For this as Polybius' primary motivation, see Plb. 1.1–1.6, noting in particular the emphasis on explaining Rome's universal dominion at 1.1.5 ("how nearly the entirety of the inhabited world fell under the sole imperial rule of the Romans"—πῶς ... σχεδὸν ἅπαντα τὰ κατὰ τὴν οἰκουμένην ... ὑπὸ μίαν ἀρχὴν ἔπεσε τὴν Ῥωμαίων, 1.2.7, and 1.3.10 ("to their full realization of empire and power over the whole world"—πρὸς τὴν συντέλειαν ... τῆς τῶν ὅλων ἀρχῆς καὶ δυναστείας).

22 The central role of *thauma* (Ion. *thōma*) in shaping Herodotean metanarrative is explained in depth by Munson 2001.

oblique criticisms of Herodotus and his self-imposed historiographical limitations, shows a strong need to defend his narrative turn.[23] He does so by emphasizing how important the *Pentekontaetia* was to the creation of the Athenian empire and her resultant conflict with the Peloponnesian League (ἅμα δὲ καὶ τῆς ἀρχῆς ἀπόδειξιν ἔχει τῆς τῶν Ἀθηναίων ἐν οἵῳ τρόπῳ κατέστη).[24] For elsewhere in his digression, he emphasizes Themistocles' role in securing power for Athens through the construction of her walls, both the reconstruction of the city walls after the Persian War (1.89–93.2) and the erecting of the long walls (1.93.3–93.8; 1.107.1), as well as the expansion of her navy which he links explicitly to her acquisition of empire (1.93.3–4; 1.99.3)[25]—all linked to the Spartan fear of the burgeoning Athenian Empire as the true cause of the Peloponnesian War (1.88).[26] Thus, what prompts a discursion from the main narrative is essentially a much fuller contextualization (*logos*) for the war's outbreak: the "beginning" (*archē*) of an "empire" (*archē*)— or, simply put, a double *archéologie*.[27]

---

23 Marincola 2001, 68: "Unlike Herodotus, Thucydides was chary of digressions, and he tended to avoid material that did not fall under the category of 'the things done in the war' (τὰ ἔργα τῶν πραχθέντων ἐν τῷ πολέμῳ, 1.22.2); for that very reason, the few places where he does allow himself to move from his stated subject matter are all the more noticeable. Earlier scholarship, in accord with its view of Thucydides as a historian with a passion for accuracy, had seen these incidents mainly as occasions for the author's correction of error on the part of others. More recently, however, scholars have suggested that these digressions are closely related to the thematic concerns of the history".
24 See also Walker 1957, 33, Stadter 1993, 38–52, Spada 2008, 70, and Pothou 2009, 120, 126–28.
25 Cf. Westlake 1955, 59–60, Rood 1998, 232, and Stadter 1993, 43–47, esp. 45.
26 Rood 1998, 226, examining Thuc. 1.88: "The passages that frame the *Pentekontaetia* suggest that it is designed as an explanation of Sparta's decision to make war, and of the perceptions that explain that decision". Similarly, Hornblower 1991, 148, writes on the reasoning for Thucydides' inclusion of 1.97 that "his motive is to amplify his statement about Athenian power at 88. This is a first-order reason for treating the period". The first to put forth such an explanation for the excursus through a connection with ἡ ἀληθεστάτη πρόφασις (1.23.6) were Westlake 1955, 66 and Walker 1957, 31. Cf. Stadter 1993, 42 and Spada 2008, 67–68.
27 Interestingly, Polybius is also quite keen to link narratology with imperial motivation. Consider, for example, the use of the similar term *epibolē* ("design") by Polybius, to refer to both the "designs" on acquiring empire (πρὸς τὴν τῶν ὅλων ἐπιβολήν, 1.3.6) and the literary "enterprise" of writing history (πρὸς τὴν ἐπιβολὴν τῆς ἱστορίας, 1.4.2). See also Hartog 2010, 38, who declares that "Polybius is the new Thucydides, or a post-Aristotelian Thucydides".

2 From Tangent to Tradition: Polybius and the Historiographical Convention of Digression

Thucydides' history as an act of historiographical reception and reconception—namely as a response to and a rejection of the expansive, more universalizing, and inherently digressive *Histories* of Herodotus—presents us with our first reformulation in the evolution of the historical digression. Indeed, the decision to limit its usage to etiologically motivated flashbacks necessitated by conflicts, either in the narrative proper or in the historiographical tradition, follows Thucydides' redefinition of history as the narrative of one substantial event in the form of the war monograph.[28] Yet, by the time Thucydides finished what he could of his *History of the Peloponnesian War* at the outset of the fourth century BCE, the digression was still not an established tradition in historical writing.[29] It was not until Polybius' employment of the digression several centuries later, and his recognition that it constituted a fundamental feature of historiography in response to his more immediate predecessors Ephorus of Cyme, Theopompus of Chios, and Timaeus of Tauromenium, that it would come to see far greater usage in a range of Roman historical subgenres.

Although Polybius had a range of historical precedents on which to model his *Histories*,[30] his avowed aim was to track Rome's steady imperial expansion

---

[28] Here, I limit my use of the label digression in Thucydides to four such excursions: the *Pentekontaetia* narrative (Thuc. 1.89–117), the biographical backstories of Pausanias and Themistocles (1.126–138), the Sicilian ethnography (6.2–5), and the digression on the tyrant slayers Harmodius and Aristogeiton (6.54–59). For a more inclusive classification of the Thucydidean digression, see Pothou 2009.

[29] In fact, a quick glance at Xenophon's two main historical works, the *Hellenica* (generally considered a continuation of Thucydides' narrative) and the *Anabasis*, feature almost none of the digressions seen in his two canonical predecessors. Nonetheless, for an analysis of digression in Xenophon, see Spada 2008, 85–111, 173–83, and Hau 2016, 241.

[30] Not only Herodotus and Thucydides, but also, based upon his own statements, the memoirs of Aratus of Sicyon, Phylarchus, Fabius Pictor, Philinus of Agrigentum, Ephorus of Cyme, Theopompus of Chios, Timaeus of Tauromenium, and likely a range of other historians and geographers. For a useful summary of these and other citations, see Walbank 1957, 2–16, and Walbank 1972, 32–46. Although Polybius never mentions Herodotus as a historical source, recent work by McGing has shown that Herodotus likely served as a model for some of his accounts (see McGing 2010, 52–58 and McGing 2012). Similarly, Thucydides is barely mentioned by name, yet arguments in favor of Thucydides' influence on Polybius abound: Ziegler 1952, 1522–24, Walbank 1972, 40–43, McGing 2010, 58–61, Hartog 2010, Rood 2012, and Longley 2012. It is worth emphasizing the strong tendency by ancient historians to cite sources only for knowledge of particular events, and to omit citations of rhetorical, stylistic, and topical influence. Excellent case studies

over several centuries, and so he opted for a more universal history which included numerous geographical settings, a temporal predilection for the *longue durée*, and plenty of digressions and backstories set in the plupast.[31] Not surprisingly, it was Polybius who first identified the digression as a necessary element in the historiographical tradition; who saw reason to define what constituted an appropriate usage of the narratological device; and who was the first writer to suggest that he perfected this historical practice that had previously been used irregularly.[32] Moreover, as *Quellenforschung* ("source criticism") and more recent developments of this comparative process have made clear, Polybius' influence on later Roman historians such as Livy was immense. Thus, his position in the development of the historiographical digression is absolutely decisive.

More than any other ancient historian, it was Polybius who made the digression a defining feature of historiography.[33] The historian himself is noted for countless, often extensive narratological excursions: his extensive Celtic backstory (2.14–35), his lengthy criticisms of Timaeus of Tauromenium (alongside praise for Aristotle, Ephorus of Cyme, and even Theopompus of Chios on occasion), which occupy almost the entirety of the fragments from a surviving book (12.3–15, 12.23–28), the similar comments on Callisthenes of Olynthus (12.17–22), his digression on the decline of Boeotia (20.4–7), and his tripartite discursion on constitutions of government (6.1–18), the Roman army (6.19–42), and further constitutional and civic ideals (6.43–57)—essentially making Book 6 in its entirety a collection of digressions.[34]

Just as important, Polybius identifies an emerging historical tradition at a pivotal moment in the historiographic corpus. The Hellenistic historians, including Polybius at the tail end, serve as a key nexus point for the canonical histories

---

in historiographical intertextuality without overt citation are given by O'Gorman 2009, Martin and Woodman 1989, Clauss 1997, and Moles 1998.

31 By "plupast", I am adopting a term developed by Grethlein and Krebs 2012, which is used to refer to the anterior, pluperfect, or more remote past when it is presented within a historical narrative that is, by default, always-already set in the past.

32 Plb. 38.6.3, discussed at length below.

33 For an overview of the Polybian digression with some ideas for classification, see Walbank 1972, 46–48.

34 Polybius, in a second preface early in Book 3, labels a number of these upcoming discussions as digressions. These include the major excursus in Book 6 on the Roman constitution—"Pausing my narrative at the point of these affairs (στήσαντες δ' ἐπὶ τούτων τὴν διήγησιν) I shall introduce an account (συστησόμεθα λόγον) concerning the constitution of the Romans (ὑπὲρ τῆς Ῥωμαίων πολιτείας)", 3.2.6—as well as his laying out (δηλώσομεν) the narrative about the fall of the dominion of Hieron of Syracuse (τὴν κατάλυσιν τῆς Ἱέρωνος τοῦ Συρακοσίου δυναστείας) "in the course of a digression (κατὰ παρέκβασιν)", 3.2.7.

of Greece and Rome. Aside from Polybius and Livy, Felix Jacoby's landmark compilation, *Die Fragmente der griechischen Historiker* (*FGrHist*), has made amply clear the high frequency with which the now fragmentary Hellenistic historians recur in Roman imperial ethnographers, geographers, historians, and encyclopedists such as Pomponius Mela, Pliny the Elder, Strabo, and Arrian—including such historians as Megasthenes (*BNJ* 715), Nearchus (*BNJ* 133), Onesicritus (*BNJ* 134), Berossus of Babylon (*BNJ* 680), and Daimachus (*BNJ* 716), to name only a few.[35] It is therefore of great significance that a Hellenistic historian is explicating digression in such detail given the frequent usage of historical texts from this period as source material for Roman imperial writings.

Consider Polybius' praise of Ephorus' usage of such asides to show the disparity with Timaeus in his extremely long criticism of the latter in his extended discursion:

> ὁ γὰρ Ἔφορος παρ' ὅλην τὴν πραγματείαν θαυμάσιος ὢν καὶ κατὰ τὴν φράσιν καὶ κατὰ τὸν χειρισμὸν καὶ κατὰ τὴν ἐπίνοιαν τῶν λημμάτων, δεινότατός ἐστιν ἐν ταῖς παρεκβάσεσι καὶ ταῖς ἀφ' αὑτοῦ γνωμολογίαις, καὶ συλλήβδην ὅταν που τὸν ἐπιμετροῦντα λόγον διατίθηται.
>
> For Ephorus, although he is admirable across the entirety of his work with respect to his diction, his literary treatment, and the inventiveness of his arguments, is most skillful in his digressions and in the collections of his maxims, and whenever, in short, he is inclined to supplement his primary narrative in some way (Plb. 12.28.10, *BNJ* 70 T 23).

What we see emerging in Polybius' praise of Ephorus is an awareness of the digression as a feature of historiography that merits discussion, just as much as literary style, treatment of subject matter, inventiveness, and personal opinion.[36] The fact that Polybius goes out of his way to stress, among other authorial and rhetorical qualities, the superlative skillfulness (δεινότατος) of the universal historian when it comes to his excursions (ἐν ταῖς παρεκβάσεσι), that is, in the supplementation of his primary narrative (τὸν ἐπιμετροῦντα λόγον), certainly marks

---

[35] Much of Jacoby's work has been translated in the development of the online *Brill's New Jacoby* (*BNJ*) edited by Ian Worthington, whose numbering I follow in the citations provided above.

[36] In terms of literary poetics, we hear mention of φράσις by the character Euripides in Aristophanes' *Frogs* (Ar. *Ran.* 1122), as well as in Longinus' *On the Sublime* (*Subl.* 8.1, 30.1); of χειρισμός in Philodemus' *On Rhetoric* (in Sudhaus 1892, Vol. 1, 371); and of ἐπίνοια, notably, in a passage in Longinus that deals with φράσις as its companion, noting that the two are "closely interlinked with one another" ('Ἐπειδὴ μέντοι ἡ τοῦ λόγου νόησις ἥ τε φράσις τὰ πλείω δι' ἑκατέρου διέπτυκται, *Subl.* 30.1).

our earliest commentary on, and therefore recognition of, the digression as a specific feature of historiography.³⁷

Even more striking, Polybius' praise of Ephorus' digressions falls in a lengthy discussion of Timaeus' failures as historian, in particular his overreliance on hearsay and his lack of experiential autopsy, in contrast to Ephorus, whom the former is said by Polybius to have criticized (12.27.4–11).³⁸

> ὧν Τίμαιος οὐδὲ τὴν ἐλαχίστην πρόνοιαν θέμενος, ἀλλὰ καταβιώσας ἐν ἑνὶ τόπῳ ξενιτεύων, καὶ σχεδὸν ὡς εἰ κατὰ πρόθεσιν ἀπειπάμενος καὶ τὴν ἐνεργητικὴν τὴν περὶ τὰς πολεμικὰς καὶ πολιτικὰς πράξεις καὶ τὴν ἐκ τῆς πλάνης καὶ θέας αὐτοπάθειαν, οὐκ οἶδ᾽ ὅπως ἐκφέρεται δόξαν ὡς ἕλκων τὴν τοῦ συγγραφέως προστασίαν.

> Of which Timaeus instilled not the least bit of concern, but spent his life in one place even though he was in exile. And so, generally speaking, even if he purposely renounced active experience in military and political affairs, as well as in wandering and sightseeing, I know not how he has eked out and amassed for himself the reputation of an expert in historiography (Plb. 12.28.6–7).

Such praise of Herodotean ideals in Ephorus (notably the wandering and sightseeing—τὴν ἐκ τῆς πλάνης καὶ θέας αὐτοπάθειαν) demonstrates a commitment to universal history, with all of its discursive implications, in a greatly expanding Roman imperial world. However, in making such a statement, Polybius also reminds readers of the Thucydidean historian—the military and political man of action (τὴν ἐνεργητικὴν τὴν περὶ τὰς πολεμικὰς καὶ πολιτικὰς πράξεις)—a model, he claims, that was also taken up by Theopompus. The idea is further complicated by Polybius' criticism of the paradox of Timaeus spending his life in one location even though he was forced into exile (ἀλλὰ καταβιώσας ἐν ἑνὶ τόπῳ ξενιτεύων).³⁹ After all, we know firsthand that Thucydides was ostracized for his military failures at Amphipolis (Thuc. 5.26.5), and, quite telling in this respect, the word he chooses for his *Pentekontaetia* "digression", *ekbolē*, originally had a

---

37 Elsewhere Polybius uses the same expression in a digression about the Sicilian tyrants Hieronymus, Hieron, and Gelon, in order to emphasize that previous historians who treated the subject devoted too much of their narrative to Hieronymus, and that any writer could have done a better narratological job (εὐλογώτερον) if he had supplemented that narrative with more about Hieron and Gelon (τὸν ἐπιμετροῦντα λόγον τῆς διηγήσεως εἰς Ἱέρωνα καὶ Γέλωνα διάθοιτο, 7.7.7).

38 For Polybius' polemical mischaracterization of Timaeus as a historian, see Baron 2013, 58–88.

39 For a summary of the historical debates regarding the dating of Timaeus departure and exile at Athens following the rise of Agathocles to power in his native city of Tauromenium, see Baron 2013, 18–22.

political denotation of exile and banishment.⁴⁰ Similarly, Polybius himself was forced to leave his own native city of Megalopolis, and it was only as a result of this that he saw much of Mediterranean world as an eyewitness to Roman geopolitics. In this respect, Timaeus' historical failures become linked to the very idea of history/*historiē* as travel-based inquiry driven by political exigency,[41] in which the digression serves as an expression of that mobile inquest.

The sea change that resulted from Philip of Macedon's conquest of the Aegean and Alexander's campaigns as far east as India lent themselves nicely to a revisiting of the digressive model of historiography. Narratives needed to travel with their far-roaming subjects, as Polybius' extensive comments in a lengthy digression make clear:[42]

> οὐ γὰρ ἀγνοῶ διότι τινὲς ἐπιλήψονται τῆς πραγματείας, φάσκοντες ἀτελῆ καὶ διερριμμένην ἡμᾶς πεποιῆσθαι τὴν ἐξήγησιν τῶν πραγμάτων, <εἴγ'> ἐπιβαλλόμενοι λόγου χάριν διεξιέναι τὴν Καρχηδόνος πολιορκίαν, κἄπειτα μεταξὺ ταύτην ἀπολιπόντες καὶ μεσολαβήσαντες σφᾶς αὐτοὺς μεταβαίνομεν ἐπὶ τὰς Ἑλληνικὰς κἀντεῦθεν ἐπὶ τὰς Μακεδονικὰς ἢ Συριακὰς ἤ τινας ἑτέρας πράξεις· ζητεῖν δὲ τοὺς φιλομαθοῦντας τὸ συνεχὲς καὶ τὸ τέλος ἱμείρειν ἀκοῦσαι τῆς προθέσεως· καὶ γὰρ τὴν ψυχαγωγίαν καὶ τὴν ὠφέλειαν οὕτω μᾶλλον συνεκτρέχειν τοῖς προσέχουσιν. ἐμοὶ δ' οὐχ οὕτως δοκεῖ, τὸ δ' ἐναντίον. μάρτυρα δὲ τούτων ἐπικαλεσαίμην ἂν αὐτὴν τὴν φύσιν, ἥτις κατ' οὐδ' ὁποίαν τῶν αἰσθήσεων εὐδοκεῖ τοῖς αὐτοῖς ἐπιμένειν κατὰ τὸ συνεχές, ἀλλ' ἀεὶ μεταβολῆς ἐστιν οἰκεία, τοῖς δ' αὐτοῖς ἐγκυρεῖν ἐκ διαστήματος βούλεται καὶ διαφορᾶς. εἴη δ' ἂν τὸ λεγόμενον ἐναργὲς πρῶτον μὲν ἐκ τῆς ἀκοῆς, ἥτις οὔτε κατὰ τὰς μελῳδίας οὔτε κατὰ τὰς λεκτικὰς ὑποκρίσεις εὐδοκεῖ συνεχῶς ταῖς αὐταῖς ἐπιμένειν στάσεσιν, ὁ δὲ μεταβολικὸς τρόπος καὶ καθόλου πᾶν τὸ διερριμμένον καὶ μεγίστας ἔχον ἀλλαγὰς καὶ πυκνοτάτας αὐτήν κινεῖ. παραπλησίως καὶ τὴν γεῦσιν εὕροι τις ἂν οὐδὲ τοῖς πολυτελεστάτοις βρώμασιν ἐπιμένειν δυναμένην, ἀλλὰ σικχαίνουσαν καὶ χαίρουσαν ταῖς μεταβολαῖς καὶ προσηνεστέρως ἀποδεχομένην πολλάκις καὶ τὰ λιτὰ τῶν ἐδεσμάτων ἢ τὰ πολυτελῆ διὰ τὸν ξενισμόν. τὸ δ' αὐτὸ καὶ περὶ τὴν ὅρασιν ἴδοι τις ἂν γινόμενον· ἥκιστα γὰρ δύναται πρὸς ἓν μένειν ἀτενίζουσα, κινεῖ δ' αὐτὴν ἡ ποικιλία καὶ μεταβολὴ τῶν ὁρωμένων. μάλιστα δὲ περὶ τὴν ψυχὴν τοῦτό τις ἂν ἴδοι συμβαῖνον· αἱ γὰρ μεταλήψεις τῶν ἀτενισμῶν καὶ τῶν ἐπιστάσεων οἷον ἀναπαύσεις εἰσὶ τοῖς φιλοπόνοις τῶν ἀνδρῶν.

---

40 Aesch. *Supp.* 421. Cf. Aesch. *Eu.* 748 for another political usage.
41 Here, we might even extend the idea to Herodotus' exemplar Solon, who, although claiming to leave Athens for sightseeing reasons (κατὰ θεωρίης πρόφασιν ἐκπλώσας, Hdt. 1.29.1), in fact does so that he might not be poltically compelled to repeal the laws he had made (ἵνα δὴ μή τινα τῶν νόμων ἀναγκασθῇ λῦσαι τῶν ἔθετο, 1.29.1). Indeed, Redfield 1985, 102, views Solon "as a kind of alter ego of the narrator himself".
42 For the role of geography in shaping this universalizing paradigm in Polybius, see Clarke 1999a, 114–28. For its role in earlier fourth century historiography, especially Theopompus, see Vattuone 2014, 15.

διὸ καὶ τῶν ἀρχαίων συγγραφέων οἱ λογιώτατοι δοκοῦσί μοι προσαναπεπαῦσθαι τῷ τρόπῳ τούτῳ, τινὲς μὲν μυθικαῖς καὶ διηγηματικαῖς κεχρημένοι παρεκβάσεσι, τινὲς δὲ καὶ πραγματικαῖς, ὥστε μὴ μόνον ἐν αὐτοῖς τοῖς κατὰ τὴν Ἑλλάδα τόποις ποιεῖσθαι τὰς μεταβάσεις, ἀλλὰ καὶ τῶν ἐκτὸς περιλαμβάνειν. λέγω δ᾽ οἷον ἐπειδὰν τὰ κατὰ τὴν Θετταλίαν ἐξηγούμενοι καὶ τὰς Ἀλεξάνδρου τοῦ Φεραίου πράξεις μεταξὺ τὰς κατὰ Πελοπόννησον Λακεδαιμονίων ἐπιβολὰς διηγῶνται, καὶ πάλιν τὰς παρὰ Θηβαίων, ἔτι δὲ τὰς κατὰ Μακεδονίαν ἢ τὴν Ἰλλυρίδα, κἄπειτα διατρίψαντες λέγωσι τὴν Ἰφικράτους εἰς Αἴγυπτον στρατείαν καὶ τὰ Κλεάρχῳ πραχθέντα παρανομήματα κατὰ τὸν Πόντον. ἐξ ὧν κεχρημένους μὲν ἅπαντας εὕροι τις ἂν τῷ τοιούτῳ χειρισμῷ, κεχρημένους γε μὴν ἀτάκτως, ἡμᾶς δὲ τεταγμένως. ἐκεῖνοι μὲν γὰρ μνησθέντες πῶς Βάρδυλλις ὁ τῶν Ἰλλυριῶν βασιλεὺς καὶ Κερσοβλέπτης ὁ τῶν Θρακῶν κατεκτήσαντο τὰς δυναστείας, οὐκέτι προστιθέασι τὸ συνεχές, οὐδ᾽ ἀνατρέχουσιν ἐπὶ τἀκόλουθον ἐκ διαστήματος, ἀλλὰ καθάπερ ἐν ποιήματι χρησάμενοι πάλιν ἐπανάγουσιν ἐπὶ τὰς ἐξ ἀρχῆς ὑποθέσεις. ἡμεῖς δὲ πάντας διῃρημένοι τοὺς ἐπιφανεστάτους τόπους τῆς οἰκουμένης καὶ τὰς ἐν τούτοις πράξεις καὶ μίαν καὶ τὴν αὐτὴν ἔφοδον ἀεὶ ποιούμενοι κατὰ τὴν τάξιν τῆς διαλήψεως, ἔτι δὲ καθ᾽ ἕκαστον ἔτος ὡρισμένως ἐξηγούμενοι τὰς καταλλήλους πράξεις ἐνεστηκυίας, ἀπολείπομεν πρόδηλον τοῖς φιλομαθοῦσι τὴν ἐπαναγωγὴν ἐπὶ τὸν συνεχῆ λόγον καὶ τὰς μεσολαβηθείσας ἀεὶ τῶν πράξεων, ὥστε μηδὲν ἀτελὲς μηδ᾽ ἐλλιπὲς γίνεσθαι τοῖς φιληκόοις τῶν προειρημένων. καὶ περὶ μὲν τούτων ἐπὶ τοσοῦτον.

I am not ignorant of the fact that some people will criticize this treatise, endlessly prattling that I have made an incomplete and disconnected narrative of events, and, although attempting for the sake of my narrative to go through in detail the siege of Carthage, thereupon I leave off from that in the midst of it, and, interrupting those very subjects, I pass over to Hellenic affairs and then to Macedonian affairs, Syrian affairs, and those of other countries. I also know that fellow scholars seek continuity and desire to hear the end of my thesis; for they desire that gratification and benefit fall readily to the lot of those who turn their attention to it. I do not think it so, but rather believe the opposite to be true. Moreover, I would call human nature as my witness to these matters, who, with respect to any of the senses, is not content to remain continuously in the same matters, but is always fond of change, and wishes to meet with the same things following an interval of time or a dislocation.

That which I speak of may first be made clear from the act of hearing, which sort of thing neither with respect to melody nor with respect to spoken tone is pleased to remain in the same positions, but rather is moved by a mutable character and, on the whole, by everything that is scattered all about and possesses the greatest and most frequent changes. One can find nearly the same thing with the sense of taste which is also incapable of sticking to the most costly of foods, but rather loathes them and delights in changes and oftentimes receives inexpensive foods more smoothly than expensive ones owing to their novelty. One can see the same thing again with vision: it is least able to remain gazing intently upon one object, whereas variety and change in what is seen stimulates it. Yet one can discern this attribute most of all with respect to the mind. For changes in the objects of one's attention and concern form a kind of reprieve for workaholics.

For which reason I suspect that the most erudite and eloquent of the ancient historians made a habit of taking a rest in advance in a manner such as this, some establishing the tradition of employing mythical and narratival digressions, while others doing so with political discursions, with the result that not only do they create shifts in their topographical settings within the Greek world, but also include events from abroad. For example, midway while recounting in detail the affairs in Thessaly and the deeds of Alexander of Pherae, they set out to recount the enterprises of the Lacedaemonians in the Peloponnese, and then those of the Thebans, and next those in Macedonia or Illyria, and after going on at length they recount the expedition of Iphicrates to Egypt and the transgressions committed by Clearchus in Pontus. From which one can deduce that all historians have employed this very literary device, but they have employed it in an irregular manner, whereas I have fixed it into a regular usage.

For those to whom I refer, after recalling how Bardyllis, the king of the Illyrians, and Cersobleptes, the king of the Thracians, acquired their dominions, no longer continue what ensues, nor do they revert to what follows after an interval, but rather, after making use of them as one would a patch,[43] lead their readers back to their initial starting point. Yet I, keeping distinct all the most notable places throughout the inhabited world and the events which took place therein, and always making one and the same approach with respect to the arrangement of my division, and moreover regularly expounding according to each year the present affairs in succession, I leave manifest in advance for fellow scholars the point of return to the continuous narrative and the interruptions of affairs at any given moment, such that nothing incomplete nor wanting results for those who were attentive to my remarks made in advance. So much, then, concerning these matters (Plb. 38.5–6).

A number of important notions stand out. First, the historian imagines that he will receive criticism for the discontinuity in his narration of events, offering as an example his abrupt shift from Punic to Illyrian narratives (μεταξὺ ταύτην ἀπολιπόντες καὶ μεσολαβήσαντες σφᾶς αὐτοὺς μεταβαίνομεν). Such a shift in geographic locale becomes a characteristic of numerous Roman annalistic historians, including Livy and Tacitus, in their moving between *res internae* (affairs at Rome) and *res externae* (foreign affairs).[44] In fact, we should not discount the significant impact Polybius had on the subsequent writing of annalistic history at Rome, especially in light of the significant parallels that have been drawn between Polybius and Livy, which David Levene has recently demonstrated to be highly nuanced in their Livian iterations.[45] Moreover, this narratological movement may function as a literary reflection of the sea change in the Hellenistic world: numerous, large empires forcing concessions from smaller, no longer autonomous city-states whose local histories could no longer stand on their own, with Rome emerging as the great unifier among them.

---

43 The translation of "patch" for ποίημα is that of Paton 1927.
44 In Tacitus these *res externae* (which, owing to circumstances in the governing of empire under the principate, have become rare indeed) take on the characteristics of digressions, in many instances offering dialogic and carnivalesque perspectives on the state of affairs in the Roman Empire. Moreover, Ginsburg 1981 has shown that Tacitus deliberately alters the annalistic framework in such a way as to suit his own thematic and political purposes.
45 Nissen 1863, Witte 1910, Klotz 1940–41, Tränkle 1977, and Levene 2010, 82–163.

In Polybius' time, however, the inclusion of separate narratives into one's primary historical sequence was still a matter of debate, as is evinced in the fact that Polybius finds even greater need than Thucydides to defend his digressive method. He begins, "I am not ignorant of the fact that some people will criticize this treatise (τινὲς ἐπιλήψονται τῆς πραγματείας), endlessly prattling that we have made an incomplete and disconnected narrative of events," before going on to explain the various geographic domains in his narrative (Καρχηδόνος ... ἐπὶ τὰς Ἑλληνικὰς ... ἐπὶ τὰς Μακεδονικὰς ἢ Συριακὰς ἤ τινας ἑτέρας πράξεις) and the regular narratological movement between them (κἄπειτα μεταξὺ ταύτην ἀπολιπόντες καὶ μεσολαβήσαντες σφᾶς αὐτοὺς μεταβαίνομεν ἐπὶ ... κἀντεῦθεν ἐπὶ).

In many ways, this seems to be not only an Ephoran but also a Theopompan thing to avow.[46] After all, Polybius at times sounds as though he is reframing his earlier rebuke of this overly digressive historian.

> Καὶ μὴν οὐδὲ περὶ τὰς ὁλοσχερεῖς διαλήψεις οὐδεὶς ἂν εὐδοκήσειε τῷ προειρημένῳ συγγραφεῖ· ὅς γ' ἐπιβαλόμενος γράφειν τὰς Ἑλληνικὰς πράξεις ἀφ' ὧν Θουκυδίδης ἀπέλιπε, καὶ συνεγγίσας τοῖς Λευκτρικοῖς καιροῖς καὶ τοῖς ἐπιφανεστάτοις τῶν Ἑλληνικῶν ἔργων, τὴν μὲν Ἑλλάδα μεταξὺ καὶ τὰς ταύτης ἐπιβολὰς ἀπέρριψε, μεταλαβὼν δὲ τὴν ὑπόθεσιν τὰς Φιλίππου πράξεις προὔθετο γράφειν. καίτοι γε πολλῷ σεμνότερον ἦν καὶ δικαιότερον ἐν τῇ περὶ τῆς Ἑλλάδος ὑποθέσει τὰ πεπραγμένα Φιλίππῳ συμπεριλαβεῖν ἤπερ ἐν τῇ Φιλίππου τὰ τῆς Ἑλλάδος. οὐδὲ γὰρ προκαταληφθεὶς ὑπὸ βασιλικῆς δυναστείας, καὶ τυχὼν ἐξουσίας, οὐδεὶς ἂν ἐπέσχε σὺν καιρῷ ποιήσασθαι μετάβασιν ἐπὶ τὸ τῆς Ἑλλάδος ὄνομα καὶ πρόσωπον· ἀπὸ δὲ ταύτης ἀρξάμενος καὶ προβὰς ἐπὶ ποσὸν οὐδ' ὅλως οὐδεὶς ἂν ἠλλάξατο μονάρχου πρόσχημα καὶ βίον, ἀκεραίῳ χρώμενος γνώμῃ.

To be sure, no one could admire the aforementioned writer when it comes to his widespread digressions. He, after setting out to write a history of Greek affairs from those events at which Thucydides left off, and as he neared the period which included the Battle of Leuctra and the most notable of Greek accomplishments, threw aside Greece and his narrative designs for it *in mediis rebus*, and altering his proposed subject matter, he set out to write about the exploits of Philip. However, it would have been far more respectable and proper to include the accomplishments of Philip within his proposed narrative about Greece than to situate those of Greece within the life of Philip. For nobody, not even one so captivated

---

[46] For Ephorus as a "universal historian", see Plb. 5.33.2 ("Ephorus, the first and only writer who succeeded in his attempt to write a universal history"—Ἔφορον τὸν πρῶτον καὶ μόνον ἐπιβεβλημένον τὰ καθόλου γράφειν), Diod. Sic. 5.1.4 ("Ephorus, who wrote up a universal history"—Ἔφορος δὲ τὰς κοινὰς πράξεις ἀναγράφων), and Barber 1993, 17–48. A different perspective on Ephorus' universal history and Polybius' assessment is given by Tully 2014. For Theopompus as a historian who combined in his history of one individual, Philip II, "nearly every variety of historical research that was then in existence", including "extensive use of digressions", see Flower 1994, 148, and also 153–60.

by kingly power, if he had obtained the authority to do so, would have in time held back from changing his work's name and title to that Greece; and no one, generally speaking, if he had an unprejudiced mind, having begun from Greek history and having proceeded so far in his narrative would have replaced it with the pomp and biography of a monarch (Plb. 8.11.3–5, *BNJ* 115 T 19).

We ought to note that Polybius, in this earlier discursion, uses the same phraseology and language that appears once more in his lengthy digression in Book 38. For example, compare the usage of the phrase μεταξὺ καὶ τὰς ταύτης ἐπιβολὰς ἀπέρριψε (8.11.3) with μεταξὺ ταύτην ἀπολιπόντες (38.5.2), and μεταξὺ τὰς ... ἐπιβολὰς διηγῶνται (38.6.2); as well as μεταλαβὼν δὲ τὴν ὑπόθεσιν (8.11.3) and ποιήσασθαι μετάβασιν (8.11.5) with καὶ μεσολαβήσαντες σφᾶς αὐτοὺς μεταβαίνομεν (38.5.2). Given the parallels between this earlier criticism, where Polybius censures Theopompus (for a similar narratological act of shifting narrative subjects), and the Book 38 digression, where he defends his own changing narratives, Polybius might in the latter instantiation be making an essential backpedal—highlighting a mobile narrative process that was, at least to some degree, forced to evolve over so lengthy and geographically expansive a historiographical endeavor, and likely motivated by contemporary historical events.[47]

Indeed, Polybius himself tells us that he altered his initial plan to conclude his work with Rome's conquest of Macedonia in 168 BCE by Aemilius Paullus, noting at the outset of his third book that he was "writing another beginning" (προήχθην οἷον ἀρχὴν ποιησάμενος ἄλλην γράφειν, 3.4.13). Even so, this modification need not alter Polybius' wide-ranging geographic history with Rome at its center, as he himself basically confirms (3.4.5–6, 12–13). He did not, after all, end up (as per his rebuke of Theopompus' *Philippica*) dropping his universal Mediterranean subject matter altogether and writing an "*Aemilia-Paullica*". In this respect, he followed through with his broader *hypothesis*, even noting in advance where some of his major digressions would occur as part of that broader historical fabric.[48]

---

[47] In this respect, it is worth noting the reply of *Cicero Pater* to an inquiry by *Cicero Filius* regarding the need to follow a preplanned narrative order. When asked by his son, "Therefore, should we always keep to the order of narration which we desire?" (*Semperne igitur ordinem collocandi quem volumus tenere possumus*), Cicero replies, "Of course not—for the ears of his audience members govern the prudent and attentive orator, and he must always alter that which they reject" (*Non sane; nam auditorum aures moderantur oratori prudenti et provido, et quod respuunt immutandum est*, Cic. *Part.* 15).

[48] See n. 34 above. It is well worth noting that Polybius' account of Ephorus as a model at 5.33 is part of a broader digression on the construction of his *Histories* (5.30.8–33) in which the historian explains that, notwithstanding his goal "not to write a history of one man, but rather an

Polybius seems to find fault with Theopompus for two interrelated reasons. First, from a narratological perspective, Theopompus did not, like Polybius, follow the general plan he had formulated for his history (μεταλαβὼν δὲ τὴν ὑπόθεσιν), and, at a superlative moment in Hellenic history, leaves off midway in his narrative (μεταξὺ ... ἀπέρριψε)—with the implication that he never returned to that original Grecian focus. Second, from a thematic perspective that touches on innovations to the genre of historiography, Theopompus abandoned what was essentially a *Hellenica* in favor of a *Philippica*, nothing short of a betrayal of Hellas and her collective past (*i.e.* a kind of Panhellenic universal history) in favor of a one-man biography of the Macedonian who conquered Greece.[49] To follow Craige Champion's model of cultural alienation—that is, to view variations in the genre of historiography in terms of cultural politics—Polybius could hardly espouse a biographical history of one Greek behaving this badly towards the collective of Hellas.[50] In fact Polybius specifically critizes the title given by Theopompus to his work, arguing that Philip's life belonged within the broader category of Hellenic history and not the other way around. As we shall see, Polybius' double-edged criticisms of Theopompus prompted a noteworthy response in the Roman digressive receptions of his *Histories*.

Yet, more noteworthy still in the lengthy Book 38 excursus are the statements in which Polybius situates his digressions not only as part of the larger historiographical tradition, but also as innovating and standardizing the position and role of the digression within that broader canon. For example, in a rather lengthy

---

account of what happened everywhere" (οὐ τινά, τὰ δὲ παρὰ πᾶσι γεγονότα γράφειν, 5.31.6), he still has to be aware of his initial plan for the work and not deviate from it until the proper time. For the use of "weaving" language as a feature of universal history, see Clarke 1999b, 265–76.

49 This question has been analyzed in depth by Vattuone 2014, 19–27, who draws a number of interesting conclusions. Two stand out in particular: first (p. 10) "the choice of embedding his Greek history into the events of Philip's times, a choice that would displease Polybius ... was a profound statement about the autonomy of the *polis* and the new era that had begun"; second (p. 26) "Polybius grants Ephorus a primacy that he denies, in order to confer it on himself, Theopompus, Timaeus, and even ... Herodotus and Thucydides, who had been epitomized or resumed by Theopompus". Indeed, we might extend this argument to note that Polybius himself, for all his criticism of Theopompus, gave a similar centrality to Rome just as Theopompus did to Philip II, in that both played a key role in unifying, through conquest, previously unconnected parts of the world.

50 Champion 2004, 34, 40–46. See also Vattuone 2014, 20, who rightly views Polybius' polemic against Theopompus' "Philippizing" to be linked to the brutal capture of Messene by his descendent, Philip V, in 213 BCE, given the close proximity of this criticism (8.11.3) to his prior rebuke of historians for their mishandling the account of the sack of Messene (8.8).

statement at the outset of chapter 6 which seems to respond to the imagined critics at the outset of chapter 5 (in fact, the latter chapter echoes many phrases in the former), our historian indicates that his actions follow those of "the most thoughtful of ancient historians" (τῶν ἀρχαίων συγγραφέων οἱ λογιώτατοι),[51] "some of whom employ mythical and narrative digressions (τινὲς μὲν μυθικαῖς καὶ διηγηματικαῖς κεχρημένοι παρεκβάσεσι), and others pragmatic digressions (τινὲς δὲ καὶ πραγματικαῖς)". Such a statement shows Polybius not only placing himself in the broader tradition of historiography, but also beginning the process of categorizing historiographical digressions into types—mythical, narrative (or descriptive; the meaning of διηγηματικός is uncertain), and factual (based on politics and having a strong didactic function)—suggesting that by the time of his *Histories* he already sees certain digressive patterns emerging in his predecessors.[52]

Polybius then illustrates how these earlier historians "shift the scene from one part of Greece to another" (κατὰ τὴν Ἑλλάδα τόποις ποιεῖσθαι τὰς μεταβάσεις), and also "include doings abroad" (τῶν ἐκτὸς περιλαμβάνειν), no doubt referring to his more recent predecessors Ephorus and Theopompus.[53] He provides a specific example of this process, noting that "midway (μεταξὺ) while recounting in detail the affairs in Thessaly ... they set out to recount the enterprises of the Lacedaemonians in the Peloponnese, and then those of the Thebans, and next those in Macedonia or Illyria (τὰς κατὰ Πελοπόννησον Λακεδαιμονίων ἐπιβολὰς διηγῶνται, καὶ πάλιν τὰς παρὰ Θηβαίων, ἔτι δὲ τὰς κατὰ Μακεδονίαν ἢ τὴν Ἰλλυρίδα, κἄπειτα διατρίψαντες). In this way, Polybius justifies his own avowedly similar process which he lays out at the beginning of his excursus: "and thereupon I leave off from that in the midst of it (κἄπειτα μεταξὺ ταύτην ἀπολιπόντες), and, interrupting those very subjects (καὶ μεσολαβήσαντες σφᾶς αὐτούς), I pass over to Hellenic affairs and then to Macedonian affairs, Syrian affairs, and those of other countries (μεταβαίνομεν ἐπὶ τὰς Ἑλληνικὰς κἀντεῦθεν ἐπὶ τὰς Μακεδονικὰς ἢ Συριακὰς ἤ τινας ἑτέρας πράξεις). Thus, Polybius explicitly

---

51 Given the derivation of the adjective *logios* from *logos*, we might also read the adjective *logiōtatos*—paired as it is with *sungrapheus*—as having a connection to narratology, as in, "the most skilled at narrative construction of the ancient historians *who wrote them into narrative sequence*".
52 Citing Plb. 38.6, Marincola 1997, 118, writes, "Eventually—we cannot pinpoint exactly when—mythical material was seen as a suitable element in digressions, where the reader might be diverted in *loci amoeni* from the more serious material of history".
53 For the argument that at the outset of 38.6 Polybius is referring exclusively to Ephorus and Theopompus, see Walbank 1979, 692.

justifies his action by claiming, with specific parallels to earlier historians, to be following existing paradigms in the historiographic tradition.

In declaring that "even the most well versed of the ancient historians" turned off the narrative highway and made rest stops (διὸ καὶ τῶν ἀρχαίων συγγραφέων οἱ λογιώτατοι δοκοῦσί μοι προσαναπεπαῦσθαι τῷ τρόπῳ τούτῳ) Polybius, I would contend, is implying that even Thucydides—the historical συγγραφεύς par excellence (Θουκυδίδης Ἀθηναῖος ξυνέγραψε τὸν πόλεμον—"Thucydides the Athenian *wrote into record* the war", 1.1.1)—made a habit of digressing, a fact that Thucydides himself would be hard pressed to disavow (1.97.2). Yet Polybius does not stop with the most erudite and eloquent (οἱ λογιώτατοι) of Greek chroniclers, which could encompass any number of his forebears. He goes on to declare that *all* historians have resorted to digressions (ἐξ ὧν κεχρημένους μὲν ἅπαντας εὕροι τις ἂν τῷ τοιούτῳ χειρισμῷ).[54] Yet where others have done so without a strong organizing principle (κεχρημένους γε μὴν ἀτάκτως), he himself has arranged his narrative excursions carefully (ἡμᾶς δὲ τεταγμένως).

This is a bold claim, for not only does it describe the act of perfecting a historiographical tradition, but it also places such an act in a stative verbal tense. Such a use of the perfect tense is telling, for it suggests present fixity through a state of past becoming, given the manner in which the Greek perfect can link a completed past action with a lasting future permanence through its stative present[55]—in the case of Polybian historiography, the reformulation of an established, already somewhat perfected usage shared by all historians, *albeit with irregularity* (ὧν κεχρημένους μὲν ἅπαντας ... κεχρημένους γε μὴν ἀτάκτως), by way of his own adverbial "perfective orderly arrangement" (ἡμᾶς δὲ τεταγμένως) of discursiveness.[56] All of this underscores the idea of Polybius leaving behind an addition to the perfected legacy of historiography, especially given the force of the stative

---

54 Miltsios 2013, 63: "Yet the fact that the target is not specified ... clearly indicates that even if Polybius, when writing these lines, had Ephorus and Theopompus in mind ... he was not seeking to castigate these two historians in particular but certain quite widespread practices".
55 The clearest overview to this phenomenon is given in Jacob Wackernagel's Lecture I, 29 on the Greek Perfect Tense, in Wackernagel 2009, 215–20, esp. 216–17.
56 Miltsios 2013, 63, sees this as an indication of Polybius' method whereby he "turns *variatio* into a structural principle of the narrative, without affecting the cohesion of the text or its reception by the reader". He then adds: "It has the further advantage of enabling Polybius to convey the process of συμπλοκή, that interweaving of geopolitical affairs throughout the Mediterranean region which ultimately led to its domination by Rome". Sacks 1981, 114–17, makes a similar claim, linking this digression to the challenge faced by Polybius in his aim of writing a universal history of events as σωματοειδής (1.3.4).

perfect on the subject (ἡμᾶς δὲ).⁵⁷ After all, this is exactly what Polybius is highlighting—the prior existence of the digression as a universal practice among historians, yet one that has until now needed standardization, which his own historical excursions as part of a carefully arranged universal history have brought to fulfillment.

3 Polybius' Discursive Legacy: Rhetoricians on Historical Narrative and Livian Counterfactuals

That Polybius was so uniquely successful in fixing the digression into a historiographical, and perhaps even a rhetorical tradition, is demonstrated by the extent to which later rhetoricians and historians sought these digressions as models for their own discursiveness and to highlight its ideal usage. Several historical figures in particular appear to have resumed the interrogation of Theopompus' digressive narratology begun by Polybius, doing so in a variety of new forms: the Roman historian Livy, the Roman statesman and man of letters Cicero, the rhetorician and antiquarian Dionysius of Halicarnassus, and the Alexandrian sophist Aelius Theon.⁵⁸

For example, we see traces of such condemnation of "Philippizing" taken up by the Roman historian Livy in his famous Alexander Digression (9.17–19). Apart from Livy's strong signposting of his upcoming discussion (*ab rerum ordine declinarem*, 9.17.1), including references to key rhetorical ideas concerning digression—especially the central notion of giving both audience and writer a respite from the primary narrative of events (*varietatibusque distinguendo opere et legentibus velut deverticula amoena et requiem animo meo quaererem*, 9.17.1)—the opening statement to his excursus also draws from Polybius' notion of having to make an unwilling, but necessary break from the original narrative plan given the greatness of the subject matter (*tamen tanti regis ac ducis mentio*, 9.17.2).

More important still, Livy's digression takes Polybius' criticisms leveled against Theopompus for abandoning Hellas in favor of Philip and reworks them

---

57 Wackernagel 2009, 216: "A second inherited feature is the use of the perfect to denote the state resulting from the performance of the action of the verb, *a state in which the effect of the performance of the action applies to the subject*" (emphasis my own).
58 Here, for the sake of brevity, I am not including the Roman historian Tacitus or the Byzantine patriarch and commentator Photius of Constantinople, even though both can be seen as engaging with these same issues in a variety of post-Polybian political and historical contexts.

by resurrecting Philip's own son in a counterfactual, discursive, historical-rhetorical exercise: imagining one great individual competing with Rome's collective history.⁵⁹ Alexander the Great, of course, far exceeded his father Philip in imperial conquests. In many ways, he was the originary cause of the globalized world of competing empires—inherited and carved out by his own generals, the Diadochi—that Polybius was to experience and historicize.⁶⁰ Yet, as Livy is keen to point out, Alexander never quite reached Italy, a fact which renders the counterfactual exercise all the more potent.⁶¹

Moreover, even as Livy is tempted, like Theopompus, by "mention of so great a king and general" in Alexander the Great, the Roman historian remains true to his Polybian paradigm of viewing universal history as triumphing over the histories of individual men, no matter how legendary. Early in his digression, he writes of Alexander, "Yet, the very fact that he was one man made him nonetheless more famous" (*sed clariorem tamen eum facit quod unus fuit*, 9.17.5), thereby suggesting that Alexander's accomplishments are exaggerated by the very fact that they are linked to his name.⁶² Later in the course of his comparisons, he declares once

---

59 A somewhat dismissive reading of the rhetorical nature of the passage and its stylistic elements is given by Anderson 1908, 94, who refers to the Alexander Digression as "a youthful dissertation, an exercise composed by Livy about the age of eighteen, when he was a pupil in the school of a *rhetor* at Patavium". For the prevalent usage of counterfactuals in the digression—itself a sign of a highly complex type of historiography—see Morello 2002.

60 In this respect, we might also note that at least one earlier Alexander historian, Anticleides of Athens, wrote a history that supposedly contained within it a lengthy digression on Egyptian antiquities. See *OCD s.v.* Anticleides, *FGrH* 140, and Pearson 1960, 252. For ancient testimonia on this history, see also D.L. 8.11, *FGrHist* 140 F 1 and Pliny, *Nat.* 7.193, *FGrHist* 140 F 11.

61 For this reason Livy seems particularly interested in the figure of Alexander of Epirus, the maternal uncle of Alexander the Great, whose campaigns in Southern Italy are documented extensively at 8.3, 8.17, and 8.24; whose death is dated to the same year as the founding of Alexandria in 331 BCE by Alexander the Great (8.24.1); and who is subsequently mentioned in the Alexander Digression as having compared, as he lay dying, his own challenging campaigns against the Italians to Alexander the Great's more favorable battles against feminine Eastern peoples (9.19.10–11).

62 In light of the "*synkrising*" of Alexander the Great and Alexander of Epirus, as well as the argument that Alexander receives too much credit owing to his fame, Livy likely has in mind Polybius' account of Philip V and his campaigns in Sicily, which alternates between Philip V (8.8, 8.12–14) and his digression on Philip II (8.9–11), in which emerges his critique of Theopompus' "Philippizing". Furthermore, these passages in Book 8 contain praise of the imperial achievements of Philip II, Alexander the Great, and the Diadochi, including the statement that Alexander alone does not deserve all the credit, but that "no less (credit is owed) to his collaborators and friends, who conquered their opponents in numerous extraordinary battles, and also endured many perilous toils, ventures, and hardships" (οὐκ ἐλάττω μέντοι γε τοῖς συνεργοῖς καὶ

more, "However great the magnitude of the man, even so will this magnitude be that of one man" (*Quantalibet magnitudo hominis ... unius tamen ea magnitudo hominis erit*, 9.18.8), and again, "The Macedonians had one Alexander" (*Macedones unum Alexandrum habuissent*, 9.18.18), contrasting, "There were many Romans equal to Alexander either in glory or in the greatness of their deeds" (*Romani multi fuissent Alexandro vel gloria vel rerum magnitudine pares*, 9.18.19).

By employing what Ruth Morello rightly sees as a *synkrisis* "between Alexander and Rome", denying Alexander a fair comparison to Rome's advantage,[63] Livy subtly shows himself beyond traditional *Quellenforschung* to be a very nuanced respondent to Polybian concerns about Theopompan digression. Not only does the comparison further weaken the image of Alexander as conqueror by introducing the tragic Italian fate of his uncle Alexander of Epirus and subtly conflating this with the myths surrounding Alexander the Great—both in the Alexander Digression and in repeated historical narrative—but it also does so through reference to different historiographical subgenres by intelligently reworking a Polybian criticism of Theopompan "great man" biographical history into a counterfactual excursus involving his nephew. Through such rhetorical positioning, Livy is able to bring a kind of counterfactual genealogy as was seen in the Homeric narratives once again into the realm of the digression.

Quite notably, this very idea of a great man historiography subsuming the broader set of contemporary events—so highly criticized by Polybius—is strongly encouraged by Cicero as the ideal form for Lucius Lucceius' history of his consulship. In Cicero's letter to Lucceius (*Fam.* 5.12), dating from well after his return from exile (12 April of 55 BCE), he discusses his hopes and ambitions regarding Lucceius' composition of a history about his triumphant defense of the Roman Republic against the Catilinarian conspiracy. Particularly notable is Cicero's deliberation regarding the best possible manner in which Lucceius ought to include him in his historiography—whether interwoven as part of a larger, more universal history following the completion of the century of the Social Wars in Italy (*sed quia videbam Italici belli et civilis historiam iam a te paene esse perfectam*, 5.12.2) and his plan to begin writing about subsequent events (*dixeras autem mihi te reliquas res ordiri*, 5.12.2); or as the subject of his own, distinct historical monograph.

φίλοις, οἳ πολλαῖς μὲν καὶ παραδόξοις μάχαις ἐνίκησαν τοὺς ὑπεναντίους, πολλοὺς δὲ καὶ παραβόλους ὑπέμειναν πόνους καὶ κινδύνους καὶ ταλαιπωρίας, 8.10.8–9). Polybius then adds: "Moreover, after the death of Alexander, when they quarreled over the greater part of the known world, they created such a distinguished, well transmitted historical record of themselves" (μετὰ δὲ τὸν Ἀλεξάνδρου θάνατον οὕτω περὶ τῶν πλείστων μερῶν τῆς οἰκουμένης ἀμφισβητήσαντες παραδόσιμον ἐποίησαν τὴν ἑαυτῶν δόξαν ἐν πλείστοις ὑπομνήμασιν, 8.10.11).

63 Morello 2002, 77.

In many ways, Cicero turns the idea of universal history on its head in his carefully chosen *exempla* and argumentation regarding how Lucceius should write a Ciceronian history. On the one hand, Cicero suggests that the historian might intertwine the events of Cicero's consulship with his account of the subsequent period (*coniunctene malles cum reliquis rebus nostra contexere*, 5.12.2). Based upon our readings of certain statements made by Polybius, this would seem to match those ideas concerning the inclusion of events into the larger narrative fabric of history. Yet, quite paradoxically given our extant Polybian corpus, Cicero cites Polybius alongside Callisthenes and Timaeus as an example of a historian who created separate histories for noteworthy subjects—what we might have earlier labeled as Theopompan and avowedly anti-Polybian.

> coniunctene malles cum reliquis rebus nostra contexere an, ut multi Graeci fecerunt, Callisthenes Phocicum bellum, Timaeus Pyrrhi, Polybius Numantinum, qui omnes a perpetuis suis historiis ea, quae dixi, bella separaverunt, tu quoque item civilem coniurationem ab hostilibus externisque bellis seiungeres.

> Whether you might prefer to weave together in a connected manner my affairs with later events. Or, you might also do as many Greek writers have done—Callisthenes for the Phocian War, Timaeus for the War of Pyrrhus, Polybius for the Numantine War, all of whom separated these wars that I have mentioned from their own continuous histories—and in a similar manner isolate the Catilinarian conspiracy from foreign enemies and external wars (*Fam.* 5.12.2).

To the reader of extant ancient histories, Cicero's choices for writers of separate historical war monographs (*qui omnes a perpetuis suis historiis ea, quae dixi, bella separaverunt*) hardly seem conventional, given that all three historians were known for some form of universal history—a *Hellenica* (Callisthenes), *Histories* that spanned Sicily and the wider Greek world (Timaeus), and *Histories* of the broader Mediterranean world (Polybius)—rather than their respective *Bellum Phocicum* (Callisthenes), *Bellum Pyrrhi* (Timaeus), and *Bellum Numantinum* (Polybius). Moreover, of the three examples, Polybius stands out especially for Cicero's citation of his other historical work. Although one need not discount Cicero's *testimonium* regarding Polybius having written a separate *Bellum Numantinum*,[64] Polybius' legacy nonetheless remains that of our universal annalistic historian par excellence (especially in light of his own statements on the topic vis-à-vis Theopompus).

For this very reason, Cicero's usage of Polybius as a model in his letter to Lucceius appears all the more noteworthy: in order to rhetorically justify being

---

[64] For a brief discussion of its possible date of composition, see Walbank 1972, 22.

the subject of his own *"Ciceronica"*—or perhaps the protagonist of his own *Bellum Catilinae* (*tu quoque item civilem coniurationem ab hostilibus externisque bellis seiungeres*), given that only one of the three titles focuses on a historical figure (Pyrrhus)—he cites three known universal Greek historians, who conveniently wrote war monographs *in addition to* these universal histories.[65]

In this respect, Cicero can be understood as attempting to redefine the known historiographical qualities of certain paradigmatic ancient historians. In fact, beyond recasting Polybius, the universal historian par excellence, into a paradigmatic writer of monographs, Cicero suggests that Lucceius not follow the strict chronology in his histories and wait until the proper time to write about Cicero (*non te exspectare dum ad locum venias*), but rather that he set about recording his accomplishments right away (*ac statim causam illam totam et tempus arripere*, 5.12.2). In an even stronger push for a *"Ciceronica"*, Cicero claims that writing a monograph about only himself and his achievements will make for a richer and more praiseworthy history: "If you turn all of your attention to a single theme and to one individual (*si uno in argumento unaque in persona mens tua tota versabitur*), I can already picture in my mind how much greater will be all the richness and the brilliance (*quanto omnia uberiora atque ornatiora futura sint*, 5.12.2)". If this were not enough, Cicero basically renounces Polybian historical aims when he subsequently demands a biased treatment from the historian: "In this thing, would that you ignore the laws of history and do not spurn that favorable partiality, and would that you yield to our affection even a little more than the truth will allow" (*in eo leges historiae neglegas gratiamque illam ... ne aspernere amorique nostro plusculum etiam quam concedet veritas largiare*, 5.12.3).[66]

---

65 That being said, we know that Callisthenes wrote firsthand accounts of Alexander's military campaigns, and in many respects might be viewed, in terms of his own historical developments, as the reverse of Theopompus—beginning in the tradition of an official court historian of a great man (writing the *Deeds of Alexander*), and transitioning to a historian of the wider Greek world (writing his own *Hellenica*).

66 Although Woodman 1988, 70–75, discusses this passage at length and cites it as part of his argument that (p. 74) "truth and falsehood were seen in terms of prejudice and bias"—namely that Cicero was addressing an implied concern on the part of Lucceius about appearing too favorable in his treatment of the orator and statesman—we cannot discount the fact that Cicero quite explicitly states that showing greater bias "even a little more than the truth will allow" (*plusculum etiam quam concedet veritas*) constitutes an act of "ignoring the laws of history" (*leges historiae neglegas*). Polybius, too, in his early polemic about Philinus and Fabius Pictor (1.14), notes a degree of difference between their unintentional misrepresentation of the truth (μὴ δεόντως ... ἀπηγγελκέναι τὴν ἀλήθειαν, 1.14.1) and intentional deceit (ἐψεῦσθαι, 1.14.2). Nev-

Nevertheless, later rhetoricians took an active interest in the digressive narratology employed by Polybius, and in some instances encouraged his historical methods quite closely. For instance, Aelius Theon in his *Progymnasmata* takes a particurly keen interest in Polybian discursive ideals, using many of the specific terms employed by Polybius in his accounts of Ephorus and Theopompus:

παραιτητέον δὲ καὶ τὸ παρεκβάσεις ἐπεμβάλλεσθαι μεταξὺ διηγήσεως μακράς. οὐ γὰρ ἁπλῶς χρὴ πᾶσαν παραιτεῖσθαι, καθάπερ ὁ Φίλιστος· ἀναπαύει γὰρ τὴν διάνοιαν τῶν ἀκροατῶν, ἀλλὰ τὴν τηλικαύτην τὸ μῆκος, ἥτις ἀπαλλοτριοῖ τὴν διάνοιαν τῶν ἀκροωμένων, ὥστε δεῖσθαι πάλιν ὑπομνήσεως τῶν προειρημένων, ὡς Θεόπομπος ἐν ταῖς Φιλιππικαῖς· δύο γάρ που καὶ τρεῖς καὶ πλείους ἱστορίας ὅλας κατὰ παρέκβασιν εὑρίσκομεν, ἐν αἷς οὐχ ὅπως Φιλίππου, ἀλλ' οὐδὲ Μακεδόνος τινὸς ὄνομά ἐστιν.

There is a need to avoid the insertion of long digressions midway through one's narrative. For one need not entirely shun every instance, as Philistus does. For it provides a rest to the thought process of one's audience. However, one must avoid one of such great length that it interferes with the comprehension by one's audience, with the result that one must remind it of matters mentioned previously, as Theopompus does in his *Philippica*. For there we encounter two and three and more entire histories within digressions, in which there is nothing whatsoever about Philip, nor the name of a single Macedonian (*Prog.* 2.80.27–81.4, BNJ 115 T 30).

On the one hand, citing the common rhetorical quality of digressions noted by Polybius and Livy, that of providing respite to the mind of one's listeners (ἀναπαύει γὰρ τὴν διάνοιαν τῶν ἀκροατῶν), Aelius Theon rebukes Philistus of Syracuse for his failure to employ digressions altogether. In fact, Philistus' *Sicelica* was highly regarded by ancient readers: by Alexander the Great, Cicero (who, in *Letter to his Brother Quintus* 2.11.4, called him "nearly a miniature Thucydides", or *paene pusillus Thucydides*), Ephorus, Dionysius of Halicarnassus, and Quintilian.[67] This suggests that in the wake of Polybian historiography, digression had come to be seen as an essential element of the genre, so much so that not even Philistus was exempt from criticism for having omitted it in his *Sicelica*.

---

ertheless, he stresses that historiography demands impartiality, concluding: "If the truth is removed from history, what is left becomes a useless tale" (ἐξ ἱστορίας ἀναιρεθείσης τῆς ἀληθείας τὸ καταλειπόμενον αὐτῆς ἀνωφελὲς γίνεται διήγημα, 1.14.6).
67 See Plut. *Alex.* 8.3 and *Dio* 36.2; Dion. Hal. *Pomp.* 5; Quint. *Inst.* 10.1.74. It is worth noting that Philistus was also criticized by some of these writers for his support of tyrants, including by Plutarch (*Dio.* 36.1) and Dionysius of Halicarnassus (*Pomp.* 5).

On the other hand, it would also seem that Aelius Theon criticizes the length of Theopompus' excursions—that is, for taking the digression to the other extreme. He reasons that one must avoid, midway through one's narrative (μεταξὺ διηγήσεως), the act of adding on overly lengthy discursions (τὸ παρεκβάσεις ἐπεμβάλλεσθαι ... μακράς). Such language clearly follows in the footsteps of Polybius' own rhetoric about digression—both his criticisms of Theopompus (μεταξὺ καὶ τὰς ταύτης ἐπιβολὰς ἀπέρριψε, 8.11.3) and his defense of his own detours (μεταξὺ ταύτην ἀπολιπόντες, 38.5.1, and μεταξὺ τὰς ... ἐπιβολὰς διηγῶνται, 38.6.2). Moreover, one of Aelius Theon's criticisms—"with the result that it becomes necessary to recall once more what was said beforehand" (ὥστε δεῖσθαι πάλιν ὑπομνήσεως τῶν προειρημένων)—supplies τῶν προειρημένων as a verbal echo of Polybius' own censure of Theopompus in that same earlier passage (οὐδεὶς ἂν εὐδοκήσειε τῷ προειρημένῳ, 8.11.3), and also likely reflects the complaints by Polybius' fellow scholars regarding the seemingly "incomplete and disconnected" nature of his *Histories*, and Polybius' response regarding the careful placement of markers to indicate in advance where the breaks and narrative returns occur.[68]

Furthermore, Aelius Theon picks up on the Polybian concern about Philippic subject matter, only in this case it is a concern for entire books of digressions that lack their eponymous leader, combined with an issue regarding the extreme length of these digressions: "For there we find two and three and more entire histories (ἱστορίας ὅλας) within the digressions (κατὰ παρέκβασιν), in which there is nothing about Philip, nor the name of any Macedonian".[69] Here, I would suggest that Aelius Theon's emphasis on Theopompus' digressions lacking the name of any Macedonian (οὐδὲ Μακεδόνος τινὸς ὄνομά ἐστιν) is meant to recall Polybius' disappointment in the work's transformation from a *Hellenica* to a *Philippica*. Furthermore, an editorializing Philip V, a descendant of the Antigonids who traced their descent back to the *Diadochi* (Antigonus I Monophthalmus and Antigonus II Gonatas, as well as Demetrius I Poliorcetes)—and the same historical figure

---

[68] Plb. 38.6.6: "I leave manifest in advance for fellow scholars the point of return to the continuous narrative and the interruptions of affairs at any given moment, such that nothing incomplete nor wanting results for those who were attentive to my remarks made in advance" (ἀπολείπομεν πρόδηλον τοῖς φιλομαθοῦσι τὴν ἐπαναγωγὴν ἐπὶ τὸν συνεχῆ λόγον καὶ τὰς μεσολαβηθείσας ἀεὶ τῶν πράξεων, ὥστε μηδὲν ἀτελὲς μηδ' ἐλλιπὲς γίνεσθαι τοῖς φιληκόοις τῶν προειρημένων).

[69] Photius likewise notes, "Theopompus therefore extends his historical narratives with the largest and most frequent digressions concerning every sort of historical topic of inquiry" (πλείσταις μὲν οὖν παρεκβάσεσι παντοδαπῆς ἱστορίας τοὺς ἱστορικοὺς αὐτοῦ λόγους Θεόπομπος παρατείνει, *Bibl.* 176, *BNJ* 115 T31).

who appears in the narrative prompting Polybius' digression on Theopompus' "Philippizing" (8.8–14)—appears to have shared that same opinion. According to Photius of Constantinople, Philip V removed substantial chunks of Theopompus' *Philippica*, including all the digressions (τῶν παρεκτροπῶν, τὰς πάσας ἀπήρτισε), preserving in sixteen books only those narratives that featured the accomplishments of Philip II (ἐξελὼν ταύτας καὶ τὰς Φιλίππου συνταξάμενος πράξεις, αἵ σκοπός εἰσι Θεοπόμπῳ εἰς ιϛ' βίβλους μόνας, *Bibl.* 176, *BNJ* 115 T31).

Finally, in Dionysius of Halicarnassus' *Letter to Pompey*, we witness instead a great deal of praise for Theopompus of Chios, and in the process see a number of digressive forms—in particular those picked up by Polybius—once again classified alongside other fundamental features of rhetoric:

γνοίη δ' ἄν τις αὐτοῦ τὸν πόνον ἐνθυμηθεὶς τὸ πολύμορφον τῆς γραφῆς. καὶ γὰρ ἐθνῶν εἴρηκεν οἰκισμοὺς καὶ πόλεων κτίσεις ἐπελήλυθε, βασιλέων τε βίους καὶ τρόπων ἰδιώματα δεδήλωκε, καὶ εἴ τι θαυμαστὸν ἢ παράδοξον ἑκάστη γῇ καὶ θάλασσα φέρει, συμπεριείληφεν τῇ πραγματείᾳ. καὶ μηδεὶς ὑπολάβῃ ψυχαγωγίαν ταῦτ' εἶναι μόνον—οὐ γὰρ οὕτως ἔχει—ἀλλὰ πᾶσαν ὡς ἔπος εἰπεῖν ὠφέλειαν περιέχει. ἵνα δὲ πάντ' ἀφῶ τἆλλα, τίς οὐχ ὁμολογήσει τοῖς ἀσκοῦσι τὴν φιλόσοφον ῥητορικὴν ἀναγκαῖον εἶναι πολλὰ μὲν ἔθη καὶ βαρβάρων καὶ Ἑλλήνων ἐκμαθεῖν, πολλοὺς δὲ νόμους ἀκοῦσαι πολιτειῶν τε σχήματα, καὶ βίους ἀνδρῶν καὶ πράξεις καὶ τέλη καὶ τύχας; τούτοις τοίνυν ἅπασαν ἀφθονίαν δέδωκεν οὐκ ἀπεσπασμένην τῶν πραγμάτων, ἀλλὰ συμπαροῦσαν. πάντα <τε> δὴ ταῦτα ζηλωτὰ τοῦ συγγραφέως ... ἔστι δὲ ἃ καὶ κατὰ τὸν πραγματικὸν τόπον ἁμαρτάνει, καὶ μάλιστα κατὰ τὰς παρεμβολάς· οὔτε γὰρ ἀναγκαῖαί τινες αὐτῶν οὔτ' ἐν καιρῷ γενόμεναι, πολὺ δὲ τὸ παιδιῶδες ἐμφαίνουσαι· ἐν αἷς ἐστι καὶ τὰ περὶ Σιληνοῦ τοῦ φανέντος ἐν Μακεδονίᾳ καὶ τὰ περὶ τοῦ δράκοντος τοῦ διαναυμαχήσαντος πρὸς τὴν τριήρη καὶ ἄλλα τούτοις οὐκ ὀλίγα ὅμοια.

Yet one might also understand his hard work if one takes into account the multiform nature of his writing. For he describes the settlements of peoples and proceeds to recount the foundations of cities, and relates the lives of kings and the peculiarities of their ways, and if any particular land or sea possesses something wondrous or bizarre, he has come to include it in his work. And let no one consider these to be merely a matter of entertainment—for it is not so—since they encompass almost every source of intellectual profit. All other topics notwithstanding, who would not agree with those practicing philosophical rhetoric that one ought to learn as much as possible about the customs of both the barbarians and the Greeks, and ought to hear about their many legal practices and constitutional forms of government, as well as the lives of their individual men, and their deeds, ends, and ultimate fates? Moreover, he provides them with all of these topics in abundance, and not separated but present together in the same narrative. To be sure, all of these things are enviable for a historian ... Yet there also those areas in which he errs in his subject matter, especially in his narrative insertions. For some of these are neither necessary nor pertinent at that given moment, but come across as jejune. Among these are the account of the Silenus that was seen in Macedonia and the legend of the sea serpent that engaged in a naval battle with a trireme, and a great many others like these (Dion. Hal. *Pomp.* 6, *BNJ* 115 T 20a).

Referring to a kind of discursive historiography that would come to be pursued by Polybius, Dionysius praises Theopompus for the "multifaceted character of his writing" (τὸ πολύμορφον τῆς γραφῆς), and for his integration of a number of additional features into the narrative proper, rather than in separate sections or different works (οὐκ ἀπεσπασμένην τῶν πραγμάτων, ἀλλὰ συμπαροῦσαν). In this respect, we see what were previously labeled as digressive elements in Polybius' *Histories*, such as legal constitutions (πολιτειῶν ... σχήματα), now viewed as material that should constitute part of (συμπαροῦσαν) the main narrative. In addition, we see a range of historical topics praised that, by the time of Roman Republican history, often feature within digressions. For example, "the settlements of peoples" and "the foundations of cities", both of which Theopompus features (καὶ γὰρ ἐθνῶν εἴρηκεν οἰκισμοὺς καὶ πόλεων κτίσεις ἐπελήλυθε), often recur in ethnographic discursions as well as digressions set in the plupast in order to explain how peoples came to inhabit particular places, came into contact with one another, and came into eventual conflict: these include Thucydides' Sicilian ethnography (6.2-5), Polybius' Celtic ethnography (2.14-35), Sallust's African ethnography (*Jug.* 17-19), the British ethnographies of Caesar (*Gal.* 5.12-14) and Tacitus (*Ag.* 10-12), and Livy's Gallo-Etruscan and Galatian digressions (5.33-35 and 38.16).[70] Likewise, his inclusion of the wondrous and paradoxographical within his narrative (καὶ εἴ τι θαυμαστὸν ἢ παράδοξον ἑκάστη γῆ καὶ θάλασσα φέρει, συμπεριείληφεν τῇ πραγματείᾳ) is in many respects what led to Herodotean *historiē* being labeled as digressive, and will eventually form the basis for numerous excursions containing dialogic subject matter in Tacitus' writings.[71]

"All of these things", writes Dionysius, "are enviable in the historian" (πάντα <τε> δὴ ταῦτα ζηλωτὰ τοῦ συγγραφέως), suggesting that the very title inherited from Thucydides and developed by Polybius (ὁ συγγραφεύς), has become transformed by discursive developments to reflect its true meaning—"one who writes what is essentially separate material into a coherent narrative unity". That this discursive narrative fusion finds much stimulus in oratory becomes even more

---

[70] The phrase ἐθνῶν ... οἰκισμοὺς seems to be a Greek equivalent of the Latin *situs gentium*, a phrase which functions as a kind of lexical marker for ethnography, often appearing at the outset of an ethnographic digression in a historical work. See Thomas 1982, 3 and Woodman and Kraus 2014, 127–28.
[71] These include the mutiny of the Usipi (*Ag.* 28), the report of the Neronian impersonator (*Hist.* 2.8-9), Mariccus' uprising (*Hist.* 2.61), Geta's masquerade (*Hist.* 2.72), the attempted assassination of Tettius Julianus (*Hist.* 2.85), Venutius' rebellion (*Hist.* 3.45), the revolt in Pontus (*Hist.* 3.47-48), the mutiny of the fleet at Misenum (*Hist.* 3.57), the account of the false Agrippa Postumus (*Ann.* 2.39-40), the Brundisian slave insurrection (*Ann.* 4.27), and the gladiatorial skirmish at Pompeii (*Ann.* 14.17).

explicit when Dionysius tells us that the "practitioners of philosophical rhetoric" (τοῖς ἀσκοῦσι τὴν φιλόσοφον ῥητορικὴν) are correct to see a benefit in learning about "the many customs of the barbarians and the Greeks" (πολλὰ μὲν ἔθη καὶ βαρβάρων καὶ Ἑλλήνων) and "their many laws and forms of government" (πολλοὺς δὲ νόμους ... πολιτειῶν τε σχήματα),[72] which not only had their origins in the Herodotean interspersing of *ethnē* and *nomoi* accounts with his Persian War *logos*, but also found a prominent place in virtually all subsequent historians.

Dionysius' only criticism leveled against Theopompus is for the one area in which he errs in his narrative (κατὰ τὸν πραγματικὸν τόπον ἁμαρτάνει),[73] "particularly in his narrative insertions" (μάλιστα κατὰ τὰς παρεμβολάς), which he labels as both untimely and infantile (οὔτ᾿ ἐν καιρῷ γενόμεναι, πολὺ δὲ τὸ παιδιῶδες).[74] Yet these are a far cry from the features Polybius labels as digressive in his own work. First, they are once more labeled in the Herodotean manner as "insertions" rather than "digressions", perhaps suggesting a different kind of discursiveness, one that is overly paradoxographical in its outlandishness and too focused on entertainment rather than intellectual profit—"the account of the Silenus that was seen in Macedonia and the legend of the sea serpent that engaged in a naval battle with a trireme" (καὶ τὰ περὶ Σιληνοῦ τοῦ φανέντος ἐν Μακεδονίᾳ καὶ τὰ περὶ τοῦ δράκοντος τοῦ διαναυμαχήσαντος πρὸς τὴν τριήρη). Second, they

---

72 Given the mention of rhetoric, it is worth noting that the passage in full mentions both Demosthenes and Isocrates. The latter's relation to historiography of the fourth century BCE is analyzed most recently by Marincola 2014, who cites as models of a more balanced approach Parmeggiani 2011, 34–36 (for Ephorus) and Flower 1994, 42–62 (for Theopompus).
73 Given the narratological subject of criticism, it is likely that the usage of the word *topos* and its pairing with *hamartanō* have connotations of narrative place and misdirected movement therein.
74 Ann Hanson has suggested to me that Polybius' earlier narrative terminology for the proper usage of digression—particularly his parrying of the charge that his history is "incomplete" (ἀτελῆ and ἀτελές) and "defective" or "wanting" (ἐλλιπές)—suggests, in light of his lengthy comparison with various senses that form a part of "human nature" (αὐτὴν τὴν φύσιν, 38.5.4), that Polybius has in mind a biological model of narrative. In this respect, he stresses that his digressions are not "abortive"—no doubt having in mind Thucydides' usage of ἐκβολή as a term for his *Pentekontaetia* digression (using the Greek term for both "abortion", LSJ IV, and "casting" of an infant left exposed to die, LSJ VIII). Moreover, the term ἀτελής can also mean "imperfect" of growth or "poorly developed" in reference to a child or minor (LSJ I 3). For Polybius, then, and Aelius Theon and Dionysius of Halicarnassus who looked to him as a model, it is important that digressions—whether due to "excessive gestation" (Aelius Theon on Theopompus) or poorly timed arrival, a narrative "miscarriage" of sorts (Dionysius on Theopompus)—do not prevent their "maternal narratives" from reaching their ultimate teleological aim of a ripe old age. Cf. Walbank 1972, 142–44 and Clarke 1999a, 124–28.

are also criticized for their lack of pertinence at that particular moment in the narrative chronology (οὔτ' ἐν καιρῷ γενόμεναι), suggesting that the placement of digressions within their respective historical narratives was just as important as the subject matter they encompassed.

This combination of praise and blame for Theopompus illustrates a number of important developments in the tradition of historical discursiveness. For example, what actually constitutes a digression versus an essential feature of historical narrative was not a static definition, and it developed with the genre over time, often preserving hints of its original discursiveness. For example, although ethnographies came to be viewed as fundamental features of historiographic narratives, as were descriptions of political constitutions and laws, we see in the phrases marking and concluding these accounts that they were still framed as digressions.[75] Moreover, as a result of universal histories and the broadening geographical scope of their inquiries, an annalistic narrative could now be inherently multifarious in both subject matter and narratological sequence—that is, "incomplete and disconnected", whether the original Polybian formulation (ἀτελῆ καὶ διερριμμένην) or an antithetical iteration by the first century BCE politician and historian Lucius Cornelius Sisenna (*ne vellicatim aut saltuatim*).[76]

Even in far more pessimistic appraisals of later historiography, Polybius' discursive legacy would continue to be reexamined. Most notably, the Roman historian Tacitus, in his lengthy digression about writing history under the principate (*Ann.* 4.32–33), would call into question Polybian and Livian annalistic models of discursivity—those writers "who composed the more distant affairs of the Roman people (*qui veteres populi Romani res composuere*, 4.32.1), and who "memorialized with substantial digression" (*libero egressu memorabant*, 4.32.1). Although Tacitus follows the Polybian model of using the digression as a space to describe one's historiographical practices, Tacitus is unable to employ the full Polybian framework inherited from Theopompus—that digressive subject matter, "the ge-

---

75 In addition to the use of ethnographic phraseology of the *situs gentium* type mentioned above at n. 70, historians from Herodotus to Ammianus Marcellinus regularly labeled their ethnographic excursions with phrases denoting a departure from and a return to the primary narrative.
76 *Item alio in loco: nos una aestate in Asia et Graecia gesta litteris idcirco continentia mandavimus, ne vellicatim aut saltuatim scribendo lectorum animos impediremus* ("Again in another place: 'We have recorded the events from one summer waged in Asia and Greece in unbroken verbal succession, lest we impede the thought processes of the readers by writing in a piecemeal and leapfrog manner'", hist. 127, Gell. 12.15.2), F130 in Cornell 2013, Vol. 2, 662. I wish here to acknowledge Dennis Pausch, whose paper drew my attention to the parallels between these two historians.

ographic locations of peoples" (*nam situs gentium*, 4.33.3), which serves to "retain and renew the mind of readers" (*retinent ac redintegrant legentium animum*, 4.33.3).⁷⁷ In the now limited space for writing history under the emperors (*nobis in arto et inglorius labor*, 4.32.2), with its "unmoved peace" (*immota quippe ... pax*, 4.32.2),⁷⁸ all that remains is "the repetitiveness and superfluity" (*rerum similitudine et satietate*, 4.33.3) of affairs at Rome, which Tacitus has convincingly transformed into a topic worthy of *historia pragmatikē*.⁷⁹

As gloomy and pessimistic as historiography became in the time of Tacitus, the Polybian tradition of digression in historiography and innovating the practice did not end with him. Historians in Late Antiquity continued to make use of this device: Ammianus Marcellinus employs a variety of discursions in his *Res Gestae*, and Procopius and Orosius make notable changes of their own. In fact, digressive innovation did not end in antiquity, but continued in the postclassical histories of the Old English and Byzantine traditions.⁸⁰ Suffice to say that the historiographical digression had a long afterlife. Foucault, no doubt, points us in the right direction when he asks of the classical historian, "On what basis, in fact, could he speak without this discontinuity that offers him history—and his own history—as an object?"⁸¹ Our answer—on almost no basis whatsoever.

---

77 Woodman 1998, 134: "We know from Quintilian and Pliny that by Tacitus' time digressions were particularly associated with the genre of historiography. Thus, by using a digression specifically to *deny* that his work contains any of the pleasurable elements of which conventional historiography was thought to consist, Tacitus could hardly have chosen a more ironically appropriate medium in which to emphasize the changed nature of his work".
78 Tacitus' use of the word *immota* ("unmoved") to describe a time with a lack of suitable material for writing discursive annalistic history underscores his emphasis on the unfortunate shift to a post-Polybian, that is, the *post-mobile*, state of Roman affairs.
79 For a discussion of the ironies and inconsistencies in this digression, see Clarke 2002. For its clear political motivations, see Moles 1998, 131–80 and Clarke 2002, 93–97. For a similar digression about the didactic value of annalistic history, see Tac. *Ann*. 3.65, with a discussion by Luce 1991 and Woodman 1998, 86–103.
80 In Old English, we see these in translations of Orosius and in the historical digressions in *Beowulf*. In the Byzantine tradition, we find numerous instances of the excursus, such as in Anna Komnene's *Alexiad*; in Symeon the Logothete's accounts of the reigns of Michael III, Basil I, and Leo VI; in Michael Psellos' *Chronographia*; and in Niketas Choniates' *History*, to name only a few examples.
81 Foucault 1972, 9.

Bibliography

Anderson, W.B. (1908), "Contributions to the Study of the Ninth Book of Livy", in: *TAPhA* 39, 89–103.
Austin, N. (1966), "The Function of Digressions in the *Iliad*", in: *GRBS* 7, 295–312.
Barber, G.L. (1993), *The Historian Ephorus*, Chicago.
Baron, C.A. (2013), *Timaeus of Tauromenium and Hellenistic Historiography*, Cambridge.
Beye, C.R. (1964), "Homeric Battle Narrative and Catalogues", in: *HSCP* 68, 345–73.
Champion, C.B. (2004), *Cultural Politics in Polybius's Histories*, Berkeley/Los Angeles/London.
Clarke, K. (1999a), *Between Geography and History: Hellenistic Constructions of the Roman World*, Oxford.
—— (1999b), "Universal Perspectives in Historiography", in: C.S. Kraus (ed.), *The Limits of Historiography: Genre and Narrative in Ancient Historical Texts*, Leiden/Boston/Cologne, 249–79.
—— (2002), "*In arto et inglorius labor*: Tacitus's Anti-history", in: A.K. Bowman/H.M. Cotton/M. Goodman/S. Price (eds.), *Representations of Empire: Rome and the Mediterranean World*, Oxford, 83–103.
Clauss, J.J. (1997), "'Domestici hostes': The Nausicaa in Medea, the Catiline in Hannibal", in: *MD* 39, 165–85.
Cornell, T.J. (ed.) (2013), *Fragments of the Roman Historians*, 3 vols., Oxford.
de Jong, I.J.F. (2002), "Narrative Unity and Units", in: E.J. Bakker/I.J.F. de Jong/H. van Wees (eds.), *Brill's Companion to Herodotus*, Leiden/Boston/Cologne, 245–66.
Foucault, M. (1970), *The Order of Things: An Archaeology of the Human Sciences*, London.
—— (1972), *The Archaeology of Knowledge*, transl. A.M. Sheridan Smith, New York.
Flower, M.A. (1994), *Theopompus of Chios: History and Rhetoric in the Fourth Century BC*, Oxford.
Ginsburg, J. (1981), *Tradition and Theme in the Annals of Tacitus*, New York.
Greenwood, E. (2006), *Thucydides and the Shaping of History*, London.
Grethlein, J. (2008), "Memory and Material Objects in the *Iliad* and the *Odyssey*", in: *JHS* 128, 27–51.
Grethlein, J./C.B. Krebs (eds.) (2012), *Time and Narrative in Ancient Historiography: The "Plupast" from Herodotus to Appian*, Cambridge.
Hartog, F. (2010), "Polybius and the First Universal History", in: P. Liddel/A. Fear (eds.), *Historiae Mundi: Studies in Universal History*, London, 30–40.
Hau, L.I. (2016), *Moral History from Herodotus to Diodorus Siculus*, Edinburgh.
Hornblower, S. (1991), *A Commentary on Thucydides*, Vol. 1, Oxford.
Jacoby, F. (1909), "Über die Entwicklung der griechischen Historiographie und den Plan einer neuen Sammlung der griechischen Historikerfragmente", in: *Klio* 9, 80–123.
Klotz, A. (1940–41), *Livius und seine Vorgänger*, Leipzig.
Lang, M.L. (1984), *Herodotean Narrative and Discourse*, Cambridge, Mass.
Larmour, D.H.J./P.A. Miller/C. Platter (eds.) (1998), *Rethinking Sexuality: Foucault and Classical Antiquity*, Princeton.
Levene, D.S. (2010), *Livy on the Hannibalic War*, Oxford.
Longley, G. (2012), "Thucydides, Polybius, and Human Nature", in: C. Smith/L.M. Yarrow (eds.), *Imperialism, Cultural Politics, and Polybius*, Oxford, 68–84.
Luce, T.J. (1991), "Tacitus on 'History's Highest Function': *praecipuum munus annalium* (*Ann.* 3.65)", in: *ANRW* 2.33.4, 2904–27.

Marincola, J. (1997), *Authority and Tradition in Ancient Historiography*, Cambridge.
— — (2001), *Greek Historians*, Oxford.
— — (2014), "Rethinking Isocrates and Historiography", in: G. Parmeggiani (ed.), *Between Thucydides and Polybius: The Golden Age of Greek Historiography*, Cambridge, Mass, 39–61.
Martin, R.H./A.J. Woodman (eds.) (1989), *Tacitus: Annals Book IV*, Cambridge.
McGing, B. (2010), *Polybius' Histories*, Oxford.
— — (2012), "Polybius and Herodotus", in: C. Smith/L.M. Yarrow (eds.), *Imperialism, Cultural Politics, and Polybius*, Oxford, 33–49.
Miltsios, N. (2013), *The Shaping of Narrative in Polybius*, Berlin/New York.
Moles, J. (1998), "Cry Freedom: Tacitus *Annals* 4.32-35", in: *Histos* 2, 95–184.
Morello, R. (2002), "Livy's Alexander Digression (9.17–19): Counterfactuals and Apologetics", in: *JRS* 92, 62–85.
Munson, R.V. (2001), *Telling Wonders: Ethnographic and Political Discourse in the Work of Herodotus*, Ann Arbor.
Nissen, H. (1863), *Kritische Untersuchungen über die Quellen der vierten und fünften Dekade des Livius*, Berlin.
O'Gorman, E. (2009), "Intertextuality and Historiography", in: A. Feldherr (ed.), *The Cambridge Companion to the Roman Historians*, Cambridge, 231–42.
Parmeggiani, G. (2001), *Eforo di Cuma. Studi di storiografia greca*, Bologna.
Parry, A. (1981), *Logos and Ergon in Thucydides*, New York.
Paton, W.R. (ed.) (1927), *Polybius. The Histories*, Cambridge, Mass.
Pearson, L. (1960), *The Lost Histories of Alexander the Great*, Oxford.
Pothou, V. (2009), *La place et le rôle de la digression dans l'œuvre de Thucydide*, Stuttgart.
Price, J.J. (2001), *Thucydides and Internal War*, Cambridge.
Redfield, J. (1985), "Herodotus the Tourist", in: *CPh* 80, 97–118.
Rhodes, P.J. (ed.) 2014. *Thucydides: History I*, Oxford.
Rood, T. (1998), *Thucydides: Narrative and Explanation*, Oxford.
— — (2012), "Polybius, Thucydides, and the First Punic War", in: C. Smith/L.M. Yarrow (eds.), *Imperialism, Cultural Politics, and Polybius*, Oxford, 50–67.
Sacks, K. (1981), *Polybius on the Writing of History*, Berkeley/Los Angeles/London.
Sammons, B. (2010), *The Art and Rhetoric of the Homeric Catalogue*, Oxford.
Spada, S. (2008), *Le storie tra parentesi. Teoria e prassi della digressione in Erodoto, Tucidide e Senofonte*, Rome.
Stadter, P.A. (1993), "The Form and Content of Thucydides' Pentecontaetia (1.89–117)", in: *GRBS* 34, 35–72.
Strasburger, G. (1954), *Die kleinen Kämpfer der Ilias*, Frankfurt am Main.
Sudhaus, S. (ed.) (1892), *Philodemi volumina rhetorica*, 2 vols., Leipzig.
Thomas, R.F. (1982), *Lands and Peoples in Roman Poetry: The Ethnographical Tradition*, Cambridge.
Thomas, R. (2000), *Herodotus in Context: Ethnography, Science and the Art of Persuasion*, Cambridge.
Tränkle, H. (1977), *Livius und Polybios*, Basel/Stuttgart.
Tully, J. (2014), "Ephorus, Polybius, and τὰ καθόλου γράφειν: Why and How to Read Ephorus and his Role in Greek Historiography without Reference to 'Universal History'", in: G. Parmeggiani (ed.), *Between Thucydides and Polybius: The Golden Age of Greek Historiography*, Cambridge, Mass., 153–95.

Vattuone, R. (2014), "Looking for the Invisible: Theopompus and the Roots of Historiography", in: G. Parmeggiani (ed.), *Between Thucydides and Polybius: The Golden Age of Greek Historiography*, Cambridge, Mass., 7–37.
Wackernagel, J. (2009), *Lectures on Syntax, with Special Reference to Greek, Latin, and Germanic*, D.R. Langslow (ed.), Oxford.
Walbank, F.W. (1957), *A Historical Commentary on Polybius*, Vol. 1, Oxford.
—— (1972), *Polybius*, Berkeley/Los Angeles/London.
—— (1979), *A Historical Commentary on Polybius*, Vol. 3, Oxford.
Walker, P.K. (1957), "The Purpose and Method of 'The Pentekontaetia' in Thucydides, Book 1", in: *CQ* 7, 27–38.
Westlake, H.D. (1955), "Thucydides and the Pentekontaetia", in: *CQ* 5, 53–67.
Witte, K. (1910), "Über die Form der Darstellung in Livius Geschichtswerk", in: *RhM* 65, 270–305.
Wood, C. (2016), "'I am going to say...': A Sign on the Road of Herodotus' *logos*", in: *CQ* 66, 13–31.
Woodman, A.J. (1988), *Rhetoric in Classical Historiography: Four Studies*, London/Sydney.
—— (1998), *Tacitus Reviewed*, Oxford.
Woodman, A.J./C.S. Kraus (eds.) (2014), *Tacitus: Agricola*, Cambridge.
Ziegler, K. (1952), "Polybios von Megalopolis", in: *RE* 21.2, 1440–578.

Christopher Baron
The Historian's Craft: Narrative Strategies and Historical Method in Polybius and Livy

The relationship between Polybius and Livy is one of the most unique and intriguing for modern scholars of ancient Greek and Roman historical writing.[1] This is a bit of a paradox, since the way Livy used Polybius is probably, in its basic tenets, very much like the way most ancient historians used their predecessors when writing about non-contemporary events. But, due to the literary tastes of the Greeks and Romans and the accidents of preservation, the survival in various forms of Polybius' and Livy's accounts of the Roman conquest of the Mediterranean allows us to glimpse aspects of the two authors' historical method in greater-than-usual detail. Especially in Livy's Fourth and Fifth Decades, we can see precisely how he handles his major source, along a spectrum of translating, paraphrasing, re-working, supplementing, and ignoring. Since these portions of Polybius' *Histories* only survive in extracts, Livy's reliance on him has allowed scholars to say much more about Polybius' work than would otherwise be possible. And, because Livy also turns to sources beyond Polybius—historians who were part of a tradition stretching back to authors prior to or contemporary with him—this unique relationship can, on a few occasions, reveal Polybius' own historical craft.

The relationship is more complicated for Livy's Third Decade, where the continuous close parallels with Polybian language and structure which characterize his treatment of Rome's Macedonian and Syrian Wars do not exist. At a fundamental level, this makes perfect sense: in Books 21–30 Livy maintains a laser-like focus on Rome's war with Carthage, while Polybius in Books 3–15 covers events in the entire *oikoumenê*, of which the battles in Italy, Spain, and Africa form just one part. However, numerous scholars over the years have held that in fact Livy used Polybius little, if at all, when writing his Third Decade, and that he only turned to him—or even "discovered" Polybius' work—as he ended Book 30 and began Book 31, when he turned to events in the Greek east. This was the position of the scholar who produced the most extensive study of the issue, Hermann Tränkle, in 1977. His findings were immediately questioned in a review the next

---

[1] My thanks to the organizers of the Thessaloniki conference, which produced much stimulating discussion; and to Erich Gruen, Lisa Hau, Brian McGing, and Nicolas Wiater for their comments on this paper (with whose conclusions they do not necessarily agree).

year by John Briscoe. When put in this extreme and concrete form, Tränkle's thesis also faced opposition from new work on Livy as a historian and the general trends of classical scholarship, which were moving away from the questions of *Quellenforschung*, so often plagued by circularity, and were discarding assumptions about method which transposed features and expectations of nineteenth and twentieth century historical writing onto the ancient Greeks and Romans.[2] The gradual rejection of Tränkle's position culminated recently in David Levene's convincing demonstration, not only that Livy used Polybius as a source and intertext already in Book 21, but also that Livy was a much more sophisticated historian (not just literary artist) than has been recognized. The latter point has also been made by Dennis Pausch in his narratological study of Livy's work, influenced by scholarship which sees Livy as a rather postmodern author in a number of ways. At the same time, though perhaps more slowly, scholars (most notably Craige Champion and Brian McGing) have begun to demonstrate that there is more to Polybius than meets the eye.[3]

If Levene and others are correct that Polybius Book 3 lies behind Book 21 of Livy, then the opening chapters of those books provide an excellent opportunity to illuminate and compare the two historians' methods. For Polybius, this is the beginning of the main body of his work; and Livy introduces his treatment of the Hannibalic War as a sort of monograph within his larger project.[4] But, before introducing the comparison with Livy, in the first part of my paper I will focus on Polybius and one of the most notorious difficulties with his account of the outbreak of the Second Punic War: the Ebro River, the agreement between Rome and Hasdrubal making it a line of demarcation, the connection of river and treaty to Rome's relationship with Saguntum, and the role Hannibal's crossing of the river played in the start of the war. I will argue that the solution to the apparent problem of the Ebro River in Polybius is to consider the whole section, from chapter 6 to 33, as a narrative and argumentative arc, crafted by the historian, in which he introduces the second-century Roman claims about the causes of the war only to undermine them, gradually bringing the reader to see their weaknesses. In the second half of the paper I will turn to a comparison of this unit in Polybius with its corresponding section of Livy (21.1–19). Dennis Pausch has shown how Livy creates suspense at the beginning of Book 21 by repeatedly delaying the outbreak

---

[2] Tränkle 1977, 193–241, Briscoe 1978. Luce 1977 marks an important milestone in approaches to Livy.
[3] Levene 2010, 126–163, Pausch 2011, Champion 2004, McGing 2010.
[4] Girod 1976 examines the very first parts of these sections with an eye toward the broader historical vision of each author.

of the war.[5] I hope to show, by comparing Livy's treatment with that of Polybius, some of the other effects Livy produces by his selection, arrangement, and emphasis of the material. At the same time, we will also see that Polybius' account is just as consciously crafted by its author.

1 Polybius and the Ebro River

In the aftermath of their defeat in the First Punic War in 241, and the disastrous rebellion of their African subjects which followed, the Carthaginians looked to Iberia as a region in which to recoup their losses. Their first commander there, Hamilcar Barca (a veteran of the war against Rome in Sicily), successfully established the Carthaginian presence in Iberia before dying in 229. His son-in-law Hasdrubal followed in that path, founding the city of New Carthage as one of his first acts. Probably in 227/226, the Romans—concerned at the growth of Carthaginian power in Iberia—concluded a treaty with Hasdrubal whose only stipulation was that the Carthaginians would not cross the Ebro River with a military purpose. Hasdrubal died in 221, and Hamilcar's son Hannibal took over command of Carthaginian forces in Iberia. At some point in that interval, the Romans had entered into some sort of protective relationship with the Iberian city of Saguntum, which lay approximately 100 miles south of the Ebro River.[6] In 219, having subdued the Iberian tribes south of the Ebro, Hannibal besieged Saguntum; after eight months, his forces captured the city and sacked it. When the Romans received this news, they sent an embassy to Carthage (early spring 218) with an ultimatum that Hannibal and his advisors be surrendered—if not, war would be declared. War it was, and, once he received news of this, Hannibal—who had spent the winter preparing an invasion force—led his army north across the Ebro and, ultimately, into Italy.

The previous paragraph is one modern attempt—my own—at summarizing the events leading up to the Second Punic War, taken mostly from Polybius' account. But the devil is in the details, and the details in this case are especially devilish. Almost every detail present in my account—chronological and causal—has been questioned, amended, or even denied by modern scholars. Now, one

---

5 Pausch 2011, 202–05.
6 Thus, well inside the Carthaginian sphere of operations allowed by the treaty but, as far as we can tell, not a technical violation of the agreement on the Romans' part (Badian 1958, 50–51).

might think that the sole detail immune to such attacks would be the basic geographical one: that Saguntum lay south of the Ebro. Here, however, it is Polybius himself who has opened the door to debate. For, on a couple occasions in this section of Book 3, he seems to imply that Hannibal, in attacking Saguntum, violated the treaty of Hasdrubal: in other words, that Saguntum lay on the other side of the Ebro River. So, let us review what Polybius says regarding this river, before turning to a close analysis of his account of the outbreak of the war as a whole.

The Ebro River first appears in Book 2 as Polybius begins his account of Rome's war with the Celts. When the Romans noticed that Hasdrubal was advancing Carthaginian interests in Iberia, they were concerned, but felt that they first had to prepare to resist an impending Celtic invasion. So, instead of aggressive action or threats against Hasdrubal, the Romans sent envoys to conclude a treaty, Polybius says, "in which no mention was made of the rest of Iberia, but the Carthaginians undertook not to cross the Ebro [*Ibêr*] River for military purposes."[7] Then, immediately after the new preface at the beginning of Book 3, the Ebro River appears again. Polybius reports that "some historians" give two causes of the Second Punic War: Hannibal's siege and sack of Saguntum, and his crossing of the Ebro River "in contravention of the treaty" (3.6). At 3.14, Polybius states indirectly that Saguntum is south of that river: after Hannibal's defeat of the Vaccaei, "all the Iberians south of the Ebro [lit. this side of], except for the Saguntines, were too cowed to resist Hannibal with any effectiveness."[8] Soon after, Roman envoys are sent to New Carthage at the request of the Saguntines; these envoys "warned [Hannibal] to leave Saguntum alone, on the grounds that it was under Roman protection, and reminded him that by the terms of their treaty with Hasdrubal he was not to cross the Ebro."[9] This is the first potential point of confusion, since one *could* read Polybius as implying that an attack on Saguntum by Hannibal would involve a breach of the Ebro treaty (or, as allowing the Roman envoys to imply this without offering a correction). Later, in Polybius' report of the Roman embassy to the Carthaginian senate after the fall of Saguntum, the Carthaginians refuse to discuss the treaty with Hasdrubal, "which they regarded either as non-existent, or as existent but irrelevant to them, since it had been entered into without their approval" and cite the Romans' actions at the end of the

---

[7] 2.13. All translations of Polybius are taken from Waterfield 2010.
[8] Polybius' language here ("this side of the Ebro") may reflect a pro-Hannibalic source (Walbank 1957, 319, Eckstein 2012, 222 n. 85), but in any case, this can only mean "south of the Ebro" given the preceding narrative.
[9] 3.15.5: Ῥωμαῖοι μὲν οὖν διεμαρτύροντο Ζακανθαίων ἀπέχεσθαι (κεῖσθαι γὰρ αὐτοὺς ἐν τῇ σφετέρᾳ πίστει) καὶ τὸν Ἴβηρα ποταμὸν μὴ διαβαίνειν κατὰ τὰς ἐπ' Ἀσδρούβου γενομένας ὁμολογίας. The text is that of Foucault 1971, but the punctuation is mine: see n. 20 below.

First Punic War as precedent for this.¹⁰ At 3.27, Polybius mentions the treaty with Hasdrubal as the last in the line of Roman-Carthaginian agreements he reviews, using the same language regarding the Ebro River as he had when introducing the treaty in Book 2. Finally, the Ebro River appears in the chapters in which Polybius adjudicates responsibility for the outbreak of the war (3.29–30). In opening, Polybius reports an argument which "one hears often" at Rome—though not an argument the Romans at the time made, he says—that the treaty with Hasdrubal could not be dismissed in the way the Carthaginians attempted (since it did not have a rider attached such as the Lutatius treaty of 241 had). Polybius goes on to discuss the merits of both sides arguments' concerning Saguntum's position in relation to the Lutatius treaty, and he appears to come down in favor of the Romans, that this treaty covered future alliances and that Rome and Saguntum had entered into such an agreement before Hannibal attacked. He concludes:

> From this it follows that [μέν] anyone who takes the cause of the war to be the destruction of Saguntum must agree that the Carthaginians were wrong to have started the war, because the treaty with Lutatius stipulated that the allies of both sides were to be immune from attack, and because the treaty with Hasdrubal stipulated that the Carthaginians were not to cross the Ebro for military purposes.¹¹

The passage continues with a very important δέ clause, which I will delay for the moment, in order to create a little suspense of my own. In the meantime, scholars have proposed a number of possibilities for these issues surrounding the Ebro in Polybius.¹²

1) The *Ibêr* River on which the treaty with Hasdrubal is based refers to a different river, running south of Saguntum, rather than the modern Ebro. This has not been widely accepted, and seems highly unlikely.¹³ We would still have Polybius writing rather carelessly (cf. 3 below) in not distinguishing this river from the Ebro, which does appear later in Book 3. And the modern Ebro makes sense,

---

10 3.21. Later in the debate, the Roman envoys state that "the violation of the treaty changed things"—but most likely this refers to the treaty of Lutatius at the end of the First Punic War.
11 3.30.3: διόπερ εἰ μέν τις τὴν Ζακάνθης ἀπώλειαν αἰτίαν τίθησι τοῦ πολέμου, συγχωρητέον ἀδίκως ἐξενηνοχέναι τὸν πόλεμον Καρχηδονίους κατά τε τὰς ἐπὶ τοῦ Λυτατίου συνθήκας, καθ' ἃς ἔδει τοῖς ἑκατέρων συμμάχοις τὴν ὑφ' ἑκατέρων ὑπάρχειν ἀσφάλειαν, κατά τε τὰς ἐπ' Ἀσδρούβου, καθ' ἃς οὐκ ἔδει διαβαίνειν τὸν Ἴβηρα ποταμὸν ἐπὶ πολέμῳ Καρχηδονίους.
12 See Hoyos 1998, 161–65 for similar discussion. For bibliography on the outbreak of the war, see Rich 1996, 1 n. 1; Schmitt 1975, no. 503, has full older bibliography.
13 See in general Rich 1996, 10–11.

physically and geopolitically, as a border chosen by both sides in 227/226, in a way that no other river in Iberia does.[14]

2) In the 1880s, Hesselbarth proposed that a phrase had dropped out of the μέν clause in 3.30.3. Most scholars are understandably reluctant to resort to this explanation with no other evidence to support it.[15]

3) Polybius was not careful or precise enough at 3.30.3 in summarizing the matter. Peter Cuff, in fact, saw this as fitting a general tendency in Polybius' non-narrative passages toward a cloudiness of language and thought. But again we have to ask whether it is likely that Polybius would have committed this sort of carelessness at this early and crucial point in his work.[16]

4) Polybius was either "momentarily" confused about the geography of Spain, due to Roman historians' manipulation of Iberian geography, or he deliberately mislocated Saguntum at these key moments. But it is difficult to see how Polybius could be confused about the relative positions of the Ebro and Saguntum at chapter 30 but not elsewhere in Book 3 on numerous occasions.[17] And given Polybius' constant criticism of those who include intentional falsehoods or geographical ignorance in their histories, it would be incredible if he began his entire main narrative with a double-whammy of this sort.

5) In a similar vein, and most commonly, scholars have argued that Polybius relied on a pro-Roman source here and did not realize the geographical problem

---

14 Derow 2015, 181–94 (a previously unpublished lecture from 1997) revives this idea in an alternate form by pointing to Polybius' language at 3.6.2, "the river whose native name is the Iber", and suggesting that Roman authors found or invented a second river (187–88). Even if accepted, this still leaves the question (as below) why Polybius left the matter obscure or neglected to draw attention to the error. On the suitability of the Ebro River as a border, see Richardson 1986, 26–27.

15 See Walbank 1957, 358.

16 Cuff 1973. Furthermore, if chapters 31 and 32 are later additions (see below, p. 211), that means he came back to this point in the text and left it the way it is. This severely weakens the claim of Badian (1958, 293) that Polybius "believed, at one time, that Saguntum lay north of the Ebro".

17 For example, five chapters later (35), when he makes Hannibal's crossing of the river in 218 (*i.e.* after the fall of Saguntum) the first action of the war; again in 3.40: the Romans discover that Hannibal has crossed the Ebro sooner than expected (thus Polybius cannot be imagining Saguntum to lie north of the river); or at 3.97, when he states that, before the naval actions of this year (218), "Never before had the Romans dared to cross the Ebro; they had been content with the friendship and alliance of the inhabitants north of the river"—but now the Scipio brothers sail south of the Ebro in order to advance toward Saguntum. Plus, in 3.17 Polybius describes the local setting of Saguntum in some detail. Can we imagine that he misplaced the city by 100 miles or so? (cf. Cuff 1973, 166).

this created. In a 2001 article, Klaus Bringmann refined this solution, and suggested that 3.30.3 reads as it does because Polybius relied on a pro-Roman source here and *neglected* to point out the geographical problem this created (rather than not realizing it).

I think Bringmann gets us close to the best explanation, but we must still ask: if Polybius realized the problem, why didn't he point it out? Given his emphasis on careful investigation throughout these opening chapters of Book 3, and his insistence throughout his work on geographical knowledge, why would he allow this error to stand? Thus, we need to draw out the full implication of Polybius' silence here for his historical method.[18]

If we take chapters 6–33 as a unit,[19] we find that Polybius has indeed left clues which indicate his *rejection* of the view he reports, not only of the Ebro's geographical position but also of its relevance for the outbreak of the war. As noted earlier, he begins chapter 6 by reporting that "some historians" give two causes of the war: Hannibal's attack on Saguntum, and his crossing of the Ebro River "in contravention of the treaty". But, Polybius continues: "In my opinion, however, the war *started* with these events, but it is quite wrong to call them the *causes* of the war …". This immediately leads him into his discussion of causes (*aitiai*) vs. beginnings (*arkhai*), and the absolute necessity of distinguishing between them if history will be useful for the reader. Thus already at the open, Polybius distances himself quite forcefully from the notion of the Ebro (or Saguntum) as a cause of the war. Later, in chapters 9 and 10, he introduces *his* three causes of the war: the anger of Hamilcar, the Roman seizure of Sardinia and imposition of an extra indemnity in 238, and Carthaginian success in Iberia.

In the mentions of the Ebro River which follow, Polybius continues to distance himself from the Roman view. Concerning the scene of the Roman embassy to New Carthage at 3.15, Polybius as narrator has just stated, a few lines earlier (3.14.9), that Saguntum lay on Hannibal's side of the Ebro. Thus, when at 3.15.5 he reports the message of the Roman envoys in indirect discourse, there is no need to read this as Polybius vouching for the notion that an attack on Saguntum involved a breach of the Ebro treaty.[20] In 3.20, as he dismisses the notion that the

---

[18] Dexter Hoyos in 1998 briefly hinted at the answer: "Clarity suffers, deliberately perhaps" (166).
[19] Pédech 1964, 179–180 notes the unity of these chapters; cf. Hess 2013.
[20] Polybius' Greek can easily be read as reporting the two warnings which the Romans wished to convey (note that Foucault's punctuation is misleading: the γάρ indicates a parenthetical clause, not the beginning of a second element—that begins only with καί). Scholars have debated the wisdom and likelihood of the Romans reminding Hannibal of his treaty obligations with respect to the Ebro, but one can imagine a situation in which the Romans felt it necessary to do so.

Romans debated war when they heard of Saguntum's fall, again he does not bring up the Ebro: he mentions only that they had warned Hannibal not to set foot in Saguntine territory. Even in reporting the exchange between the Roman envoys and the Carthaginian senate (3.21), the Ebro does not come up directly. The Carthaginians refuse to discuss the treaty with Hasdrubal, on the grounds that they did not approve of it; and they argue that the treaty after the Sicilian war ignored Iberia, nor was Saguntum a Roman ally at that time. The Romans, too, refer to "the treaty" being broken, but this is most easily taken as a reference to the treaties in the aftermath of the First Punic War.[21] In 3.27, when Polybius mentions the final treaty between Rome and Carthage (the one with Hasdrubal), the only clause he reports is about crossing the Ebro, and he does not bring up Saguntum.

In the key passage beginning at 3.29, Polybius continues to make more or less explicit distinctions between the Ebro and Saguntum. He introduces the arguments as those often heard from the Romans of his time—it was not necessarily the Roman response in 218, he says, because they were too angry about Saguntum. The Romans say the Carthaginians could not dismiss *the treaty with Hasdrubal* because it did not have a rider requiring confirmation by the government (as Lutatius' treaty in 241 did have); and one of the clauses in this treaty was that the Carthaginians would not cross the Ebro. Then, Polybius continues, the Romans also argue against the Carthaginian interpretation of the mention of allies in *the Sicilian treaty* (i.e. the Lutatius treaty of 241), and here Polybius states that this interpretation is the most plausible. The Saguntines had become Roman allies before Hannibal's time, as the Carthaginians themselves (implicitly) acknowledged by referring to Roman arbitration in the city's internal disputes (cf. 3.15). Then, 3.30.3, the culmination of Polybius' attitude toward the Ebro: *anyone who sees the cause of the war as the destruction of Saguntum* must place the blame on the Carthaginians, since the Sicilian treaty made each side's allies immune from attacks by the other, and since the Hasdrubal treaty made the Ebro a line not to be crossed. But—and here is the all-important δέ clause I left hanging earlier—*anyone who sees the seizure of Sardinia and the extra indemnity as the cause of the war* must admit that the Carthaginians were justified in fighting back. Who sees Sardinia and the extra indemnity as the cause of the war? Polybius does, as he told us in 3.10. Logically, then, at 3.30.3, Polybius does *not* see Saguntum and the Ebro as causes of the war. This also closes the circle of Polybius' argument, since back in 3.6, it was with exactly those two supposed but erroneous "causes" that

---

21 Though Walbank (1957, 336) finds it remaining perfectly ambiguous.

Polybius began his discussion.[22] In the meantime, nowhere has he himself used the crossing of the Ebro as a justification for Rome's declaration of war.[23]

But we are still justified in asking why, if Polybius knew the relative locations of the Ebro and Saguntum, he did not simply say that the attempt to link the two was wrong.[24] I would draw attention to the following two chapters (3.31–32), in which Polybius digresses in order to defend the need for him "to go into these matters with such precision and at such length". The second of these chapters, with its reference to "40 books", must have been added at a later date, after his revision of the overall plan for the work, and indeed it seems to respond to complaints about the length of the *Histories*. But at the end of this chapter, Polybius re-states in summary form his view of the causes of Rome's wars, among which "the war with Hannibal ... in turn arose out of the war with Sicily" (3.32.7)—the same view he held when he first wrote Book 3. Could this later addition reflect criticism, not just of his historical method or the length of the work, but of his discussion of the subject itself? Was his account of the outbreak of the war with Hannibal seen as being too favorable to Carthage, or not pro-Roman enough? I would suggest that in answering the question about why Polybius does not point out the error surrounding Saguntum's location, we must keep in mind how comfortable he might have felt openly challenging the dominant Roman narrative of the outbreak of the war. John Thornton has recently proposed a reading of the *Histories* as a "diplomatic speech" in order to "take into account the constraints imposed on its author by the real power relations" between Rome and Greece in the mid-second century.[25] Polybius was not necessarily as interested in speaking on behalf of the Carthaginians as he was for his fellow Greeks, but as a member of a subordinate group in relation to Rome, he may very well have felt that there were limits on the type of narrative he could publicize regarding the dominant group's past. In other words, did Polybius *have* the option of simply saying, "The Ebro lies north of Saguntum, therefore Romans who link the two are wrong

---

22 Eckstein 1989, 5, Hess 2013, 20.
23 Walbank 1957, 323, on 3.15.10: "here and in 30.3–4 P[olybius] writes as if it [the cession of Sardinia] were the only cause" of the war. See also Rich 1996, 8–9.
24 Cf. Halfmann 2013, 55–56, on 2.13: Polybius' specification is meant to reject the (unstated here) position of Fabius Pictor that the Ebro treaty included Saguntum. Indeed, the opening section of Book 3 is filled with censure of those unconcerned with accuracy or facts (note here also 3.33 and Polybius' claim to have read Hannibal's inscription on Cape Lacinium, which immediately follows the narrative unit dealing with the causes and outbreak of the war).
25 Thornton 2013, 214 (my thanks to Brian McGing for this reference); see also Hess 2013, 21, on the "complex ... manner in which Polybius builds his argument", wherein blame for the war falls on Rome, though Polybius never says so explicitly.

and/or lying"? If not, his treatment of the Ebro may represent an attempt at subtle correction of an erroneous tradition.

2 Livy and Polybius

As I noted at the opening of the paper, the relationship between Livy Book 21 and Polybius Book 3 has received a great deal of attention from scholars over the years—though, for many of those years, the prevailing opinion was that Livy had not consulted Polybius directly for the outbreak and early years of the Second Punic War. That is no longer the case, and scholars have begun to pay closer attention to the similarities and divergences in the two accounts on the assumption that Livy knew Polybius' text. Hannibal's crossing of the Alps, and the events surrounding the battle at the Trebia, have been the major beneficiaries of this attention. But, as I hope to show here, if we take the unit of Polybius we have just been considering (3.6–33) and compare it with the corresponding portion of Livy (21.1–19),[26] we find some intriguing structural features which help illustrate how each historian created the narrative of his choosing, by arranging and selecting from the same fundamental set of components. My concern here is not to gauge which chapters of Livy "come from" Polybius, but to illuminate the two authors' historical methods.

Table 1: Comparison of Polybius 3.6–33 and Livy 21.1.–19

Polybius Book 3	Livy Book 21
Plb. chs. 6–12 Beginning of the war (Ebro, Saguntum) not the same as causes Causes include anger of Hamilcar Barca *Story of Hannibal's oath at the altar (A)*	Livy chs. 1–2 Preface to "most memorable war in history" flows into *Hannibal's oath at the altar (A)* Anger of Hamilcar Barca Hasdrubal signs treaty with Rome (Ebro, Saguntum)
Plb. 13.1–4 After Hasdrubal's death, Hannibal elected by army, approved unanimously at Carthage	Livy ch. 3 After Hasdrubal's death, Hannibal elected by army, approved by popular vote at Carthage (despite previous opposition from some nobility including Hanno - speech)

---

26 Good analysis of this unit can be found in Burck 1950, 57–64 and Pausch 2011, 202–05.

Polybius Book 3	Livy Book 21
	Livy ch. 4 *Character sketch of Hannibal (B)*
Plb. 13.5–14.3 (*War in Spain, C*) Hannibal's first action is to invade Olcades; success Winters at New Carthage, rewards soldiers Next summer, Hannibal invades Vaccaei; takes Helmantica easily, Arboucalê after fierce resistance	Livy 5.1–8 (*War in Spain, C*) Hannibal attacks Iberian tribes in order to isolate Saguntum (with eye already on Rome); his first action is to invade Olcades; success Winters at New Carthage, rewards soldiers Next summer, Hannibal invades Vaccaei; takes Helmandica easily, Arbocala after fierce resistance
Plb. 14.4–10 Forced to fight at *Tagus River (D)* by Carpetani All Iberia south of Ebro in his power except Saguntum	Livy 5.9–17 Forced to fight at *Tagus River (D)* by Carpetani All Iberia south of Ebro in his power except Saguntum
Plb. ch. 15 Saguntines send to Rome for help *Roman embassy to Spain, rebuffed by Hannibal on specious pretexts, sails on to Carthage (E)* *Comments on Hannibal's irrational anger (B)*	Livy ch. 6 Saguntines send to Rome for help Romans vote embassy to Spain, but then hear that siege of Saguntum has begun; embassy voted again, with instructions to proceed to Carthage afterward
Plb. ch. 16 Roman action in Illyria	
Plb. ch. 17 Hannibal besieges Saguntum and captures it after eight months *(F)*	Livy chs. 7–9 Hannibal begins siege of Saguntum *(F)* Hannibal refuses to meet Roman envoys *(E)*
	Livy 10.1–11.2 *Roman envoys at Carthage (G?) hear Hanno's speech in favor of surrendering Hannibal to Romans and ending siege of Saguntum*
Plb. chs. 18–19 Roman action in Illyria	
	Livy 11.1–15.2 *Dramatic end to siege of Saguntum (F)*

Polybius Book 3	Livy Book 21
	Livy 15.3–6 *Confusion over date of siege (F)*
Plb. ch. 20 *Reaction at Rome to news of Saguntum (H)* Comments on bad historians inventing speeches Roman envoys sent to Carthage (G?), instructed to demand surrender of Hannibal	Livy ch. 16 *Reaction at Rome to news of Saguntum (H)*
	Livy ch. 17 Details of troop levies and consular armies
Plb. 21.1–8 *Arguments of Carthaginian senate and Roman envoys (J)*	Livy ch. 18 *Arguments of Carthaginian senate (speech) (J)* *Fabius' toga-fold offer, declaration of war (K)*
Plb. 21.8–27.10 Examination of Roman-Carthaginian treaties	
Plb. chs. 28–30 *Assessment of blame for war (L)*	Livy 19.1–5 *Comments on the merits of each side's arguments (L)*
Plb. chs. 31–32 Digression on the importance of history, rebuttal of complaints about the length of his work	
Plb. 33.1–4 *Senior Roman envoy's toga-fold offer, declaration of war (K)*	

In Table 1, I have assigned a letter (A–L) to each of the parallel components appearing in both historians' accounts. This highlights some of the major differences in arrangement. But a glance down the columns shows that there are many more basic items, forming the backbone of the narrative, which Livy shares with Polybius. In fact, the only units missing in Livy are the Roman actions in Illyria (Plb. 16, 18–19) and Polybius' methodological discussions: the nature of causes, bad historians inventing speeches, the examination of the Roman-Carthaginian treaties, and the importance of reading in-depth history. Livy, for his part, in terms of narrative components, has only added the character sketch of Hannibal (but more on this below), the discussion on the chronology of the siege of Saguntum, and the details of Roman troop levies, as well as several direct speeches.[27] The differences between the two accounts are often emphasized: Livy's immediate focus on Hannibal and his virtues and vices, the dramatic and drawn-out siege of Saguntum, the speeches in the Carthaginian senate; and on Polybius' side, his recurring insistence on proper methodology. But that emphasis masks the fundamental similarity in content with regard to the building blocks of the narrative: Hannibal's oath (A), his first campaign in Spain (C/D), the siege of Saguntum (F), reaction at Rome to news of the city's fall (H), arguments between the Carthaginian senate and Roman envoys (J), and the historian's assessment of responsibility for the war (L).

The similarity in content makes the differences in each historian's structural choices all the more interesting. I will not go through each narrative unit in detail here, but will focus on areas where divergence in placement, presentation, or emphasis reveals something important about the two authors' approaches to writing history.[28]

A: Hannibal's oath.[29] For Livy, clearly, placing the story in the first chapter serves to highlight the hatred of the two opposing sides, which he has just listed in the preface as one of the factors in this war being "the most momentous war ever fought".[30] The story also introduces the indisputable major figure of the entire Third Decade.[31] For Polybius, the famous scene of the young Hannibal taking

---

27 Cf. Pausch 2011, 204, who emphasizes Livy's creation of suspense by announcing the war in chapter 1 but only reaching its declaration in 19. Some information similar to Livy 21.17 appears in Polybius 3.40, but not in nearly as much detail. Polybius, of course, has his own detailed troop list—for Hannibal, based on documentary evidence (3.33).

28 Hoyos 2006, 417–21, uses a similar approach to analyze the two authors' treatments of events around the Rhone (Livy 21.26–32, Plb. 3.41–50) and Hannibal's victory at the Tagus (see below, n. 33).

29 See Cipriani 1984, 15–32 for analysis. There are slight differences in the presentation, but note the interesting common detail of Hannibal's "boyish insistence" (Plb. 3.11.7: καί τι καὶ προσαξιώσαντος παιδικῶς; Livy 21.1.4: *pueriliter blandientem*). Girod 1976, 123–28, shows how Livy draws on Polybius for the scene but also adjusts it to his own purposes (cf. Livy 35.19).

30 All translations of Livy are taken from Yardley 2006.

31 Luce 2009 (orig. 1971), 155 n. 13, notes the technique here—and the difference with Polybius—in his discussion of Camillus in Book 5: "The use of a prefatory anecdote, chiefly to foreshadow and to characterize". Cf. Moore 2010, 154–55, who notes how the oath story and Hannibal's dream (21.22.6–9) are both introduced with *fama est*, which he sees as Livy "framing his account

the oath at the altar is perhaps unavoidable, but he maneuvers it to serve his purpose—which is to explain the true causes of the war (none of which involve Hannibal!)—by embedding the story within a larger discussion of causes (3.6–12). Moreover, rather than insisting on Hannibal's character, Polybius draws a more general lesson from the anecdote: that statesmen must pay attention to the psychological state of their former enemies (3.12.5). In fact, in the end he uses the story to clinch his argument about *Hamilcar's* anger (one of his causes for the war), not Hannibal's. This emphasis on Hamilcar is enhanced not only by Polybius' explicit statements to this effect as he introduces and concludes the story (3.10.7, 12.2–3), but by his choice to focalize the tale through the court of Antiochus III, at the end of Hannibal's life rather than as the initial element in a biographical sketch of Hannibal.

B: Hannibal's character. The next component provides a starker difference between the two authors. Polybius does not give the sort of character sketch which Livy (21.4) famously provides upon Hannibal being chosen to command the army in Spain. But Polybius does pause to examine Hannibal's mind and soul at a later point in his narrative, when the first Roman embassy arrives at New Carthage in the winter of 220/219 and demands that he stay away from Saguntum. Here, Polybius criticizes Hannibal for being "wholly gripped by irrational and uncontrollable anger" (3.15.9). While this is presumably a negative character trait, Polybius emphasizes its impact on Hannibal's ability to recognize causes versus pretexts—which the historian himself has just done with impeccable precision. In this case, then, even though Livy has not adopted his character sketch directly from Polybius, we can see each author choosing where to place their comments on a similar narrative component—Hannibal's psyche—and these choices match the overall emphasis of their treatment.[32]

Table 2: Comparison of Polybius and Livy on Hannibal's first Spanish campaign

Polybius 3.13–14 (Waterfield 2010)	Livy 21.5 (Yardley 2006)
	[From day 1, Hannibal sought war with Rome, and decided to attack Saguntum]

---

of the events leading up to the war ... with reminders that much of what he reports is the product of a tradition of doubtful authority".

32 See Levene 2010, 99–104, Will 1983, 158–60.

Polybius 3.13–14 (Waterfield 2010)	Livy 21.5 (Yardley 2006)
The first thing Hannibal did after assuming command was set out to subdue the Olcades.	… he first led his army into the territory of the Olcades … [south of the Ebro, a pretext for getting drawn into conflict with Saguntum]
He invested Althaea, their principal city, which soon fell to the rapid series of terrifying assaults he launched against it.	Hannibal took by storm and pillaged the rich city of Cartala, the tribal capital,
At this, the rest of the Olcades surrendered in fear to the Carthaginians.	and the fear this inspired drove the smaller communities to capitulate and accept the imposition of an indemnity.
He levied money from the towns and cities, captured a great many valuables, and then went to winter at New Carthage.	The triumphant army, rich with booty, was led back to winter in New Carthage.
He was generous with the men under his command, and he paid their wages and promised more later, which went down very well with them and left them raring to go.	There, by generously dividing up the booty and scrupulously discharging any arrears in pay, Hannibal consolidated the loyalty of all, citizens and allies alike,
(14) The following summer, Hannibal set out again, this time against the Vaccaei.	and in the early spring he marched on the Vaccaei.
Helmandica fell straight away to his assault, but he had to besiege Arboucale and take it by storm, which proved to be no easy task: it was a large and populous city, and the inhabitants resisted bravely.	Hermandica and Arbocala, cities of the Vaccaei, were taken by storm, but there was prolonged resistance from Arbocala, thanks to the townspeople's courage and their large population.
Later, on his way back, he suddenly found himself in extreme danger, when the Carpetani, virtually the strongest tribe in the region, massed against him, and were joined by the neighboring tribes. Their hostility had been kindled above all by the Olcadian refugees, and then the survivors from Helmandica had added more fuel to the fire.	The refugees from Hermandica then joined forces with exiles of the Olcades, the tribe that had been crushed the previous summer. They roused the Carpetani to action and, not far from the River Tagus, launched an attack on Hannibal…
… After this defeat, all the Iberians south of the Ebro, except for the Saguntines, were too	… And now everything south of the Ebro was under Carthaginian control – except Saguntum.

Polybius 3.13–14 (Waterfield 2010)	Livy 21.5 (Yardley 2006)
cowed to resist Hannibal with any effectiveness.	

C and D: Hannibal's first campaign in Spain. These two components reveal how closely Livy and Polybius can match at a detailed level (Table 2). This applies not only to the events and their sequence, but the characters' motivation for action: in both authors' accounts, Hannibal lavishes his troops with booty in order to consolidate their willingness to follow him, and the Carpetani are stoked to resistance by refugees from places previously attacked by Hannibal. The subsequent battle at the Tagus River (Plb. 3.14.4–8; Livy 21.5.9–16) has been studied closely over the years as part of the debate over each author's sources. There are extra elements in Livy, but we find basically the same details in terms of troop and elephant numbers, tactics, and outcome.[33] Of course a hypothetical, lost common source can never be ruled out completely; but given the close similarities throughout this narrative unit, it seems rather perverse to claim that Livy was not reading Polybius. At the same time, Livy adds a subtle framing device by mentioning Saguntum twice at the beginning in order to mirror its appearance at the end.

Moving forward[34] to component F, the siege of Saguntum, the different level of detail is generally typical of each historian's work. Polybius' account is very brief, contained within one chapter—in fact, the action of the siege itself is barely narrated, just seven lines of Greek (3.17.8–9), and the rest of the chapter concerns the geography of Saguntum, Hannibal's reasoning for his attack, and the end result. Furthermore, the events at Saguntum are surrounded by Polybius' narrative of Roman actions in Illyria. This sequence fits Polybius' concern for chronology as well as the buildup toward the interweaving of Mediterranean affairs.[35] Livy, on the other hand, plays up the siege to its full dramatic potential. But the attention devoted to the siege also matches each historian's outlook on the causes of the war. Livy, adopting the view of the Roman tradition, saw Hannibal's attack

---

33 See Witte 1910, 415–17 for analysis; Walbank 1957, 318–19, Hoyos 2006, 420.
34 On my component (E), the Roman embassy to Hannibal, see Walbank 1957, 319–24. Livy seems to have misunderstood or been misled by one of his sources concerning the timing of the embassy.
35 See Miltsios 2013, 58–64, on the importance of synchronicity for Polybius' work; at 65–68 he discusses how these chapters in Polybius (3.15–17) highlight the Roman error in looking to the east first in 219.

on Saguntum (supposedly a Roman ally) as the key moment.[36] Polybius, having emphasized that the causes of the war lay farther back in time, has no reason to spend more time on this siege than on any other.[37]

H: Reaction at Rome to the news that Saguntum had fallen. Polybius (3.20) attacks earlier historians who claimed that the Senate assembled in order to debate going to war, and who invented "gloomy" speeches attended by the children of the senators (who then kept quiet about the result). Perhaps Livy slyly alludes to Polybius' criticism when he says, "Various emotions gripped the senators at the same moment"—sorrow, pity, fear, anger—and continues, "So many emotions arising together threw them off balance, making them dither rather than deliberate" (21.16.2). Livy foregoes the speeches themselves, but still paints a gloomy picture, going on to describe just how difficult Rome's situation was, and ending the chapter with the image of Rome having "to fight the whole world, and [to] do so in Italy and before their city walls". However, he then moves directly into the consular arrangements and troop levies for 218 and notes that the Roman people approved war with Carthage (21.17). In the end, Livy has his cake and eats it too: Rome takes decisive action, as Polybius would have it, but not before a bit of emotion-wrought hand-wringing and dramatic buildup.[38]

Finally, J and K: The Roman declaration of war. Polybius goes out of his way to create his own suspense by postponing the culmination of the Roman embassy to Carthage, the scene of the toga-fold offer. The embassy is described in 3.20–21, including the Roman refusal to talk about anything other than their ultimatum that Hannibal be handed over. Polybius then embarks on his investigation of the Roman-Carthaginian treaties, assesses each side's responsibility for the war, digresses on the importance of history, and rebuts complaints about the length of his work—before finally, a full twelve chapters later, returning to the scene in the Carthaginian senate-house: "the Roman envoys listened to the speeches in silence. Then ..." (3.33.1). One may perhaps argue that Polybius, the plodding and pedantic historian, cannot help interrupting his own narrative to address the

---

[36] It is immediately followed (21.16) by his depiction of the reaction of the Romans, who now see themselves at war (and Hannibal is already crossing the Alps). Cf. however Pausch 2011, 144–48, on how Livy's focalization of two key events before the war (Eryx, 244–241 and Sardinia, 238) impresses upon the reader "ein Bewusstsein für die Relativität historischer Urteile im allgemeinen" (148).

[37] Hoffmann 1942, 24–25, Walbank 1957, 329. Pausch 2011, 203 n. 72, notes the drastically different attention given to the siege by each author (see also Pausch 2014, 295–96).

[38] Cf. Levene 2010, 81, on how Livy "communicates particular interpretations of the war" via juxtaposition.

technical political details. But is not this deliberate deferral of the climax an attempt at an artful narrative maneuver? Livy's attempt within his chapter 18 may be more obviously artful: a finely crafted and passionate direct speech by the Carthaginians, followed by an exchange of shouts and a declaration of war. But when Polybius could just as easily have placed this scene in his chapter 21, *before* his digression, I think we must give him credit for producing drama within the constraints for historical writing he had set himself.[39]

Bibliography

Badian, E. (1958), *Foreign Clientelae*, Oxford.
Bringmann, K. (2001), "Der Ebrovertrag, Sagunt und der Weg in den Zweiten Punischen Krieg", in: *Klio* 83.2, 369–376.
Briscoe, J. (1978), "Livy and Polybius" (review of Tränkle 1977), in: *CR* 28.2, 267–269.
Burck, E. (1950), *Einführung in die dritte Dekade des Livius*, Heidelberg.
Champion, C.B. (2004), *Cultural Politics in Polybius's Histories*, Berkeley/London.
Cipriani, G. (1984), *L'epifania di Annibale: Saggio introduttivo a Livio*, Annales XXI, Bari.
Cuff, P.J. (1973), "Polybius, III, 30, 3: A Note", in: *RSA* 3, 163–170.
Derow, P. (2015), *Rome, Polybius and the East*, Oxford.
Eckstein, A.M. (1989), "Hannibal at New Carthage. Polybius 3.15 and the Power of Irrationality", in: *CPh* 84.1, 1–15.
—— (2012), "Polybius, the Gallic Crisis, and the Ebro Treaty", in: *CPh* 107.3, 206–229.
Girod, R. (1976), "Les origines de la deuxième guerre punique chez Polybe (III, 1–12) et Tite-Live (XXI, 1–5)", in: *Aiôn: le temps chez les Romains*, 119–135.
Halfmann, H. (2013), "Livius und Polybios," in: V. Grieb/C. Koehn (eds.), *Polybios und seine Historien*, Stuttgart, 49–57.
Hess, L. (2013), "Functions of Polemic in the Composition of Polybius, Books I–V", in: *Palamedes* 8, 1–26.
Hoffmann, W. (1942), *Livius und der zweite Punische Krieg* (Hermes Einzelschriften 8), Berlin.
Hoyos, B.D. (1998), *Unplanned Wars: The Origins of the First and Second Punic Wars*, Berlin/New York.
—— (2006), "Crossing the Durance with Hannibal and Livy: the Route to the Pass", in: *Klio* 88.2, 408–465.
Foucault, J. de (ed.) (1971), *Polybe: Histoires Livre III*, Paris.
Levene, D.S. (2010), *Livy on the Hannibalic War*, Oxford/New York.
Luce, T.J. (2009) (1971), "Design and Structure in Livy: 5.32–55", in: J.D. Chaplin/C.S. Kraus (eds.), *Livy: Oxford Readings in Classical Studies*, Oxford, 148–187.
—— (1977), *Livy: The Composition of his History*, Princeton.
McGing, B.C. (2010), *Polybius' Histories*, New York.
Miltsios, N. (2013), *The Shaping of Narrative in Polybius*, Berlin/Boston.

---

[39] Pédech 1964, 180 n. 405, notes the "great relief" produced by 3.33.1 after the suspense of the previous chapters.

Moore, T.J. (2010), "Livy's Hannibal and the Roman Tradition", in: W. Polleichtner (ed.), *Livy and Intertextuality. Papers of a Conference Held at the University of Texas at Austin, October 3, 2009*, Trier, 135–167.
Pausch, D. (2011), *Livius und der Leser: narrative Strukturen in Ab Urbe Condita*, Munich.
— — (2014), "Livy Reading Polybius: Adapting Greek Narrative", in: D. Cairns/R. Scodel (eds.), *Defining Greek Narrative*, Edinburgh, 279–297.
Pédech, P. (1964), *La méthode historique de Polybe*, Paris.
Rich, J. (1996), "The Second Punic War: A Reappraisal", in: T. Cornell/B. Rankov/P. Sabin (eds.), *The Origins of the Second Punic War*, London, 1–37.
Richardson, J.S. (1986), *Hispaniae: Spain and the development of Roman Imperialism, 218–82 BC*, Cambridge.
Schmitt, H. (ed.) (1975), *Die Staatsverträge des Altertums*, Vol. 3, Munich.
Thornton, J. (2013), "Polybius in Context: The Political Dimension of the *Histories*", in: T. Harrison/B. Gibson (eds.), *Polybius and his World. Essays in Memory of F.W. Walbank*, Oxford, 213–229.
Tränkle, H. (1977), *Livius und Polybios*, Basel.
Walbank, F.W. (1957), *A Historical Commentary on Polybius*, Vol. 1, Oxford.
Waterfield, R. (transl.) (2010), *Polybius: The Histories*, Oxford.
Will, W. (1983), "Mirabilior adversis quam secundis rebus: Zum Bild Hannibals in der 3. Dekade des Livius", in: *WJA* 9, 157–171.
Witte, K. (1910), "Über die Form der Darstellung in Livius Geschichtswerk", in: *RhM* 65, 270–305 & 359–419.
Yardley, J.C. (transl.) (2006), *Livy: Hannibal's War, Books 21–30*, Oxford.

Part III: Intertextual Relationships

Maria Seretaki and Melina Tamiolaki
Polybius and Xenophon: Hannibal and Cyrus the Great as Model Leaders

Polybius' relationship with his predecessors has not been fully explored.[1] Although it has been more customary to compare Polybius with Thucydides, especially regarding their common methodological principles and narrative techniques, current scholarship underlines Polybius' close(r) engagement with fourth-century historiography.[2] This study follows this recent trend: it aims at formulating a working hypothesis and at prompting further reflection on the relationship between Polybius and the Athenian historian of the fourth century BCE, Xenophon. This comparison has not attracted much scholarly attention. Brian McGing notes some parallels between the presentation of Scipio in Polybius and that of Agesilaus in Xenophon and observes: "it is hard to imagine that Xenophon did not provide some sort of model for Polybius to follow when writing himself into the story of Rome ... Perhaps there are more parallels than has been generally thought".[3] Bruce Gibson has also convincingly analyzed the episode of the Mercenary War in the first book of Polybius' *Histories* in the light of Xenophon's *Anabasis*,[4] while F. Walbank has spotted some indirect allusions to the *Hellenika* and the *Anabasis* in Polybius' work.[5] This paper will focus on the third book of Polybius' *Histories* and will propose a comparison with Xenophon's *Cyropaedia*. It will suggest that Polybius' presentation of Hannibal could have been inspired by Xenophon's portrayal of Cyrus the Great.

---

[1] McGing 2010, 52–66 sketches out his debt to the classical historians (Herodotus, Thucydides, Xenophon, and Ephorus).
[2] In fact, Polybius mentions Thucydides only once, when he refers to the authors who wrote Greek history *after Thucydides* (Plb. 8.11.3): Καὶ μὴν οὐδὲ περὶ τὰς ὁλοσχερεῖς διαλήψεις οὐδεὶς ἂν εὐδοκήσειε τῷ προειρημένῳ συγγραφεῖ· ὅς γ' ἐπιβαλόμενος γράφειν τὰς Ἑλληνικὰς πράξεις ἀφ' ὧν Θουκυδίδης ἀπέλιπε ... For the relationship of Polybius with Thucydides, see Rood 2012 and Miltsios 2013b, on the relationship between Thucydides Book 1 and Polybius' narrative of *prokataskeue* (Book 1). Cf., however, Parmegianni and Scardino (this volume) who stress Polybius' (greater) dependence on fourth-century historiography, the latter denying Thucydides' influence altogether.
[3] McGing 2010, 61.
[4] Gibson 2013.
[5] Walbank 1957 *ad* Plb. 2.37.4 and 4.26.2. Cf. also Gibson 2013, 164, who views the phrase μετὰ ταῦτα and the word ταραχῆς in Plb. 3.14.12–13 as indirect allusions to Xenophon's *Hellenika*.

https://doi.org/10.1515/9783110584844-012

Before proceeding to our analysis, two methodological questions should be addressed: first, to what extent can we assume Polybius' knowledge of Xenophon? Second, since Xenophon presents several efficient leaders in his works, why are we singling out Cyrus the Great? In order to answer the first question, it is necessary to examine Polybius' references to Xenophon. Polybius mentions the Athenian historian three times. The first occurrence is found in an intriguing passage of the third book: Polybius hints here at Xenophon's *Anabasis*, by interpreting the successful return of Greek mercenaries to Greece through the hostile Persian Empire as the initial cause of the war between Greeks and Persians:

> The first (*i.e.* initial cause) was the retreat of the Greeks *under Xenophon* (ἡ τῶν μετὰ Ξενοφῶντος) from the upper satrapies, in which, though they traversed the whole of Asia, a hostile country, none of the barbarians ventured to face them.[6]

Bruce Gibson remarks that Polybius refers here to Xenophon, although Xenophon himself refrains from revealing that he is the author of the *Anabasis* and uses the pseudonym Themistogenes (Xen. *Hell*. 3.1).[7] It could be further assumed that the expression "under Xenophon" testifies specifically to an established reception of Xenophon's *Anabasis* during the Hellenistic period.

In the sixth book of his *Histories* Polybius mentions Xenophon again, together with other authors of the fourth century BCE (such as Ephorus, Plato, and Callisthenes) who wrote about the Cretan constitution:

> To pass to the constitution of Crete, two points here demand our attention. How was it that *the most learned of the ancient writers*—Ephorus, Xenophon, Callisthenes, and Plato— (πῶς οἱ λογιώτατοι τῶν ἀρχαίων συγγραφέων, Ἔφορος, Ξενοφῶν, Καλλισθένης, Πλάτων) state in the first place that it is one and the same with that of Lacedaemon and in the second place pronounce it worthy of commendation?[8]

---

6 Plb. 3.6.10. Translations of Polybius in this paper are from the Loeb edition (Paton 2001). All emphases in italics are ours. This passage forms part of a wider argument of causation regarding the Second Punic War and the war between Greeks and Persians more generally, from the expedition of the Greek Mercenaries until Alexander the Great. The expedition of the so-called Ten Thousand is perceived as a successful operation against the Persians already in the fourth century BCE. Cf. Isocr. *Paneg*. 145–149, *Phil*. 90. See Walbank 1957 *ad loc*.
7 Cf. Gibson 2013, 163.
8 Plb. 6.45.1.

Leaving aside the problematic character of this reference,⁹ the fact that Polybius lists Xenophon among the λογιώτατοι ("most erudite", "most learned") of the ancient authors betrays an appreciation of his predecessor.

Finally, in the tenth book of his *Histories*, Polybius cites a famous phrase from Xenophon's *Hellenika* and *Agesilaus* when he describes Scipio's ardent preparations for war:

> So with the infantry exercising and drilling on the ground outside the town, with the fleet at sea practicing manoeuvres and rowing, and with the men in the town sharpening weapons, forging brass or carpentering, in a word, with everyone busily engaged upon the preparation of weapons, *no one could have helped when he saw that town saying, in the words of Xenophon, that it was "a workshop of war"* (οὐκ ἔσθ' ὃς οὐκ ἂν εἶπε κατὰ τὸν Ξενοφῶντα τότε θεασάμενος ἐκείνην τὴν πόλιν ἐργαστήριον εἶναι πολέμου).¹⁰

Besides these references, which could testify to Polybius' (direct or indirect) awareness of Xenophon's works, the two authors also have several biographical features in common: their separation from their motherland, their educational standards, their interest in riding and hunting, their high political and social position in the new land in which they lived (Rome and Scillous respectively), their personal participation in military activities, and their friendship with great political men of their time (such as Scipio, Agesilaus, and Cyrus the Younger).¹¹ Consequently, it is not improbable that Polybius might have felt a kind of affinity with the Athenian historian.

Concerning the second methodological issue, our focus on the *Cyropaedia*: the *Cyropaedia* is the first extensive biographical treatment of a leader. According to Arnaldo Momigliano, it paved the way for the emergence of the genre of biography, having exerted a considerable influence both in Antiquity and in modern

---

9 Xenophon had not dealt with the Cretan constitution in his works, so Polybius wrongly cites him among the authors who have praised the Cretan constitution. For the various problems raised by this passage and the proposed solutions, see Walbank 1957 *ad loc.*
10 Plb. 10.20.7. Cf. Xen. *Hell.* 3.4.17–18 (ἀξίαν δὲ καὶ ὅλην τὴν πόλιν ἐν ᾗ ἦν [τὴν Ἔφεσον] θέας ἐποίησεν· ἥ τε γὰρ ἀγορὰ ἦν μεστὴ παντοδαπῶν καὶ ἵππων καὶ ὅπλων ὠνίων, οἵ τε χαλκοτύποι καὶ οἱ τέκτονες καὶ οἱ χαλκεῖς καὶ οἱ σκυτοτόμοι καὶ οἱ ζωγράφοι πάντες πολεμικὰ ὅπλα κατεσκεύαζον, ὥστε τὴν πόλιν ὄντως οἴεσθαι πολέμου ἐργαστήριον εἶναι) and Xen. *Ages.*1.26 (ἀξίαν δὲ καὶ ὅλην τὴν πόλιν ἐν ᾗ ἦν θέας ἐποίησεν. ἥ τε γὰρ ἀγορὰ μεστὴ ἦν παντοδαπῶν καὶ ὅπλων καὶ ἵππων ὠνίων, οἵ τε χαλκοτύποι καὶ οἱ τέκτονες καὶ οἱ σιδηρεῖς καὶ σκυτεῖς καὶ γραφεῖς πάντες πολεμικὰ ὅπλα κατεσκεύαζον·ὥστε τὴν πόλιν ὄντως ἂν ἡγήσω πολέμου ἐργαστήριον εἶναι).
11 For the life of Polybius, see Walbank 1972, 1–31. For the life of Xenophon, see Délébecque 1957 and Anderson 1974.

times.¹² Interestingly, the third book of Polybius' *Histories* revolves around the personality and military qualities of a famous leader, Hannibal, Rome's great enemy;¹³ it thus evokes in many ways the biographical track, which Xenophon followed concerning Cyrus the Great. Of course, Xenophon praises several leaders in his works (Agesilaus, Cyrus the Younger, Epaminondas, Jason of Pherae, etc.). However, Cyrus the Great, like Hannibal, was not Greek. From this perspective, he could have served as a more convenient paradigm for Polybius. Moreover, given that Polybius had a growing interest in the rise and fall of empires, it is very probable that he was fascinated by Cyrus' successes and domination of the vast Persian empire. Finally, and perhaps more tellingly, the legendary nature of Cyrus' leadership[14] could be another factor that would justify Polybius' modeling of his hero on the famous Persian king.

In what follows we will highlight some parallels (linguistic and thematic) between the narratives of the two authors with regards to the presentation of their model leaders (Hannibal and Cyrus the Great respectively). We will dwell on the following topics: family bonds, strategic qualities, and the leaders' character. In our opinion, the accumulation of these parallels allows us to make a case for a possible influence of Xenophon on Polybius.

1 Family bonds

Polybius seems to be motivated by a biographical interest when he relates Hannibal's close bond with his father, Hamilcar. In a vivid narrative in the third book of his *Histories*, he describes how Hamilcar inspired Hannibal with hatred against the Romans. Similarly, in the first book of the *Cyropaedia*, Xenophon narrates the encounter between the Persian King Cambyses and his young son, Cyrus (Xen. *Cyr.* 1.6.1–44). The two scenes share several common motifs. In both episodes paternal advice is linked with young age. Polybius states that Hannibal was nine years old when he received the first advice from his father:

> At the time when his father was about to start with his army on his expedition to Spain, he himself, then nine years of age, was standing by the altar, while Hamilcar was sacrificing to Zeus (καθ' ὃν καιρὸν ὁ πατὴρ αὐτοῦ τὴν εἰς Ἰβηρίαν ἔξοδον μέλλοι στρατεύεσθαι μετὰ

---

[12] Momigliano 1993, 55–57, Haegg 2012, 51–66.
[13] Miltsios 2013a, 68–70.
[14] Xenophon emphasizes Cyrus' great reputation at the beginning of the *Cyropaedia* (*Cyr.* 1.4.25): "Cyrus was on the tongues of all ... both in story and in song".

τῶν δυνάμεων, ἔτη μὲν ἔχειν ἐννέα, θύοντος δ' αὐτοῦ τῷ Διὶ παρεστάναι παρὰ τὸν βωμόν). When, on the omens being favourable, Hamilcar had poured a libation to the gods and performed all the customary rites, he ordered the others who were attending the sacrifice to withdraw to a slight distance and calling Hannibal to him asked him kindly if he wished to accompany him on the expedition. On his accepting with delight, and, like a boy, even begging to do it besides (καί τι καὶ προσαξιώσαντος παιδικῶς), his father took him by the hand, led him up to the altar, and bade him lay his hand on the victim and swear never to be the friend of the Romans.[15]

When Cyrus meets Cambyses, he is around twenty-seven years old, but the whole conversation greatly relies on his recollections about the education he received *during his childhood* (Xen. *Cyr.* 1.6.3: μέμνημαι, 1.6.5: μέμνησαι, 1.6.7: ἐπελάθου, 1.6.8: μέμνημαι, 1.6.12: μέμνησαι); Xenophon has also already informed us that the Persians begin their education both in family and at schools at a very young age (Xen. *Cyr.* 1.2.3–8; cf. Xen. *Anab.* 1.9.4).

Furthermore, both authors stress the piety of the father: Polybius presents Hamilcar sacrificing to Zeus and it is only when he receives favorable omens that he proceeds to give his advice to Hannibal. Similarly, the encounter between Cambyses and Cyrus in the first book of the *Cyropaedia* is preceded by good omens, and Cambyses also gives Cyrus detailed advice on the importance of securing the goodwill of the gods and being pious (Xen. *Cyr.* 1.6.1–2).

More importantly, both Polybius and Xenophon suggest that the success of a leader can be partly conceived as (and depends upon) the implementation of paternal advice. Polybius states:

> Hannibal tried as far as he could to keep his hands off this city, wishing to give the Romans no avowed pretext for war, until he had secured his possession of all the rest of the country, *following in this his father Hamilcar's suggestions and advice* (κατὰ τὰς Ἁμίλκου τοῦ πατρὸς ὑποθήκας καὶ παραινέσεις)".[16]

Similarly, Xenophon presents Cyrus taking into account and implementing his father's suggestions on various occasions and on a wide range of topics: providing soldiers with supplies, military preparations, tactics, taking care of the soldiers' health, fostering discipline, gaining advantage over the enemy.[17] In sum,

---

15 Plb. 3.11.5–8.
16 Plb. 3.14.10.
17 Providing soldiers with supplies (Xen. *Cyr.* 1.6.7: advice, Xen. *Cyr.* 4.5.58: implementation), military preparations (Xen. *Cyr.* 1.6.10: advice, Xen. *Cyr.* 2.1.21: implementation), tactics (Xen. *Cyr.* 1.6.14: advice, Xen. *Cyr.* 2.1.20: implementation), taking care of the soldiers' health (Xen. *Cyr.* 1.6.16: advice, Xen. *Cyr.* 2.1.20: implementation), fostering discipline (Xen. *Cyr.* 1.6.20: advice,

although Xenophon's narrative of the encounter between father and son is more detailed than Polybius', it could have served as a kernel, which Polybius reworked and adapted in his *Histories* with the aim of presenting a more complete portrait of Hannibal.

Both authors also present their model leaders collaborating with their relatives. In these contexts the superiority of model leaders is brought to the fore. For instance, Polybius presents Hannibal giving orders to his elder brother Hasdrubal and also summoning his younger brother Mago:

> After two days' march he halted and, constructing a bridge of boats, ordered Hasdrubal to see to the passage of the army and he himself crossing at once (καταλύσας δὲ δευτεραῖος καὶ γεφυρώσας τοῖς ποταμίοις πλοίοις τὴν διάβασιν <u>Ἀσδρούβᾳ μὲν ἐπέταξεν</u> διακομίζειν τὸ πλῆθος).[18]

> The Carthaginian general now consulted with his brother Mago and the rest of the staff about the coming battle, and on their all approving of his plan, after the troops had had their supper, he summoned Mago, who was still quite young, but full of martial enthusiasm and trained from boyhood in the art of war, and put under his command a hundred men from the cavalry and the same number of infantry (πλὴν ὅ γε τῶν Καρχηδονίων στρατηγὸς κοινολογηθεὶς Μάγωνι τἀδελφῷ καὶ τοῖς συνέδροις περὶ τοῦ μέλλοντος ἀγῶνος, συγκατατιθεμένων αὐτῷ πάντων ταῖς ἐπιβολαῖς, ἅμα τῷ δειπνοποιήσασθαι τὸ στρατόπεδον <u>ἀνακαλεσάμενος Μάγωνα τὸν ἀδελφόν</u>, ὄντα νέον μὲν ὁρμῆς δὲ πλήρη καὶ παιδομαθῆ περὶ τὰ πολεμικά, συνέστησε τῶν ἱππέων ἄνδρας ἑκατὸν καὶ πεζοὺς τοὺς ἴσους).[19]

The words ἐπέταξε and ἀνακαλεσάμενος are telling in these contexts. In the *Cyropaedia* Xenophon presents Cyrus collaborating with his uncle, the Median King Cyaxares. Cyaxares initially invites Cyrus to join the battle against the Assyrians (Xen. *Cyr.* 1.5.4: ἔπεμπε δὲ καὶ πρὸς Κῦρον, δεόμενος αὐτοῦ πειρᾶσθαι ἄρχοντα ἐλθεῖν τῶν ἀνδρῶν). However, Cyrus manages to gain the goodwill of the Medes and, despite the fact that he is not yet king, he is eventually treated and respected by the Medes *as if he were king*, thus supplanting Cyaxares and provoking his envy (Xen. *Cyr.* 4.1.13, 5.5.25–26).[20] The motif of the leader surpassing his relatives in military qualities and talent is another idea that Polybius may have borrowed from Xenophon.

Xen. *Cyr.* 2.4.10: implementation), taking advantage of the enemy (Xen. *Cyr.* 1.6.27: advice, Xen. *Cyr.* 7.5.21: implementation).
18 Plb. 3.66.6.
19 Plb. 3.71.5.
20 For Cyaxares' envy, see Tatum 1989, 115–33, Gray 2011, 267–76, Tamiolaki 2016, 54–57.

2 Strategy

Competent strategy is an important component of good leadership. Both Polybius and Xenophon depict their model leaders as perceptive and successful generals. We will first present some common motifs regarding the leaders' attitude towards their enemies and potential allies and we will then turn to their attitude towards their soldiers inside their camps.

A common motif of the two leaders regarding their attitude towards their enemies is the appeal to fear. Polybius underlines time and again that Hannibal had recourse to fear and that fear was an important root of his success. For instance, he describes Hannibal's plan to attack Saguntum as follows:

> ... he was convinced that by this blow he would inspire universal terror, and render the Iberian tribes who had already submitted more orderly (καταπληξάμενος ἅπαντας εὐτακτοτέρους μὲν ἐπέπειστο παρασκευάσειν τοὺς ὑφ' αὑτὸν ἤδη ταττομένους) and those who were still independent more cautious, while above all he would be enabled to advance safely with no enemy left in his rear.[21]

The motif of universal terror appears in exactly the same wording at the beginning of the *Cyropaedia* and is again combined with an image of universal orderliness and obedience:

> He (sc. Cyrus) was able to cover so vast a region with the fear which he inspired, that he struck all men with terror and no one tried to withstand him (καὶ ὅμως ἐδυνάσθη ἐφικέσθαι μὲν ἐπὶ τοσαύτην γῆν τῷ ἀφ' ἑαυτοῦ φόβῳ, ὥστε καταπλῆξαι πάντας καὶ μηδένα ἐπιχειρεῖν αὐτῷ).[22]

Polybius also remarks that the conquest of the Allobroges proved of great service to Hannibal, because "he struck such terror into the next tribes that none of those in the neighborhood of the ascent were likely to venture to molest him" (φόβον ἐνειργάσατο τοῖς ἑξῆς πρὸς τὸ μὴ τολμᾶν αὐτῷ ῥᾳδίως ἐγχειρεῖν μηδένα τῶν παρακειμένων ταῖς ἀναβολαῖς).[23] Similarly, when Hannibal massacres the Taurini, Polybius again notes that "he struck such terror into the neighboring tribes of barbarians that they all came in at once and submitted to him" (τοιοῦτον ἐνειργάσατο φόβον τοῖς σύνεγγυς κατοικοῦσιν τῶν βαρβάρων ὥστε πάντας ἐκ

---

21 Plb. 3.17.5.
22 Xen. *Cyr.* 1.1.5. Translations of the *Cyropaedia* are from Ambler 2001 and Miller 1994 (sometimes adapted).
23 Plb. 3.51.13.

χειρὸς παραγίνεσθαι).²⁴ Xenophon's Cyrus employs similar tactics. For example, Xenophon relates in detail how Cyrus greatly terrified the Armenian King who deserted from him by not paying the tribute:

> When the Armenian heard from the messenger what Cyrus had said, he was stunned (ἐξεπλάγη), as he reflected that he had been unjust in neglecting the tribute and in not sending the army. The greatest problem, which he especially feared (ἐφοβεῖτο), was that he was about to be discovered in the early stages of fortifying his palace so as to make it sufficient for armed resistance. Hesitating (ὀκνῶν) because of all these things, he sent around to gather his own power ... At this point the Armenian no longer dared (οὐκέτι ἔτλη) to come to blows, so he withdrew.²⁵

The Armenian King's son, Tigranes, also explicitly states that his father is greatly terrorized by Cyrus and presents this fear as the worst kind of enslavement (Xen. *Cyr.* 3.1.23). In a similar vein, in the fourth book of the *Cyropaedia*, Cyrus orders the enemy soldiers to surrender their arms, otherwise they will lose their heads (Xen. *Cyr.* 4.2.32).²⁶ Cyrus can also appear harsh even towards his own men. Xenophon states in the fourth book of the *Cyropaedia* that he issues a proclamation to all his commissaries to come to him and that "to anyone who should dare to disobey he threatened direst punishment" (Xen. *Cyr.* 4.2.35). It thus becomes obvious that both Polybius and Xenophon consider fear an indispensable prerequisite of a leader's success. Although fear plays an important role in all historiographical texts,²⁷ we would like to suggest that Polybius could have been inspired precisely by Xenophon's treatment of fear in the *Cyropaedia*, not least since in this work the appeal of fear is more clearly and positively linked with good leadership and the consolidation of power.

Fear is not, of course, the sole basis of a leader's success. Hannibal and Cyrus can also display kindness. We observe again a similarity in the vocabulary employed by the two authors. The term used by Polybius to describe Hannibal's kindness is φιλανθρωπία (Plb. 3.77.3: <u>ἐν τῇ πάσῃ φιλανθρωπίᾳ διεξῆγεν</u>). Φιλανθρωπία is also one of Cyrus' cardinal virtues: Xenophon characterizes him as φιλανθρωπότατος (Xen. *Cyr.* 1.2.1). Moreover, Xenophon emphasizes that the

---

24 Plb. 3.60.10.
25 Xen. *Cyr.* 3.1.1–3.
26 Cf. also Xen. *Ages.* 1.33: Agesilaus burns Sardis and invites its inhabitants to become his allies; otherwise he will have recourse to arms.
27 See, for instance, Hdt. 4.126–127 (Darius threatens the Scythians), 5.106.3 (Darius threatens Histiaeus), 8.111–112 (Themistocles threatens the Andrians), Thuc. 5.85–112 (the Athenians threaten the Melians).

practice of kindness has important political connotations and constitutes a significant organizational principle of the Persian empire (Xen. *Cyr.* 8.2.1).[28] It is interesting that both Hannibal and Cyrus exploit the political potential of φιλανθρωπία: they display kindness in order to achieve better political results. Polybius recounts that Hannibal treated the Celtic prisoners with kindness, because he wished to get them on his side against the Romans (Plb. 3.77.3–4). In another instance, Hannibal refrains from killing the captives (Plb. 3.77.3–4). Cyrus the Great also releases prisoners because he considers this tactic more profitable (Xen. *Cyr.* 4.4.6: σύμφορον). Moreover, he treats the Armenian captives with mercy, again because he is convinced by Tigranes that this policy will be more advantageous to his empire (Xen. *Cyr.* 3.1.16).

Military tactics is another field in which we observe noteworthy similarities between the two leaders. For example, both Hannibal and Cyrus are interested in mixing cavalry with infantry. Polybius describes Hannibal's array in battle as follows:

> on his left close to the river he placed his Spanish and Celtic horses facing the Roman cavalry, next these half his heavy-armed Africans ... (ἐτίθει δ' ἐπ' αὐτὸν μὲν τὸν ποταμόν, ἐπὶ τῶν εὐωνύμων, τοὺς Ἴβηρας καὶ Κελτοὺς <u>ἱππεῖς</u> ἀντίους τοῖς τῶν Ῥωμαίων ἱππεῦσι, <u>συνεχεῖς</u> δὲ τούτοις πεζοὺς τοὺς ἡμίσεις τῶν ἐν τοῖς βαρέσι καθοπλισμοῖς Λιβύων).[29]

This scene recalls a similar episode of the *Cyropaedia*, when Cyrus offers shields and swords to his taxiarchs and orders them to carry them, following after the horses (note the words συνεχεῖς and ἕπωνται in the two authors):

> And leading them off right away, he assigned them to their captains. He ordered that they give them their shields and their light swords, so that they might follow with these behind the horses (καὶ εὐθὺς ἄγων πρὸς τοὺς ταξιάρχους συνέστησεν αὐτούς, καὶ ἐκέλευσε τά τε γέρρα καὶ τὰς ψιλὰς μαχαίρας τούτοις δοῦναι, ὅπως ἔχοντες σὺν τοῖς ἵπποις <u>ἕπωνται</u>).[30]

Another similar scene concerns the leaders' tactics towards the enemy: both Hannibal and Cyrus are presented preparing their troops for battle and then withdrawing them, because their enemies (Favius Maximus and the Assyrian King respectively) are not eager to fight (the linguistic and thematic parallels are again worth noticing: παρετάξατο/παραταξάμενος, οὐδενὸς ἐπεξιόντος/οὐκ ἀντεξῆσαν, ἀνεχώρησεν/ἀπήγαγε τὸ στράτευμα):

---

[28] For Cyrus' φιλανθρωπία, see Azoulay 2004, 318–26, Noël 2009, Sandridge 2012, 79–96. Agesilaus also shows kindness, but Xenophon uses the word πραότης for him (Xen. *Ages.* 1.20–21).
[29] Plb. 3.113.7.
[30] Xen. *Cyr.* 4.5.58.

When he learnt that Fabius had arrived, Hannibal, wishing to strike such a blow as would effectually cow the enemy, led his forces out and drew them up in order of battle at a short distance from the Roman camp, but after waiting some time, as nobody came out to meet him, he retired again to his own camp (Ἀννίβας δὲ συνεὶς τὴν παρουσίαν τοῦ Φαβίου καὶ βουλόμενος ἐξ ἐφόδου καταπλήξασθαι τοὺς ὑπεναντίους, ἐξαγαγὼν τὴν δύναμιν καὶ συνεγγίσας τῷ τῶν Ῥωμαίων χάρακι παρετάξατο. χρόνον δέ τινα μείνας, οὐδενὸς ἐπεξιόντος αὖθις ἀνεχώρησεν εἰς τὴν ἑαυτοῦ παρεμβολήν).[31]

After this he went to Babylon, keeping the same order as when the battle was fought. When the Assyrians did not come out in opposition, Cyrus...had the army draw back (Ἐκ τούτου δὴ ᾔει πρὸς Βαβυλῶνα παραταξάμενος ὥσπερ ὅτε ἡ μάχη ἦν. ὡς δ' οὐκ ἀντεξῇσαν οἱ Ἀσσύριοι ... ὁ δὲ Κῦρος ... ἀπήγαγε τὸ στράτευμα).[32]

Furthermore, we find several thematic parallels between Polybius and Xenophon's *Cyropaedia* with regards to the strategy of the two leaders. For example, both leaders put forward new ways of fighting: Cyrus familiarizes the Persians with cavalry fighting (Xen. *Cyr.* 4.3.4–15), while Hannibal introduces complex manoeuvres in his fighting against the Romans (Plb. 3.115.9–10).[33] F. Walbank also notes that both Polybius and Xenophon use the term πελτοφόροι (Plb. 3.75.7 and Xen. *Cyr.* 7.1.24).[34] Moreover, the two leaders mix up different nations in their armies and try to foster a harmonious collaboration between them: Hannibal mixes Africans and Spaniards, while Cyrus encourages cooperation between the Persians, the Medes, the Hyrcanians, the Armenians, and the Chaldaeans. Both leaders are also depicted as intelligent and foreseeing the enemy's actions: they surprise the enemy at night, they send envoys to spy on the enemy, they try to learn the topography of the enemy land, which they exploit by opening roads and trenches, and they are capable of choosing the appropriate occasion for battle.[35]

It goes the same with the leaders' attitude towards their potential allies. Polybius' *Histories* and the *Cyropaedia* again contain similar scenes. For instance, Polybius informs us that Hannibal was initially distrustful towards the barbarians who came to him and willingly offered their friendship, but then decided to accept their alliance, because he thought that this attitude would make them more pacific and less eager to attack him (Plb. 3.52.6–7). This scene evokes Cyrus' alliance with the Hyrcanians, described in the fourth book of the *Cyropaedia*: the

---

[31] Plb. 3.89.1–2.
[32] Xen. *Cyr.* 5.3.5–8.
[33] Cf. Xen. *Ages.* 1.23, 2.5: Agesilaus introduces horsemanship.
[34] Walbank 1957, 409.
[35] Plb. 3.93.2, Xen. *Cyr.* 7.5.21; Plb. 3.50.7, Xen. *Cyr.* 5.3.56; Plb. 3.79.1, Xen. *Cyr.* 4.4.4; Plb. 3.55.6–7, Xen. *Cyr.* 7.5.9; Plb. 3.14.5, Xen. *Cyr.* 3.3.32.

Hyrcanians express their wish to become Cyrus' allies; Cyrus is initially suspicious of them, but eventually becomes their ally and uses them profitably in subsequent expeditions (Xen. *Cyr.* 4.2.7). Furthermore, both authors present their model leaders fostering alliances with the enemies of their enemies: Hannibal cooperates with the Celts, who have a long-standing conflict with the Romans (Plb. 3.34.2–3), while Cyrus the Great allies himself to Gobryas and Gadatas, who deserted from the Assyrian King, the Persians' greatest enemy (Xen. *Cyr.* 4.6.2). These similarities could be considered coincidental, simply attesting to a kind of intertextuality of characters or a repetition of historical circumstances. However, if these scenes are studied together with the linguistic parallels noted above, they constitute cumulative evidence and hence, in our opinion, reinforce the possibility that Polybius could have modeled his presentation of Hannibal on Cyrus the Great.

As for the leaders' attitude towards their soldiers, we again observe some remarkable parallels between Hannibal and Cyrus. First of all, both leaders are interested in the provisions and armament of their soldiers. Polybius notes:

> not only did he (*sc.* Hannibal) furnish the army with plenty of corn and other provisions (τοῖς ἄλλοις ἐπιτηδείοις), but he replaced all their old and worn weapons by new ones, thus freshening up the whole force very opportunely.[36]

Similarly, Cyrus constantly shows concern about the provisions of his soldiers and also takes the bold initiative to create new arms for the Persian commoners (Xen. *Cyr.* 2.1.9; cf. Xen. *Cyr.* 4.5.58). Caring for provisions is, according to Cambyses' advice, the most significant means of securing the perpetual goodwill of a leader's subordinates (Xen. *Cyr.* 4.5.57–58; cf. Xen. *Cyr.* 1.6.9: "if your army does not receive its provisions, your authority will collapse"). The frequent use of the word τὰ ἐπιτήδεια both in Polybius' *Histories* and in the *Cyropaedia* is important in these contexts.[37]

The two leaders also exploit captured arms. Polybius notes that when Hannibal encamped near the Adriatic with a large booty, "he re-armed the Africans in the Roman fashion with select weapons, being, as he now was, in possession of a very large quantity of captured arms".[38] Similarly, Xenophon mentions that Cyrus, after his conquest of the Phrygians, the Cappadocians and the Arabians, "secured armor for not less than forty thousand Persian horsemen" (Xen. *Cyr.* 7.4.16).

---

36 Plb. 3.49.11.
37 Cf. Xen. *Ages.* 2.8: Agesilaus' concern about his soldiers.
38 Plb. 3.87.3–4.

Furthermore, both leaders are depicted as ready to make good use of the high morale of their soldiers and lead them to battle. Polybius states: "Hannibal was anxious to force a battle on the enemy, wishing in the first place to avail himself of the enthusiasm of the Celts while still fresh".[39] Xenophon also notes that Cyrus decides to attack the enemy, as soon as he realizes that his soldiers are in good physical and psychological condition (Xen. *Cyr.* 3.3.9).[40] Both leaders also reward their soldiers according to merit in order to make them fight more bravely (Plb. 3.17.10, Xen. *Cyr.* 2.2.20; cf. Xen. *Ages.* 2.8).

Finally, we note a similarity in the vocabulary used by the two historians regarding the disposal of the plunder. Polybius notes that the plunder helped Hannibal to accomplish many things which were *of service to* him, while Xenophon presents Cyrus as stating that the plunder will always be *at the service* of anyone who needs it (note the words χρησίμων and χρήσεται in the two passages below):

> by setting aside these funds, he (*sc.* Hannibal) was able to accomplish many things of much service to him (αὐτός τε πολλὰ τῶν χρησίμων μετὰ ταῦτα κατειργάσατο διὰ τῆς τῶν χορηγιῶν παραθέσεως).[41]

> καὶ ὅσα δὲ ἐμοὶ δίδοτε, ἡδέως, ἔφη, δέχομαι· χρήσεται δ' αὐτοῖς ὑμῶν ὁ ἀεὶ μάλιστα δεόμενος ("I accept with pleasure what you are giving me", he said. "Whoever among you is especially in want of them may use them").[42]

3 Character

Hannibal and Cyrus share some common features with regards to their character as well. First of all, they are both presented as being carried away by juvenile enthusiasm. On the one hand, Polybius notes that Hannibal, at a very young age, was full of martial ardor and was greatly motivated by his hatred against the Romans:

> Hannibal, being young, full of martial ardour, encouraged by the success of his enterprises, and spurred on by his long-standing enmity to Rome (ὁ δ' Ἀννίβας, ἅτε νέος μὲν ὤν, πλήρης

---

[39] Plb. 3.70.9–10.
[40] Cf. Xen. *Anab.* 1.7.8: Cyrus the Younger is also capable of raising the morale of his soldiers.
[41] Plb. 3.17.11
[42] Xen. *Cyr.* 5.1.1.

δὲ πολεμικῆς ὁρμῆς, ἐπιτυχὴς δ' ἐν ταῖς ἐπιβολαῖς, πάλαι δὲ παρωρμημένος πρὸς τὴν κατὰ Ῥωμαίων ἔχθραν ...).⁴³

Xenophon also describes Cyrus' enthusiasm in the *Cyropaedia* during his childhood in a boar-hunting scene:

> But when he perceived a shout, he leaped up on his horse as would one possessed; and when he saw a boar bearing down upon them, he rushed straight toward it, poised [his spear], and with a good aim struck the boar in the forehead and brought it down (ὁ οὖν Κῦρος ... ὡς δ' ᾔσθετο κραυγῆς, ἀνεπήδησεν ἐπὶ τὸν ἵππον ὥσπερ ἐνθουσιῶν, καὶ ὡς εἶδεν ἐκ τοῦ ἀντίου κάπρον προσφερόμενον, ἀντίος ἐλαύνει καὶ διατεινάμενος εὐστόχως βάλλει εἰς τὸ μέτωπον καὶ κατέσχε τὸν κάπρον).⁴⁴

Furthermore, both leaders are pious: in his speech in front of his soldiers Hannibal states that they should be thankful to the gods, because the gods help them attain victory over the enemies (Plb. 3.111.3–4). Similarly, Cyrus is presented as very pious throughout the *Cyropaedia*, making sacrifices to the gods, paying attention to omens, and often requesting the help of Zeus (Xen. *Cyr.* 7.1.11).⁴⁵

Another common feature of the two leaders is their great concern about their soldiers. For instance, they take care of their soldiers and horses. Polybius notes:

> He (sc. Hannibal) now encamped near the Adriatic in a country abounding in all kinds of produce, and paid great attention to recruiting the health of his men as well as of his horses by proper treatment (ἐν ᾧ καιρῷ καταστρατοπεδεύσας παρὰ τὸν Ἀδρίαν ἐν χώρᾳ πρὸς πάντα τὰ γεννήματα διαφερούσῃ μεγάλην ἐποιεῖτο σπουδὴν ὑπὲρ τῆς ἀναλήψεως καὶ θεραπείας τῶν ἀνδρῶν, οὐχ ἧττον δὲ καὶ τῶν ἵππων).⁴⁶

Similarly, Cyrus states that he will take care of the health of his soldiers (Xen. *Cyr.* 1.6.15) and also shows concern about men and horses:

> ἔχειν δὲ χρὴ καὶ ἱμάντας· τὰ γὰρ πλεῖστα καὶ ἀνθρώποις καὶ ἵπποις ἱμᾶσιν ἤρτηται (We must also have straps, for most things, for both human beings and horses, are attached with straps).⁴⁷

---

43 Plb. 3.15.6–7.
44 Xen. *Cyr.* 1.4.8. Cyrus the Younger is also depicted as "most fond of hunting" (φιλοθηρότατος) and "prone to danger when hunting wild animals" (φιλοκινδυνότατος).
45 Piety is an important quality of leaders in Xenophon (see also Xen. *Ages.* 1.13). See Flower 2016.
46 Plb. 3.87.1–2.
47 Xen. *Cyr.* 6.2.32.

Furthermore, both Hannibal and Cyrus the Great confer honor on people who have offered services to them. F. Walbank notes the use of the verb τιμάω (honor) in Polybius and Xenophon's *Cyropaedia* (Plb. 3.69.4; Xen. *Cyr.* 3.3.6). Both leaders also constitute models for imitation for their followers. Polybius observes about Hannibal: "he was now setting an example to the soldiers by sharing personally the fatigue of the battering operations, now cheering on the troops and exposing himself recklessly to dangers".[48] Similarly, Cambyses advises Cyrus as follows: "I think that the leader ought to surpass those under his rule not in self-indulgence, but in taking forethought and willingly undergoing toil ... And in his campaigns also, if they fall in the summer time, the general must show that he can endure the heat of the sun better than his soldiers can, and that he can endure cold better than they if it be in winter; if the way lead through difficulties, that he can endure hardships better".[49] Cyrus follows his father's advice since he sets himself as a paradigm of self-restraint and moderation (Xen. *Cyr.* 8.1.37, 39: παράδειγμα μὲν δὴ τοιοῦτον ἑαυτὸν παρείχετο).

Both leaders also place great importance on discipline. Hannibal encourages his soldiers as follows: "He begged them therefore to be at their ease about details, but to obey orders and behave like brave men and in a manner worthy of their own record in the past".[50] Cyrus gives a similar advice to his soldiers: "to be brave men, knowing that obedience, perseverance, and the endurance of toil and danger at the critical time bring the great pleasures and the great blessings".[51] Finally, although both Hannibal and Cyrus the Great are generally depicted as brave, Polybius and Xenophon demonstrate instances of their weakness as well: for example, the troops of Hannibal are presented as afraid of the Roman legions and that is why they decide to bring the battle to a close (Plb. 3.105.7). Similarly, Cyrus is afraid of the large numbers of the Assyrians and orders the retreat of his men (Xen. *Cyr.* 3.3.69–70).

4 Conclusion

Scholars have already noted some parallels between Polybius' *Histories* and Xenophon's works. Our investigation expands this research by focusing on the third

---

48 Plb. 3.17.18–19.
49 Xen. *Cyr.* 1.6.8, 1.6.25.
50 Plb. 3.44.12–13.
51 Xen. *Cyr.* 3.3.8.

book of Polybius' *Histories* and by offering a comparison with Xenophon's *Cyropaedia*. The focus on Hannibal and the detailed analysis of his plans, strategic qualities, and character strongly evoke Xenophon's treatment of Cyrus in the *Cyropaedia*. In our opinion, the accumulation of common themes and linguistic parallels regarding the two leaders renders plausible the hypothesis that a possible source of influence for Polybius' representation of Hannibal could have been Cyrus the Great, the hero of Xenophon's *Cyropaedia*. It is further hoped that this study will encourage more scholars to undertake a systematic comparison between Polybius and Xenophon on other aspects of their works as well.

Bibliography

Ambler, W. (2001), *Xenophon. The Education of Cyrus*, Ithaca/London.
Anderson, J.K. (1974), *Xenophon*, New York.
Délébecque, É. (1957), *Essai sur la vie de Xénophon*, Paris.
Flower, M. (2016), "Piety in Xenophon's Theory of Leadership", in: R. Buxton (ed.) *Aspects of Leadership in Xenophon*, Histos Suppl. 5, 85–119.
Gera, D.L. (1993), *Xenophon's Cyropaedia. Style, Genre, and Literary Technique*, Oxford.
Gibson, B. (2013), "Polybius and Xenophon: The Mercenary War", in: B. Gibson/T. Harrison (eds.), *Polybius and his World. Essays in Memory of F.W. Walbank*, Oxford, 159–179.
Gray, V. (2011), *Xenophon's Mirror of Princes. Reading the Reflections*, Oxford.
Haegg, T. (2012), *The Art of Biography in Antiquity*, Cambridge.
McGing, B. (2010), *Polybius' Histories*, Oxford.
Miller, W. (1994), *Xenophon. Cyropaedia*, 2 Vols., Cambridge, Mass. (1st edn 1914).
Miltsios, N. (2013a), *The Shaping of Narrative in Polybius*, Berlin.
—— (2013b), "The Narrative Legacy of Thucydides: Polybius, Book I", in: A. Tsakmakis/M. Tamiolaki (eds.), *Thucydides Between History and Literature*, Berlin/Boston, 329–349.
Momigliano, A. (1993), *The Development of Greek Biography*, Cambridge, Mass.
Noël, M.-P. (2006), "Symposion, philanthropia et empire dans la *Cyropédie* de Xénophon", in: P. Brillet-Dubois (ed.), *Philologia: Mélanges offerts à M. Casevitz*, Lyon, 133–146.
Paton, W.R. (2001), *Polybius. The Histories*, Vol. II, Cambridge, Mass. (1st edn 1922).
Rood, T. (2012), "Polybius, Thucydides, and the First Punic War", in: C. Smith/L.M. Yarrow (eds.), *Imperialism, Cultural Politics, and Polybius*, Oxford, 50–67.
Sandridge, N. (2012), *Loving Humanity, Learning and Being Honored. The Foundations of Leadership in Xenophon's Education of Cyrus*, Washington, DC.
Tamiolaki, M. (2016), "Emotion and Persuasion in Xenophon's *Cyropaedia*", Phoenix 70, 40–63.
—— (2017), "Xenophon's Cyropaedia. Tentative Answers to an Enigma", in: M. Flower (ed.), *The Cambridge Companion to Xenophon*, Cambridge, 174–194.
Tatum, J. (1989), *Xenophon's Imperial Fiction*, Princeton.
Walbank, F.W. (1957), *A Historical Commentary on Polybius*, Vol. 1 (Commentary on Books I–VI), Oxford.
—— (1972), *Polybius*, Berkeley.

Evangelos Alexiou
Τόπος ἐγκωμιαστικός (Polybius 10.21.8): The Encomium of Philopoemen and its Isocratic Background

In the tenth book of his *Histories* Polybius makes some interesting observations about the relationship between his biographical digression on Philopoemen and the work that he had already written in three books about his life (10.21.1–8 = *FGrHist* 173 T 1). This programmatic passage tells us much about Polybius' relationship with literary genres. Although the text is often recalled by scholars, in order to throw light on the distinction between related genres such as historiography and biography,[1] what Polybius emphatically stresses is the τόπος ἐγκωμιαστικός (10.21.8); this means that he describes his earlier work as an encomium, in which the encomiastic motifs—presumably similar to those of a rhetorical epideictic speech—are predominant. Considering that the term τόπος ἐγκωμιαστικός refers to rhetorical theory and practice, William Fortenbaugh and Stefan Schorn have argued that Polybius was working in line with the tradition of rhetorical treatises of the 4th century BCE, such as the *Rhetoric to Alexander* or the *Rhetoric* of Aristotle, or with actual encomia such as the *Evagoras* of Isocrates.[2]

Taking the above observation as a starting point, in this article I will make a systematic comparison between the introductory remarks of Polybius at 10.21 and the encomiastic motifs found in real epideictic speeches, such as those of Isocrates. The comparison with Isocrates is worth pursuing at first for its own sake: His *Evagoras*, the first prose encomium of a non-mythical person (*Evag.* 8), was well known in the fourth century, and it had a huge impact on the evolution of the genre.[3] On the other hand, Isocrates advertises his encomiastic approach across his whole corpus and develops epideictic *topoi*, which are not limited to *Evagoras*, as they are also attested in the encomium of Alcibiades in *De bigis* and in mythical encomia, such as *Helen* and *Busiris*. Moreover, texts like Xenophon's *Agesilaus* or *Cyropaedia* have also been influenced by Isocrates.

---

[1] See e.g. Steidle 1963, 40, Sonnabend 2002, 4f., Gallo 2005, 11. Cf. also the discussion in Momigliano 1983, 82f., Dihle 1987, 11–16; 1998, 127–30, Schorn 2014a, 689.
[2] Fortenbaugh 2007, 60–71, Schorn 2014b. Cf. Schepens 2007, 342–44, who refers to the difference between historiography and encomium; Lucian *Hist. conscr.* 7; Tuplin 2000, 128, Farrington 2011, 325–27.
[3] See Alexiou 2014, 796.

1

It is important that Polybius' characterization of his earlier work on Philopoemen as τόπος ἐγκωμιαστικός makes a clear distinction between encomium and historiography, which is not only of theoretical but also of practical importance. Polybius is aware of the πρέπον: the proper character of each work has to be preserved (10.21.7: ἵνα τὸ πρέπον ἑκατέρᾳ τῶν συντάξεων τηρῶμεν). In fact, Polybius attributes to an encomium a focus on essentials, a brief and concise manner, and the amplification of virtues, while historiography involves both praise and blame, which makes for a true and conclusive account, supported by relevant considerations:[4]

> ὥσπερ γὰρ ἐκεῖνος ὁ τόπος, ὑπάρχων ἐγκωμιαστικός, ἀπῄτει τὸν κεφαλαιώδη καὶ μετ' αὐξήσεως τῶν πράξεων ἀπολογισμόν, οὕτως ὁ τῆς ἱστορίας, κοινὸς ὢν ἐπαίνου καὶ ψόγου, ζητεῖ τὸν ἀληθῆ καὶ τὸν μετ' ἀποδείξεως καὶ τῶν ἑκάστοις παρεπομένων συλλογισμῶν.
>
> For just as the former work, being in the form of an encomium, demanded a summary and somewhat exaggerated account of his achievements, so the present history, which distributes praise and blame impartially, demands a strictly true account and one which states the ground on which either praise or blame is based (Plb. 10.21.7–8, transl. W.R. Paton).

The adjective ἐγκωμιαστικός is a technical term, which recalls rhetorical treatises such as the *Rhetoric to Alexander*. Scott Farrington has argued convincingly that the adjective ἐγκωμιαστικός does not mean "encomium-like" but rather "belonging to the encomiastic class or τέχνη".[5] It has to be noted, furthermore, that Polybius uses the adjective together with the word τόπος (topic), which is also a technical term.[6] Moreover, the whole phrase ἐγκωμιαστικὸς τόπος, in the plural form, is a common rhetorical term in later rhetorical treatises.[7]

I will first make a general remark on the awareness of the overlapping between related literary genres and Polybius' attempt to clarify the lines of his own

---

[4] Schorn 2014b, 150–55 emphasizes that Polybius, like Diodorus, Ephorus or Timaeus, uses the theory of encomium in defining his own concept of historiography. Polybius does not, however, adopt the classification of later rhetoricians, whereby an encomium as species of epideictic oratory includes praise and blame. See Nicol. *Progymn.* 54.1–6 (Felten): τῶν γὰρ ἐγκωμίων τὸ μέν ἐστιν ἔπαινος τὸ δὲ ψόγος.
[5] Farrington 2011, 326f. Cf. Fortenbaugh 2007, 68; Anax. *Ars rhet.* 1.1; 3.1; 35.1.
[6] So Arist. *Rhet.* 1362a 13–14: ὁ περὶ τοὺς ἐπαίνους τόπος. Cf. 1358a 12; 1401b 3; 1403a 23; 1419b 18–19.
[7] So [Dion. Hal.] *Ars rhet.* 5.3 (p. 274 Us.-Rad.): χρηστέον δὲ καὶ ἐνταῦθα τοῖς ἐγκωμιαστικοῖς τόποις, ἀπὸ γένους, ἀπὸ φύσεως, ἀπὸ ἀνατροφῆς. See also [Hermog.] *Progymn.* 7.5; 8.2 (Patillon).

work. Encomium, historiography and biography have common generic features, so it is no coincidence that the biographer Plutarch in the second century AD tries to explain that the *Lives of Alexander and Caesar* are βίοι and not ἱστορίαι (*Alex.* 1.2) and why his *Life of Lucullus* is not an encomium but a biography (*Cim.* 2.2).[8] The *Lives* are related to encomium in that the biographer is engaged in making evaluative comments. Polybius finds it natural to discuss the relationship between literary genres—to broach *Gattungsfragen*—and this discussion can be compared with related questions about the development of the epideictic speech in other authors, beginning with Isocrates.

Isocrates himself would have approved of such a comparison, which takes the encomium as a starting point. His speeches are often linked to a specific relationship/distinction of literary genres, such as that between an encomium and an apology. The forensic speeches played an important role in the development of the prose encomium in *De bigis* as well, a defense in a racing-team trial against charges brought by one Tisias against the younger Alcibiades on the grounds that his father had robbed him of a team of horses. Isocrates takes the opportunity, in the early stage of his authorship, to present a very positive portrayal of the famous Athenian Alcibiades as an outstanding individual.[9] This speech shows generic resemblances to an encomium; actually it was transformed from an apology to an encomium of a non-mythical person—a rhetorical innovation.[10] In a significant passage in *Helen* (14–15), an encomium of a mythical person closely connected with *Helen* of Gorgias, Isocrates signals certain generic barriers, separating encomium from defense. Isocrates praises his teacher for the choice of subject; he criticizes him, however, because he declares that he has written an encomium about Helen, but has actually composed a defense (*apologia*) for what she did. Praise is a feature and privilege of the encomium: it is fitting to make a defense for those who have been accused of injustice, but one praises those who excel in some good (15: ἐπαινεῖν δὲ τοὺς ἐπ' ἀγαθῷ τινὶ διαφέροντας). In *Busiris* Isocrates raises again a question of genre and sharply criticizes Polycrates, who worked on difficult issues such as Ἀπολογία Βουσίριδος and Κατηγορία Σωκράτους. The contrast here is between apology/laudation and charge/accusation: Isocrates wants to show Polycrates how to compose a real laudation (10–29) and a real apology (30–43). In each of these three texts Isocrates elaborates the differences between related genres and applies the basic principle of laudatory

---

[8] Cf. Piccirilli 1990, xxxiii, Alexiou 2007, 29–31, 47; 2010, 43f.
[9] The speech is to be dated after 397 BCE, possibly at 396/5. See Flacelière 1961, 95, Gribble 1999, 111–17, Alexiou 2011, Eck 2015, Alexiou 2016, 186–95.
[10] See Alexiou 2011, 333f.

rhetoric, the ability to praise and to "make larger" (in rhetorical terminology αὔξησις, *amplificatio*) as a distinctive characteristic of the encomiastic speech:

> Ἁπάντων γὰρ εἰδότων ὅτι δεῖ τοὺς μὲν εὐλογεῖν τινὰς βουλομένους πλείω τῶν ὑπαρχόντων ἀγαθῶν αὐτοῖς τὰ προσόντ' ἀποφαίνειν, τοὺς δὲ κατηγοροῦντας τἀναντία τούτων ποιεῖν.[11]

> Everyone knows that those who want to eulogize people must point out more good attributes than they actually have, and those who want to prosecute them must do the opposite (*Bus.* 4, transl. D. Mirhady).

The ability to present some traits as bigger than they really are, the amplification of virtues, is the common point shared by Isocrates and Polybius, indicative of the ἐγκωμιαστικὸς τόπος, which brings Isocrates and Polybius close together. Polybius' earlier work is closely connected with an encomium and recalls Anaximenes (*Ars rhet.* 3.1): συλλήβδην μὲν οὖν ἐστιν ἐγκωμιαστικὸν εἶδος προαιρέσεων καὶ πράξεων καὶ λόγων ἐνδόξων αὔξησις καὶ μὴ προσόντων συνοικείωσις (To speak generally, the eulogistic kind is the amplification of creditable purposes, deeds, and words, and the attribution of qualities which do not exist, transl. E.S. Forster).[12]

It is time, then, to examine *Evagoras*, a novelty in Isocrates' writing task, as he asserts himself to be the first to write a prose encomium on a contemporary political figure, the dead Cyprian king Evagoras I (*Evag.* 8). In *Evagoras* 5, Isocrates strongly criticizes the lack of encomia on the achievements of outstanding contemporaries. Isocrates' starting point is, indeed, the historical events; he stays within the confines of credibility, but chooses to interpret them in such a way that, in the end, Evagoras is not represented as a historical figure but as a political ideal.[13] It is an idealized representation of a personality incarnating a list of praiseworthy virtues, which Isocrates based on selected actions and deemed far more important than the development of the personal life of the person praised. Isocrates implements a series of rhetorical encomiastic *topoi*, such as *amplificatio* (αὔξησις) and *praeteritio* (παράλειψις), which show strong resemblances with the κεφαλαιώδη καὶ μετ' αὐξήσεως ἀπολογισμόν of Polybius.

Amplification can take various forms, aiming to encourage a particular interpretation by the reader. Isocrates uses the Homeric heroes as an expedient foil,

---

[11] Cf. *Paneg.* 8: τά τε μεγάλα ταπεινὰ ποιῆσαι καὶ τοῖς μικροῖς μέγεθος περιθεῖναι; *Panath.* 36: τὰ μὲν μικρὰ τῶν πραγμάτων ῥᾴδιον τοῖς λόγοις αὐξῆσαι.
[12] Cf. 3.6–12; Quint. 8.4. For Auxesis, see Plöbst 1911, Buchcheit 1960, 15–26, Bauer 1992, Pernot 1993, 675–80.
[13] See Alexiou 2015.

juxtaposing them with Evagoras (*Evag.* 6, 65) in order to highlight the king's qualities as well as his achievements. Indeed, Evagoras surpasses the heroes of the Trojan War in his exploits.[14] Isocrates exploits the mythical exempla rhetorically in order to compare them with contemporaries and to create space for an increased performance of a protagonist of his own era, such as Evagoras. This also applies to the comparison of Evagoras with Cyrus (*Evag.* 37–38), the founder of the Persian Empire.[15] Cyrus the Great is an important example for the rhetorical *topos* of the σύγκρισις πρὸς ἐνδόξους. Isocrates compares the protagonist with the most honourable heroes in order to magnify his achievements. His focus is the amplification of Evagoras' achievements. Aristotle in his *Rhetoric* (1368a 19–22) uses Isocrates' writing as a typical example of this technique. As he puts it, "if you cannot find enough to say of a man himself, you may pit him against others, which is what Isocrates used to do owing to his want of familiarity with forensic pleading. The comparison should be with famous men; that will strengthen your case; it is a noble thing to surpass men who are themselves great. It is only natural that methods of 'heightening the effect' should be attached particularly to speeches of praise".[16]

The construction of the comparison between Cyrus and Evagoras highlights the *topos* of μόνος,[17] namely the contrast between Cyrus' significant military forces and Evagoras' almost exclusively individual success (37).[18] Furthermore, to prove Evagoras' political virtues, Isocrates bases his argument on the τόπος ἐκ κρίσεως, referring to those who showed their appreciation of Evagoras by settling in Cyprus: for instance, the Athenian general Conon (*Evag.* 52–57).[19] After the military disaster of the Athenians at Aegospotamoi, Conon's decision to steer for Cyprus was a conscious one, a choice made from a range of options that were open

---

[14] Their demythologization is already found among historians, such as Herodotus and Thucydides. Hdt. 7.20.2; Thuc. 1.10.3; 1.11.2; 1.21.1. Cf. Pallantza 2005, 187–200.
[15] See further Alexiou 2010, 120–23. For Isocrates and the past, see the recent study of Brunello 2015.
[16] Cf. Anaxim. *Ars rhet.* 3.7; Menand. *De epid.* 421.8–10 Russ./Wils. Compare also Isocrates *Panath.* 39–41, 238; Roth 2003, 107–08, Blank 2014, 515–18. See also the comparison between Heracles and Theseus (*Hel.* 23–25) and between Egypt and Lacedaemon (*Bus.* 17–20).
[17] Arist. *Rhet.* 1368a 10–11; Quint. 3.7.166; Cic. *De or.* 2.347; Theon *Progymn.* 9 (110.22–26 Pat./Bol.); Pernot 1993, 705–08, Rapp 2002, 428f.
[18] Cf. *Evag.* 32: καὶ μόνος πρὸς πολλοὺς καὶ μετ' ὀλίγων πρὸς ἅπαντας. See also *Evag.* 29 and 61.
[19] Aristotle (*Rhetoric* 1399a 1–6) also mentions Conon's judgement about Evagoras. Cf. 1398b 21–26; *Top.* 100b 18–23; Anaxim. *Ars rhet.* 1.13; Quint. 5.11.36–44; [Hermog.] *Progymn.* 3.9 (Patillon).

to the virtuous Athenian general. Nonetheless, some typically Isocratean techniques of historical manipulation emerge here, in order to serve the practical needs of the encomium. Isocrates refers to the same subject in *Philippus* 62, but in a substantially different way. Conon did not return to Athens because of the shame he felt. Diodorus (13.106.6) mentions Conon's fear of the Athenians' wrath and his friendship with Evagoras.[20] It is obvious that Isocrates, while retaining the historical core of what happened, interprets the historical facts according to the specific encomiastic objectives of his speech.

Polybius observes (10.21.7) that in the former description of Philopoemen the achievements of his riper years were presented κεφαλαιωδῶς (briefly summarized, focusing on the most important), which is the proper character of the encomiastic speech (τὸν κεφαλαιώδη ἀπολογισμόν) but not of a historiographic work, in which he has to add details to the earlier summary account (τοῖς δὲ κατὰ τὴν ἀκμὴν αὐτοῦ κεφαλαιωδῶς ἐκεῖ δεδηλωμένοις ἔργοις προσθεῖναι καὶ κατὰ μέρος).[21] This distinction recalls the rhetorical device of *praeteritio* (παράλειψις), wherein the speaker brings up a subject without full details, by stating or drawing attention to something in the very act of pretending to pass it over.[22] It is used by Isocrates throughout his speeches, and Aristotle is also familiar with it (*Rhet.* 1416b 22–23: ἐνίοτε οὐκ ἐφεξῆς δεῖ διηγεῖσθαι πάντα). The brevity of the narration is an Isocratean virtue, commonly expressed with the stereotypic statement τί δεῖ λέγοντα διατρίβειν.[23] A particularly fine example is the battle of Salamis in *Panegyricus* 97, where Isocrates makes the statement that he does not need to spend time describing the uproar arising from that battle and the shouts and the encouragements that are common to all naval battles. The same applies with *Evagoras* 31, where Isocrates does not describe in detail the battle between Evagoras and the usurper: "Why should I spend time speaking of the confusion at such moments, the fear of the other men, and his exhortations?" Equally, in *Evagoras* 51–52 the *praeteritio* supports the amplification. Even though many distinguished

---

20 See also Laistner 1927, 144, Alexiou 2010, 144.
21 The use of the word κεφαλαιωδῶς recalls Aristotle; in *Rhet.* 1415b 7–9 he observes that in the proem of a speech a summary statement (κεφαλαιωδῶς) of the subject is only wanted, to put a sort of head on the main body of the speech. Cf. Plb. 1.13.1: ἐπὶ βραχὺ καὶ κεφαλαιωδῶς; 3,1,5: κεφαλαιωδῶς ἐπιμνησθῆναι καὶ προεκθέσθαι; 6.5.2–3: τοῦτο πειρασόμεθα κεφαλαιωδῶς διελθεῖν.
22 Lausberg 1960, 436–37. In *Evag.* 21 Isocrates tells us that he elects to omit the rumors, prophecies, and dreams about Evagoras, which made him appear superhuman.
23 Not only limited to warfare; cf. *Ad Nic.* 45; *Nicocl.* 35; *Archid.* 21; *Hel.* 59; *Panath.* 105, 201; *Plat.* 7; *Ad Loch.* 10. This principle attaches Quintilian to the Isocratean school (4.2.31). See also Usher 1990, 172.

Greeks left their own countries to live in Cyprus, Isocrates names only Conon, because it would be a large task to name all the others. For the encomiastic speech, what is unsaid is as important as what is said (cf. *Evag.* 34).

2

The beginning of Polybius' introductory remarks on Philopoemen is marked by his wish to highlight the training (ἀγωγή) and nature (φύσις) of the Achaean general (10.21.1). But in the *Histories* Polybius will omit details concerning Philopoemen's training and ambitions of his youth, since in his former work he had dealt in detail with Philopoemen himself, his family and his training (10.21.5: καὶ τίς ἦν καὶ τίνων καὶ τίσιν ἀγωγαῖς ἐχρήσατο νέος ὤν). That Polybius has discussed these subjects elaborately in his encomiastic text is very important, leading straight into well-known encomiastic *topoi*:

εἰ μὲν οὖν μὴ κατ' ἰδίαν ἐπεποιήμεθα τὴν περὶ αὐτοῦ σύνταξιν, ἐν ᾗ διεσαφοῦμεν καὶ τίς ἦν καὶ τίνων καὶ τίσιν ἀγωγαῖς ἐχρήσατο νέος ὤν, ἀναγκαῖον ἦν ὑπὲρ ἑκάστου τῶν προειρημένων φέρειν ἀπολογισμόν· ἐπεὶ δὲ πρότερον ἐν τρισὶ βυβλίοις ἐκτὸς ταύτης τῆς συντάξεως τὸν ὑπὲρ αὐτοῦ πεποιήμεθα λόγον, τήν τε παιδικὴν ἀγωγὴν διασαφοῦντες καὶ τὰς ἐπιφανεστάτας πράξεις, δῆλον ὡς ἐν τῇ νῦν ἐξηγήσει πρέπον ἂν εἴη τῆς μὲν νεωτερικῆς ἀγωγῆς καὶ τῶν νεωτερικῶν ζήλων κατὰ μέρος ἀφελεῖν.

Now had I not dealt with Philopoemen in a special work in which I explain who he and his family were, and the nature of his training when young, I should be compelled to give an account of all these matters here. Since, however, I have formerly in three books, which do not form a part of the present work, treated of him, stating what was his training as a boy and enumerating his most famous actions, it is evident that in the present narrative my proper course is to omit details concerning his early training and the ambitions of his youth (Plb. 10.21.5, transl. W.R. Paton).

Isocrates' literary portrayal of the King of Cyprus begins with the formulation (*Evag.* 12) περὶ τῆς φύσεως τῆς Εὐαγόρου καὶ τίνων ἦν ἀπόγονος. The *physis* can mean the origin (12, 54), his disposition (24, 81), his personality on the whole (45, 49, 59), his almost divine status (72) or his physical appearance (75). In this sense the phrase τίνων ἦν ἀπόγονος at *Evagoras* 12 explains the φύσις and signifies the nobility of birth (εὐγένεια), which is a basic encomiastic *topos*.[24] It is one of the *argumenta a persona* (Quint. 5.10.24; cf. 3.7.10), and is found often in Isocrates

---

24 Rightly Clarke 1885, 35. See also Arist. *Rhet.* 1360b 31–38; 1367b 30–32.

and is directly linked to the growth of epideictic literature.²⁵ Anaximenes (*Ars rhet.* 35.3–5) classifies it among the ἔξω τῆς ἀρετῆς ἀγαθά, exposed immediately after the proem.

Isocrates devotes extensive praise to the famous mythical ancestors of Evagoras, the Aeacids, *i.e.* the descendants of Aeacus down to Teucer who settled Salamis in Cyprus (*Evag.* 12–18),²⁶ but is not interested in the most recent ancestors of Evagoras who probably were not well known. Isocrates presents Evagoras as an idealized *agathos*, possessing the highest possible level of virtues (23), such as courage, wisdom and justice, corresponding to mythical figures that appear in other speeches: Agamemnon possesses all the virtues in an excessive degree (*Pan.* 72), just as Theseus does (*Hel.* 21). Evagoras' claims to the ruling power are in line with the superiority of his talented personality, namely the φύσις (*Evag.* 24); nevertheless, Isocrates does not blindly applaud competitive aspirations. Evagoras is suited to be not only a hero of Homeric competitive values, but also an example of the acknowledged cooperative virtues of a city-state citizen, who knows to avoid internal conflicts (23–24).²⁷

In his commentary on Polybius (10.21.5) Walbank refers to Isocrates' *Evagoras*, but observes that Isocrates, differing from Polybius, covers only the first two points in his encomium, the character and the origin of Evagoras, while the king's training is not cited—the ἀγωγή according to Polybius' terminology.²⁸ This is only partially right. Isocrates does not describe the education of Evagoras as a child (in *Evag.* 22 he only makes a reference to his fellow students), but in *Evag.* 41 the Isocratean educational ideal of constant concern and systematic devotion to the subject is transferred to the political level and is ideally exemplified by the Cyprian king.²⁹ What is important, I believe, is that Evagoras rejects the αὐτοσχεδιάζειν, which in conjunction with ὀλιγωρεῖν ("take no heed", "neglect"; *Areop.* 46, 51; *De pac.* 96) has a very negative meaning: it is the lack of systematic care and concern for public affairs, exactly the opposite point of the Isocratean ideal in δόξα-oriented education. This central term is a *terminus technicus* for a

---

25 Cf. *Demon.* 12; *Phil.* 79, 115, 127; *Evag.* 80–81; *Nicocl.* 29, 42; *Archid.* 8; *Hel.* 16, 23; *Panath.* 206; *Bus.* 10, 35; *Antid.* 308; *De big.* 25, 31, 33; Pernot 1993, 154–56.
26 Cf. the inscription of the last King of Salamis Nicocreon (IG IV 583): ματρ[όπο]λίς μοι χθὼν Πέλοπος τὸ Πελαζγικὸν Ἄργος, / Πνυταγόρας δὲ πατὴρ Αἰάκου ἐκ γενεᾶς. See also Christodoulou 2009.
27 On the topic "competitive-cooperative" values, see the classical work of Adkins 1960.
28 Walbank 1967, 222.
29 Cf. the parallel between rhetoric and politics in *Epist.* 6.8–9 and the encomium on the Isocratean student and Athenian general Timotheus (*Antid.* 128). For a fuller discussion of Isocrates' digression on Timotheus, see Alexiou 1995, 68–87, Too 2008, 153–56.

dispute between Alcidamas and Isocrates. Alcidamas (*Soph.* 9–14, 16, 30, 33–34) criticizes epideictic speech and the written style, while emphasizing the importance of improvisation in forensic and deliberative oratory.[30] Isocrates praises Evagoras because of the exercise of his intellect and the cultivation of the virtues instilled in him. This means that the exercise of the mind represents an effort to improve outstanding physical abilities and implies Evagoras' relationship with Isocratean education.[31]

The extensive praise of the famous mythical ancestors of Evagoras, the Aeacids, and the absence of any reference to the most recent famous ancestors is probably the reason why Isocrates does not insist on the training of Evagoras. However, this encomiastic *topos* is already found in *De bigis*, which is formally a forensic speech but constitutes an encomium of Alcibiades and is to be dated possibly in 396/5 BCE, before *Evagoras* (370 BCE). Alcibiades had often been criticized for his anti-democratic sentiments,[32] but Isocrates presents him and his ancestors as figures who established democracy. He is set up as an extraordinary character: his birth and his training are praised consistently (25–29) with the aim of highlighting the close ties of Alcibiades, as great individual, with the traditional values of the city.[33] Alcibiades' ancestors, including the reformer of the Athenian constitution Cleisthenes, symbolize the glorious *patrios politeia* and the idealized democracy before the Persian Wars (26–27). The most interesting aspect of this presentation is the term ἐπαιδεύθησαν (were educated): the citizens were brought to virtue through the establishment of an ideal constitution by Alcibiades' ancestors.[34] The idea of the politician-educator is central to Isocrates,[35] for whom it is very important to show that the moral legitimacy of Alcibiades has

---

30 See O'Sullivan 1992, 23–62, Mariss 2002, 26–55, Alexiou 2010, 128–29; 2016, 90–104.
31 Cf. Sykutris 1927, 32, Schiappa 1999, 171. Against Mason 1975, 80 and Eucken 1983, 265f., who focus on the natural intelligence of Evagoras. However, nature and education are for Isocrates inseparable (see *Antid.* 187, 274–275).
32 See *De big.* 38; Thuc. 6.16.4; Xenoph. *Mem.* 1.2.14; [Plat.] *Alc.* 1105a-3; Demosth. 21.143; Plut. *Alc.* 16,7; 34,7–35,1; Nepos *Alc.* 7.3; Seager 1967, 6–18, Alexiou 2011, 319f., 327f.
33 Cf. Gribble 1999, 121.
34 This educational process, which was implemented by the political leaders, is repeated in the description of the Athenian democracy before the Persian Wars in *Panegyricus* (82 and thoroughly discussed in paragraphs 75–81). Isocrates does not focus on the rather general education of the *polis*, as Thucydides (2.36ff.), but on the spirit of the political leaders who acted as educators. Using such ideas and teaching the young such habits (82: καὶ τοὺς νεωτέρους ἐν τοῖς τοιούτοις ἤθεσιν παιδεύοντες), they created men to fight against those from Asia, cf. Alexiou 2011, 322f.
35 See *Ad Nic.* 31: τὸ τῆς πόλεως ὅλης ἦθος ὁμοιοῦται τοῖς ἄρχουσιν. Cf. *Evag.* 48; *Hel.* 37; *De pac.* 126.

been achieved through Pericles, an idealized *agathos*, possessing the highest possible level of virtue (28: σωφρονέστατος, δικαιότατος καὶ σοφώτατος). By linking Alcibiades to the virtues of Pericles and the ancestral constitution, Isocrates associates the birth and the training of Alcibiades with the paradigmatic role of his ancestors (ἡγοῦμαι γὰρ καὶ τοῦτ' εἶναι τῶν καλῶν, ἐκ τοιούτων γενόμενον ὑπὸ τοιούτοις ἤθεσιν ἐπιτροπευθῆναι καὶ τραφῆναι καὶ παιδευθῆναι). They cultivated his character and steered him to virtue in the same way as the political leaders, who lived before the Persian Wars, prepared those who followed.

Inasmuch as Alcibiades is represented in a very positive light as a child of Athens, Isocrates asserts that Alcibiades' achievements were inextricably tied to the welfare of the *polis*. This message comes from the comparison with his ancestors and his personal effort (29). Isocrates states that Alcibiades wanted to emulate his ancestors and compare himself with them, as a basis for moral action. In rhetorical terminology this is the προσῆκον (Arist. *Rhet.* 1367b 12–13), the appropriate noble actions which are worthy of his ancestry. For Aristotle good birth and education contribute to the credibility of the encomium; good fathers are likely to have good sons, and good training is likely to produce good character (*Rhet.* 1367b 30–32). Indeed, in *Evagoras* Isocrates uses the Aeacids as a model for the king who lived up to the greatest and finest examples left to him as an inheritance (*Evag.* 12: καλλίστων καὶ μεγίστων παραδειγμάτων καταλειφθέντων οὐδὲν καταδεέστερον αὐτὸν ἐκείνων παρέσχεν).

This paradigmatic element is also attested in the observations of Polybius. It applies to the ethical improvement of the readers who will be able to emulate and imitate the great individuals of the past, since Polybius has introduced them to the character, training and ambitions of these great men:

καὶ γὰρ ἄτοπον τὰς μὲν τῶν πόλεων κτίσεις τοὺς συγγραφέας, καὶ πότε καὶ πῶς καὶ διὰ τίνων ἐκτίσθησαν, ἔτι δὲ τὰς διαθέσεις καὶ περιστάσεις μετ' ἀποδείξεως ἐξαγγέλλειν, τὰς δὲ τῶν τὰ ὅλα χειρισάντων ἀνδρῶν ἀγωγὰς καὶ ζήλους παρασιωπᾶν, καὶ ταῦτα τῆς χρείας μεγάλην ἐχούσης τὴν διαφοράν· ὅσῳ γὰρ ἄν τις καὶ ζηλῶσαι καὶ μιμήσασθαι δυνηθείη μᾶλλον τοὺς ἐμψύχους ἄνδρας τῶν ἀψύχων κατασκευασμάτων, τοσούτῳ καὶ τὸν περὶ αὐτῶν λόγον διαφέρειν εἰκὸς (πρὸς) ἐπανόρθωσιν τῶν ἀκουόντων.

It is indeed a strange thing that authors should narrate circumstantially the foundations of cities, telling us when, how, and by whom they were founded, and detailing the precise conditions and the difficulties of the undertaking, while they pass over in silence the previous training and the objects of the men who directed the whole matter, though such information is more profitable. For inasmuch as it is more possible to emulate and to imitate living men than lifeless buildings, so much more important for the improvement of a reader is it to learn about the former (Plb. 10.21.3–4, transl. W.R. Paton).

Polybius' exempla are based on the conception of emulation, which is developed for the moral improvement of the readers. His protagonists provide models to his readers and Polybius treats them with respect. Albrecht Dihle rightly observes that Polybius pursues ethical goals in his biographical excursus (ζηλῶσαι, μιμήσασθαι, πρὸς ἐπανόρθωσιν τῶν ἀκουόντων), an element that is consistent with the purposes of Plutarch's *Lives* (*Aem.* 1: πρὸς ἐπανόρθωσιν ἠθῶν) and with the ultimate goal of praise in Isocrates and Xenophon.[36] Given the different conception of what influence living men (ἔμψυχοι ἄνδρες) can have on the readers and lifeless buildings (ἄψυχα κατασκευάσματα), Polybius seems to adopt a concept of oratory that we find at the end of Isocrates' *Evagoras* (73–75). By recalling the opening of Pindar's *Nemean Ode* 5 (1–2),[37] Isocrates states that statues necessarily remain among those who set them up, while speeches can move throughout all of Greece. Polybius refers to cities, not to statues like Isocrates, but both of them share the sense of the audience's ethical encouragement, and such a role can only be assigned to living men in texts, not lifeless buildings or motionless statues. A similar idea is also present in Polybius 6.47.9–10: the comparison of a lifeless statue with living and breathing men would seem to spectators to be entirely problematic.[38]

For Isocrates, moral conduct is obtained through the imitation of the character and the thought of others that are represented in encomia, not through statues or paintings:

> τοῖς μὲν πεπλασμένοις καὶ γεγραμμένοις οὐδεὶς ἂν τὴν τοῦ σώματος φύσιν ὁμοιώσειεν, τοὺς δὲ τρόπους τοὺς ἀλλήλων καὶ τὰς διανοίας τὰς ἐν τοῖς λεγομένοις ἐνούσας ῥάδιόν ἐστιν μιμεῖσθαι τοῖς μὴ ῥᾳθυμεῖν αἱρουμένοις, ἀλλὰ χρηστοῖς εἶναι βουλομένοις.[39]
>
> No one would be able to make their own body resemble a statue or a painting, but it is easy for those who wish to take the trouble and are willing to be the best to imitate the character and thoughts of others that are represented in speeches (Isocr. *Evag.* 75, transl. Y.L. Too).

Τρόποι, διάνοιαι, μιμεῖσθαι are key terms, a product of an efficient moral instruction, which elaborate prose encomia can provide. Indeed, the paradigm is so central in Isocrates' educational model that it leads him to compose a speech as a

---

[36] Dihle 1987, 10. For some modifications on this kind of ethical improvement, see Schorn 2014b, 152f.
[37] Pindar *Nem.* 5.1–2: οὐκ ἀνδριαντοποιός εἰμ', ὥστ' ἐλινύσοντα ἐργάζεσθαι ἀγάλματ' ἐπ' αὐτᾶς βαθμίδος / ἑσταότα. See Pfeijffer 1999, 62, 99-108, Steiner 2001, 136–45, Burnett 2005, 63f., Alexiou 2010, 177f.
[38] Cf. Alexiou 2000, 109f., Schorn 2014b, 151 n. 54.
[39] For the arguments of Isocrates, see in detail Alexiou 2000, 103–17, Benediktson 2000, 35–37.

basis for moral action, to regard his writings as exempla to be used by students and as the best advice for people's lives, much like the precepts (ὑποθῆκαι) of the earlier poets such as Theognis or Hesiod (*Ad Nic.* 3, 43). They are used as teaching models (παραδείγματα) for his own pupils.⁴⁰

Isocrates assigns a central role to imitation, as it already emerges in the proem of *Evagoras*, where he argues that other authors should have praised good men among their contemporaries so that the youth could strive harder to achieve virtue (5: φιλοτιμοτέρως διέκειντο πρὸς τὴν ἀρετήν). In the epilogue Evagoras seems to be the appropriate παράδειγμα for imitation. Isocrates says that he is writing this speech considering that it will be by far the best encouragement (76: καλλίστην παράκλησιν) for Nicocles and Evagoras' other descendants, if someone assembles his virtues and imparts them to the younger. Isocrates next proceeds to define the imitation of others as an educational process of significance and benefit for the students, so that they will desire the way of life of those praised (77: ἵνα ζηλοῦντες τοὺς εὐλογουμένους τῶν αὐτῶν ἐκείνοις ἐπιτηδευμάτων ἐπιθυμῶσιν). In other words, Isocrates establishes the view that the encomium on Evagoras is therefore part of an educational process in which Nicocles also participates. The encomium of Evagoras has been transformed into an exhortation to Nicocles and recalls Aristotle, who observes the analogy between praise and advice.⁴¹ The praise of Evagoras corresponds with the advice that Isocrates offers to the monarch in the speeches *To Nicocles* and *Nicocles*. Supporting the differences between encomiastic writings and statues, Isocrates addresses Nicocles, Evagoras' son, advising him as follows: "Prefer to leave artistic images of your excellence rather than of your body as your memorial" (*Ad Nic.* 36).⁴²

In sum, it is the case that the basic encomiastic *topoi* established in the tradition of epideictic speeches, such as Isocrates' *De bigis* and *Evagoras*, help to make meaningful sense of Polybius' programmatic remarks in the tenth book of his *Histories*. If these remarks are interpreted in the light of the rhetorical ἐγκωμιαστικὸς τόπος, they suggest that Polybius had a thorough knowledge of the rhetorical background of the encomium. Whatever the concrete differences between related literary genres might be, Polybius uses the influential isocratic epideictic tradition in defining his own concepts of encomium, biography or historiography, and writes according to specific literary rules.

---

40 Cf. Papillon 1998, 52, Collins Edwards 2010, 377–400, esp. 383, Collins 2015, 219–28.
41 So Arist. *Rhet.* 1367b 37–39: ἔχει δὲ κοινὸν εἶδος ὁ ἔπαινος καὶ αἱ συμβουλαί. ἃ γὰρ ἐν τῷ συμβουλεύειν ὑπόθοιο ἄν, ταῦτα μετατεθέντα τῇ λέξει ἐγκώμια γίγνεται. Cf. Quint. *Inst. Or.* 3.7.28; Pernot 2015, 93f.
42 Cf. Ford 1993, 47.

Bibliography

Adkins, A.W.H. (1960), *Merit and Responsibility. A Study in Greek Values*, Oxford.
Alexiou, E. (2000), "Enkomion, Biographie und die 'unbeweglichen Statuen': Zu Isokrates *Euagoras* 73–76 und Plutarch *Perikles* 1–2", in: *C&M* 51, 103–117.
—— (2007), *Πλουτάρχου Παράλληλοι Βίοι. Η προβληματική των θετικών και αρνητικών παραδειγμάτων*, Thessaloniki.
—— (2010), *Der Euagoras des Isokrates. Ein Kommentar*, Berlin.
—— (2011), "Isokrates De bigis und die Entwicklung des Prosa-Enkomions", in: *Hermes* 139, 316–336.
—— (2014), "Die Rhetorik des 4. Jahrhunderts", in: B. Zimmermann/A. Rengakos (eds.), *Handbuch der griechischen Literatur der Antike: II. Die Literatur der klassischen und hellenistischen Zeit*, Munich, 734–859.
—— (2016), *Η ρητορική του 4ου αι. π.Χ. Το ελιξίριο της δημοκρατίας και η ατομικότητα*, Athens.
Bauer, B. (1992), "Amplificatio", in: *Hist. Wört. der Rhet.* 1, 445–471.
Blank, T. (2014), *Logos und Praxis. Sparta als politisches Exemplum in den Schriften des Isokrates*, Berlin.
Benediktson, T.D. (2000), *Literature and the Visual Arts in Ancient Greece and Rome*, Norman, OK.
Brunello, C. (2015), *Storia e paideia nel Panatenaico di Isocrate*, Rome.
Buchheit, V. (1960), *Untersuchungen zur Theorie des Genos Epideiktikon von Georgias bis Aristoteles*, Munich.
Burnett, A.P. (2005), *Pindar's Songs for Young Athletes of Aigina*, Oxford.
Christodoulou, P. (2009), "Nicocréon, le dernier roi de Salamine de Chypre: discours idéologique et pouvoir politique", in: *CCEC* 39, 235–258.
Clarke, H. (1885), *The Evagoras of Isocrates. With an Introduction and Notes*, London.
Collins, J.H. (2015), *Exhortations to Philosophy. The Protreptics of Plato, Isocrates, and Aristotle*, Oxford.
Collins Edwards, L. (2010), "Shifting Paradigms. Mimesis in Isocrates", in: P. Mitsis/C. Tsagalis (eds.), *Allusion, Authority, and Truth. Critical Perspectives on Greek Poetic and Rhetorical Praxis*, Berlin/New York, 377–400.
Dihle, A. (1987), *Die Entstehung der historischen Biographie*, Heidelberg.
—— (1998), "Zur antiken Biographie", in: W.-W. Ehlers (ed.), *La biographie antique*, Vandœuvres/Genève, 119–146.
Eck, B. (2015), "Alcibiade dans le Sur l'Attelage d'Isocrate", in: C. Bouchet/P. Giovannelli-Jouanna (eds.), *Isocrate. Entre jeu rhétorique et enjeux politiques*, Lyon, 33–46.
Eucken, C. (1983), *Isokrates. Seine Positionen in der Auseinandersetzung mit den zeitgenössischen Philosophen*, Berlin/New York.
Farrington, S.T. (2011), "Polybius and the Gap between Encomium and History", in: *CPh* 106, 324–342.
Flacelière, R. (1961), *Isocrate cinq discours. Éloge d'Hélène, Busiris, Contre les Sophistes, Sur l'attelage, Contre Callimachos*, Paris.
Ford, A. (1993), "The Price of Art in Isocrates. Formalism and the Escape from Politics", in: T. Poulakos (ed.), *Rethinking the History of Rhetoric. Multidisciplinary Essays in Rhetorical Tradition*, Boulder, 31–52.
Fortenbaugh, W.W. (2007), "Biography and the Aristotelian Peripatos", in: M. Erler/S. Schorn (eds.), *Die griechische Biographie in hellenistischer Zeit*, Berlin/New York, 45–78.

Gallo, I. (2005), *La biografia greca. Profilo storico e breve antologia di testi*, Soveria Mannelli.
Gribble, D. (1999), *Alcibiades and Athens. A Study in Literary Presentation*, Oxford.
Laistner, M. (1927), *Isocrates De Pace and Philippus, Edited with a Historical Introduction and Commentary*, New York/London.
Lausberg, H. (1960), *Handbuch der literarischen Rhetorik*, Munich.
Mariss, R. (2002), *Alkidamas. Über diejenigen, die schriftliche Reden schreiben, oder über die Sophisten. Eine Sophistenrede aus dem 4. Jahrhundert v. Chr. eingeleitet und kommentiert*, Münster.
Mason, D.K. (1975), *Studies in the Evagoras of Isocrates*, Chapel Hill.
Momigliano, A. (1993), *The Development of Greek Biography. Expanded Edition*, 2nd edn, Cambridge, Mass./London.
O'Sullivan, N. (1992), *Alcidamas. Aristophanes and the Beginnings of Greek Stylistic Theory*, Stuttgart.
Pallantza, E. (2005), *Der Troische Krieg in der nachhomerischen Literatur zum 5. Jahrhundert v. Chr.*, Stuttgart.
Papillon, T. (1998), "Isocrates and the Greek Poetic Tradition", in: *Scholia* 7, 41–61.
Pernot, L. (1993), *La rhétorique de l'éloge dans le monde gréco-romain*. I: *Histoire et technique*, II: *Les valeurs*, Paris.
—— (2015), *Epideictic Rhetoric. Questioning the Stakes of Ancient Praise*, Austin.
Pfeijffer, I.L. (1999), *Three Aeginetan Odes of Pindar. A Commentary on Nemean V, Nemean III, & Pythian VIII*, Leiden.
Piccirilli, L. (1990), "Introduzione", in: C. Carena/M. Manfredini/L. Piccirilli, *Plutarco Le vite di Cimone e di Lucullo*, Milan.
Plöbst, W. (1911), *Die Auxesis (Amplificatio). Studien zu ihrer Entwicklung und Anwendung*, Munich.
Roth, P. (2003), *Der Panathenaikos des Isokrates. Übersetzung und Kommentar*, Munich/Leipzig.
Schepens, G. (2007), "Zum Verhältnis von Biographie und Geschichtsschreibung in hellenistischer Zeit", in: M. Erler/S. Schorn (eds.), *Die griechische Biographie in hellenistischer Zeit*, Berlin/New York, 335–361.
Schiappa, E. (1999), *The Beginnings of Rhetorical Theory in Classical Greece*, London.
Schorn, S. (2014a), "Biographie und Autobiographie", in: B. Zimmermann/A. Rengakos (eds.), *Handbuch der griechischen Literartur der Antike: II. Die Literatur der klassischen und hellenistischen Zeit*, Munich, 678–733.
—— (2014b), "Historiographie, Biographie und Enkomion. Theorie der Biographie und Historiographie bei Diodor und Polybios", in: *RSA* 44, 135–162.
Seager, R. (1967), "Alcibiades and the Charge of Aiming at Tyranny", in: *Historia* 16, 6–18.
Sonnabend, H. (2002), *Geschichte der antiken Biographie. Von Isokrates bis zur Historia Augusta*, Stuttgart/Weimar.
Steidle, W. (1963), *Sueton und die antike Biographie*, 2nd edn, Munich.
Steiner, D.T. (2001), *Images in Mind. Statues in Archaic and Classical Greek Literature and Thought*, Princeton.
Sykutris, J. (1927), "Isokrates' Euagoras", in: *Hermes* 62, 24–53 (= F. Seck [ed.], *Isokrates*, Darmstadt 1976, 74–105).
Tuplin, C. (2000), "Nepos and the Origins of Political Biography", in: C. Deroux (ed.), *Studies in Latin Literature and Roman History X*, Bruxelles, 124–161.
Usher, S. (1990), *Isocrates. Panegyricus and To Nicocles*, Warminster.

Walbank, F.W. (1967), *A Historical Commentary on Polybius*. Vol. 2: *Commentary on Books* vii–xviii, Oxford.

Antonis Tsakmakis
Polybius and Biography

Discussion of Polybius' views about biography has been monopolized by the interpretation of the historian's reference to his lost work on Philopoemen in chapter 10.21 of his *History*. While earlier scholars, among them Momigliano and Dihle,[1] were mostly concerned with the possible importance of the lost work for the development of Greek biography, Fortenbaugh, Schepens and Farrington have convincingly argued that Polybius' characterization of it as λόγος ἐγκωμιαστικός has to be taken more seriously.[2] Accordingly, the σύνταξις in three books which dealt in more detail with Philopoemen's family, character and education and only briefly mentioned (κεφαλαιώδη... ἀπολογισμόν) the deeds of his political and military career, was an encomium. More recently, Stephan Schorn has pointed out that Polybius' distinction between the genres of his two works relies on Isocrates' theory of the *encomium* as it is developed in his *Evagoras*.[3]

However, the partial thematic overlapping between encomium, historiography and biography, and the fact that Polybius' does not devote a separate discussion to biography as a genre, neither minimizes a priori the importance of biographical elements in his work, nor anticipates that their function and importance is exhausted in the suggestion of praise and blame. This may hold for Diodorus, for whom Schorn has stated, "daß die Theorie der Biographie und ein Teil der Theorie der Historiographie bei Diodor in Auseindandersetzung mit der Theorie des Enkomions entstanden ist, wobei diese um den Aspekt der Kritik für schlechtes Handeln erweitert wurde".[4] Unlike Diodorus or Plutarch, Polybius' stance towards biography cannot be discussed exclusively against the backdrop of rhetorical theory.

---

[1] Momigliano 1993, 116 acknowledges the character of the work as an encomium but supposes "a connection with Xenophon's *Cyropaedia*". For Dihle 1987, 9–22, the common elements of encomium and biography are signs of influence of the former genre on the latter; Dihle imputes too much importance to the moral content and its edifying character in both genres.
[2] Fortenbaugh 2007; Schepens 2007; Farrington 2011. The key passage is 10.21.8: "For just as that work, being an encomium, demands a summary narration with amplification of the accomplishments, so does this work of history, impartial concerning praise and blame, demand a true account and one supported by a demonstration of the reasoning accompanying each action" (Transl. from Farrington 2011; all other translations are from Paton).
[3] Schorn 2014. On the influence of Isocrates' *Evagoras* on Polybius, see also the contribution of Alexiou in the present volume.
[4] Schorn 2014, 147.

In this paper it will be argued not only that Polybius occasionally resorts to biographical methods of representation, but also that these methods are organically integrated into the concept of his historiography. Furthermore, we suggest that even if it cannot be proved that Polybius contributed significantly to the development of Greek political biography, he is a valuable witness of the literary-cultural process which would later lead to Plutarchean biography.

The pre-history of Greek political biography is an ardently debated issue. Geiger has rightly pointed out that there is no evidence for the fully developed genre in Greek literature before Plutarch and he regards Nepos as a main source of inspiration for the prolific Boeotian's biographic endeavor.[5] On the other hand, Geiger's theory equally diminishes the impact of a Greek tradition of biographical writing on the formation of *Lives* of political and military leaders.[6] Yet even if Geiger is right in observing that essential traits of Plutarchean biography are for the first time traceable in Nepos, still Nepos is not necessary to explain the emergence of Plutarchean biography.

At this point some further preliminary clarifications about the essence of biography and what can be called typical for this genre (the "biographical") are needed. Biography is not to be equated with prosopography; the focus on an individual or the inclusion of information about a person's private life and character do not suffice to make a text or passage biographical, as some modern scholars have too readily assumed.[7] Distinctions such as that between complete biography, partial biography and biographical material are of equally little use. Nor does the area in which the protagonist of a given biography excelled seem to have any special significance for a definition of biography in literary terms.[8] Least decisive for establishing the genre "biography" is the purpose or effect of a text, intended or not, despite the didactic, moralizing, or paradigmatic tendency of a great part of ancient biographies.[9] All this may be part of literary history, but it is not enlightening from a theoretical perspective.

Is it possible to advance beyond a historical and descriptive approach of ancient biography and also to determine what distinguishes prosopographical in-

---

[5] Geiger 1985.
[6] See most recently Adams 2013, 81, who rightly refuses to examine political biography independently from the biographies of other categories of people. On the existence of an already formed tradition of literary biography in the third century BCE, see Knöbl 2010, 37.
[7] See also the cautious remarks by Schepens 1998, xvi–xviii.
[8] Against restrictive definitions and subdivisions of the genre, see Luke 2015, xciv–xcvi.
[9] On the exemplary character of biography, cf. Stem 2012, 128–61 (for further literature 132 with n. 12).

formation from biographical elements found in other works such as Polybius' history? Momigliano's famous compact and minimal definition of biography, "an account of the life of a man [sic] from birth to death",[10] may be applicable to modern biography, but in the context of ancient texts called a *bios*, each tenet of this definition would require endless adaptations and modifications.[11] It ultimately relies on the assumption of an one-to-one correlation between reality and its linguistic expression; but a literary genre is more than a sum of referential statements: it is a complex conceptual frame which can only be defined through the study of the mental representations that find an expression through it.

The term *bios* was invariably used by the Greeks for a person's life and for any verbal representation of it. Let us first focus on the latter. *Bioi* could constitute narratives, but could also be condensed reports about a person and his/her deeds.[12] Eventually, ancient Greek *bioi* varied considerably: Lives of poets could be selective and unbalanced, full of antiquarian material including alternative versions of various details; lives of poets and philosophers could be full of quotes and doxography. Fictional anecdotes and historical material could co-exist in the same text. Some very brief *bioi* could look like an entry in an encyclopedia. One could argue that these *Lives* are so different that they cannot be treated in common, but this argument would entail a *petitio principii*. Nobody in antiquity seems to have been annoyed by the diversity of length, relative completeness, historicity and literary characteristics of *bioi* as would, say, a modern publisher who would deny to publish a biography which was evidently fictional or covered with extreme unevenness the various stages of a person's life. The expectations of ancient readers were considerably different from those of today. Our working hypothesis is that in antiquity even in the case of concise texts which left much to be desired, a kernel of biographical essence justified their inclusion into rather than exclusion from an ideal community of texts regarded as "biographical".

A cognitive definition may enable us to provide a sufficient explanation for the multiple instantiations of *bios* in antiquity and cover, *a fortiori*, any other manifestation of biography, including of course modern biography. All uses of the term cohere in that they activate a prototypical mental structure which governs both the production and the way a reading community looks at a text. In the following we will try to define biography in cognitive terms and subsequently ex-

---

10 Momigliano 1993, 11.
11 A title, as any other formal element, is not a sufficient criterion for the definition of genre; cf. Schepens 1998, xvi–xvii; yet, the ancient use of the term cannot be ignored altogether.
12 On the distinction between narrative and report, see Smith 2003.

amine the mental representations associated with the notion of βίος in Greek; finally, we will focus on sections of Polybius' work that share typical features with biography.

Bios as a generic term (and any text which is recognized as biographical) activates a set of assumptions which in turn determine the frame for the interpretation of the text.

1. A single person is foregrounded as a sole protagonist and subject of the text. From this results the monographic character of the text. Digressions and independent sections whose function may temporarily remain unclear are avoided, so that the reader's attention remains constantly fixed on the protagonist.
2. The protagonist is supposed to have been an important figure for reasons that the audience (are supposed to) know in advance and share. The protagonist's field of activity and excellence (politician, lawgiver, philosopher, poet, saint etc.) usually corresponds to the priorities and interests of specific reading communities.
3. As every detail has to be related to the protagonist, irrelevant material is excluded.[13] The extraordinary importance of relevance further suggests a hierarchy of readings of individual sections. An anecdote about a philosopher's miraculous birth is not necessarily scrutinized in terms of its historicity; instead, it may be primarily regarded as relevant for the evaluation of the protagonist.
4. The work relates virtually all the available information pertaining to the protagonist; if, however, too much information is available to the author, the most salient and appropriate items can be selected, as Plutarch makes clear in the preface to his *Life of Alexander*. Serial biographies are most likely to seek uniformity and thus require serious cuts where more material is at the author's disposal.[14] Here we grasp a difference between ancient and modern biography; in ancient biography the parts are dispensable, they have relative importance; their meaning depends on the whole.
5. Information is arranged so as to fit a familiar pattern which ideally reproduces the narrative structure of a human life. The content consists in

---

13 Cf. Späth 2000, 58–60.
14 Nepos' *Lives of foreign generals* and Plutarch's *Parallel Lives* are good examples; on the contrary, the encyclopedic perspective of Diogenes Laertius, whose standard practice is to exploit the available material to the highest degree makes shorter lives appear poorer, compared to the more complete ones, and creates on the whole a feeling of formal asymmetry.

a so-called "world schema" (a conceptual structure which expresses what everybody understands as human life), and this content is adapted into a text schema, a literary construct with distinct characteristics.[15] The world schema produces a literary schema (a prototypical pattern which consists in a sequence of constant elements such as family, parents, birth, formation—which includes natural characteristics, education, initiation—beginning of career, deeds, representative actions and sayings, death). Even if a *bios* is brief, incoherent, lacking information about most stages of a person's life, the overall schema assures the orientation of the reader. On the other hand, the enactment of the schema of biography ("biographical" schema) is the essential criterion to decide whether information about a person in a non-biographical context (e.g. historiography) can be labelled as biographical.

6. The audience's perception and definition of the self by means of experiences framed within the conceptual framework of the human life helps establish connections between the world of the text (which is structured around a person's life) and the reality of the audience. The way the texts are related to the readers' lives enrich their meanings and dictate their uses (as sources of information, instruction, moral improvement etc.). Various responses to biographical texts can be cued, depending on the merits of the main figure. In the Plutarchean version of morally-oriented biography the prospective emulation of virtue by the reader is foregrounded (*Aem. Paul.* 1; *Arat.* 1). *Lives* of poets may entail keys for the interpretation of the poets' work, *Lives* of philosophers and saints may serve the purpose of indoctrination and initiation of the readers into a higher way of life etc.

While some texts may have a prototypical character, others occupy a position in the periphery. But even texts which conform to a limited degree with the pattern are appropriately understood as *bioi*.

---

15 Cf. Stockwell 2002, 77: "The conceptual structure drawn from memory to assist in understanding utterances is a schema that was first called a script". Biography transforms a world schema (a content organized according to a pattern familiar to everybody from his/her world experience), and a text schema, which, according to Peter Stockwell "represent[s] our expectations of the way that world schemas appear to us in terms of their sequencing and structural organization" (80). The Greek term *bios* accounts for both the world schema, the typical notion of human life, and for the textual genre, a work illustrating the life of an important personality according to a constitutive pattern. This pattern can be negotiated, confirmed, revised, enriched in almost every work.

This discussion would be incomplete without an examination of the mental representations of βίος as the notion of human life. In Greek, as in most languages, expressions about life usually exploit two conceptual metaphors. In the first place, life is associated with the idea of the continuous flow of time; accordingly, the image activated by the term *bios* is that of movement: either movement of life itself, or movement within time. A common associated metaphor is that of life as a journey. In various languages there exist several metaphorical expressions about life in terms of movement: life has a beginning and an end (cf. Greek: καταστρέφω τὸν βίον, τελευτὴ τοῦ βίου etc.), it "goes on", "elapses", during our life we "pass" across/through stages or events (such as a war) etc. Alternatively, life is frequently objectified, it is treated as a single object of thought and discourse, even as one moves *through* it. In these cases, the evoked image is that of a demarcated space, sometimes thought of as a container: one moves *through life* (διάγω, διεξέρχομαι τὸν βίον, literally: "go through"; διὰ βίου); we leave life or exchange it for another location (ἐκλείπειν, ἀπολείπειν, μεταλλάσσειν τὸν βίον).[16] While in these schemas no energetic participation of the involved person is foregrounded, in Greek some peculiar expressions treat life as the object of an activity: a person follows a way towards a life, education "leads" to it (ἀγωγὴ ἐπὶ τὸν βίον—or into life: εἰς τὸν βίον), life can be "filled with" a content (cf. Plut. *Alex.* 23.2: πλείστων καὶ μεγίστων πράξεων ἐνέπλησεν; on the contrary, we mostly talk of a life which *is* "full" of adventures, experiences etc.), humans can make a choice of βίος in advance (αἵρεσις τοῦ βίου)[17]—in this case βίος (viewed as a whole) is understood as the way of life (this meaning occurs mostly in constructions with an adjective or genitive: e.g. δίκαιος, ἄλυπος, ἀσφαλής, παράνομος, λέοντος, Τίμωνος etc.).[18]

It is this objectified notion of life which mostly occurs in the main Greek biographical corpus of political biographies, the *Parallel Lives* of Plutarch; the idea of life as an object, which can be thought of or observed as a whole, characterized, emulated etc., is common throughout Plutarchean biography. As a unique object, a person's life can be seized in its totality by an external observer (Polybius' term *synopsis* could adequately be used to do justice to this idea). It can be

---

[16] Similar expressions for the stages of life: ἐπὶ γήραος οὐδῷ, "at the threshold of old age"; cf. Pl. *Rep.* 328e.

[17] The term βίος is also used metonymically for the material means that secure existence (literally: what is needed πρὸς τὸν βίον).

[18] In this sense, βίος is for the individual the equivalent of πολιτεία for the state; see esp. Pl. *Leg.* 858c–858e; Plut. *Is.* 47.

conceptualized, metaphorically, as a visual image which, like the image of a material monument, appears in a mirror (Plut. *Timol.* 1; *Aem. Paul.* 1). More generally, in ancient biography the narrative about a person's life is equivalent to the demonstration of an edifice which consists of various parts. A biography (*bios*) is a representation of a life (*bios*) which in a way reveals the soul of the person behind it.[19] Thus, it provides the framework which guarantees the meaning of each part of it. The value of the parts is derived from the structure, not *vice versa*. Anecdotes, quotes, miraculous stories in lives of poets and philosophers are not included in a biography for their own sake, but as manifestations of the person's most characteristic traits. This idea of life as a meaningful, accomplished structure elicits the idea that the ancient approach to biography is teleological. While in a life which is understood as a journey change can be associated with reversal and tragic effects, change in ancient biography brings the protagonist closer to the accomplishment of his characteristic image.

According to these considerations, a historiographical passage can be regarded as biographical if it evokes the literary schema of biography (which, *a fortiori*, has to be accompanied, at least partly, by the further traits of biography we have enumerated) and—in the particular Greek understanding of the genre—treats individual episodes or stages of life as instrumental for the accomplishment of character. Among earlier historians, Herodotus occasionally adopts a biographical perspective, especially in his references to Persian monarchs. In doing so he is most likely to reflect the form of his sources (in Oriental monarchies, history was the history of monarchs)—than to assign programmatically to the biographical approach a specific importance. On the other hand, the biographical arrangement does not have an essential impact on the construction of meaning or modify the interpretation of any part of the work—it lacks the typically Greek component. Thucydides' obituary of Pericles (2.65) includes many references to his mental and moral qualities; nevertheless, they are not framed as biographical: they do not bring the reader closer to Pericles as a person and to his life; they belong to the image of a leader and contain the necessary information for a better understanding of the political life and history of Athens before and after Pericles' death. References to Pericles' moral qualities do not serve as a guide for the reader's education, but as a contribution to the delineation of ideal leadership. When one comes to Xenophon, although his model in the *Cyropedia* is characteristically biographical, the presentation of the main figures in his *Hellenica* is not: family and education, details which are not interesting for political and military

---

[19] Even in the case of divine immortality cognition is what distinguishes βίος from χρόνος (time); Plut. *Is.* 1.

history, are ignored in the latter. Explicit or implicit characterization of political personalities is not understood as a contribution to a comprehensive representation of their life, but as means better to expound the dynamics of a historical situation. Xenophon's emphasis on individuals in the *Hellenica* is analogous to his evaluation of the importance of charismatic leadership, especially in his mature age. Taking this into account, we can concede that the detailed presentation of individual leaders, e.g. Jason of Pherae, could be easily associated with a biographical frame; such passages confirm the existence and importance of the biographical prototype for the Athenian historian.

Polybius' world is quite different. In his model of historiography knowledge and information serve the reader's self-improvement. Thus, a fundamental affinity to biography seems to be taken for granted. In addition, the conceptual frame and the teleological perspective of biography, elements which guarantee unity and coherence, are characteristically evoked through Polybius' vision of history, as he, at least in retrospect, interprets the Roman conquest of the world as the result of a movement towards unity and integration. In contrast, however, with this concept of macro-history, where a force beyond the control of individual actors (*tyche*) is constantly at work,[20] outstanding individuals can leave their imprints on the lives of their communities at certain historical periods. External and superior forces do not deprive these persons of the opportunity to influence actively the course of events and excel. In the following we will demonstrate that the treatment of these individuals in many cases displays some characteristic features of Greek biography.

Most characteristically, personal excellence awakes the people's desire to learn more about an outstanding personality. In a passage which announces the detailed account of the deeds of a most illustrious man, Scipio Africanus, this desire is notably expressed in a way which evokes the familiar schema of biography: people appear to enquire into Scipio's nature and education in order to better understand his achievements. Scipio clearly is the focus of attention of writers and common people alike, and this interest in his person grows beyond the details of his public career. Polybius eagerly acknowledges this interest and integrates the special treatment of the issue into his historiography:

> Now that I am about to recount Scipio's exploits in Spain, and in short everything that he achieved in his life, I think it necessary to convey to my readers, in the first place, a notion of his character and natural parts. For the fact that he was almost the most famous man of

---

[20] Cf. 1.1.2: In the context of world history the individual can only use knowledge in order to "endure bravely the changes of fortune".

all time makes everyone desirous to know what sort of man he was, and what were the natural gifts and the training which enabled him to accomplish so many great actions. But none can help falling into error and acquiring a mistaken impression of him, as the estimate of those who have given us their views about him is very wide of the truth. That what I myself state here is sound will be evident to all who by means of my narrative are able to appreciate the most glorious and hazardous of his exploits. As for all other writers, they represent him as a man favored by fortune, who always owed the most part of his success to the unexpected and to mere chance, such men being, in their opinion, more divine and more worthy of admiration than those who always act by calculation. They are not aware that one of the two things deserves praise and the other only congratulation, the latter being common to ordinary men, whereas what is praiseworthy belongs alone to men of sound judgment and mental ability, whom we should consider to be the most divine and most beloved by the god (10.2.1–7).

To satisfy the people's desire and explain Scipio's success, the historian promises a detailed narrative which gives a complete picture of the man's character and virtues and associates his exploits with his mental and moral qualities. In advance, however, he pointedly amends existing biographical traditions (written, but possibly oral as well) insisting particularly on one point which is crucial for the overall evaluation of Scipio. Scipio was believed to have been guided by god and favored by chance; according to Polybius, this view is mistaken, as Scipio's success was not due to chance or any other irrational and unintelligible factors (ἐπιτυχῆ τινα καὶ τὸ πλεῖον αἰεὶ παραλόγως καὶ ταὐτομάτῳ κατορθοῦντα);[21] in fact he was exceptionally prudent. This point will be later exemplified by the way Scipio captured New Carthage (10.14). He had based his stratagem on his understanding of the phenomenon of ebb and flow, which he took into account in elaborating his plan;[22] to his troops, however, he had announced in advance that Neptune had appeared in his dream and promised his assistance (10.11.7). Scipio was aware of the mentality of his troops. He thus manipulates them in order to assure that they execute willingly and bravely his own plan. Before, however, the narrative commences, Polybius points to a historical parallel from Greek history, which was known only through legend and was part of local Spartan history:

> To me it seems that the character and principles of Scipio much resembled those of Lycurgus, the Lacedaemonian legislator. For neither must we suppose that Lycurgus drew up the constitution of Sparta under the influence of superstition and solely prompted by the Pythia, nor that Scipio won such an empire for this country by following the suggestion of dreams and omens. But since both of them saw that most men neither readily accept any-

---

[21] Cf. also 36.17.1. On *tyche* in Polybius, cf. Brouwer 2011.
[22] On the problems of this account, cf. Walbank 1957–1979, ii.192–93.

thing unfamiliar to them, nor venture on great risks without the hope of divine help, Lycurgus made his own scheme more acceptable and more easily believed in by invoking the oracles of the Pythia in support of projects due to himself, while Scipio similarly made the mane under his command more sanguine and more ready to face perilous enterprises by instilling into them the belief that his projects were divinely inspired. That everything he did was done with calculation and foresight, and that all his enterprises fell out as he had reckoned, will be clear from what I am about to say (10.2.8–13).

The parallelism emphasizes that it was Scipio himself who, being aware of the ideology of ordinary people, endorsed the erroneous interpretation of his deeds. While the projection of a dis-illusionist rationalism upon Scipio himself maximizes the effect of the narrative on the reader,[23] the parallelism functions as a persuasion device which provides further support to Polybius' theoretical expositions.

The illustration of theory and praxis as a unity, exemplified through a characteristic episode of the life of the protagonist, is a trademark of biographical writing which surfaces in this Polybian passage. The historical parallelism further suggests to the reader the idea that history can be made useful and comprehensible, if one is able to recognize recurrent patterns and interpret historical incidents correctly. On the whole, the enactment of the "biographical" schema which was suggested by the people's desire to enquire into Scipio's character and education is utilized in a way that enhances a certain involvement of the reader in interpretation and increases the persuasiveness and instructive effectiveness of the passage in a way that serves the historian's ultimate aims: to establish the correct association of causes and effects,[24] the appreciation of personal excellence—moral as well as mental—as a moving force in history, and the fruitful correlation of remote historical examples as a tool of historical interpretation.[25]

Scipio belongs to the persons who deserve special attention, like the heroes of biography, due to his extraordinary achievements and due to the fact that these deeds reveal remarkable personal qualities. The *raison d'être* of a biographical outlook—the coherent representation of the character of powerful personalities

---

[23] For a similar use of focalization in Polybius to maximize the persuasiveness of the narrative, see Tsakmakis 2015, 45–51. For Polybius' suggestive writing as a means to achieve the intended effect of the work, cf. Guelfucci 2005.
[24] Cf. also 11.19a.1–4; 11.25b.1.
[25] The *synkrisis* of emblematic figures from Greek and Roman history on the grounds of similarities which are not self-evident but presuppose characterization based on a particular interpretation of their deeds, and not in order to explain the one through the other, but in order to endorse a more abstract alignment of different strands of history, clearly anticipates the compositional principle of Plutarch's *Parallel Lives*.

and its expression in their actions—is further safeguarded by passages such as 32.4.1–2, where Polybius illustrates an opposite example: how a single person can exercise a negative influence on the course of military and political events and the fortune of a whole nation.

> Lyciscus the Aetolian was a turbulent and noisy man, and after he was slain, the Aetolians from this time forward lived in unison and concord, simply owing to the removal of this one man. So great it seems is the power exercised by men's natures that not only armies and cities, but national groups and in fact all the different peoples which compose the whole world, experience the extremities sometimes of misfortune and sometimes of prosperity, owing to the good or bad character of a single man.

A further passage, 30.9.20–21, shows an independent interest in the behavior of certain historical persons as an instructive case study for readers. Polybius admits that he is not following his usual standards, but aims at the full demonstration of a paradigmatic story, so that the reader can share the protagonists' experience:

> If I am asked why I have dealt at length with the case of Polyaratus and Deinon, it was not in order to exult over their misfortunes, which would be indeed outrageous, but that I might by clearly exhibiting their lack of wisdom render such as find themselves placed by circumstance in a similar situation better prepared to act advisedly and wisely.

We notice again, that Polybius' decision to organize his narrative around the activities of specific persons serves a double goal: to demonstrate the agreement of character and action and to provide the reader with instructive case studies for better preparation for his own life.

Polybius acknowledges the existence of various types of readers, and he is also sensitive to the various responses triggered by different kinds of writing.[26] As some historical works approach the specialized monographic sub-genres in the periphery of historiography, they respond to the needs of different types of readers. In 9.1.4 the historian distinguishes between a φιλήκοος who is attracted more by the γενεαλογικός τρόπος, the πολυπράγμων and περιττός who prefers stories about colonisation, foundations and local traditions and mythography about the ancestors, and the πολιτικός who has an interest in the deeds of nations, cities and leaders:

> The genealogical side appeals to those who are fond of a story, and the account of colonies, the foundation of cities, and their ties of kindred, such as Ephorus, also remarks somewhere

---

[26] Cf. 12.26.1–6.

or other, attracts the curious and lovers of recondite lore, while the statesman is interested in the doings of nations, cities, and monarchs.

While Polybius gives the last type of historiography, which corresponds to the πραγματική ιστορία, the absolute priority (9.1.5–6), other authors show a preference for specific parts (μέρη) of historiography; in doing so, they each become more appealing to a different type of reader. Polybius neither excludes these readers from his target audience[27] nor is indifferent toward the historical material which is included in certain "partial" genres.[28] His objections to these sub-genres are related to their limited scope of presentation. The "mode" (τρόπος) of partial historiography does not allow for a synoptic view of history in its totality (1.4.6); those who believe that they can have access to the knowledge of history as a whole by studying exclusively a part of history resemble people who claim to have the impression of a living animal when they take into sight some of its members and parts (1.4.7). When Polybius criticizes Theopompus for making Philip the center of a historical work, his principal objection does not stem from what this historian includes in his major work (although he may largely disagree with Theopompus' evaluation of Philip), but from what he leaves out. Theopompus' flaw is that he loses the wider perspective of Greek history. Polybius does not reject biographical writing as such, provided that it does not undermine the aims of historiography. On the contrary, the two prove compatible in many aspects. According to Polybius, the didactic purposes of his work are better served through empathy: readers are not detached analysts concerned with theoretical understanding; they are encouraged to imagine themselves living in the world of history and to imagine how they would act in various circumstances.[29] By comparison with Thucydides' expectations about the use of his own work (e.g. 1.22.4; 1.23.5; cf. 2.48.3), we notice a shift of priorities, from the dominance of the intellectual component to the implementation of practical and moral tasks into the

---

[27] Polybius can sometimes write in a more epideictic manner (38.4.1), and he also writes for both the φιλήκοοι and the φιλομαθοῦντες alike (10.21.3; 38.6.6).
[28] Polybius (who devotes a whole book, 34, to geography) praises Eudoxus for his treatment of Greek history, but especially Ephorus, who stands out for his foundations, genealogies, colonisations and presentations of leaders; he claims to be by far superior in geographical and topographical documentation (34.1.3–4). On the other hand (12.26.1–6) Timaios is criticized for the inaccuracy of his colonization and foundation stories and genealogies.
[29] 11.25b.3. On the reader's ἐπανόρθωσις or διόρθωσις, cf. 1.35.1–10; 10.21.4. As an instructor of political and military leaders, the historian has to avail of experiences in public life in order to better understand the events he describes. The lack of αὐτοπάθεια is condemning for Timaeus and other "armchair" historians: 12.25h.1–6; cf. also 12.25c.4–5. On Polybius' bias against Timaeus and its motivation, see Baron 2009.

communicative situation of the historian who addresses his audience. In Thucydides, human nature assured the appropriate scale for the presentation and evaluation of historical events; in Polybius the commensurability between the narrated story and the reader's reality enriches the latter's experience. Herein lies a characteristic similarity to a cognitive process which is fundamental for biography: the framing of the story in terms of everyone's experience of human life—which is ultimately internalized and becomes part of our understanding of the self.

Certainly, biography, like other μέρη of historiography, cannot supply a complete vision of the organic whole which is history in the eyes of Polybius. But as the complete vision of Polybius' historiography is the result of a comprehensive composition which, necessarily, consists of parts, the particular, individual μέρη of historiography can be useful within a historical composition, under the condition that it uphold the holistic perspective of the work.[30] But this holistic approach which makes the components cohere and agree with the whole in a meaningful structure is also a characteristic of Greek biography.

Unlike classical historians, we notice that in several passages of his work Polybius devotes special attention to individual stages of a person's life in a way which evokes both the "biographical" schema and the holistic perspective of the Greek biographical tradition.[31] In the following we will discuss in some detail a passage of this kind: it presents a private discussion between two persons who, at this stage of their life, have no public duties and would otherwise not be the focus of historiographical attention: the almost eighteen year old Scipio the younger and the author of the text, Polybius.

> Now that the progress of my narrative and the date call our special attention to this family, I wish in order to satisfy the reader's curiosity to execute a promise I made in the previous book and left unfulfilled, and this was that I would tell how and why the fame of Scipio in Rome advanced so far and became so brilliant more quickly than it should, and to tell also how his friendship and intimacy with the author grew so great that this report about them not only spread to Italy and Greece, but that even further afield their liking and intercourse

---

[30] This approach is endorsed by passages such as 10.40.7: a brief glance at the end of life can confirm the characterization suggested by a person's deeds; cf. Pomeroy 1996, esp. 410–411. See also 11.10.1–8: a speaker is more persuasive if his way of life (βίος) provides a telling example for the truth of his words.

[31] See e.g. 10.21.2–5. He similarly does not hesitate to make the entire life or activity of a person the subject of a section of his work; cf. 10.2.1; for biographical details and focus on a person, cf. 13.4 on Heracleides of Tarentum; 27.15 on Charops; 36.15 on Prousias. These passages may reflect Polybius' sources, which are also indicative of the development of a certain model of historiographical presentation of individuals.

were a matter of common knowledge. Now I have already explained that their acquaintance took its origin in the loan of some books and conversation about them. But as their intimacy grew, and when the Achaeans in detention were sent off to provincial towns, Fabius and Scipio, the sons of Lucius Aemilius, urgently begged the praetor to allow Polybius to remain in Rome. This was done, and their intercourse now becoming much closer, the following incident took place. On one occasion when they were all coming out together from the house of Fabius, the latter happened to take a turning leading to the forum, while Polybius and Scipio turned off in the opposite direction. As they advanced Scipio, addressing Polybius in a quiet and gentle voice, and blushing slightly said: "Why, Polybius, since there are two of us, do you constantly converse with my brother and address to him all your questions and explanations, but ignore me? Evidently you also have the same opinions of me that I hear the rest of my countrymen have. For, as I am told, I am believed by everybody to be a quiet and indolent man, with none of the energetic character of a Roman, because I don't choose to speak in the law courts. And they say that the family I spring from does not require such a protector as I am, but just the opposite; and this is what I feel most".

Polybius was surprised at the way in which the young man opened the conversation; for he was then not more than eighteen years old. "For goodness' sake, Scipio," he said, "don't talk in that way, or get any such notion into your head. I don't, I assure you, do this because I have a low opinion of you or ignore you, but because your brother is your senior. I both begin conversation with him and finish with him, and as for any explanations and advice, I address myself especially to him in the belief that your opinions are the same as his. However, now I admire you when you say that you are pained to think that you are of a milder character than becomes members of this family; for that shows that you have a high spirit. I myself would be delighted to do all in my power to help you to speak and act in a way worthy of your ancestors. For as those studies which I see now occupy and interest you, you will be in no want of those ready to help both of you; so great is the crowd of such men that I see flocking here from Greece at present. But as regards what you say now troubles you I don't think you could find anyone more efficient than myself to forward your effort and help you". Before Polybius ceased speaking, Scipio, grasping his right hand in both his own and pressing it warmly, said: "Would I could see the day on which you, regarding nothing else as of higher importance, would devote your attention to me and join your life with mine; for then I shall at once feel myself to be worthy of my house and my forefathers". Polybius was on the one hand very happy to see the enthusiasm and affection of the young man, yet was embarrassed when he reflected on the high position of the family and the wealth of its members. However, after this mutual explanation the young man never left his side, and preferred his society to anything else (31.23–24).

The unusual character of the episode leads Polybius to a double justification in a preface; one is text-internal (he had promised to illustrate the reasons of Scipio's fame, which was disproportional to his age), the other text-external (the story is already in circulation). Only the second reason is evidently related to the story that follows; the first is not directly related to its content, thus it rather serves as a hint for its intended interpretation: Polybius' company was instrumental for

Scipio's acquisition of fame at a remarkably early age. This interpretation is supported by the vivid characterization of the two persons. Scipio's zeal to prove worthy of his family, his noble, proud soul, his sociable character, his frankness and his sensitivity become evident through the episode. In parallel, Polybius appears loyal, respectful, prudent, honest and modest; he is not an opportunist.

The episode displays the typical structure of anecdotes:

- Delineation of an initial setting (general historical frame: it occurred after the relocation of many Greeks from Rome to the provinces; on the request of Scipio and his brother, Polybius had been exempted; precision of a specific scene: Polybius and Scipio were left alone while they were walking in Rome).
- Introduction of the protagonists and background of their relationship ("their acquaintance took its origin in the loan of some books and conversation about them") which also implicitly provides cues about their personality.
- "Crisis": Scipio complains about Polybius' behavior (Scipio feels that Polybius shows a preference for his elder brother).
- Solution consisting in the protagonist's remarkable words; Polybius' reply leads to the peak, Scipio's enthusiastic reaction. Polybius not only puts an end to Scipio's uncomfortable feeling and restores his self-esteem, but he is also characterized positively in the eyes of the reader (he had paid the due respect to Fabius because of his seniority). Regarding the future, however, he is now equipped with sufficient reasons to become Scipio's mentor.
- Epilogue (consequences: a new order is established).

The typology of the anecdote is reminiscent of biographical anecdotes about people who are admired for their intellectual superiority: the core of the narrative consists in a person's inspired and instructive words.[32] But this is only a superficial impression. Scipio also performs a characteristic speech act (a promise), accompanied by a symbolic gesture, which displays the young man's decision to attach himself to Polybius' as a mentor. In turn, this action is beneficial for Polybius, too: It confirms that his social position (which had been presented as threatened from the outset) is safe. Thus, a complex structure of reciprocity emerges. Nonetheless, there is a detail which seems out of place: Polybius' reference to the many Greek teachers who could equally become Scipio's instructors.

---

[32] Quotes originally belonged to what can be labeled a literary portrait rather than to biographies; cf. Wehrli 1973, 194.

Scipio's tone does not suggest that he considered the possibility of replacing him; on the contrary, together with his brother, he had energetically proved his faithfulness to Polybius. Still, the apparently redundant detail contributes to the meaning of the story: it makes the beginning of the new phase in the relationship between Scipio and Polybius appear as a choice with important consequences. For Scipio, it is the self-conscious choice of a guide who will have the opportunity to influence his way of life; for Polybius, Scipio's choice means distinction and social ascent; for both, it is a moment of symbolic change of status, a passage from one stage to another, which brings them closer to the fulfilment of their respective missions in life. Polybius' reaction, presented through the reading of his mind ("on the one hand very happy to see the enthusiasm and affection of the young man, yet was embarrassed when he reflected on the high position of the family and the wealth of its members") confirms the significance of Scipio's reply for both the Roman and the Greek.

While, however, at the beginning, the dominant role was that of the intellectual authority (Polybius is Greek, older, educated, experienced as a commander), whose favor Scipio is seeking, in the end, Polybius' social distinction and his selection among numerous potential candidates is equally emphasized to suggest balance and reciprocity. The young statesman now has the ideal mentor, an important element in a complete biography. In turn, Polybius' position at Scipio's side secures the privilege of access to first-hand information and increases his authority as a historian; thus, it maximizes the educational value of his work.

Anecdotes are a typical element of biography. They usually convey a meaning which is representative for the text as a whole; at an early stage, they were part of the oral biographical tradition and circulated independently; (as Polybius characteristically stated in the preface, this was the case with the present anecdote, as well—a declaration which, initially, may have sounded rather curious). In biographical literature, anecdotes are likely to mark important changes in a person's status, such as initiation, conversion, absolving education, making an important decision, entering a new phase of life etc.

In the present episode, Scipio chooses a spiritual guide and, by implication, a way of life, and lays the foundation for a splendid career; this moment is highlighted as the true beginning of the most important stage in his life which assured him the admiration of his contemporaries and of subsequent generations. Very much in the spirit of traditional Greek reciprocity, his *laudator*, Polybius, like a new Pindar, emphasizes his own role as the author of a trustworthy account about Scipio's life and deeds, but above all, he claims an essential role within the story itself: he is presented as the key figure in Scipio's formation. Polybius' position as a teacher is reflected in his right to praise and evaluate Scipio's character and his response to μαθήματα.

We thus see that the impact of this biographical anecdote is twofold: it can be read both as part of Scipio's biography as well as of Polybius' autobiography. Scipio's zeal is also an example for Polybius' readers, who wish to learn from him through his work. Scipio's life is worth studying and imitating, and Polybius' company proved beneficial for Scipio; in consequence, the recommendation of Polybius' history is, for those who would like to emulate Scipio, reduplicated.

Individual episodes and especially anecdotes performed a key function in Greek biography as an essential constituent of the literary schema of the genre. Their meaning is not restricted in their immediate context. They usually reveal central aspects of one's personality. They are associated with pivotal elements of the "biographical" schema, such as initiation, transition from one temporal phase or stage of career to another, expression of moral and mental qualities, manifestation of intellectual, political or social skills, and accomplishment of important achievements. These traits are pertinent to Polybius' account of his conversation with Scipio Aemilianus. They evoke the "biographical" schema and thus testify not only that Polybius was acquainted with the tradition of Greek biographical writing, directly or indirectly, but also that he made use of it in a passage whose importance cannot be underestimated, as it is connected with the assessment of a major figure of Roman history and Polybius' patron, and constitutes Polybius' most extensive autobiographical passage in the surviving parts of his work.

Other parts of his work also show a wide-ranging affinity of Polybius' theory of historiography and biography, especially political biography. Both aim at the reader's instruction through the study of historical examples. They invite the reader to emulate the virtues of their protagonists and to enrich his historical experience through the study of significant historical events. Although they consist of individual narratives, their perspective is—unlike other historiographical subgenres—holistic. They never lose sight of the big picture: they are both studies of human morality in a macro-historical framework.

The history of Greek political biography before Plutarch remains obscure, and Polybius' discussion of other historiographical genres did not survive. Thus, we are not able to know whether the historian included biographical literature in his treatment. However, our analysis has shown that some prototypical characteristics of biography can be traced in both his theory and literary praxis. Especially passages whose interpretation cues the enactment of the "biographical" schema show that Polybius, together with some of the lost representatives of Hellenistic historiography,[33] in a sense paved the way for Plutarch.

Bibliography

Adams, S.A. (2013), *The Genre of Acts and Collected Biography*, Cambridge.
Baron, C. (2009), "The Use and Abuse of Historians: Polybios' Book XII and Our Evidence for Timaios", in: *AncSoc* 39, 1–34.
Brouwer, R. (2011), "Polybius and Stoic Tyche", in: *GRBS* 51, 111–132.
Dihle, A. (1956), *Studien zur griechischen Biographie*, Göttingen.
—— (1987), *Die Entstehung der historischen Biographie*, Heidelberg.
Farrington, S.T. (2011), "Action and Reason: Polybius and the Gap between Encomium and History", in: *CPh* 106, 324–342.
Fortenbaugh, W.W. (2007), "Biography and the Aristotelian Peripatos", in: M. Erler/S. Schorn (eds.), *Die griechische Biographie in hellenistischer Zeit*, Berlin, 45–78.
Geiger, J. (1985), *Cornelius Nepos and Ancient Political Biography*, Stuttgart.
Guelfucci, M.-R. (2005), "La vérité, la rhétorique et l'histoire: les forms de la persuasion dans les *Histoires* de Polybe", in: *CEA* 42, 237–253.
Knöbl, R. (2010), "Talking about Euripides: Paramimesis and Satyrus' Bios Euripidou", in: P. Borghard/K. de Temmerman (eds.), *Biography and Fictionality in the Greek Literary Tradition, Phrasis. Studies in Language and Literature*, Vol. 51.1, 37–58.
Luke, T. (2015), "Review—Discussion: *Nepos as a political Biographer*", (Review of Stem 2012), in: *Histos* 9, XCI–C.
Momigliano, A. (1993), *The Development of Greek Biography. Expanded edition*, Cambridge, Mass.
Pomeroy, A.J. (1996), "Polybius' Death Notices", in: *Phoenix* 40, 407–423.
Schepens, G. (1998), "Prolegomena", in: F. Jacoby, *Die Fragmente der Griechischen Historiker, continued*, IV A 1, Leiden/Boston/Köln, vii–xviii.
—— (2007), "Zum Verhältnis von Biographie und Geschichtsschreibung in hellenistischer Zeit", in: M. Erler/S. Schorn (eds.), *Die griechische Biographie in hellenistischer Zeit*, Berlin, 335–361.
Schorn, S. (2014), "Historiographie, Biographie und Enkomion. Theorie der Biographie und Historiographie bei Diodor und Polybios", in: *RSA* 44, 137–164.
Smith, C. (2003), *Modes of Discourse: The Local Structure of Texts*, Cambridge.
Späth, T. (2000), "Camillus: Ein Held zwischen griechischer Biographie und römischer Geschichtsschreibung", in: I. Gallo/C. Moreschini (eds.), *I generi letterari in Plutarco. Atti del VII Convegno plutarcheo*, Pisa, 2–4 giugno 1999, Naples, 47–79.
Stem, R. (2012), *The Political Biographies of Cornelius Nepos*, Ann Arbor.
Stockwell, P. (2002), *Cognitive Poetics. An Introduction*, London/New York.

---

[33] Cf. Schepens 2007, 354: "Mit ihren Charakteranalysen der politisch-militärischen Handlungsträger übernahm die Geschichtsschreibung teilweise Funktionen der Biographie".

Tsakmakis, A. (2015), "Polybius between Linguistics and Narratology. An Analysis of 1.6–12", in: G.A. Xenis (ed.), *Literature, Scholarship, Philosophy, and History. Classical Studies in Memory of Ioannis Taifacos*, Stuttgart, 37–51.
Walbank, F.W. (1957–1979), *A Historical Commentary on Polybius*, 3 vols., Oxford.
Wehrli, F. (1973), "Gnome, Anekdote und Biographie", in: *MH* 30, 193–208.

Giovanni Parmeggiani
Polybius and the Legacy of Fourth-Century Historiography

> M. Momigliano: "Il est ... intéressant de se demander ce qu' un historien connaît, mais dont il ne parle pas: dans le cas de Polybe: Thucydide et Caton (comme historien)."
>
> M. Walbank: "Ne peut-on admettre que la cause de cette lacune, c'est que Polybe ne s'intéressait pas à l'histoire du Ve siècle, mais bien à celle du IVe?"
>
> M. Pédech: "M. Walbank a raison. De toute évidence, la culture historique de Polybe ne remonte guère jusqu' au Ve siècle: elle a son point de départ chez les historiens du IVe siècle, Ephore et Théopompe."
>
> *Polybe. Entretiens sur l'Antiquité classique* XX, Vandoeuvres—Genève 1974, 62–63

Thucydides lived in the second half of the fifth century BCE; he was a politician, a military man, and also a historian. Polybius lived in the second century BCE; he too was a politician, a military man, and a historian. Thucydides chose to write contemporary history, and so did Polybius. Thucydides has gained admiration from modern academics for his advanced thought in research methodology. So has Polybius. In the modern imagination, Thucydides and Polybius are naturally linked to each other: many critics, while reading some of Polybius' most important statements about both the nature and the practice of history, as well as the aims of historical research, often got the impression that they had before their eyes an "ideal pupil" of Thucydides, or an exegete of the Thucydidean text.[1]

Such an impression is rooted, at least in part, in the idea that the historians "in between" held quite a different view of history and historical research than Thucydides and Polybius: fourth- and third-century historians—it has long been said—chose non-contemporary and antiquarian history instead of contemporary history, *akoe* instead of *opsis*, rhetoric instead of truth. The fact that some of Polybius' methodological statements recalled, more or less, those of Thucydides,

---

[1] On Polybius' familiarity with Thucydides' work and historiographical principles, see, among others, Ziegler 1952, 1503ff., 1522–24, 1557 and 1564, Avenarius 1956, 22ff., Walbank 1972, 40–43, Lehmann 1974, 165ff., Derow 1994, Nicolai 1995 and 1999, Musti 2001, 17ff., Canfora 2006, 724–27, Foulon 2010, McGing 2010, 58ff., Longley 2012, Rood 2012, Miltsios 2013. For a more cautious approach, see Hornblower 1994, 60–61, and 1995, 59, considering certain only Polybius' familiarity with Thucydides' Book 1. Quite sceptical Pédech 1964, 95, and 1969, xli-xlii. See also Scardino's paper in this volume.

and at the same time the fact that the historians "in between" seemed so different, gave rise to the idea that Polybius "jumped back" directly to the fifth century to imitate Thucydides, an act itself condemning the fourth- and third-century predecessors to a "diversity status" for which they deserved only to be despised—as indeed has happened until the present day.²

Now we have the possibility to see things rather differently. New inquiries into fragmentary historians of the fourth century BCE show that the development of Greek historiography after Thucydides should be conceived in terms of continuity and progress, rather than discontinuity and regress.³ This obviously has serious implications when one deals with such issues as the roots of Polybius' historiographical thought and Polybius' relationship with his predecessors.

Who was Polybius more indebted to, Thucydides or fourth-century historians? We will not answer by saying "fourth-century historians", stating that they are quoted by Polybius far more frequently than Thucydides, whom Polybius quotes only once and in a very cursory way:⁴ in fact, "no mention of" does not mean "no knowledge of"; moreover, what has been transmitted to us is only part of Polybius' work,⁵ and no one could claim with certainty that Polybius had never read Thucydides, whose *Histories*, in the Hellenistic age, were part of the rhetorical studies of well trained Greeks—of whom Polybius was one. To be sure, we will not question that Polybius knew Thucydides; rather, we will show that Polybius got most—if not all—of his view on history and historical methodology not from Thucydides, but from fourth-century historians. We shall do this in the four points below: the first deals with the aims of history writing, the second and the third with the methodology of research, and the fourth with aetiology. As we shall see, those very instances in which Polybius seems to echo Thucydides, are in reality adaptations of fourth-century historians.

---

2 See e.g. Jacoby 1926, 27, Avenarius 1956, Will 1991, Momigliano 1992, 49ff., Meister 1992, 183ff.
3 See Vattuone 1991, Flower 1994, Lenfant 2004, Schepens/Bollansée 2005, Parmeggiani 2011 and 2014.
4 Plb. 8.11.3: ὅς (sc. Theopompus) γ' ἐπιβαλόμενος γράφειν τὰς Ἑλληνικὰς πράξεις ἀφ' ὧν Θουκυδίδης ἀπέλιπε ... Here Polybius does not focus on Thucydides, but on Theopompus (*FGrHist* 115 T 19).
5 Cf. Hornblower 1994, 60, and 1995, 59.

1 History writing and its aims

Let us first examine Polybius' preface to Book 9, which is famous because of Polybius' distinction between different branches of history (*tropoi*), and for the explanation he gives for his decision to write only contemporary history.

> ... I am not unaware that my work owing to the uniformity of its composition has a certain severity, and will suit the taste and gain the approval of only one class of reader. For nearly all other writers, or at least most of them, by dealing with every branch of history, attract many kinds of people to the perusal of their works (οἱ μὲν γὰρ ἄλλοι συγγραφεῖς σχεδὸν ἅπαντες, εἰ δὲ μή γ', οἱ πλείους, πᾶσι τοῖς τῆς ἱστορίας μέρεσι χρώμενοι πολλοὺς ἐφέλκονται πρὸς ἔντευξιν τῶν ὑπομνημάτων). The genealogical side appeals to those who are fond of a story, and the account of colonies, the foundation of cities, and their ties of kindred, such as Ephorus (*FGrHist* 70 T 18b) also remarks somewhere or other, attracts the curious and lovers of recondite lore, while the statesman is interested in the doings of nations, cities, and monarchs (τὸν μὲν γὰρ φιλήκοον ὁ γενεαλογικὸς τρόπος ἐπισπᾶται, τὸν δὲ πολυπράγμονα καὶ περιττὸν ὁ περὶ τὰς ἀποικίας καὶ κτίσεις καὶ συγγενείας, καθά που καὶ παρ' Ἐφόρῳ λέγεται, τὸν δὲ πολιτικὸν ὁ περὶ τὰς πράξεις τῶν ἐθνῶν καὶ πόλεων καὶ δυναστῶν). As I have confined my attention strictly to these last matters and as my whole work treats of nothing else, it is, as I say, adapted only to one sort of reader, and its perusal will have no attractions for the large number. I have stated elsewhere at some length my reason for choosing to exclude other branches of history and chronicle actions alone, but there is no harm in briefly reminding my readers of it here in order to impress it on them. Since genealogies, myths, the planting of colonies, the foundation of cities an their ties of kinship have been recounted by many writers and in many different styles, an author who undertakes at the present day to deal with these matters must either represent the work of others as being his own, a most disgraceful proceeding, or if he refuses to do this, must manifestly toil to no purpose, being constrained to avow that the matters on which he writes and to which he devotes his attention has been adequately narrated and handed down to posterity by previous authors. So omitting these things for the above and various other reasons, I decided on writing a history of actual events; firstly because there is always something fresh in them which demands novel treatment—since it was not in the power of the ancients to narrate events subsequent to their own time—and secondly, owing to the great practical utility of such a history, both formerly and especially at the present day, when the progress of the arts and sciences has been so rapid, that those who study history are, we may almost say, provided with a method for dealing with any contingency that may arise. My aim, therefore, being not so much to entertain readers as to benefit those who pay careful attention (διόπερ ἡμεῖς οὐχ οὕτως τῆς τέρψεως στοχαζόμενοι τῶν ἀναγνωσομένων ὡς τῆς ὠφελείας τῶν προσεχόντων), I disregarded other matters and was led to write this kind

of history. The best testimony to the truth of what I say will be that of those who study this work with due application.[6]

Polybius distinguishes, firstly, a "genealogical side", which "appeals to those who are fond of a story"; secondly, "the account of colonies, the foundation of cities, and their ties of kindred", which "attracts the curious and lovers of recondite lore"; and thirdly, "the doing of nations, cities, and monarchs", in which "the statesman is interested". Then Polybius explains his choice to confine himself to contemporary history (therefore to "the doing of nations, cities and monarchs"), by stating that there is always something new to find and to tell for those who deal with contemporary events, unlike what happens to writers of non-contemporary history, who, instead, are compelled to repeat—Polybius states, quite maliciously—what others have already found and recounted. A reference to Ephorus appears, while Polybius is talking about the second *tropos* of history (*i.e.* "the account of colonies, the foundation of cities, and their ties of kindred"): Ephorus is highly appreciated by Polybius for his excellent treatment of ancient Greek history,[7] and, as a consequence, an implicit contrast arises in the reader's mind, between Ephorus on the one hand, as the historian of non-contemporary events whose science is principally built on *akoe*, and Polybius on the other, as the contemporary historian whose science is principally built on *opsis*. Furthermore, Polybius stresses the importance of contemporary history by contrasting *terpsis* with *opheleia*: "My aim, therefore, being not so much to entertain readers as to benefit those who pay careful attention, I disregarded other matters and was led to write this kind of history (that is, history of actual events)".[8] Such distinction is reminiscent of the most famous statement of Thucydides 1.22.4:

> And it may well be that the absence of the fabulous from my narrative will seem less pleasing to the ear; but whoever shall wish to have a clear view both of the events which have happened and of those which will some day happen again—in the same or similar way, because of human nature—for these to adjudge my history profitable will be enough for me. And, indeed, it has been composed, not as a prize-essay to be heard for the moment, but as a possession for all time (καὶ ἐς μὲν ἀκρόασιν ἴσως τὸ μὴ μυθῶδες αὐτῶν ἀτερπέστερον φανεῖται· ὅσοι δὲ βουλήσονται τῶν τε γενομένων τὸ σαφὲς σκοπεῖν καὶ τῶν μελλόντων ποτὲ

---

[6] Plb. 9.1.2–2.7, transl. Paton, Walbank and Habicht. Schepens 2010, 128–29, rightly argues against the ordinary view that Polybius here is contrasting history with "antiquarianism".
[7] See Plb. 34.1.3 *apud* Strab. 10.3.5 = Ephor. *FGrHist* 70 T 18a. Jacoby's selection ought to be read in light of Strabo's full context: see Parmeggiani 2011, 31–32.
[8] Plb. 9.2.6, transl. Paton, Walbank and Habicht.

αὖθις κατὰ τὸ ἀνθρώπινον τοιούτων καὶ παραπλησίων ἔσεσθαι, ὠφέλιμα κρίνειν αὐτὰ ἀρκούντως ἕξει. κτῆμά τε ἐς αἰεὶ μᾶλλον ἢ ἀγώνισμα ἐς τὸ παραχρῆμα ἀκούειν ξύγκειται).[9]

As a consequence, in the reader's mind the already established opposition between Ephorus and Polybius subtly develops into another opposition, this time, between Ephorus as the master of non-contemporary and antiquarian history on the one hand, and Thucydides and Polybius as masters of contemporary history on the other.

Polybius' preface, at first sight, would seem to suggest that Polybius is both consciously imitating Thucydides and setting himself in opposition with Ephorus as well as, generally speaking, with fourth-century historians.[10] But a closer reading of both Polybius' preface and Thucydides 1.22.4 can lead to different conclusions. Firstly, Thucydides in 1.22.4 contrasts *terpsis* with *ophelimon* much more harshly than Polybius does (as we understand also by the famous opposition Thucydides draws in 1.21.1 between his own historical reconstruction of the past on the one side, and the way both poets and logographers deal with the past on the other).[11] Polybius, for his part, conceives *terpsis* as admissible in history writing, although inferior to *opheleia* ("not so much to entertain readers as to benefit", says Polybius[12]): it is clear that Thucydides and Polybius use the very same concepts, but their perspectives are not quite the same. Secondly, Polybius mentions Ephorus after having stated that "nearly all other writers, or at least most of them, by dealing with every branch of history ...":[13] it is clear that Ephorus, in Polybius' view, was one of those previous historians who did not write only ancient history, *but contemporary history too*—as is also demonstrated by recent surveys of Ephorus' fragments.[14] Thus Polybius' text doesn't support the view of an opposition between Ephorus as a mere historian of non-contemporary events on the one hand, and Polybius as a contemporary historian on the other.[15]

---

9 Thuc. 1.22.4, transl. Forster Smith, partly revised.
10 See e.g. Ziegler 1952, 1522–23; Canfora 2006, 724–26.
11 See Parmeggiani 2003.
12 Plb. 9.2.6. See Saïd 2010, 172–74, who rightly emphasizes that such an attitude by Polybius is not confined to the preface to Book 9. As pointed out by Walbank 1957, 7, according to Polybius "both aims, pleasure and profit, are admissible", although "the scale comes down very sharply on the side of profit". On *terpsis* and *ophelimon* in Polybius, see also Walbank 1990.
13 Plb. 9.1.3.
14 See Parmeggiani 2011. Twenty-one books of Ephorus' work (Books 10–30) indeed covered modern and contemporary history (ca. 489–341 BCE), *i.e.* 149 on a total of 730 years (Ephor. *FGrHist* 70 T 8, F 223).
15 See also Parmeggiani 2011, 46–47.

Polybius is clearly in debt to Ephorus for his distinction of the three branches of history:[16] without any doubt, he did not have Thucydides in mind here. Furthermore, as we have seen above, Polybius is not saying the same about *terpsis* and *opheleia/ophelimon* as Thucydides. In this regard, one may ask: could it be that Polybius is independently developing Thucydides' ideas in 1.22.4?

One could answer "yes", if themes such as *terpsis* and *ophelimon* were not the object of meditation by post-Thucydidean historians, *but they were*—as happens to be proven, incidentally, by Polybius himself, when he states, in the preface to the whole work, that "all previous historians, so to speak", praised history because they conceived the study of history as the perfect training for an active politician.[17] Now, we know that Ephorus was far more "Thucydidean" than Polybius for what he regarded as *terpsis*: in Ephorus' view, *terpsis*, *apate*, *mythos* and *ekplexis* have no place in history writing (see e.g. TT 8, 18b; FF 8, 31b [πανταχοῦ ἄριστον τἀληθές, "the truth is best in all cases"], 42).[18] Theopompus, on the other hand, expressly recognized that he was going to insert fabulous accounts in his history, as we read in F 381:

> It is self-evident that they (*sc.* Homer, Alcman, and so on) are weaving in myths intentionally, not through ignorance of the facts, but through an intentional invention of the impossible, to gratify the taste for the marvellous and the entertaining (φαίνεται γὰρ εὐθὺς ὅτι μύθους παραπλέκουσιν ἑκόντες οὐκ ἀγνοίᾳ τῶν ὄντων, ἀλλὰ πλάσει τῶν ἀδυνάτων τερατείας καὶ τέρψεως χάριν). But they give the impression of doing this through ignorance, because by preference and with an air of plausibility they tell such tales about the unfamiliar and the unknown. Theopompus (*FGrHist* 115 F 381) expressly acknowledges the practice when he says that he intends to narrate myths too in his History—a better way than that of Herodotus, Ctesias, Hellanicus, and the authors of the Histories of India (Θεόπομπος δὲ ἐξομολογεῖται φήσας ὅτι καὶ μύθους ἐν ταῖς ἱστορίαις ἐρεῖ, κρεῖττον ἢ ὡς Ἡρόδοτος καὶ Κτησίας καὶ Ἑλλάνικος καὶ οἱ τὰ Ἰνδικὰ συγγράψαντες).[19]

Once we read Theopompus' quotation in Strabo's full context, it appears that Theopompus considered *terpsis* not as *the* aim of historical inquiry (Theopompus'

---

[16] See Parmeggiani 2011, 150ff.
[17] Plb. 1.1.2. On this passage, see Parmeggiani 2014b. Note that Thucydides is hardly among Polybius' πάντες, since Thucydides gives no praise of history in his work: see Schweighäuser 1792, 117, Walbank 1957, 39. Against the conventional view that Ephorus was uninterested in political history and wanted to impart moral lessons, see now Parmeggiani 2011, 47ff., 150ff.
[18] Respectively Diod. 4.1.2–3; Plb. 9.1.4 and 4.20.5; Strab. 9.3.11–12 and 7.3.9. See Parmeggiani 2011, 74–78, 87–95, 139–146, 150–153, and *passim*.
[19] Strab. 1.2.35, transl. Jones. The right interpretation of Theopompus' fragment in light of Strabo's context is given by Flower 1994, 34–35; Biraschi 1996.

admission speaks for his awareness that the first aim of historical inquiry is, rather, *aletheia*), but as something which could legitimately be part of the historical narrative.[20] This concept is very close to that which we find in Polybius' preface to Book 9.

In light of this, it is safe to conclude that Polybius, while talking about *terpsis* and *ophelimon* in his preface to Book 9, did not have the statements of Thucydides in his mind, but the statements of post-Thucydidean historians.

A general observation should now be made. After Thucydides, historians like Ephorus and Theopompus considered contemporary history to be part of their historiographical plans, and since their narratives extended to non-contemporary events, they made both *terpsis* and *opheleia/ophelimon* the objects of further speculation. As I have demonstrated elsewhere, Ephorus started his meditation on historical methodology from Thucydides' methodological section (1.20–22).[21] Not by chance, Ephorus' statements of research were used by the Hellenistic authors of *hypomnemata* for their comments on crucial methodological statements by Thucydides, including that contained in 1.22.4: this is philologically shown by some lexical links between Ephorus' fragments (FF 8, 110) and Dionysius of Halicarnassus' treatise *On Thucydides*.[22] An example, concerning specifically Ephorus F 8, follows:

---

[20] On Theopompus as "a lover of truth" (*philalethes*: Theopomp. *FGrHist* 115 TT 28a–b; F 181a), see now Vattuone 2014. That Theopompus' first aim was *aletheia*, rather than pleasing the reader by narrating myths, is also suggested by Diod. 4.1.3 (Theopomp. *FGrHist* 115 T 12). See especially Dion. Hal. *Pomp.* 6, ii.244.11ff. U–R (Theopomp. *FGrHist* 115 T 20a), on the nature of Theopompus' historical work, the wide variety of its subject-matter (including pragmatic history), and also the *opheleia* it grants to the reader.
[21] Parmeggiani 2011, 99ff. (on Ephor. *FGrHist* 70 FF 8, 9, 110 and 111) and 148–149.
[22] Dion. Hal. *De Thuc.* 6, i.333.3–12 U-R, and 7, i.333.24–334.12 U-R ~ Ephor. *FGrHist* 70 F 8; Dion. Hal. *De Thuc.* 6, i.332.20–23 U-R ~ Ephor. *FGrHist* 70 F 110. See Parmeggiani 2011, 119–20 (on Ephor. F 110) and 141ff. (on Ephor. F 8).

> **Thuc. 1.22.4**
> ... καὶ ἐς μὲν ἀκρόασιν ἴσως <u>τὸ μὴ μυθῶδες αὐτῶν ἀτερπέστερον φανεῖται</u>· ὅσοι δὲ βουλήσονται τῶν τε γενομένων τὸ σαφὲς σκοπεῖν καὶ τῶν μελλόντων ποτὲ αὖθις κατὰ τὸ ἀνθρώπινον τοιούτων καὶ παραπλησίων ἔσεσθαι, <u>ὠφέλιμα</u> κρίνειν αὐτὰ ἀρκούντως ἕξει. κτῆμά τε ἐς αἰεὶ μᾶλλον ἢ ἀγώνισμα ἐς τὸ παραχρῆμα ἀκούειν ξύγκειται.

> **Ephor. FGrHist 70 F 8**
> (general proem of the *Histories*)
>
> ... μουσικὴν <u>ἐπ' ἀπάτῃ καὶ γοητείᾳ</u> παρεισῆχθαι τοῖς ἀνθρώποις.

> **Dion. Hal. De Thuc. 6, i.333.3–12 U–R:**
>
> ἔπειτα <u>κατὰ τὸ μηδὲν αὐτῇ μυθῶδες προσάψαι</u> (*sc.* Thucydides), <u>μηδ' εἰς ἀπάτην καὶ γοητείαν τῶν πολλῶν ἐκτρέψαι τὴν γραφήν</u>, ὡς οἱ πρὸ αὐτοῦ πάντες ἐποίησαν, Λαμίας τινὰς ἱστοροῦντες ἐν ὕλαις καὶ νάπαις ἐκ γῆς ἀνιεμένας, κτλ.
>
> **Dion. Hal. De Thuc. 7, i.333.24–334.12 U–R:**
>
> Θουκυδίδῃ δὲ τῷ προελομένῳ μίαν ὑπόθεσιν, ᾗ παρεγίνετο αὐτός, <u>οὐχ ἥρμοττεν ἐγκαταμίσγειν τῇ διηγήσει τὰς θεατρικὰς γοητείας οὐδὲ πρὸς τὴν ἀπάτην ἁρμόττεσθαι τῶν ἀναγνωσομένων, ἣν ἐκεῖναι πεφύκασι φέρειν αἱ συντάξεις, ἀλλὰ πρὸς τὴν ὠφέλειαν</u>, ὡς αὐτὸς ἐν τῷ προοιμίῳ τῆς ἱστορίας δεδήλωκε κατὰ λέξιν οὕτως γράφων (full quotation of Thuc. 1.22.4 follows)· "καὶ ἐς μὲν ἀκρόασιν τὸ μὴ μυθῶδες αὐτῶν ἀτερπέστερον φαίνεται ... ξύγκειται".

Moreover, one should recall that Polybius endorsed Ephorus' distinction between *logos historikos* and *logos epideiktikos* (F 111), this being a clear instance of the definition of history as a genre, for both theory and practice.[23] Polybius had no need to "jump back" to Thucydides, for Thucydides had already been well digested by historians of the fourth-century BCE, who were also the first to provide a definition of *genos historikon*.[24]

---

[23] Plb. 12.28.10–11 = Ephor. *FGrHist* 70 F 111: ὁ γὰρ Ἔφορος ... κατὰ δέ τινα συντυχίαν εὐχαριστότατα καὶ πιθανώτατα περὶ τῆς συγκρίσεως εἴρηκε τῆς τῶν ἱστοριογράφων καὶ λογογράφων. On Ephorus' *synkrisis* of historiography and epideictic speeches, see Parmeggiani 2011, 124ff. On the meaning of κατὰ δέ τινα συντυχίαν, see Chávez Reino 2005, 35 n. 38.
[24] The preface to Book 9 is not the only *locus* where Polybius reasons about *terpsis* and *ophelimon*: see e.g. 2.56.10–12; 3.31.11–13; 38.4.8. Cf. Walbank 1957, 7, and 1990. Polybius' view looks

2 Methodology of research of the facts

In his polemic against Timaeus in Book 12, Polybius criticizes his predecessor for both his neglect of direct inquiry and the preference he accorded to written sources: Polybius stresses Timaeus' faults by stating the importance and the methodological need for both the autopsy of events and places, and the interview of direct informants:

> Nature has given us two instruments, as it were, by the aid of which we inform ourselves and inquire about everything. These are hearing and sight, and of the two sight is much more veracious according to Heracleitus (22 B 101a D–K). "The eyes are more accurate witnesses than that ears", he says. Now, Timaeus (*FGrHist* 566 T 19) enters on his inquiries by the pleasanter of the two roads, but the inferior one. For he entirely avoids employing his eyes and prefers to employ his ears. Now the knowledge derived from hearing being of two sorts, Timaeus diligently pursued the one, the reading of books, as I have above pointed out, but was very remiss in his use of the other, the interrogation of living witnesses. It is easy enough to perceive what caused him to make this choice. Inquiries from books may be made without any danger or hardship, provided only that one takes care to have access to a town rich in documents or to have a library near at hand ... Personal inquiry, on the contrary, requires severe labor and great expense, but is exceedingly valuable and is the most important part of the historical research. This is evident from expressions used by historians themselves. Ephorus (*FGrHist* 70 F 110) says that if it could be possible to all writers of history be personally present at all events, this would be by far the best among "empeiriai" (ὁ μὲν γὰρ Ἔφορός φησιν, εἰ δυνατὸν ἦν αὐτοὺς παρεῖναι πᾶσι τοῖς πράγμασι, ταύτην ἂν διαφέρειν πολὺ τῶν ἐμπειριῶν). Theopompus (*FGrHist* 115 F 342) says that the man who has the best knowledge of war is he who has been present at the most battles, that most capable speaker is he who has taken part in the greatest number of debates, and that the same holds good about medicine and navigation (ὁ δὲ Θεόπομπος τοῦτον μὲν ἄριστον ἐν τοῖς πολεμικοῖς τὸν πλείστοις κινδύνοις παρατετευχότα, τοῦτον δὲ δυνατώτατον ἐν λόγῳ τὸν πλείστων μετεσχηκότα πολιτικῶν ἀγώνων. τὸν αὐτὸν δὲ τρόπον συμβαίνειν ἐπ' ἰατρικῆς καὶ κυβερνητικῆς). Homer has been still more emphatic on this subject than these writers.

---

more "Thucydidean", so to speak, in 3.31.11–13 (see Ziegler 1952, 1503, Avenarius 1956, 26, Walbank 1957, 359, Hornblower 1994, 60, Nicolai 1995, 17–18, Foulon 2010, 143–46, Rood 2012, 52, Longley 2012, 70, Miltsios 2013, 332) and 38.4.8 (Ziegler 1952, 1503, Walbank 1957, 359, Derow 1994, 84–85, Nicolai 1995, 17–18, Foulon 2010, 143–46, McGing 2010, 58–59). However, since we know that lost historians after Thucydides dwelt with *terpsis* and *ophelimon* in their works in a "Thucydidean manner" (e.g. Ephorus), and they were also very well known to Polybius, it is quite hurried to conclude that Polybius ought his notions to Thucydides and no one else. On Plb. 2.56.10–12 and its links with Thucydides, see especially Ziegler 1952, 1503–1504, Avenarius 1956, 26, Nicolai 1995, 17, Foulon 2010, 143–46 and Longley 2012, 70–72. On the very same *locus* and its links with Ephorus, see Wehrli 1972, 132ff., Parmeggiani 2011, 139, 146 and 148.

Wishing to show us what qualities one should possess in order to be a man of action he says (quotation of *Od.* 1.1–3 follows) and further on (quotation of *Od.* 1.3–4 and 8.183 follows).[25]

Polybius defends the primacy of direct inquiry by quoting several witnesses. Among them, we find only two historians, namely Ephorus (F 110) and Theopompus (F 342). Needless to say that a modern reader would have expected to find here a quote from Thucydides 1.22.2 (somewhat a "cornerstone", in the modern imaginary, of methodological statements about direct inquiry):

> As to the facts of the occurrences of the war, I have thought it my duty to give them, not inquiring by chance nor as seemed to me probable, but only after investigating with the greatest possible accuracy each detail, in the case both of the events in which I myself participated and of those regarding which I got my information from others (τὰ δ' ἔργα τῶν πραχθέντων ἐν τῷ πολέμῳ οὐκ ἐκ τοῦ παρατυχόντος πυνθανόμενος ἠξίωσα γράφειν, οὐδ' ὡς ἐμοὶ ἐδόκει, ἀλλ' οἷς τε αὐτὸς παρῆν καὶ παρὰ τῶν ἄλλων ὅσον δυνατὸν ἀκριβείᾳ περὶ ἑκάστου ἐπεξελθών).[26]

But Thucydides is not found in Polybius' passage, and the reader is left with the following question: why does Polybius quote Ephorus and Theopompus here, and not Thucydides?

Polybius' choice is not so difficult to understand. In 1.22.2 Thucydides stresses that his history relies on direct inquiry, but also states that he checked *both* what his informants saw with their eyes and what he himself saw: Thucydides is sceptical about *opsis* as an independent means for reaching truth.[27] Polybius instead—as we have seen above—stresses the unquestioned primacy of autopsy. This puts him on the very same line as Ephorus and Theopompus, both of whom, after Thucydides' criticism, restated the superiority of autopsy not because they did not understand Thucydides or were against his conclusions, but because the geography and the time they covered with their narratives were much more extensive than those covered by Thucydides, who confined himself to the description of a contemporary war. Moreover, we see that Polybius stresses the importance of "experience" in historical research (*empeiria*): this point is also in the statements of both Ephorus and Theopompus, as they are preserved by Polybius, not in Thucydides 1.22.2. This is not by chance: Theopompus' analogy in F 342, between the practice of history on the one hand, and the practice of medicine and navigation on the other, describes historical inquiry as an "empirical

---

25 Plb. 12.27, transl. Paton, Walbank and Habicht, partly revised.
26 Thuc. 1.22.2, transl. Forster Smith, partly revised.
27 See Parmeggiani 2018.

science", and this very approach is also found in Polybius' own definition of *pragmatikon meros* in 12.25d–e.²⁸

Chapters 27, 28 and 28a, which are at the core of Polybius' own historiographical theory, are full of references to key concepts of Theopompus' historiographical theory as Dionysius of Halicarnassus describes it in the letter *Ad Pompeium Geminum* 6.2ff., ii.245.1ff. U–R (T 20a) on the basis of Theopompus' own words in the general proem of *Philippika*. Such concepts include the necessity of great expenses for collecting material (Plb. 12.27.6, ἡ δὲ πολυπραγμοσύνη πολλῆς μὲν προσδεῖται ταλαιπωρίας καὶ δαπάνης [cf. 28a.4] ~ Dion. Hal. *Pomp.* 6.2, ii.245.3–4 U–R, μεγίστας δὲ δαπάνας εἰς τὴν συναγωγὴν αὐτῶν τετελεκώς); the importance of being *autoptes* (Polyb. 12.28a.4, τὸ πειραθῆναι τῶν πλείστων ἐθνῶν καὶ τόπων αὐτόπτην γενέσθαι ~ Dion. Hal. *Pomp.* 6.3, ii.245.4–5 U–R, πολλῶν μὲν αὐτόπτης γεγενημένος); the conception of the historiographical task not as something marginal to life, but as the most crucial thing (Plb. 12.28.4, μὴ ... παρέργως ~ Dion. Hal. *Pomp.* 6.3, ii.245.7–8 U–R, οὐ γὰρ ὥσπέρ τινες πάρεργον τοῦ βίου).²⁹ Generally speaking, Polybius' focus on such concepts as the preparation required for research (12.28.8ff.: παρασκευή), industry (*ibid.*: φιλοπονία) and necessity of the historical research (see 12.28.3–4: οἱ πραγματικοὶ τῶν ἀνδρῶν γράφειν ἐπιχειρήσωσι τὰς ἱστορίας, μὴ καθάπερ νῦν παρέργως, νομίσαντες δὲ καὶ τοῦτ' εἶναι σφίσι τῶν ἀναγκαιοτάτων καὶ καλλίστων) is evidence for Polybius' debt to Theopompus (see Dion. Hal. *Pomp.* 6.2–3, ii.245.1–9 U–R [T 20a]: δῆλος γάρ ἐστιν, εἰ καὶ μηδὲν ἔγραψε, πλείστην μὲν παρασκευὴν εἰς ταῦτα παρεσκευασμένος ... οὐ γὰρ ὥσπέρ τινες πάρεργον τοῦ βίου τὴν ἀναγραφὴν τῆς ἱστορίας ἐποιήσατο, ἔργον δὲ τὸ πάντων ἀναγκαιότατον),³⁰ and especially to Ephorus, for it was Ephorus who first argued—by means of highly commendable remarks, according to

---

28 In sections 25d–e Polybius draws a parallel between history, medicine and navigation, as Theopompus did before him. *Contra* Longley 2012, 79–80, who mentions Thucydides as inspiring Polybius' analogy in 12.25d–e, but ignores Theopomp. F 342. Note Dion. Hal. *Pomp.* 6.8, ii.246.22ff. U–R (Theopomp. *FGrHist* 115 T 20a) on Theopompus acting, by his criticism of famous persons, like "*surgeons who cut and cauterise the morbid parts of the body, operating to a certain depth, but not encroaching upon the healthy and normal parts*" (Transl. Usher).
29 See Pédech 1961, 146, Sacks 1983, 72.
30 See Bearzot 2005, 64–65. Note that Polybius' reference to Odysseus as the model of the perfect inquirer (12.27.10–11) may have been inspired by Theopompus: see Dion. Hal. *Pomp.* 6.3, ii.245.4–6 U–R (Theopomp. *FGrHist* 115 T 20a), πολλῶν μὲν αὐτόπτης γεγενημένος (sc. Theopompus), πολλοῖς δ' εἰς ὁμιλίαν ἐλθὼν ἀνδράσι τοῖς τότε πρωτεύουσι, and cf. Hom. *Od.* 1.3, πολλῶν δ' ἀνθρώπων ἴδεν ἄστεα καὶ νόον ἔγνω (sc. Odysseus), with Chávez Reino 2007, 137a. The conclusion by Sacks 1983, 73, "it is reasonable to assume that Dionysius at some point read Polybius XII and took the theoretical arguments of Polybius, applying them to his own favorite,

Polybius himself (12.28.10–11)³¹—that *logos historikos* required greater talent (φύσις), more industry (φιλοπονία), and more preparation (παρασκευή) than *logos epideiktikos* (F 111). No doubt that such concepts—φύσις, φιλοπονία, and παρασκευή—were fully explained by Ephorus in his original *synkrisis*, which Polybius admired so much.

To sum up, the link between Polybius and fourth-century historians is far more direct, as well as more apparent, than the link between Polybius and Thucydides. As further evidence for our conclusion, we recall Polybius 12.4c.4–5:

> For since many events occur at the same time in different places, and one man cannot be in several places at one time, nor is it possible for a single man to see with his own eyes every place in the world and all the peculiar features of different places, the only thing left for an historian is to inquire from as many people as possible, to believe those worthy of belief and to be an adequate critic of the reports that reach him (ἐπειδὴ γὰρ αἱ μὲν πράξεις ἅμα πολλαχῇ συντελοῦνται, παρεῖναι δὲ τὸν αὐτὸν ἐν πλείοσι τόποις κατὰ τὸν αὐτὸν καιρὸν ἀδύνατον, ὁμοίως γε μὴν οὐδ' αὐτόπτην γενέσθαι πάντων τῶν κατὰ τὴν οἰκουμένην τόπων καὶ τῶν ἐν τοῖς τόποις ἰδιωμάτων τὸν ἕνα δυνατόν, καταλείπεται πυνθάνεσθαι μὲν ὡς παρὰ πλείστων, πιστεύειν δὲ τοῖς ἀξίοις πίστεως, κριτὴν δ' εἶναι τῶν προσπιπτόντων μὴ κακόν).³²

One may think, while reading such a methodological statement, that Polybius got inspiration from Thucydides, who is renowned for his care for accuracy in selecting information (1.22.2). Instead, Polybius' statement is modelled after Ephorus' own statement in F 110: since the historian cannot be everywhere, full autopsy of both events and places is a dream; therefore he must avail of the best informants, to gain the truth.³³ Polybius, as a universal historian, was quite sensitive to such an issue, as, before him, was Ephorus, whom Polybius, not by chance, considered to be the first and the only one among his predecessors to have written a truly universal history.³⁴

Theopompus", is unconvincing (Dionysius was inspired by Theopompus' own words, as he himself admits in *Pomp.* 6.2, ii.245.1ff. U–R: δῆλος γάρ ἐστιν, εἰ καὶ μηδὲν ἔγραψε [sc. Theopompus], πλείστην μὲν παρασκευὴν κτλ. See especially Vattuone 1997, 92ff., with reference to further Theopompean fragments), and is somewhat symptomatic of the influence of the *communis opinio* neglecting, *a priori*, that Polybius may be taught by his fourth-century predecessors.
31 See n. 23 above for the Greek text.
32 Plb. 12.4c.4–5, transl. Paton, Walbank and Habicht, with minor changes.
33 Cf. Parmeggiani 2011, 120.
34 See Plb. 5.33.2 = Ephor. *FGrHist* 70 T 7.

3 Methodology of record of the speeches

In his methodological polemic against Timaeus in Book 12, and also elsewhere in his *Histories*, Polybius talks fluently about how speeches of historical characters should be recorded by historians:

> The peculiar function of history is <u>to discover, in the first place, the words actually spoken, whatever they were</u> (αὐτοὺς τοὺς κατ' ἀλήθειαν εἰρημένους, οἷοί ποτ' ἂν ὦσι, γνῶναι λόγους), and next to ascertain the reason why what was done or spoken led to failure or success. For the mere statement of a fact may interest us but is of no benefit to us: but when we add the cause of it, study of history becomes fruitful ... A writer who passes over in silence the speeches made and the cause and in their place introduces false rhetorical exercises and discursive speeches, destroys the peculiar virtue of history.[35]

The historian must write the truth of what was really spoken, that is, he must record both the actual words and the real sense of what was said.[36]

One may think that Thucydides 1.22.1 stands behind Polybius' remarks:

> Of the various speeches made either when war was imminent or in the course of the war itself, it was hard to reproduce the exact words used either when I heard them myself or when they were reported to me by other sources. I made each speaker say broadly what I supposed would have been needed on any given occasion, while keeping as closely as I could to the overall sense of what was actually said (ὡς δ' ἂν ἐδόκουν ἐμοὶ ἕκαστοι περὶ τῶν αἰεὶ παρόντων τὰ δέοντα μάλιστ' εἰπεῖν, ἐχομένῳ ὅτι ἐγγύτατα τῆς ξυμπάσης γνώμης τῶν ἀληθῶς λεχθέντων, οὕτως εἴρηται).[37]

Still, Polybius rejects invention, and—to quote John Marincola—"postulates a relationship," between "speeches" and "facts", which is "much closer" than that suggested by Thucydides.[38] In Polybius' view, "speeches" and "facts" are almost on the same level (both require *akribeia*); moreover, "a historical character's advice is bound up in a causal relationship with the action that follows from that advice".[39] As we shall see now, the reason for this difference is that fourth-century

---

[35] Plb. 12.25b, transl. Paton, Walbank and Habicht, with minor changes.
[36] See also 2.56.10; 3.20.1–5; 29.12.9; 36.1.
[37] Thuc. 1.22.1, transl. Hammond, partly revised. On this passage as inspiring Polybius directly, see Canfora 2006, 724–26, Foulon 2010, 146–47; and especially Nicolai 1999, who describes Polybius as an exegete of Thucydides.
[38] Marincola 2007a, 123.
[39] Marincola 2007a, 123, following Sacks 1981, 79–96, particularly 91ff. Such aetiological link between speeches and deeds well explains, in my opinion, why Polybius appears to be more sensible than Thucydides to the issue of recording the actual words.

historians obviously reflected on speeches in historical writing, and therefore mediated between Thucydides and Polybius.

We read in Callisthenes F 44:

> The historian Callisthenes says: "Anyone attempting to write something must not fail to hit upon the character, but must make speeches appropriate to the persons and the circumstances" (δεῖ τὸν γράφειν τι πειρώμενον μὴ ἀστοχεῖν τοῦ προσώπου, ἀλλ' οἰκείως αὐτῷ τε καὶ τοῖς πράγμασι τοὺς λόγους θεῖναι).[40]

This is very reminiscent of Thucydides' stress on the role of invention in the recording of the speeches,[41] and we are sure that Ephorus too conformed to this norm, while writing down the speeches of historical characters, as did other fourth-century colleagues such as Theopompus and Anaximenes.[42] Still, in Ephorus F 9 we read:

> ... with regard to ancient events, those who proceed in a similar way [i.e. report the events in the most detailed way], we consider them absolutely unreliable, for we believe that one can remember neither all facts nor the majority of speeches after so much time has gone by [or: in so detailed way] (περὶ δὲ τῶν παλαιῶν τοὺς οὕτω διεξιόντας [i.e. τοὺς ἀκριβέστατα λέγοντας] ἀπιθανωτάτους εἶναι νομίζομεν, ὑπολαμβάνοντες οὔτε τὰς πράξεις ἁπάσας οὔτε τῶν λόγων τοὺς πλείστους εἰκὸς εἶναι μνημονεύεσθαι διὰ τοσούτων).[43]

Ephorus distinguishes between "facts" and "speeches", as did Thucydides 1.22.1–2; he is also fully aware of Thucydides' advice, since he stresses that recording speeches is a more complicated matter than recording facts (Ephorus says, τὰς πράξεις <u>ἁπάσας</u> and τῶν λόγων <u>τοὺς πλείστους</u>). Yet he does not talk of invention, and makes both "facts" and "speeches" the object of one and the same thought on the limits of *akribeia* in historical research, that is, he puts "facts" and "speeches" on the same level. This is exactly what we see happen in Polybius.

Also Theopompus T 20a⁺, from the epitome of Dionysius of Halicarnassus' lost treatise *De imitatione*, is noteworthy:

> (Theopompus) ... does not conceal the unspoken causes of events or speeches, but aims at detecting exactly the thought of those who have spoken or acted (τοῦ μηδὲ τὰς ἀπορρήτους

---

40 Athen. Mechan. 7 = Callisth. *FGrHist* 124 F 44. Transl. Marincola 2007a, 122.
41 See Marincola 2007a, 122.
42 See now Parmeggiani 2012.
43 Harp. s.v. ἀρχαίως = Ephor. *FGrHist* 70 F 9. Transl. mine. On this fragment, see Parmeggiani 2011, 99ff.

τῶν γενομένων ἢ λεχθέντων αἰτίας ἀποκρύψασθαι, στοχάσασθαι δ' ἀκριβῶς τῆς τῶν εἰπόντων ἢ πεποιηκότων γνώμης.⁴⁴

The words μηδὲ τὰς ἀπορρήτους τῶν γενομένων ἢ τῶν λεχθέντων αἰτίας ἀποκρύψασθαι are a parallel of ἐξετάζειν τὰς ἀφανεῖς αἰτίας τῶν πράξεων καὶ τῶν πραξάντων αὐτὰς in Theopompus T 20a (Dion. Hal. *Pomp*. 6.7, ii.246.12–13 U–R: see below § 4). Beside the problem of the relationship between the two texts and the lost treatise *De imitatione*,⁴⁵ it seems that Theopompus too did put "facts" and "speeches" on the very same level (τὰς τῶν γενομένων ἢ τῶν λεχθέντων αἰτίας … τῆς τῶν εἰπόντων ἢ πεποιηκότων γνώμης), and also believed, like Polybius did later, that speeches were not less important than facts on the aetiological side. In this regard, if the words μηδὲ τὰς ἀπορρήτους τῶν γενομένων ἢ <u>τῶν λεχθέντων αἰτίας ἀποκρύψασθαι</u> paraphrase ἐξετάζειν τὰς ἀφανεῖς αἰτίας τῶν πράξεων καὶ <u>τῶν πραξάντων αὐτὰς</u> (T 20a), one may ask whether Theopompus too emphasized that the historical character's speeches explain the deeds he performs. Furthermore, the words στοχάσασθαι δ' ἀκριβῶς τῆς τῶν εἰπόντων ἢ πεποιηκότων γνώμης, while recalling Thucydides 1.22.1, ἐχομένῳ ὅτι ἐγγύτατα τῆς ξυμπάσης γνώμης τῶν ἀληθῶς λεχθέντων, may suggest that Theopompus, again like Polybius, was very sensible to the issue of recording the actual words: like the reconstruction of the facts, also that of the speeches requires *akribeia*.

Both Ephorus F 9 and Theopompus T 20a⁺ are very important documents for the reconstruction of the development of the theory of speeches in ancient historiography, since they help to explain the subtle differences which occur between Thucydides' remark in 1.22.1 and Polybius' later remarks: they show that a link exists between Polybius and Thucydides, and that this link is due to fourth-century historiography.

4 Aetiology

Some critics believe that Polybius' famous distinction between *aitia* (the cause of the action), *arche* (the beginning of the action) and *prophasis* (the pretext for the action) is a redefinition/refinement of Thucydides' older distinction between

---

44 Dion. Hal. *De imit*. 3.3, ii.209.17–20 U–R = Theopomp. *FGrHist* 115 T 20a⁺. Transl. mine.
45 See Weaire 2002, with bibliography.

aitia and *prophasis* (cf. 1.23.5–6).⁴⁶ As we shall see, things are far more complex, if we consider, once again, the mediation of fourth-century historians.

In Book 3 of his *Histories*, Polybius defines *aitia*, *arche*, and *prophasis* and gives an example:

> By the beginning of anything I mean the first attempt to execute and put in action plans on which we have decided, by its causes what is leading up to decisions and judgments, that is to say our notions of things, our state of mind, our reasoning about these, and everything through which we reach decisions and projects (αἰτίας δὲ τὰς προκαθηγουμένας τῶν κρίσεων καὶ διαλήψεων· λέγω δ' ἐπινοίας καὶ διαθέσεις καὶ τοὺς περὶ ταῦτα συλλογισμοὺς καὶ δι' ὧν ἐπὶ τὸ κρῖναί τι καὶ προθέσθαι παραγινόμεθα) ... It is easy for anyone to see the real causes and origin of the war against Persia. The first was the retreat of the Greeks under Xenophon ... The second was the crossing of Agesilaus, king of Sparta, to Asia ... From both of these facts Philip perceived and reckoned (ἐξ ὧν Φίλιππος κατανοήσας καὶ συλλογισάμενος) on the cowardice and indolence of the Persians as compared with the military efficiency of himself and his Macedonians, and further fixing his eyes on (πρὸ ὀφθαλμῶν θέμενος) the splendor of the great prize which the war promised, he lost no time ... seizing on the pretext that he was eager to take vengeance on the Persians for their injurious treatment of the Greeks, he bestirred himself and decided to go to war, beginning to make every preparation for this purpose (εὐθέως προφάσει χρώμενος ὅτι σπεύδει μετελθεῖν τὴν Περσῶν παρανομίαν εἰς τοὺς Ἕλληνας, ὁρμὴν ἔσχε καὶ προέθετο πολεμεῖν, καὶ πάντα πρὸς τοῦτο τὸ μέρος ἡτοίμαζε).⁴⁷

Paul Pédech thought that Polybius' theory was inspired by Theopompus, since Polybius' example concerns Philip II, who was the most important character in Theopompus' *Philippika*.⁴⁸ Indeed, one can think of Theopompus as a model for Polybius, but in a different sense. Polybius exemplifies the concept of *"cause"* by focusing his attention on Philip's own strategies, and, most importantly, by showing Philip's *"secret" reasoning*: Polybius looks at Philip's *psyche*, clearly emphasizing the concept of *aitia*, *"cause"*, as an intimate *aphanes* (something *"unapparent"* to common view). This has much to do with Theopompus' approach to aetiology, as is described by Dionysius of Halicarnassus in his letter *Ad Pompeium Geminum* 6.7, ii.246.10–16 U–R (T 20a):

> His final and most characteristic accomplishment is something which no other historian, either before or since, has achieved with comparable exactness or effect. And what is this

---

46 See Ziegler 1952, 1553, Lehmann 1974, 167–68, Derow 1994, Hornblower 1994, 60, and 1995, 59, McGing 2010, 59, Longley 2012, 72–73, Miltsios 2013, 332. Walbank 1957, 306, observes: "Though he [*sc.* Polybius] makes no reference to Thucydides' system, his silence spells criticism of it, for in 31.12f. he shows by reminiscence his familiarity with his predecessor".
47 Plb. 3.6.7–13, transl. Paton, Walbank and Habicht. Cf. 22.18.6ff.
48 Pédech 1964, 95ff., also noticing Isocratean echoes in Polybius' discourse.

quality? It is the ability, in the case of every action, not only to see and to state what is appearing to most people, but to examine even the hidden reasons for actions and the motives of their agents, and the feelings in their hearts (which most people do not find it easy to discern), and to reveal all the mysteries of apparent virtue and of the unrevealed vice (τὸ καθ' ἑκάστην πρᾶξιν μὴ μόνον τὰ φανερὰ τοῖς πολλοῖς ὁρᾶν καὶ λέγειν, ἀλλ' ἐξετάζειν καὶ τὰς ἀφανεῖς αἰτίας τῶν πράξεων καὶ τῶν πραξάντων αὐτὰς καὶ τὰ πάθη τῆς ψυχῆς, ἃ μὴ ῥᾴδια τοῖς πολλοῖς εἰδέναι, καὶ πάντα ἐκκαλύπτειν τὰ μυστήρια τῆς τε δοκούσης ἀρετῆς καὶ τῆς ἀγνοουμένης κακίας).[49]

Dionysius detects in Theopompus' aetiological approach something new, and he is right. Theopompus' distinction between *aphanes* ("unapparent") and *phaneron* ("apparent") clearly recalls Thucydides' most famous distinction in 1.23.5–6;[50] but some differences are notable. Thucydides made a distinction between "*historical* causes" on the one hand (the events of Corcyra and Potidaea, that provoked the war in 431 BCE), and a "*philosophical* cause" on the other (a war between Sparta and Athens was inevitable because of the growing power of Athens, which inspired fear in Sparta): the former causes were apparent, the latter cause was unapparent.[51] Theopompus, for his part, makes a distinction between apparent and unapparent causes of the action, as well as apparent and unapparent causes of the man who did it: he therefore conceives two spheres, the actions on the one hand, and the men who did them on the other, and, while discussing the *historical* causes, brings Thucydides' original distinction between *phaneron* and *aphanes* into each sphere.

Theopompus emphasized the difference between the apparent causes of men's deeds and their unapparent reasons. This approach to aetiology is to be seen as a necessary premise to the distinction we find later in Polybius between *aitia* as the "*real cause*" for the man's action, which is mostly left unspoken and which the historian must show his reader, and *prophasis* as the spoken reason, which covers the man's real aim and, as such, is to be intended as the "*pretext*".

---

49 Dion. Hal. *Pomp.* 6.7, ii.246.10–16 U-R = Theopomp. *FGrHist* 115 T 20a. Transl. Usher, partly revised.
50 Thuc. 1.23.5–6: διότι δ' ἔλυσαν, τὰς αἰτίας προύγραψα πρῶτον καὶ τὰς διαφοράς, τοῦ μή τινα ζητῆσαί ποτε ἐξ ὅτου τοσοῦτος πόλεμος τοῖς Ἕλλησι κατέστη. τὴν μὲν γὰρ ἀληθεστάτην πρόφασιν, ἀφανεστάτην δὲ λόγῳ, τοὺς Ἀθηναίους ἡγοῦμαι μεγάλους γιγνομένους καὶ φόβον παρέχοντας τοῖς Λακεδαιμονίοις ἀναγκάσαι ἐς τὸ πολεμεῖν· αἱ δ' ἐς τὸ φανερὸν λεγόμεναι αἰτίαι αἵδ' ἦσαν ἑκατέρων, ἀφ' ὧν λύσαντες τὰς σπονδὰς ἐς τὸν πόλεμον κατέστησαν. See Vattuone 2007, 151b–152a, and 2014, 16ff.; Ottone 2010, 319–20.
51 See Parmeggiani 2014a, 115–17, and 2018.

5 Conclusions

We have examined three main items in four points: conception of history (§ 1), methodology (§§ 2 and 3) and aetiology (§ 4). As we have seen, Polybius' historiographical culture derived mainly from fourth-century historians, Ephorus and Theopompus to be precise. A wider-ranging examination than the one we have conducted here would suggest the same: to give just a few examples, Polybius' comparison of constitutions in Book 6 would be unthinkable without the comparison of constitutions in Ephorus' Book 4 as a premise;[52] the concept itself of "universal history" in Polybius would be unthinkable without that of Ephorus as a premise, for Ephorus was the very first historian who stressed the dramatic impact of Western events on Greek affairs, and therefore also stressed the necessity of a wider view of events as a means for correctly understanding and describing each of them;[53] Polybius' "contemporary universal history" focused on the extraordinary ascent of Rome, and is conceptually close to Theopompus' own "contemporary universal history", which focused on the extraordinary ascent of Philip II.[54] Without any doubt, the links between fourth-century historians and Polybius prove to be very strong and pervasive: Polybius knew Thucydides, but fourth-century historians were far more important to him, and in a positive sense.[55] All this makes us see the general development of Greek historiography from the fifth century BCE to the age of Polybius in a new way.

For many years, Thucydides and Polybius have both been conceived as models of "good historiography"; the fourth- and third-century historians, by contrast, as models of "bad historiography". Thucydides, the "best historian" because he was a contemporary historian, represents the "Classical Age" of Greek historiography; the fourth- and third-century historians, because they were mostly writers of non-contemporary events, represent the dark "Middle Ages"; Polybius, as an imitator of Thucydides and also a contemporary historian, and

---

[52] See Parmeggiani 2011, 220–52, 714.
[53] See Parmeggiani 2011, 711ff.
[54] See Marincola 2007b, 174–76; Vattuone 1998, 83, and 2014, 26–27.
[55] Scholars often emphasize instances of criticism toward Ephorus and Theopompus in Polybius' work (on Ephorus, see Plb. 4.20.5 [F 8]; 6.45–46.10 [F 148]; 12.25f [T 20]; on Theopompus, see Plb. 8.8.7–11.8 [T 19 + FF 27, 225a]; 12.25f [T 32], 16.12 [F 343], and 38.6 [T 29 + F 28]. See e.g. Meister 1975, 56ff.), therefore neglecting the nature of Polybius' approach to his predecessors in general (on such topic, see the various papers collected in Schepens/Bollansée 2005) and instances of appreciation of both Ephorus and Theopompus in particular. In 1974 Paul Pédech asked: "Les historiens que Polybe a critiqués n'ont-ils pas exercé sur lui quelque influence?" (Gabba 1974, 202). My answer is "yes".

therefore a "great historian", represents the "Renaissance". Such a picture, schematic and simplistic as it may appear, does illustrate the way in which the history of Greek historiography from the fifth century BCE to the age of Polybius has often been conceptualized in modern scholarship from the beginning of the nineteenth century until today; and it is wrong. If Polybius appears to be unthinkable without Thucydides, it is only because of fourth-century historians, who made Thucydides' statements the object of fruitful insight: they did not forget Thucydides' intuitions, rather they embodied such intuitions in full theory in both historical research and historical writing. In this way, they were the first to give birth to the *genos historikon*.

Polybius was a self-aware professional of history writing. He consciously worked within the tradition of *genos historikon*. He looked at fourth-century historians, and treated them as models of comparison: it could not have been otherwise, for they were the first professional historians, who theorized the practice of history not as a *parergon*, something marginal to their lives, but as the most necessary thing to carry out—the most meaningful pursuit to which their lives should be devoted.

Bibliography

Bearzot, C. (2005), "Polibio e Teopompo: osservazioni di metodo e giudizio morale", in: Schepens/Bollansée (2005) 55–71.

Biraschi, A.M. (1996), "Teopompo e l'uso del mito. A proposito di FGrHist 115 F 381", in: *Hermes* 124, 160–169.

Canfora, L. (2006), "Thucydides in Rome and Late Antiquity", in: A. Rengakos/A. Tsakmakis (eds.), *Brill's Companion to Thucydides*, Leiden/Boston, 721–754.

Chávez Reino, A.L. (2005), "Los claroscuros del Éforo de Polibio", in: Schepens/Bollansée (2005) 19–54.

—— (2007), "αὐτόπτης", in: *LHG&L* 2, 123b–146a.

Derow, P. (1994), "Historical Explanation: Polybius and His Predecessors", in: S. Hornblower (ed.), *Greek Historiography*, Oxford, 73–90.

Flower, M.A. (1994), *Theopompus of Chios: History and Rhetoric in the Fourth Century BC*, Oxford.

Foulon, É. (2010), "Polybe a-t-il lu Thucydide?", in: V. Fromentin/S. Gotteland/P. Payen (eds.), *Ombres de Thucydide. La réception de l'historien depuis l'Antiquité jusqu' au début du XXe siècle*. Actes des colloques de Bordeaux, les 16–17 mars 2007, Bordeaux, 141–153.

Gabba, E. (1974), *Polybe. Entretiens sur l'Antiquité classique XX*, Vandoeuvres, Genève.

Hornblower, S. (1994), "Introduction", in: *id*. (ed.), *Greek Historiography*, Oxford, 1–72.

—— (1995), "The Fourth-Century and Hellenistic Reception of Thucydides", in: *JHS* 115, 47–68.

Jacoby, F. (1926), "Griechische Geschichtsschreibung", in: *Die Antike* 2, 1–29. (Now H. Bloch [ed.], *Abhandlungen zur griechischen Geschichtsschreibung von Felix Jacoby zu seinem achtzigsten Geburtstag am 19 März 1956*, Leiden 1956, 73–99).

Lehmann, G.A. (1974), "Polybios und die ältere und zeitgenössische griechische Geschichtsschreibung: Einige Bemerkungen", in: Gabba (1974) 147–200.
Lenfant, D. (2004), *Ctésias de Cnide, La Perse. L'Inde. Autres fragments*, texte établi, traduit et commenté par D. Lenfant, Paris.
Longley, G. (2012), "Thucydides, Polybius, and Human Nature", in: C. Smith/L.M. Yarrow (eds.), *Imperialism, Cultural Politics, & Polybius*, Oxford/New York, 68–84.
McGing, B. (2010), *Polybius' Histories*, Oxford.
Marincola, J. (2007a), "Speeches in Classical Historiography", in: J. Marincola (ed.), *A Companion to Geeek and Roman Historiography*, I, Malden, 118–132.
—— (2007b), "Universal History from Ephorus to Diodorus", in: J. Marincola (ed.), *A Companion to Greek and Roman Historiography*, I, Malden, 171–179.
Meister, K. (1975), *Historische Kritik bei Polybios*, Wiesbaden.
—— (1992), *La storiografia greca. Dalle origini alla fine dell'Ellenismo*, It. transl. by M. Tosti Croce, Rome/Bari.
Miltsios, N. (2013), "The Narrative Legacy of Thucydides: Polybius, Book I", in: A. Tsakmakis/M. Tamiolaki (eds.), *Thucydides between History and Literature*, Berlin/Boston, 329–352.
Momigliano, A. (1992), *Le radici classiche della storiografia moderna*, It. transl. by R. Di Donato, Firenze.
Musti, D. (ed.) (2001), *Polibio, Storie (libri I-II)*, Milan.
Nicolai, R. (1995), "Κτῆμα ἐς αἰεί. Aspetti della fortuna di Tucidide nel mondo antico", in: *RFIC* 123, 5–26.
—— (1999), "Polibio interprete di Tucidide: la teoria dei discorsi", in: *SemRom* 2, 281–301.
Ottone, G. (2010), "Scrivere la storia dopo Tucidide: Teopompo di fronte all'Ateniese dalla prospettiva di Polibio e Dionigi di Alicarnasso", in: V. Fromentin/S. Gotteland/P. Payen (eds.), *Ombres de Thucydide. La réception de l'historien depuis l'Antiquité jusqu' au début du XXe siècle*. Actes des colloques de Bordeaux, les 16–17 mars 2007, Bordeaux, 307–323.
Parmeggiani, G. (2003), "L'εὑρεῖν senza σαφές. Tucidide e la conoscenza del passato", in: *AncSoc* 33, 253–283.
—— (2011), *Eforo di Cuma. Studi di storiografia greca*, Bologna.
—— (2012), "Plutarco sulle arringhe dei generali nelle opere storiche di Eforo, Teopompo e Anassimene (Plut. *Praec. ger. reip.* 6, Mor. 803b = Ephor. *FGrHist* 70 T 21 = Theopomp. *FGrHist* 115 T 33 = Anaxim. *FGrHist* 72 T 15)", in: *RSA* 42, 27–40.
—— (2014a), "The Causes of the Peloponnesian War: Ephorus, Thucydides and Their Critics", in: *id.* (ed.), *Between Thucydides and Polybius: The Golden Age of Greek Historiography*, Washington D.C., 115–132.
—— (2014b), "On the Translation of Polybius 1.1.2", in: *Histos* 8, 180–188.
—— (2018),"Thucydides on Aetiology and Methodology and Some Links with the Philosophy of Heraclitus", in: *Mnemosyne* 71, forthcoming.
Pédech, P. (1961), *Polybe, Histoires, Livre XII*, texte établi, traduit et commenté par Paul Pédech, Paris.
—— (1964), *La méthode historique de Polybe*, Paris.
—— (1969), *Polybe, Histoires, Livre I*, texte établi et traduit par Paul Pédech, Paris.
Rood, T. (2012), "Polybius, Thucydides, and the First Punic War", in: C. Smith/L.M. Yarrow (eds.), *Imperialism, Cultural Politics, & Polybius*, Oxford/New York, 50–67.
Sacks, K.S. (1981), *Polybius on the Writing of History*, Berkeley.

—— (1983), "Historiography in the Rhetorical Works of Dionysius of Halicarnassus", in: *Athenaeum* 61, 65–87.

Saïd, S. (2010), "La condamnation du μυθῶδες par Thucydide et sa postérité dans l'historiographie grecque", in: V. Fromentin, S. Gotteland, and P. Payen (eds.), *Ombres de Thucydide. La réception de l'historien depuis l'Antiquité jusqu' au début du XXe siècle*. Actes des colloques de Bordeaux, les 16–17 mars 2007, Bordeaux, 167–189.

Schepens, G. (2010), "Thucydide législateur de l'histoire? Appréciations antiques et modernes", in: V. Fromentin/S. Gotteland/P. Payen (eds.), *Ombres de Thucydide. La réception de l'historien depuis l'Antiquité jusqu' au début du XXe siècle*. Actes des colloques de Bordeaux, les 16–17 mars 2007, Bordeaux, 121–140.

Schepens, G./J. Bollansée (eds.) (2005), *The Shadow of Polybius: Intertextuality as a Research Tool in Greek Historiography*, Proceedings of the International Colloquium. Louvain, 21–22 September 2001, Louvain/Paris/Dudley.

Schweighäuser, J. (1792), *Polybii Megalopolitani Historiarum quidquid superest. Recensuit, digessit, emendatiore interpretatione, varietate lectionis, adnotationibus, indicibus illustravit Johannes Schweighäuser*, Vol. 5, Leipzig.

Vattuone, R. (1991), *Sapienza d'Occidente. Il pensiero storico di Timeo di Tauromenio*, Bologna.

—— (1997), "Una testimonianza dimenticata di Teopompo (Phot., *Bibl.*, 176, p. 121 A, 30-34). Note sul proemio dei *Philippika*", in: L. Criscuolo/G. Geraci/C. Salvaterra (eds.), *Simblos. Scritti di storia antica*, II, Bologna, 85–106.

—— (1998), "Koinai Praxeis. Le dimensioni «universali» della storiografia greca fra Erodoto e Teopompo", in: L. Aigner Foresti et al. (eds.), *L'ecumenismo politico nella coscienza dell'Occidente*. Bergamo, 18–21 settembre 1995, Roma, 57–96.

—— (2007), "ἀφανής", in: *LHG&L* 2, 146a–152b.

—— (2014), "Looking for the Invisible: Theopompus and the Roots of Historiography", in: G. Parmeggiani (ed.), *Between Thucydides and Polybius: The Golden Age of Greek Historiography*, Washington D.C., 7–37.

Walbank, F.W. (1957), *A Historical Commentary on Polybius*, I, Oxford.

—— (1972), *Polybius*, Berkeley/Los Angeles/London.

—— (1990), "Profit or Amusement: Some Thoughts on the Motives of Hellenistic Historians", in: H. Verdin/G. Schepens/E. De Keyser (eds.), *Purposes of History: Studies in Greek Historiography from the 4th to the 2nd Centuries BCE*. Proceedings of the International Colloquium, Louvain 24–26 May 1988, Louvain, 253–266.

Weaire, G. (2002), "The Relationship between Dionysius of Halicarnassus' *De imitatione* and *Epistula ad Pompeium*", *CPh* 97, 351–359.

Will, W. (1991), "Die griechische Geschichtsschreibung des 4. Jahrhunderts. Eine Zusammenfassung", in: J.M. Alonso-Núñez (ed.), *Geschichtsbild und Geschichtsdenken im Altertum*, Darmstadt, 113–135.

Ziegler, K. (1952), "Polybios", in: *RE* 21.2, 1440–1578.

Carlo Scardino
Polybius and Fifth-Century Historiography: Continuity and Diversity in the Presentation of Historical Deeds

Most scholars have accepted that—in the organization and presentation of his ἱστορία—Polybius was influenced by Herodotus and Thucydides, the two father-figures of ancient historiography.[1] In his entry on Polybius in Pauly's *Realenzyklopädie* (1952), Konrat Ziegler summed up contemporary academic opinion, concluding that Polybius "ihn [*sc.* Thucydides] gut gekannt und in vieler Hinsicht an ihn Anschluß genommen hat" (knew [Thucydides] well and followed him in many respects).[2] Similarly Luschnat, in the "Nachwirkung" section of his monograph on Thucydides, argued that, at least in some respects, Thucydides' history had inspired Polybius.[3] Today, the question of how Polybius' forerunners may have influenced his work has again become a topic of debate. This renewed interest is due to some extent to the development of intertextual approaches, which in addition to clear echoes can also point to deeper structural parallels between two texts.

Comparison with Herodotus and Thucydides (and Xenophon) is inevitable given the fragmentary nature of historians from the fourth and third centuries BCE, and our subsequent lack of knowledge regarding the structure of their work. These include Ephorus, Theopompus, Callisthenes, Duris, Phylarchus, and Timaeus. The fragments of these authors are included in the writings of later historians, biographers, geographers, antiquarians, and grammarians who generally cite merely a few lines, and then only in support of their own arguments. This leads to an incomplete and distorted image of the original works, and makes comparison with Polybius largely unfeasible. And while it is true that many of these lost historians were also sources for Diodorus, who produced his monumental history in the first century BCE, this author's relatively free and creative exploitation of earlier historians also makes his *Bibliotheca historica* unsuitable for reconstituting the works of, for example, Ephorus or Timaeus.[4] These issues make a

---

[1] I would like to thank Jasper Donelan for translating this contribution from German into English.
[2] Ziegler 1952, 1523.
[3] Luschnat 1970, 1294–97.
[4] On the question of Diodorus' sources, see the summary in Scardino 2014, 607f. (with further bibliography).

structural and thematic comparison of Polybius' history with the extant works of Herodotus and Thucydides attractive.

Unlike earlier studies, which had denied Herodotus' influence on Polybius, McGing was the first scholar to investigate the relationship between the two historians in detail.[5] He rightly concludes "that Polybius' apparent failure to mention Herodotus (or Thucydides) is not proof that he was ignorant of his work".[6] And even though McGing is unable to provide any examples of a direct influence of Herodotus on Polybius, he suspects "that familiarity with Herodotus provided Polybius with a model of historical presentation which suited his character and which, to a certain extent, he reproduced, perhaps at times only unconsciously".[7] There is of course a significant difference between detailed knowledge of a given work and "unconscious use as a model or as an intertext"—unconscious use is namely difficult to prove.

The first point of contact that McGing identifies between the two historians is that in:

> "his [sc. Polybius'] persona as a historian, particularly the persistent intrusiveness of the narrator, and his centralizing of geography in the historical enterprise and manner of visualizing the physical environment, Polybius can trace a real, if thin, line of descent from Herodotus".[8]

For the idea of an "intrusive narrator", one who comments in the first person singular on his narrative or makes geographic and ethnographic digressions in his own voice, there can be no doubt that Herodotus "displays his control over his material simply by announcing what he is going to say, by cutting a story short, by explaining his reasons for narrating something, or by expressing which criteria govern his whole work".[9] Herodotus confidently offers his opinion (1.5.3) as to

---

[5] Murray 1972, for example, found no influence of Herodotus on Polybius and states (p. 210) that "only in the late Hellenistic period does Herodotus seem to have suffered a slight eclipse as a serious writer to be studied". As Hornblower 1974, 60 and Hornblower 1995, 49 emphasizes, it is important to realize that "'not mentioned' is not the same as 'not read'. Even in the fifth century BC the same principle applies: it would be wrong to argue that, merely because Thucydides does not mention Herodotus by name, he did not know Herodotus' work well. When dealing with a period like the fourth century, and especially the Hellenistic period when our literary evidence survives in such tatters (even Polybius is far from complete), it is even more true that we must proceed indirectly, and be ready to detect oblique influences, influences exerted in ways which do not immediately jump on to computer screens".
[6] McGing 2012, 34.
[7] McGing 2012, 37.
[8] McGing 2012, 49.
[9] Munson 2001, 30.

who is to blame for the Persian War, pointing out that the Lydian king Croesus was responsible for the first ἀδικήματα between Europe and Asia. In other instances, too, Herodotus provides his readers with authorial glosses, guiding their interpretation of his account.[10] Thucydides takes a different approach, and seldom speaks in the first person as author of his history. Rare examples include the preface (σκοποῦντί μοι, 1.1.3) or the chapter on methodology (ἠξίωσα γράφειν, 1.22). Generally, however, Thucydides "lets the facts speak for themselves".[11] As for Xenophon, he regularly (although not always) speaks in the first person when making authorial comments or explicative glosses.[12] Gray therefore concludes rightly that his "conversationalised narrative" recalls Herodotus' technique.[13] The fragmentary nature of the fourth- and third-century historians does not permit us to evaluate confidently their influence on Polybius' level of authorial intrusiveness into his narrative.

More so than Herodotus, Polybius passes judgment on his narrative in the form of asides, commentary, and interpretative notes. These are almost always highlighted by markers in the first person. Regarding Polybius' interest in geography, McGing identifies various Herodotean echoes, including the vivid description of countries and of the fertility of the regions discussed. McGing believes, for example, that Polybius' description of the Euphrates (9.43) recalls Herodotus' description of the Nile (2.19–34).[14] The same is supposed to be true for the fertility of Po Valley (2.15), reminiscent of "Herodotus' assessment of Babylonia's rich land" (1.93).

---

[10] Similar too is Herodotus' assessment that the Athenian contribution was decisive for Greece's salvation (7.139).

[11] Unlike in Herodotus, verbs and pronouns in the first person (referring to the narrator) are relatively rare in Thucydides. Note, however, the description of the plague: ἐγὼ δὲ οἷον ἐγίγνετο λέξω (2.48.3), and the second preface, a passage in which Thucydides says that he remembers both the beginning and the end of the war: ἔγωγε μέμνημαι (5.26.4). In authorial passages, we also frequently find the expression (ὡς) ἐμοὶ δοκεῖ (e.g. 1.10.4, 22.1, 93.7).

[12] In the *Hellenica*, Xenophon comments on the death of Theramenes: τοῦτο μὲν οὐκ ἀγνοῶ, ὅτι ... (2.3.56), explains the end of Spartan hegemony νῦν γε μὴν λέξω ... (5.4.1), praises Iphicrates ἀλλὰ τοῦτο ἐπαινῶ, ὅτι ...(6.2.32), and honors Epameinondas ἔγωγε φήσαιμι ...(7.5.8). Glosses in the first person that structure the narrative and lend emphasis to particular points occur at e.g. 4.8.1, 6.1.19, 7.4.1.

[13] Gray 1989, 11ff.

[14] McGing 2012, 43: "Just describing the characteristics of the Euphrates in the way Polybius does, even if it did not correct Herodotus or reflect his account of the Nile, is Herodotean". Murray 1972, 206, on the other hand, emphasizes the similarities between Herodotus' description of Egypt with Nearchus' description of India (*FGrHist* 133 F 17–20).

For technical details, McGing compares Hannibal's crossing of the Rhone with Xerxes' bridging of the Hellespont, noting that "the repetition of technical details—binding the rafts together, anchoring them to the land, numbers, distances, measurements, dealing with the current, covering the pontoon with soil, bringing the animals across—gives the two accounts a very similar feel, but is this just an accident of their authors' similar interests", whereby "familiarity with one of the most technological descriptions in Herodotus ... has unconsciously suggested to Polybius a model for his own account".[15]

However, if we take the fragments of Ephorus into consideration, we also find a number of descriptions comparable with those from Polybius. Ephorus shares Polybius' interest in geography, for example, and in the description of different countries along with their distinctive features and inhabitants. Fragment 30 reveals Ephorus' interest in the various peoples who inhabit the οἰκουμένη. In this fragment, Ephorus locates and describes the environments of the Indians, Ethiopians, Celts, and Scythians. Compare also Fragment 119, in which Ephorus outlines the geographical and ethnographical peculiarities of Boeotia, underscoring that region's wealth. Ephorus suggests that geographical factors caused the Boeotians to become leaders (τὴν μὲν οὖν χώραν ἐπαινεῖ διὰ ταῦτα, καί φησι πρὸς ἡγεμονίαν εὐφυῶς ἔχειν), citing the Theban Epaminondas as proof of this. This is highly reminiscent of Ionic historiography and the followers of Hippocrates, who themselves influenced Herodotus.[16]

The same is true for Timaeus who, although heavily criticized by Polybius, in some respects assuredly served as a model. Timaeus' description of Sicily (F 164) reveals an interest in dimensions and distances, and highlights the island's fertility.[17] Indeed, Timaeus' emphasis on the fertility of the Plain of Catania recalls Polybius' description of northern Italy (2.15). Timaeus may well have been the prototype here, and as such, it is not always necessary to look to Herodotus (e.g. 1.193) for Polybius' inspiration. This is especially true given that Timaeus' work itself betrays a Herodotean influence; it is not without reason that Baron, in his monograph, refers to Timaeus as the "Herodotus of the West".[18]

---

15 McGing 2012, 41f.
16 Cf. Hippocrates *Aër.* 12ff., esp. ch. 16 and 23, and Hdt. e.g. 1.71, 3.20ff. Cf. Scardino 2007, 79f.
17 F 164: ... καὶ τὸν τοῦ σίτου καρπὸν ταύτην πρώτην ἀνεῖναι διὰ τὴν ἀρετὴν τῆς χώρας ... ἔν τε γὰρ τῶι Λεοντίνωι πεδίωι καὶ κατὰ πολλοὺς ἄλλους τόπους τῆς Σικελίας μέχρι τοῦ νῦν φύεσθαι τοὺς ἀγρίους ὀνομαζομένους πυρούς. καθόλου δὲ {πρὸ τῆς εὑρέσεως τοῦ σίτου} ζητουμένου κατὰ ποίαν τῆς οἰκουμένης γῆς πρῶτον ἐφάνησαν οἱ προειρημένοι καρποί, εἰκός ἐστιν ἀποδίδοσθαι τὸ πρωτεῖον τῆι κρατίστηι χώραι.
18 Baron 2013, 235.

Whereas prior to McGing, no one had worked through the parallels between Polybius and Herodotus, the relationship between Polybius and Thucydides has long been a topic of discussion. Konrat Ziegler, in the *RE* article cited above, argued that Polybius knew Thucydides' work well.[19] However, he later revised this position, claiming that no direct Thucydidean influence on Polybius could be established.[20] Gelzer too was skeptical about the influence of Thucydides on Polybius' methodology, preferring to emphasize the importance of later historians: "Polybios—wo nicht überhaupt—zum mindestens auch noch durch entsprechende Erörterungen in der nachthukydideischen Historiographie angeregt wurde" (Polybius was at least also—if not wholly—inspired by relevant discussions from historiographical works later than Thucydides).[21] Hornblower, on the other hand, although conceding that Polybius' reception of Thucydides is problematic and inconsistent, has nevertheless argued the influence of the earlier historian on Polybius' methodology is manifest.[22] A thorough evaluation of the relationship between the two authors is complicated by the fact that Polybius' work has not survived extant.

Rood has taken a different, intertextual approach, attempting to show that "Polybius engaged with Thucydides in a far more extensive and suggestive way than has been appreciated".[23] In particular, Rood supports the idea that Polybius' opening book, which covers the First Punic War, picks up Thucydides' description of the Sicilian Expedition from Books 6 and 7: "Polybius also uses language found in Thucydides' Sicilian narrative to emphasize the shifting fortunes experienced by both sides during the long war".[24] The examples that Rood provides in support of his argument have failed to convince many scholars working on the topic.

---

19 Ziegler 1952, 1523. Walbank 1972, 41 and Mohm 1977, 134 also lean toward the idea that Polybius knew Thucydides' work.
20 Ziegler 1956, 163f.
21 Gelzer 1955, 279f.
22 Cf. Hornblower 1974, 1994, and finally 1995, 58: "Polybius may have had better recall of the methodological chapters of Thucydides, especially those early in Book One, than of routine Thucydidean narrative and particular speeches. In this he is perhaps unlike Callisthenes and other Aristotelians, who *were* interested in Thucydides' speeches and in his principles in composing them. In any case it did not for whatever reason occur to Polybius that Thucydides was a stick with which to beat Timaeus. A final and obvious warning: Polybius is not fragmentary like Hieronymus or Agatharchides, but nor is he complete either, in the sense that Herodotus or Thucydides were complete. A papyrus find tomorrow might disclose Polybius in explicit dialogue with the dead Thucydides, and we should look appropriately foolish".
23 Rood 2012, 51.
24 Rood 2012, 59.

Rood suggests, for instance, that the depicted fear of the Romans in the face of growing Carthaginian power (1.10.5–6) contains an explicit echo of Alcibiades' speech in Sparta (Thuc. 6.90.2–3):

Plb. 1.10.5–6	Thuc. 6.90.2–3
οὐ μὴν ἀγνοοῦντές γε τούτων οὐδέν, θεωροῦντες δὲ τοὺς Καρχηδονίους οὐ μόνον τὰ κατὰ τὴν Λιβύην, ἀλλὰ καὶ τῆς Ἰβηρίας ὑπήκοα πολλὰ μέρη πεποιημένους, ἔτι δὲ τῶν νήσων ἁπασῶν ἐγκρατεῖς ὑπάρχοντας τῶν κατὰ τὸ Σαρδόνιον καὶ Τυρρηνικὸν πέλαγος, ἠγωνίων, εἰ Σικελίας ἔτι κυριεύσαιεν, (μὴ) λίαν βαρεῖς καὶ φοβεροὶ γείτονες αὐτοῖς ὑπάρχοιεν, κύκλῳ σφᾶς περιέχοντες καὶ πᾶσι τοῖς τῆς Ἰταλίας μέρεσιν ἐπικείμενοι.	ἐπλεύσαμεν ἐς Σικελίαν πρῶτον μέν, εἰ δυναίμεθα, Σικελιώτας καταστρεψόμενοι, μετὰ δ' ἐκείνους αὖθις καὶ Ἰταλιώτας, ἔπειτα καὶ τῆς Καρχηδονίων ἀρχῆς καὶ αὐτῶν ἀποπειράσοντες. εἰ δὲ προχωρήσειε ταῦτα ἢ πάντα ἢ καὶ τὰ πλείω, ἤδη τῇ Πελοποννήσῳ ἐμέλλομεν ἐπιχειρήσειν, κομίσαντες ξύμπασαν μὲν τὴν ἐκεῖθεν προσγενομένην δύναμιν τῶν Ἑλλήνων, πολλοὺς δὲ βαρβάρους μισθωσάμενοι καὶ Ἴβηρας καὶ ἄλλους τῶν ἐκεῖ ὁμολογουμένως νῦν βαρβάρων μαχιμωτάτους, τριήρεις τε πρὸς ταῖς ἡμετέραις πολλὰς ναυπηγησάμενοι, ἐχούσης τῆς Ἰταλίας ξύλα ἄφθονα, αἷς τὴν Πελοπόννησον πέριξ πολιορκοῦντες καὶ τῷ πεζῷ ἅμα ἐκ γῆς ἐφορμαῖς τῶν πόλεων τὰς μὲν βίᾳ λαβόντες, τὰς δ' ἐντειχισάμενοι, ῥᾳδίως ἠλπίζομεν καταπολεμήσειν καὶ μετὰ ταῦτα καὶ τοῦ ξύμπαντος Ἑλληνικοῦ ἄρξειν.

There are some obvious points of contact between the two passages, such as the encirclement of Sparta/Italy or the idea of expansion toward the west. Rood's conclusion is unconvincing, however, when he argues that Polybius exaggerates the Romans' fear or that the intentions of the Carthaginians are anachronistic, and that the text therefore consciously follows Thucydides' model:

> "Alcibiades' exaggerated presentation of Athens' ambitions undermines the authority of the Roman perceptions of Carthage. It hints that the Romans exaggerated the scope of Carthaginian ambitions in order to justify to themselves their own morally dubious intervention in Sicily".[25]

In context, it is clear that Alcibiades' plan—presented in *oratio recta*—goes beyond what he had earlier advised (Thuc. 6.16–18). As such, it represents a rhetorical exaggeration, one that Alcibiades exploits to rouse the Spartans by drawing a link between the Sicilian Expedition and the security of the Peloponnese. And while Polybius hints at a similar dynamic for the Romans, this is nowhere made

---

[25] Rood 2012, 56.

explicit (for example via an authorial note suggesting that the Romans' superiority was exaggerated). The similarities between the two passages may be striking, but there is no indication in the text itself that Polybius was alluding to the Thucydidean episode. Note also that the idea of encircling one's opponent was an established *topos* already in the fifth century. The strategic importance of Cythera and of Pylos for encircling the Spartans, for example, appears in Herodotus and Thucydides.[26]

Polybius' mention of the lunar eclipse reported by Thucydides (7.50.4) is an important argument for Rood's thesis. And yet, whereas in Thucydides the eclipse takes place prior to the battle in the harbor and leads to a delay of twenty-seven days, in Polybius (who discusses the same event at 9.19.1–4), the delay lasts merely a day. Rood explains that:

> "Rather than assuming ignorance of Thucydides, it seems better to posit a simple slip: the delay of a single day that Polybius places after the eclipse may be a mistaken recollection of the delay that Thucydides places after the final sea-battle (7.74.1) ... Polybius' gaffe about Nicias can in any case be set against an apparently clear echo of Thucydides".[27]

Yet it is unclear why Polybius needed to use Thucydides as a model here. It is entirely possible that Polybius was relying on a different source, since Thucydides is not the only historian to have discussed the Sicilian expedition; Philistus of Syracuse, Ephorus, and Timaeus all also covered the same period. Polybius often criticizes the versions of other historians and improves on them with his own interpretation. In his account of the eclipse, however, neither Thucydides nor any other source is named and there can, therefore, be no certainty as to the origin of the information.

It is interesting to note which historians Polybius cites in his work:

Historians	Citations	In Book 12
Herodotus	0	
Thucydides	1	
Ctesias	0	

---

[26] Cf. Hdt. 7.235 and the entire fourth book of Thucydides with the Pylos episode (1–41) and the Athenians' capture of Cythera (53–57). Plans for expansion to the West can already be detected in Herodotus (7.8y) where Xerxes promises his audience that after Greece, he will then conquer not only the West, but the entire world. For the idea that an enemy's growth poses a threat, compare Thuc. 1.23.6.
[27] Rood 2012, 52.

Historians	Citations	In Book 12
Cratippus	0	
Philistus	0	
Xenophon	3	
Ephorus	17	11
Theopompus	8	4
Callisthenes	12	10
Duris	0	
Timaeus	68	63
Phylarchus	6	
Demochares	3	1
Philinus	7	
Chaireas	1	
Sosilus	1	
Fabius Pictor	6	
Hieronymus of Cardia	0	
Aratus of Sicyon	6	
Silenus of Caleacte	0	
Non-historians		
Plato	5	1
Aristotle	12	12
Theophrastus	2	2

Polybius almost never cites historians from the fifth century, while he often engages with those from the fourth and third centuries, such as Ephorus, Theopompus, and (particularly) Timaeus. Polybius is highly critical of the last of these, who was his immediate predecessor for the history of the West and with whom he was competing.[28]

For the periods covered by Herodotus and Thucydides (the Persian and Peloponnesian Wars), other contemporary or later historians were also available to

---

[28] Miltsios 2013, 332 is of the opinion that in Book 12 Polybius only wishes to rehabilitate those historians (who did not include Thucydides) who had been attacked by Timaeus, and that is why Thucydides is not mentioned. Due to the highly fragmentary nature of Timaeus' work, this cannot be confirmed.

those working in Hellenistic or Roman times. Plutarch, writing in the second century CE, demonstrates this in his *De malignitate Herodoti* (869 A) when he prefers Hellanicus' and Ephorus' reports on the number of Naxian triremes over that of Herodotus.[29] Similarly, in his *Life of Pericles*, Plutarch mentions that Duris of Samos detailed many gruesome events from Pericles' quelling of the Samian revolt, events missing from the works of Thucydides, Ephorus, and Aristotle.[30] Alternative reports to those of Herodotus and Thucydides were clearly at hand. Such reports were used in particular by Diodorus (first century BCE), whose version of the Persian and Peloponnesian Wars regularly differs from that of Herodotus and Thucydides.

Similar to Rood, Miltsios also argues that Polybius borrowed elements from Thucydides in the organization of his first book. One of these elements is the excursus on earlier historical events that appears at the beginning of both historians' works (for Thucydides, this is the *Pentecontaetia*, for Polybius the προκατασκευή). Here, information is presented that will be crucial for understanding subsequent events and that helps "the reader to understand the basis of the protagonists' supremacy, as well as the inadequacy of the historians that had attempted to record these events in the past".[31] We should note, however, that for Thucydides, the *Pentecontaetia* forms part of a subtle explanation that correlates with chapter 1.23 and explains the true causes of the Peloponnesian War (with the conflicts in Corcyra and Potidaea being simply the more immediate provocations).[32] In Polybius, on the other hand, the προκατασκευή is in no way separated or distinct from other explanatory passages.

Further parallels for Miltsios include the importance of sea battles,[33] and the opposition between sea and land powers (Athens/Sparta and Carthage/Rome). In

---

[29] Plut. *De Herod. mal.* 869 A: "Νάξιοι γὰρ τρεῖς ἔπεμψαν τριήρεις συμμάχους τοῖς βαρβάροις, εἷς δὲ τῶν τριηράρχων Δημόκριτος ἔπεισε τοὺς ἄλλους ἑλέσθαι τὰ τῶν Ἑλλήνων (= Hdt. 8.46)" ... <ἀντι>μαρτυρεῖ δ' αὐτῶι τῶν μὲν πρεσβυτέρων Ἑλλάνικος (4 F 183), τῶν δὲ νεωτέρων Ἔφορος, ὁ μὲν ἓξ ὁ δὲ πέντε ναυσὶν αὐτοὺς Ναξίους ἐλθεῖν τοῖς Ἕλλησι βοηθοῦντας ἱστορήσας.

[30] Plut. *Pericles* 28 : ἐνάτωι δὲ μηνὶ τῶν Σαμίων παραστάντων ὁ Περικλῆς τὰ τείχη καθεῖλε καὶ τὰς ναῦς παρέλαβε καὶ χρήμασι πολλοῖς ἐζημίωσεν ... Δοῦρις δ' ὁ Σάμιος (76 F 67) τούτοις ἐπιτραγωιδεῖ πολλὴν ὠμότητα τῶν Ἀθηναίων καὶ τοῦ Περικλέους κατηγορῶν, ἣν οὔτε Θουκυδίδης (1.117) ἱστόρηκεν οὔτ' Ἔφορος οὔτ' Ἀριστοτέλης.

[31] Miltsios 2013, 334: "Like the Pentekontaetia, the prokataskeue has an introductory and analeptic character, since it deals with events that took place prior to those presented in the main part of the work, and covers a period of similar length (forty-eight years in the case of Thucydides [479–431] and forty-four in the case of Polybius [264–220]). The two historians also employ exactly the same arguments to justify the inclusion of these narrative sections in their works".

[32] Cf. Scardino 2007, 385f.

[33] Miltsios 2013, 337.

each case, the side that was originally the weaker sea power defeats the other with the aid of technical advances.[34] But Thucydides' narrative is more complex than this. Whereas in Polybius, the Romans transform themselves from a land to a sea power in the First Punic War, in Thucydides, the Corinthians and the Syracusans (a population akin to the Athenians) played an important role in the loss of Athenian sea dominance after the Sicilian Expedition.[35] The differences between Thucydides' narrative of the Corcyrean conflict and Polybius' account of Rome's intervention in Messana offset the similarities identified by Miltsios (e.g. the Athenians' and the Romans' focus on potential benefits during their respective deliberations). Whereas in Thucydides the Corcyreans and the Corinthians speak in Athens and put forward their concerns, this is missing from Polybius, where the Romans debate the Marmertines' request for help alone.[36] Some of the more striking parallels fulfill different functions in the two works. So, for example, whereas in Thucydides (1.10) the *topos* of the conflict's amplitude relates to the war about to be narrated, in Polybius (1.63.5) it looks back to the First Punic War.[37] In the end, Miltsios reaches a similar conclusion to that of McGing, asserting that "Thucydides' work forming part of Polybius' intellectual heritage has been absorbed into his historical vision, even if unconsciously or not fully consciously".[38]

It is difficult to assess the popularity of Herodotus and Thucydides in the second century BCE. In what comes across almost as a deconstructivist understanding of intertextuality, Miltsios emphasizes the role of the reader in the recognition of analogies: "the creation of intertextual links, as well as the means of using these in the interpretive process, depends not only on the author of the text but also on the readers".[39] When we look at Polybius' contemporaries, however, we find almost no authors writing about either Herodotus or Thucydides. This is of course complicated by the fact that the majority of writers from this period exist

---

34 Miltsios 2013, 340.
35 Miltsios 2013 343 does not emphasize this enough: "Just as Thucydides' readers wonder how the Lacedaemonians will be able to offset the naval supremacy of the Athenians in order to achieve victory, Polybius' readers cannot help doing the same when they read about the Romans' decision to compete against their foes in their natural element".
36 Thus Miltsios 2013, 346 notes: "The most noticeable difference is that Polybius does not include the envoys' speech but merely makes a brief allusion to its content (1.10.2). But this is a choice evidently connected with the summary form of the *prokataskeue*".
37 The *topos* of the conflict's amplitude is employed with regard to the Battle of Hyria (φόνος Ἑλληνικὸς μέγιστος, Hdt. 7.170.3).
38 Miltsios 2013, 349.
39 Miltsios 2013, 348.

only in fragments or paraphrases from later compilers. It is virtually impossible, for example, to determine to what extent the geographer Agatharchides (paraphrased by Diodorus and contrasted with Herodotus) in fact made use of Herodotus' work.[40] The same holds true for contemporary grammarians and scholars such as Aristophanes of Byzantium or Apollodorus, whose work only survives in the form of fragments and quotes. In terms of commentaries on Thucydides and Herodotus, we can assume that both historians were studied for their linguistic and grammatical idiosyncrasies.[41] Yet only traces of these commentaries survive in the scholia and the works of later grammarians, such as Dionysius of Halicarnassus.[42] Since almost no second-century author explicitly cites either Herodotus or Thucydides, it is difficult to reconstruct the level of engagement with those historians, especially in terms of their readers. It seems likely that scholarly work on Herodotus and Thucydides abated in the Hellenistic Period,[43] and rose again only in the first century BCE with the advent of Atticism and the works of Diodorus, Dionysius of Halicarnassus, or Cicero and Livy in Rome.[44] From this time on, and throughout the Roman Empire, numerous authors (once again) directly and explicitly worked with both historians (e.g. Plutarch and Lucian). We cannot, therefore, readily assume that Polybius' contemporary readers would have recognized (possible) implicit references to Thucydides.

We have no positive evidence that at the time of Polybius either Herodotus or Thucydides played any significant role in discussions of history. Polybius' own decision not to cite historians from the fifth century would be a further sign that Herodotus and Thucydides occupied a marginal role in the second century. Polybius mentions Thucydides just once, *en passant*, when he informs us that Theopompus began his work at the point where Thucydides left off.[45] This is in no

---

40 In contrast, Photius *Bibl.* 213.6 (= *FGrHist* 86 T2) says that Agatharchides was an emulator of Thucydides (ζηλωτὴς μέν ἐστι Θουκυδίδου).
41 The remains of a commentary on Herodotus by Aristarchus survive in papyri fragments; see Paap 1948, 37f.
42 For Alexandrian interpretations of Thucydides, probably still detectable in the scholia, see Strebel 1935, 24f. and especially Luschnat 1954, 22–26. It is, however, not possible to determine when exactly the Thucydidean scholia were first drafted. On the basis of the papyri, Malitz 1990, 343 dates the comments to the second century BCE. On the difficulty involved in dating Egyptian papyri to either the Ptolemaic or the Roman Period, see however Murray 1972, 203.
43 Thus Strebel 1935, 26 with regard to Thucydides: "so erkennen wir in der hellenistischen Epoche ein merkliches Nachlassen des Interesses ans Thukydides' Geschichtswerk".
44 Rightly Strebel 1935, 50: "Im ersten vorchristlichen Jahrhundert ist Thukydides zum Klassiker geworden".
45 Plb. 8.11.3: ὅς γ' ἐπιβαλόμενος γράφειν τὰς Ἑλληνικὰς πράξεις ἀφ' ὧν Θουκυδίδης ἀπέλιπε, καὶ συνεγγίσας τοῖς Λευκτρικοῖς καιροῖς καὶ τοῖς ἐπιφανεστάτοις τῶν Ἑλληνικῶν ἔργων.

way evidence for a deeper familiarity with Thucydides, and could have been gleaned from Theopompus himself.

Modern scholars have often projected Thucydides' status as a canonical author for Dionysius of Halicarnassus (first century BCE), and later Lucian (second century CE), onto earlier writers. This process has been aided by the presence of comparable statements in the works of Thucydides and Polybius, even if these are not explicit. Canfora confidently states:

> "Polibio cita e critica i suoi predecessori a partire dalla generazione di Teopompo, ma non più indietro. Prima, evidentemente, ci sono i 'modelli': Tucidide è il 'canone' ed al suo pensiero e alla sua prassi si rinvia come a regole, senza neanche nominarlo. Fenomeno significativo anche da un punto di vista generale: si ipostatizza un determinato autore fino ad assumerlo come canone, e così vi si può fare riferimento senza nominarlo ma senza danno per la chiarezza" (Polybius quotes and criticizes his predecessors, starting from Theopompus' generation, but no earlier. Before that, there are obviously "models": Thucydides represents the "canon" and one refers to his thinking and to his practice as if to rules, although without naming him. This is a significant phenomenon also from a general point of view: one hypostatizes a particular author until he becomes canonical, and thus one can refer to him without naming him and with no loss of clarity).[46]

However, close inspection of the parallels in fact leads to a different conclusion. This is particularly true for the supposed parallels between the last paragraphs of Thucydides' methodological chapter and Polybius' own excursus on methodology:

Plb. 3.31.12–13	Thuc. 1.22.4
ἱστορίας γὰρ ἐὰν ἀφέλῃ τις τὸ διὰ τί καὶ πῶς καὶ τίνος χάριν ἐπράχθη τὸ πραχθὲν καὶ πότερον εὔλογον ἔσχε τὸ τέλος, τὸ καταλειπόμενον αὐτῆς ἀγώνισμα μὲν μάθημα δ' οὐ γίνεται, καὶ παραυτίκα μὲν τέρπει, πρὸς δὲ τὸ μέλλον οὐδὲν ὠφελεῖ τὸ παράπαν.	καὶ ἐς μὲν ἀκρόασιν ἴσως τὸ μὴ μυθῶδες αὐτῶν ἀτερπέστερον φανεῖται· ὅσοι δὲ βουλήσονται τῶν τε γενομένων τὸ σαφὲς σκοπεῖν καὶ τῶν μελλόντων ποτὲ αὖθις κατὰ τὸ ἀνθρώπινον τοιούτων καὶ παραπλησίων ἔσεσθαι, ὠφέλιμα κρίνειν αὐτὰ ἀρκούντως ἕξει. κτῆμά τε ἐς αἰεὶ μᾶλλον ἢ ἀγώνισμα ἐς τὸ παραχρῆμα ἀκούειν ξύγκειται.

---

[46] Canfora 1977, 325. See also Hornblower 1995, 49, for whom Thucydides clearly influenced Polybius' methodology.

The most important Thucydidean echoes would seem to be reinforced by the appearance of similar concepts and vocabulary,[47] such as the rarely attested ἀγώνισμα.[48] However, given that Thucydides is not mentioned here, while Thucydides' immediate successors did make a point of discussing his methodology,[49] Polybius may be recalling something from his own education or an intermediate source (for example Ephorus).

It is striking that, when Polybius criticizes Timaeus' way of writing history and his treatment of Hermocrates' speech in Gela from the year 424 BCE (12.25),

---

[47] This is the opinion of most modern authors, thus e.g. Strebel 1935, 23: "Wem fiele beim Lesen dieser Stelle nicht der vielzitierte Schlußsatz des thukydideischen Proömiums ein? Ich stehe nicht an, diese Worte als Kompliment gegen seinen großen Vorgänger zu deuten, mit dessen Programm er sich im wesentlichen eins weiß" (In reading this passage, who would not think of the oft-quoted closing phrase of Thucydides' proem? I would not hesitate to interpret these words as a compliment to his great predecessor, with whose program he largely agrees). Also Canfora 1977, 324: "Da Polibio a Dionisio si intravede dunque una durevole e corretta interpretazione del programma tucidideo" (From Polybius to Dionysius, there is thus a lasting and accurate interpretation of the Thucydidean program), and Nicolai 1995, 17, who admits however that: "Polibio, che non fa esplicito riferimento alle parole di Tucidide, allude chiaramente alle sue dichiarazioni programmatiche, in vari luoghi della sua opera ... Le parole di Tucidide sembrano risuonare anche 3,31,12 sg." (Polybius, who does not explicitly refer to Thucydides' words, alludes clearly to his programmatic statements in various places of his work ... He seems to refer to Thucydides' words also at 3.31.12ff).

[48] Cf. Hornblower 1974, 60f., for whom "the reference to ἀγώνισμα seems decisive evidence that Polybius knew Thucydides". See also Rood 2012, 52.

[49] Cf. the rightly skeptical Miltsios 2013, 333: "But even these similarities in arguments and in language are perhaps not of such decisive importance to our subject as at first appears. Since they come from methodological chapters in the two historians' works, they may not be due to an immediate reception of Thucydides by Polybius". For parallels with fourth-century historians (especially Ephorus), see Parmeggiani's contribution to the present volume.

which Polybius believes Timaeus to have misrepresented, he does not offer Thucydides' version as an alternative.[50] This is particularly surprising given that Thucydides likely served as Timaeus' model.[51] When he is aware of a second version, Polybius normally cites it. In the same book, for example, he twice relies on Aristotle to refute Timaeus on matters concerning the colonization of Locri.[52] Polybius' failure to cite Thucydides in chapter 12.25, even if this represents an *argumentum ex silentio*, is significant.

Although in the extant sections of Polybius' work the historian only rarely deals with events also covered by Herodotus and Thucydides, he does find the occasion to discuss matters from the fifth century (especially in excurses). According to Herodotus (7.145.2), the Greek *poleis* which wished to oppose the Persians sought allies prior to Xerxes' invasion. Among those petitioned was the Syracusan tyrant Gelon, and Herodotus reproduces the conversation between the two parties (7.157). On the condition that he be given ultimate command over the army or the fleet, Gelon offers the following support (7.158.4): ἀλλ' ἕτοιμός εἰμι βοηθεῖν παρεχόμενος διηκοσίας τε τριήρεας καὶ δισμυρίους ὁπλίτας καὶ δισχιλίην ἵππον καὶ δισχιλίους τοξότας καὶ δισχιλίους σφενδονήτας καὶ δισχιλίους ἱπποδρόμους ψιλούς· σῖτόν τε ἁπάσῃ τῇ Ἑλλήνων στρατιῇ, ἔστ' ἂν διαπολεμήσωμεν, ὑποδέκομαι παρέξειν (I am ready to send to your aid two hundred triremes, twenty thousand men-at-arms, two thousand horsemen, two thousand archers, two thousand slingers, and two thousand light-armed men to run

---

50 Gomme 1956, 523 is surprised by "the nearly complete silence about Thucydides in what remains to us of ancient writers before the age of Cicero and Dionysios of Halikarnassos ... is anyhow remarkable, nowhere more so than in the pages of Polybios who was of course aware of Thucydides' work (8.11.3)". Walbank 1985, 251–53, on the other hand, believes that Polybius fails to mention Thucydides here because he does not want to criticize Thucydides vis-à-vis the speeches, which Polybius organizes according to very different principles. Hornblower 1974, 61 argues that Polybius' knowledge of Thucydides was perhaps "uneven": "The early, methodological, chapters of Thucydides were striking and memorable, part of a post-classical prose writers's mentale furniture—the detailed narrative, including eben pivotal episodes like the Gela conference, was perhaps something to read once and no more". Also Hornblower 1995, 58: "It is possible that Timaeus' different handling of Hermocrates' speech was offered as silent polemic against Thucydides".
51 If we believe Plut. *Nicias* 1, Timaeus wanted to outdo Thucydides in terms of δεινότης.
52 Plb. 12.5.4–5: ἀλλ' ὅμως οὐκ ὤκνησα καὶ λέγειν καὶ γράφειν ὅτι τὴν ὑπ' Ἀριστοτέλους παραδιδομένην ἱστορίαν περὶ τῆς ἀποικίας ἀληθινωτέραν εἶναι συμβαίνει τῆς ὑπὸ Τιμαίου λεγομένης. σύνοιδα γὰρ τοῖς ἀνθρώποις ὁμολογοῦσιν ὅτι παραδόσιμος αὐτοῖς ἐστιν αὕτη περὶ τῆς ἀποικίας ἡ φήμη παρὰ πατέρων, ἣν Ἀριστοτέλης εἴρηκεν, οὐ Τίμαιος. And 12.6a.1: Ἐκ τούτων ἄν τις συλλογιζόμενος Ἀριστοτέλει πρόσσχοι μᾶλλον ἢ Τιμαίῳ· καὶ μὴν τὸ συνεχὲς τούτῳ τελέως ἄτοπον.

with horsemen. I also pledge to furnish provisions for the whole Greek army until we have made an end of the war). When he is rebuffed by the Greek envoys, who are unwilling to relinquish control over either the army or the fleet, Gelon curtly dismisses them.

Polybius, however, records that it was Gelon who sent an envoy to the Greeks in Corinth. There, Gelon promises (12.26b.1) τοῖς Ἕλλησι δισμυρίοις πεζοῖς, διακοσίαις δὲ ναυσὶ καταφράκτοις βοηθήσειν, ἐὰν αὐτῶι τῆς ἡγεμονίας {ἢ τῆς ἡγεμονίας} ἢ τῆς κατὰ γῆν ἢ τῆς κατὰ θάλατταν παραχωρήσωσι, φασὶ τοὺς προκαθημένους ἐν Κορίνθωι τῶν Ἑλλήνων πραγματικώτατον ἀπόκριμα δοῦναι τοῖς παρὰ τοῦ Γέλωνος πρεσβευταῖς (to send to the assistance of the Greeks twenty thousand infantry and two hundred warships, if they would grant him the command either on land or at sea, they say that the representatives of Greece sitting in council at Corinth gave a reply to Gelon's envoys which was much to the point). Polybius goes on to record the debate over supreme command (ἡγεμονία, §§2–3). He criticizes Timaeus' version for its rhetorical embellishment of praise for Sicily (τοσούτους ἐντείνει λόγους καὶ τοσαύτην ποιεῖται σπουδὴν περὶ τοῦ τὴν μὲν Σικελίαν μεγαλομερεστέραν ποιῆσαι τῆς συμπάσης Ἑλλάδος), which he says is reminiscent of rhetorical school exercises (§§4–5). But Polybius does not question the rest of the account, including differences with Herodotus in terms of the amount and kind of assistance being offered, or the location of the negotiations (Corinth as opposed to Syracuse). Polybius does not refute Timaeus' underlying information. Indeed, he bases his censure on it. Criticism via a contrast with Herodotus is absent.[53]

There is nothing to show convincingly that Polybius was influenced by either Herodotus or Thucydides. There is, however, a different explanation for Polybius' supposed "unconscious use" of the first historians: namely that there existed, relatively early in the development of historiography, an awareness of the genre and of its written and unwritten norms. In Aristotle's *Poetics*, for example, the philosopher is fully aware of the concept of a literary genre, deploying history writing (ἱστορία) as a foil to epic and dramatic poetry (1451b1–11). It is not the form that is important for Aristotle (Herodotus in verse would still be history), but rather the relationship to reality (τῷ τὸν μὲν τὰ γενόμενα λέγειν, τὸν δὲ οἷα ἂν γένοιτο). Aristotle draws a clear distinction between the two genres. History is the science that looks at τὰ γενόμενα or τὰ καθ' ἕκαστον.[54] Awareness of genre,

---

[53] Hornblower 1974, 61 is of a similar opinion with regard to the historical period treated by Thucydides: "Polybius must ... have had a working knowledge of the fifth century ...; but if so, it was perhaps mediated through Ephorus, a more palatable drink than neat Thucydides".
[54] Cf. Scardino 2007, 29–35 with further bibliography.

and the attempt to define history writing as such, can be found elsewhere as well. Hecataeus (*FGrHist* 1 F1) and particularly Thucydides (esp. 1.20–22 in the distinction between logographers and poets), as well as, for instance, Duris (*FGrHist* 76 F 1) with his criticism of Ephorus and Theopompus, all attempt to establish the rules and boundaries of historiography. Polybius' extensive disapproval of his predecessors Phylarchus and Timaeus shows that the debate was still lively in his time.[55] Writing on Timaeus, Baron's reflections on genre could easily be extended to include Polybius:

> "At the same time, our notion of genre depends on innovation as a key component in the continual re-formation of generic categories. The pre-existing structure is a guide, a set of suggestions, rather than an inflexible and all-powerful restraining force. Each new author makes decisions on how to position himself or herself vis-à-vis the existing tradition, which aspects to borrow wholesale, which to adapt, which to discard".[56]

Polybius contributes to the debate and distinguishes himself from his immediate predecessors, with whom he is in competition. Yet unlike later authors, such as Dionysius of Halicarnassus or Lucian, Polybius feels no need to include Herodotus and Thucydides in his discussion. Similar content, thematic or methodological echoes, and the supposed "unconscious use" of the first two historians are better understood as innate aspects of the genre rather than the result of explicit influence. Participation in the debate does not require knowledge of Herodotus and Thucydides; the historians named by Polybius suffice.

Polybius' characteristic manner of writing history and thus of establishing his own niche within the genre will be illustrated here with an example. The third book (in which Hannibal begins his campaign against Italy) lends itself to the following analysis, since it is structurally and thematically comparable with similar portrayals by other historians.

In his own voice, Polybius opens the book with a summary of a) the συμμαχικόν, and b) the Hannibalic war and the fifty-three years up to 168 BCE. As mentioned above, Polybius is a highly intrusive narrator who consistently informs his readers of his intentions and guides their reactions. This manifests itself first and foremost in the authorial summaries and transitions located at the be-

---

[55] Lossau 1990 assumes an indirect influence of Aristotle on Polybius. This is entirely plausible, but by no means necessary given the lively debate within the genre of historiography itself.
[56] Baron 2013, 233. For similar comments on the genre of poetry, see the fundamental study by Rossi 1971.

ginnings of his books. These are wholly absent from both Herodotus and Thucydides, who could not therefore have been their inspiration, as McGing rightly notes.[57]

Particularly interesting is the long section on the causes of the war (6–10), where Polybius discusses the attempts of his predecessors and gives his own opinion. In Chapter 6, he distinguishes between the causes (αἰτίαι), that is, the motives, intentions and deliberations (ἐπίνοιαι, διαθέσεις, συλλογισμοί) preceding the decision to go to war, from the beginnings themselves (ἀρχαί), that is, the first steps and actions following the decision, as well as from the pretense (πρόφασις). Although distinguishing between the different causes of the war recalls Thucydides' comments at 1.23.6, Polybius differs not only in his tripartite division, but also in the semantics of the terms employed. So while in Polybius πρόφασις means "pretense" or "excuse", in Thucydides the phrase ἀληθεστάτη πρόφασις refers to the "truest cause".[58] For Thucydides, the reason for the war is Sparta's fear of growing Athenian strength. In Polybius' aetiology, the influence of Thucydidean categories and definitions (such as αἰτίαι καὶ διαφοραί or ἀληθεστάτη πρόφασις) is minimal. Polybius takes a different approach, differentiating between events (ἀρχαί) and their causes (αἰτίαι). This is illustrated in Polybius via a comparison with Alexander's campaign against the Persians. In the following chapters he identifies personal motivations as the underlying cause for Hannibal's resentment toward the Romans after the loss of Sicily (3.9.6: νομιστέον πρῶτον μὲν αἴτιον γεγονέναι τὸν Ἀμίλκου θυμὸν τοῦ Βάρκα μὲν ἐπικαλουμένου, πατρὸς δὲ κατὰ φύσιν Ἀννίβου γεγονότος). For ancient historians, human emotions are frequently taken as the real cause of a given event. Polybius is no different. Negative impulses such as anger (θυμός) or hatred (μῖσος)

---

57 McGing 2012, 36: "At the beginning of book 2 he summarizes what he has said in book 1; at the beginning of book 3 he looks ahead to all the major events he will be covering in the rest of his work ... There is nothing quite like this in Herodotus, who does not make the same organized attempt to clarify the overall structures of his work".
58 See also Plb. 4.13.6, where αἰτίαι, ἀφορμή (likely the equivalent of πρόφασις), and ἀρχή all appear, and also 22.18.6ff. On this vocabulary, see Pédech 1964, 57, 202 and Meister 1990, 158: "Während Thukydides die Begriffe Anlaß bzw. Ursache präzise definiert und verwendet, bleibt deren Bestimmung bei Polybios (3,6ff.; 22,18) vordergründig und oberflächlich" (Whereas Thucydides defines and uses the terms "cause" and "reason" precisely, Polybius' definition of them (3.6ff.; 22.18) remains sketchy and superficial).

dictate the actions of individuals like Hamilcar Barca or Hannibal. This is dramatically depicted by Polybius in the oath-scene.[59] In the case of Hannibal, the *topos* of youthful ambition is added.[60] The losses of Sardinia and of Corsica, on the other hand, represent only secondary motives for the Carthaginians.

The repeated authorial interventions (reflections, commentary, and interpretative glosses in the first person) represent a further peculiarity of Polybius' account. These occur throughout the narrative. For the Siege of Saguntum, Polybius argues that there was no deliberation in Rome (διαβούλιον), as other historians (ἔνιοι τῶν συγγραφέων) claim; Polybius links his stance to the polemic surrounding the Hannibal-historians Chaireas and Sosilus (3.20.5). In an authorial analepsis, Polybius also discusses the agreements between Rome and Carthage, refuting the complaints of the Carthaginians. In this way, he steers his readers' interpretation vis-à-vis responsibility for the war's outbreak (3.21.9f.). An excursus on the usefulness of Polybius' history for interpreting causal relationships follows (3.31). After Hannibal's departure from Spain (36–39), there is then a further authorial excursus on names and geographical features of the West unfamiliar to the (Greek) reader, but which are necessary for understanding Hannibal's route to Italy. Polybius re-emphasizes the importance of familiarity with geographical features when Hannibal arrives in Italy (3.57).

Polybius relates anecdotes too. Out of fear for the Celts, Hannibal is supposed to have employed a bizarre trick involving wigs to unsettle his adversaries (3.78.1–4). Similar to Herodotus and Thucydides, Polybius' narrative is also enlivened thanks to "if-not" situations, for example in the account of the Alpine ascent.[61] Harsh criticism of his predecessors, such as Chaireas and Sosilus, is another feature (3.20.5). For Polybius, Chaireas and Sosilus are not historians, but rather transmitters of gossip and nonsense (ἀλλὰ κουρεακῆς καὶ πανδήμου λαλιᾶς

---

59 Plb. 3.11.7: λαβόμενον τῆς δεξιᾶς προσαγαγεῖν αὐτὸν πρὸς τὸν βωμὸν καὶ κελεύειν ἁψάμενον τῶν ἱερῶν ὀμνύναι μηδέποτε ῾Ρωμαίοις εὐνοήσειν. The same is true for the Roman Flaminius: εὐθέως μετέωρος ἦν ὁ Φλαμίνιος καὶ θυμοῦ πλήρης (3.82.2).
60 Plb. 3.15.6: ὁ δ᾽ Ἀννίβας, ἅτε νέος μὲν ὤν, πλήρης δὲ πολεμικῆς ὁρμῆς. The topos is discussed by Aristotle at *Rhet.* 1389a3ff., and, in addition to epic and drama, appears already in both Herodotus (Xerxes at 7.13.2) and Thucydides (Alcibiades at 6.12f.).
61 Plb. 3.53.1: ἐν ᾧ καιρῷ πάντας ἄρδην ἀπολέσθαι συνέβη τοὺς περὶ τὸν Ἀννίβαν, εἰ μὴ δεδιότες ἀκμὴν ἐπὶ ποσὸν καὶ προορώμενοι τὸ μέλλον τὰ μὲν σκευοφόρα καὶ τοὺς ἱππεῖς εἶχον ἐν τῇ πρωτοπορείᾳ, τοὺς δ᾽ ὁπλίτας ἐπὶ τῆς οὐραγίας. We find "if-not" situations in Herodotus (7.10γ2; 9.113.2) and Thucydides (1.74.4; 7.2.4; 7.42.4) too. Ultimately, the trope can be traced back to epic poetry (see Nesselrath 1992).

ἔμοιγε δοκοῦσι τάξιν ἔχειν καὶ δύναμιν). The tone of this criticism goes far beyond anything found in Herodotus or Thucydides.⁶²

As Bruns recognized, Polybius' approach is thus a subjective one and much closer to modern historiography than that of his predecessors.⁶³ In his presentation of the Punic Wars, Polybius combines an indirect, dramatic style, employing shifting points of view with indirect speeches as well as analepses and prolepses, which all serve to break up the rhythm of his narrative. These changes in pace and the switching between annalistic and synchronistic accounts of (geographically diverse) events result in a complex narrative structure. Whereas analepses often provide background information and employ a moralistic and didactic tone (9.9.1–4: Nicias' refusal to sail was a mistake), internal prolepses prepare the reader's response (e.g. the Carthaginian defeat is foretold at 3.11; Rome's global dominance is confirmed despite defeat at Cannae and the subsequent loss of Tarentum at 3.118).

An important aspect of Polybius' narrative style is the *récit motivé* in which the historian tells the reader what his protagonists see, think, plan, etc. Perceptions and plans are treated as equal if not more important than the action itself. This is another way in which Polybius guides the reader, clearly informing him whether a plan was good or bad, successful or unsuccessful. We see this in the story of Roman considerations about the East after the Illyrian War (3.16.4–6). With a series of participles, Polybius depicts the events from the point of view of the Romans, but intervenes to highlight how they were, in fact, mistaken: εἰς ἃ βλέποντες Ῥωμαῖοι καὶ θεωροῦντες ἀνθοῦσαν τὴν Μακεδόνων οἰκίαν ἔσπευδον ἀσφαλίσασθαι τὰ πρὸς ἕω τῆς Ἰταλίας πεπεισμένοι καταταχήσειν διορθωσάμενοι μὲν τὴν Ἰλλυριῶν ἄγνοιαν, ἐπιτιμήσαντες δὲ καὶ κολάσαντες τὴν ἀχαριστίαν καὶ προπέτειαν τὴν Δημητρίου. διεψεύσθησαν δὲ τοῖς λογισμοῖς· κατετάχησε γὰρ αὐτοὺς Ἀννίβας, ἐξελὼν τὴν Ζακανθαίων πόλιν (The Romans, in view of those proceedings and of the flourishing fortunes of the Macedonian kingdom, were anxious to secure their position in the lands lying east of Italy, feeling confident that they would have time to correct the errors of the Illyrians and rebuke and chastise Demetrius for his ingratitude and temerity. But in this calculation they were deceived; for Hannibal forestalled them by taking Saguntum). This method of dramatizing and steering the narrative via focalization is typical of Herodotus,

---

62 Compare McGing 2012, 37: "There are certain opinions offered by Polybius that go beyond what we find in Herodotus—praise and blame ... judgments on other historians, instructions on how to write history...".
63 Bruns 1896 *passim*. See also Strebel 1935, 24 (who notes differences between Polybius' and Thucydides' methods) and Miltsios 2013, 330.

Thucydides, Xenophon, and later historians who, unlike their modern counterparts, are all representative of the narrative style of history writing.[64] The siege of Saguntum (3.17.4–11) provides a further example:

> Ἀννίβας ἐνεργὸς ἐγίνετο περὶ τὴν πολιορκίαν, πολλὰ προορώμενος εὔχρηστα πρὸς τὸ μέλλον ἐκ τοῦ κατὰ κράτος ἑλεῖν αὐτήν. (5) πρῶτον μὲν γὰρ ὑπέλαβε ... δεύτερον δὲ ... ἐπέπειστο... (6) τὸ δὲ μέγιστον... (7) χωρίς τε τούτων... ὑπελάμβανεν...
> (8) τοιούτοις δὲ χρώμενος διαλογισμοῖς ἐνεργῶς προσέκειτο τῇ πολιορκίᾳ...
> (9) ... τέλος ἐν ὀκτὼ μησὶ κατὰ κράτος εἷλε τὴν πόλιν...
> (11) ταῦτα δὲ πράξας οὐ διεψεύσθη τοῖς λογισμοῖς οὐδ' ἀπέτυχε τῆς ἐξ ἀρχῆς προθέσεως, ἀλλὰ...

> Hannibal ... set himself to besiege it vigorously, foreseeing that many advantages would result from its capture. (5) First of all he thought ... and secondly he was convinced... (6) while above all... (7) Besides, he would...
> (8) From all these considerations he actively pursued the siege...
> (9) At length after eight months ... he took the city by storm ...
> (11) The result did not deceive his expectations, nor did he fail to accomplish his original purpose; but...

Everything is reported from the point of view of the protagonist Hannibal, who appears as the *spiritus rector* of the siege and who is responsible for all aspects of it, from its planning right through to the capture of the city. With his πολλὰ προορώμενος εὔχρηστα, Polybius emphasizes the merit of Hannibal's judgment. Hannibal's plan and deliberations are more important than the result itself. Polybius repeats his positive assessment of Hannibal's counsel at the narrative's close (§11). And with a conditional syllogism (3.48) employed at the moment of Hannibal's crossing of the Rhone, Polybius shows, there too, that Hannibal's calculations were accurate, while other historians offer unrealistic reports of the crossing (for example that divine intervention or a *deux ex machina* were needed).

Regarding speeches, Polybius prefers authorial summaries and indirect focalization to speeches in *oratio recta*.[65] In Hannibal's and Publius' advice, only a few sentences are given from Publius' speech (3.64.5–7), in *oratio recta* in an internal analepsis related to the Rhone crossing narrated chapter 45. On the other hand, parts of the speeches of Lucius Aemilius (3.108.8–109.12) and of Hannibal (3.111.3–10) before the Battle of Cannae—the historical and dramatic climax of the narrative—are given in *oratio recta*. These offer strategic considerations and en-

---

[64] See e.g. Montgomery 1965 and Schneider 1974.
[65] On speeches, see Scardino 2007, 754–69 and Nicolai in the present volume.

couragement to the soldiers. Polybius' direct speeches, which dramatize the narrative and characterize its historical protagonists, are not significantly different from the speeches of Herodotus and Thucydides, even if they take up much less space in Polybius' work. It is, therefore, noteworthy that Polybius does not emphasize the consequences of the Battle of Cannae in the form of speeches, but rather intervenes as author to identify the decisive factor in Rome's victory: Rome's constitution (3.118.9).

This brief survey of Polybius' third book has demonstrated how the historian developed his own style within the genre of historiography. Some aspects and techniques find parallels in Herodotus and Thucydides (and later historians), while others reveal Polybius' innovative contribution. Polybius' history contains no implicit or explicit reference to Herodotus or Thucydides, however.

In summary, we can draw the following conclusions:

- No direct influence of Herodotus or Thucydides on Polybius' work can be ascertained (as a model or an intertext). It is doubtful that either was used by Polybius as a source.
- Similarities with Herodotus and Thucydides can be put down to Polybius' writing in the same genre (ἱστορία).
- Polybius' πραγματικὴ ἱστορία represents an innovative way of writing history compared with the contemporary trend of "rhetorical" (or "tragic") historiography (whose proponents include Phylarchus and Timaeus).
- The need to establish a new paradigm shows that Herodotus and Thucydides were no longer considered influential figures in the second century BCE.

Bibliography

Baron, C.A. (2013), *Timaeus of Tauromenium and Hellenistic Historiography*, Cambridge/New York.
Bruns, I. (1896), *Das literarische Porträt der Griechen im fünften und vierten Jahrhundert vor Christi Geburt*, Berlin.
—— (1898), *Die Persönlichkeit in der Geschichtsschreibung der Alten*, Berlin.
Gelzer, M. (1955), "Die Pragmatische Geschichtsschreibung des Polybios", in: G. Bruns (ed.), *Festschrift fuer C. Weickert*, Berlin, 87–91.
Canfora, L. (1977), "Storiografia", in: R. Bianchi Bandinelli (ed.), *Storia e civiltà dei Greci 9: La cultura ellenistica, Filosofia, scienza, letteratura*, Milan, 315–340.
Gomme, A.W. (1956), *A Historical Commentary on Thucydides, The Ten Years' War*, Vol. 3: Books IV-V24, Oxford.

Gray, V. (2004), "Xenophon", in: I.J.F. De Jong/R. Nünlist/A. Bowie (eds.), *Narrators, Narratees, and Narratives in Ancient Greek Literature. Studies in Ancient Greek Narrative*, Leiden/Boston, 129–146.
Hornblower, S. (1994), "Introduction", in: *id.* (ed.), *Greek Historiography*, Oxford, 1–72.
— — (1995), "The Fourth-Century and Hellenistic Reception of Thucydides", in: *JHS* 115, 47–68.
Lossau, M. (1990), "Ἱστορία Ποίησις. Aristotelisches im Polybios", in: P. Steinmetz (ed.), *Beiträge zur Hellenistischen Literatur und ihrer Rezeption in Rom*, Stuttgart, 109–122.
Luschnat, O. (1954), "Die Thukydidesscholien: Zu ihrer handschriftlichen Grundlage, Herkunft und Geschichte", in: *Philologus* 98, 14–58.
— — (1970), "Thukydides", in: *RE* Suppl. 12, Stuttgart, 1085–1354.
Malitz, J. (1990), "Das Interesse an der Geschichte. Die griechischen Historiker und ihr Publikum", in: H. Verdin/G. Schepens/E. de Keyser (eds.), *Purposes of History. Studies in Greek Historiography from the 4th to the 2nd Centuries B.C. Proceedings of the International Colloquium Leuven, 24–26 May 1988*, Louvain, 323–349.
McGing, B. (2012), "Polybius and Herodotus", in: C. Smith/L.M. Yarrow (eds.), *Imperialism, Cultural Politics, and Polybius*, Oxford, 33–49.
Meister, K. (1990), *Die griechische Geschichtsschreibung. Von den Anfängen bis zum Ende des Hellenismus*, Stuttgart.
Miltsios, N. (2013), "The Narrative Legacy of Thucydides: Polybius, Book I", in: A. Tsakmakis/M. Tamiolaki (eds.), *Thucydides Between History and Literature*, Berlin/Boston, 329–349.
Mohm, S. (1977), *Untersuchungen zu den historiographischen Anschauungen des Polybios*, PhD diss., Saarbrücken.
Montgomery, H. (1965), *Gedanke und Tat: Zur Erzähltechnik bei Herodot, Thukydides, Xenophon und Arrian*, Lund.
Munson, R. (2001), *Telling Wonders. Ethnographic and Political Discourse in the Work of Herodotus*, Ann Arbor.
Murray, O. (1972), "Herodotus and Hellenistic Culture", in: *CQ* 22, 200–213.
Nesselrath, H.G. (1992), *Ungeschehenes Geschehen. "Beinahe"-Episoden im griechischen und römischen Epos von Homer bis zur Spätantike*, Stuttgart.
Nicolai, R. (1995), "Κτῆμα ἐς αἰεί. Aspetti della fortuna di Tucidide nel mondo antico", in: *RFIC* 123, 5–26.
Paap, A.H.R.E. (1948), *De Herodoti reliquiis in papyris et membranis Aegyptiis servatis*, Leiden.
Pédech, P. (1964), *La méthode historique de Polybe*, Paris.
Rood, T. (2004), "Polybius", in: I.J.F. De Jong/R. Nünlist/A. Bowie (eds.), *Narrators, Narratees, and Narratives in Ancient Greek Literature. Studies in Ancient Greek Narrative*, Leiden/Boston, 147–164.
— — (2012), "Polybius, Thucydides, and the First Punic War", in: C. Smith/L.M. Yarrow (eds.), *Imperialism, Cultural Politics, and Polybius*, Oxford, 50–67.
Rossi, L.E. (1971), "I generi letterari e le loro leggi scritte e non scritte nelle letterature classiche", in: *BICS*, 69–94.
Scardino, C. (2007), *Gestaltung und Funktion der Reden bei Herodot und Thukydides*, Berlin/New York.
— — (2014), "V. Historiographie—Griechische Literaturgeschichte II", in: B. Zimmermann/A. Rengakos (eds.), *Handbuch der griechischen Literatur der Antike*, Vol. 2, Munich, 617–677.

Strebel, H.G. (1935), *Wertung und Wirkung des Thukydideischen Geschichtwerkes in der griechisch-römischen Literatur*, PhD diss., Munich, Speyer.
Walbank, F.W. (1972), *Polybius*, Berkeley/Los Angeles/London.
—— (1985), "Speeches in Greek Historians", in: id. (ed.), *Selected Papers. Studies in Greek and Roman History and Historiography*, Cambridge, 242–261.
Ziegler, K. (1952), "Polybios", in: *RE* 21.2, 1440–1578.
—— (1955/1956), "Thukydides und Polybios", *Wissenschaftliche Zeitschrift der E.M. Arndt-Universität Greifswald. Gesellschafts- und sprachwissenschaftliche Reihe*, Nr. 2/3, Jahrgang V, 161–170.

Part IV: **Reception**

Nikos Miltsios
Polybius and Arrian: The Cases of Philip V and Alexander the Great

For reasons not difficult to discern, the relationship between Polybius and Arrian has never seriously preoccupied classical scholarship. Arrian opens his *Anabasis* by stating that the sources he used for his history of Alexander were Ptolemy Lagos and Aristobulus of Cassandreia, since he regarded their texts as more reliable than others on the subject (1.praef.1–2); and though he often makes frequent reference to other authors, Polybius does not number among them. For his part, though Polybius speaks of Alexander on a fair number of occasions, he usually does so when aiming to compare his behavior with that of the kings who succeeded him.[1] At least as far as the extant part of his work is concerned, he does not initially give the impression of being a source of inspiration and information for writers interested in working on Alexander. Besides, it is well known that our other surviving sources on the man—Plutarch, Curtius and Diodorus—chose to rely more on the biographical tradition than on the general or universal historians, who would also definitely have had plenty to say about the Macedonian king.[2] All of the above might have been more than enough to dissuade me from investigating how Polybius may possibly have been received by Arrian, and from looking at the intertextual relations between their works. Yet while studying the way Polybius presents Philip V in Books 4 and 5, where he records the early years of the Social War, the similarities I could see with Arrian's presentation of Alexander on the narrative and thematic level led me to set my doubts aside, and to reflect that a parallel reading of the two texts might be worth the effort, or even prove to be truly promising.

    This article is divided into two parts. In the first I shall offer a comparative examination of how Polybius presents Philip V in Books 4 and 5 of the *Histories* and how Arrian portrays Alexander in the *Anabasis*. In particular, I shall argue that the two narratives are identical not only as regards the motifs that sketch out the protagonists' personalities and skills, but also in relation to the narrative devices used to highlight these motifs. In the second part I shall attempt to clarify the extent to which any intertextual affinity between the two texts might result either from the use of common sources or from Polybius' presentation as received by Arrian. To that end, I shall argue that the narrative in Books 4 and 5 of the

---

[1] Cf. e.g. 4.23.8–9, 5.10.6–9, 18.3.2–5.
[2] See Billows 2000, 287.

Histories shows clear signs of how Polybius creatively reworked the historical material he drew from his sources, and I shall cite a number of additional points of contact with Arrian's text.

1 Speed and effectiveness

Perhaps the most fundamental feature of the way Polybius presents Philip in the early years of his career is the special emphasis placed upon the speed and effectiveness of his actions and movements.[3] The first reference to this theme is in 4.22.6, where Philip's great speed in reaching the Peloponnese from Macedonia (ἔτι θᾶττω τὴν παρουσίαν) is pointed out. The same theme is elaborated thereafter, functioning as a recurring motif that lends the narrative structure and shape, and becoming an integral part of Philip's behavior and success. Thus when he learns that the Dardani are preparing to invade Macedonia in his absence, Philip judges it essential to return as fast as possible (κατὰ τάχος, 4.66.2) to fend off the danger, and rapidly heads back with his army (μετὰ σπουδῆς ἐποιεῖτο τὴν ἐπάνοδον, 4.66.3). The march to Macedonia is executed in the same decisive manner as it starts, as Polybius notes that Philip advances without stopping (προῆγε κατὰ τὸ συνεχὲς εἰς τὸ πρόσθεν, 4.66.5). Later on, when Philip's allies in the Peloponnese have despaired of his returning after the onset of winter, he reaches Corinth from Thessaly so rapidly that none of the Peloponnesians are aware of the fact (ὥστε μηδένα Πελοποννησίων ὑπονοῆσαι τὸ γεγονός, 4.67.7). The speed of Philip's movements is also clearly apparent from the fact that while still following his initial plan at an unaltered pace, he catches up with the Aetolian general Euripidas, even though the latter has got wind of the Macedonians' arrival, and makes every effort to cross the territory of Stymphalus and gain high, difficult ground before the enemy reaches him (4.68–69). Many of Philip's adversaries are routed, only having realized at the eleventh hour that they are up against the Macedonians. This success amazes the Peloponnesians, who learn of Philip's arrival and his victory at the same time (ἅμα γὰρ ἤκουον τὴν παρουσίαν καὶ τὴν νίκην τοῦ βασιλέως, 4.69.9).

Philip's conduct at the start of the Social War is relentless. Wishing, as Polybius characteristically puts it, "to leave nothing unattempted or half-accomplished" (μηδὲν ἀβασάνιστον μηδ' ἀπέραντον ἀπολιπεῖν, 4.75.3), Philip takes one

---

[3] As McGing 2010, 116 acutely pointed out: "Speed, combined with youthful helplessness misidentified, is the theme Polybius has developed to portray the beginnings of Philip's reign".

city after another. He conquers all of Triphylia in six days (4.80.14). His speed takes friends and foes by surprise, leaving them behind, while his arrival at Limnaea is so sudden (διὰ τὸ τῆς παρουσίας αἰφνίδιον, 5.6.3) that it leaves his Epirot allies no time to muster their forces, despite their willingness to harm the Aetolians. In order to invade the district of Thermus suddenly and unexpectedly (ἄφνω καὶ παραδόξως, 5.6.6), he forces his army to march all through the night up to the Achelous river, and from there, without resting his soldiers, advances briskly (προῆγε συντόνως, 5.7.6). The Macedonians' achievement in crossing such a long and difficult distance in so short a time (5.8.1–3) is further amplified by the detailed description of the ascent to Thermus containing references to the length and ruggedness of the route and the high cliffs extending on both sides. Like Euripidas earlier on in the Peloponnese, the opposing Aetolian general Dorimachus has no hope in the face of Philip's speed. Although he rushes to assist on learning that Aetolia has been invaded, he cannot catch the Macedonians, who have already left.

Speed and vigor are likewise the hallmarks of Philip's march to Sparta. Although the Messenians hasten eagerly (ὁρμῇ) and immediately (μετὰ σπουδῆς) in response to Philip's call to meet up with him and the other Peloponnesian allies at Tegea, they miss him (5.20.1–2). But it is the Spartans themselves who are the most amazed and dismayed at Philip's sudden arrival outside their city. News of his invasion of Thermus has only just got around when they suddenly see the Macedonian army before them (5.18.5). Having employed internal focalization to present the thoughts and feelings of the Spartans at this development, Polybius gives a detailed description of the Macedonian army's march to Sparta, so as to stress its difficulties, highlight Philip's determination in pursuing it and account for the surprise and bewilderment felt by his adversaries (5.18.6–10):

> ὑπὲρ δὲ τοῦ τὸ δεινὸν ἥξειν ἐπὶ σφᾶς οὕτως ὀξέως ἐκ τηλικούτου διαστήματος οὐδὲ διενοεῖτο παράπαν αὐτῶν οὐδείς, ἅτε καὶ τῆς ἡλικίας ἐχούσης ἀκμὴν εὐκαταφρόνητόν τι τῆς τοῦ βασιλέως. διὸ καὶ παρὰ δόξαν αὐτοῖς τῶν πραγμάτων συγκυρούντων εἰκότως ἦσαν ἐκπλαγεῖς. ὁ γὰρ Φίλιππος τολμηρότερον καὶ πρακτικώτερον ἢ κατὰ τὴν ἡλικίαν χρώμενος ταῖς ἐπιβολαῖς εἰς ἀπορίαν καὶ δυσχρηστίαν ἅπαντας ἦγε τοὺς πολεμίους. ἀναχθεὶς γὰρ ἐκ μέσης Αἰτωλίας, καθάπερ ἐπάνω προεῖπον, καὶ διανύσας ἐν νυκτὶ τὸν Ἀμβρακικὸν κόλπον, εἰς Λευκάδα κατῆρε. Δύο δὲ μείνας ἡμέρας ἐνταῦθα, τῇ τρίτῃ ποιησάμενος ὑπὸ τὴν ἑωθινὴν τὸν ἀνάπλουν, δευτεραῖος πορθήσας ἅμα τὴν τῶν Αἰτωλῶν παραλίαν ἐν Λεχαίῳ καθωρμίσθη. μετὰ δὲ ταῦτα κατὰ τὸ συνεχὲς ποιούμενος τὰς πορείας ἑβδομαῖος ἐπέβαλε τοῖς ὑπὲρ τὴν πόλιν κειμένοις παρὰ τὸ Μενελάϊον λόφοις, ὥστε τοὺς πλείστους ὁρῶντας τὸ γεγονὸς μὴ πιστεύειν τοῖς συμβαίνουσιν.

No one ever imagined that the danger would descend on their heads so swiftly from such a long distance, the king's extreme youth still tending to inspire contempt for him. Consequently, as things fell out quite contrary to their expectations, they were naturally much dismayed; for Philip had shown a daring and energy beyond his years in his enterprises, and reduced all his enemies to a state of bewilderment and helplessness. For putting to sea from the centre of Aetolia, as I above narrated, and traversing the Ambracian Gulf in one night, he had reached Leucas, where he spent two days, and setting sail on the morning of the third day he came to anchor next day in Lechaeum after pillaging the coast of Aetolia on his voyage. After thus marching without a break he gained upon the seventh day the hills near the Menelaïum that look down on Sparta. So that most of Spartans though they saw what had happened, could not believe their eyes.[4]

Polybius takes care to underscore the surprise and fear Philip strikes into the hearts of his enemies. In the most categorical way, Philip's achievements refute the widely held impression that his youth would stand in the way of him posing a substantial threat to his enemies' plans. Philip's age and the way others view it is a theme that gains in significance throughout the narrative of Books 4 and 5, where it is presented as ranking among the causes of the Social War (4.3.3), and recurs with remarkable frequency (4.5.3–4, 4.22.5, 4.24.1, 4.82.1, 5.16.2).[5] At least to some degree, and with the safety of distance, the emphasis Polybius creates via repetition enables readers to experience something of the surprise felt by historical characters when they see their plans and expectations of Philip being overturned.

Up to this point, the way Polybius presents Philip's doings and behavior readily brings to mind Alexander the Great, Philip's most famous predecessor on the Macedonian throne and the epitome of a young king distinguished by his determination and vigor. Yet this association is almost inevitable for readers of Arrian in particular, since the speed with which Alexander moves, reacts and carries out his plans is one of the most fundamental features of the way he is presented in the *Anabasis*. In different forms and various combinations (e.g. σπουδῇ, κατὰ σπουδήν, σπουδῇ εἶμι, σπουδῇ ἄγω, σπουδῇ ἐλαύνω, σπουδῇ προχωρῶ, σπουδῇ πλέω), the term σπουδή is used over twenty times in reference to Alexander, in parallel with other expressions used to denote the speed with which he leads his army and pursues his enemies, such as δρόμῳ ἡγεῖτο (3.21.8) and ὀξείας τὰς διώξεις ποιησάμενος (3.25.7).[6]

Yet beyond this common motif, which is vital in sketching the personalities of the protagonists in the two works and accounting for their success, it is particularly interesting to note that Arrian uses the same narrative devices as Polybius

---

4 My translations of Polybius are taken from the Loeb edition of W.R. Paton, and those of Arrian from the Loeb edition of E.I. Robson.
5 Cf. McGing 2010, 116, *id.* 2013.
6 Cf. e.g. 3.8.1, 4.4.7, 5.14.1, 6.17.5.

to highlight Alexander's speed and render it all the more impressive. One of these is the emphasis laid in some instances on the ruggedness and difficulty of the route, which we saw Polybius doing in characteristic fashion when describing Philip's ascent to Thermus. For instance, when narrating the assault on the Uxian villages, Arrian stresses that the route taken by Alexander was rough and difficult, and that he managed to cover it in one day (διελθὼν ὁδὸν τραχεῖαν καὶ δύσπορον ἐν μιᾷ ἡμέρᾳ, 3.17.3). Rather than being forced by the rugged terrain to slow his pace, Alexander continues to move fast (ᾔει σπουδῇ ἐπὶ τὰ στενά, 3.17.3; πολλῷ τάχει ᾔει, 3.17.4). He even manages to take some key advantageous positions before the Uxians, despite their being more familiar with the area (3.17.4–5). Similarly, when Arrian describes the detour Alexander takes to avoid the wall built at the Persian Gates by Ariobarzanes, the satrap of Persia, he once again points out the ruggedness and difficulty of the route, so as to highlight the fact that the Macedonian leader covered most of the ground at a fast pace (τραχεῖαν τὴν ὁδὸν καὶ στενὴν ἐπύθετο, 3.18.4; ᾔει ὁδὸν χαλεπὴν καὶ τραχεῖαν καὶ ταύτην δρόμῳ τὸ πολὺ ἦγε, 3.18.6).

One further way in which Arrian draws attention to Alexander's speed is by comparison with other characters in his work. Like Polybius in Books 4 and 5, he too makes it clear that none of the other characters is worthy of comparison with the protagonist in his narrative as regards speed. When part of the Persian cavalry is put to flight during the battle of Gaugamela, pursued by Alexander and the men under Simmias, Arrian notes that nobody in Simmias' phalanx is capable of keeping up with Alexander's speed (οὐκέτι συνεξορμῆσαι Ἀλεξάνδρῳ δυνατοὶ ἐγένοντο ἐς τὴν δίωξιν, 3.14.4). Later, when Alexander sets out from Ecbatana to capture Darius, Arrian mentions that the rapid pace of pursuit forces many soldiers to lag behind due to tiredness, and even exhausts the horses (καὶ αὐτῷ κατὰ τὴν ὁδὸν σπουδῇ γιγνομένην τῶν τε στρατιωτῶν πολλοὶ κάμνοντες ὑπελείποντο καὶ ἵπποι ἀπέθνησκον, 3.20.1). That Darius repeatedly escapes capture (e.g. 2.11.4, 3.15.5, 3.20.2) in no way alters or undermines the image cultivated in readers' minds as to Alexander's unrivalled speed of movement, since the Persian king's escape is at no point associated with his skill—in fact, after the battle of Issus it is explicitly attributed to luck (2.11.4). Rather, his resorting to flight is explicitly presented as a shameful choice (αἰσχρᾷ φυγῇ ἔφυγε, 3.1.2; ἔφυγέ τε ἐν πρώτοις αἰσχρῶς, 3.22.4), and one resulting from fear of Alexander's vigor (πάντα ὁμοῦ τὰ δεινὰ καὶ πάλαι ἤδη φοβερῷ ὄντι Δαρείῳ ἐφαίνετο, 3.14.3).

Darius is not the only one to fear Alexander. Many characters in the *Anabasis* are presented as being forced to flee on hearing news of his approach, and in some cases the speed at which their opponent moves is mentioned as giving rise to their fear. Thus the third technique Arrian employs to underline Alexander's speed is to record the emotions and reactions it provokes in others. One characteristic case in point is the reaction of Arsames, satrap of Cilicia: on learning of the Macedonian king's rapid advance on Tarsus (δρόμῳ ἦγεν), he hurriedly abandons the city without plundering or laying waste to it (2.4.6). Likewise, in the incident mentioned earlier, the Uxians are so amazed by the speed at which Alexander moves (τῷ τε τάχει Ἀλεξάνδρου ἐκπλαγέντες, 3.17.5) that they depart without even giving battle.[7] Something similar also occurs with Satibarzanes, satrap of the Arians. On learning that Alexander is close at hand, he is so astounded at the swiftness of his approach (τῇ ὀξύτητι τῆς ἐφόδου ἐκπλαγέντες, 3.25.7) that he flees with what soldiers remain to him, since most have abandoned him for fear of Alexander.[8] Just as in Polybius, then, the emphasis Arrian places on the way others learn of and are affected by Alexander's remarkable speed allows the narrator to elaborate his theme more fully, highlight its importance and arouse surprise and wonder in his readers similar to that felt by the characters in his work.

2 Achieving difficult goals

Though speed may be a basic hallmark of the two Macedonian kings' mentalities and strategies, it is certainly not the only attribute they share. The two accounts also contain other features that are stressed to show the protagonists' skills and determination. For example, one further feature the two kings have in common is their keenness to set difficult goals, to be inspired rather than deterred by their difficulty, and to make every possible effort to achieve them. This zeal is perhaps nowhere more apparent than in the descriptions of sieges against towns and positions regarded as impregnable on account of their exceptional defences. In the account of the early years of the Social War, the most memorable instance is the capture of Psophis, which Polybius describes in detail in 4.70–72. The *Anabasis* contains several cases of apparently impregnable cities and fortresses taken by Alexander, such as Tyre (2.18–24), Gaza (2.26–27), the Rock of Sogdiana (4.18.4–19), the Rock of Chorienes (4.21) and Aornos (4.28–30.4). The frequent recurrence of this theme in the *Anabasis* serves to add to the image Arrian cultivates of Alexander's skills and determination, showcasing, as he characteristically states in

---

[7] It is worth noting that the reference to the amazement of the Uxians occurs only in Arrian. The other sources on the episode are not equally emphatic in pointing out Alexander's speed.
[8] The other writers who describe the incident (Diodorus 17.78, Curtius 6.6.20–34) do not mention in what way Alexander's speed affects Satibarzanes.

4.21.7, that "nothing could not be taken by force by Alexander and his army". In what follows I shall argue that in narrative terms, the way Arrian handles such descriptions closely resembles the manner in which Polybius describes the taking of Psophis by Philip in Book 4 of his *Histories*.

Polybius employs two basic techniques to highlight the significance of Philip's success. He begins with a detailed description of the position's natural and man-made fortifications, so as to stress the difficulty involved in besieging it and to arouse reader interest (4.70.7–11):

> συνθεωρῶν δὲ τὴν ὀχυρότητα τῆς Ψωφῖδος ὁ βασιλεὺς ἠπορεῖτο τί χρὴ ποιεῖν. τὴν γὰρ ἀφ' ἑσπέρας πλευρὰν αὐτῆς καταφέρεται λάβρος χειμάρρους ποταμός, ὃς κατὰ τὸ πλεῖστον μέρος τοῦ χειμῶνος ἄβατός ἐστι, ποιεῖ δὲ καὶ τὸ παράπαν ἐχυρὰν καὶ δυσπρόσοδον τὴν πόλιν διὰ τὸ μέγεθος τοῦ κοιλώματος, ὃ κατὰ βραχὺ τῷ χρόνῳ κατείργασται φερόμενος ἐξ ὑπερδεξίων τόπων. παρὰ δὲ τὴν ἀπ' ἠοῦς πλευρὰν ἔχει τὸν Ἐρύμανθον, μέγαν καὶ λάβρον ποταμόν, ὑπὲρ οὗ πολὺς καὶ ὑπὸ πολλῶν τεθρύληται λόγος. τοῦ δὲ χειμάρρου προσπίπτοντος πρὸς τὸν Ἐρύμανθον ὑπὸ τὸ πρὸς μεσημβρίαν μέρος τῆς πόλεως, συμβαίνει τὰς μὲν τρεῖς ἐπιφανείας αὐτῆς ὑπὸ τῶν ποταμῶν περιλαμβανομένας ἀσφαλίζεσθαι τὸν προειρημένον τρόπον· τῇ δὲ λοιπῇ, τῇ πρὸς ἄρκτον, βουνὸς ἐρυμνὸς ἐπίκειται τετειχισμένος, ἄκρας εὐφυοῦς καὶ πραγματικῆς λαμβάνων τάξιν. ἔχει δὲ καὶ τείχη διαφέροντα τῷ μεγέθει καὶ ταῖς κατασκευαῖς. πρὸς δὲ τούτοις βοήθειαν συνέβαινε παρὰ τῶν Ἠλείων εἰσπεπτωκέναι, καὶ τὸν Εὐριπίδαν ἐκ τῆς φυγῆς διασεσωσμένον ὑπάρχειν ἐν αὐτῇ.

> On its western side there descends a violent torrent, impassable for the greater part of the winter, and rendering the city very strongly protected and difficult of approach on this side, owing to the depth of the bed it has gradually formed for itself, descending as it does from a height. On the eastern side of the town flows the Erymanthus, a large and rapid stream of which many fables are told by various authors. The torrent falls into the Erymanthus to the south of the city, so that three faces of the city are surrounded and protected by the rivers in the manner I have described. On the fourth or northern side rises a steep hill protected by walls, serving very efficiently as a natural citadel. The town has also walls of unusual size and admirable construction, and besides all these advantages it had just received a reinforcement of Eleans, and Euripidas was present having taken refuge there after his flight.

The detailed description of the city's excellent fortifications and natural advantages leaves readers to wonder whether and how it will be possible to take it. Polybius intensifies suspense by recording the anxiety Philip feels when faced by the scale of the task, and his dilemma over whether to undertake it or not. The features rendering the city immune to enemy assault are deliberately presented from Philip's perspective (συνθεωρῶν, 4.70.6; ταῦτ' οὖν πάντα συνορῶν καὶ συλλογιζόμενος, 3.71.1); he seriously contemplates abandoning the attempt, but on considering the city's exceptional strategic significance eventually decides to cast doubt aside (4.71.1–2). Of course, the suspense created does not so much concern whether the siege will take place or not, since Philip's decision is rapidly announced, but how an undertaking that disconcerts such a capable military leader can be achieved.[9]

Polybius further stresses the difficulty of the endeavor by describing the considerable surprise felt by the besieged at Philip's decision to press ahead. The king soon reaches the town, since the incursion is so unexpected that there is no-one to block the way (διὰ τὸ παράδοξον τῆς ἐπιβολῆς), and everyone is amazed (4.71.4). Having absolute confidence in the town's fortifications, the enemy is taken aback by events (διηπόρουν ἐπὶ τοῖς συμβαίνουσι), for they cannot contemplate anyone venturing to storm Psophis or launch a lengthy siege (4.71.5). Their sense of wonder and surprise is so intense that they begin to suspect Philip has arranged with people inside the town to take it by betrayal. The emphasis placed on how the defenders of Psophis are wrongfooted not only highlights the enormity of the endeavor, but also accounts for its outcome. Despite their valiant attempts to fight off the assault, Philip's enemies ultimately fail for lack of suitable preparation (ὡς ἂν ἐκ τοῦ καιροῦ τῆς παρασκευῆς γεγενημένης, 4.71.10; οὐδεμιᾶς σφίσι παρασκευῆς ὑπαρχούσης, 4.72.2). The notion that seemingly impregnable cities end up being taken precisely because their inhabitants are complacent about their fortifications, and do not take necessary precautionary measures, is a frequently recurring topos in Polybius.[10] Indeed, as the historian stresses in 7.15.3–4, such cities are often taken at their most fortified points, which the defenders think there is no chance of the enemy using.

Arrian employs both of the above narrative techniques in the same manner when describing sieges against towns and positions famed for their exceptional fortifications. Like Polybius, he lays great emphasis on the difficulty involved in these endeavors, so as to highlight Alexander's determination to undertake them, and his ability to complete them successfully. In particular, on some occasions Arrian stresses the site's excellent fortifications (2.18.2, 2.26.1), on others the difficulty of ascending (4.28.3), and on others the special prevailing conditions that complicated the siege (4.18.5). For instance, the description of the Rock of Chori-ene in 4.21.2 is particularly impressive:

ἦν δὲ τὸ μὲν ὕψος τῆς πέτρας ἐς σταδίους εἴκοσι, κύκλος δὲ ἐς ἑξήκοντα· αὐτὴ δὲ ἀπότομος πάντοθεν, ἄνοδος δὲ ἐς αὐτὴν μία καὶ αὐτὴ στενή τε καὶ οὐκ εὔπορος, οἷα δὴ παρὰ τὴν φύσιν τοῦ χωρίου πεποιημένη, ὡς χαλεπὴ εἶναι καὶ μηδενὸς εἴργοντος καὶ καθ' ἕνα ἀνελθεῖν, φάραγξ τε κύκλῳ περιεῖργε τὴν πέτραν βαθεῖα, ὥστε ὅστις προσάξειν στρατιὰν τῇ πέτρᾳ

---

[9] On suspense in ancient historiography, see Rengakos 2006, 293, de Jong 2013, 281–84, and in Polybius, in particular, Miltsios 2009.
[10] Cf. e.g. 8.14.5 (Acrolissus) and 10.8.4 (New Carthage) with Davidson 1991, 17–18.

ἔμελλε, πολὺ πρόσθεν αὐτῷ τὴν φάραγγα εἶναι χωστέον, ὡς ἐξ ὁμαλοῦ ὁρμᾶσθαι προσάγοντα ἐς προσβολὴν τὸν στρατόν.

> The height of this rock was about twenty stades, its circuit, some sixty; it was sheer on all sides, and there was only one way up to it, and this narrow and difficult, made as it was despite the nature of the ground, so that it was difficult, even if no one prevented, to ascend even in single file. A deep ravine also protects the rock all round, so that anyone desiring to bring up an army against the rock would be obliged beforehand to do much filling up of the ravine, so that he might start from level ground when bringing up his force to the assault.

In two cases Arrian even mentions certain characteristic details that assist him in further clarifying his message and communicating it more effectively. In the first instance, when describing the siege at the Rock of Sogdiana, he narrates that when Alexander calls on the Sogdians to propose a surrender they urge him to find winged soldiers to take their stronghold, as they think no man capable of doing so (4.18.6). In the second, when describing the conquest of Aornos, Arrian cites a rumor that not even Hercules managed to conquer it (4.28.1).[11] Both of these details are highly significant not only because they eloquently highlight the difficulty of the respective tasks at hand, but also because Arrian presents them as the incentives that spur Alexander into action (4.18.6, 4.28.4). Moreover, in the same manner as Polybius, Arrian uses the motif of the surprise felt by the besieged (e.g. ἐκπλαγεὶς ὁ Χοριήνης πρὸς τὰ γιγνόμενα, 4.21.6; πρός τε τὴν ἀδιήγητον τόλμαν τῶν ἐς τὸν γήλοφον βιασαμένων Μακεδόνων ἐκπλαγέντες, 4.30.2), who are either frightened into abandoning their position and surrendering (4.21.10, 4.30.2), or who cannot properly comprehend what they see, as happens to the defenders at the Rock of Sogdiana when they are confronted by the handful of Macedonians who have taken the rock's summit (4.19.4).

Such frequent descriptions of sieges against apparently impregnable towns and positions in the *Anabasis* clearly show Alexander's determination, dynamism and keenness to fight on, investing superhuman efforts so as to achieve even the most difficult goals. Arrian explicitly acknowledges this when, in connection with the siege at the Rock of Choriene, he mentions Alexander's belief that "everything should be accessible to him, and that everything could be captured" (πάντα ᾤετο χρῆναι βατά τε αὐτῷ καὶ ἐξαιρετέα εἶναι, 4.21.3). This particular observation immediately calls to mind the note we have already seen Polybius making about Philip in a similar instance, when he also is attacking an inaccessible, impregnable position: Philip's opinion was that he should never leave anything untried or incomplete (μηδὲν ἀβασάνιστον μηδ' ἀπέραντον

---

[11] Cf. 5.26.5.

ἀπολιπεῖν, 4.75.3). Given the image of the protagonists' mentalities and behaviors cultivated in the two texts, it is hardly surprising that both Macedonian kings are presented as intending to expand their dominions beyond the bounds of Greece, and lay claim to ruling the world. Polybius presents Philip as developing the ambition to extend his sovereignty in the West as the upshot of Hannibal's repeated successes in Italy, and of Demetrius of Pharos' arguments aimed at pointing him in that direction. He does however take pains to stress how easily such words found fertile ground, not only on account of Philip's character, but also due to his coming from a line of kings long interested in world domination, thus essentially alluding to Alexander (5.101.8–102.1):[12]

> ὃς καὶ λαβόμενος τῆς ἀφορμῆς ταύτης τὸν μὲν πρὸς τοὺς Αἰτωλοὺς ᾤετο δεῖν τὴν ταχίστην ἀπορρῖψαι πόλεμον, ἀντέχεσθαι δὲ τῶν κατὰ τὴν Ἰλλυρίδα πραγμάτων ἠξίου καὶ τῆς εἰς Ἰταλίαν διαβάσεως. τὰ μὲν γὰρ κατὰ τὴν Ἑλλάδα πάντα καὶ νῦν ἤδη ποιεῖν αὐτῷ τὸ προσταττόμενον ἔφη καὶ μετὰ ταῦτα ποιήσειν, Ἀχαιῶν μὲν ἐθελοντὴν εὐνοούντων, Αἰτωλῶν δὲ καταπεπληγμένων ἐκ τῶν συμβεβηκότων αὐτοῖς κατὰ τὸν ἐνεστῶτα πόλεμον· τὴν δ' Ἰταλίαν ἔφη καὶ τὴν ἐκεῖ διάβασιν ἀρχὴν εἶναι τῆς ὑπὲρ τῶν ὅλων ἐπιβολῆς, ἣν οὐδενὶ καθήκειν μᾶλλον ἢ 'κείνῳ τὸν δὲ καιρὸν εἶναι νῦν, ἐπταικότων Ῥωμαίων. τοιούτοις δὲ χρησάμενος λόγοις ταχέως παρώρμησε τὸν Φίλιππον, ὡς ἄν, οἶμαι, καὶ νέον βασιλέα καὶ κατὰ τὰς πράξεις ἐπιτυχῆ καὶ καθόλου τολμηρὸν εἶναι δοκοῦντα, πρὸς δὲ τούτοις ἐξ οἰκίας ὁρμώμενον τοιαύτης, ἣ μάλιστά πως ἀεὶ τῆς τῶν ὅλων ἐλπίδος ἐφίεται.

Demetrius seized on this opportunity to advise him to get the Aetolian war off his shoulders as soon as possible, and to devote himself to the reduction of Illyria and a subsequent expedition to Italy. The whole of Greece, he said, was even now and would be in the future subservient to him, the Achaeans being his partisans by inclination and the spirit of the Aetolians being cowed by what had happened during the war. An expedition, however, to Italy was the first step towards the conquest of the world, an enterprise which belonged to none more properly than to himself. And now was the time, after this disaster to the Roman arms. By such words as these he soon aroused Philip's ambition, as I think was to be expected in the case of a king so young, who had achieved some much success, who had such a reputation for daring, and above all who came of a house which we may saw had always been inclined more than any other to covet universal dominion.

---

[12] As Nicholson 2015, 223 observes: "While each Macedonian ruler appears to have attempted to implement an aggressive expansionist policy in as much as his circumstances would allow, it is difficult to accredit Antigonos II Gonatas, Demetrios II and Antigonos Doson, whose reigns were much more defensive, with the explicit pursuit of the grander aim".

Arrian describes the equivalent ambitions harbored by Alexander more emphatically, presenting them as the consequence of his constant desire for new conquests, *i.e.* as a personality trait (7.1.4):[13]

> Ἐγὼ δὲ ὁποῖα μὲν ἦν Ἀλεξάνδρου τὰ ἐνθυμήματα οὔτε ἔχω ἀτρεκῶς ξυμβαλεῖν οὔτε μέλει ἔμοιγε εἰκάζειν, ἐκεῖνο δὲ καὶ αὐτός ἄν μοι δοκῶ ἰσχυρίσασθαι, οὔτε μικρόν τι καὶ φαῦλον ἐπινοεῖν Ἀλέξανδρον οὔτε μεῖναι ἄν ἀτρεμοῦντα ἐπ' οὐδενὶ τῶν ἤδη κεκτημένων, οὐδὲ εἰ τὴν Εὐρώπην τῇ Ἀσίᾳ προσέθηκεν, οὐδ' εἰ τὰς Βρεττανῶν νήσους τῇ Εὐρώπῃ, ἀλλὰ ἔτι ἄν ἐπέκεινα ζητεῖν τι τῶν ἠγνοημένων, εἰ καὶ μὴ ἄλλῳ τῳ, ἀλλὰ αὐτόν γε αὑτῷ ἐρίζοντα.

> As for what was in Alexander's mind, I for my part have no means of conjecturing with any accuracy, nor do I care to guess; this, however, I think I can for my own part asseverate, that Alexander had no small or mean conceptions, nor would ever have remained contented with any of his possessions so far, not even if he had added Europe to Asia, and the Britannic islands to Europe; but would always have searched far beyond for something unknown, being always the rival, if of no other, yet of himself.

The comments on the two kings' expansionist ambitions, in both cases made by the primary narrator, appear reasonable and persuasive in the light of what has preceded. By this point it is clear to readers of both Polybius and Arrian that the two Macedonian kings not only had grand ambitions, but also the skills to realize them.

3 Common sources or reception?

Thus far we have seen that the way Polybius presents Philip V bears several striking resemblances to Arrian's portrayal of Alexander. Both historians place particular emphasis on the determination and martial prowess of their protagonists via incidents illustrating the vigor and speed at which they move, as well as their willingness to undertake the riskiest of endeavors. One possible objection at this point might be that these similarities do not stand as evidence of an intertextual relationship between the *Histories* and the *Anabasis*, but point to Polybius' conscious intention to present Philip as a new Alexander. Comparison with Alexander was a favorite theme in the propaganda of his successors, and Philip was certainly no exception to that rule; we know that he was keen to appear as the perpetuator of traditions associated with the politics of the Argead royal house.[14]

---

[13] Cf. 7.19.6: ἄπληστος ἦν τοῦ κτᾶσθαί τι ἀεὶ Ἀλέξανδρος ("Alexander was always insatiate in winning possessions").
[14] See Dreyer 2013, 204, 206.

Nevertheless, even if we accept that Polybius consciously chose to describe the beginning of Philip's career so as to evoke the image his readers had of Alexander, that in no way weakens or rules out the view that Arrian knew of the description or used it in his own work. In fact, it probably adds weight to such a hypothesis, unless we believe that both historians merely had the same sources. On the other hand, supporting the view that the narrative in Books 4 and 5 of the *Histories* advances the link between Philip and Alexander is not entirely unproblematic. For when dealing with the Macedonian outrages at Thermus, Polybius draws a clear distinction between the two men: "But instead of this, though all through his life he [sc. Philip V] was at great pains to prove that he was allied in blood to Alexander and Philip, he was not in the least anxious to show himself their emulator" (5.10.10). In the remaining section of my paper I would like to respond to the above objections, and cite evidence in further support of my view that the similarities between the two texts are not due to common sources, but rather to Arrian's reception of Books 4 and 5 of the *Histories*.

The question of the degree to which Polybius reproduces his sources when narrating the early years of the Social War may not be entirely unanswerable, as usually applies in such instances. The two main themes we have seen being used to underscore Philip's abilities and the effectiveness of his actions (his astounding speed and the unanticipated capture of fortified Psophis) are motifs recurring in the same characteristic manner elsewhere in the *Histories*. Thus Hannibal's march from Spain to Italy is likewise pursued at such high speed that, as in the case of Philip, it surprises and confounds his enemies. For instance, when P. Cornelius learns of Hannibal's arrival at the Rhone, he can scarcely believe it (ἀπιστῶν διὰ τὸ τάχος τῆς παρουσίας, 3.41.8). The inhabitants of Rome are similarly amazed (παραδόξου φανέντος αὐτοῖς τοῦ γινομένου, 3.61.9) on hearing that Hannibal is in Italy. Indeed, Polybius stresses their reaction with the same narrative device used to describe the consternation felt by the Spartans when they see Philip's army outside their city. Having learnt of the fall of Saguntum, the Romans are preparing to face the Carthaginians in Spain, only to learn that Hannibal has already arrived in Italy and is laying siege to some cities (3.61.8). The incident concerning the taking of Psophis is similarly typical in the *Histories*. Polybius frequently describes impressive instances of sieges against apparently impregnable cities such as Dimale (3.18.3–5) and Sardis (7.15–18).[15] Far from being deterred by the reputation attached to such cities, the would-be besiegers exploit the trust placed by the defenders in their excellent fortifications so as to surprise them with risky endeavors and emerge victorious.

---

15 See above, n. 10.

Furthermore, the description of how Philip's reign begins is carefully planned and orchestrated so as to serve the story's general economy. As recounted by Polybius, the king's career does not develop in the auspicious manner it begins. For all the initial encouraging signs of leniency and determination, Philip's subsequent course takes a very different turn, which not only prevents him from achieving his ambitious aims as regards routing the Romans and expanding his sovereignty to the West, but renders him detestable even among his compatriots. Although the text has not survived in its entirety, so as to permit in-depth observation of this interesting transformation, the existing fragments do offer us an idea of its features and causes. To a great extent, Polybius attributes them to the corrosive influence exercised on the king by his poor counsellors (7.14.6, 9.22.10). In 16.10 he comments on Philip's failure to exploit the major opportunity to attack Egypt that presented itself after the Battle of Lade, thus underlining an important aspect of the negative direction in which his career was heading:

Ὅτι μετὰ τὸ συντελεσθῆναι τὴν περὶ τὴν Λάδην ναυμαχίαν καὶ τοὺς μὲν Ῥοδίους ἐκποδὼν γενέσθαι, τὸν δ' Ἄτταλον μηδέπω συμμεμιχέναι, δῆλον ὡς ἐξῆν γε τελεῖν τῷ Φιλίππῳ τὸν εἰς τὴν Ἀλεξάνδρειαν πλοῦν. ἐξ οὗ δὴ καὶ μάλιστ' ἄν τις καταμάθοι τὸ μανιῶδη γενόμενον Φίλιππον τοῦτο πρᾶξαι. Τί οὖν ἦν τὸ τῆς ὁρμῆς ἐπιλαβόμενον; οὐδὲν ἕτερον ἀλλ' ἡ φύσις τῶν πραγμάτων. ἐκ πολλοῦ μὲν γὰρ ἐνίοτε πολλοὶ τῶν ἀδυνάτων ἐφίενται διὰ τὸ μέγεθος τῶν προφαινομένων ἐλπίδων, κρατούσης τῆς ἐπιθυμίας τῶν ἑκάστου λογισμῶν· ὅταν δ' ἐγγίσωσι τοῖς ἔργοις, οὐδενὶ λόγῳ πάλιν ἀφίστανται τῶν προθέσεων, ἐπισκοτούμενοι καὶ παραλογιζόμενοι τοῖς λογισμοῖς διὰ τὴν ἀμηχανίαν καὶ τὴν δυσχρηστίαν τῶν ἀπαντωμένων.

After the sea-fight at Lade was over, the Rhodians being out of the way and Attalus not yet having joined, it was evidently quite possible for Philip to sail to Alexandria. This is the best proof that Philip had become like a madman when he acted thus. What was it then that arrested his impulse? Simply the nature of things. For at a distance many men at times strive after impossibilities owing to the magnitude of hopes before their eyes, their desires getting the better of their reason: but when the hour of action approaches they abandon their projects again without any exercise of reason, their faculty of thought being confused and upset by the insuperable difficulties they encounter.

The contrast could hardly be starker between the above passage and the image cultivated of Philip in the early years of his reign, when he let no opportunity go to waste and astounded enemies and allies alike with the speed at which he carried out his plans. Polybius deliberately emphasizes Philip's determination in the Social War to such an extent as to render the subsequent change in his behavior and the way he handles power all the more striking, and to highlight just how crucial his immediate environment was in bringing about this change.[16] It is thus evident that the narrative on the start of the Social War is structured with material, scenes, motifs and themes heavily colored by Polybius, and ties in perfectly with the remainder of Philip's story, serving the historian's thematic concerns and the goals he sets when presenting the story. Thus even if Polybius used pro-Philip sources in his description of the early years of Philip's reign, it would appear that he subjected his material to detailed, systematic revision so as to compose a masterfully structured narrative that placed emphasis where and how he pleased.

I considered it appropriate to discuss the organic link between the description of Philip's early years as king and the account of how his story subsequently unfolds, in order to show that the similarities in Polybius' presentation of Philip and Arrian's portrayal of Alexander do not appear to be due merely to the use of common sources. Rather, in describing Alexander's amazing speed and ability to conquer the most inaccessible positions, Arrian is relying on ground meticulously prepared by Polybius. This view is further reinforced by the fact that, in addition to the above, a number of other characteristic themes in the Polybian presentation of Philip's early years are encountered in Books 3 and 4 of the *Anabasis*, from which the overwhelming majority of my examples derive. One such theme concerns the conspiracies hatched against the two kings by their own men. In Book 5 Polybius makes repeated, detailed reference to the plot by Apelles, Leontius and Megaleas against Philip, while Arrian mentions Philotas' conspiracy against Alexander in Book 3 (26–27), and gives an analytical account of the one involving the royal pages in Book 4 (13–14). Furthermore, the symposium scene in the *Anabasis*, where Cleitus reproaches Alexander for his weakness for flattery and barbarian living (4.8.4), calls to mind the equivalent scene in the *Histories*, where in the course of a symposium Leontius and Megaleas evince no hesitation in openly expressing their displeasure at Philip's favoritism towards Aratus (5.15). Needless to say, I am not claiming that Arrian drew his material for the conspiracies and symposium scene from Polybius rather than from his sources on Alexander; indeed, in the case of the royal pages he highlights specific points on which relevant sources disagree (4.14.3–4). However, if Polybius' account of the early years in Philip's reign really did influence the way Arrian presents Alexander, as I am arguing here, then it is only reasonable for it also to have influenced the criteria with which Arrian chose the source material for inclusion and use in his own history.

---

16 On Polybius' dramatic presentation of Philip's last years, cf. most recently Dreyer 2013, Nicholson 2015, 203–55.

A final common point between Polybius and Arrian's accounts I would like to discuss is, in my view, highly interesting, since at first sight it would seem to counterdict the notion that Polybius associates Philip with Alexander. In 5.9.1–5 Polybius mentions that when the Macedonians under Philip invaded Thermus in Aetolia, they burnt the valuable votive offerings and demolished the thousands of statues at the site. He even notes that Philip was of the opinion that this was right and fair, as it was retaliation for the Aetolian outrages at Dium and Dodona (5.9.6). The historian does not share this view, however, and has no hesitation in interrupting the narrative flow to express openly his disagreement (ἐμοὶ δὲ τἀναντία δοκεῖ τούτων, 5.9.7), contrasting Philip's behavior with the considerable self-restraint shown in similar situations by Antigonus III, Philip II and Alexander, three of his predecessors on the Macedonian throne (5.9.7–10.9). A striking parallel is to be found in Book 3 of the *Anabasis*, where Arrian relates how Alexander burnt down the royal palace at Persepolis, despite Parmenion's advice to retain whatever was then in his possession and not to give the Asians the impression that he was a transient conqueror (3.18.11–12). Here it is worth stressing that there is no conflict between this and the comment Polybius makes when comparing Philip's behavior to that of Alexander, since to his mind Alexander's self-restraint lies in the fact that he avoided sacrilegious acts even when punishing enemies.[17] Rather, what is noteworthy is the similarity between the two incidents with regard both to the events recounted and to the way the authors handle them on the narrative level. Like Philip, Alexander justifies his actions by presenting them as constituting fair recompense for the evils committed by his enemies in the past. And as in the *Histories*, so in the *Anabasis*, this view prompts an immediate reaction from the narrator, who intervenes in the first person to refute it (ἀλλ' οὐδ' ἐμοὶ δοκεῖ σὺν νῷ δρᾶσαι τοῦτό γε Ἀλέξανδρος οὐδὲ εἶναί τις αὕτη Περσῶν τῶν πάλαι τιμωρία, 3.18.12).

In this paper I have offered a comparative examination of Philip as presented by Polybius in Books 4 and 5 of the *Histories* and Alexander as portrayed by Arrian in the *Anabasis*, especially in Books 3 and 4, where there is a high density of features common to both texts. More specifically, I have argued that in order to highlight the strong points and diverse merits of their protagonists, Polybius and Arrian do not simply rely on identical themes and motifs, such as their incomparable speed and almost superhuman ability to capture impregnable positions, but also present them using the same narrative strategies. In addition, I have attempted to clarify whether these striking similarities between the two texts are

---

[17] Importantly, too, later on in the *Anabasis* Alexander is presented as regretting his decision to burn down the Persian palace (6.30.1).

due to common sources or to Arrian's reception of Polybius. I have maintained that the presentation of Philip's early reign shows clear marks of Polybian fashioning, as it is carefully reworked so as to fit in organically with the subsequent development of his history and the remaining work. The material with which Arrian highlights Alexander's uniqueness is of a distinctly Polybian hue, involving motifs and patterns that recur in the same manner in various incidents in the *Histories*. In any case, even if this accumulation of features common to both narratives cannot confirm whether and to what extent Arrian read and used the *Histories* in his *Anabasis*, it shows that Polybius' influence on subsequent historians, whether directly or indirectly exercised on Arrian, is profounder than usually acknowledged.

Bibliography

Billows, R. (2000), "Polybius and Alexander Historiography", in: A.B. Bosworth/E.J. Baynham (eds.), *Alexander the Great in Fact and Fiction*, Oxford, 286–306.

Davidson, J. (1991), "The Gaze in Polybius' *Histories*", in: *JRS* 81, 10–24.

Dreyer, B. (2013), "Frank Walbank's *Philippos Tragoidoumenos*: Polybius' Account of Philip's Last Years", in: B. Gibson/T. Harrison (eds.), 201–11.

Gibson, B./T. Harrison (eds.) (2013), *Polybius and his World. Essays in Memory of F.W. Walbank*, Oxford.

de Jong, I.J.F. (2013), "Narratological Aspects of the *Histories* of Herodotus", in: R.V. Munson (ed.), *Herodotus, Vol. 1. Herodotus and the Narrative of the Past*, Oxford, 253–91.

McGing, B. (2010), *Polybius'* Histories, Oxford.

—— (2013), "Youthfulness in Polybius: The Case of Philip V of Macedon", in: B. Gibson/T. Harrison (eds.), 181–99.

Miltsios, N. (2009), "The Perils of Expectations: Perceptions, Suspense and Surprise in Polybius' *Histories*", in: J. Grethlein/A. Rengakos (eds.), *Narratology and Interpretation. The Content of Narrative Form in Ancient Literature*, Berlin, 481–506.

Nicholson, E.L. (2015), "A Reassessment of Philip V. of Macedon in Polybios' *Histories*", PhD diss., Newcastle University.

Rengakos, A. (2006), "Thucydides' Narrative: The Epic and Herodotean Heritage", in: A. Rengakos/A. Tsakmakis (eds.), *Brill's Companion to Thucydides*, Leiden, 279–300.

Brian McGing
Appian, the Third Punic War and Polybius

Polybius' admiration for Rome in its prime, or at least his admiring statements, need no detailed exposition. The passages praising individual Romans or state institutions and collective virtues are well known and much quoted, as are the rather fewer negative statements (in the surviving text) about particular Roman actions. Over the years there has been a wide range of modern scholarly opinion about Polybius' views of Roman imperialism, whether he was a supporter, even spokesman, or opponent and critic.[1] The four Greek reactions to Rome's destruction of Carthage preserved from Book 36 (Plb. 36.9) are a good litmus test of scholarly positions. Donald Baronowski, along with Walbank, Ferrary and others, believes that Polybius shared the view that Rome was justified in acting as she did, while harbouring sufficient worries to include the negative opinions.[2] And at least one of the major strands of scholarship has been to ascribe to Polybius a fundamentally benign interpretation of Rome's expansion and domination, allowing for the occasional critique of Roman self-interests. The Romans, in Polybius' opinion, according to Baronowski, "generally treated other nations with moderation and beneficence at all stages of their imperial evolution".[3] I have serious doubts that this was Polybius' overall judgement on Roman imperialism,[4] but in this paper I limit myself to consideration of the Third Punic War. My focus is less on Polybius, necessarily, given that his account is preserved only in a few fragments of Books 36 and 38, more on Appian, and in particular his long narrative of the preliminaries before the fighting started (*Lib*. 67.301–94.447). In spite of the fact that Appian is generally viewed as "above all an ardent admirer of Rome",

---

[1] The scholarship is reviewed most helpfully, and thoroughly, by Baronowski 2011, 5–11. Whether we can accept what Polybius says on the subject as a reflection of what he really thought, however, is doubted by Thornton 2013, 213–29, who treats the *Histories* as diplomatic, or figured, speech: Polybius was sending a message to the world's new imperial masters, rather than simply writing history, in an attempt to win the best possible conditions for his homeland. What he wrote, therefore, represents what he thought were the best arguments, not necessarily what he himself believed.
[2] Baronowski 2011, 101–06.
[3] Baronowski 2011, 113. For a much darker interpretation of Polybius' (and Josephus') views on the nature of Roman imperialism, see Gruen 2013.
[4] It seems to me that Polybius' criticisms of Roman policy and individuals in the very meagre remains after Book 6 are more numerous than one would expect from a historian supposed to be well disposed to Roman imperialism: McGing 2010, 157–64.

his description of Roman behaviour in this matter is unrelentingly negative.[5] Since his main source was Polybius, this obviously has potential consequences for our assessment of Polybius' attitude towards Rome's treatment of Carthage. To what extent did Appian inherit his hostility from Polybius?[6]

The dangers of reconstructing what a lost, or fragmentary, source said, and the tone in which he said it, from a later author are obvious: we cannot be sure to what extent the surviving author manipulated, built on or otherwise interpreted his source. Study of Appian's use of his sources yielded for a long time very small returns on a huge investment of ink.[7] The situation is changing, however. The new Budé editions of Appian, for example, have demonstrated much good sense and greatly advanced the subject; Richard Westall has recently demonstrated how it is still possible to say important things even about the sources of the *Civil Wars*, an admittedly difficult topic;[8] and John Rich's detailed study of Appian's use of Polybius for his account of Antiochus III's war against Rome is a model of what can be achieved.[9] These advances both reflect and result from a sea-change in the way Appian has been approached by contemporary scholars. It has been accepted since the time of Niebuhr, Nissen and others that Appian relied heavily on Polybius for his account of the years 200–146 BCE, and Rich makes a most convincing case that he used Polybius directly, not through some later and mysterious early imperial intermediary, an idea promoted primarily by Schwartz in his influential Paully-Wissowa entry of 1896.[10] The theory grew, not entirely but largely, out of the dominant late 19th and early 20th century view that Appian was an incompetent historian, almost without value in his own right, who did little more than stitch together his sources. So, if his account diverged from, or had more material than, what remains in, for example, Polybius, he must have been following another source who used Polybius, but had other material as well.

---

5 *OCD³* sv. Appian. See also, for example, Brodersen 1993, 355, Bucher 2000, 443–44. That Appian was an admirer of the Rome of his day is undoubtedly correct, but he was not impeded by the same sort of political pressures Polybius faced, from criticizing, fiercely if necessary, Roman behaviour in the past.
6 Polybius' position on the causes and pretexts of the war has been carefully studied by Baronowski 1995.
7 On the study of Appian's sources see, for example, McGing 1993, 498, Westall 2015, 125–26.
8 Westall 2015, 125–67.
9 Rich 2015, 65–123.
10 Schwartz 1896, 217–22, Rich 2015, 65–69. Rich's arguments should rout the opposition, but as he notes himself (Rich 2015, 67), the intermediary theory has always attracted powerful support. See also Baronowski 1995, 18 n. 8.

Research over the last 30 years or so, however, including most recently the important volume edited by Kathryn Welch, has shown repeatedly that Appian had ideas, interests, rhetorical talent and a historical plan of his own, and that he pursued his own agenda in his own way.[11] It does not make him a brilliant historian all of a sudden, but it certainly makes him considerably more interesting, and important, than previous generations thought.[12]

Appian had little time for worrying about Polybius' famous distinction between the real cause of wars, the starting point and the pretext (Plb. 3.6–7), although he was very interested in pretexts, and did like to identify the real causes: it is just that he found it all much simpler than Polybius.[13] The cause of the Second Punic War, for example, discussed at great length and inconclusively by Polybius (Plb. 3.6–32), was straightforward for Appian. By attacking Saguntum, which was north of the river Ebro, Hannibal broke the treaty and thus caused the war. He got the Turbulates to complain that the Saguntines were attacking their territory, giving a pretext for the war, but Appian has no difficulty in attributing sole responsibility to Hannibal (*Ib.* 9.33–10.39, *Hann.* 3.10–12). For Appian the real cause of the Third Punic War is also clear—Roman fear of Carthage played up particularly by Cato on his return from the embassy Rome sent in 152 (*Lib.* 69.312–315)—and although, as we will see, Appian is less comfortable with it, the pretext is fairly clearly the accusation that by fighting Massinissa, king of Numidia, the Carthaginians had broken their treaty with Rome (*Lib.* 74.339–340). What I want to draw attention to is the extremely hostile critique of Roman actions.

Right from the beginning, the Romans were duplicitous in their relationship with Carthage by secretly doing everything to favour Massinissa (*Lib.* 68.307):

---

[11] Welch 2015. Welch's own introduction to that volume (Welch 2015a, 1–13) highlights the main change in the modern approach to Appian: the readiness to treat him as an author in his own right, not just as a receptacle of superior, but now lost predecessors.

[12] I regret, in a previous article (McGing 1993, 520), falling into the modern trap of "ranking" Appian, when I raised him, rather condescendingly, from Nissen's third rank of sources into the second rank. It would have been more profitable just to say that he wrote an independent work of history that deserved far more serious treatment than it had received.

[13] On Appian's tendency to simplify, see particularly Goldmann 1988. Bucher 2005, 62–63 shows Appian simplifying the narrative of the battle of Pharsalus. I would argue that this tendency extends beyond narrative to Appian's mode of explanation as well.

There were many other acts of war committed by both sides, until eventually new Roman envoys arrived to negotiate a settlement. But, as before, they had been told to support Massinissa's cause secretly.[14]

Interestingly, one of the few fragments of Polybius' account overlaps here with Appian (Plb. 31.21).[15] Massinissa cast envious eyes on Carthaginian territory and tried to take it away from them. He got control of the countryside but the towns were too well guarded, and both sides sent embassies to Rome. The Carthaginians, however, always came off second best at Rome, not because they did not have justice on their side, but because "the judges were convinced it was in their own interest to decide againt them".[16] And Polybius emphasizes that Massinissa himself recognised that he had no valid claim to the territory under dispute. So Appian got a clear direction from Polybius about Rome's deceit and dishonest treatment of the Carthaginians with regard to Massinissa.[17]

Polybius does not specifically refer to Roman secrecy in favouring Massinissa, or in deciding to go to war, but it is the clear implication of the important fragment dealing with the Roman decision to go to war with Carthage (Plb. 36.2):

> They had long ago made up their minds to act thus, but they were looking for a suitable opportunity and a pretext that would appeal to the world at large. For the Romans very rightly paid great attention to this matter, since, as Demetrius says, when the inception of a war seems just, it makes victory greater and ill-success less perilous, while if it is thought

---

[14] ἄλλα τε πολλὰ αὐτοῖς ἔργα πολέμων ἐς ἀλλήλους γίγνεται, μέχρι Ῥωμαίων ἕτεροι πρέσβεις ἐπῆλθον ἐς διαλύσεις, οἷς ὁμοίως εἴρητο Μασσανάσσῃ βοηθεῖν ἀδήλως. This support for Massinissa is also noted at *Lib*. 67.302, 69.311.

[15] ἀμφοτέρων δὲ ποιουμένων τὴν ἀναφορὰν ἐπὶ τὴν σύγκλητον ὑπὲρ τῶν ἀμφισβητουμένων, καὶ πρεσβευτῶν πολλάκις ἐληλυθότων διὰ ταῦτα παρ' ἑκατέρων, αἰεὶ συνέβαινε τοὺς Καρχηδονίους ἐλαττοῦσθαι παρὰ τοῖς Ῥωμαίοις, οὐ τοῖς δικαίοις, ἀλλὰ τῷ πεπεῖσθαι τοὺς κρίνοντας συμφέρειν σφίσι τὴν τοιαύτην γνώμην, ἐπείτοι χρόνοις οὐ πολλοῖς ἀνώτερον αὐτὸς ὁ Μασαννάσας διώκων τὸν Ἀφθῆρα τὸν ἀποστάτην μετὰ στρατοπέδου δίοδον ᾐτήσατο τοὺς Καρχηδονίους διὰ ταύτης τῆς χώρας [οἱ δ' οὐχ ὑπήκουσαν], ὡς οὐδὲν αὐτῷ προσηκούσης ("Both parties appealed to the senate about their differences, and numerous embassies had come from both on the subject, but the Carthaginians always came off second best at Rome, not because they had not right on their side, but because the judges were convinced that it was in their own interest to decide against them. Their claim to the country was evidently just; for Massinissa himself not many years previously, while pursuing with an army Aphther who had rebelled against him, had begged permission from them to pass through this district, thus acknowledging that he had no claim to it").

[16] This is, of course exactly the same sort of Roman self-interest Polybius famously identifies elsewhere in Book 31, in relation to the Ptolemies (31.10.6–7) and the Seleucids (31.11.11).

[17] Appian did, however, have a special interest in deceit, as Cowan 2015 demonstrates clearly in the context of the *Civil Wars*.

to be dishonorable and wrong it has the opposite effect. So on this occasion their disputes with each other about the effect on outside opinion very nearly made them desist from going to war.[18]

Obviously the pretext they were seeking was not the real reason for making the decision to go to war with Carthage, and equally obviously, if they did not know what pretext they were going to present, they must have kept their decision to go to war secret. Appian reflects this secret decision and search for a pretext repeatedly:

> Cato in particular said that Rome's freedom would never be secure until Carthage had been destroyed. When the senate heard this, they decided on war, but, still needing a pretext, kept their decision secret (*Lib.* 69.314).[19]

> As soon as the Romans learnt of the previous conflict, they began to recruit an army throughout Italy, not specifying its purpose, but to have for immediate use in executing orders (*Lib.* 74.340).[20]

> The senate, who had in fact long ago decided on war and were looking for any old excuse... (*Lib.* 74.343).[21]

Appian is not interested in Polybius' observation about how attentive the Romans were to appearing to have right on their side, or in his citation of Demetrius of Phalerum on the strategic advantages of fighting a war that seemed to be just, and the disadvantages of the opposite. Appian does not want the Romans even to appear to have right on their side, and therefore makes no reference either to Polybius' further observation that the Romans disagreed with each other so strenuously about outside opinion, presumably about the pretext they would offer,

---

18 πάλαι δὲ τούτου κεκυρωμένου βεβαίως ἐν ταῖς ἑκάστων γνώμαις καιρὸν ἐζήτουν ἐπιτήδειον καὶ πρόφασιν εὐσχήμονα πρὸς τοὺς ἐκτός. πολὺ γὰρ δὴ τούτου τοῦ μέρους ἐφρόντιζον Ῥωμαῖοι, καλῶς φρονοῦντες· ἔνστασις γὰρ πολέμου κατὰ τὸν Δημήτριον δικαία μὲν εἶναι δοκοῦσα καὶ τὰ νικήματα ποιεῖ μείζω καὶ τὰς ἀποτεύξεις ἀσφαλεστέρας, ἀσχήμων δὲ καὶ φαύλη τοὐναντίον ἀπεργάζεται· διὸ καὶ τότε περὶ τῆς τῶν ἐκτὸς διαλήψεως πρὸς ἀλλήλους διαφερόμενοι παρ' ὀλίγον ἀπέστησαν τοῦ πολέμου.
19 καὶ ὁ Κάτων μάλιστα ἔλεγεν οὔ ποτε Ῥωμαίοις βέβαιον οὐδὲ τὴν ἐλευθερίαν ἔσεσθαι, πρὶν ἐξελεῖν Καρχηδόνα. ὧν ἡ βουλὴ πυνθανομένη ἔκρινε μὲν πολεμεῖν, ἔτι δ' ἔχρῃζε προφάσεων, καὶ τὴν κρίσιν ἀπόρρητον εἶχον.
20 αὐτίκα γὰρ οἱ Ῥωμαῖοι πυθόμενοι στρατὸν ἐπήγγελλον ἐς ὅλην τὴν Ἰταλίαν, τὴν μὲν χρείαν οὐ λέγοντες, ὡς δ' ἂν ὀξέως ἔχοιεν ἐς τὰ παραγγελλόμενα χρῆσθαι.
21 ἡ δὲ βουλὴ πάλαι διεγνωκυῖα πολεμῆσαι καὶ προφάσεις ἐρεσχηλοῦσα...

that they nearly desisted from war.[22] This might imply that they had moral doubts about their decision.

There is nothing necessarily improper, as far as Polybius is concerned, about an imperial power looking for a sound pretext—it helps to win wars—but it does bring into play the much discussed fragment 99 B–W (101 Loeb), which is usually thought to belong in this context:

> For the Romans took extra care not to appear to be the first to act unjustly, or to attack their neighbors when they undertook their wars, and tried instead to seem to be defending themselves and to be entering their wars under compulsion.[23]

It is, of course, dangerous to build too much on a disembodied fragment, and it needs very special pleading to interpret it as benignly as Baronowski, who thinks it means that "the Romans took great care not to commit injustice and aggression, but to make people see that they were in fact acting in self-defence".[24] On the contrary, it surely concerns what Walbank calls "public relations", and the contrast between appearance and reality: the Romans avoid the appearance of being the first to offer violence unjustly, or of using wars to lay hands on their neighbours.[25] It was important for military success to seem to be acting in self-defence and under compulsion, which is another way of stating the position argued by

---

[22] I disagree with Baronowski 1995, 19 that the Roman failure to agree a pretext implies that the senate cannot have been satisfied with the Massinissa pretext alone, and must have found something else to complain about. The Romans had already decided on war by 152, after Cato's return from Africa, but the Carthaginians had not yet done anything that could be cited as a pretext: hence the Roman difficulty. By the end of 150, however, as Walbank 1979, 655 notes, the war between Carthage and Numidia provided the perfect pretext. But Baronowski 1995, 18 is surely right that Diodorus 32.5 seems to have picked up Polybius on this point and assigned the reality, not just the appearance, of moral wars to Rome—that is, if the fragment belongs in this context: "The Romans aspire to embark only upon wars that are just, and to make no casual or precipitate decisions about such matters" (Ὅτι σφόδρα οἱ Ῥωμαῖοι φιλοτιμοῦνται δικαίους ἐνίστασθαι τοὺς πολέμους καὶ μηδὲν εἰκῇ καὶ προπετῶς περὶ τῶν τοιούτων ψηφίζεσθαι).

[23] οἱ γὰρ Ῥωμαῖοι οὐ τὴν τυχοῦσαν πρόνοιαν ἐποιοῦντο τοῦ μὴ κατάρχοντες φαίνεσθαι χειρῶν ἀδίκων, μηδ' ἀναιρούμενοι τοὺς πολέμους τὰς χεῖρας ἐπιβάλλειν τοῖς πέλας, ἀλλ' ἀεὶ δοκεῖν ἀμυνόμενοι καὶ κατ' ἀνάγκην ἐμβαίνειν εἰς τοὺς πολέμους. See Walbank 1979, 653–55, Baronowski 2011, 73–74 for discussion.

[24] Baronowski 2011, 73, who seeems to have substantially changed his earlier position on the fragment (Baronowski 1995, 21–22).

[25] Walbank 1979, 653. And like Walbank and Habicht in the new Loeb translation, I take φαίνεσθαι to govern the verb ἐπιβάλλειν in the second clause: the Romans avoid the appearance of initiating unjust war, and they avoid the appearance of attacking their neighbours.

Demetrius of Phalerum, whom, as we have seen, Polybius (36.2) cited approvingly. It is about the appearance of holding the high moral ground, not about the actuality of doing so. And it clearly allows for the possibility that Rome did initiate unjust aggression, but tried to hide it—which is certainly what happened, according to Appian, in the Third Punic War.

The pretext for war that Rome eventually adopted is clearly stated in Diodorus (32.1), who is also agreed to have used Polybius for this period:[26] by warring with Massinissa the Carthaginians were considered to have broken their treaty with Rome. And Appian (*Lib.* 74.339–40) confirms this, although somewhat reluctantly. The Carthaginians, he says, were afraid of Roman ill-will towards them and of the Roman intention to make Massinissa their excuse. And they were right on both counts. For as soon as they learnt of the war with Massinissa, Rome began to recruit an army, although they kept the reason secret. But Appian plays down the credibility of the pretext. In order to make the Roman excuse redundant, the Carthaginians condemned to death the commanders in the war against Massinissa. And later, after they have handed over 300 children as hostages and have presented themselves at Utica for further instructions, their envoys give a speech in which they bring the pretext up again (*Lib.* 79.365–370). We have done everything you have told us, they say, so what part of the treaty do you accuse us of violating, that you vote for war so suddenly and march against us without even declaring it? You say we have been at war with Massinissa, but he has behaved so unjustly towards us that he has dissolved (συνέχεεν) our treaty with you. "If this is the excuse for this war", the envoys say, we have condemned the commanders and explained ourselves. The argument that the Carthaginians did not break the treaty with Rome by fighting against Massinissa, because his outrageous behaviour (consistently but secretly supported by Rome) vitiated it, is not in any of the surviving Polybius or Diodorus, and may well be Appian's own invention. In spite of, or perhaps because of, the doubt cast by the envoys on the validity of the Massinissa pretext, it is clear that Appian knew this was the pretext, and its presence in both Appian and Diodorus confirms that it was in Polybius too.[27] Appian has, however, done his best to demonstrate how weak it was, the Romans knowing perfectly well that Massinissa had wronged Carthage, and done so with Roman connivance.

One of the strong narrative lines in Appian's account is how the Carthaginians are constantly perplexed by Rome's unreasonable stance and misled by the

---

26 On Diodorus' use of Polybius, see Rich 2015, 74 with 116 n. 27.
27 Polybius was certainly aware of the Roman accusation that Carthage had broken its treaty: see Plb. 36.9.16.

Roman refusal to speak unambiguously. Their embassy to Rome after they had executed the generals responsible for fighting Massinissa provides a good example (*Lib.* 74.342–346). Their ambassadors complain of Massinissa and the hastiness of their own commanders, now executed, but the senate do not accept their defence. These negotiations are, however, not negotiations at all, because Rome has already made up its mind to go to war and was looking for any old excuse (ἐρεσχηλοῦσα).[28] In distress (ἀγωνιῶντες), the ambassadors ask how, if they were considered to have committed an offence, they could get the charge dismissed. The reply is that they must satisfy Rome (εἰ τὸ ἱκανὸν ποιήσετε Ῥωμαίοις). Unable to decide what this means, the Carthaginians send another embassy to Rome asking for clarity (σαφῶς), only to be told that they knew perfectly well (οἳ δὲ αὖθις ἔφασαν εἰδέναι Καρχηδονίους καλῶς). Interestingly, Diodorus (32.1–3) also emphasizes the Roman refusal to talk straight: the senate give a reply that was unclear (ἀσαφῆ), and then make a statement that was intractable and difficult to understand (δυστράπελος καὶ δυσκατανόητος), for they declared that they knew what they had to do.[29]

Astonished at the Roman declaration of war, and completely unprepared for it, the Carthaginians send yet another mission to Rome to settle the matter on any terms they can get (*Lib.* 76.352–355). Once again, however, the senate is deceitful in their apparent readiness to negotiate, as they had no interest in compromise: the consuls of 149 had already been dispatched with secret orders not to stop fighting until they had razed Carthage to the ground (*Lib.* 75.348). It is at this point that Appian introduces the first of the demands issued by Rome (although the senate has already decided to destroy Carthage): if they hand over 300 of their children as hostages within thirty days, Rome will guarantee their freedom and autonomy, and the Carthaginians will retain their territory in Africa. This was passed by public vote, although "in secret a message was sent to the consuls instructing them to follow the orders given to them in private". In Diodorus (32.6), the Romans also suppress their decision to destroy Carthage, while guaranteeing the people their laws, territory, sanctuaries, tombs, freedom and property. Diodorus highlights the Roman failure to say anything about the city itself (as they

---

[28] ἐρεσχηλοῦσα is a rare word, used only one other time by Appian to describe L. Licinius Murena's search for an excuse to attack Mithradates VI of Pontus in 83 BCE (*Mith.* 64.265)—another instance where, for Appian, the Romans are solely responsible for the dispute.

[29] But something has presumably gone wrong in Diodorus, as the text actually says, "for the senate declared that the Romans knew what they had to do" (ἐδογμάτισε γὰρ γινώσκειν τοὺς Ῥωμαίους ὃ δεῖ πράττειν αὐτούς). This scarcely makes sense as an explanation for a reply that was difficult for the Carthaginians to understand.

have secret plans to destroy it), a detail that he got from, and that features prominently in, another surviving passage of Polybius: the Carthaginians were very anxious at the fact that no mention was made of the city (Plb. 36.4.9).[30] Curiously Appian seems to ignore this—one would have thought it was an opportunity to highlight Roman dishonesty—and emphasizes instead that Carthaginian suspicion and unease were caused by the fact that nothing was said about the return of the hostages (*Lib.* 77.356). In Diodorus, by complying with the demand to give 300 hostages, the Carthaginians thought (obviously incorrectly) they were quit of the war, and so complied, with much wailing. He took this too from Polybius who says that the Carthaginians thought they got quite a good deal just having to hand over hostages, although at their departure there were great lamentations and tears, as each was accompanied by their family, with women inflaming the situation (36.4–5). At the very least, then, Polybius acknowledged that the Carthaginians did not understand the Roman intention and that the Romans made no attempt to clarify this. Appian does not directly take up the Roman silence about the city, because evidently he is much more interested in the dramatic possibilities offered by the departure scene of the 300 children, which he builds up with heart-rending detail (*Lib.* 77.356–358):

> Parents and relatives wept over them, especially their mothers, who with frenzied cries clung to their children, to the ships transporting them, to the commanders taking them away, and in their efforts to stop the ship sailing they even laid hold of the anchors, tried to pull at the ropes, and embraced the sailors. There were even some who swam beside the ship far out to sea, weeping and trying to keep their children in view. Others on land tore their hair and beat their breasts, as if in mourning for the dead. For they thought that because they had handed over their children without an agreement, the word "hostage" was just a euphemism that in fact meant giving up the city. Many also predicted in their lamentations that delivering up their children would be of no benefit to the city.[31]

That the future of the city itself, however, is somehow connected with the demand for the hostages perhaps indicates that Appian has either forgotten exactly

---

30 περὶ δὲ πόλεως μὴ γεγονέναι μνείαν εἰς μεγάλην ἐπίστασιν αὐτοὺς ἦγε καὶ πολλὴν ἀμηχανίαν.
31 γονέων τε αὐτοῖς ἐπικλαιόντων καὶ οἰκείων καὶ μάλιστα τῶν μητέρων, αἳ σὺν ὀλολυγῇ μανιώδει τῶν τέκνων ἐξήπτοντο καὶ νεῶν τῶν φερουσῶν αὐτὰ καὶ στρατηγῶν τῶν ἀγόντων ἀγκυρῶν τε ἐπελαμβάνοντο καὶ καλῴδια διέσπων καὶ ναύταις συνεπλέκοντο καὶ τὸν πλοῦν ἐκώλυον. εἰσὶ δ', αἳ καὶ μέχρι πολλοῦ τῆς θαλάσσης παρένεον, δεδακρυμέναι τε καὶ ἐς τὰ τέκνα ἀφορῶσαι. αἱ δ' ἐπὶ τῆς γῆς τὰς κόμας ἐτίλλοντο καὶ τὰ στέρνα ἔκοπτον ὡς ἐπὶ πένθει· ἐδόκουν γὰρ ὄνομα μὲν ἐς εὐπρέπειαν εἶναι τὴν ὁμηρείαν, ἔργῳ δὲ τῆς πόλεως ἔκδοσιν, ἐπ' οὐδεμιᾷ συνθήκῃ τῶνδε τῶν παίδων διδομένων. καὶ πολλαὶ καὶ τοῦτο ἐν ταῖς οἰμωγαῖς κατεμαντεύοντο τῇ πόλει, μηδὲν αὐτὴν ὀνήσειν τοὺς παῖδας ἐκδιδομένους.

what Polybius wrote, or has chosen to incorporate it differently into his version.[32] After the children have been sent off, the senate continue to deceive the Carthaginians by informing them that in relation to the end of the war (ἐς τὸ τέλος τοῦ πολέμου), they would tell them the rest in Utica.

At Utica the Carthaginians begin a series of long exchanges with the Romans that ends with the decision to go to war (*Lib.* 78–93). The Carthaginian speakers invariably get the stronger rhetorical arguments, and the reader's sympathies are enlisted solely on the Carthaginian side. The first speech (*Lib.* 78.362–79.370)[33] asks for Roman compassion, a fitting response for the mighty, who place their hope in not wronging others and claim special preeminence in piety, but concentrates on Carthaginian compliance with their treaty requirements and with Roman demands. They have paid the tribute, and given up their ships and elephants, and although they fought with Massinissa, his actions dissolved their treaty with Rome, and if this was wrong, they have condemned the generals responsible and shown themselves ready to comply with all Roman demands. The evidence of their readiness to comply is their handing over of the hostages, even before the deadline. The agreement was that if they delivered the hostages, Rome would allow Carthage to be free and autonomous, and retain possession of her territories. For Appian, the Carthaginians have done nothing wrong, or if they have, they have made amends, and they have carried out all Roman orders.

The reply of the consul L. Marcius Censorinus is brief and nit-picking, and introduces a new Roman demand—for the Carthaginians to give up all their weapons (*Lib.* 80.371–374). Strangely, Censorinus does not say, "you broke the treaty", but reverts to the previous opaque Roman response that the Carthaginians know perfectly well what has caused the war. He picks them up, however, on one lie they have told (*Lib.* 80.372): "for the decree makes clear, and we explained this to you before in Sicily when we received the hostages, that we would give you additional orders about the rest of what we decided at Utica". This is not actually what Appian had reported earlier, where the Romans said they would tell the Carthaginians about the end of the war, not about their further decisions. The Carthaginians immediately agree to give up their arms. Appian makes a more dramatic scene of it than Diodorus (32.6.2), but the report in both, of 200,000 sets of armour and 2,000 catapults, presumably goes back to Polybius. Appian also dramatises

---

[32] On Appian's working methods, in particular his use of drafts, and the consequences for the nature of the finished product, see the important analysis of Rich 2015, 69–72.
[33] "An annalistic confection" according to Walbank 1979, 658, but the confection is surely Appian's own.

at greater length than Diodorus the extreme emotional response of the Carthaginian envoys to the final Roman demand that they must settle inland, as the city of Carthage is to be razed to the ground (*Lib.* 81.378). For Appian even the Romans shed tears at such a pitiable sight. Diodorus says that everyone was moved to pity at the subsequent speech of the Carthaginian ambassador, Blanno (Banno in Appian), and the idea of Roman sympathy for the Carthaginian situation may have come from Polybius himself, if fragment 192 B–W (195 Loeb), which reports members of the senate being "stunned and crazed, since they shared the overwhelming grief of those who had nothing", belongs in this context.[34]

The speech of Banno (*Lib.*83–85) repeats at greater length the arguments already set out by the Carthaginians. The once great rulers of Africa deserve compassion, they did nothing to break their existing treaty with Rome, and they have complied with all the present demands made of them. The Carthaginian case may contain a fudge on the matter of going to war against Massinissa—and Banno just asserts that they have not violated the treaty—but for Appian it is clear that they have the high moral ground, because there is a central dishonesty in the Roman position, which Banno spells out. The deal was a free and autonomous Carthage in return for the hostages: you cannot promise that Carthage will be free and autonomous if it is razed to the ground. He also returns to the theme of Rome's reputation for piety in dealings of this sort, another awkward point for the Romans to face if they go ahead with their plan. And to show how reasonable they are, the Carthaginians ask for an opportunity to send another diplomatic mission to Rome.

The consuls scowled sullenly (ἐσκυθρωπακότες) through Banno's speech, thus showing they were not going to yield, and Censorinus gives the Roman response (*Lib.* 86–89). Rhetorically, it is a general disquisition on the imperial dangers and temptations of people who live beside the sea, the Athenians being cited as a warning for the Carthaginians: it will be better for everyone, the Carthaginians included, if Carthage is destroyed and its people move inland. The speech makes virtually no attempt to answer the awkward case put forward by Banno, and ends with the manifest sophistry that Rome regards Carthage as its people, not the physical city itself: they can be free and autonomous, as promised, if they build a new settlement inland. The Carthaginian response is stunned silence, before they make one more plea demonstrating how reasonable they are: they ask the Romans to send a fleet to make sure that the Carthaginians bow before the

---

34 ὥστε καὶ τοὺς ἐν τῷ συνεδρίῳ ἀχανεῖς γενέσθαι καὶ παρεκστῆναι ταῖς διανοίαις, συμπάσχοντας τῇ τῶν ἀκληρούντων ὑπερωδυνίᾳ. Nissen's assignment to this context was accepted, with reservations, by Walbank 1979, 754.

inevitable (*Lib.* 90.432–435). Appian's account then deals with the drama of the ambassadors' return to Carthage and report of what had happened, the madness and grief of the people, and their decision to fight and preparations (*Lib.* 91–93). In contrast to the frenzy of action at Carthage, the consuls delayed, perhaps hesitating, Appian suggests, to commit an act of such perversity (ἔργον ἀλλόκοτον, *Lib.* 94.442). Later, when the fighting was already under way, and not going very well for Rome, even the Romans realized that they could not expect peace, as they had been the first to break faith in their demands (*Lib.* 112.558).[35]

There is no redeeming feature about Roman behaviour in this account. They have brutally and dishonestly forced Carthage into war, because they are afraid of it and want the opportunity to destroy it once and for all. The Carthaginians have done nothing at all contrary to their oaths and agreements, and they have done everything required by Rome, until they have no course open but to fight. There is no equivocation on Appian's part. How much of his hostile analysis of Roman behaviour goes back to Polybius, and how much is the product of his own interpretation of events?

If we were continuing to regard Appian as little more than a stitcher-together of his sources, we would have to think that what he wrote is largely what Polybius wrote. It is clear beyond doubt now that we cannot treat Appian in this way. There does seem to be a degree of similarity in the way that Appian treats Rome's behaviour in relation to other enemies in wars of the second and first centuries BCE. This would point to his own fashioning of events. His version of what happened, for example, before the outbreak of the Third Macedonian War (*Mac.* 11.1–9) and First Mithradatic War (*Mith.* 12.38–14.49) bear some close resemblances to what we have seen at Carthage. Rome was suspicious of the growing power of Perseus, king of Macedon (Ῥωμαῖοι ταχέως αὐξανόμενον τὸν Περσέα ὑφεωρῶντο, *Mac.* 11.1), just as they were of the growing city of Carthage (πόλεως … εὐχερῶς οὕτως αὐξανομένης, *Lib.* 69.314) and the great empire of Mithradates (τὸ μέγεθος τῆς ἀρχῆς τοῦ Μιθριδάτου πολλῆς οὔσης ὑφορώμενοι, *Mith.* 10.31). The Roman ambassadors to the Bastarnae reported their observations on the rich resources of Macedon in much the same way as Cato's embassy reported on the strengths of Carthage (*Lib.* 69.312–315), and as the Bithynian envoys in Asia Minor describe, in greater detail, the strengths of the kingdom of Pontus (*Mith.* 13.42–45). Eumenes, king of Pergamum, and Nicomedes of Bithynia do not act in exactly the same way as Massinissa, but functionally they have the same sort of role in the narrative, provoking war. As in the case of Carthage, so too with Macedon, the Romans decide to go to war, but

---

35 οὐ γάρ τινα διάλυσιν προσεδόκων, ἄπιστα πρότεροι κελεύσαντες.

keep their decision secret, a point repeated twice subsequently by Appian.[36] In Asia Minor the Roman envoys order Ariobarzanes and Nicomedes to invade Pontus and stir up a war in which Rome will help them (τὴν γῆν τὴν Μιθριδάτου κατατρέχειν καὶ ἐς πόλεμον ἐρεθίζειν, ὡς Ῥωμαίων αὐτοῖς πολεμοῦσι συμμαχησόντων, *Mith*. 11.38). So whatever negotiations go on, the Romans on the spot have already decided they want a war.[37] In what sounds like an originally Polybian critique, Appian says of the situation in Macedon that it was not Roman policy "to allow the sudden rise to preeminence on their flanks of a sensible, hard-working and widely generous king who was a hereditary enemy".[38] Their pretext was the allegations made by Eumenes. And Perseus' ambassadors, in seeking to allay Roman fears, make the same sort of thoroughly reasonable points as the Carthaginian envoys, explaining all Perseus' actions: he has done nothing wrong, broken no treaty, so why are you going to war against him, you Romans, who set such store by your respect for treaties? Just as the Romans have no valid response to the accusation that they are abusing their treaty of alliance with Carthage, so too they can find nothing to say to Perseus' ambassadors, and respond with silence, merely announcing their declaration of war. In the diplomatic stand-off before the First Mithradatic War, the Pontic envoy Pelopidas makes many of the same points as the Carthaginians and Macedonians, particularly playing on the awkward fact of the treaty of alliance between Rome and Pontus. Pelopidas highlights the insoluble dilemma faced by Rome: as friends and allies the Romans are obliged by the terms of the treaty to protect Pontus against the aggression of Nicomedes, or hold him back (*Mith*. 12.41, 14.48). As before in Macedon and Carthage, the Roman ambassadors have no answer: they had long before decided to help Nicomedes, and were only pretending to listen to Pelopidas' arguments. Yet they were shamed by Pelopidas' words and by the existence of the treaty, and for a long time did not know what to say. In the end they came up with what Appian calls "the following sophistry" (*Mith*. 14.49): "We neither want Mithridates to suffer any unpleasantness at the hands of Nicomedes, nor will we

---

36 Polybius (27.6.3) too says that Rome had long decided to go to war with Perseus when they were supposedly negotiating with Macedonian ambassadors.
37 Appian is also well aware that Mithradates was looking for a war, but that he wanted to have right on his side (*Mith*. 12.38). On Mithradates' aggression, see McGing 2009.
38 ἡ δ' ἔργῳ μὲν οὐκ ἀξιοῦσα βασιλέα σώφρονα καὶ φιλόπονον καὶ ἐς πολλοὺς φιλάνθρωπον, ἀθρόως οὕτως ἐπαιρόμενον καὶ πατρικὸν ὄντα σφίσιν ἐχθρόν, ἐν πλευραῖς ἔχειν. As Walbank 1979, 300 points out, however, Polybius, unlike Appian, did not regard Rome as responsible for the Third Macedonian War, which had been planned by Philip and inherited by Perseus.

allow war to be waged against Nicomedes. For we do not believe it is in Rome's best interests for Nicomedes to be harmed".[39]

To such narrative patterns, one might add Appian's description of Roman behaviour in their wars in Spain in the second century BCE: he has no hesitation in castigating the treachery of, for example, L. Licinius Lucullus (*Ib*. 52.218–221), Servius Sulpicius Galba (*Ib*. 59.249–60.255) or Quintus Pompeius (*Ib*. 79.338–345) and praising the Spaniards, most notably Viriathus (*Ib*. 75.317–321) and the people of Numantia (*Ib*. 97.419–423). The enemies of Rome tend to get very favourable coverage from Appian. Even Mithradates Eupator, who committed unprecedented atrocities against Romans and Italians, especially during the infamous Asian Vespers, gets a warm summary from Appian (*Mith*. 112.540–550).

If Appian had his own agenda in his account of the Third Punic War, at least many of the important seeds of his narrative are there in the slender remains of Polybius, and others implied by their presence in Diodorus: the Roman support for Massinissa, purely out of self-interest and flying in the face of justice; the secret Roman decision to wage war on Carthage without a respectable pretext; the secret decision to destroy the city; the perplexity of the Carthaginians at deliberately opaque and evasive Roman answers to their questions and at the piecemeal, climactic, Roman revelation of their intentions. What we do not really get from the fragments is the flavour of how Polybius judged all this. Which, if any, of the four Greek opinions about the destruction of Carthage expressed at 36.9 did Polybius subscribe to? There is no definite answer possible, but it is perhaps worth pointing out the uncharacteristically weak arguments Walbank makes for supporting the view that Polybius favoured the first and fourth opinions, the ones that said Rome acted completely properly in relation to Carthage and in no way immorally or unjustly.[40] His reasons were as follows. First, the chiastic arrangement of the opinions—pro-Rome one and four, anti-Rome two and three—shows he favoured one and four. This can scarcely be any firm indication at all. Second, the pro-Roman views get 36 lines, the anti-Roman views 30 lines, "a clear weighting in favour of the pro-Roman view". I would suggest this is not a clear weighting at all. Third, Polybius was with Scipio Aemilianus at Carthage, and it is unlikely that he condemned the policy that Scipio was carrying out. This is a more important point. In fact, even Appian is

---

39 μετὰ σοφίας ὧδε ἀπεκρίναντο· οὔτε Μιθριδάτην ἄν τι βουλοίμεθα πάσχειν ἄχαρι πρὸς Νικομήδους, οὔτε Νικομήδους ἀνεξόμεθα πολεμουμένου· οὐ γὰρ ἡγούμεθα Ῥωμαίοις συμφέρειν βλάπτεσθαι
Νικομήδη.
40 Walbank 1979, 663–64.

very well disposed to Scipio, while condemning Roman behaviour before the war actually started. But both Polybius and Appian in his wake can afford to be nice to Scipio, because Scipio was not the problem: he was not part of the duplicitous Roman behaviour beforehand that drove the Carthaginians to desperate resistance. He was just the Roman general arriving on the scene and doing what a Roman general was supposed to do—winning the war. Fourth, Polybius is very hostile to the men who led the opposition to Rome in Achaea, Macedonia and Carthage. Obviously this is correct in relation to Achaea, and Polybius is very negative about the Carthaginian commander Hasdrubal, but we do not have enough to say that he was ill-disposed to the Carthaginians who opposed Rome. Walbank does bring into play the comment of Polybius at 38.1 that the fate of Greece in 146 was in some ways even worse than Carthage, because at least "the Carthaginians left some ground to posterity, however slight, for defending their cause, but the Greeks gave no plausible pretext to anyone who wishes to support them and acquit them of error".

This brings us into the realm of general, overarching statements as opposed to detailed narrative. It is interesting, as I pointed out at the beginning, that Appian is usually thought of as a great admirer of Rome, and the preface of his work gives good reason to think this (e.g. *Proem* 11.43). I believe his preface owes much to Polybius' preface, which is also full of admiration for Rome. But these are very general, editorial statements, just like Polybius' grudging allowance that the Carthaginians had some small justification for fighting, and it seems to me quite possible that Appian was both a great admirer of the overall Roman imperial achievement and the contemporary Roman empire, while at the same time a severe critic of particular parts of the Roman story and Roman rule of the past. Erich Gruen has argued this distinction between general opinion and specific detail for Polybius and Josephus, and is prepared to see both of them as much more hostile to Rome than others have argued.[41] Appian stands in a very similar relationship to Polybius as Josephus, and is unhesitatingly critical of Rome at times, in much the same way as Josephus. The question I posed earlier is, does Appian's hostile interpretation of Rome's behaviour with regard to the Third Punic War mirror Polybius? My answer is that in Appian there may well be different emphases, and details elaborated differently, to illustrate particular

---

41 Gruen 2013, 258–65.

concerns of his, but there is enough to suggest that they are merely developments of the hostile account he found in Polybius.⁴²

Bibliography

Baronowski, D.W. (1995), "Polybius on the Causes of the Third Punic War", in: *CPh* 90, 16–31.
— — (2011), *Polybius and Roman Imperialism*, Bristol.
Brodersen, K. (1993), "Appian und sein Werk", in: *ANRW* II 34.1, 339–363.
Bucher, G.S. (2005), "Fictive Elements in Appian's Pharsalus Narrative", in: *Phoenix* 59, 50–76.
— — (2000), "The Origins, Program, and Composition of Appian's *Roman History*", in: *TAPhA* 130, 411–458.
Cowan, E. (2015), "Deceit in Appian", in: K. Welch (ed.), 185–203.
Gibson, B./T. Harrison (eds.) (2013), *Polybius and his World. Essays in Memory of F.W. Walbank*, Oxford.
Goldmann, B. (1988), *Einheitlichkeit und Eigenständigkeit der Historia Roman des Appian*, Hildesheim.
Gruen, E.S. (2013), "Polybius and Josephus on Rome", in: B. Gibson/T. Harrison (eds.), 255–265.
McGing, B.C. (1993), "Appian's *Mithridateios*", in: *ANRW* II 34.1, 496–522.
— — (2009), "Mithridates VI Eupator: Victim or Aggressor?", in: J.M. Hojte (ed.), *Mithridates VI and the Pontic Kingdom*, Aarhus, 203–216.
— — (2010), *Polybius' Histories*, Oxford.
Rich, J. (2015), "Appian, Polybius and the Romans' War with Antiochus the Great: A Study of Appian's Sources and Methods", in: K. Welch (ed.), 65–123.
Schwartz, E. (1896), "Appianus" (No.2), in: *RE* 2, 1.216–237.
Thornton, J. (2013), "Polybius in Context: The Political Dimension of the *Histories*", in: B. Gibson/T. Harrison (eds.), 213–229.
Walbank, F.W. (1979), *A Historical Commentary on Polybius*, Vol. 3, Oxford.
Welch, K. (ed.) (2015), *Appian's Roman History. Empire and Civil War*, Swansea.
— — (2015a), "Appian and the Roman History: A Reappraisal", in: K. Welch (ed.), 1–13.
— — (2015b), "Programme and Narrative in Civil Wars 2.118–4.138", in: K. Welch (ed.), 277–304.
Westall, R. (2015), "The Sources for the *Civil Wars* of Appian of Alexandria", in: K. Welch (ed.), 125–167.

---

42 To some extent my conclusion echoes that of Welch 2015b, whose study of Appian's coverage of the period after the assassination of Julius Caesar argues, among much else, that Appian inherited at least some of his attitudes from his sources.

Dennis Pausch
Lost in Reception? Polybius' Paradoxical Impact on Writing History in Republican Rome

1 Introduction: Polybius in Rome

Polybius would not have liked a sword and sandal movie about Hannibal nor an "infotainment" production on his crossing of the Alps. This at least is the impression the author wants his reader to get from his *Histories*.[1] The Hellenistic equivalents to these modern devices of making history popular and comprehensible to a larger audience come easily to mind. Polybius' narrator does, in fact, distance himself many times from the ways of writing history that have been collectively branded as tragic or rhetorical or with whichever other label one may prefer.[2] This will have been obvious to his Roman readers as well. Thus, it comes as no surprise that after his involuntary stay in Rome as an exile in the middle of the second century BCE[3] Roman historians are influenced by his promotion of a more serious, more "scientific" way to reconstruct the past. Yet, precisely at the same time, authors of historiographical works at Rome also commit themselves to a more literary, a more entertaining, a more reader-friendly way of writing history.

Admittedly, the reason for these parallel-but-opposing developments could also be explained, at least in part, by the simultaneous influence of Greek historians other than Polybius on Roman writers. But I think it plausible that Polybius with his detailed and emphatic description of the "dos and don'ts" in writing history properly not only had the effect which he intended on his Roman contempo-

---

1 It is very pleasant to recall those days at Thessaloniki, especially with regard to the warm atmosphere of the conference itself, for which I would like to thank Nikos Miltsios above all. I feel obliged, however, also to all participants of the discussion and among them particularly to Nicolas Wiater, who also afterwards did his very best to prevent me from many mistakes and to improve my English.
2 On the long-lasting debate, if these labels are suitable to describe the developments Hellenistic historiography, see e.g. Walbank 1960, Marincola 2003, Rutherford 2007, Chaniotis 2013 and Parmeggiani 2014.
3 On his detention from a historical point of view, see now Erskine 2012; on his famous acquaintance with Scipio Aemilianus, see Sommer 2013.

https://doi.org/10.1515/9783110584844-018

raries, but also the paradoxical impact of opening their eyes for other recent evolutions of how to represent the past. In fact, the negative examples which Polybius cites as warnings might have been as influential as the positive precepts he gives to the historians who are willing to learn from him. No less important might have been the circumstance that Polybius—as has been noted by many of his readers—does not always seem to practise what he preaches, but appears to offer against his own doctrine more than a few samples of highly dramatic and truly entertaining passages using rhetorical devices and all the other techniques that he excluded from his ideal conception of historiography. To be sure, recent research has convincingly argued that this contradiction between theory and practice in Polybius appears as the result of a superficial reading to a large degree, and that it can be resolved by adopting a more refined interpretative approach.[4] Nevertheless, the *prima facie* impression that there is one Polybius who talks about writing history and another who actually does it, surely was an important way of reading his work.

Both directions of his impact on Roman historical writing are, in my reading at least, nicely illustrated in Livy's *ab urbe condita*,[5] a work whose relationship with Polybius' *Histories* has often been discussed.[6] My aim in this chapter, by contrast, is to go one step back and look at the Roman historians from the middle of the second to the middle of the first centuries BCE, who are both Livy's predecessors and Polybius' more or less immediate successors. How did they react to the "push for modernisation" brought into the historical scene at Rome by the exile from Megalopolis? The main problem with this approach is, of course, that contrary to Livy's *magnum opus*, a large part of which survives today, the works of the earlier historians are lost except for individual fragments. These invaluable "snippets" of the historians from the time of the Roman Republic have garnered considerable attention over last two decades and have been edited, translated

---

[4] See e.g. McGing 2010, 71–75, Marincola 2013, Grethlein 2013, 224–267, esp. 249–263, and now Wiater 2017, esp. 210–212, who argues that these "sensational" passages are themselves designed to encourage the reader to reflect on the dangerous power of emotions that drives the historian agents and, thus, cause a rational distance to the events, rather than emotional involvement as Polybius regards it as typical of "tragic" historians.

[5] See Pausch 2011, 46–74 (with further references).

[6] The whole affair has been set on a new basis by the arguments put forward by David Levene that Livy uses Polybius not only as his source, but also establishes an intertextual dialogue with his Greek predecessor (see Levene 2010, esp. 126–163); for more traditional approaches, see now e.g. Briscoe 2013a and Halfmann 2013.

and commented upon respectively in French,[7] German[8] and most recently in English.[9] In most cases, however, they are simply too short to provide much significant insight into their narrative technique. This is one of the reasons why Polybius' influence on the historical method of his Roman contemporaries—in contrast to his impact as a source[10]—is rarely studied on a broader basis and with regard to more than one author.[11]

Yet some observations are possible, most notably, as I will argue in this chapter, regarding the individual historian's choice of a particular subgenre (*i.e.* universal history or historical monograph), the relation between reason and emotion in the explanation of events, and the use of speeches as a tool of the didactic function of historical writing. But before starting with the Roman fragments, I will have a quick look back at some passages in Polybius' *Histories* that were all but bound to have the aforementioned paradoxical impact on Roman writers.

2 Polybius' precepts and their possible side effects

How to cross the Alps properly and other advice

Before describing the actual crossing of the mountains, Polybius uses Hannibal's crossing of the Alps for one his longer statements on how and how not to write history:

> ἔνιοι δὲ τῶν γεγραφότων περὶ τῆς ὑπερβολῆς ταύτης, βουλόμενοι τοὺς ἀναγινώσκοντας ἐκπλήττειν τῇ περὶ τῶν προειρημένων τόπων παραδοξολογίᾳ, λανθάνουσιν ἐμπίπτοντες εἰς δύο τὰ πάσης ἱστορίας ἀλλοτριώτατα· καὶ γὰρ ψευδολογεῖν καὶ μαχόμενα γράφειν αὑτοῖς ἀναγκάζονται. ἅμα μὲν γὰρ τὸν Ἀννίβαν ἀμίμητόν τινα παρεισάγοντες στρατηγὸν καὶ τόλμῃ καὶ προνοίᾳ τοῦτον ὁμολογουμένως ἀποδεικνύουσιν ἡμῖν ἀλογιστότατον, ἅμα δὲ καταστροφὴν οὐ δυνάμενοι λαμβάνειν οὐδ' ἔξοδον τοῦ ψεύδους θεοὺς καὶ θεῶν παῖδας εἰς πραγματικὴν ἱστορίαν παρεισάγουσιν. ὑποθέμενοι γὰρ τὰς ἐρυμνότητας καὶ τραχύτητας

---

7 See Chassignet 1996–2004.
8 See Beck/Walter 2001–2004 (= *FRH*).
9 See Cornell 2013a (= *FRHist*).
10 A recent and detailed overview of this vast topic is provided by the entries under the heading "Polybius" in the *index rerum* of the *Fragments of the Roman Historians* (*FRHist*): see Cornell 2013, Vol. III, 749.
11 See, however, Ziegler 1952, 1572–74, and Davidson 2009. For the particular impact Polybius had on Roman historians in terms of the choice of titles for their works, see now Krebs 2015.

τῶν Ἀλπεινῶν ὀρῶν τοιαύτας ὥστε μὴ οἷον ἵππους καὶ στρατόπεδα, σὺν δὲ τούτοις ἐλέφαντας, ἀλλὰ μηδὲ πεζοὺς εὐζώνους εὐχερῶς ἂν διελθεῖν, ὁμοίως δὲ καὶ τὴν ἔρημον τοιαύτην τινὰ περὶ τοὺς τόπους ὑπογράψαντες ἡμῖν ὥστ', εἰ μὴ θεὸς ἤ τις ἥρως ἀπαντήσας τοῖς περὶ τὸν Ἀννίβαν ὑπέδειξε τὰς ὁδούς, ἐξαπορήσαντας ἂν καταφθαρῆναι πάντας, ὁμολογουμένως ἐκ τούτων εἰς ἑκάτερον τῶν προειρημένων ἁμαρτημάτων ἐμπίπτουσι. ... [48.8] ἐξ ὧν εἰκότως ἐμπίπτουσιν εἰς τὸ παραπλήσιον τοῖς τραγῳδιογράφοις. καὶ γὰρ ἐκείνοις πᾶσιν αἱ καταστροφαὶ τῶν δραμάτων προσδέονται θεοῦ καὶ μηχανῆς διὰ τὸ τὰς πρώτας ὑποθέσεις ψευδεῖς καὶ παραλόγους λαμβάνειν, τούς τε συγγραφέας ἀνάγκη τὸ παραπλήσιον πάσχειν καὶ ποιεῖν ἥρωάς τε καὶ θεοὺς ἐπιφαινομένους, ἐπειδὰν τὰς ἀρχὰς ἀπιθάνους καὶ ψευδεῖς ὑποστήσωνται. πῶς γὰρ οἷόν τε παραλόγοις ἀρχαῖς εὔλογον ἐπιθεῖναι τέλος; Ἀννίβας γε μὴν οὐχ ὡς οὗτοι γράφουσιν, λίαν δὲ περὶ ταῦτα πραγματικῶς ἐχρῆτο ταῖς ἐπιβολαῖς. καὶ γὰρ τὴν τῆς χώρας ἀρετήν, εἰς ἣν ἐπεβάλετο καθιέναι, καὶ τὴν τῶν ὄχλων ἀλλοτριότητα πρὸς Ῥωμαίους ἐξητάκει σαφῶς, εἴς τε τὰς μεταξὺ δυσχωρίας ὁδηγοῖς καὶ καθηγεμόσιν ἐγχωρίοις ἐχρῆτο τοῖς τῶν αὐτῶν ἐλπίδων μέλλουσι κοινωνεῖν. ἡμεῖς δὲ περὶ τούτων εὐθαρσῶς ἀποφαινόμεθα διὰ τὸ περὶ τῶν πράξεων παρ' αὐτῶν ἱστορηκέναι τῶν παρατετευχότων τοῖς καιροῖς, τοὺς δὲ τόπους κατωπτευκέναι καὶ τῇ διὰ τῶν Ἄλπεων αὐτοὶ κεχρῆσθαι πορείᾳ γνώσεως ἕνεκα καὶ θέας.

Some of the writers who have described this passage of the Alps, from the wish to impress their readers by the marvels they recount of these mountains, are betrayed into two vices ever most alien to true history; for they are compelled to make both false statements and statements which contradict each other. While on the one hand introducing Hannibal as a commander of unequalled courage and foresight, they incontestably represent him to us as entirely wanting in prudence, and again, being unable to bring their series of falsehoods to any close or issue they introduce gods and the sons of gods into the sober history of facts. By representing the Alps as being so steep and rugged that not only horses and troops accompanied by elephants, but even active men on foot would have difficulty in passing, and at the same time picturing to us the desolation of the country as being such, that unless some god or hero had met Hannibal and showed him the way, his whole army would have gone astray and perished utterly, they unquestionably fall into both the above vices. ... [48.8] The natural consequence is that they get into the same difficulties as tragic dramatists all of whom, to bring their dramas to a close, require a *deus ex machina*, as the data they choose on which to found their plots are false and contrary to reasonable probability. These writers are necessarily in the same strait and invent apparitions of heroes and gods, since the beginnings on which they build are false and improbable; for how is it possible to finish conformably to reason what has been begun in defiance of it? Of course Hannibal did not act as these writers describe, but conducted his plans with sound practical sense. He had ascertained by careful inquiry the richness of the country into which he proposed to descend and the aversion of the people to the Romans, and for the difficulties of the route he employed as guides and pioneers natives of the country, who were about to take part in his adventure. On these points I can speak with some confidence as I have inquired about the circumstances from men present on the occasion and have personally inspected the country and made the passage of the Alps to learn for myself and see.[12]

This notorious attack against some of his predecessors is, of course, one-sided and surely overstated, as polemic tends to be both in general and no less a part of Polybius' strategy to claim authority as a historian.[13] Nevertheless, his main point about the adverse consequences of writing history in a dramatic manner becomes unmistakably apparent here and is further supported by several similar passages that criticize the use of literary devices in a historiographical narrative proper.[14] All of these verdicts, however, not only bring across the negative message intended by their author, but also inform his readers about exactly the recent developments in historical narrative that Polybius rejects and, thus, help to promote indirectly the whole variety of contemporary historical writing in Rome. Most of these approaches, of course, have not passed unnoticed by earlier Roman historians. During the following decades, however, the adoption of these ideas seems to have been intensified (at least this is suggested by the surviving fragments).

That one ought to read Polybius' verdicts against the grain, so to say, is suggested by two features of the *Histories*. On the one hand, as mentioned above, the Polybian narrator seems to contradict his own methodological precepts repeatedly in the narrative portions of his work. This is the case even in the actual description of the crossing of the Alps immediately following the passage cited above, for example, when he remarks that the Allobroges would have defeated Hannibal, if they only had managed to keep their intentions secret, and is thus using a typical technique to create suspense in an historiographical text.[15] On the other hand, Polybius is not everywhere as strict in his verdicts as he is here.[16] On the contrary, his ideal conception of πραγματικὴ ἱστορία,[17] for all its focus on util-

---

12 Cf. Plb. 3.47.6–9 and 48.8–12. The Greek text—here as well as in the following—depends on Büttner-Wobst (1882-1904), the translation is by Paton et al. 2010.
13 See Marincola 1997, esp. 229–32, and Dreyer 2011, 123–31.
14 See e.g. Meister 1975, 109–26; Schepens 2005; Marincola 2013 and Grethlein 2013, 245–48, Wiater 2017 (all of them including in their general discussion of the issue many of the relevant passages).
15 See Plb. 3.50.4 with Maier 2012, 109–10.
16 See e.g. Plb. 1.4.11; 3.31.12–13; 3.57.7–9 and 16.17.9–11. His methodological statements as a whole are discussed by Dreyer 2011, 69–120, and Miltsios 2013, 113–32.
17 See e.g. Walbank 1993 and Marincola 2001, esp. 121f.

ity (τὸ χρήσιμον) in the tradition of Thucydides, does in fact incorporate the pleasure of the reader (τὸ τερπνόν) as a "modern" or Hellenistic element as well.[18] Once again, recent research has shown that this seeming conflict can be resolved and, thus, that for Polybius himself no such contradiction existed at all.[19]

Despite his general preference of utility, therefore, some of his statements— and especially when read separately—leave room for a re-evaluation and thus for an increased consideration of the entertainment of the reader, too. A good example is provided by the thoughts he exposes in Book 38, when he tries to justify his use of an annalistic layout in the larger part of his work. In doing so, he aims above all at defending this decision against the criticism that this would lead to too much disorder in the narration and disruption on part of the reader:

ἐμοὶ δ' οὐχ οὕτως δοκεῖ, τὸ δ' ἐναντίον. μάρτυρα δὲ τούτων ἐπικαλεσαίμην ἂν αὐτὴν τὴν φύσιν, ἥτις κατ' οὐδ' ὁποίαν τῶν αἰσθήσεων εὐδοκεῖ τοῖς αὐτοῖς ἐπιμένειν κατὰ τὸ συνεχές, ἀλλ' ἀεὶ μεταβολῆς ἐστιν οἰκεία, τοῖς δ' αὐτοῖς ἐγκυρεῖν ἐκ διαστήματος βούλεται καὶ διαφορᾶς. εἴη δ' ἂν τὸ λεγόμενον ἐναργὲς πρῶτον μὲν ἐκ τῆς ἀκοῆς, ἥτις οὔτε κατὰ τὰς μελῳδίας οὔτε κατὰ τὰς λεκτικὰς ὑποκρίσεις εὐδοκεῖ συνεχῶς ταῖς αὐταῖς ἐπιμένειν στάσεσιν, ὁ δὲ μεταβολικὸς τρόπος καὶ καθόλου πᾶν τὸ διερριμμένον καὶ μεγίστας ἔχον ἀλλαγὰς καὶ πυκνοτάτας αὐτὴν κινεῖ. παραπλησίως καὶ τὴν γεῦσιν εὕροι τις ἂν οὐδὲ τοῖς πολυτελεστάτοις βρώμασιν ἐπιμένειν δυναμένην, ἀλλὰ σικχαίνουσαν καὶ χαίρουσαν ταῖς μεταβολαῖς καὶ προσηνεστέρως ἀποδεχομένην πολλάκις καὶ τὰ λιτὰ τῶν ἐδεσμάτων ἢ τὰ πολυτελῆ διὰ τὸν ξενισμόν. τὸ δ' αὐτὸ καὶ περὶ τὴν ὅρασιν ἴδοι τις ἂν γινόμενον· ἥκιστα γὰρ δύναται πρὸς ἓν μένειν ἀτενίζουσα, κινεῖ δ' αὐτὴν ἡ ποικιλία καὶ μεταβολὴ τῶν ὁρωμένων. μάλιστα δὲ περὶ τὴν ψυχὴν τοῦτό τις ἂν ἴδοι συμβαῖνον· αἱ γὰρ μεταλήψεις τῶν ἀτενισμῶν καὶ τῶν ἐπιστάσεων οἷον ἀναπαύσεις εἰσὶ τοῖς φιλοπόνοις τῶν ἀνδρῶν.

My opinion is just the reverse of this; and I would appeal to the testimony of Nature herself, who in the case of any of the senses never elects to go on persistently with the same allurements, but is ever fond of change and desires to meet with the same things after an interval and a difference. What I mean may be illustrated in the first place from the sense of hearing, which never either as regards melodies or recitation readily consents to give ear persistently to the same strain, but is touched by a diversified style and by everything that is disconnected and marked by abrupt and frequent transitions. Take again the sense of taste. You will find that it is incapable of constantly enjoying the most luxurious viands but becomes

---

[18] For Polybius' position in regard to the historiographic theory in Hellenistic times, see e.g. Walbank 1990.
[19] See e.g. Marincola 2001, 126–28, and Wiater 2017, 205–09, esp. 207: "The alternative is not, then, between true and useful, but unexciting, and entertaining, but invented and, hence, useless, narratives. Polybius' point is, rather, that a true narrative offers as much pleasure as an invented one, even though, unlike its 'tragic' counterpart, it has not been specifically designed to please, and *also* enables successful action in the present. Polybius is redefining truth as an aesthetic phenomenon".

disgusted with them and likes change, often preferring quite simple dishes to expensive ones merely owing to their novelty. And the same holds good as regards the sense of sight. For it is quite incapable of gazing constantly at one object, but requires variety and change to captivate it. But this is especially true as regards the intellect. For hard workers find a sort of rest in change of the subjects which absorb and interest them.[20]

The number of relevant passages could easily be increased, but I think that what I aim to show has become apparent: it must have been possible to understand Polybius' precepts of how to write history not only in the way he intended, but also to read between their lines and thereby use them as a window, as it were, into the latest developments in Hellenistic literary trends.[21] His influence, therefore, can be seen in the intensification of the theoretical debates on the proper writing of history that can be observed in Rome from the second half of second century BCE onwards.[22] In the remainder of this chapter, I will demonstrate this paradoxical influence of Polybius' methodological remarks on Roman historians by discussing their choices pertaining to the design and function of their works. In doing so, I will not take into consideration Cato the Elder and his *Origines*. Admittedly, we know that he met Polybius personally at least once and thus it cannot be excluded that they exchanged their views on historiography, too.[23] Yet, as was argued, for example, by James Davidson, it is not likely that Cato was influenced by the Greek detainee to a larger degree.[24]

---

[20] Cf. Plb. 38.5.4–9 (Translation by Paton 1995 [1927]); see further e.g. Meister 1975, 77–80, Sacks 1981, 114f., Levene 2010, 2f., and Miltsios 2013, 62f.
[21] See e.g. Marincola 2003, 293–302, and Pausch 2011, 49–52.
[22] See e.g. Ziegler 1952, 1572: "Without doubt, the *Histories* of Polybius, the friend and confidant of the leading men of the empire, had been acknowledged to be important already during his lifetime—at least among his closer circle, whose members surely knew the work, eagerly read and discussed it and criticised it disparagingly at times, as is shown by several passages that sound apologetic—and was ranked among the classics of historiography soon afterwards and until the end of antiquity. It will have been part of the liberal education to know him. That is not to say, of course, that everyone will have studied the big work—which must have comprised, judged by the length the remaining five books, much more than 4000 pages of a Teubner-edition—in its entirety".
[23] For a plausible reconstruction of such discussions, see e.g. *FRHist* 5 M. Porcius Cato F148, Vol. III, S. 157f.
[24] Cf. Davidson 2009, 127–128: "… a number of parallels in the content of the two œuvres have been adduced and it is rather more likely that the influence went from the older Roman to the younger Greek, from the more finished to the less finished text, than the other way round".

The choice of the subgenre: universal history vs. monographs

One important issue in the theoretical debate in Rome on how to write history intensified by Polybius was the choice of the appropriate subgenre or—to put it the other way around—the appropriate period of the past to deal with. Polybius, of course, insisted on the greater usefulness of universal history, namely in his methodological remarks.[25] Yet, once more, his own work can be read against him. By designing his first two books as a prehistory to the main topic, he followed Thucydides closely and, thus, repeated the classical example of a monograph focused on one distinct period. Both ways of writing history will be embraced by Roman historians during the following decades.

To be sure, they regarded universal history as the default mode of writing about the past anyway, not least since chronological completeness formed an integral part of the traditional annalistic layout. Nevertheless, Polybius' promotion of the idea that the historical events of the whole *oecumene* are interwoven since the Second Roman-Carthaginian War and that the events of and after this period should be presented in this way apparently resulted in an enhanced interest in foreign affairs on the part of Roman historians.[26] This seems to have been the case not least for those authors who continued to write in the annalist tradition, so that even Claudius Quadrigarius, Valerius Antias, Licinius Macer and Aelius Tubero, who have often been criticised for clinging to an old-fashioned model (or even for returning to it against contemporary tendencies)[27] could claim to follow Polybius' example in this as well as in other regards, in particular in the increased room they made for contemporary, especially political and military, history).[28]

Given the fact that the universal approach to history was deeply rooted in Roman tradition, it is even more surprising that despite Polybius' work Roman historians started to write the first historical monographs as well. One could even go so far as to say that the monograph with a focus on political and military events advanced to being the pinnacle of modern historical writing in Rome during the following decades. This might have been the case right up to the middle of the first century BCE, when with Sallust's *The Conspiracy of Catiline* and *The War against Jugurtha* respectively, two prime examples of this genre, were written.

---

[25] Cf. esp. Plb. 3.32.1–3 and further 1.4.7–11; 5.33.1–8; 8.3–4; 8.13; 29.12; for recent discussions, see e.g. Rood 2007, Pitcher 2009, 116–17, Dreyer 2011, 91–92, and Kloft 2013.
[26] See. Plb. 1.3.3–6; 4.28; 15,24a and 38,5–6.
[27] For a re-evaluation of their decision as well-conceived choice, see Timpe 1979, 101, and Walter 2003, 143–47.
[28] See e.g. Timpe 1979, 99–102, and Walter 2003, 143–55.

Shortly afterwards, Livy was to change the trend again by returning successfully to the fully fledged annalistic layout. The first Roman author, however, who is known to have written a work in this (at the time) new and fashionable genre is L. Coelius Antipater.[29] Around 120–110 BCE, he chose the most obvious and most suitable period of the entire Roman history for a work of this kind, namely the war against Hannibal. This event he described in seven books of which roughly sixty fragments survive.[30] We will come across him and his work, probably called *Histories* or *Bellum Punicum*, repeatedly in the following sections, since he is a paramount example of a Roman historian who is influenced by Polybius in both ways: He claimed to be more "scientific" than his predecessors and to have used only the works of those historians who could be regarded as truthful,[31] yet in his narrative portions he apparently also was more "literarily inclined" than previous writers.

At his point, however, we will take a quick look at some of the other authors who seem to have envisaged themselves as part of the *avant-garde* of history-writing in Rome: Sempronius Asellio, Cornelius Sisenna and, once more, Sallust, albeit now with regard to the other side of his oeuvre, the *Histories*. The format which they preferred was neither universal history nor the historical monograph in the strict sense, but a detailed, year-by-year account with a focus on contemporary political and military events. They usually wrote about a period they had witnessed themselves and, to some degree, even contributed to shaping as office-holders. Moreover, they adopted the habit of continuing the works of their predecessors, thus creating a collaborative description of Roman history from roughly 130 to 67 BCE,[32] that is, to the presumed ending of Sallust's unfinished *Histories*.[33] Sempronius Asellio's starting point might even have been the year 146 BCE; his entire historical project might then have been designed as a sequel to

---

29 Little is known about the author and his background. He seems to have been a member of the Roman nobility, but apparently held no offices. For recent discussions of his life and work, see e.g. Mutschler 2000, 118–21; Kierdorf 2003, 35–38; Beck/Walter 2004, 35–39; Briscoe 2013b.
30 They amount to 67 (= *FRH*) or 65 (= *FRHist*; including three marked as doubtful); their attribution to his work is largely uncontroversial, even if some of them, inevitably, give rise to discussion.
31 See *FRHist* 15 F 62 / *FRH* 11 F 1 (= Prisc. *GL* 2, p. 383): *ex scriptis eorum, qui veri arbitrantur* ("... from the writings of those who are regarded as truthful ..." [Transl. Briscoe 2013b]).
32 On the general habit of historians to continue the work of a predecessor, see Marincola 1997, 237–41.
33 For a recent edition of Sallust' *Histories*, see now La Penna/Funari 2015.

Polybius' *Histories*.[34] To be sure, this is nothing more than a reasonable surmise based primarily on the fact that both men are likely to have met at least once, namely in the entourage of Scipio Aemilianus during the siege of Numantia (133 BCE).[35] More important to the present argument, however, is the fact that the surviving fragments of their works seem to share the same combination of different influences that appears to be characteristic also of the narrative of Coelius Antipater. So let us now examine these literary techniques in the following section.

The explanation of events: reasons vs. emotions

We will start with another, admittedly rather wide-ranging question: how did these historians view the relation between reasons and emotions in their explanation of past events? This is a particularly good place to start as the most obviously "Polybian" statement is found in none other than Sempronius Asellio and is quoted by Aulus Gellius in his *Attic Nights*, a miscellany work written around the middle of second century CE:

> [F 1 = Gell. 5.18.8] "verum inter eos", inquit, "qui annales relinquere voluissent, et eos, qui res gestas a Romanis perscribere conati essent, omnium rerum hoc interfuit: annales libri tantummodo, quod factum quoque anno gestum sit, ea demonstrabat, id est quasi qui diarium scribunt, quam Graeci ἐφημερίδα vocant. nobis non modo satis esse video, quod factum esset, id pronuntiare, sed etiam, quo consilio quaeque ratione gesta essent, demonstrare".

> [F 2 = Gell. 5.18.9] paulo post idem Asellio in eodem libro: "namque neque alacriores", inquit, "ad rempublicam defendundam neque segniores ad rem perperam faciundam annales libri commovere quicquam possunt. scribere autem bellum initum quo consule et quo confectum sit, et quis triumphans introierit ex eo, quae<que> in bello gesta sint non praedicare aut interea quid senatus decreverit aut quae lex rogatiove lata sit, neque quibus consiliis ea gesta sint iterare, id fabulis pueris est narrare, non historias scribere".

[F 1 = Gell. 5.18.8] But between the sort of writer, he says, who wished to leave behind annals and the sort who tried to write a thorough account of the things accomplished by the Romans, there was above all the following difference: books of annals showed only what was

---

34 For arguments in favour of this assumption, see e.g. Gotter et al. 2003, 33, but the *communis opinio* opts for a more sceptical view e.g. Beck/Walter 2004, 84 (n. 4), Pobjoy 2013, 276.
35 Cf. FRHist 20 T 2 (= Gell. 2.13.3): is Asellio sub P. Scipione Africano tribunus militum ad Numantiam fuit resque eas, quibus gerendis ipse interfuit, conscripsit ("That Asellio was tribune of the soldiers under Publius Scipio Africanus at Numantia, and wrote an account of those affairs in which he himself participated" [Transl. Pobjoy 2013]); see e.g. Davidson 2009, 128, Pobjoy 2013, 276, Krebs 2015, 503f.

done and in which year it was accomplished—in other words, in the manner of those who write a journal, which the Greeks call an "ephemeris". For me, I do not see it as satisfactory simply to announce what was done: it is necessary also to show with what purpose and according to what plan things were accomplished.

[F 2 = Gell. 5.18.9] A little later in the same book Asellio continues: for books of annals cannot do anything to make people more keen to defend the commonwealth or less ready to do something wrong. And indeed, to write in whose consulship a war was undertaken and in whose it was ended, and who entered the city in triumph thereafter, <and> not to declare what was accomplished in the war, and meanwhile what the senate decreed or what law or bill was put forward, nor to recount with what purposes those things were accomplished, is to tell stories to children, not to write histories.[36]

Although Sempronius Asellio does not mention Polybius by name here or anywhere in the remaining fragments of his work, written, presumably, during the first decades of the first century BCE, many readers have noticed that this passage follows closely the ideas expounded by the Greek writer.[37] Even more than the concept of πραγματικὴ ἱστορία which usually comes to mind first, these remarks fit very well with Polybius' programmatic adoption of the concept of ἀποδεικτικὴ ἱστορία with clear focus on a rational explanation of past events.[38] One might even argue that Sempronius has not only adopted the content from his Greek predecessor, but also the polemical tone that is so characteristic of Polybius' confrontational presentation of his work and method.[39] A closer analysis of this much-discussed text, however, has revealed that it is more likely directed against the Roman annalistic tradition (or, more precisely, a simplified concept of it) rather than offering a clear commitment to a specific new way of writing history.[40] Therefore, it seems probable that Asellio, too, integrated a large range of different influences in his narrative, rather than simply adopting Polybius' principles of

---

36 *FRHist* 20 F 1–2 / *FRH* 12 F 1–2 (= Gell. 5.18.8–9). The translation is the one of Pobjoy 2013. For a number of suggestions to improve the reading of the Latin text, see Woodman 2015, 29–37.
37 E.g. Davidson 2009, 128: "… whose opening statements of principle, with their focus on explaining causes rather than merely recording events, have been universally seen as both assuredly Polybian in character—'wie eine Übersetzung'—and as a watershed in Roman historiography, the Greek guest the catalyst, according to his narrative, for a decisive transformation in the character of the histories written by his host"; Pobjoy 2013, 276, Woodman 2015, 32. See also now the detailed discussion by Krebs 2015, esp. 507–515 (with further references).
38 See esp. Plb. 1.1.5; 2.1.1–2; 3.1.3–5; 3.4.4–8; 3.20.5; 11.19a and 12.25b.
39 See Krebs 2015, 504.
40 For the problems related to the terminology of *annales* and other titles of works of historiography used here, see esp. Verbrugghe 1989 and Scholz 1994, but now also the engaged reading by Krebs 2015, who argues for a programmatic use of the title *res gestae* by Asellio.

historical method and writing.⁴¹ Unfortunately, we cannot go beyond speculation on this point since most of the fifteen fragments that have survived of his work are too short to allow any in-depth analysis.

The evidence is better, however, for the work of Asellio's younger contemporary L. Cornelius Sisenna, who was praetor in 78 BCE⁴² and probably wrote his *Histories* during the following years. It is likely that Sisenna started his work exactly where Asellio's ended (probably due to his death), namely in 91 BCE.⁴³ Admittedly, it is not necessarily the case that Sisenna, by continuing Asellio's account, intended to present himself as the elder historian's successor also in terms of style and method.⁴⁴ But given that Sallust, in turn, continued Sisenna in style and method,⁴⁵ it might be surmised that the *historia continua* written by these three authors did, in fact, share some fundamental ideas of how to narrate the past.⁴⁶ Sallust, however, would lead us beyond the scope of the present discussion, so we will focus on Sisenna for now.

Regarding Sisenna, Cicero, in the proem of his dialogue *de legibus* (ca. 52 BCE), has Atticus remark that of all Greek historians Sisenna seemed to have read only Cleitarchus and, as a consequence, wrote in same "childish" manner (*puerile quiddam*).⁴⁷ This harsh critique of Sisenna's narrative technique as lacking in seriousness and being—in a way—akin to the novel, is at odds with the much

---

41 For good observations on some of the longer fragments, see e.g. Woodman 2015, 37–39; for the seamless integration of non-Polybian elements in Asellio's work, see also Krebs 2015, 510f.
42 See *FRHist* F 26 T 1 (= *ILLRP* 513 = *CIL* 12.2.589).
43 For this conclusion, see Rawson 1979, esp. 331.335, see further e.g. Krebs 2015, 519, and Briscoe 2013c, 308.
44 For this general caveat, see Marincola 1997, 238–40. On continuations among Greek historians, see further Mehl 2013.
45 Most prominently, both of them had a tendency for archaizing style; see Rawson 1979, 342–45.
46 So, for instance, both of them seem to have had a tendency to archaisation: see Rawson 1979, 342–45.
47 See *FRHist* 26 T 6 (= Cic. leg. 1.7): is tamen neque orator in numero vestro umquam est habitus, et in historia puerile quiddam consectatur, ut unum Clitarchum neque praeterea quemquam de Graecis legisse videatur, eum tamen velle dumtaxat imitari: quem si adsequi posset, aliquantum ab optumo tamen abesset. quare tuum est munus hoc, a te exspectatur; nisi quid Quinto videtur secus ("But he has never been regarded as an orator in your [sc. Cicero's] class, and in historiography his aim is something immature, so that he seems to have read Clitarchus and no other Greek historian, and to have no other wish than to imitate him; and even were he able to emulate him, he would still be some distance from what is best" [Transl. Briscoe 2013c]).

more positive judgement on Sisenna's skills as a historian expressed by both Cicero[48] himself and other authors.[49] This contradiction can be explained quite convincingly by the observation that Cicero's surveys of Latin historiography before him are all highly idiosyncratic and obviously aimed not least at paving the way for his own work in this field (even though the latter remained unrealized).[50] The two different views about Sisenna's work by Atticus and Cicero, respectively, do suggest, in any case, that Sisenna was not only a "critical" historian in the Polybian fashion, but also incorporated entertaining elements into his work. This impression is confirmed up to a point by a closer look at the almost 150 fragments of Sisenna's *Histories*, despite the fact that most of them are cited by grammarians in search of pre-classical words alone and thus are often too short to allow any inferences about his narrative technique.

Particularly relevant to the present discussion is yet another passage in Cicero. It comes from the first book of his dialogue *de divinatione* (45/44 BCE), and thus is put into the mouth of his brother Quintus. Quintus, after stating that Sisenna was sceptical about the reliability of dreams of historical figures,[51] observes that he had failed to apply the same methodological principle to other supernatural phenomena:

> idem contra ostenta nihil disputant, exponitque initio belli Marsici et deorum simulacra sudavisse, et sanguinem fluxisse, et discessisse caelum, et ex occulto auditas esse voces, quae pericula belli nuntiarent, et Lanuvii clipeos—quod haruspicibus tristissumum visum esset—a muribus esse derosos.

> The same man makes no arguments against prodigies, and narrates that at the beginning of the Marsic War the images of the gods sweated, and blood flowed, and sky split apart, and voices announcing the dangers of war were heard coming from a hidden place, and at Lanuvium shields were gnawed away by mice—this the soothsayers regarded as the grimmest omen.[52]

Sisenna's inconsistency in dealing with different forms of prodigies that attracted Cicero's attention here can be seen against the larger background of the dichot-

---

48 See e.g. *FRHist* 26 T 7 (= Cic. *Brut.* 228) together with Rawson 1979, 339f., and Beck/Walter 2004, 242f.
49 So, for instance, Varro named his theoretical work on historiography after him; regrettably the title *Sisenna vel de historia* is the only thing surviving: see *FRHist* 26 T 18 (= Gell. 16.9.5).
50 This applies also to his remarks in *de oratore* (cf. Cic. *de orat.* 2.51–52); see esp. Beck/Walter 2001, 19–21.
51 See *FRHist* 26 T 9 (= Cic. *div.* 1.99).
52 *FRHist* 26 F 6 / *FRH* 16 F 5 (= Cic. *div.* 1.99). The translation is the one of Briscoe 2013c.

omy which, I have argued above, is typical of many of the Roman historians writing in the double-sided shadow of Polybius: on the one hand, they claim to be more "scientific", which indeed does hold true for large parts of their work, and on the other hand they also want to be more entertaining. They are equally successful in that respect, too.

This is borne out even by several of the shorter fragments from Sisenna's *Histories*, especially when read in sequence: one inevitably gets the impression that his narrative contained a lot of highly dramatic action, as these extracts, brief as they are, contain a surprisingly large number of words belonging to the semantic field of scheming, fighting and suffering. Consider the following quote, for example, which is preserved by Priscian (regrettably without any indication as to its historical context): *vitam cum dolore et insigni cruciatu carnificatus amisit* ("he lost his life, butchered with pain and extraordinary agony").[53] That passages such as this one might have been representative of Sisenna's work as a whole is suggested by a passage in Gellius again. Pursuing his interest in pre-classical words, so much in vogue during the second century AD, Gellius scanned Sisenna's *Histories* not for their content but for adverbs with the archaic ending "*–im*". He presents his findings in chapter 15 of the twelfth book of his *Attic Nights*. And even though Gellius provides only a list of words, the words themselves do provide a certain insight into the kind of historical actions that Sisenna must have been narrating and, thus, the way in which he narrated them.

[F 129] cum lectitaremus historiam Sisennae adsidue, huiuscemodi figurae adverbia in oratione eius animadvertimus cuimodi sunt haec: "cursim," "properatim," "celatim," "vellicatim," "saltuatim".

[12.15.2] ex quibus duo prima, quia sunt notiora, exemplis non indigebant, reliqua in historiarum sexto sic scripta sunt: "quam maxime celatim poterat, in insidiis suos disponit".

[F 130] item alio in loco: "nos una aestate in Asia et Graecia gesta litteris idcirco continentia mandavimus, ne vellicatim aut saltuatim scribendo lectorum animos impediremus".

[F 129] While repeatedly and carefully reading the *History* of Sisenna, I noticed adverbs formed in this way, as follows: *cursim* ("hurriedly"), *properatim* ("rapidly"), *celatim*, *vellicatim*, *saltuatim*.

[12.15.2] Of these the first two, being well known, do not need examples. The rest are written in the sixth book of the *Histories* thus: "he placed his men in ambush as secretly as he could".

---

[53] *FRHist* 26 F 141 / *FRH* 16 F 140 (= Prisc. *GL* 2, p. 546). The translation is the one of Briscoe 2013c.

[F 130] Again in another place: "I have described without interruption events which occurred in Asia and Greece in one summer, my reason being to avoid impending the reader's mind by writing piecemeal or jumping from one matter to another".[54]

Whereas Sisenna's methodological remark in the second part of this collection closely resembles Polybius' justification for adopting the annalistic scheme (see above), the adverbs cited in the first part all betray signs of an emotional way of writing history. Thus Gellius' reading of Sisenna, limited in scope as it might have been, further corroborates the twofold influence that Polybius' *Histories* exerted on later Roman writers.

This holds true no less for other historians of this period who formed no part of the *historia continua* those three writers established. That might be especially obvious for those authors who continued to use the traditional annalistic layout, but, of course, claimed to write serious and up-to-date history nevertheless. They have been blamed, however, already by their contemporaries for placing too much value on the entertainment of their readers. Afterwards, it was primarily Livy who again and again referred to their exaggerations and, in doing so, incorporated many such examples of emotional manipulation into his own work. But even Coelius Antipater, for the emphasis he seems to have placed on the search for truth and for the importance of causes in his methodological remarks (see above), apparently included several literary elements in the narrative portions of his work. Livy cites a prominent example of this dramatization, falling within his account of Scipio's crossing of the Mediterranean in order to face Hannibal in his North-African homeland (204 BCE), which eventually results in the decisive battle of Zama:

[F 36] Coelius ut abstinet numero, ita ad immensum multitudinis speciem auget: [4] volucres ad terram delapsas clamore militum ait tantamque multitudinem conscendisse naves ut nemo mortalium aut in Italia aut in Sicilia relinqui videretur.

[F 37] prosperam navigationem sine terrore ac tumultu fuisse permultis Graecis Latinisque auctoribus credidi. [14] Coelius unus, praeterquam quod non mersas fluctibus naves, ceteros omnes caelestes maritimosque terrores, postremo abreptam tempestate ab Africa classem ad insulam Aegimurum, inde aegre correctum cursum exponit, [15] et prope obrutis navibus iniussu imperatoris scaphis, haud secus quam naufragos, milites sine armis cum ingenti tumultu in terram evasisse.

---

54 *FRHist* 26 F 129–130 / *FRH* 16 F 128–129 (= Gell. 12.15.1–2). The translation is the one of Briscoe 2013c.

[F 36] Coelius does not commit himself to a figure, but nevertheless increases the appearance of a great number to an enormous degree; [4] he says that the shouts of the soldiers caused the birds to fall to the ground, and that so great a crowd boarded the ships that not a single person seemed to be left in Italy or Sicily.

[F 37] I have believed the very large number of both Greek and Latin writers who say that the voyage was successful and accomplished without panic or confusion. [14] Coelius alone describes all the terrors that sky and sea can produce, refraining only from saying that the ships were overwhelmed by the waves. At the end, he says, the fleet was torn away from Africa by a storm to the island of Aegimurus; from there their course was corrected with difficulty, [15] and when the ships had almost been overwhelmed, the soldiers, without the command of the general, escaped to the land on skiffs in great confusion and without their arms, just like victims of shipwreck.[55]

Attempts have been made to attribute this passage to Claudius Quadrigarius rather than Coelius Antipater because in another fragment, which without doubt belongs to his sixth book, Coelius describes a landing without any complications. This passage is generally identified with Scipio's arrival in North Africa, since in the period covered by Book 6 no other major naval operations took place.[56] Furthermore, some manuscripts read Caecilius instead of Coelius in the second part of the quotation, which some scholars have regarded as a corruption of Claudius (sc. Quadrigarius).[57] Nevertheless, one cannot avoid the impression that one of the reasons behind these efforts is the reluctance to accept that Coelius shared with other historians an interest in dramatic depictions. The weight of evidence, however, does point to Coelius as the source of Livy's description and the methodologically sound position would seem to be to see Coelius as yet another example of a Roman historian influenced by Polybius' historical method in more ways than Polybius intended.

The usage of speeches: plausibility vs. impact

This general observation can be further substantiated by looking at the speeches in the works of the Roman historians from the middle of the second century onwards. Here, too, we find a certain discrepancy already present in Polybius, between the condemnation of invented speeches in his theoretical remarks, on the

---

[55] *FRHist* 15 F 36–37 / *FRH* 11 F 46–47 (= Liv. 29.25.3–4; 29.27.13–15). The translation by Briscoe 2013b.
[56] See *FRHist* 15 F 38 / *FRH* 11 F 48 (= Non. p. 137) together with e.g. Beck/Walter 2004, 72f.
[57] Cf. F 37 = Liv. 29.27.14; this solution is favoured by Briscoe 2013c *ad loc.*

one hand,[58] and the regular use of invented speeches in his actual narrative, on the other.[59] Such an ambivalent attitude towards speeches is, of course, a problem Polybius shares with many of his predecessors, including Thucydides.[60] It is, thus, probable, that his *Histories* offered to prospective Roman historians not so much definitive answers, but rather a fresh look on both sides of an ongoing discussion.

Although the highly fragmentary transmission of the early Roman historians does not allow firm conclusions, it is not unlikely that already Fabius Pictor and the other writers of the first generation made use of the narrative technique of inserting speeches and, thus, had to face the problems related to this practice, especially regarding the plausibility of the words put into the mouths of historical figures.[61] The first solid evidence for speeches in Roman historical works, however, comes from Cato the Elder, who is known to have incorporated his own discourses in his *Origines*.[62] Speeches uttered by Romans seem to have been part of the works of the other historians of this period as well, although for unknown reasons these left but meagre traces in the surviving fragments.[63]

Nevertheless, it can be argued that it was, again, Coelius Antipater who played an important role in the further development of this device.[64] The tiny fragments surviving of his *bellum Punicum* allow neither an analysis of an entire speech nor a comparison between the amount of text occupied by the discourses of the historical figures with that occupied by the author's own remarks. But, as

---

[58] See esp. Plb. 2.56.1–13; 12.25a; 36.1.1–2 together with e.g. Ziegler 1952, 1524–27, Pédech 1964, 254–302, Sacks 1981, 79–96, Marincola 2001, 128–33, McGing 2010, 86–91, Dreyer 2011, 71–73, and Wiater 2014.

[59] See esp. Wiater 2010; for their contribution to the effect of "sideshadowing", see Maier 2012, 119–29.

[60] On speeches in ancient historiography in general, see e.g. Walbank 1965, Marincola 2007, Laird 2009 and Pitcher 2009, 103–11.

[61] For a recent discussion of the design of his work and likely impact of Greek historiography probably on him, see Bispham/Cornell 2013, 169–76 (though their focus for the latter is mainly on the content).

[62] See *FRHist* 5 F 87–93 / *FRH* 3 F 100–106 (his speech in defence of the Rhodians) and *FRHist* 5 F 104–107 / *FRH* 3 F 121–123 (his speech against Ser. Sulpicius Galba); and for further discussion, see Cornell 2013b, esp. 213f.: "If he included others, and if so which ones, is entirely uncertain".

[63] For L. Cassius Hemina, see esp. *FRHist* 6 F 15 / *FRH* 6 F 25 (= Serv. *Aen.* 1.55f.); for C. Fannius *FRH* 12 T 2 / *FRH* 9 F 5 (= Cic. *Brut.* 81) and for Cn. Gellius *FRHist* 14 F 4 / *FRH* 10 F 14 (= Charis. 67–68).

[64] Not as important, however, as assumed by Peter 1914, ccxviii, who claimed that Coelius was the first Roman historian at all who inserted invented speeches into his narrative.

chance would have it, thanks to late-antique grammarians, especially Priscian and Nonius, we do have a number of citations that seem to stem from speeches in *oratio recta*. Some of them appear to have been put not only into the mouths of Romans[65] but also into those of their opponents, in this case of the Carthaginians.[66] The latter point is particularly significant as there is no hint that earlier historians attributed complete speeches to non-Romans,[67] even though this might, of course, be due to coincidences of transmission.[68]

Be that as it may, the three most significant examples from what remains of Coelius' work on the Hannibal War are the following:[69]

> Coelius in i: neque ipsi eos alii modi esse atque Amilcar dixit ostendere possunt aliter.
>
> Coelius in Book 1: nor can they themselves demonstrate otherwise, namely that those people are of a different kind from that stated by Hamilcar.[70]
>
> Coelius annali libro i: cum iure sine periculo bellum geri poteratur.
>
> Coelius in the *Annals*, Book 1: at a time when the war could be [or could have been] waged justly and without danger.[71]
>
> Coelius in i: qui cum is ita foedus icistis.
>
> Coelius in Book 1: you who concluded a treaty with them in such a way.[72]

According to the *communis opinio* these fragmentary passages all belong to the debate in Carthage around 220 BCE about whether a new war against Rome should be risked or not. If the context of these fragments is thus rightly restored

---

65 See e.g. *FRHist* 15 F 45 / *FRH* 11 F 55 (= Fest. 482).
66 See Beck/Walter 2004, esp. 38: "Die Prägekraft, die vom coelianischen Werk auf die weitere Tradition ausging ..., dürfte in dieser Hinsicht mithin am größten gewesen sein".
67 Pointed sayings and famous *dicta*, by contrast, were attributed to non-Romans, for example by Cato: *FRHist* 5 F 78–79 / *FRH* 3 F 4.14 (= Gell. 10.24.6–7).
68 See e.g. Briscoe 2013b, 262.
69 For a further extract from a speech presumably directed to a Roman audience by a non-Roman speaker, see *FRHist* 15 F 24 / *FRH* 11 F 28 (= Prisc. *GL* 2, p. 198): *Coelius: nullae nationi tot tantas tam continuas victorias tam brevi spatio datas arbitror quam vobis* ("Coelius: I think that no nation has been given so many, so great, and so continuous victories in so short a time as you have" [Transl. Briscoe 2013b]).
70 *FRHist* 15 F 3 / *FRH* 11 F 4 (= Prisc. *GL* 3, p. 8). The translation is by Briscoe 2013b, as in the following.
71 *FRHist* 15 F 4 / *FRH* 11 F 8 (= Non. 508).
72 *FRHist* 15 F 5 / *FRH* 11 F 7 (= Prisc. *GL* 2, p. 510).

(and I think it is), this illustrates an important step in the use of speeches in Roman historiography: as it is not very likely that Coelius had access to the protocols of orations delivered in the Carthaginian senate, these examples constitute a significant shift from historically proven, or at least provable, "facts" to the inclusion of such elements into the narrative for primarily literary motives.

The reasons for this procedure are not difficult to guess: by presenting the decisive discussion in Carthage of whether to wage war against Rome or not in the highly dramatic mode of a real debate with speeches rendered in *oratio recta* instead of a matter-of-fact report by the narrator the literary character of the text is increased. In this case, the intended effect on the reader was most likely the creation of suspense: a Roman reader, of course, will have known the result of this discussion already and been aware of the fact that his ancestors would have to face the war against Hannibal with all its defeats and catastrophes before their eventual win in the end. Nevertheless, a reader's reaction to a text and the level of his involvement is enhanced by such elements, which can be subsumed under the heading of anomalous suspense[73] or of sideshadowing.[74] Such a way of telling the story, however, affects not only the entertainment of the reader, but also the didactic impact of the narrative: by including possible alternative developments of the past in the narrative, attention is drawn to the fact that the actual outcome was not a given, but the result of decisions taken by the protagonists.[75]

The assumption that Coelius was the *first* Roman historian to use speeches in exactly this way rests on shaky ground, since the few fragments from earlier authors are simply too scarce to grant us insight into their practice. What we do see, however, is that Sallust and Livy employ speeches of historical figures to such ends, among others, in a sophisticated and obviously well-established manner (Livy even presents the same debate among the Carthaginians, probably influenced by Coelius).[76] It is, therefore, likely that the usage of this technique was introduced into Roman historical writing well before their time. That said, the idea that Coelius Antipater and what he learned from Polybius played an important role in this process seems at least a reasonable guess.

---

[73] See Gerrig 1989; for an application on Livy, see Pausch 2011, esp. 193–200 (with further references).
[74] See Morson 1994; for an application on Polybius, see Maier 2012, 119–29, and Grethlein 2013, 243f., 255f.
[75] See e.g. Pausch 2011, 249–51.
[76] See Liv. 21.10.1–11.2. Interestingly enough, there is no counterpart in Polybius: see Händl-Sagawe 1995, 76.

3 Conclusion: History and Its Readers

This assumption, of course, would also fit nicely with the general picture of Polybius' twofold influence on Roman historiography that I have tried develop in this chapter. On the one hand, he surely was successful in promoting what he would have called serious history. On the other, he seems to have opened the eyes of his younger Roman contemporaries to the whole variety of different ways of writing history. In the end, this paradoxical impact is perhaps not too surprising after all. Not only did Polybius make use of a wide range of narrative techniques in his narrative, he also discussed the latest developments in Hellenistic historiography in his theoretical remarks. That most of them are presented in polemical form evidently was no obstacle for his Roman readers to take them as prompts to re-evaluate the "state of the art" and as starting points for a renewed discussion about the relationship between history and literature.

This holds especially true for one aspect of this broader picture, namely the historian's enhanced consideration of his readers and their interests. Polybius has quite lot to say about this topic.[77] I will confine myself to one last passage, his well-known differentiation of the various types of readers of historiography at the beginning of the ninth book:

> οὐκ ἀγνοῶ δὲ διότι συμβαίνει τὴν πραγματείαν ἡμῶν ἔχειν αὐστηρόν τι καὶ πρὸς ἓν γένος ἀκροατῶν οἰκειοῦσθαι καὶ κρίνεσθαι διὰ τὸ μονοειδὲς τῆς συντάξεως. οἱ μὲν γὰρ ἄλλοι συγγραφεῖς σχεδὸν ἅπαντες, εἰ δὲ μή γ', οἱ πλείους, πᾶσι τοῖς τῆς ἱστορίας μέρεσι χρώμενοι πολλοὺς ἐφέλκονται πρὸς ἔντευξιν τῶν ὑπομνημάτων. τὸν μὲν γὰρ φιλήκοον ὁ γενεαλογικὸς τρόπος ἐπισπᾶται, τὸν δὲ πολυπράγμονα καὶ περιττὸν ὁ περὶ τὰς ἀποικίας καὶ κτίσεις καὶ συγγενείας, καθά που καὶ παρ' Ἐφόρῳ λέγεται, τὸν δὲ πολιτικὸν ὁ περὶ τὰς πράξεις τῶν ἐθνῶν καὶ πόλεων καὶ δυναστῶν. ἐφ' ὃν ἡμεῖς ψιλῶς κατηντηκότες καὶ περὶ τοῦτον πεποιημένοι τὴν ὅλην τάξιν, πρὸς ἓν μέν τι γένος, ὡς προεῖπον, οἰκείως ἡρμόσμεθα, τῷ δὲ πλείονι μέρει τῶν ἀκροατῶν ἀψυχαγώγητον παρεσκευάκαμεν τὴν ἀνάγνωσιν.

> I am not unaware that my work owing to the uniformity of its composition has a certain severity, and will suit the taste and gain the approval of only one class of reader. For nearly all other writers, or at least most of them, by dealing with every branch of history, attract many kinds of people to the perusal of their works. The genealogical side appeals to those who are fond of a story, and the account of colonies, the foundation of cities, and their ties of kindred, such as we find, for instance, in Ephorus, attracts the curious and lovers of recondite longer, while the student of politics is interested in the doings of nations, cities, and

---

[77] See e.g. Plb. 16.17.9–11 (impact of diction) or 38.5–6 (impact of structure); on Polybius' reasoning about the effect his narrative will have on its readers in general, see now Miltsios 2013, 115–46.

monarchs. As I have confined my attention strictly to these last matters and as my whole work treats of nothing else, it is, as I say, adapted only to one sort of reader, and its perusal will have no attractions for the larger number.[78]

I have argued elsewhere that this passage, too, had some influence on the subsequent development of historical writing in Rome.[79] One reason for this is, once more, that despite the fact that Polybius' own preferences are very clear, his discussion sets out a whole range of possibilities which, in turn, could be taken up by the Romans who read his work. The most important effect, however, seems to have been that the idea that historiography was not simply the transmission of useful knowledge to an anonymous posterity but also a dialogue with actual readers in the present. This will have been of even greater interest to Roman writers in the second half of the second and the first half of the first century BCE, as this is precisely the period in which the expansion of the Roman Empire and the spread of the Latin language significantly increased the number of potential readers for their works. But the social diversity of readers of historiography was growing even within the city of Rome itself: works of history were no longer written exclusively for senators or active politicians.[80] Rome, therefore, in that period was repeating the development that had taken place in the Hellenistic world some time before and that is reflected, albeit only indirectly, in Polybius' theoretical remarks.

One could therefore say, perhaps, that the same process would have unfolded at Rome even without Polybius' stay and the reception of his *Histories*. But Tyche would have that Polybius and his work were in right place at the right time and could thus have a paradoxical impact on Roman history.

Bibliography

Beck, H./H. Walter (eds.) (2001), *Die Frühen Römischen Historiker*, Vol. 1, Darmstadt (= *FRH*).
—— (eds.) (2004), *Die Frühen Römischen Historiker*, Vols. 2, Darmstadt (= *FRH*).
Bispham, E./T.J. Cornell (2013), "Q. Fabius Pictor", in: T.J. Cornell (ed.), *The Fragments of the Roman Historians*, Vol. 1, Oxford (= *FRHist*), 160–178.
Briscoe, J. (2013a), "Some Misunderstandings of Polybius in Livy", in: B. Gibson/T. Harrison (eds.), *Polybius and his World. Essays in Memory of F.W. Walbank*, Oxford, 117–124.
—— (2013b), "L. Coelius Antipater", in: T.J. Cornell (ed.), *The Fragments of the Roman Historians*, Vol. 1, Oxford (= *FRHist*), 256–263.

---

[78] Cf. Plb. 9.1.2–5 [Translation by Paton 1993 (1925)]; see further Näf 2010, 185–87, and Dreyer 2011, 92f.
[79] See Pausch 2011, 38–45.
[80] See e.g. Timpe 1979, 113–115, and Beck/Walter 2004, 23f.

── (2013c), "L. Cornelius Sisenna", in: T.J. Cornell (ed.), *The Fragments of the Roman Historians*, Vol. 1, Oxford (= *FRHist*), 306–319.
Büttner-Wobst, T. (1882–1904), *Polybii Historiae*. 5 vols., Leipzig.
Chaniotis, A. (2013), "Empathy, Emotional Display, Theatricality, and Illusion in Hellenistic Historiography, in: *id.*/P. Ducrey (eds.), *Unveiling Emotions II. Emotions in Greece and Rome: Texts, Images, Material Culture*, Stuttgart, 53–84.
Chassignet, M. (1996–2004) *L'annalistique romaine*, 3 vols., Paris.
Cornell, T.J. (ed.) (2013a), *The Fragments of the Roman Historians*, 3 vols., Oxford (= *FRHist*).
── (2013b), "M. Porcius Cato", in: *id.* (ed.), *The Fragments of the Roman Historians*, Vol. 1, Oxford (= *FRHist*), 191–218.
Davidson, J. (2009), "Polybius", in: A. Feldherr (ed.), *The Cambridge Companion to The Roman Historians*, Cambridge, 123–136.
Dreyer, B. (2011), *Polybios. Leben und Werk im Banne Roms*, Darmstadt.
Erskine, A. (2012), "Polybius Among the Romans: Life in the Cyclops' Cave", in: C. Smith/L.M. Yarrow (eds.), *Imperialism, Cultural Politics, and Polybius*, Oxford, 17–33.
Gerrig, R.J. (1989), "Suspense in the Absence of Uncertainty", in: *Journal of Memory and Language* 28, 633–648.
Gotter, U./N. Luraghi/U. Walter (2003), "Einleitung", in: U. Eigler *et al.* (eds.), *Formen römischer Geschichtsschreibung von den Anfängen bis Livius*, Darmstadt, 9–38.
Grethlein, J. (2013), *Experience and Teleology in Ancient Historiography. "Futures Past" from Herodotus to Augustine*, Cambridge.
Händl-Sagawe, U. (1995), *Der Beginn des 2. Punischen Krieges. Ein historisch-kritischer Kommentar zu Livius Buch 21*, Munich.
Halfmann, H. (2013), "Livius und Polybios", in: V. Grieb/C. Koehn (eds.), *Polybios und seine Historien*, Stuttgart, 49–58.
Henderson, J.G.W. (2001), "From Megalopolis to Cosmopolis: Polybius, or There and Back Again", in: S. Goldhill (ed.), *Being Greek under Rome. Cultural Identity, the Second Sophistik and the Development of Empire*, Cambridge, 29–49.
Kierdorf, W. (2003), *Römische Geschichtsschreibung in republikanischer Zeit*, Heidelberg.
Kloft, H. (2013), "Polybios und die Universalgeschichte", in: V. Grieb/C. Koehn (eds.), *Polybios und seine Historien*, Stuttgart, 13–24.
Krebs, C. (2015), "The Buried Tradition of Programmatic Titulature Among Republican Historians: Polybius' Πραγματεία, Asellio's *Res Gestae*, and Sisenna's Redefinition of *Historiae*", *AJPh* 136, 503–524.
Laird, A. (2009), "The Rhetoric of Roman Historiography", in: A. Feldherr (ed.), *The Cambridge Companion to The Roman Historians*, Cambridge, 197–213.
La Penna, A./R. Funari (2015), *C. Sallusti Crispi Historiae I: fragmenta 1.1–146*, Texte und Kommentare 51, Berlin 2015.
Levene, D.S. (2010), *Livy on the Hannibalic War*, Oxford.
Maier, F.K. (2012), *'Überall mit dem Unerwarteten rechnen'. Die Kontingenz historischer Prozesse bei Polybios*, Vestigia 65, Munich.
Marincola, J. (2001), *Greek Historians*, Greece & Rome: New Surveys in the Classics 31, Oxford.
── (2003), "Beyond Pity and Fear: The Emotions of history", in: *AncSoc* 33, 285–315.
── (2007), "Speeches in Classical Historiography", in: *id.* (ed.), *A Companion to Greek and Roman Historiography*, 2 vols., Malden, 118–144.

—— (2013), "Polybius, Phylarchus, and 'Tragic History': A Reconsideration", in: B. Gibson/T. Harrison (eds.), *Polybius and his World. Essays in Memory of F.W. Walbank*, Oxford, 73–90.

Mehl, A. (2013), "Geschichte in Fortsetzung: wie, warum und wozu haben Autoren wie Polybios und Thukydides/Xenophon auf ein Ziel hin geschriebene Geschichtswerke fortgesetzt?", in: V. Grieb/C. Koehn (eds.), *Polybios und seine Historien*, Stuttgart, 25–48.

Meister, K. (1975), *Historische Kritik bei Polybios*, Palingensia 9, Wiesbaden.

McGing, B. (2010), *Polybius' Histories*, Oxford.

Miltsios, N. (2013), *The Shaping of Narrative in Polybius*, Trends in Classics—Supplementary Volumes 23, Berlin.

Morson, G.S. (1994), *Narrative and Freedom. The Shadows of Time*, New Haven.

Mutschler, F.-H. (2000), "Norm und Erinnerung. Anmerkungen zur sozialen Funktion von historischem Epos und Geschichtsschreibung im 2. Jh. v. Chr.", in: M. Braun et al. (eds.), *Moribus antiquis res stat Romana. Römische Werte und römische Literatur im 3. und 2. Jh. v. Chr.*, Beiträge zur Altertumskunde 134, Munich, 87–124.

Näf, B. (2010), *Antike Geschichtsschreibung: Form—Leistung—Wirkung*, Stuttgart.

Parmeggiani, G. (2014), "Introduction", in: id. (ed.), *Between Thucydides and Polybius. The Golden Age of Greek Historiography*, Washington, 1–6.

Paton, W.R. (1993) (1925), *Polybius. The Histories. Vol. IV, Books 9-15*. The Loeb Classical Library 159, London.

—— (1995) (1927), *Polybius. The Histories. Vol. VI, Books 28-39*. The Loeb Classical Library 159, London.

Paton, W.R./F.W. Walbank/C. Habicht (2010), *Polybius: The Histories. Vol. II, Books 3-4 (revised edition)*. The Loeb Classical Library 137, London.

Pausch, D. (2011), *Livius und der Leser. Narrative Strukturen in ab urbe condita*, Munich.

Pédech, P. (1964), *La méthode historique de Polybe*, Paris.

Peter, H. (1914), *Historicorum Romanorum Reliquiae*, Vol. 1, Leipzig ²1914.

Pitcher, L.V. (2009), *Writing Ancient History: An Introduction to Classical Historiography*, London.

Pobjoy, M. (2013), "Sempronius Asellio", in: T.J. Cornell (ed.), *The Fragments of the Roman Historians*, Vol. 1, Oxford (= *FRHist*), 274–277.

Rawson, E. (1979), "L. Cornelius Sisenna and the Early First Century BCE", in: *CQ* 29, 327–346 (= in: id. [ed.] 1991. *Roman Culture and Society: Collected Papers*, Oxford, 363–388).

Rood, T. (2007), "The Development of the War Monograph", in: J. Marincola (ed.), *A Companion to Greek and Roman Historiography*, 2 vols., Malden, 147–158.

Rutherford, R. (2007), "Tragedy and History", in: J. Marincola (ed.), *A Companion to Greek and Roman Historiography*, 2 vols., Malden, 504–514.

Sacks, K.S. (1981), *Polybius on the Writing of History*, Berkeley.

Schepens, G. (2005), "Polybius on Phylarchus' 'Tragic' Historiography", in: id./J. Bollansée (eds.), *The Shadow of Polybius. Intertextuality as a Research Tool in Greek Historiography*. Proceedings of the International Colloquium Leuven, 21–22 September 2001, Leuven, 141–164.

Scholz, U.W. (1994), "*Annales* und *historia(e)*", in: *Hermes* 122, 64–79.

Sommer, M. (2013), "Scipio Aemilianus, Polybius, and the Quest for Friendship in Second-Century Rome", in: B. Gibson/T. Harrison (eds.), *Polybius and his World. Essays in Memory of F.W. Walbank*, Oxford, 307–318.

Timpe, D. (1979), "Erwägungen zur jüngeren Annalistik", in: *A&A* 25, 97–119 (= in: *id.* [ed.] 2007. *Antike Geschichtsschreibung. Studien zur Historiographie*, Darmstadt, 209–236).

Verbrugghe, G.P. (1989), "On the Meaning of Annales, on the Meaning of Annalists", in: *Philologus* 133, 192–230.

Walbank, F.W. (1960), "History and Tragedy", in: *Historia* 9, 216–234 (= in: *id.* [ed.] 1985. *Selected Papers: Studies in Greek and Roman History and Historiography*, Cambridge, 224–241).

—— (1965), *Speeches in Greek Historians*. The Third J.L. Myres Memorial Lecture, Oxford 1965 (= in: *id.* [ed.] 1985. *Selected Papers: Studies in Greek and Roman History and Historiography*, Cambridge, 242–261).

—— (1990), "Profit or Amusement: Some Thoughts on the Motives of Hellenistic Historians", in: H. Verdin/G. Schepens/E. de Keyser (eds.), *Purposes of History. Studies in Greek Historiography from the 4th to the 2nd Centuries BCE*, Studia Hellenistica 30, Leuven, 253–266 (= in: *id.* [ed.] 2002. *Polybius, Rome and the Hellenistic world: essays and reflections*, Cambridge, 231–241).

—— (1993), "Polybius and the Past", in: H.D. Jocelyn (ed.), *Tria Lustra. Essays and Notes presented to John Prinsent*, Liverpool, 15–23 (= in: *id.* [ed.] 2002. *Polybius, Rome and the Hellenistic world: essays and reflections*, Cambridge, 178–192).

Walter, U. (2003), "Opfer ihrer Ungleichzeitigkeit. Die Gesamtgeschichten im ersten Jahrhundert v. Chr. und die fortdauernde Attraktivität des 'annalistischen Schemas'", in: U. Eigler et al. (eds.), *Formen römischer Geschichtsschreibung von den Anfängen bis Livius*, Darmstadt, 135–156.

Wiater, N. (2010), "Speeches and Historical Narrative in Polybius' Histories: Approaching Speeches in Polybius", in: D. Pausch (ed.), *Stimmen der Geschichte: Funktionen von Reden in der antiken Historiographie*, Beiträge zur Altertumskunde 284, Berlin, 67–107.

—— (2014), "Polybius on Speeches in Timaeus: Syntax and Structure in Histories 12.25a", in: *CQ* 64, 121–135.

—— (2017), "The Aesthetics of Truth. Narrative and Historical Understanding in Polybius' *Histories*", in: I. Ruffell/L.I. Hau (eds.), *Truth and History in the Ancient World. Pluralising the Past*, London, 202–225.

Woodman, A.J. (2015), *Lost Histories: Selected Fragments of Roman Historical Writers*, Histos—Supplement 2, Newcastle.

Ziegler, K. 1952. "Polybios", in: *RE* 21.2, 1440–1578.

Thomas Biggs
Odysseus, Rome, and the First Punic War in Polybius' *Histories*

This chapter explores several speculative aspects of the *Odyssey*'s presence in Polybius' *Histories*, beyond the well-known roles Odysseus plays as a model for autopic inquiry, historiographical method, and Polybius' own wandering life. The framework against which I read Polybius' narrative of the First Punic War is largely formed from Latin literary perspectives that predate his take on the conflict, since it is within possible Roman receptions that my interpretations of the *Histories* are most likely to have occurred. Accordingly, I devote not insignificant space to the Latin texts that first depicted the First Punic War, explicitly and allegorically, since their novel modes of casting Roman affairs are at the core of what I think a Roman reader could have done with certain elements of the Polybian narrative.

Odysseus is Polybius' methodological symbol, the figure chosen to represent his approach to historiography, and he is one carefully selected for a polyvalent, multicultural resonance. He could speak to Greek and Roman audiences in the same terms with a wide array of meanings. At the top of this list, Odysseus communicated historiographic authority of the Hellenic tradition both to Greeks and to Romans who read Greek—a well-known aspect of the genre since Hecataeus and Herodotus and in little need of explication within this volume. Of primary importance, I submit, is how Odysseus will have evoked a character with a deep local legacy for Roman audiences, particularly one whose narrative defined Latin literature of the First Punic War era. It is within the contexts of reception that my readings will diverge from scholars who imagine Polybius' impact to have been more restricted. Whether or not Polybius knew of Odysseus' role in Rome's literary and cultural innovations of the late third century, I contend that the reception of his text's use of Odysseus, especially at pointed moments in the narrative, will have been able to privilege local semantics over other interpretative paradigms.[1]

---

[1] Several studies have addressed Odysseus in historiography with focus on Polybius' *Histories*. For example, Hartog 2001 deals with Polybian self-characterization via Odysseus, while Marincola 2007 focuses on the methodological implications of Odysseus for Polybius' method. Cf. also Montiglio 2011; Stanford 1954 is still worthy of consultation. Most scholars have little to say regarding the implications of Roman contexts and conceptions of Odysseus for the reception of Polybius' project (*i.e.* his Italic prehistory as traveler and founder, and his First Punic War role as *the* figure from the age of *nostoi* for thinking about Roman experience).

1

Much changed at Rome in the late third century BCE. In the course of the First Punic War, Rome left the mainland and embraced the ideology and iconography of naval power. The city of Rome experienced what Matthew Leigh has dubbed Rome's "Maritime Moment".[2] Latin literature first emerged in the shadow of the war, and within the epic genre, Latins' first two texts contributed to the larger cultural moment, shaping the war's reception in different ways. The first, the *Odusia* of Livius Andronicus, was a Roman Odyssey for a naval generation. Andronicus, a Greek from southern Italy, created a markedly relevant work for the Romans: journeys at sea and imperial adventures in Italy and Sicily were right at home in the late third century. Places like Tusculum, Praeneste, and Circeii had also been pronouncing Odyssean origins and connections for centuries, hence Hellenistic Latium was clearly a landscape marked by Odysseus.[3] The *Odusia's* successor, Naevius' *Bellum Punicum* (c. 220 BCE), first turned to Roman affairs and crafted a narrative arch from Aeneas to Romulus, to Rome at sea in its first war against Carthage. The First Punic War is, then, undoubtedly an era of extreme cultural significance, in addition to its political and military importance. It was a moment in which a world war at sea created new experiences, and a narrative (the *Odyssey/Odusia*) and some well-known heroes of the *nostoi* calqued on the *aner polytropos* allowed a generation to conceive of these experiences and set these changes into an intelligible system, rendering Roman history understandable in literary forms.[4]

For all this, however reflective he was of Rome's maritime expansion in the third century, Odysseus and his *Odyssey* soon accrued further symbolic roles within the cultural production of the second century BCE. Italic and especially Etruscan visual art show a deep interest in the exploits of Odysseus in the years before the Second Punic War, but in the late third and second centuries BCE, perhaps in the light cast by Hannibal's Carthage, the negative Odysseus also known from earlier Greek literature emerges. For instance, Roman comedy often casts him as a trickster, no longer a hero whose exploits could well represent the Roman collective's success at sea. Consider briefly the comparisons with the base Odysseus that Chrysalus and Pseudolus engage in throughout Plautus' *Bacchides* and *Pseudolus* (*Bacch.* 940, 945–49, *Pseud.* 1063–64 and 1243–44):

---

[2] Leigh 2010.
[3] Cf. e.g. Malkin 1998, Farrell 2004.
[4] One can compare the role I propose for the *Odyssey* at Rome at this point in time with its status as an epic of exploration, expansion, and colonization, as explored by e.g. Dougherty 2001.

... ego sum Vlixes, quoius consilio haec gerunt.
nostro seni huic stolido, ei profecto nomen facio ego Ilio;
miles Menelaust, ego Agamemno, idem Vlixes Lartius,
Mnesilochust Alexander, qui erit exitio rei patriae suae;
is Helenam avexit, cuia causa nunc facio obsidium Ilio.
nam illi itidem Vlixem audivi, ut ego sum, fuisse et audacem et malum:

I am Ulysses, according to whose plan they're doing this.
This stupid old man of ours, I'll definitely give him the name Ilium. The soldier is Menelaus,
I am Agamemnon, but also Ulysses, son of Laertes. Mnesilochus is Alexander, who will be
the end of his father's wealth. He carried off Helen, for whose sake I'm now besieging Ilium.
Well, I've heard that Ulysses there was bold and bad, just as I am.

Viso quid rerum meus Vlixes egerit,
iamne habeat signum ex arce Ballionia

I'm checking what my Ulysses has been up to,
whether he already has the image from the Ballionian citadel

nimis illic mortalis doctus, nimis vorsutus, nimis malus;
superavit dolum Troianum atque Vlixem Pseudolus

He's a very smart, very clever, very wicked fellow;
Pseudolus has surpassed the Trojan trick and Ulysses.[5]

The Odysseus of the lying tale, crafty deception, and marauding expedition emerges as the Odysseus of the Roman second century, not the naval explorer who appeared as the first hero of Latin literature and whose journey home from Troy allowed Romans to interpret their own experience at sea.[6] Nevertheless, and this is key, he remains a model for historians, especially Greek historians, both in narratives of the past and in narratives of these authors' own lives.

---

[5] Transl. De Melo 2011 and 2012.
[6] This is seen in second century tragedy as well. Consider how "the unfaithfulness and unreliability of Ulixes as well as other negative characteristics are mentioned" in Accius' corpus (Acc. *Trag.* Ribbeck 131–32, 133–34). Manuwald 2011, 136.

2 The First Punic War in the *Histories*

Polybius knew that a global, interconnected state of affairs had come into existence (the *symploke* of the Mediterranean world). It was imperative for him to understand it, not only for the sake of his readers, but also to figure out who he had become—an exile in a foreign land, split between cultural tendencies and points of view that had been impossible only a generation before.[7] Indeed, although writing from Rome with access to Rome's elite, Polybius retains the perspective of an outsider.[8] This conception is not formulated solely on language. Although writing in Greek aligns the text with his historiographical predecessors back east, it also, one must recall, aligns it with Roman "annalistic" tradition (*i.e.* the histories of Fabius Pictor and his pre-Catonian successors). So too, writing Roman history in Greek at Rome in the mid-second century sits in opposition to the new face of Latin historiography that Cato introduced at this same time. Yet Polybius' "outsider" perspective emerges mainly from the anthropological lens of his narrative style and from his *Histories'* configuration of a complex audience, sometimes made up of Romans with knowledge of Greek and at other times consisting of readers whose acculturation was Hellenic and whose knowledge of Rome was at least superficially projected to be minimal.[9] Although many scholars have attempted to highlight Polybius' intended audience as *either* Greek *or* Roman, contexts of reception show the *Histories'* afterlife in both languages and cultures. Even more to the point, as Champion reminds us, Polybius

---

[7] Hartog 2001, 165: "a new world deserved a new history". Although earlier in the preface Polybius states that the Hannibalic War was the game changer for the Mediterranean, his comments throughout the *Histories* make it clear that he understood the process of change to begin with the First Punic War and Rome's first sea crossing.

[8] Cf. Allen 2006, 206–07: "As a detainee in Italy and companion of the well-connected consular [Scipio Aemilianus], Polybius had close access to Roman power at home and abroad, and he clearly developed important friendships. It is important to note that Polybius's exposure to Roman politics and culture did not spell an unquestioning loyalty or dependence".

[9] Audience is a thorny issue. My present reading is entirely predicated on the conclusion that Polybius' audience is figured to be made up of both Greeks and Romans. For audience, cf. Champion 2004, 4 n. 5. As a parallel, consider Dillery's arguments for Fabius Pictor's audience in Dillery 2009.

explicitly states that he writes for both a Greek and a Roman readership. In particular, Polybius writes for aristocratic statesmen, the Greek and Roman ruling elite; and in this regard, I believe, we may safely concentrate on Polybius's audience as the dominant culture of the political elite.[10]

Space and scope prohibit further consideration of this important issue. For what follows it is essential to understand that I will mainly approach the text from Roman eyes, a perspective I think the text invites, but one that will have happened all the same, with or without "permission".

Now, at the outset it is necessary to highlight the emphasis Polybius places on the overall centrality of the First Punic War to the entire historical movement he depicts. Consider several marked expressions from throughout the text:[11]

ἡ μὲν οὖν πρώτη Ῥωμαίων ἐκ τῆς Ἰταλίας διάβασις μετὰ δυνάμεως ἥδε καὶ διὰ ταῦτα καὶ κατὰ τούτους ἐγένετο τοὺς καιρούς, ἣν οἰκειοτάτην κρίναντες ἀρχὴν εἶναι τῆς ὅλης προθέσεως, ἀπὸ ταύτης ἐποιησάμεθα τὴν ἐπίστασιν, ἀναδραμόντες ἔτι τοῖς χρόνοις τοῦ μηδὲν ἀπόρημα καταλιπεῖν ὑπὲρ τῶν κατὰ τὰς αἰτίας ἀποδείξεων (1.12.5).

Such then was the occasion and motive of this, the first crossing of the Romans from Italy with an armed force, an event which I take to be the most natural starting-point of this whole work. I have therefore made it my serious base, but went also somewhat further back in order to leave no possible obscurity in my statements of general causes.

Ὁ μὲν οὖν Ῥωμαίοις καὶ Καρχηδονίοις συστὰς περὶ Σικελίας πόλεμος ἐπὶ τοιούτοις καὶ τοιοῦτον ἔσχε τὸ τέλος, ἔτη πολεμηθεὶς εἴκοσι καὶ τέτταρα συνεχῶς, πόλεμος ὧν ἡμεῖς ἴσμεν ἀκοῇ μαθόντες πολυχρονιώτατος καὶ συνεχέστατος καὶ μέγιστος (1.63.4–5).

Such then was the end of the war between the Romans and Carthaginians for the possession of Sicily, and such were the terms of peace. It had lasted without a break for twenty-four years and is the longest, most unintermittent, and greatest war we know of.

---

10 Champion 2004, 27. Walbank saw the reality of Polybius' multiple audiences but bent the text to conform to his expectations that Greeks were the only readers towards whom it truly had an internal orientation. Cf. esp. Walbank 1972, 3 for this far too rigid viewpoint: "Polybius writes with both a Greek and a Roman public in mind. His Roman readers are mentioned here and there. For instance, in his account of the Punic treaties he specifically hints at the need felt by Roman senators for accurate information; and he excuses himself for any shortcomings in his account of the Roman constitution that may be apparent to those brought up at Rome. But these passages are on the whole exceptional … It is surely apparent that in this passage [Book 31 on the death of Aemilius Paulus] Polybius is addressing a Greek audience, and mentions his Roman readers only as a kind of guarantee that what he is saying about Rome is the plain unvarnished truth: as he goes on to add, 'this should be borne in mind throughout the whole work'".
11 All translations of Polybius, unless stated otherwise, are from the updated Loeb of Paton 2010.

> καίτοι διότι πλεῖσται μὲν καὶ μέγισται τότε περί τε τὴν Ἰβηρίαν καὶ Λιβύην, ἔτι δὲ τὴν Σικελίαν καὶ Ἰταλίαν ἐπετελέσθησαν πράξεις, ἐπιφανέστατος δὲ καὶ πολυχρονιώτατος ὁ κατ' Ἀννίβαν πόλεμος γέγονε πλὴν τοῦ περὶ Σικελίαν, πάντες δ' ἠναγκάσθημεν πρὸς αὐτὸν ἀποβλέπειν διὰ τὸ μέγεθος, δεδιότες τὴν συντέλειαν τῶν ἀποβησομένων, τίς οὕτως ἐστὶν ἀδαὴς ὃς οὐκ οἶδεν (5.33.4–6).

> Yet no one is so ignorant as not to know that many actions of the highest importance were accomplished then in Spain, Africa, Italy, and Sicily, that the war with Hannibal was the most celebrated and longest of wars if we except that for Sicily, and that we in Greece were all obliged to fix our eyes on it, dreading the results that would follow.

To these authorial proclamations of importance, of which there are many more,[12] we must add the essential point made by Miltsios concerning the content of the narrative and its particular casting. As he notes, "it would be no exaggeration to say that the joints in the account of the First Punic War are essentially constructed with material relating to the Romans' adventures at sea".[13]

We have before us, then, a narrative of the war of extreme significance to the entire historical project, one that marked an era of change and expansion; one that was the necessary starting point for the whole work, and that was the greatest and most intense war of all time. So too, this war is defined by the Romans' "adventures at sea". Perhaps unsurprisingly, the unique combination seen here leads us to the "adventure at sea" par excellence.

3 Polybius' First Punic War and the *Odyssey*

Polybius recounts that in 253 BCE the consuls Gnaeus Servilius and Gaius Sempronius sailed through unfamiliar waters on their way to campaign off of Africa and hit upon the island of the Lotus-eaters (τὴν τῶν Λωτοφάγων νῆσον), soon becoming lost through their ignorance of the geography (διὰ τὴν ἀπειρίαν) (1.39.1–4):[14]

---

[12] It is a *topos* within the genre but still significant.
[13] Miltsios 2013, 33.
[14] Now called Djerba. The formula for introducing the names of places is somewhat common, especially when they are considered foreign or notable, but there are no exact parallels in the first book: cf. e.g. 1.44, "he came to anchor off the islands called Aegusae, which lie between Lilybaeum and Carthage".

κομιζόμενοι δὲ παρὰ τὴν χώραν ἐποιοῦντο καὶ πλείστας ἀποβάσεις, ἐν αἷς οὐδὲν ἀξιόλογον πράττοντες παρεγίνοντο πρὸς τὴν τῶν Λωτοφάγων νῆσον, ἣ καλεῖται μὲν Μῆνιγξ, οὐ μακρὰν δ' ἀπέχει τῆς μικρᾶς Σύρτεως. ἐν ᾗ προσπεσόντες εἴς τινα βράχεα διὰ τὴν ἀπειρίαν, γενομένης ἀμπώτεως καὶ καθισάντων τῶν πλοίων εἰς πᾶσαν ἦλθον ἀπορίαν.

> ... and sailing along the coast, [they] made a number of descents in which they accomplished nothing of importance, and finally reached the isle of the Lotus-eaters, which is called Meninx and is not far distant from the lesser Syrtis. Here, owing to their ignorance of the seas, they ran on to some shoals, and, on the tide retreating and the ships grounding fast, they were in a most difficult position.

The consuls' further tactical blunders in their attempt to return to Rome via Panormus resulted in the loss of more than one hundred and fifty ships (πλείω τῶν ἑκατὸν καὶ πεντήκοντα πλοίων), a trauma with great impact back home.

How is the reader of a pragmatic history to grapple with the presence of Homeric geography within the narration of a catastrophic event of Roman history?[15] Polybius largely avoids using a mythic register in narrative passages, and he explicitly charges a historian to explain events as they are, even rationalizing the island here by immediately relating its current name (Meninx).[16] Elsewhere he enjoins the reader (4.40.1–3),

> But since our attention is now fixed on this subject, I must leave no point unelaborated and barely stated, as is the habit of most writers, but must rather give a description of the facts supported by proofs, so that no doubts may be left in the reader's mind. <u>For this is the characteristic of the present age, in which, all parts of the world being accessible by land or sea, it is no longer proper to cite the testimony of poets and mythographers regarding matters of which we are ignorant</u>, as my predecessors have done on most subjects, "offering", as Heraclitus says, "untrustworthy sureties for disputed facts", but we should aim at laying before our readers a narrative resting on its own credit.[17]

---

15 Cf. e.g. 1.1, 2.56, 9.1.
16 A point Polybius makes repeatedly throughout Book 12, although a modern reader must be at odds with this ontological and representational crux. While the entire method of geographical exposition here is not unique in the histories, the context subjects it to greater scrutiny, coming as it does at the outset of the work and in a key context for characterizing the Roman people. Compare the geographic remarks with e.g. 4.39.6: ἀπὸ δὲ τοῦ Πόντου τὸ καλούμενον Ἱερόν, ἐφ' οὗ τόπου φασὶ κατὰ τὴν ἐκ Κόλχων ἀνακομιδὴν Ἰάσονα θῦσαι πρῶτον τοῖς δώδεκα θεοῖς ("On the side of the Pontus it begins at the so-called Holy Place, where they say that Jason on his voyage back from Colchis first sacrificed to the twelve gods").
17 Of course, a verse philosopher is quoted in this passage itself, a further interpretive complexity: ἐπεὶ δ' ἐπὶ τὸν τόπον ἐπέστημεν, οὐδὲν ἀφετέον ἀργὸν οὐδ' ἐν αὐτῇ τῇ φάσει κείμενον, ὅπερ οἱ πλεῖστοι ποιεῖν εἰώθασι τῶν συγγραφέων, ἀποδεικτικῇ δὲ μᾶλλον τῇ διηγήσει χρηστέον, ἵνα μηδὲν ἄπορον ἀπολείπωμεν τῶν ζητουμένων τοῖς φιληκόοις. τοῦτο γὰρ ἴδιόν ἐστι τῶν νῦν

So what is one to make of the passage's momentary depiction of Romans at sea during the First Punic War in contact with and viewing the world through features of the *Odyssey's* geography, separated from Rome and confronted with the violence of the sea within sight of the Lotophagoi?

As I have already suggested, after Livius Andronicus a new connection existed for Roman audiences between the narrative of the *Odyssey* and the experience of the First Punic War. That Polybius in his attempt to access and explain the war composed a similar conflation of mythic and historic space is suggestive of this intellectual phenomenon as well, whether intentional or not. Throughout Polybius' narrative of the First Punic War, Homeric material—indeed what we would call mythic material in general—is completely absent. Nowhere else outside of this mention of the Lotus-eaters does any non-historic element play an explicit role in the discussion of the war.

Explicit is key, however, since his account surrounding the creation and training of Rome's first fleet has a markedly mythic, even Argonautic tone.[18] As Walbank notes on the episode, Polybius' "account—perhaps from Fabius—reinforces the intended expression of wonder at the Roman achievement".[19] Nevertheless, beyond the quizzical usage of Odyssean geography in Book 1, Odysseus himself and the poetic text of the *Odyssey* play a relatively large role in other sections of the *Histories*, especially in relation to defining Polybius' historical method (in Book 12) and his allegiance to rationalizing Homeric geography (in Book 34; the lotus itself is discussed in 12 and 34).[20] Concerning the lotus in Polybius, we likely can see the influence of Eratosthenes in particular; consider Pliny, who engages with the same sources (*NH* 5.41):

> These seas do not contain very many islands. The most famous is Zerba, 25 miles long and 22 miles broad, called by Eratosthenes Lotus Eaters' Island. It has two towns, Meninx on the

---

καιρῶν, ἐν οἷς πάντων πλωτῶν καὶ πορευτῶν γεγονότων οὐκ ἂν ἔτι πρέπον εἴη ποιηταῖς καὶ μυθογράφοις χρῆσθαι μάρτυσι περὶ τῶν ἀγνοουμένων, ὅπερ οἱ πρὸ ἡμῶν πεποιήκασι περὶ τῶν πλείστων, ἀπίστους ἀμφισβητουμένων παρεχόμενοι βεβαιωτὰς κατὰ τὸν Ἡράκλειτον, πειρατέον δὲ δι' αὐτῆς τῆς ἱστορίας ἱκανὴν παριστάναι πίστιν τοῖς ἀκούουσιν.

18 A quick qualification: Polybius does quote Euripides to highlight Regulus' reversal of fortune at 1.35 and includes similes to boxing and cockfighting to depict battle. These are momentary insertions of other genres and registers, but they are not mythical.

19 Walbank 1957, 74 (*ad* 1.20.13).

20 12.2.1, 34.3.12.

side of Africa and Thoar on the other side, the island itself lying off the promontory on the right-hand side of the Lesser Syrtis, at a distance of a mile and a half away.²¹

While such passages are surely relevant to certain interpretations of the passage in Book 1, recourse to Polybius' interest in Eratosthenes and Homeric geography, especially as reported by Strabo, does not fully explain this isolated diversion into Homeric territory. Or, if it does, it still cannot account for all possible readings of the feature, hence the importance of reception to the current line of argumentation.

To my mind, the narrative jump from historic to mythic geography emerges, at the very least, as a highly marked mode of description. But is Polybius' narrative voice anomalously, yet "objectively", reporting this piece of mythical, geographic information? Meninx, after all, did have numerous monuments of Odysseus' voyage there for the traveler or historian to observe and analyze (Strabo 17.17):

> Continuous with these is the Little Syrtis, which is also called the Syrtis of the Lotus-eaters. The circuit of this gulf is one thousand six hundred stadia, and the breadth of the mouth six hundred; and at each of the two promontories which form its mouth are islands close to the mainland—the Cercinna above-mentioned and Meninx, which are about equal in size. Meninx is regarded as the land of the Lotus-eaters mentioned by Homer; and certain tokens of this are pointed out—both an altar of Odysseus and the fruit itself; for the tree which is called the lotus abounds in the island, and its fruit is delightful.²²

This later-attested promotion of the Odyssean past by the island's inhabitants may have helped to prolong the vitality of the island's claims to authoritative status as the site from Homer's text, but there is perhaps more at stake in Polybius' narrative from a Roman point of view. Might we ask if Polybius is focalizing the Roman commanders lost at sea, or depicting the probable mappings that a Roman (or a Roman audience) might turn to when presented with a narrative of

---

21 Transl. Rackham 1942. Insulas non ita multas complectuntur haec maria. clarissima est Meninx, longitudine XXV, latitudine XXII, ab Eratosthene Lotophagitis appellata; oppida habet duo, Meningen ab Africae latere et altero Thoar, ipsa a dextro Syrtis Minoris promunturio passibus MD sita.

22 Transl. Jones 1932. Συνεχὴς δ' ἐστὶν ἡ μικρὰ Σύρτις, ἣν καὶ Λωτοφαγῖτιν Σύρτιν λέγουσιν. ἔστι δ' ὁ μὲν κύκλος τοῦ κόλπου τούτου σταδίων χιλίων ἑξακοσίων, τὸ δὲ πλάτος τοῦ στόματος ἑξακοσίων· καθ' ἑκατέραν δὲ τὴν ἄκραν τὴν ποιοῦσαν τὸ στόμα προσεχεῖς εἰσι τῇ ἠπείρῳ νῆσοι, ἥ τε λεχθεῖσα Κέρκιννα καὶ ἡ Μῆνιγξ, πάρισοι τοῖς μεγέθεσι. τὴν δὲ Μήνιγγα νομίζουσιν εἶναι τὴν τῶν Λωτοφάγων γῆν τὴν ὑφ' Ὁμήρου λεγομένην, καὶ δείκνυταί τινα σύμβολα, καὶ βωμὸς Ὀδυσσέως καὶ αὐτὸς ὁ καρπός· πολὺ γάρ ἐστι τὸ δένδρον ἐν αὐτῇ τὸ καλούμενον λωτόν, ἔχον ἥδιστον καρπόν.

maritime wandering on the western sea? After all, in the mid-second century most Romans would not have been privy to the landscapes of Meninx noted by Eratosthenes and Strabo. And in fact, we know well that Romans employed such a mythic lens at the time, notably in contexts much closer to the present one than the comic examples we saw already from Plautus. For instance, it is as Odysseus that Cato the Elder is said by Polybius to have characterized the author of the *Histories* himself, a view surely shaped by Polybius' own self-depiction, but still suggestive of a contemporary Roman's ability to probe and exploit the nuances of the characterization (Plb. 35.6 = Plutarch, *Cato Maior*, 9.3):

> Cato was approached by Scipio on behalf of the Achaean exiles through the influence of Polybius, and when there was a long debate in the senate, some advocating their return and others opposing it, Cato rose and said, "Just as if we had nothing to do we sit here all day disputing about some wretched old Greeks whether they shall be carried to their graves by bearers from Rome or from Achaea". And when their restitution was voted, and a few days afterwards Polybius intended to enter the house to demand that the exiles should recover the honours they had previously enjoyed in Achaea, and asked Cato's advice, Cato smiled and said that Polybius, like Ulysses, wanted to enter the cave of the Cyclops again, because he had forgotten his cap and belt.[23]

Let's now return to Book 1. The passage concerning the Lotus-eaters describes events of 253, but looking back only a few sections in the *Histories* to the year 254 presents a reader with a significant event that colors any view of the momentary Odyssean scene. This event was the largest loss of Roman life during the war, a loss suffered at the hands of the Sicilian sea itself. Polybius begins his narrative at 1.37.1–3 and expends no effort to soften the blows while reporting the specifics and reflecting on their magnitude:

> διάραντες δὲ τὸν πόρον ἀσφαλῶς καὶ προσμίξαντες τῇ τῶν Καμαριναίων χώρᾳ τηλικούτῳ περιέπεσον χειμῶνι καὶ τηλικαύταις συμφοραῖς ὥστε μηδ' ἂν εἰπεῖν ἀξίως δύνασθαι διὰ τὴν ὑπερβολὴν τοῦ συμβάντος. τῶν γὰρ ἑξήκοντα καὶ τεττάρων πρὸς ταῖς τριακοσίαις ναυσὶν ὀγδοήκοντα μόνον συνέβη περιλειφθῆναι σκάφη, τῶν δὲ λοιπῶν τὰ μὲν ὑποβρύχια

---

[23] ὑπὲρ δὲ τῶν ἐξ Ἀχαΐας φυγάδων ἐντευχθεὶς διὰ Πολύβιον ὑπὸ Σκιπίωνος, ὡς πολὺς ἐν τῇ συγκλήτῳ λόγος ἐγίνετο, τῶν μὲν διδόντων κάθοδον αὐτοῖς, τῶν δ' ἐνισταμένων, ἀναστὰς ὁ Κάτων "ὥσπερ οὐκ ἔχοντες" εἶπεν "ὃ πράττωμεν, καθήμεθα τὴν ἡμέραν ὅλην περὶ γεροντίων Γραικῶν ζητοῦντες, πότερον ὑπὸ τῶν παρ' ἡμῖν ἢ τῶν ἐν Ἀχαΐᾳ νεκροφόρων ἐκκομισθῶσι". ψηφισθείσης δὲ τῆς καθόδου τοῖς ἀνδράσιν, ἡμέρας ὀλίγας οἱ περὶ τὸν Πολύβιον διαλιπόντες αὖθις ἐπεχείρουν εἰς τὴν σύγκλητον εἰσελθεῖν, ὅπως ἃς πρότερον εἶχον ἐν Ἀχαΐᾳ τιμὰς οἱ φυγάδες ἀναλάβοιεν, καὶ τοῦ Κάτωνος ἀπεπειρῶντο τῆς γνώμης. ὁ δὲ μειδιάσας ἔφη τὸν Πολύβιον, ὥσπερ τὸν Ὀδυσσέα, βούλεσθαι πάλιν εἰς τὸ τοῦ Κύκλωπος σπήλαιον εἰσελθεῖν, τὸ πιλίον ἐκεῖ καὶ τὴν ζώνην ἐπιλελησμένον. On the passage, see Erskine 2012.

γενέσθαι, τὰ δ' ὑπὸ τῆς ῥαχίας πρὸς ταῖς σπιλάσι καὶ τοῖς ἀκρωτηρίοις καταγνύμενα πλήρη ποιῆσαι σωμάτων τὴν παραλίαν καὶ ναυαγίων. ταύτης δὲ μείζω <u>περιπέτειαν</u> ἐν ἑνὶ καιρῷ κατὰ θάλατταν οὐδ' ἱστορῆσθαι συμβέβηκεν.

> The passage was effected in safety, and the coast of Camarina was reached: but there they experienced so terrible a storm, and suffered so dreadfully, as almost to beggar description. The disaster was indeed extreme: for out of their three hundred and sixty-four vessels eighty only remained. The rest were either swamped or driven by the surf upon the rocks and headlands, where they went to pieces and filled all the seaboard with corpses and wreckage. No greater <u>catastrophe</u> is to be found in all history as befalling a fleet at one time.

Polybius makes clear that no event in history at sea (κατὰ θάλατταν) was worse than this. The tragic coloring of the lines (he uses the word περιπέτεια) intensifies the effect on a reader, activating latent emotional connections between event, text, and audience.[24] In fact, Polybius had already flagged reversals of fortune as key to his narrative of the First Punic War in an introductory discussion (1.13.10–13):[25]

> βραχὺ δ' ἐπιμελέστερον πειρασόμεθα διελθεῖν ὑπὲρ τοῦ πρώτου συστάντος πολέμου Ῥωμαίοις καὶ Καρχηδονίοις περὶ Σικελίας. οὔτε γὰρ πολυχρονιώτερον τούτου πόλεμον εὑρεῖν ῥάδιον οὔτε παρασκευὰς ὁλοσχερεστέρας οὔτε συνεχεστέρας πράξεις οὔτε πλείους ἀγῶνας <u>οὔτε περιπετείας μείζους</u> τῶν ἐν τῷ προειρημένῳ πολέμῳ συμβάντων ἑκατέροις. αὐτά τε τὰ πολιτεύματα κατ' ἐκείνους τοὺς καιροὺς ἀκμὴν ἀκέραια μὲν ἦν τοῖς ἐθισμοῖς,

---

[24] Polybius elsewhere, for example at 1.59.3 and 4.59.11, uses secondary focalization, thought expressed by the characters (here it is the Romans). See Miltsios 2013. Polybius was also quite interested in changes of fortune. Tyche is one of the guiding principles of historical events in his work. His Preface to Book 1 indicates a clear focus on changed circumstances and the knowledge gained from adversity. His work is replete with this type of *peripeteiai*, but the tragic focus on individual suffering devoid of moral or intellectual purpose is far less common, which is one part of what is explicitly denounced. The issue, however, is complex. Cf. Marincola 2007, 45f. He discusses the problems with "tragic" historiography (2007, 46): "... it would be absurd for Polybius to fault Phylarchus for narrating *peripeteiai* when Polybius himself throughout his work focuses on reversals and gives them a prominent role in his preface ... an interest in reversals themselves can in no way be posited as a distinguishing mark of so-called 'tragic' historians". Plb. 3.4.4–6 also contains a strong defense of the role *peripeteia* plays in the *Histories*. See Baron 2013 for recent discussion and bibliography on Hellenistic "Tragic Historiography", Polybius, and his predecessors.

[25] With different language Polybius also indicates this unexpected quality of Rome's story at the outset of the work (1.1.4): αὐτὸ γὰρ τὸ παράδοξον τῶν πράξεων, ὑπὲρ ὧν προῃρήμεθα γράφειν, ἱκανόν ἐστι προκαλέσασθαι καὶ παρορμῆσαι πάντα καὶ νέον καὶ πρεσβύτερον πρὸς τὴν ἔντευξιν τῆς πραγματείας ("For the very element of unexpectedness in the events I have chosen as my theme will be sufficient to challenge and incite everyone, young and old alike, to peruse my systematic history").

μέτρια δὲ ταῖς τύχαις, πάρισα δὲ ταῖς δυνάμεσι. διὸ καὶ τοῖς βουλομένοις καλῶς συνθεάσασθαι τὴν ἑκατέρου τοῦ πολιτεύματος ἰδιότητα καὶ δύναμιν οὐχ οὕτως ἐκ τῶν ἐπιγενομένων πολέμων ὡς ἐκ τούτου ποιητέον τὴν σύγκρισιν.

I shall, however, attempt to narrate somewhat more carefully the first war between Rome and Carthage for the possession of Sicily; since it is not easy to name any war which lasted longer, nor one which exhibited on both sides more extensive preparations, more unintermittent activity, more battles, and greater changes of fortune. The two states were also at this period still uncorrupted in morals, receiving but modest help from fortune, and equal in strength, so that a better estimate of the peculiar qualities and gifts of each can be formed by comparing their conduct in this war than in any subsequent one.

Moreover, the description of the traumatic naval event in the diction of *peripeteiai* may also signal a primary connection to the narrative of the *Odyssey* before the Lotus-eaters are evoked. As Marincola remarks, "the more long-lasting historiographical influence of the narrating Odysseus on ancient historiography may be found in the prevalence of reversals of fortune".[26] And in a recent piece, Rood has shown how often Thucydides' use of paradox and reversal of fortune in the Sicilian expedition is allusively evoked in Polybius' First Punic War narrative, especially concerning maritime events.[27]

When a reader, then, reaches the description of the consuls lost at sea, anxiety emerges constructed from intertextual and mythological resonance that is difficult to suppress: "The Romans are at war with the Carthaginians, yet at the same time they are at war with the sea".[28] An elemental conflict emerges that reaches deep into Rome's cultural memory. The textual dynamics of the passage that tap into these features depend on a convergence of elements. The scene featuring the Lotus-eaters is still redolent of the previous passage's maritime reversal, one that

---

[26] Marincola 2007, 37. He cites Aristotle, *Poetics* 1453a 30–35 to highlight the Greek conception of the *Odyssey* as an epic of *peripeteia*, and further defines its role in Herodotus. The use of *peripeteia* was, from a certain perspective, commonplace by Polybius' day.

[27] Rood 2012. The waters of the western Mediterranean, especially off of Sicily, are the setting for these famous moments of loss. It is interesting that Thucydides, a historian also focused on pragmatics and detail, turns to *peripeteia* when faced with his city's loses in the same geographic region, one which he also explicitly linked to Odysseus' travels and misfortunes. For example, Rood remarks on 4.24.5, "[w]hen the Thucydidean narrator reports what 'is said' (*legetai*) to have happened in a place in the distant past, he exploits the mythical aura of that place—of the strait between Italy and Sicily, say, 'the so-called Charybdis past which Odysseus is said to have sailed' (4.24.5)" (Rood 2004, 119). Yet the distancing employed here by Thucydides is not found in Polybius' scene, and the vividness of the ties between "Odyssey" and Sicilian exploit shaped by his Latin epic predecessors freights such geography with additional weight.

[28] Miltsios 2013, 34.

was worthy of Odyssean *peripateia* in both tone and diction, but Polybius amplifies the connection and provides the link lexically with the mention of the Lotus-eaters.[29]

Polybius' passage in Book 1 soon appears to transition from "mythic" back into "historic" space when the consuls get their fleet off the shoals and head back towards Sicily. There, again, *peripeteia*: they are met by the force of the sea, and a storm destroys more than 150 ships. These episodes of disaster, subjected to a Roman reading, may recall other parallel scenes from the era such as Naevius' surely emotive depiction in the *Bellum Punicum* of the storm at sea off of Sicily that afflicted Aeneas (a model for Vergil according to Servius and Macrobius).[30] In the same vein, we read a line from Andronicus' *Odusia* depicting Odysseus' fear in the midst of a storm at sea (Blänsdorf 30 = Flores XV) *igitur demum Ulixi cor frixit prae pavore*, "then at last Ulysses' heart went cold with fear".[31] Roman readers, as well as Polybius himself, could easily have been drawn to such images to conceive of and depict traumatic scenes of maritime disaster. We should also note that Varro tells us Naevius related in his epic that he was a veteran of the war he narrates, making him an autopic historian of the first order in Polybius' view, one who felt the sea on his face and the fear in his heart.[32] Indeed, Naevius'

---

29 The tragic coloring of historical narration, especially a sea disaster, recalls not only generic predecessors such as Thucydides' description of the Sicilian expedition, but also Aeschylus' *Persians* and the emotional impact Phrynichus' *Sack of Miletus* had on its Athenian audience (Hdt. 6.21.1).
30 Macrob. *Sat.* 6.2.30–31 (Blänsdorf 14 = Flores X): in principio Aeneidos tempestas describitur et Venus apud Iovem queritur ... hic locus totus sumptus a Naevio est ex primo libro Punici belli. Illic enim atque Venus Troianis tempestate laborantibus cum Iove queritur, et secuntur verba Iovis filiam consolantis spe futurorum ("In the first book of the *Aeneid* a storm is depicted and Venus complains to Jupiter ... this entire passage is taken from the first book of Naevius' *Bellum Punicum*. For in that poem Venus complains to Jupiter while the Trojans labor in a storm; Jupiter's words follow, consoling his daughter with the expectation of the future"). Transl. is my own. Seru. ad Aen. 1.198, Thilo (Blänsdorf 13 = Flores XVII)): et totus hic locus de Naevio belli Punici libro translatus est ("even this entire passage has been taken from Naevius' poem, the *Bellum Punicum*"). Transl. is my own.
31 And consider its later Vergilian recasting as a point of contextual comparison: *Aeneid* 1.92: extemplo Aeneae solvuntur frigore membra. Cf. Leigh 2010 for more passages and discussion concerning Roman historical experience and literary production.
32 Blänsdorf 2 = Gell. 17, 21, 45: eodemque anno (235 BCE) Cn. Naevius poeta fabulas apud populum dedit, quem M. Varro in libro de poetis primo stipendia fecisse ait bello Poenico primo, idque ipsum Naevium dicere in eo carmine, quod de eodem bello scripsit ("In the same year Gnaeus Naevius put on plays for the people; in his book *de Poetis*, Marcus Varro notes that Naevius had served in the First Punic War, and he says that Naevius himself relates this in his poem, which he wrote about the same war"). Transl. is my own. Marincola 1997, 137: "It is possible—

epic certainly depicted the Romans of his day tossed on the waves as well, but the extant fragments of these episodes are rather poor.

The geography at *Histories* 1.29 can thus been seen to shift into the Odyssean at exactly the point when it is in the midst of two major maritime disasters, and, I suggest, it taps into the undercurrent of literary thinking about such experiences at Rome to elevate the narrative. Recall how Livius Andronicus renders Laodamas' words from *Odyssey* 8, and consider the resonance the verses could have had among Roman audiences in the shadow of the First Punic War (Blänsdorf 18 = Flores XIX),

> namque nullum peius macerat humanum
> quamde mare saeuum: uires cui sunt magnae
> <...> topper confringent inportunae undae
>
> For nothing wounds a mortal worse than
> a savage sea: he whose strength is great,
> the remorseless billows shatter at once.[33]

Now, to revise something from earlier: while Homeric geography is absent from the First Punic War narrative aside from the Lotus-eaters, some readers might perceive at least one other prominent Odyssean feature. At 1.29, Marcus Atilius Regulus' invasion of Africa reaches shore at the "Headland of Hermes", perhaps Cap Bon. And at 1.36, when the survivors of that disastrous campaign are rescued, it occurs thanks to a Roman naval victory at this same Cape of Hermes. If the Romans are on their own "Odyssey", Hermes, as the well-known guide of Odysseus and recently also of Aeneas in Naevius' *Bellum Punicum*,[34] may even be brought into play by the topography of the scene. While Mediterranean Capes of Hermes are somewhat common, this one in particular plays a major role in Greco-Roman sources. And Hermes' prominence as a key divine aid for the journeys of epic heroes, but also as psychopomp, makes his evocation here quite intriguing.[35]

---

indeed, it is likely—that the early Hellenophone historians of Rome adopted Greek conventions in addressing their Greek audiences and that (e.g. Fabius) mentioned his participation and presence at events. It is noteworthy that the poet Naevius, perhaps influenced by historians, mentioned in his *Punic War* that he had served in the war, and it is hardly to be doubted that this served as an important validation for his credibility".

33 Transl. is Goldberg 1995. Cf. *Odyssey* 8.138–9.
34 Seru. Dan. *ad Aen.* 1.170 Thilo = Blänsdorf 7 = Flores XVI: novam tamen rem Naevius Bello Punico dicit, unam navem habuisse Aeneam, quam Mercurius fecerit ("Naevius relates a novel thing in his *Bellum Punicum*, that Aeneas had one ship, which Mercury made").
35 For those issues, I have a piece in the works for an Oxford volume focused on Hermes/Mercury, edited by Jenny Strauss Clay and John Miller. When the *Histories'* ties to the *Odyssey* are

4

To recap briefly, Polybius' narration of traumatic maritime loss during the First Punic War (at 1.37) prompts the transition to a mode of discourse and thought that processed such experience through *nostos* myth (1.39). The island viewed from the sea is seen to exist within Odyssean geography, a slippage (both visual and narrative) that follows the just reported Odyssean *peripateia* of the fleet. Regardless of Polybius' intentions, whether the reading I have proposed was caused by Greek views of the *Odyssey* or Rome's own *Odusian* view of their wartime misfortune, a Roman reader would have ultimately been able to receive the passage in the latter way, prioritizing local semantics over other interpretive categories, such as reference to Eratosthenes or other rationalizing geographic debates. This scene of Polybius' history of the First Punic War thus emerges as markedly expressive when read though the epics of Andronicus and Naevius.

When Polybius narrates the First Punic War or views Roman history through Odyssean language or imagery, a separate Roman semantics is potentially activated. This is possible because the memory of Odysseus' integral role earlier in Roman history and collective memory, especially during the First Punic War, did

---

viewed more widely (something there is not enough space for at present), a structural comparison between the order of events in the *Odyssey* and in Polybius' First Punic War narrative suggests a more integral and pervasive relationship. Consider how the *Histories* mark their true beginning in the 140th Olympiad, essentially the outbreak of the Second Punic War, but must then backtrack. A universal history, like the epic cycle, requires an impossible task—choosing a beginning. In turn, narrative techniques such as invocations, proems, starting *in medias res*, and use of analepsis (flashback) abound in both. Like the *Odyssey*, the true beginning requires a reset of the narrative opening. Both plotlines, too, are overshadowed by the great conflict of the prior generation—the First Punic war and the Trojan War. Polybius turns his gaze back so as to build ties between First and Second Punic Wars, and Homer obliquely does the same for the events at Troy throughout the *Odyssey*; Odysseus himself as bard-historian tells his voyages in flashback in a delayed *prokataskeue* of a sort. On an even wider view, readers meet Odysseus after his great struggles and trauma in war and especially at sea. His first task, to enable success and achieve his homecoming, is to build a boat. Rome's wartime experience, its journey from landlubber to naval power responds well to this Homeric plot structure. Telemachus' entry onto the world stage also consists of fitting out a boat for the first time, the key event in a Bildungsroman with clear overlap with Rome during the First Punic War; each come of age in their own ways and on their own journeys to sea. Loose analogies like these can be seen in even more suggestive ways within the *Histories*. Consider how Polybius actually begins the work at 1.6 with the year 387/6, the sack of Rome. This moment activates themes of destruction, imperial rise and fall (Troy's or Rome's? See the *anacyclosis* in Book 6), and the newly expounded Roman mythological self-conception as Troy's descendants.

not completely die out.³⁶ What I mean here is that Odysseus had the potential to symbolize many differing, culturally determined modes of thought in the second century. For a Roman, he might convey what he generally did among Greeks: Greek historiography and the knowledge of travel, cunning intelligence, or even just Homer.³⁷ He might also strike some as an odd choice, especially those who knew him mainly from comedy, but his role in the *Odusia* and in Rome's First Punic War moment was still an active one, and for a Roman audience it is one that was likely evoked by Polybius' text. Polybius is thus quite unique. His position at Rome and tendency to view affairs *from* Rome coalesce with his Greek linguistic and cultural heritage and the distinct authorizing functions of each category.

In sum, Polybius' reference to and use of Odysseus in Book 1 and throughout the histories more widely activates both the Greek historiographical tradition going back at least to Hecataeus and Herodotus, and for a Roman audience it additionally taps into the collective cultural and literary moment that led to the relevance of the *Odusia* during the First Punic War. Odysseus' role in the western Mediterranean before and beyond the *Odusia* clearly conveyed a significance that would not have been lost on Polybius—that is to say, on a learned Greek set upon observing and recording Roman culture. This Odyssean significance extends from the tomb paintings of Tarquinia to the foundation legends of Circeii, Tusculum, and Praeneste, to the epics of Livius and Naevius. The *polytropos aner* was the polyvalent symbol a Greek historian at Rome needed when writing of this Mediterranean world at this time. Polybius' text appears simultaneously attuned to these seemingly contradictory conceptions of Odysseus while actively performing its own *synkrisis* of the hero's significatory potential. He is at once Homer's *andra polytropon* and Livius Andronicus' *virum versutum*, the turned about man, or, the "translated man" as he is famously rendered in the first line of the epic (Blänsdorf 1 = Flores I): *virum mihi, Camena, insece versutum*.

---

36 Although Hartog 2001, 162 is incorrect to ascribe the suppression of Odyssean variants to such an early date, the following quotation does hint at the nature of Odysseus' Roman status in the second century—bearing in mind that the widespread cultural relevance of Odysseus for the First Punic War is not something Hartog has considered: "It is also worth noting that even if the Romans did not consider the pious Aeneas to be the official founder of Rome, he nevertheless remained closely associated with its foundation, whereas the memory of Odysseus lived on only in the margins of Latium". It must be remembered, however, that the margins are consistently there on the side of any other narrative.
37 In Polybius, "the *Odyssey* thus establishes a certain hierarchy of knowledge; travel ensures eyewitness testimony, which provides the most reliable form of knowledge; reports from eyewitnesses constitute a second method of knowledge". Marincola 2007, 5. Cf. Marincola 1997, 63–85.

5

By way of conclusion I want to turn to Appian. Jumping ahead in time can help further develop the issues introduced in this chapter. Appian's narrative of the Roman civil wars contains a detailed description of Octavian and Agrippa's defeat of Sextus Pompey at Mylae (only a short while before their crippling defeat of Sextus a stone's throw away at Naulochus in 36 BCE). And the specific ways Appian depicts Sicilian geography can nicely wrap up the present discussion.

To best Pompey's fleet Octavian employs the *corvus* (6.106), a plank-like grappling hook first used by Gaius Duilius to win the first large scale naval battle of the First Punic War (in 260 BCE) at this same location off of Sicily. The victory resulted in Rome's first naval triumph and the erection of Duilius' influential *columna rostrata*, which Octavian later restored and duplicated with his own rostral column for Naulochus in the Forum, solidifying a bond between these moments in time.[38] The textual connection between the First Punic War and Octavian's victory is also impossible to miss here, since the *corvus* as such had been out of use for quite some time before the war between Sextus and Octavian—a striking anachronism. Yet Appian takes things even further and taps into the comparative web Polybius had spun, inserting Homeric geography at a moment that elevates it beyond the more standard inclusion of such geographic features by authors of the genre.

At 6.116, Agrippa leads Sextus' fleet away from Mylae and Octavian occupies the region, at which point Appian relates the following:

> Ἀγρίππου δὲ νομισθέντος ἐπελεῖν ἐς Πελωριάδα μετεπήδησεν, ἐκλιπὼν τὰ στενὰ περὶ Μύλας· καὶ ὁ Καῖσαρ αὐτῶν τε κατέσχε καὶ Μυλῶν καὶ Ἀρτεμισίου, πολίχνης βραχυτάτης, ἐν ᾗ φασι τὰς Ἡλίου βοῦς γενέσθαι καὶ τὸν ὕπνον Ὀδυσσεῖ.

> Believing that Agrippa was moving his fleet against him, Pompeius changed his position to Pelorus, abandoning the defiles around Mylae; and Octavian occupied them and also Mylae and Artemisium, a very small town, in which, they say, were the cattle of the Sun and where Odysseus fell asleep.[39]

Appian only mentions Odysseus by name at one other point in all of his extant writings.[40] And although he hedges here with *phasi*, the nature of this transition

---

38 Cf. Roller 2013, Biggs 2018.
39 Transl. White 1912.
40 *Mithridatic Wars* 8.53 contains mention of Odysseus and the Palladium during the narrative of Fimbria at Troy. Odyssean features are also somewhat rare. He begins the *Illyrian Wars* (Book

from late Republican civil war to a First Punic War battle waged in a landscape redolent of Odysseus is rather marked. The same temporal black hole we entered by sailing with the consuls of Polybius' narrative appears again when Agrippa and Octavian enter an identical space and perform deeds of the exact same type. Appian's move renders Octavian's *Bellum Siculum* a replay of the First Punic War, and he further evokes established modes of thinking about that Republican conflict by inserting the Odyssean into the mix. Octavian and Agrippa now can be seen defeating a new Carthaginian enemy on Homeric seas, replaying Rome's first overseas conflict in the epic tone within which it was cast by Latin's first authors in the late third century.

As we have seen, this marked connection between the world of the *Odyssey* and the First Punic War is neither arbitrary nor found for the first time in Appian. Perhaps Greek historiographical interest in melding Homeric geography with narratives of Rome's wars around Sicily can fully be explained with recourse to Hellenic traditions, but for Roman readers of such episodes, especially in Polybius, the impact early Latin epic had on shaping the First Punic War's reception as a "Roman Odyssey" would have been unavoidable and, I suggest, could have played a role in the reception of the text at Rome.

Bibliography

Allen, J. (2006), *Hostages and Hostage-Taking in the Roman Empire*, Cambridge.
Baron, C.A. (2013), *Timaeus of Tauromenium and Hellenistic Historiography*, Cambridge.
Biggs, T. (2018), "A Second First Punic War: Re-Spoliation of Republican Naval Monuments in the Urban and Poetic Landscapes of Augustan Rome", in: M. Loar/C. MacDonald/D. Padilla Peralta (eds.), *Rome, Empire of Plunder: The Dynamics of Cultural Appropriation*, Cambridge, 47–68.
Blänsdorf, J./K. Büchner/W. Morel (eds.) (2010), *Fragmenta poetarum Latinorum epicorum et lyricorum*, Berlin.
Champion, C. (2004), *Cultural Politics in Polybius's Histories*, Berkeley.
Dillery, J. (2009), "Roman Historians and the Greeks: Audiences and Models", in: A. Feldherr (ed.), *The Cambridge Companion to the Roman Historians*, Cambridge, 77–107.
Dougherty, C. (2001), *The Raft of Odysseus: The Ethnographic Imagination of Homer's Odyssey*, Oxford.
Erskine, A. (2012), "Polybius among the Romans: Life in the Cyclops' Cave", in: C. Smith/L.M. Yarrow (eds.), *Imperialism, Cultural Politics, and Polybius*, Oxford, 17–32.

1.2) with a genealogy from Polyphemus: "They say that the country received its name from Illyrius, the son of Polyphemus; for the Cyclops Polyphemus and his wife, Galatea, had three sons, Celtus, Illyrius, and Galas, all of whom migrated from Sicily, and ruled over the peoples called after them Celts, Illyrians and Galatians". Transl. White 1912.

Farrell, J. (2004), "Roman Homer", in: R.L. Fowler (ed.), *The Cambridge Companion to Homer*, Cambridge, 254–71.
Flores, E. (2011), *Livi Andronici Odusia: introduzione, edizione critica e versione italiana*, Naples.
—— (2014), *Commentario a Cn. Naevi Bellum Poenicum*, Naples.
Goldberg, S.M. (1995), *Epic in Republican Rome*, Oxford.
Hartog, F. (2001), *Memories of Odysseus: Frontier Tales from Ancient Greece*, Chicago.
Jones, H.J. (1932), *Strabo. Geography, Volume VIII: Book 17. General Index*. Loeb Classical Library 267, Cambridge, Mass.
Leigh, M. (2010), "Early Roman Epic and the Maritime Moment", in: *CPh* 105.4, 265–280.
Malkin, I. (1998), *The Returns of Odysseus: Colonization and Ethnicity*, Berkeley.
Manuwald, G. (2011), *Roman Republican Theatre*, Cambridge.
Marincola, J. (1997), *Authority and Tradition in Ancient Historiography*, Cambridge.
—— (2007), "Odysseus and the Historians", in: *SyllClass* 18, 1–79.
de Melo, W.D.C. (2011), *Plautus. Amphitryon, The Comedy of Asses, The Pot of Gold, The Two Bacchises, The Captives*. Loeb Classical Library, 60, Cambridge, Mass.
—— (2012), *Plautus. The Little Carthaginian, Pseudolus, The Rope*. Loeb Classical Library, 260, Cambridge, Mass.
Miltsios, N. (2013), *The Shaping of Narrative in Polybius*, Trends in Classics. Supplementary Volume 23, Berlin.
Montiglio, S. (2005), *Wandering in Ancient Greek Culture*, Chicago.
—— (2011), *From Villain to Hero: Odysseus in Ancient Thought*, Ann Arbor.
Paton, W.R./F.W. Walbank/C. Habicht (2010), *Polybius. The Histories, Volume I: Books 1–2*, Cambridge, Mass.
Paton, W.R./F.W. Walbank/C. Habicht/S.D. Olson (2012), *Polybius. The Histories*, Volume VI: Books 28-39. Fragments. Loeb Classical Library 161, Cambridge, Mass.
Rackham, H. (1942), *Pliny. Natural History, Volume II: Books 3–7*. Loeb Classical Library 352, Cambridge, Mass.
Ribbeck, O. 1897–8), *Scaenicae Romanorum Poesis Fragmenta*, Leipzig.
Roller, M. (2013), "On the Intersignification of Monuments in Augustan Rome", in: *AJPh* 134.1, 119–31.
Rood, T. (2004),"Thucydides", in: I.J.F. De Jong et al. (eds.), *Narrators, Narratees, and Narratives in Ancient Greek Literature*, Leiden, 115–28.
—— (2012), "Polybius, Thucydides, and the First Punic War", in: C. Smith/L.M. Yarrow (eds.), *Imperialism, Cultural Politics, and Polybius*, Oxford, 50–67.
Stanford, W.B. (1954), *The Ulysses Theme: A Study in the Adaptability of a Traditional Hero*, Oxford.
Walbank, F.W. (1957), *A Historical Commentary on Polybius*, Oxford.
—— (1972), *Polybius*, Berkeley.
White, H. et al. (1912), *Appian's Roman History*. Loeb Classical Library, 2–5, London.
Wiseman, T.P. (2015), *The Roman Audience: Classical Literature as Social History*, Oxford.

Evangelos Karakasis
Silius Italicus and Polybius: *Quellenforschung* and Silian Poetics

Quellenforschung has long been a favorite approach to Silius Italicus' *Punica*, since it is a historical epic narrating a major historical event, for the Roman mind in any case: the Second Punic War. As early as Ruperti's commentary (1795–8) and Heynacher's (1877) seminal study on Silius' historical sources, it is a *communis opinio* that Silius often sets in epic hexameters historical data as narrated in his main historiographical source: the third decade of Livius' immense opus (*Books* 21–30), although the possibility of a shared unknown source in several cases is by no means to be rejected.[1] Even so, various narrative sequences, historical details and indications of linguistic assimilation support the view of Livy as Silius' main historiographical source, though often one may discern a noteworthy change of focus between the Livian and the Silian narrative.[2]

In these cases Silius may diverge from Livius' narrative towards different versions, including that of Polybius.[3] These secondary sources are often highly debated, especially in the case of the so-called "annalistic tradition", i.e., a chiefly single story-line allegedly exemplified by various reports of the Hannibalic War.[4] What is more, many sources of the Hannibalic War have been largely lost (Silenus, Fabius Pictor, L. Cincius Alimentus, Coelius Antipater, Valerius Antias); therefore, it is not possible to determine with any accuracy the degree of Silius' access to these narratives of the Second Punic War. The Greek historian seems, however, to be noticeably affecting Silius from the very beginning of his work. A reference in vv. 7–8 of his προοίμιον to a competition over world dominion, for example, a detail crucially absent from Livius' relevant account, points to a possible influence of Polybius (1.3.7) on Silius, as Gibson 2010, 51–54 has compellingly argued.[5] Or at least this may signal a historiographical tradition on which Polybius also draws. It is quite possible that Silius had direct access to Polybius' histories, if one takes into account both the wealth of Silius' libraries and his extended literary interests as attested, for example, by Pliny's obituary (cf. *Ep.*

---

1 Cf. Nicol 1936, 19.
2 Cf. Pomeroy 2010, 27–45, especially pp. 31–32, also Augoustakis 2010, 12, Stocks 2014, 35–36. See, however, the reservations voiced by Nicol 1936, 17–19.
3 *Pace* Miniconi and Devallet 1979, xliv–xlvi.
4 Cf. Pomeroy 2010, 29–30.
5 Vs. von Albrecht 1964, 19, Marks 2005, 69 and n. 21; see also Gibson 2010, 52 and n. 18.

3.7.4), and the affluent *doctrina* of the Flavian educational system, as suggested by the rich curriculum of Statius' father's teaching.[6]

1 Methodological Remarks Aims/Objectives of the Present Paper

It is true that much of the non-Livian material in Silius may be explained as a conscious authorial invention / alteration due to specific compositional demands or for generic reasons (cf. especially Klotz 1933, Venini 1972, 1972a, Nesselrath 1986, Lucarini 2004, Spaltenstein 1986; 1990, 2006[7]); however, the view adopted in this paper is that incorporation of Polybian information and the implementation of generically imposed requirements should not, in principle, be read as mutually exclusive, especially when particular details in the Polybian and the Silian narratives point to their association. An alternative source, Polybius himself or Polybius' historiographical tradition for the interests of this paper (see above), may occasionally help Silius implement his poetic and poetological objectives, and this seems to be evidenced on the level of Silian intertextual poetics as well.

From this perspective, the present paper aims to re-assess some possible Polybian influences on the *Punica* from the perspective of Silian poetics and Flavian ideology in particular. In more detail, I shall be examining instances where Silius diverges from his main, Livian model by incorporating in his narrative details of a historiographical tradition, largely represented by Polybius (Nicol 1936 is still at this point highly invaluable[8]). My intention is to examine:

a) possible patterns in the distribution of these likely Polybian reminiscences within Silius' epic.

b) the way these probable recollections of Polybius' account are incorporated in narratives evoking Roman literary intertexts, from the Augustan, the Neronian as well as the Flavian period, for producing intertextual meaning as part of Silius' overall authorial intertextual poetics and epic objectives,

---

[6] Cf. Gibson 2010, 43 and n. 6, Pomeroy 2010, 31.
[7] For a concise yet informed literature review of scholarship on Silian *Quellenforschung*, cf. Pomeroy 2010, especially p. 29.
[8] Nicol 1936 is also significantly informed by and capitalizes on the important *Quellensforschung* scholarship on Silius of the late eighteenth century, when this scholarly trend was fashionable (e.g. Heynacher 1877, Bauer 1883, Schlichteisen 1881, van Veen 1884); see Nicol 1936, *preface*, Dominik 2010, 429 and nn. 145, 146, Pomeroy 2010, 29 and n. 7.

c) and to contextualize, when applicable, these references to Polybius in the Flavian literary milieu and ideology as promoted by Flavian epic, and Silius' narrative in particular.

2 *Punica* 1—Polybius, Vergil and Lucan

Let us start with the Silian lines of the first book devoted to Hasdrubal, who succeeded Hamilcar, his father-in-law, in the command of Spain (vv. 56–181). In vv. 146 ff. Silius draws a negative portrait of Hasbrubal as a cruel commander-in-chief, prone to violent rages, avid for power simply for the sake of his malice. This bloodthirsty Hasdbrubal is depicted as crediting himself with glory just for his ability to provoke fear, against the Roman ideal of glory as the result of military success; the latter is an ideal promoted by the *bellatrix gens* of the Flavian emperors as evidenced, *inter alia*, by Flavian coinages[9] and disclosed in Jupiter's prophecy (*Pun.* 3.595–6) and, therefore, up to a point, by the Silian epic as a whole. According to Silius, it was Hasdrubal's brutality and savage punishments that led to Hasdrubal's conquest of Spain (the cruel execution of the king Tagus is a clear example). But the Livian account (21.2.5) tells a rather different story, and commends the reconciliatory politics of Hasbrubal through which he secured the expansion of Carthaginian sway over Spain. Nicol 1936, 21–2 is right in bringing to the fore a similar account offered by Polybius who, even if mentioning Hasdrubal's diplomacy and restraint, also cites Hasdrubal's unfavorable portrayal by Fabius Pictor, a further alleged source of Livius. The Fabian narrative adapted by Polybius (3.8) also underlines Hasdrubal's despotic politics in Spain which he ruled κατὰ τὴν αὐτοῦ προαίρεσιν. What is more, as a result of king Tagus' horrifying crucifixion, mentioned above, and the equally abhorrent parading of his unburied corpse to the grieving citizens, Silius describes the revenge of a slave who snatches the sword from his master's unburied body still hanging on the tree, rushes into the palace and kills Hasdrubal (vv. 165–8). Again, there is sufficient evidence to suggest (Nicol 1936, 22–3) that the narrative of Tagus' death and its avenging also associates the Silian account with Polybius' storyline (1.166), which describes the murder of Hasdrubal by an avenger who forces an entry into the commander's lodging. Livy, on the contrary, only mentions an attack by the murderer who is easily captured by those witnessing the scene (21.2.6).

---

9 Cf. Tuck 2016, 111–12, 116.

Silius gathers together Livian material, so as to give a particular importance to Carthaginian drawbacks of character, such as their proverbial deceitfulness and vindictiveness.[10] A similar narrative technique seems to be developed here, with Silius preferring the Polybian alternative in order to underline the typical Punic vice of cruelty,[11] commented upon in Roman literature as early as Ennius' *Annales* (cf. 287 Skutsch and the ham-stringing of a Punic foe; see also Liv. 21.4.9, 24.45.12–4). Not only is Hasdrubal depicted as cruel, but he also falls victim to the very cruelty he inspires. This is depicted in a scene intensifying the pathos of the narrative, an additional apparent reason for inclusion of Polybian material. What is more, the emphasis of these Polybius-inspired lines on Punic malice is underscored on the intertextual level as well, as the Silian Hasdrubal's harshness evokes intertexts from Vergil and Lucan. Hasdrubal's cruelty, a side issue in the Livian narrative, is in the Silian lines suggested also by the detail of the Carthaginian leader's rejoicing in the fear he can arouse as proof of personal glory. This attitude is criticized by the epic narrator who calls Hamilcar's son-in-law insane (*demens*). This combination of the motif of pride in being fearsome along with its condemnation by the epic storyteller calls to mind a similar attitude of Lucan's Caesar, who, in a passage where he is portrayed as a pitiless tyrant and a foreign foe marching to Rome, similarly (3.82–3) *gaudet ... esse timori tam magno populis*, thus provoking Lucan's criticism (cf. 3.71–97).[12]

As to the pitiless execution of Tagus, Silius creates the image of a nature sympathetic to the handsome ruler's death; the Nymphs of Spain are presented as bewailing his loss in their grottos and banks (vv. 155–6). This image of the Nymphs representing the natural world and mourning, following the pathetic fallacy motif, the cruel passing of a handsome young man evokes the Nymphs of the fifth Vergilian eclogue, who similarly lament the death of the beautiful Daphnis, the archetypical bucolic singer. Daphnis of the fifth Vergilian bucolic, however, has long been compellingly read, as already by ancient scholiasts, as standing for a positively focalized, deified Caesar. In the case of both figures of the Silian narrative (Hasdrubal and Tagus) one thus can argue for an intertextual association with Caesar through the intertexts evoked by a narrative deviating from the main Livian account towards Polybius' handling of historical material. Nonethe-

---

10 Cf. e.g. Pomeroy 2010, 36.
11 Despite a more sympathetic overall view of Hannibal offered by Polybius (cf. Plb. 3.13.8, 9.22.8), in opposition to Roman sources emphasizing the Carthaginian leader's viciousness; see Stocks 2014, 16, 18, 21 (with bibliography).
12 Cf. Hunink 1992, 65.

less, a negatively focalized Silian Hasdrubal is crucially linked to Caesar as a symbol of tyrannical conduct in Lucan's epic, similarly received and re-appropriated in the tyrannical figures of the Flavian epic.[13] This is occasionally the case with the incontrollable and "ambivalent"[14] Silian Hannibal as well, fraught with evident Caesarian undertones (Marks) and crucially described as a Tyrian tyrant (cf. 1.239–79). Silius presents Caesar disparagingly as well, as a tyrannical character, through Sibyl's prophecy concerning civil war in the *nekyia* of *Punica* 13 (vv. 850– 67), i.e., in yet another passage intertextually conversing with Lucan's epic and unfavorable Caesarian moments (Tipping). In any case, Hasdrubal's attitude towards fear also alludes to the proverbial, by the Flavian age, phrase *oderint dum metuant*, used of the tyrant Atreus in Accius (*trag.* 203) and later as his motto by the emperor Caligula (cf. Suet. *Cal.* 30). That latter, of course, was not a much favored Julio-Claudian emperor, as were Augustus and Claudius, for example. While the Carthaginian commander is associated with a negatively focalized Caesar, the victim of Hasdrubal's vindictiveness is, on the other hand, associated with a positively focalized Caesar, also the martyr of a cruel assassination. Thus, Silius seems to be capitalizing on the various focalizations of Caesar evoked by a narrative incorporating what is probably Polybian material.

3 *Punica* 4, 5 and 7—Polybius, Lucan and Statius

Further instances of a probable Polybian influence occur in Books 4, 5 and 7. Among Silius' objectives one should include not only his desire to call attention to the alleged vices of the Carthaginians but also to highlight the positive qualities of Hannibal as a military leader as well as those of his men; abilities generally acclaimed in the case of the Punic commander-in-chief as the "synecdochic hero" (term of Hardie 1983) of the Carthaginians, as early as, e.g., Antiochus at Enn. *Ann.* 371–3 Skutsch, and enhanced by Polybius (9.22) and Livy (cf. e.g. 21.4.8, 24.45.12–4) too. This occurs especially in the narration of that part of the war when, despite an apparent climax of the Roman *mores*, a Punic final victory seemed quite likely. Therefore, the Carthaginians in the Silian narrative are occasionally portrayed as the apposite opponents of the Romans, destined to function as a test which will eventually bring into being great Roman warriors; the poet

---

13 Cf. e.g. Bernstein 2016, 398–99.
14 For Silian Hannibal's "ambivalence", see especially Stocks 2014, 232. Positive delineation of Silian characters is by no means strictly conditioned upon ethnic associations; cf. Bernstein 2016, 404–05.

thus programmatically declares (4.603) "manhood is tested by adversities" (*explorant adversa viros*). On the other hand, Silius also negatively remarks on the lack of the necessary military expertise on the part of the defeated Romans during the adverse years of the war. This intention has been compellingly shown to account for the transposition of Livian material and the change of focus of the Silian narrative in relation to its main, Livian model. A similar intention seems to be discerned in the case of "Polybian" digressions as well.

In his seventh book, Silius depicts Hannibal largely positively as a far-sighted general, watchful and vigilant, tormented by the difficult situation he faces, ambushed as he is among the Formian hills and the swamps at Liternum, when trying to find an escape through Mount Callicula. This gateway was eventually materialized through the stratagem of the blazing cattle (cf. Liv. 22.16.7), crucially domestic just like in Polybius (cf. 3.93.3–10).[15] Thus, in *Punica* 7 (cf. vv. 279–81) Hannibal has to cope with a tougher situation than in Livy, since Silius' Hannibal faces the prospect of starvation and total ruin in opposition to his Livian counterpart, who simply realizes his strenuous wintering with insufficient supplies against the Roman troops (22.16.4–5).[16] In terms of this positive, up to a point, coloring of Hannibal and his men, one should also interpret the favorable presentation of Acherras, a Punic fighter, who, in vv. 340–2, is depicted as taking care of a worn out horse, giving it a rub and washing his sour mouth. Littlewood 2011, xxiv is right in associating Silius' emphasis on the Punic treatment of domesticated animals with a Polybian influence. A similar emphasis on the treatment of horses, paramount for the Carthaginians in opposition to the Romans for their military movements, is narrated by Polybius (3.74.11). The emphasis on the rubbing down of the steed's coat and the healing of its sores brings the Silian lines close to Polybius' account of the Carthaginians when reaching the Adriatic after Trasimene: Polybius similarly stresses the use of antiseptic material (wine-vinegar) for the various lesions the horses suffer from and the rubbing of their coat with oil. Acherras, a notable Gaetulian officer of the Carthaginian army, is also represented as keeping vigil during the night, in opposition to younger soldiers

---

[15] For this rather Polybian information and its (intertextual) implications as well, cf. esp. Littlewood 2011, xxv, 2013, 281 and n. 10.

[16] Cf. Spaltenstein 1986, 465. For a further possible influence of Polybius here, cf. also Nicol 1936, 37–38, who discusses the Polybian Fabius' belief (3.93.1) that, due to the privileges of the Roman positioning, he could bring the whole campaign to an end, victorious for the Roman side. Polybius' emphasis on Hannibal's absolutely critical situation is, however, given through Fabius' perspective whereas in Silius this is brought to the fore by means of Hannibal's anxiety. This further highlights the quite dramatic circumstances of which a positively focalized Carthaginian leader is markedly conscious.

like Maraxes and Mago, whom Hannibal, also on his guard, found sleeping; in this Acherras is a double of the Carthaginian leader. This is a rather Roman military virtue, as deduced by classical Roman historiographical discourses such as those of Sallust (cf. *Cat.* 5.3) and Livy (cf. 21.4.6). This Roman asset is here transferred, through the Polybian reference, to the Carthaginian warrior; Hannibal himself is characterized by the same virtue in the first programmatic book, when Hannibal's excellence once more consists in his refusal of sleep, his being armed and ready against any menace (vv. 245–6; see also Liv. 21.4.6). In terms of intertextual poetics, the motif of martial wakefulness along with the wording of the relevant line (v. 390: *parca quies minimumque soporis*), evoke Lucan's similar description of Cato as *somni parcissimus* (9.590). Whereas a negatively focalized Hasdrubal is, in terms of a passage of Polybian undertones, intertextually associated with the conceited, tyrannical Caesar of Lucan's epic, a positively portrayed Carthaginian official, again in a part of a narrative influenced by Polybius is, on the other hand, linked to the real hero of Lucan's *Bellum Civile*, the true representative of the Stoic ideal: Cato is wakeful in his march through Libya, often conclusively read as an allegory of the trials of the Stoic sage. Acherras is thus associated with Stoic ideals, crucially promoted by Silius and, up to point, accepted by Domitian with his Stoic Herculean associations.[17] Polybian data and Lucanian intertexts are in this way associated in Silian poetics with varying effect.

Polybian reminiscences and their intertextual associations are occasionally, on the other hand, used as a means for denigrating the lack of traditional military valor and expertise, i.e., a further major Flavian ideal. C. Flaminius, the consul of 217 BCE and the Roman leader in the battle at lake Transimene, is a rather negative exemplum in both Livy (21.3.4–5) and Polybius as well as in Silius, where the officer and his doomed, foolhardy rush are condemned in contrast to the positive paradigm of Fabius (7.229–31).[18] Be that as it may, when introducing Flaminius' advance, Silius reports on the positioning of the hasty Roman commander as a precursor, in front of his standards, and in charge of an undisciplined army, followed by numerous camp groups (vv. 5.28–33); such an army inevitably falls into the trap of the Carthaginians hidden along the hills over Trasimene. A similar emphasis on the position of the leader, his impetuosity and rashness as well as on his followers, occurs in the relevant description of the incident by Polybius

---

[17] Domitian should not be read as an enemy of Stoicism in general (cf. Jones 1992, 121–22), despite the so-called "Stoic opposition" to the emperor.
[18] Cf. also Ariemma 2010, 250.

(3.82.7, 8). Scholars may therefore be right in detecting here a likely Polybian influence. This Polybian allusion is further combined with an intertext from Statius' *Thebaid*: the detail of the warriors entering the battle as fugitives (v. 33: *pugnam fugientum more petebant*) evokes a similar attitude of another negatively depicted army, that of the equally hasty Argives of the seventh book in Statius' long epic. The Argives do not pay the appropriate heed to the omens of disaster, but instead rapidly take up arms against the Thebans, spurred by Hermes, Jupiter's messenger, who re-ignites the polemic disposition after his visit to Mars' abode. The warriors are again represented as rushing to face their opponent as if they were fugitives (vv. 401–2: *properatur in hostem / more fugae*). Polybian allusions and their intertextual associations, used in the case of Acherras as a means for praising his Roman values are, instead, employed, in the case of the Roman general, for censuring hasty military tactics which do not follow tried and tested strategic plans such as, for example, the *cunctatio* policy of Fabius Maximus in *Pun.* 7. Flaminius is not patient enough[19] to await encouraging omens, despite the augur Corvinus' counsel, or to wait for Servilius' auxiliary army, and is thus led into disaster (5.53–189). Thus Flaminius, a chiefly negatively focalized *exemplum* of a contemptuous, disrespectful attitude towards divine signs, may be historically contextualized as following in the steps of a similarly disrespectful Galba, one of the emperors responsible for the historical chaos of 69 AD to which the Flavians and Domitian in particular (cf. e.g. Suet. *Dom.* 13.1)[20] give an end: Flaminius, on the other hand, is accordingly set in opposition to Vespasian, the founder of the Flavian dynasty, reverential in public, who during Domitian's reign paid heed to gods' will (cf. Tac. *Hist.* 1.18, 2.78, 4.81–4)[21]. Despite some differences in points of detail between the Polybian and the Silian narrative, several scholars[22] identify a further Polybian allusion as having previously been employed by Silius in Book 4 for underscoring Flaminius' lack of the necessary military proficiency against opponents like the Carthaginians; these are furthermore contrasted to the fickle Gallic tribe of the Boii conquered by the Roman general.[23] Silius thus likens Flaminius, a bad general rushing on the way to Trasimene, an instrument of Juno to destroy Rome from the outset of his consular office, to the totally inexperienced

---

19 For rashness as Flaminius' character-trait, cf. also Pomeroy 2010, 40 and n. 42, Gibson 2013, 81, Fucecchi 2013, 114–15 and n. 16. For Flaminius as a double-sided, "ambivalent" character, equally pious and impious, cf. Chaudhuri 2013, 379–97.
20 Cf. Galimberti 2016, 92.
21 Cf. Bernstein 2016, 400.
22 Cf. Nicol 1936, 35, Marks 2005, 18 and n. 12, Gibson 2010, 51 and n. 12; see, on the other hand, the reservations by Sapaltenstein 1986, 323.
23 Cf. Gibson 2010, 51.

pilot of a ship (a simple landsman) unable to properly steer a vessel (vv. 4.713–7) tossed about in mid-ocean. This in opposition to the delayer Fabius (also contrasted in Livy, 22.12.5) who, on the other hand, is measured against a vigilant helmsman (1.687–89) pulling in the sails due to an impending tempest.[24] Haste on the whole is certainly detrimental to Romans in Silius, when associated either with the victorious Carthaginians (Hannibal is a classical example of such a quick action) or the defeated Romans (cf. also Varro at Cannae in *Pun.* 8)[25]. Likewise Polybius (3.81.11) associates the absence of a competent general, something which Flaminius is not (cf. 2.31.1, 7–9, 2.21.8–9, 3.80.3), with lack of a helmsman. The simile of course does, in addition, fit the epic generic identity of Silius' lines, assimilating an epic *topos*, that of a helmsman in stormy weather.[26]

4 *Punica* 14—Polybius and the epic Vergil (*Aeneid*)

In line with the overall "pathetic" character of Silius' epic narrative, the Flavian epic poet is quite dramatic in tone and largely exaggerating when focusing on Archimedes, who appears as a predominantly positive figure in the Silian narrative, especially when describing the fatal effects Archimedes' war devices (the *ferrea manus* of Livy) had upon Marcellus' Roman forces attacking Syracuse in *Punica* 14, vv. 320–32. Yet again, in opposition to Livy and in keeping with Polybius' account (8.7(9).4), Silius seems to be amplifying the makings of the martial machine and speaks of an engine able to lift soldiers up in the air and have them

---

[24] Cf. also Ariemma 2010, 267.
[25] Cf. also Bernstein 2016, 400, 402–03.
[26] In large part generic/plot demands may account for the presence in Silius (7.409–11) of the Punic fleet in the bay of Naples, allegedly absent from Livius as opposed to Polybius, i.e., a further likely Silian source at this point; cf. Nicol 1936, 39. This assumed "Polybian addition" results in an embedded narrative chiefly of the epic kind, namely Proteus' prophesy as to the outcome of the Punic Wars. However, a reference to a Punic naval incursion which the Roman commander, Servilius, was responsible to counter-attack does appear in Livy as well (22.11.6–7). He, however, locates the Carthaginian convoy to the north of Caieta, namely Cosa; see also Spaltenstein 1986, 473. Livy thus may compellingly be read here as yet again Silius' primary source, especially if one takes into account the well-documented Silian method of locally and chronologically transposing Livian material (cf. e.g. Gibson 2010, 49–51). In any case, in Polybius (3.96.8–10) there is not a specific reference to Formiae or Caieta, unlike in the Silian report; Polybius simply gives an account of the fleet's route to Pisa whence, due to the awaiting grave Roman danger it had to cope with, the Punic navy sailed back to Carthage through Sardinia; see also Nicol 1936, 39, Littlewood 2011, 169.

fall down again. The quite lethal character of Archimedes' war engine in Silius, following the Polybian version, is further underscored by its intertextual association with Aeneas' deadly trophy to Mars, a notably polished trunk, upon which the arms, the *spolia opima* of the slain Mezentius, are hung by the Vergilian hero, at the beginning of the eleventh book of the Vergilian epic, cf. *A.* 11.5: *ingentem quercum decisis undique ramis:*[27] the Silian emphasis on the notion of a rounded off war structure along with the formulation of this information, namely an ablative temporal complement in the last metrical part of the line, where the participle is separated by its subject through an *undique* in the middle, *erasis undique nodis* (v. 320), points to the intertextual linking of the Silian line with the Vergilian model. The engine of Silius thus assumes the intertextual status of an unmistakable token of a Roman-vanquishing conqueror, as Aeneas' tree-trunk trophy is indicative of contemporary Roman military practice.[28] In the Silian narrative, however, it is an opponent of the Romans, in particular Archimedes with his celebrated outstanding mastermind (cf. also *Pun.* 14.341–52), who acquires the intertextual standing of the Roman military defeater. Vergilian intertextuality, along with Polybian information, are here used as a means for extolling Archimedes' praised genius. This near-death experience for the Roman troops and their commander, Marcellus, intertextually associated as they are with the defeated Mezentius, Turnus' ally,[29] eventually becomes the trial for the transformation of Marcellus to a largely positively focalized paradigm of a general with Fabian traits.[30] The Roman general shows notable conceit and contempt for his opponents at the beginning of the Sicilian enterprise (14.237) and is in the miniature *epos* of *Punica* 14, to a certain extent, intratextually related to Hannibal at Saguntum.[31] The intertextual Mezentian connotations this Silian passage is fraught with calls for a further intratextual association: The un-Fabian Flaminius, up to a point modeled on Vergilian Mezentius,[32] eventually loses the battle and is slain; an also un-Fabian Marcellus of Mezentian undertones, on the other hand, in due course adopts Fabian features and is finally the champion of the enterprise.

---

27 Cf. Spaltenstein 1990, 310.
28 Cf. Gransden 1991, 70.
29 Mezentius is a notable contemptuous and arrogant figure of the Vergilian *Aeneid* (cf. *A.* 7.647–8, 11.15–6), occasionally re-appropriated in the tyrannical figures of the Neronian and Flavian literature as well. Cf. Basson 1984, 58–59, Bernstein 2016, 309.
30 Cf. Fucecchi 2010, 237.
31 Cf. Stocks 2014, 147–66.
32 Cf. Ripoll 1998, 341–42.

5 Punica 17—Polybius, Propertius and Seneca

A further telling difference between the Second Punic War-narratives of Livy and Polybius relates to the presence of Syphax, the Numidian king, in the triumph conducted by Scipio Aemilianus (17.625–54). In opposition to Livy (33.45), for whom Syphax died at Tibur shortly before the celebratory event of the final Roman victory, Silius presents Syphax, just like Polybius (16.23.6; see also V. Max. 6.2.3, Tac. *Ann.* 12.38.1), as a prominent captive of Scipio's victorious parade. King Syphax, furthermore, is in Silius (17.629–30) presented as also chained in golden shackles, according to the established pattern of captive officials in imperial triumphs. Be that as it may, the very image of the golden chains of a prisoner king in a triumphal procession (cf. Sil. 14.629–30: *ante Syphax, feretro residens, captive premebat / lumina, et auratae servabant colla catenae*) allude to Seneca's *Troades* (vv. 153–6 in particular),[33] where, availing herself on the *topos* of the misfortunes a dead person has avoided as also known from Roman *consolations*,[34] Hecuba presents Priam as *felix* (v. 144). He is a classical example of human misfortune, however, for the chorus in conversation with the Trojan queen, slain as he was with his sons having lost their lives before him (vv. 132–42). For Hebuca, the Phrygian king is *felix*, because he has escaped the disgrace of participating with golden chains, burdening his hand, in the triumph of the Greek leader, Agamemnon, at Argos or Mycenae. Syphax is thus intertextually depicted as more ill-fated than the exemplum par excellence of human wretchedness, Priam. All at once the ally of the Carthaginians is also thus intertextually associated with the royal captives in the triumphs of Augustus' era, a connection to which cogency is further lent by the likewise intertextual correlation of Scipio's triumph to Augustus' triple *triumphus* in Verg. A. 8.714–20 (see also 6.801–5);[35] Syphax's vanquisher, Scipio, is thus linked to Augustus himself. The triumph Seneca's Priam is presented to escape, unlike the Silian Syphax, is crucially depicted, as Fantham 1982, 230–1 convincingly remarks, as an Augustan triumphal procession (cf. also Hor. *Carm.* 2.12.11–2). Scipio Africanus, the main Silian persona of a "proto-*princeps*" (Bernstein 2016, 400), of Domitian Germanicus in particular (cf. Marks

---

33 Cf. Spaltenstein 1990, 481.
34 Cf. Fantham 1982, 230.
35 Cf. Tipping 2010, 213–14 with the bibliography cited; see also Tipping 2010a 187, Lovatt 2016, 372–73.

2005, 209–44, especially p. 218)³⁶ is thus intertextually portrayed as a new Augustus, in line with the Flavian imperial propaganda;³⁷ the emperor promotes his image as a "new Augustus" and crucially adopts the "Julio-Claudian portraiture"³⁸ as well as the first imperial dynasty's public discourse of a tranquil and merciful emperor.³⁹ Similar Augustan undertones, promoting the public image of Domitian, may be discerned in a further literary intertext of the imprisoned Syphax's golden chains in Silius' Scipionic triumph, namely Propertius (2.1.33),⁴⁰ where kings with golden chains around their necks, just like in Silius, are also presented as Octavian's captives; both the image and the wording of the Silian line (see above) are reminiscent of Propertius' picture and diction (v. 33: *regum auratis circumdata colla catenis*). This image is part of a Propertian *recusatio*, where the poet of the *genus tenue* excuses himself to Maecenas for not being able to praise in epic lines Octavian's deeds and Maecenas' devoted assistance to the *princeps*; the list of Octavian's victories include Mutina (43 BCE), Philippi (42 BCE), Naulochus (36 BCE), Perusia (41 BCE), Actium (31 BCE), and the subsequent Alexandrian War, rounded off by a reference to Octavian's triumph in 29 BCE after the subjugation of Egypt,⁴¹ in which the chained kings of v. 33 take part. In this way yet again Scipio / Domitian *triumphans* is linked with his imperial model, Augustus *triumphator*.

6 Conclusions

To conclude: on the basis of the analysis offered above, the main reasons for the incorporation of likely Polybian information in the Silian narrative, evidently put in the service of Silian poetics, include the following or a combination thereof:
  a) emphasis on the typical, for the Roman mind, negative features of the Carthaginians,

---

36 For a more reserved view, cf. Tipping 2007, 235–39, 2010, 185–92, Jacobs 2010, 137–39, Chaudhuri 2013, 396 and n. 42.
37 Cf. Tuck 2016, 109–10 (with bibliography).
38 Cf. especially Marks 2005, 236 and n. 93, 243, see also Karakasis 2014, 263; for an account of Scipio's Domitianic associations in the triumph-passage of *Pun.* 17 in particular, see also Tipping 2010, 213–15, 2010a 188–89.
39 Cf. Tipping 2010a, 163–64.
40 Cf. Spaltenstein 1990, 481.
41 Cf. Camps 1985, 65, 69–70.

b) focus on the superior military strategy of the Carthaginians, the most suitable enemies of the Romans, who ultimately will bring to light the Roman valor of the last books in the *Punica*, after the defeat of the Romans in the disastrous battle of Cannes in each case,
c) a negative comment, on the other hand, on the lack of the appropriate martial tactics on the part of the Romans, chiefly in the first part of the epic,
d) intensification of the *pathos* of the epic narrative, and
e) integration of key generic, epic features such epic similes.

Silius' assimilation and reworking of Polybius' material is occasionally combined with intertexts reinforcing the point of borrowed Polybian content and associating it with Flavian concerns and interests; the cruelty and the tyrannical character of Hasdrubal, for example, as in both Silius and Polybius and unlike Livy, is also enhanced by his intertextual association with a cruel Lucanian Caesar. The present paper does not have as its ambition to exhaust the issue of Polybius' influence on Silius, but simply hopes to have showcased the way Silian deviations towards the Greek historiographer or, in any case, a tradition which includes him, becomes part of Silius' intertextual poetics. This ultimately accentuates the need for a research method which is not simply interested in detecting Silius' historiographical sources, Polybius included, but which instead combines *Quellenforschung* with an attention to Silius' sophisticated and complex means of producing meaning.

Bibliography

von Albrecht, M. (1964), *Silius Italicus: Freiheit und Gebundenheit Römischer Epik*, Amsterdam.
Ariemma, E.M. (2010), *"Fons Cuncti Varro Mali*: The Demagogue Varro in *Punica* 8–10", in: A. Augoustakis (ed.), *Brill's Companion to Silius Italicus*, Leiden, 241–76.
Augoustakis, A. (ed.) (2010), *Brill, Companion to Silius Italicus*, Leiden.
Basson, W.P. (1984), "Vergil's Mezentius: a Pivotal Personality", *AClass* 27, 57–70.
Bauer, L. (1883), *Das Verhältnis der Punica des C. Silius Italicus zur dritten Dekade des T. Livius*, PhD diss., Erlangen.
Bernstein, N.W. (2016), "Epic Poetry: Historicizing the Flavian Epics", in: A. Zissos (ed.), *A Companion to the Flavian Age of Imperial Rome*, Malden/Oxford/Chichester, 395–411.
Camps, W.A. (1985), *Propertius. Elegies II*, London.
Chaudhuri, P. (2013), "Flaminius' Failure?", in: G. Manuwald/A. Voigt (eds.), *Flavian Epic Interactions*, Berlin, 379–97.
Dominik, W.J. (2010), "The Reception of Silius Italicus in Modern Scholarship", in: A. Augoustakis (ed.), *Brill, Companion to Silius Italicus*, Leiden, 425–47.
Fantham, E. (1982), *Seneca, Troades: A Literary Introduction with Text, Translation, and Commentary*, Princeton.

Fucecchi, M. (2010), "The Shield and the Sword: Q. Fabius Maximus and M. Claudius Marcellus as Models of Heroism in Silius' *Punica*", in: A. Augoustakis (ed.), *Brill's Companion to Silius Italicus*, Leiden, 219–39.
—— (2013), "Looking for the Giants: Mythological Imagery and Discourse on Power in Flavian Epic", in: G. Manuwald/A. Voigt (eds.), *Flavian Epic Interactions*, Berlin, 107–22.
Galimberti, A. (2016), "The Emperor Domitian", in: Zissos (ed.), *A Companion to the Flavian Age of Imperial Rome*, Malden/Oxford/Chichester, 92–108.
Gibson, B. (2010), "Silius Italicus: A Consular Historian", in: A. Augoustakis (ed.), *Brills Companion to Silius Italicus*, Leiden, 47–72.
—— (2013), "Praise in Flavian Epic", in: G. Manuwald/A. Voigt (eds.), *Flavian Epic Interactions*, Berlin, 67–86.
Gransden, K.W. (1991), *Virgil. Aeneid, Book XI*, Cambridge.
Heinacher, T.M. (1877), *Die Stellung des Silius Italiens unter den Quellen zum zweiten punischen Kriege*, Berlin.
Hunink, V. (1992), *M. Annaeus Lucanus. Bellum Civile, Book III. A Commentary*, Amsterdam.
Jacobs, J. (2010), "From Sallust to Silius Italicus: *Metus Hostilis* and the Fall of Rome in the *Punica*", in: J. Miller/A. Woodman (eds.), *Latin Historiography and Poetry in the Early Empire: Generic Interactions*, Leiden, 123–40.
Jones, B.W. (1992), *The Emperor Domitian*, London.
Karakasis, E. (2014), "Homeric Receptions in Flavian Epic: Intertextual Characterization in *Punica* 7", in: A. Augoustakis (ed.), *Flavian Poetry and its Greek Past*, Leiden, 251–66.
Klotz, A. (1933), "Die Stellung des Silius Italicus unter den Quellen zur Geschichte des zweiten punischen Krieges", *RhM* 82, 1–34.
Littlewood, R.J. (2011), *A Commentary on Silius Italicus' Punica 7*, Oxford.
Lovatt, H. (2016), "Flavian Spectacle: Paradox and Wonder", in: A. Zissos (ed.), *A Companion to the Flavian Age of Imperial Rome*, Malden/Oxford/Chichester, 361–75.
Lucarini, C.M. (2004), "Le fonti storiche di Silio Italico", *Athenaeum* 92, 103–26.
Marks, R.D. (2005), *From Republic to Empire. Scipio Africanus in the Punica of Silius Italicus*, Frankfurt a.M.
Miniconi, P./Devalle, G. (1979), *Silius Italicus, La Guerre Punique*, livres I-IV, Paris.
Nesselrath, H.G. (1986), "Zu den Quellen des Silius Italicus", *Hermes*, 114, 203–30.
Nicol, J. (1936), *The Historical and Geographical Sources Used by Silius Italicus*, Oxford.
Pomeroy, A.J. (2010), "To Silius through Livy and his Predecessors", in: A. Augoustakis (ed.), *Brill's Companion to Silius Italicus*, Leiden, 27–46.
Ripoll, F. (1998), *La morale héroïque dans les épopées latines d'époque flavienne. Tradition et Innovation*, Louvain.
Ruperti, G.A. (1795–8), *Caii Silii Italici Punicorum libri septemdecim varietate lectionis et perpetua adnotatione illustrati*, 2 vols., Göttingen.
Schlichteisen, J. (1881), *De fide historica Silii Italici quaestiones historicae et philologicae*, Königsberg.
Spaltenstein, F. (2006), "A propos des sources historiques de Silius Italicus. Une réponse à Lucarini", *Athenaeum* 94, 717–8.
—— (1986–1990), *Commentaire des Punica de Silius Italicus*, 2 vols., Geneva.
Stocks, C. (2014), *The Roman Hannibal: Remembering the Enemy in Silius Italicus' Punica*, Liverpool.

Tipping, B. (2007), "*Haec tum Roma fuit*: Past, Present, and Closure in Silius Italicus' *Punica*", in: S.J. Heyworth/P.G. Fowler/S.J. Harrison (eds.), *Classical Constructions. Papers in Memory of Don Fowler. Classicist and Epicurean*, Oxford, 221–41.
—— (2010), "Virtue and Narrative in Silius Italicus' *Punica*", in: A. Augoustakis (ed.), *Brill's Companion to Silius Italicus*, Leiden, 193–218.
—— (2010a), *Exemplary Epic. Silius Italicus' Punica*, Oxford.
Tuck, S.L. (2016), "Imperial Image-Making", in: A. Zissos (ed.), *A Companion to the Flavian Age of Imperial Rome*, Malden/Oxford/Chichester, 109–28.
van Veen, J.S. (1884), *Quaestiones Silianae*, Leiden.
Venini, P. (1972), "Cronologia e composizione nei *Punica* di Silio Italico", *RIL* 106, 518–31.
—— (1972a), "Tecnica allusiva in Silio Italico", *RIL* 106, 532–42.

Luke Pitcher
Polybius and Oscar Wilde: *Pragmatike Historia* in Nineteenth Century Oxford

For Jennifer Ingleheart

1 Introduction

In 1879 Oscar Wilde, then twenty-four, prepared an essay for the Chancellor's English Essay Prize on the theme of "Historical Criticism Among the Ancients". This prize was one of the many which the University of Oxford annually awarded, and still awards. Wilde, as we shall see, relished ironies of collocation throughout his life. He might have appreciated the fact that the 2016 notice for this prize on the Oxford University website appears two entries after that for the Newdigate Prize, which he won with his poem "Ravenna" in 1878,[1] and immediately before that for the Lord Alfred Douglas Memorial Prize.[2]

Wilde had graduated from Magdalen College, Oxford, on the 28th of November 1878,[3] after sitting the examinations for the Final Honour School of *Literae Humaniores* in June of that year. Having matriculated in 1874,[4] he fell easily within the requirements of eligibility for the Chancellor's English Essay Prize.[5] The title of the essay was not Wilde's choice. It had been announced "in the same issue of the *Oxford University Gazette* as that which recorded the winners of the 1878 prizes".[6]

---

[1] Ellmann 1987, 93.
[2] (consulted on 20.04.2016).
[3] Ellmann, 1987, 100.
[4] Ellmann 1987, 36.
[5] For details on the Prize, see Mason 1914, 470. Ellmann 1987, 102 seems to imply that Wilde was exploiting a constitutional loophole by entering the competition as a graduate: "By a quirk of the Oxford statutes he was *still* eligible" [my italics]. In fact candidates for the Prize in this period would typically have graduated or at the very least finished their studies, as only students who had exceeded four years but not seven of their matriculation were eligible (so correctly Guy 2007, xx); matriculation occurs at the beginning of the student's course, and *Literae Humaniores* usually takes four years.
[6] Guy 2007, xx.

Wilde did not win the 1879 Prize. It was not awarded to any of the candidates, a withholding which seems to have happened on only one previous occasion (1871) since the Prize was founded in 1768.[7] Wilde never published the essay, which has subsequently become known as both *Historical Criticism* and *The Rise of Historical Criticism*,[8] in his lifetime. There is no strong evidence that he ever intended to do so.[9]

The publication history of the essay after Wilde's death in 1900 is a long and rather complicated affair. It is explained with admirable clarity by the essay's most recent editor.[10] Until the Twenty-First Century, the version of *Historical Criticism* in common circulation was one that had been subjected to considerable editorial intervention by Wilde's friend Robert Ross. Josephine Guy's 2007 edition of the essay from the original manuscript, which is now held in the Clark Library,[11] has therefore inaugurated a new age in the study of *Historical Criticism*.[12] Even more recently, Philip E. Smith II has published a manuscript book of Wilde's containing notes and drafts of language for the text.[13] The labours of Guy and Smith in their editions and commentaries, and Horst Schroeder's articles in response to Guy's edition, have contributed very greatly to our understanding of the text.

Historical Criticism has met with a somewhat mixed critical response in the one hundred and thirty-eight years since Wilde wrote it. J.W. Mackail, whose opinion on the piece Wilde's bibliographer Hugh Mason sought in the early Twentieth Century, said that "the essay, young as it is, is quite up to the general level of that sort of thing" and did not know why the prize had not been awarded.[14] Wilde's entry in the *Dictionary of National Biography* says that it shows

---

[7] So Mason 1914, 470.

[8] The three manuscript books in which the text is preserved bear slight variations on the title *Historical Criticism: Ἀλήθεια*. See Guy 2007, xxiii. In what follows, I call the essay *Historical Criticism*, and the notebook in which Wilde recorded notes and drafts of language for it the *Historical Criticism Notebook*, following the practice of Guy 2007 and Smith 2016.

[9] Ellmann 1987, 102 speculates that the essay might have been amongst the essays about "Greek matters" which Wilde envisaged publishing in 1880, but Guy 2007, xx–xxi, notes that it was never mentioned in his correspondence after the summer of 1879; see also Schroeder 2009, 64.

[10] Guy 2007, xxiv–xxvii.

[11] MS Wilde W6721M3 R595 [1879?]. I have not personally inspected this MS, a fact which will be of significance with regard to a textual point (see n. 58 below).

[12] Guy 2007, 3–67. All references to *Historical Criticism* in what follows are keyed to Guy's text. It is worth stressing my debt to the achievements of Guy's edition at this point, as I shall be differing substantially from her interpretations of several passages in what follows.

[13] Smith 2016.

[14] Mason 1914, 470.

"a remarkable grasp of historiography, a subject then in its infancy".[15] Philip E. Smith II and Michael S. Helfand identified what they saw as "the centrality of Wilde's synthesis and its components (mind, imagination, race, evolution) as guiding ideas" in the essay.[16]

By contrast, the most recent editor of the text is keener to stress the derivative elements of Wilde's argument.[17] Several readers have criticized its turgid and ponderous style, especially surprising in light of its authorship.[18] Above all, its deficiencies of structural organization have met with general censure.[19] These are particularly obvious in the recent Oxford edition of the essay, which returns to Wilde's autograph rather than the version which Robert Ross had tidied up. Indeed, Horst Schroeder has recently expressed scepticism that a piece so manifestly ramshackle (and leaving so little subsequent archival trace) could ever actually have been submitted for the Chancellor's English Essay Prize at all.[20] Even a cursory reading of *Historical Criticism* in the 2007 edition reveals the force of this point. To take one example among many, Wilde, in defence of his claim that Livy has no powers of critical thinking, claims: "I append three instances as a proof". Not only does Wilde not produce his three instances, he moves immediately on to talk (briefly and elliptically) about Tacitus instead.[21]

One may think that the text of *Historical Criticism* as it now remains for us was indeed submitted for the Prize (which to me, as to Schroeder, seems unlikely). One may think that Wilde never entered the competition at all (a more likely hypothesis). One may think that what we have now is a penultimate draft and that the version which Wilde ultimately submitted is lost to time (this seems to me a hypothesis with more to recommend it than Schroeder allows). Whatever the truth of the matter, the essay retains an arresting interest. Quite apart from

---

15 [consulted 18.05.2016].
16 Smith and Helfand 1989, 37.
17 Guy 2007, xxviii.
18 Ellmann 1987, 102: "The essay he offered was longer than anything he would ever write in the discursive mode, and did not escape an uncharacteristic tediousness"; Kohl and Wilson 1989, 70: "its somewhat heavy, long-winded style is totally uncharacteristic of Wilde's later work".
19 Ellmann 1987, 102: "Otherwise, the organization of this essay was rickety, a defect which Wilde attempted to override by frequent references to his structural 'plan'"; Dowling, 2001, xx, sees the essay as "Arnoldian but disorganized".
20 Schroeder 2009, 64. We may note, however, that the absence of a copy of Wilde's essay in the University Archives is not, in fact, at all suspicious. The University Archives at Oxford do not generally seem to retain copies of the entries for the Chancellor's English Essay Prize (as I ascertained in correspondence with the Keeper, Simon Bailey, 26/06/17).
21 Guy 2007, 65.13.

the later glories of its author, it is (as the *Dictionary of National Biography*, quoted above, notes)[22] an exercise in the comparative study of classical historiography from a time when such enterprises were less fashionable in England and Ireland than they have subsequently become.

There is a particular aspect to the enduring interest of *Historical Criticism* which makes a study of it well-fitted to the concerns of the present volume. This is the exceptionally prominent place which Wilde gives Polybius in his discussion of ancient historical thought. Richard Ellmann noted this unusual prominence in his 1987 life of Wilde.[23] Josephine Guy, in the 2007 Oxford edition, does a good job of tracking down Wilde's Polybian references, supplemented and corrected at some points by the indefatigable subsequent researches of Horst Schroeder and Philip Smith II.[24] Outside the recent Wildean editions and *adversaria* relating directly to them, however, the importance of Polybius in *Historical Criticism* has not received much critical attention, with the exception of J.A. Garcia Landa's brief examination of Wilde's use of Polybius in relation to his parallel treatment of Vico.[25] This applies even to modern synoptic treatments of Wilde's relationship to classical authors.[26] The absence from the scholarly literature is understandable. Wilde did not make much use of Polybius in later life. Yet the prominence of Polybius in this item of Wildean juvenilia remains of interest.

In what follows, I shall begin by looking at Wilde as a student of classical historiography in general in *Historical Criticism*. I shall suggest that, while he certainly shows numerous weaknesses in his interpretations, his work in this vein is more up-to-date, and more alive to contemporary debates about ancient history, than some of the recent scholarship has suggested. I shall examine the question of why Polybius enjoys this somewhat surprising visibility in Wilde's unsuccessful prize essay. I shall argue that Polybius' usefulness to Wilde may be considered under three main headings: historiographical methodology; structural transition within the over-arching argument of *Historical Criticism*; and, perhaps most interestingly, Polybius as a predecessor to Wilde's own practice in writing the essay. In connexion with the last point, I shall conclude with the argument that the use of Polybius in *Historical Criticism*, for all the work's manifest flaws, shows,

---

[22] P. 417.
[23] Ellmann 1987, 102: "His praise of Polybius, unusual for the time, showed his independence …".
[24] As, for example, at Schroeder 2013a, 72–73, Schroeder 2013b, 63–64.
[25] Garcia Landa 2013.
[26] In Ross 2013, for example, Polybius is mentioned once (134), to illuminate Wilde's view of Alexandria. K. Riley, A. Blanshard, and I. Manny (eds.), *Oscar Wilde and Classical Antiquity* (Oxford, 2017), appeared just as this volume went to print, so unfortunately no account could be taken of it in this discussion.

occasionally, the self-reflexive wit and slyness of argument that would come to the fore in Wilde's later prose works.

2 Wilde as a student of classical historiography in *Historical Criticism*

Wilde makes a fair few missteps while analysing the classical historians in the pages of *Historical Criticism*. At the very least, he indulges in some misleading emphases. The Oxford edition notes several examples of these delinquent moments. For instance, Wilde slightly mixes up the epigraphic evidence alleged by Thucydides for one of his arguments about earlier Athenian history.[27] Some other cases of Wildean errancy or *suggestio falsi* in *Historical Criticism*, however, perhaps deserve some treatment here, as they are not altogether apprehended in the current scholarly literature.

These blemishes vary in severity. Sometimes Wilde is simply a little disingenuous. Such is the case when he asserts, alluding to Thucydides 1.22.1,[28] that "Thucydides states clearly that where he was unable to find out what people really said, he put down what they ought to have said".[29] In fact, Thucydides does not say that his policy on speeches (whatever it was) applied where he was *unable* to find out what "people really said". Rather, he speaks of the *difficulty* that he and his informants had in remembering exactly what was said.[30] Wilde also quietly omits any discussion of the notorious ἐχομένῳ ὅτι ἐγγύτατα τῆς ξυμπάσης γνώμης τῶν ἀληθῶς λεχθέντων clause, which is not especially easy to reconcile with his interpretation of the passage.

In fairness to Wilde, the exact meaning of Thucydides 1.22.1 is still a notorious crux. Christopher Pelling has observed that "no sentence in the Greek language

---

[27] Guy 2007, 16.23–5: "This view he [*sc.* 'Thucydides'] further corroborates by another inscription on the altar of the Apollo, which mentions the children of Hippias and not those of his brothers". As Guy 2007, 302 notes, Thuc. 6.55.1 actually attributes this inscription to a stele concerning the wrongdoings of the tyrants, not the altar of Pythian Apollo which he has mentioned earlier in the same passage (Thuc. 6.54.6–7).
[28] The reference is not noted in the commentary on this passage at Guy 2007, 345, but is picked up at Schroeder 2013a, 74; neither comments on the minutiae of Wilde's rather creative translation.
[29] Guy 2007, 55.28–9.
[30] Thuc. 1.22.1: χαλεπὸν τὴν ἀκρίβειαν αὐτὴν τῶν λεχθέντων διαμνημονεῦσαι ἦν ἐμοί τε ὧν αὐτὸς ἤκουσα καὶ τοῖς ἄλλοθέν ποθεν ἐμοὶ ἀπαγγέλλουσιν.

can have been taken quite so variously".³¹ Some of Wilde's other missteps are less justifiable. It is a little hard on Livy to assert that "his method as a rule is merely to mention all the accounts, and to decide in favour of the most probable sometimes, but usually not to decide at all".³² One of the examples Wilde alleges of a crux where Livy will not make up his mind, "who was the first dictator",³³ is actually one where Livy reasons out a decision, and not merely on the grounds of probability.³⁴ Pursuing from Thucydides his discourse on the nature of speeches in ancient historiography, Wilde remarks that "we find that one of the most celebrated speeches in Tacitus[,], that in which the Emperor Claudius gives the Gauls their freedom[,] is shown by an inscription discovered recently at Lugdunum to be entirely fabulous".³⁵ This is a dubious and hyperbolic characterization of the relationship between the speech recorded on the Lyons tablet and Tacitus *Annals* 11.24.³⁶ The nadir is probably Wilde's assertion, earlier in the same passage, that "the speeches given in the senate on the occasion of the Catilinarian Conspiracy are very different from the same orations as they appear in Cicero".³⁷ In fact, Sallust notoriously does not give any rendering of a speech by Cicero at all in the *Bellum Catilinae*. The nearest he ever approaches to doing so is a single sentence: "*Tum M. Tullius consul, sive praesentiam eius timens sive ira conmotus, orationem habuit luculentam atque utilem rei publicae, quam postea scriptam edidit*" (Then M. Tullius the consul, whether because he was unnerved by his [*sc.* "Catiline's"] presence or because he was overcome by anger, delivered a speech that was beautiful and of service to the state, which he subsequently wrote down and circulated).³⁸ This describes the delivery of the speech that we know as the *First Catilinarian*.³⁹

---

31 Pelling 2000, 115. I am indebted to Professor Pelling for his helpful comments on this.
32 Guy 2007, 64.32–65.2.
33 Guy 2007, 64.31.
34 Livy 2.18.4–7, which brings in not only appeals to probability (why choose Manius Valerius rather than his more experienced father?) but also analysis of the comparative antiquity of sources (the oldest authorities plump for Larcius). The precise reference to Livy, omitted at Guy 2007, 357, is identified at Smith 2016, 179 n. 195.
35 Guy, 2007, 56.4–7, with the commentary at 347.
36 Contrast, for example, the more subtle argumentation of Martin 1981, 149, Griffin 1982, 405, and Woodman in Kraus and Woodman 1997, 98–99. It is also a little odd for Wilde to describe the Lyons Tablet, which was found in 1528 (so Martin 1981, 147; not, *pace* Guy 2007, 347, in 1524) as "an inscription discovered recently".
37 Guy 2007, 55.31–3.
38 Sall. *BC* 31.6 (my translation).
39 Guy 2007, 346 does not note quite how glaring the mismatch between Wilde's claims and what the sources actually say is here.

It is tempting to read significance into the fact that Wilde's more obvious errors tend to congregate in his discussion of Latin sources. Ellmann notes that "Wilde did not care much for Latin, having absorbed Mahaffy's contempt 'for any Roman thing'".[40] The meagre allotment of space to the Roman historians in *Historical Criticism* is also, at first blush, suggestive. Wilde's whistle-stop tour of Latin historiography takes up about three and a half pages of a sixty-four page essay.

One should, however, sound a note of caution here. As often with Wilde, the reality of his taste was a little more complex than his resonant declarations would sometimes seem to suggest. Much later, in Reading Prison, he requested and received the *Corpus Poetarum Latinorum* as reading matter.[41] The verbal texture of *Historical Criticism* is enriched, at one point, by a casual allusion to Horace's *Odes*, though the phrase in question is, to be sure, a fairly famous one.[42] More significantly, Smith's edition of Wilde's notes towards the *Historical Criticism* essay reveals that Wilde actually amassed several pages of material on Tacitus, which did not find their way into the text of *Historical Criticism* as we now have it.[43] Whatever Wilde's reasons were for omitting this material from *Historical Criticism* (a question that is obviously bound up with that of the exact textual status of the draft we currently possess), he had, at least, done the ground-work.

The fact remains, however, that Wilde makes a fair few mistakes in *Historical Criticism*. The general tenor of the Oxford edition is to suggest that the essay is not merely sloppy but also derivative.[44] Once more, however, caution is in order. We have already seen that the Oxford edition, while it does, on the whole, a sound job of tracking down many of Wilde's allusions, also misses quite a few of them.[45]

---

[40] Ellmann 1987, 42, quoting Stanford and McDowell 1971, 31. J.P. Mahaffy had been Wilde's tutor at Trinity College, Dublin.
[41] Ellmann 1987, 465.
[42] Guy 2007, 10.1: "There were heroes before the son of Atreus". This translates Hor. *Od.* 4.9.25: "*vixere fortes ante Agamemnona*", which, appropriately, is in a context about the importance of having an author to write up one's deeds if one wishes to enjoy a posthumous reputation. The allusion is not noted at Guy 2007, 292.
[43] Smith 2016, 122–27. Smith notes and examines the disparity between the material on Tacitus in the *Historical Criticism Notebook* and Wilde's much more brief and dismissive treatment of that historian in *Historical Criticism* as it stands at Smith 2016, xxvi–xxviii.
[44] Guy 2007, xxviii: "The Commentary to the present edition will also make readers more alert to the frequently derivative elements of Wilde's argument ...": Guy 2007, 270: "There are several instances in *Historical Criticism* where the particular textual examples which Wilde gives, and the particular contexts in which he discusses them, suggest that his knowledge was often second-hand, and thus that the range of classical allusions in his work is not all that it seems".
[45] As, for example, in the case described in n. 42 above.

As a result, the reader of the Oxford edition may easily take away the impression that Wilde's range and facility of allusion was more constrained than it really was.

There are also some methodological issues to ponder. The Oxford edition explicitly tries to relate what Wilde says in *Historical Criticism* to the coverage of such matters in a small number of secondary sources which Wilde is known (or overwhelmingly likely) to have read: Mommsen's *History of Rome*; Hegel's *Lectures on the Philosophy of History*; Symonds' *Studies of the Greek Poets*: and Grote's *History of Greece*.[46] The editor defends this procedure on the grounds that "Of course these were not the only general books on classical culture to which Wilde may have had access; nevertheless they provide a useful reference point by which to judge the novelty (or otherwise) of his particular observations...".[47] The texts in question are certainly well-chosen. Mommsen, for example, was, beyond doubt, an important figure in Wilde's classical scholarship: Mommsen's *History of Rome* would ultimately be another of the books that Wilde would request while serving his penal term for gross indecency in the 1890s (at Pentonville, this time, rather than Reading, but the book accompanied him throughout his changes of prison).[48] "Dr. Mommsen" is also mentioned by name towards the end of *Historical Criticism*.[49]

The problem with this method is that the Oxford edition sometimes cites "cross-references" to these secondary sources for passages of *Historical Criticism* which are not, in fact, based upon, or allusions to, these secondary sources at all. The effect of this is to reinforce the impression that Wilde's argument in the essay is informed only by a small number of well-worn authorities. In fact, Wilde's range of scholarly reference is demonstrably both wider and more up-to-date on contemporary strands of ancient historical scholarship in the late 1870s than the Commentary to the Oxford Edition suggests.

The most significant example of this up-to-dateness is to be found in Wilde's remarks on what we might now call "revisionist" historiography:

> Similar ethical canons are applied to the accounts of the heroes of the days of old, and by the same a-priori principles Achilles is rescued from the charges of avarice and insolence in a passage [Rep. Bk. III. 391] which may be ranked as the earliest instance of that "whitewashing of great men", as it has been called, which is so popular in our own day when

---

46 Guy 2007, 273.
47 Guy 2007, *ibid*.
48 Ellmann 1987, 456.
49 Guy 2007, 64.11: "...Dr. Mommsen's view of him [*sc.* 'Sallust'] as merely a political pamphleteer...".

Catiline and Clodius are represented as honest and far-seeing politicians, when "ein edle [sic] und gute natur" is claimed for Tiberius, and Nero rescued from his heritage of infamy, as an accomplished dilettante whose moral aberrations are more than excused by his exquisite artistic sense; and charming tenor voice (Guy 2007, 7.23–32).

What leads Wilde to choose the examples of Catiline, Clodius, and Tiberius in this passage? The Oxford Edition sees the remark about "whitewashing" as "probably an allusion to Mommsen's comments on the partisan nature of Sallust's *Belllum Catilinae*".[50] Wilde does indeed speak about "Dr. Mommsen's view of him [sc. 'Sallust'] as a merely a political pamphleteer", with the clear implication that he does not whole-heartedly agree, towards the end of the essay.[51] But it will not do to detect Mommsen's views on the *Bellum Catilinae* as the subject of allusion in this portion of *Historical Criticism*. This passage is concerned with perverse (in Wilde's view) interpretations of particular historical miscreants. Sallust paints Catiline as prodigiously talented, but a dyed-in-the-wool villain.[52] He does not mention Clodius in his extant works or fragments at all, although the full text of the *Historiae* would, no doubt, have been a different matter.[53] Nor is it likely that Sallust saw a need to whitewash the infant Tiberius.

In fact, one can make a good case that, by picking the sequence of Catiline, Clodius, and Tiberius (in that order, and together), Wilde is pointedly setting himself in opposition to a position taken in a freshly-published and controversial piece of English historical scholarship. In 1878, the year before Wilde prepared *Historical Criticism*, E.S. Beesly, Professor of Latin at Bedford College, London, published *Catiline, Clodius, and Tiberius*.[54] This was, indeed, a notably revisionist take on three traditionally despised historical characters.

The sequence, the concinnity of dates, and Beesly's notably heterodox stance on his eponymous subjects are enough in themselves to suggest that Wilde has Beesly in mind for this stretch of *Historical Criticism*. But we can also establish that Beesly was running through Wilde's mind at another point in his essay. Consider the following passage:

---

50 Guy 2007, 285.
51 See n. 49 above.
52 As, for example, at Sall. *BC* 5.1.
53 See Tatum 1999, 46–47 for the argument that Plut. *Luc.* 34.3–4, giving a speech of Clodius at the Nisibis mutiny, is derived from Sallust's *Historiae*.
54 Beesly, 1878. For an assessment of Beesly's work on the late Roman Republic, see Wiseman 1998, 121–34.

> No canon of historical criticism can be said to be of more real value than that involved in this distinction: and the overlooking of it has filled our histories with the contemptible accounts of the intrigues of courtiers and of kings, and the petty plottings of back-stair influence, particulars interesting no doubt to those who would ascribe *the Reformation to Anne Boleyn's pretty face*, *the Persian war* to the influence of a doctor or *a curtain-lecture from Atossa*, or the French Revolution to Madame de Maintenon, but without any value for those who aim at any scientific treatment of history (Guy 2007, 50.1–9; my italics).

Guy observes that Wilde's allusion to "Anne Boleyn's pretty face" in the above extract is "puzzling, since she was not generally considered to have great beauty".[55] Schroeder subsequently notes that the notion of Anne Boleyn as a beauty probably has its origin in Shakespeare and Fletcher's *Henry the Eighth*.[56] However, while that play may be the ultimate authority for the queen's pulchritude, we are justified, I think, in detecting a more proximate source for Wilde's passage:

> If there is a childish way of explaining a political movement, a literary man will generally adopt it. He is irresistibly attracted by what is petty and personal, as he is repelled and alarmed by the idea of an orderly evolution of human affairs. It is so easy, and to the vulgar mind so agreeable, to attribute *the Persian invasion of Greece to a curtain lecture of Atossa's, or the English Reformation to the pretty face of Anne Boleyn* (Beesly 1878, 67; my italics).

Wilde, it seems, liked Beesly's fulminations against those who would ignore the possibility that greater forces than individuals shape historical events enough to import it (without acknowledgment, and with some additions and modifications) into his own essay. This demonstration of his acquaintance with Beesly's text makes it all the more probable that he includes the examples of Catiline, Clodius, and Tiberius earlier in *Historical Criticism* as a deliberate shot across the Professor's bows. He may even have made this challenge explicit: Wilde produces, amongst what look like his verso notes to the main text,[57] a list of writers who have indulged in the "whitewashing" that he denigrates, one of which, a name

---

55 Guy 2007, 340.
56 Schroeder 2009, 69.
57 Guy 2007, xc.

of five or six characters beginning with "B", has perplexed the readers of the manuscript.[58] Wilde certainly accuses these named authors of being "paradoxical";[59] the charge of "paradox" is one which Beesly's *Catiline, Clodius, and Tiberius* anticipates.[60] In any event, Beesly's contemporary book has had a palpable effect on the genesis of *Historical Criticism*.

The example is instructive. If one avowedly seeks to relate Wilde's text only to a handful of well-worn authorities, then *Historical Criticism* will naturally present a hackneyed and derivative aspect. But sometimes, if one is in a position to chase down the precise sources of Wilde's allusions, the aspect changes. Wilde on historical revisionism is not, in fact, reheated Mommsen. Rather, he is pointedly dissenting from one of the latest English works on Roman history. Moreover, once we realize that Beesly is appropriated with approval elsewhere in the text (that is, in the denial that grand historical events can be explained solely in terms of the caprices of individuals), we can see that Wilde's response to Beesly is necessarily a complex one. On the one hand, Wilde wants to refute Beesly's heterodox readings of historical individuals: Catiline, Clodius, and Tiberius are not the heroes of the people that Beesly desires them to be. On the other hand, Beesly's Positivist insistence on the applicability of general laws to historical development ("an orderly evolution of human affairs") is in tune with *Historical Criticism*'s own take on historical (and historiographical) development, where, as we shall see later, Comte is very much in mind.[61] Wilde is not simply swallowing or rejecting past texts wholesale. His response is, at least in the case of Beesly, more nuanced than that. In fact, despite the disagreements about other individuals, the interpretation of the career of Julius Caesar which emerges from the pages of *Historical Criticism* is not very far away from Beesly's.[62]

---

[58] Wilde's handwriting is not always easy to elucidate. Guy 2007, 7, 32 opts tentatively for "Besler[?]", but notes (286) that it is hard to see the significance of that name in this context. Schroeder 2009, 65, speculates that the name might be "Beulé" (that is, Charles Ernest Beulé, who, as well as being an archaeologist, wrote several works of popular ancient history), but adds that this suggestion is made *"faute de mieux"*. I have not, however, scrutinized the autograph myself to determine my suggestion's plausibility.

[59] *Historical Criticism* is censorious (amusingly so, to a reader familiar with its author's later literary output) about purveyors of paradoxography. Wilde attributes to Polybius (with apparent approval) the stance that the ideal historian is not "to falsify *truth* for the sake of a paradox or an epigram" (Guy 2007, 57.15–16).

[60] Beesly 1878, 86: "Do not suppose that I take a perverse pleasure in maintaining a paradox".

[61] Guy 2007, 29.25–6, in conjunction with the excellent note at 319–20.

[62] Guy 2007, 58.23–5: "... culminated, as all democratic movements *do* culminate, in the supreme authority of one man, the Lordship of the world under the world's rightful Lord, Gaius Julius Caesar". Cf. e.g. Beesly 1878, 71.

Historical Criticism, then, shows rather more width and discrimination in its use of sources, ancient and modern, than one might at first expect. It is against such a background of philological discrimination that we should consider the unusual prominence of Polybius in the essay. Whatever the reason for this prominence, it should not be ascribed merely to unthinking assimilation of a limited number of authorities on Wilde's part.

3 Polybius and Methodology

If Wilde's enthusiasm for Polybius in *Historical Criticism* is not merely a matter of his sources, what other plausible reasons can we give for it? One explanation is, to a modern student of ancient historians, very obvious. Writers of history in antiquity vary a great deal in the extent to which they are prepared to meditate explicitly upon their own methodology. This can easily lead to a situation, in modern treatments of ancient historiography, where the prominence of a given historian in the treatment is proportional to his willingness to issue such meditations.[63]

Historical Criticism, to an extent, falls in line with this observation. This helps to explain why Xenophon, alone among the substantially extant Greek historians writing before the first century BCE, is barely represented in the extant text of *Historical Criticism* at all,[64] and does not appear in the *Historical Criticism Notebook* either.[65] Xenophon, notoriously averse to making explicit statements about historiographical methodology,[66] simply does not give Wilde enough material to work with. Such taciturnity leaves him prey to the dictum by which Wilde executes his transition from Thucydides to Polybius: "As my aim is not to give an account of historians, but to point out *those great thinkers whose methods* have *furthered the advance of this spirit* of historical criticism, I shall pass over those annalists and chroniclers who intervened between Thucydides and Polybius".[67]

Of course, it was not just practising historians in the ancient world who were willing to discuss how to write history. Modern writers looking for theoretical

---

[63] Cf. Pitcher 2009, 28.
[64] Guy 2007, 293, notes a possible reference to Xen. *Mem.* 3.9.2 (not one of Xenophon's historiographical works, of course) at 10.19–21; otherwise, the Xenophontic cupboard is bare.
[65] The only appearance of Xenophon in Smith 2016 is in a discussion of a phrase that comes up in an unrelated notebook (xxx).
[66] Marincola 1997, 69.
[67] Guy 2007, 41.13–17. The italics here represent Wilde's own underlining (Guy 2007, xc).

works on historiography from antiquity itself do not find many extant candidates. Scholars therefore tend to fall back on a limited number of texts: passages from Cicero's *De Oratore* and *De Legibus*; Plutarch's treatise *On the Malice of Herodotus*, and Lucian's *How History Ought To Be Written*. Wilde certainly availed himself of most of these texts in his preparation for writing *Historical Criticism*. This is another case where (as in that of Tacitus, mentioned above)[68] material from the *Historical Criticism Notebook* did not make its way into the surviving version of the essay itself: there are two pages of notes on *How History Ought To Be Written* in the *Notebook* of which no trace survives in *Historical Criticism*, where Lucian is no longer mentioned.[69] Plutarch *On the Malice of Herodotus* retains a mention in *Historical Criticism*, though only as a note to a discussion of Herodotus himself,[70] and Wilde does allude rather obliquely to the beginning of *De Legibus* in his brief comments about Cicero's views on the status of myths in writing history,[71] and the orator's conviction that he was well-fitted to be a historiographer.[72] On the whole, however, Wilde does not use these texts to anything like the extent that one might expect in an essay on ancient history-writing. For example, Cicero *De Oratore* 2.62–3, which customarily plays an important role in modern discussions of the subject,[73] does not appear at all. In general, *Historical Criticism*, as compared with the *Historical Criticism Notebook*, seems to move away from allotting as much importance to the views of ancient writers who were neither philosophers (since Wilde sees the gradual perfection of historical method as a manifestation of wider tendencies in rigorous thought)[74] nor historians (in the strictest sense) in their own right: Smith perceptively notes that Wilde "reduces Plutarch

---

[68] P. 421 with n. 43.
[69] Smith 2016, 128–29, with Smith's note on this material at xxix.
[70] Guy 2007, 11.27–32. Other works of Plutarch do appear later in the essay: Guy 2007, 60.
[71] Guy 2007, 64.14–16: "Cicero had a good many qualifications for a scientific historian and (as he usually did) thought very highly of his own powers." Cic. *Leg.* 1.5: "*potes autem tu profecto satis facere in ea, quippe cum sit opus, ut tibi quidem uideri solet, unum hoc oratorium maxime*" ("Moreover, you are assuredly able to do justice on that score, since this is an enterprise, at least in your habitual opinion, uniquely and pre-eminently worthy of an orator"—my translation). Guy's commentary at 357 is not explicit on this allusion.
[72] Guy 2007, 64.16–17: "On passages of ancient legend however he [sc. Cicero] is rather unsatisfactory. For while he is too sensible to believe them he is too patriotic to reject them". This seems to be an allusion to the discussion between Cicero and Atticus at Cic. *Leg.* 1.3–4 (again, Guy's commentary at 357 is not explicit on this allusion).
[73] As most famously in Woodman 1988.
[74] Note, for example, the prominence of Aristotle at Guy 2007, 24–26.

from historian to biographer" in the transition from the notebook to the essay.⁷⁵ Wilde may simply have preferred to stick, by and large, to what practising historians had to say about historiography.⁷⁶

Against this background, the prominence of Polybius becomes readily explicable. Polybius talks longer, more thoroughly, and more clearly about the nature and practice of historiography than any other practising historian of the Greco-Roman world. Indeed, Wilde openly acknowledges this characteristic:

> And to Polybius belongs the office—how noble an office he made it his writings show—of making more explicit the ideas that were implicit in his predecessors, of showing that they were of wider applicability and perhaps of deeper meaning than they had before seemed, of examining with more minuteness the laws which they had discovered, and finally of pointing out more clearly than anyone had done before the range of the science, and the means it offered for analysing the present and predicting what was to come (Guy 2007, 40.16–23).

The sheer volume and range of quotable passages about historiography within Polybius' oeuvre make him indispensable to Wilde's enterprise. Polybius' willingness to talk about methodology also helps to explain the distribution of the passages within his corpus which Wilde is most interested in discussing. As one might expect, Wilde makes particular use of Book 12—the traditional hunting-ground of students of historiography, where Polybius sets out many of his objections to the practices of other historians. Polybius' strictures on Timaeus form the back-bone for Wilde's discussion of Polybian methodology.⁷⁷

In line with the practice of most students of historiography before or since (including the present writer), Wilde's picture of Polybius is given a certain homogeneous quality by his decisions about which passages he cites and which he omits. Wilde's Polybius, for example, has an enthusiasm for the control of historical hypotheses through comparison with documents that Ranke would have approved, and which pointedly contrasts with the epigraphic carelessness of Wilde's Tacitus:⁷⁸ "In other cases he [sc. 'Polybius'] appeals to public documents *the importance of which he was always most foremost in recognising*; showing for instance by a document in the public archives of Rhodes how inaccurate were the

---

75 Smith 2016, xxxi. Plutarch was more fortunate than his fellow biographer Suetonius, however. Suetonius is mentioned once in the *Historical Criticism Notebook* (Smith 2016, 126), but not at all in the essay.
76 Cf. Marincola 2014, 39–40.
77 Guy 2007, 53–55.
78 See p. 420 above.

accounts given of the battle of Ladé by Zeno and Antisthenes".⁷⁹ Wilde's allusion to Polybius 15.8 here is shrewd (although Polybius does not claim to have seen the document himself).⁸⁰ But Wilde arguably does not do full justice to Polybius' sniffiness elsewhere about epigraphic investigations if Polybius was not the one who was conducting them.⁸¹

In similar vein, Wilde portrays Polybius as a courteous critic, in contrast to what he sees as the prevailing tendencies of the ancient world: "But in Polybius there is I think little of that bitterness and pettiness of spirit which characterises most other writers, and an incidental story he tells of his relations with one of the historians he criticised shows that he was a man of a great courtesy and refinement of taste as indeed befitted one who had lived always in the society of those who were great and of noble birth".⁸² As Schroeder notes, this is an allusion to Polybius' account of how he wrote to Zeno in a friendly manner to correct Zeno's mistakes about Laconia.⁸³ While subsequent students of historiography have differed as to their assessment of Polybius' ingenuousness in that passage,⁸⁴ the allusion is, once again, a shrewd one, and Wilde's picture of Polybius as a critic is one that some modern scholars would certainly endorse.⁸⁵ All the same, it would be fair to say that some passages of Polybius on his predecessors (above all, perhaps, his treatment of Callisthenes) would produce a rather different impression.⁸⁶

Wilde's quotations of Polybius on historiographical ways and means show, then, a thoughtful, if slightly partial, fashioning of Polybius as something close

---

79 Guy 2007, 53.20–3 (my italics). Guy 2007, 344 seems a little surprised by Wilde's decision to accentuate the latter syllable of "Ladé", but he was, of course, trying to replicate the final eta of the island's name in Greek.
80 On Polybius and documents, see Pitcher 2009, 200 n. 24.
81 Plb. 12.11.2. Wilde does, however, allude more obliquely to this passage in his discussion of how Polybius criticizes Timaeus for not giving accurate citation details for one of his alleged inscriptions (Guy 2007, 55.18–22).
82 Guy 2007, 53.6–10.
83 Plb. 16.20.5–9, as identified at Schroeder 2013a, 72–3.
84 Marincola 1997, 230 takes it as being sincere and notes the tradition of lauding courteous correction elsewhere in classical historiography. Contrast von Scala 1890, 294 and Walbank 1972, 54–55.
85 Marincola 1997, 230: "In practice, he [sc. 'Polybius'] is a sensible and (on the whole) mild critic, despite the prevalent view of him as unfair and captious".
86 As conceded at Marincola 1997, 230. Marincola notes (n. 72) that Callisthenes "treated a time that had nothing to do with Polybius' chosen theme", but this does not seem to me pertinent to the issue of Polybian bad faith in how Callisthenes is treated in his text. Polybius does not say, at 16.20.5–9, that courtesy is subject to a statute of limitations.

to a methodological paragon amongst the historians of antiquity. For Wilde, Polybius is not necessarily a great innovator. But he is a writer who expounds and takes to their logical conclusion the discoveries of his predecessors.

Polybius is not alone in generating historiographical precepts, of course, even if he is particularly fertile in them. Other historians might not have been as chatty as Polybius on such matters, but, equally, they were not all as silent as Xenophon. Wilde can, and does, make use of such precepts from the other historians who are the principal focus of his concern. We have already seen him taking a stance on the meaning of a famous and controversial methodological moment in Thucydides. Wilde similarly deploys other key disquisitions on method from the history of the Peloponnesian War, making particular use (as one might readily expect) of the celebrated passage on the likelihood of the reiteration of something like the sufferings generated by the stasis at Corcyra "ἕως ἂν ἡ αὐτὴ φύσις ἀνθρώπων ᾖ".[87] The *Historical Criticism Notebook* makes it clear that he also gathered together authorial statements from the text of Tacitus, though these tend more to express Tacitus' own views on particular metaphysical issues than historiographical method *per se* and (as noted above) this material did not make it into the present text of *Historical Criticism* itself.[88]

However, Wilde's deployment of Polybius is not merely quantitatively, but qualitatively, different from the use he makes of the other classical historians. The volume of useful material is a consideration, but it is not the only one. There is merit in exploring why this is the case.

4 Polybius and the Structure of *Historical Criticism*

Polybius' significance to Wilde is structural as well as evidential. The structure of *Historical Criticism*, as we have seen, has not won many plaudits from critics.[89] It would be fair to say that some elements of Wilde's handling of Polybius bear out that criticism. In particular, there is the oddity that Polybius is effectively introduced *twice*, a couple of pages apart in the essay.[90] Wilde is clearly aware of this awkwardness, and makes a game attempt to smooth it out ("the man of genius

---

[87] Thuc. 3.82, with Guy 2007, 29.1–11 and 319.
[88] Smith 2016, 124–25.
[89] Above, n. 19.
[90] Guy 2007, 40.9, 42.23.

whose influence in the evolution of the philosophy of history I have a short time ago dwelt on").⁹¹ The effect remains a little jarring.

All the same, *Historical Criticism* does have a structure, and one in which Polybius is the lynch-pin. Some aspects of this centrality are obvious. Indeed, Wilde himself spells some of them out. We have already seen that, in Wilde's developmental model of Greek historiography, Polybius represents a sort of culmination, the codifier and thorough exponent of what has gone before.⁹² Wilde also, at one point, formalizes the progression from Herodotus through Thucydides to Polybius in terms of Comte:

> Perhaps we may say that with him the philosophy of History is partly in the metaphysical stage, and see in the progress of this idea from Herodotus to Polybius, the exemplification of the Comtian law of the three stages of thought, the theological, the metaphysical, and the scientific: for truly out of the vagueness of theological mysticism this conception, which we call the Philosophy of History, was raised to a scientific principle according to which the past was explained, and the future predicted, by reference to general Laws (Guy 2007, 23–30).

Polybius works pretty well as the culmination to a sequence of this sort. Thucydides does allude to the possibility of past events recurring in some form or another in future time.⁹³ But Polybius speaks more explicitly than Thucydides ever does about the possibility of predicting future events in a way that may actually be tangibly profitable to his reader.⁹⁴

There are, however, other movements in *Historical Criticism*, beyond those that Wilde explicitly acknowledges. He claims, as we have seen, to be giving an account of *"those great thinkers whose methods have furthered the advance of this spirit* of historical criticism". In practice, however, *Historical Criticism* is not simply a work on the history of history. It perpetually teeters on the edge of becoming a work of history in its own right, exemplifying the historiographical principles it spends the rest of its time describing. This, of course, is a not uncommon move when literary writers, even nascent ones such as the young Wilde, venture

---

91 Guy 2007, 42.23.
92 Above, p. 428.
93 See n. 87 above. Scholarship is still divided on the question of what, if anything, Thucydides thinks that such predictions might achieve. See, for example, Raaflaub 2013, especially 6–7 and Stahl 2013, especially 314. Wilde seems to have felt that Thucydides was at least trying to prepare readers for future recurrences, "in order that on a recurrence of the same crises men may know how to act" (Guy 2007, 17.29–30).
94 See, for example, Plb. 12.25b.3, with Miltsios 2016, especially 117–18.

a treatise on a subject. The treatise begins, often self-consciously, to display the very qualities that it describes.[95]

To this enterprise, the city of Rome is key. Wilde paints the initial rise of Rome in lush colours: "the gradual rise of this Italian city, from the day when the first legion crossed the narrow strait of Messene to the fertile fields of Sicily…".[96] The city's evolution from city-state to dominant Republic to Empire is an underlying theme as the essay progresses, with Wilde obeying his own dictum that the "spirit of the age" is more important in a work of a history than "the intricate details of sieges and battles".[97] Above all, Rome is then pivotal in the triumph of Christianity:

> Nations may not have missions but they certainly have functions: and the function of ancient Italy was not merely to give us what is statical in our institutions and rational in our law but to blend into one elemental creed the spiritual aspirations of Aryan and of Semite: Italy was not a pioneer in intellectual progress, nor a motive power in the evolution of thought. The owl of the goddess of wisdom traversed over the whole land and found nowhere a resting place. The dove which is the bird of Christ flew straight to the city of Rome and the new reign began (Guy 2007, 65.25–31).

The religious turn of this latter passage, enhanced, perhaps, by sidelong Biblical allusion,[98] is fundamental to Wilde's treatment of Rome in the essay. The present disposition of Roman monuments becomes a symbol for the failure of paganism to prevail against Christianity: "… in what vain defence the statue of Mary set in the heart of the Pantheon can best tell us".[99] (The *Historical Criticism Notebook* is, once again, illuminating here on Wilde's evolving intentions as he wrote the essay, since he originally seems to have intended to use very similar phrasing about

---

[95] Compare Alexander Pope (equally self-reflexively) on Longinus in *An Essay on Criticism* (3.679–80): "Whose own example strengthens all his laws; / And is himself that great sublime he draws".
[96] Guy 2007, 43.18–19.
[97] Guy 2007, 17.7, 9.
[98] The owl that cannot find a resting place evokes, perhaps, the dove of *Genesis* 8:9 (not noted at Guy 2007, 358), as well as Hegel (which Guy does note). Wilde produces an equally pointed allusive incongruity earlier in the essay (10.15–16), when Herodotus' intellectual aspirations ("his eyes are ever strained to discern the Spirit of God moving over the face of the waters of Life") are described in the language of *Genesis* 1:2 (not noted at Guy 2007, 293, perhaps on the grounds that the allusion is a very obvious one).
[99] Guy 2007, 9.

the Athenian Parthenon instead, but apparently changed his mind).[100] Such ironies of collocation appeal to Wilde. He even pulls off a particularly adroit example in a glance at the textual transmission of Polybius: "But perhaps there is no passage which breathes such a manly and splendid spirit of rationalism in the whole of ancient and modern history as one preserved to us in the Vatican—strange resting place for it!".[101]

When one notes this narrative of Rome as a recurrent theme in *Historical Criticism*, Polybius' structural importance within the essay becomes obvious. As well as being the preeminent source for historiographical methodology in antiquity, Polybius affords Wilde an excellent means by which he can effect a transition to Roman history without having to talk much about Roman historians. We have already noted Wilde's rather erratic and jejune treatment of Sallust, Livy, and Tacitus in *Historical Criticism*. The situation with regard to Tacitus, as we have seen, might have been a little better if Wilde had seen fit to include the Tacitean material from the *Historical Criticism Notebook*, but the impression even from that is that Wilde finds Tacitus rather interesting than wholly admirable: "all three questions Tacitus poses in his history, like many a wiser man he has no answer for them ...",[102] "... it would be wrong to call it [*sc.* "Tacitus' interest in crime"] morbid for it is essentially intellectual and yet it is too analytical to be really healthy ...".[103] By contrast, Wilde's focus on Polybius means that Tacitus can be reduced, in the main narrative of *Historical Criticism*, to little more than a vector for Polybius' views on the Roman constitution, while enabling Wilde himself to discourse upon Roman history.

> Polybius ends this great diapason of Greek thought: when the philosophy of history appears next, as in Plutarch's tract on "Why God's anger is delayed", the pendulum of thought has swung back to where it began.
>
> His theory was introduced to the Romans under the cultured style of Cicero and was welcomed by them as the philosophical panegyric of their state.
>
> The last notice of it in Latin Literature is in the pages of Tacitus who alludes to the stable polity formed out of these elements as a constitution easier to commend than to produce,

---

100 Smith 2016, 85: "the statue of Mary sits the heart of the Parthenon, how vain a method of defence it was...". Smith 2016, 186 n. 246 does not note that Wilde replaces the Athenian Parthenon in the notebook with the Roman Pantheon in the essay.
101 Guy 2007, 46.
102 Smith 2016, 124.
103 Smith 2016, 126.

and in no case lasting. Yet Polybius had seen the future with no uncertain eye and had prophesied the rise of the Empire from the unbalanced power of the ochlocracy...[104]

Wilde does not do himself or his interpreters any favours with his clarity of expression at this point in the essay. The introduction of Plutarch in the first sentence of the extract above means that "His..." at the beginning of the second could grammatically refer either to Polybius or to Plutarch.[105] Wilde does not spell out to what exactly "his theory" and the "last notice of it" refers.

The context, however, makes it clear that the theory in question is Polybius' characterization of the Roman state in Book 6 of his history.[106] Tacitus is talking about the theory of the mixed constitution, of which Polybius was by far the most notable exponent, in the passage of the *Annals* which Wilde is freely translating in the penultimate sentence of the extract above.[107] One also notes that Polybius is the subject of the final sentence of the extract. (We may further observe that the earlier reference to Cicero is probably to the constitutional passage in the *De Re Publica* rather than to the general historiographical one in the *De Legibus* that the Oxford editor suggests).[108] Polybius, then, enables Wilde to manage a segue from Greek historiography to Roman history, with only a minimum of dalliance on the less congenial topic of Latin literature.

5 Wilde's Polybius; Polybius' Wilde

In its treatment of Rome, *Historical Criticism* reveals its pretensions to consideration as a work of history in its own right. The essay paradigmatically displays, or seeks to display, those virtues in the development of historiographical method which it simultaneously traces through the ancient Greek historians. This brings us to the third way in which, one might argue, Polybius was a particularly tempting subject for Wilde. Wilde, in the writing of his essay, goes out of his way to demonstrate virtues as a historian that are eminently Polybian.

---

104 Guy 2007, 40.25–41.1.
105 Guy 2007, 331: "W's syntax does not make it absolutely clear whether it is the work of Plutarch or Polybius which he claims to find 'in the pages of Tacitus'...".
106 *Pace* Guy 2007, 331, who seems to lean towards Plutarch on stylistic grounds, although she does not try to identify the passage.
107 Tac. *Ann.* 4.33.1 ("*delecta ex iis et consociata rei publicae forma laudari facilius quam evenire, vel si evenit, haud diuturna esse potest*"), translated by Wilde as "the stable polity formed out of these elements as a constitution easier to commend than to produce, and in no case lasting".
108 Cic. *Rep.* 1.34, *pace* Guy 2007, 331.

Wilde's Polybius is a man who "employs his own geographical ... knowledge", particularly with regard to mainland Greece.[109] Polybius' ideal historian, as Wilde puts it, is "no bookworm, living aloof from the experiences of the world in the artificial isolation of a university town but a politician, a soldier, and a traveller".[110] Wilde is true to the spirit of Polybius in this summation. One might recall, for example, what Polybius himself has to say about Odysseus.[111]

Rather as in the case of Polybius's own remarks, however, it is hard not to suspect a certain element of self-reflexiveness here. A very prominent characteristic of Wilde's depiction of Polybius is the importance that he allots to the historian's native land, and the elaboration with which he describes it. "Born in the serene and pure air of the clear uplands of Arkadeia Polybius may be said to reproduce in his work the character of the place which gave him birth".[112] "For he is connected with another idea whose course is as the course of that great river of his native Arcadia which springing from some arid and sun bleached rock gathers strength and beauty as it flows till it reaches the asphodel meadows of Olympia and the light and laughter of Ionian waters".[113] In 1877, two years before composing *Historical Criticism*, Wilde had flouted Oxford rules by visiting, in term-time, both Greece and Rome. He explored the area of ancient Arcadia at the beginning of April, and met Gustav Hirschfeld, director of the German excavations at Olympia.[114] In describing the area of Polybius' upbringing, then, Wilde is showing himself true to the Polybian precept that the proper historian must be a traveller—rather than one who loiters in a "University town", as Wilde twice puts it in the

---

109 Guy 2007, 53.11–19.
110 Guy 2007, 56.31–57.1. Wilde is even more expansive on Polybius the traveller in the *Historical Criticism Notebook*: "(for he had travelled from Gaul & the Atlantic to the Nile & Euxine often as he tells us in grievous perils)" (Smith 2016, 31).
111 Plb. 12.27.10–12.28.1.
112 Guy 2007, 42.26–8.
113 Guy 2007, 59.19–23.
114 Ellmann 1987, 69–70; Ross 2013, 46–47. Smith 2016, 187 n. 250 notes that Wilde visited Mycenae with Mahaffy as well, and that, while Mycenae appears in the *Historical Criticism Notebook* (Smith 2016, 86), it is absent from the parallel passage in *Historical Criticism*. See also Smith 2016, n. 419 on the likely relationship between Wilde's own visit to Athens and what he says about it in *Historical Criticism* and the *Historical Criticism Notebook*.

essay, such as Alexandria,[115] or (dare one say it?) such as Oxford. *Historical Criticism* likes to stress the virtues of such autopsy, and, often, does so with reference to areas which Wilde himself has personally seen.[116]

Such sly self-reflexiveness may have been only for Wilde's own benefit. Essays for Oxford prizes are, at least in principle, anonymous. Wilde's primary (and perhaps only) intended readership should not have been aware of how thoroughly *Historical Criticism* was informed by the personal experiences of its author. All the same, the decision to dwell upon the Arcadia with which Wilde had made himself personally familiar is suggestive. Even if only for his own amusement, Wilde fashions a vision of himself as the adventurous and experienced historian, in contradistinction to the bookworm who languishes in a library. For such a self-fashioning, Polybius was the ideal ancient model.

6 Conclusion

It is difficult to disagree with the verdict that *Historical Criticism*, in the form that has come down to the present day, is a scrappy affair. It does, indeed have a rickety structure. Its claims about ancient historiography (especially where that ancient historiography is in Latin) are occasionally wide of the mark, or even (though seldom) simply mistaken.

On the other hand, we have seen that Wilde's engagement with both ancient and contemporary authors is far from being a dull and chaotic rehash of a limited number of stale secondary authors. In fact, Wilde, in *Historical Criticism*, is demonstrably interacting with the latest trends in ancient historical scholarship. There is a dialogue with Beesly happening at a couple of points in the essay, which is all the sharper for the fact that the conception of history which *Historical Criticism* articulates is itself in many respects a Positivist one; Wilde appropriates Beesly's insistence that historical forces go beyond the personal passions of individuals, while denying the details of the older scholar's reading of the careers of Catiline, Clodius, and Tiberius. Wilde's prentice work is a livelier affair, and more in tune with current historical debates, than some elements of recent scholarship have suggested.

---

115 Guy 2007, 42.16–17: "The narrow, artificial atmosphere of that University town as we may call it ...". For the other instance, see n. 110 above.
116 As for example at Guy 2007, 20.22–3: "...any one who has compared the waste fields of the Eurotas plain, with the lordly monuments of the Athenian acropolis".

In particular, Wilde's use of Polybius has all the interest which Ellmann's passing remark in his biography suggests. Polybius is a fertile source of historiographical data for Wilde. But he is also something more. The Greek historian of Rome gives Wilde a handy means to expatiate upon the subject of that city without having to devote too much space to Latin writers. And Polybius the traveller, with his easy contempt for the stay-at-home historian, proves a very congenial model to the man who bunked off Greats to visit Greece.

Appendix: A Supplementary List of Classical Allusions in Wilde's Historical Criticism and Historical Criticism Notebook

As the reader will have seen, Wilde alludes to a wide range of passages from ancient authors in both his *Historical Criticism* essay and the *Notebook* which he used to put the essay together. Wilde does not make the precise source for many of these allusions explicit in either text. Josephine Guy, Philip E. Smith II, and Horst Schroeder track down the vast majority of these allusions in their valuable commentaries and articles on the two works.[117] Some, however, remain as yet unidentified in print.[118]

The present Appendix seeks to identify the provenance of some of these unidentified left-overs, supplementing (and, rarely, correcting) this previous work. Beside this labour's general utility to future scholars, it helps to clarify our picture of Wilde's habits of allusion.[119] What follows is keyed to the texts of *Historical Criticism* and the *Historical Criticism Notebook* as presented in Guy 2007 and Smith 2016, respectively. References to Guy give page and line number in her edition and page numbers for her commentary; references to Smith exclude line numbers, which the *Notebook* itself, as a working document, lacks, but include, where relevant, the numeration of notes in Smith's commentary. Spelling mistakes and oddities of expression in the lemmas are Wilde's own; these are so common, particularly in the *Historical Criticism Notebook*, that I have not bothered to sprinkle *sics*.

---

117 Guy 2007, 269–360; Smith 2016, 149–225; Schroeder 2009, 64–70, Schroeder 2013a, 62–77, Schroeder 2013b, 57–76.
118 Schroeder 2013a, 77: "…there are, metaphorically speaking, still many keys which need to be retrieved, many passages to be explored, many lumber-rooms to be turned upside down".
119 Cf. Guy 2007, 269–72.

Historical Criticism

6.24–5: "the arrows which rattled in the quiver of the 'Far Darter'" The reference to Apollo's arrows rattling in this passage makes it an allusion to Hom. *Il.* 1.46.

10.1: "There were heroes before the son of Atreus" Hor. *Od.* 4.9.25 (which confirms Guy's hypothesis (292) that the 'son of Atreus' in this passage is Agamemnon rather than Menelaus).

27.10: "the elaborate researches of Mr Taylor and Sir John Lubbock have done little more than verify the theories put forward in the *Bound Prometheus* and the *De Rerum Natura*". Lucretius' account of the rise of humanity from barbarism is at Lucretius 5.925–1457; at *Historical Criticism Notebook* 6, which corresponds to this section, Wilde misidentifies the passage as coming from Book Four.

40.30–2: "His theory was introduced to the Romans under the cultured style of Cicero and was welcomed by them as the philosophical panegyric of their state". Cic. *Rep.* 1.34, rather than *Leg.* 1.5. See the discussion in the text of the main essay above (p. 434 with n. 108).

40.34: "the stable polity formed out of these elements as a constitution easier to commend than to produce, and in no case lasting". Tac. *Ann.* 4.33.1, and see the discussion in the main text of the article above (p. 434 with n. 107).

62.10: "Like Apollo it [sc. 'the Greek spirit'] had lost none of its divinity through its long servitude". Guy seems to understand this as a reference to the on-going popularity of Apollo's cult.[120] It is more likely that Wilde is alluding to the fact that Apollo was a god who, in myth, was constrained on a number of occasions to serve mortals ("servitude") on account of his transgressions, although it is not easy to determine whether Wilde principally has in mind Apollo's service to Admetus, whom he served as a shepherd (compare, for example, Eur. *Alc.* 6–9), or his work with Poseidon at Troy for Laomedon (as at Hom. *Il.* 7.452–3, 21.441–57).

64.14–16: "Cicero had a good many qualifications for a scientific historian and (as he usually did) thought very highly of his own powers". Cic. *Leg.* 1.5 (see p. 427 and n. 71 in the main article above).

64.16–17: "On passages of ancient legend however he is rather unsatisfactory. For while he is too sensible to believe them he is too patriotic to reject them". Cic. *Leg.* 1.3–4 (see p. 427 and n. 72 in the main article above).

64.31: "how many tribunes there were". Livy 2.33.2–3.

---

[120] Guy 2007, 353.

Historical Criticism Notebook
6 "the 4th book De Rerum Natura". See my note on *Historical Criticism* 27.10 above.

28 "Thucydides had indeed recognized the essential by πρόφασις and αἰτία". Thuc. 1.23.6, as in the passage of *Historical Criticism* that corresponds to it, which, contra Smith,[121] is 49.19–20 ("Thucydides had pointed out the difference between the real and alleged cause")[122] rather than 49.23–5, which is about causal vocabulary in Polybius instead. Smith does not, I think, realize that Thucydides, too, has a vocabulary of *aitia* and *prophasis*, which he uses rather differently to Polybius. Subsequent scholarship has tended to understand the explanatory power which Thucydides allots to these two concepts somewhat differently from Wilde.[123]

31 "(for he had travelled from Gaul & the Atlantic to the Nile & Euxine often as he tells us in grievous perils)". Polybius mentions the hazards that he faced in travelling to Gaul and the Atlantic at Plb. 3.59.7; his visit to Alexandria (and so the Nile delta) is mentioned at Plb. 34.14.6. It is more difficult to back up Wilde's assertion that Polybius personally visited the Euxine, although the historian does say that he has gone to Sardis in Asia Minor (Plb. 21.38.7) and gives a detailed account of Sestos and Abydos at Plb. 16.9.3.

59 "but as far as a military training is concerned we are not disposed to regard as in any way ae necessary qualification for a historian, or indeed a useful occupation training for any intellectual man: Gibbon indeed says somewhere that … but then he was…". Wilde's jottings are quite elliptical at this point, but it is clear that he has just been talking about the usefulness or otherwise of military training to an historian. The way in which the reference to Gibbon is structured ("indeed … but") suggests that Wilde is thinking of a passage where Gibbon asserts the position, contrary to Wilde's, that such training *is* useful to a practising historian. It is therefore likely that what Wilde has in mind is a famous passage from Gibbon's *Memoirs of my Life and Writing*, recalling his commission in the Hampshire Militia: "The discipline and evolutions of a modern battalion gave me a clearer notion of the phalanx and the legion; and the captain of the Hampshire grenadiers (the reader may smile) has not been useless to the historian of the Roman empire".[124]

---

121 Smith 2016, 160 n. 80.
122 Schroeder 2013b, 64–65 identifies the relationship of *Historical Criticism* 49.19–20 to Thuc. 1.23.6.
123 Hornblower 1991, 65.
124 Murray 1897, 190.

66 "Livy had spoken of Brutus & Cassius with respect, under Tiberius men were murdered for daring to praise their hero". Wilde is alluding here to Tacitus' handling of the death of Cremutius Cordus, who was put on trial under Tiberius for praising Brutus and calling Cassius the "last of the Romans" (Tac. *Ann.* 4.34.1); Tacitus has Cremutius Cordus defend himself by mentioning that Livy often treated Cassius and Brutus with respect (Tac. *Ann.* 4.34.5). Note that this passage appears in the *Annals* very shortly after the discourse on the longevity or otherwise of mixed constitutions which Wilde uses elsewhere in his work (*Historical Criticism* 40.34, *Historical Criticism Notebook* 114; see my notes on these passages).

90 "till in the vain sceptics of S. E. it wasted its strength fruitlessly in the barren attacks of". Smith correctly notes that this passage informs *Historical Criticism* 62.28–32, which concerns the three philosophical systems (Stoicism, Epicureanism, and Scepticism) which Wilde sees as influential in classical Rome.[125] However, Smith's hypothesis that "S. E." "might be taken as abbreviations for Stoicism and Epicureanism" does not really work: Wilde speaks of the "vain sceptics of S. E.", and would have known that neither Stoics nor Epicureans were Sceptics (contrast, for example, D. L. 10.146). It seems more likely that "S. E." stands for "Sextus Empiricus", the most substantial extant source for the doctrines of ancient Scepticism.

91 "Daedalus was a good looking sailor boy". Palaephatus 12 (Brodersen 2002, 50). Wilde has crossed out a great deal here, and his train of thought is once again quite elliptical. I suspect, *pace* Smith,[126] that Wilde was actually thinking of the young Icarus (who also appears in that section of Palaephatus) as the "good-looking sailor *boy*" rather than his father, who would not be in the right age category for such an appellation.

114 "Tac alludes to the fact of Empire having succeeded the Rep as a proof of the unsoundness of the theory." The allusion here is to Tac. *Ann.* 4.33.1, as in the passage of *Historical Criticism* that corresponds to it. See my note on *Historical Criticism* 40.34 above.

125 "Agrippina's guilty love for Nero corroborated by authors a popular belief as well as by the psychological probabilities afforded by her previous career". Smith, noting the reference "IV*lx" after this passage, correctly sees "IV*lx" as pointing to Tac. *Ann.* 4.60, which mentions Agrippina's partiality to Nero.[127] At that point in Tacitus' narrative, however, Agrippina's love is not yet explicitly

---

[125] Smith 2016, 188 n. 261.
[126] Smith 2016, 189 n. 262: "his notebook reference to Daedalus as a good-looking sailor boy".
[127] Smith 2016, 209 n. 369.

"guilty", nor is there any corroboration by "authors" or resort by the narrator to psychological probabilities. The key passage for Agrippina's *guilty* love for her son is Tac. *Ann.* 14.2, where Tacitus recounts the versions of the story that Agrippina offered herself to Nero. This not only contains corroborating references to authors (Cluvius at 14.2.1; Fabius Rusticus at 14.2.3), but also delves into the question of what version of the story is most in line with Agrippina's character as revealed by her past career (14.2.4); one may also note that two earlier attributed passages on this page of the *Notebook* are also from *Annals* Book Fourteen.[128] Wilde's mention of *Annals* 4.60 is thus more in the nature of an afterthought mentioning a prior place where Agrippina is mentioned in an emotional connexion to Nero than the claimed provenance for the whole passage that precedes it.

Bibliography

Beesly, E.S. (1878), *Catiline, Clodius, and Tiberius*, London.
Brodersen, K. (2002), *Die Wahrheit über die griechischen Mythen: Palaiphatos' Unglaubliche Geschichten*, Stuttgart.
Dowling, L. (ed.) (2001), *The Soul of Man Under Socialism and Selected Critical Prose*, Harmondsworth.
Ellmann, R. (1987), *Oscar Wilde*, London.
Garcia Landa, J.A. (2007), "Benefit of Hindsight: Polibio, Vico, Wilde y el emergentismo critico", available at https://zaguan.unizar.es/record/3215?ln=en.
Griffin, M.T. (1982), "The Lyons Tablet and Tacitean Hindsight", in: *CQ* 32, 404–418.
Guy, J.M. (ed.) (2007), *The Complete Works of Oscar Wilde, Volume Four: Criticism: Historical Criticism, Intentions, The Soul of Man*, Oxford.
Hornblower, S. (1991), *A Commentary on Thucydides* Volume 1: Books I-III, Oxford.
Kraus, C.S./A.J. Woodman 1997, *Latin Historians*, Cambridge.
Marincola, J. (1997), *Authority and Tradition in Ancient Historiography*, Cambridge.
—— (2014), "Rethinking Isocrates and Historiography", in: G. Parmeggiani (ed.), *Between Thucydides & Polybius: The Golden Age of Greek Historiography*, Cambridge, Mass., 2014, 39–62.
Martin, R.H. (1981), *Tacitus*, Berkeley.
Mason, S. (1914), *Bibliography of Oscar Wilde*, London.
Miltsios, N. (2016), "Knowledge and Foresight in Polybius", in: A. Lianeri (ed.), *Knowing Future Time In and Through Greek Historiography*, Berlin, 117–130.
Murray, J. (ed.) (1897), *The Autobiographies of Edward Gibbon*, 2nd edn, London.
Pelling, C.B.R. (2000), *Literary Texts and the Greek Historian*, London.
Pitcher, L.V. (2009), *Writing Ancient History: An Introduction to Classical Historiography*, London.

---

[128] Cf. Smith 2016, 208 nn. 366–67.

Raaflaub, K. (2013), "*Ktēma es aiei*: Thucydides' Concept of 'Learning Through History' and Its Realization in His Work", in: A. Tsakmakis/M. Tamiolaki (eds.), *Thucydides Between History and Literature*, Berlin, 3–21.

Ross, A. (2013), *Oscar Wilde and Ancient Greece*, Cambridge.

Schroeder, H. (2009), "Volume IV of the OET Edition of The Complete Works of Oscar Wilde, I. Historical Criticism and The Soul of Man Under Socialism", in: *The Wildean* 34, 61–76.

—— (2013a), "*Historical Criticism* Revisited", in: *The Wildean* 42, 62–78.

—— (2013b), "*Historical Criticism* Yet Again", in: *The Wildean* 43, 57–76.

Smith, P.E. (ed.) (2016), *Oscar Wilde's* Historical Criticism Notebook, Oxford.

Smith, P.E./M.S. Helfand (1989), *Oscar Wilde's Oxford Notebooks*, New York.

Stahl, H.-P. (2013), "The Dot on the 'I': Thucydidean Epilogues", in: A. Tsakmakis/M. Tamiolaki (eds.), *Thucydides Between History and Literature*, Berlin, 309–328.

Stanford, W.B/R.B. McDowell (1971), *Mahaffy: A Biography of an Anglo-Irishman*, London.

Tatum, W.J. (1999), *The Patrician Tribune: Publius Clodius Pulcher*, Chapel Hill/London.

von Scala, R. (1890), *Die Studien des Polybios*, Stuttgart.

Walbank, F.W. (1972), *Polybius*, Berkeley.

Wiseman, T.P. (1998), "E.S. Beesly and the Roman Revolution", in: *id.* (ed.), *Roman Drama and Roman History*, Exeter, 121–134.

Woodman, A.J. (1988), *Rhetoric in Classical Historiography*, London/Sydney.

List of Contributors

Evangelos Alexiou is Associate Professor of Ancient Greek Literature at the Aristotle University of Thessaloniki. His research interests include Rhetoric, Plutarch and Biography, Second Sophistic, Ethics and History of Ideas in Antiquity. He is the author of the following books: *Ruhm und Ehre. Studien zu Begriffen, Werten und Motivierungen bei Isokrates*, Heidelberg 1995; *Der Euagoras des Isokrates. Ein Kommentar*, Berlin 2010, and of the chapter "Die Rhetorik des 4. Jahrhunderts", in: B. Zimmermann/A. Rengakos (eds.), *Handbuch der griechischen Literatur der Antike*, II, Munich 2014, 734–859. He has published articles on Isocrates, Plutarch, Thucydides, Lysias, Xenophon, Dio Chrysostom, and Julian.

Christopher Baron is an Associate Professor of Classics at the University of Notre Dame (South Bend, IN). He specializes in the study of the historical writing of ancient Greece and Rome as well as the history of the Greek world after Alexander. He is the author of *Timaeus of Tauromenium and Hellenistic Historiography* (Cambridge University Press, 2013) as well as a series of articles on Duris of Samos. He is also General Editor of *The Herodotus Encyclopedia* (Wiley, forthcoming). His next large-scale project concerns the Greek historians under the Roman Empire.

Cinzia Bearzot is Full Professor of Greek History in the Catholic University of Milan. She is director of the journal "Erga/Logoi. Rivista di storia, letteratura, diritto e culture dell'antichità" and of the series "Quaderni di Erga/Logoi"; co-director of the journal "Politica antica" and of the series "Contributi di storia antica". She is the author of several books and of more than 150 minor essays: her research interests regard political and institutional history of the Greek world, history of ancient political thought, history of ancient historiography.

Thomas Biggs is Assistant Professor of Classics at the University of Georgia. His research focuses on Roman epic and historiography. He has recently published in *Classical Philology, Classical Journal, American Journal of Philology*, and *Classical Review*. In addition to several forthcoming articles and chapters, he is currently co-editing a volume on the epic journey and writing a monograph on Naevius' *Bellum Punicum* and the First Punic War.

Craige B. Champion is Professor of Ancient History and Classics in the Maxwell School of Citizenship and Public Affairs at Syracuse University. He is the author of *Cultural Politics in Polybius's Histories* and *The Peace of the Gods: Elite Religious*

Practices in the Middle Roman Republic; editor of *Roman Imperialism: Readings and Sources*; and one of the General Editors of Wiley-Blackwell's *Encyclopedia of Ancient History*.

Bruce Gibson is Professor of Latin at the University of Liverpool. His publications include a text, commentary and translation of Statius, *Silvae 5* (Oxford 2006), *Polybius and his World: Essays in Memory of Frank Walbank* (co-edited with Thomas Harrison, Oxford 2013), and *Pliny the Younger in Late Antiquity* (*Arethusa* 46.2, 2013, co-edited with Roger Rees), as well as articles and chapters on a wide range of Latin texts in prose and verse. He is currently writing a commentary on Pliny's *Panegyricus*.

Erich S. Gruen is Wood Professor of History and Classics, Emeritus, University of California, Berkeley. His books include *The Hellenistic World and the Coming of Rome* (1984), *Studies in Greek Culture and Roman Policy* (1990), *Images and Ideologies: Self-Definition in the Hellenistic World* (ed.) (1993), *Hellenistic Constructs: Essays in Culture, History, and Historiography* (ed.) (1997), *Rethinking the Other in Antiquity* (2011).

Lisa Irene Hau is Lecturer in Classics at the University of Glasgow. Her research centres on (Greek) historiography as a literary genre, and she has published articles on Thucydides, Xenophon, Polybius, and Diodorus of Sicily. She is the author of the monograph *Moral History from Herodotus to Diodorus Siculus* (Edinburgh 2016) and co-editor of *Beyond the Battlefields. New Perspectives on Warfare and Society in the Graeco-Roman World* (with E. Bragg and E. Macaulay-Lewis, Cambridge 2008) and *Truth and History in the Ancient World* (with I. Ruffell, London 2016). Currently she is working on a re-evaluation of so-called tragic history.

Evangelos Karakasis studied Classics at the University of Ioannina, Greece (BA, 1995) and Pembroke College, University of Cambridge (MPhil, 1997; PhD 2001) and taught Latin Language and Literature at the Aristotle University of Thessaloniki (Lecturer in Latin 2004–11); at present he is Associate Professor of Latin at the University of Ioannina. He is the author of *Terence and the Language of Roman Comedy*, Cambridge 2005 (hardback), 2008 (paperback); *Song-Exchange in Roman Pastoral*, Berlin 2011; *T. Calpurnius Siculus. A Pastoral Poet in Neronian Rome*, Berlin 2016, and of various papers on Roman comedy, elegy, epic, novel and pastoral. He is currently completing a monograph on Post-Calpurnian Roman Pastoral.

Kyle Khellaf is currently a doctoral candidate in classical philology at Yale University, where he is completing a dissertation entitled *The Paratextual Past: Digression in Classical Historiography*.

Felix K. Maier is Associate Professor at the University of Freiburg (Germany) at the Department of Ancient History. After studying in Eichstätt, Freiburg and Oxford, he completed his PhD with a book on Polybius (*Überall mit dem Unerwarteten rechnen—die Kontingenz historischer Prozesse bei Polybios*). He has published several articles on Polybius afterwards. His second book, which is now in press, deals with the self-representation of Roman Emperors in the fourth century CE. Together with Prof. Dr. Hans-Joachim Gehrke, Felix K. Maier is co-editor of the *Fragmente der griechischen Historiker V: Die Geographen*.

Brian McGing is Regius Professor of Greek at Trinity College Dublin. He is primarily a Greek papyrologist and historian of the Hellenistic period. His research spans a fault line between east and west that runs from Asia Minor down the east coast of the Mediterranean and on into Egypt. Major interests include the Hellenistic kingdoms of Asia Minor; Jewish history; the history of Egypt after Alexander the Great; Greek papyrology; Polybius of Megalopolis; Appian of Alexandria. He is a Senior Fellow of Trinity College, a Member of the Royal Irish Academy, a Foreign Member of the Royal Flemish Academy of Belgium, and a Trustee of the Chester Beatty Library.

Nikos Miltsios obtained his PhD from the Aristotle University of Thessaloniki, where he has been recently elected Assistant Professor of Classics. He specializes in Greek historiography and has published monographs and articles in the area.

Roberto Nicolai is Full Professor of Greek literature at the University of Rome "La Sapienza". He is the author of many contributions on Greek historical and geographical literature and on Attic tragedy. In 1992 he published *La storiografia nell'educazione antica* and in 2004 *Studi su Isocrate*. He has contributed to a handbook on Greek literature by L.E. Rossi (1995) and in 1998 he edited an Italian translation of Polybius. He is director of "Seminari Romani di cultura greca" and he is also participating in the editorial board of several scientific journals and is member of the board of GAHIA (Geography and Historiography in Antiquity).

Giovanni Parmeggiani holds a PhD from the University of Bologna and is a Visiting Professor of Greek History at the Universities of Ferrara and Trieste. He is the author of *Eforo di Cuma. Studi di storiografia greca* (Bologna, Pàtron, 2011) and also the editor of *Between Thucydides and Polybius: The Golden Age of Greek Historiography* (Washington DC, Center for Hellenic Studies, 2014).

Dennis Pausch was Assistant Professor of Latin at Giessen University from 2000 to 2011. During this time and during his research stay in Edinburgh as Feodor Lynen Fellow of the Humboldt Foundation he wrote his first book (*Biographie und Bildungskultur: Personendarstellungen bei Plinius dem Jüngeren, Gellius und Sueton*, Berlin: de Gruyter 2004) and his second book (*Livius und der Leser: Narrative Strukturen in Ab urbe condita*, Munich: Beck 2011), which was awarded the Bruno Snell Prize of the Mommsengesellschaft in 2011. After three years as a teaching professor at the University of Regensburg, he now holds the chair of Latin at the Technische Universität Dresden.

Luke Pitcher is Fellow and Tutor in Classics at Somerville College, Oxford. His publications include *Writing Ancient History: An Introduction to Classical Historiography* (London, 2009) and contributions to *Brill's New Jacoby* and the *Studies in Ancient Greek Narrative* sequence.

Carlo Scardino studied Ancient Greek, Latin, Ancient History, and Islamic Sciences at the Universities of Basel and Freiburg i. Br. He completed in 2006 his PhD in Greek Philology with a thesis on the speeches in Herodotus and Thucydides. He also participated in the research Project "Iulius Africanus, *Kestoi*" (2007–2012). In 2012 he earned his Habilitation at the Philipps-Universität Marburg with an interdisciplinary Graeco-Arabic thesis on the transmission of ancient agricultural writers in Arabic. Currently, he is working as senior researcher at the University of Düsseldorf in the long-term project "Minor and Fragmentary Historians of Late Antiquity" (KFHist).

Maria Seretaki holds a BA in Classics from the University of Crete. She has also studied journalism.

Melina Tamiolaki is Assistant Professor of Classics at the University of Crete (Department of Philology) and specializes in Greek historiography. She is the author of *Liberté et esclavage chez les historiens grecs classiques* (Paris 2010). She has also edited the volumes: (with Antonis Tsakmakis) *Thucydides Between History and Literature* (Berlin 2013), *Comic Wreath. New Trends in the Study of Ancient Greek Comedy* (Rethymnon 2014-in modern Greek), and *Methodological Perspectives in Classical Studies. Old Problems and New Challenges* (Heraklion 2017-in modern Greek).

Antonis Tsakmakis is Associate Professor of Greek in the Department of Classical Studies and Philosophy, University of Cyprus. His research interests are Greek historiography, Old comedy, The sophists, Greek stylistics, Greek particles, Pragmatic and cognitive approaches to literature, The reception of antiquity in modern times, Greek in Secondary Education. He is the author of *Thukydides über die Vergangenheit*, Tübingen 1995 and co-editor of *Brill's Companion to Thucydides*, Mnemosyne Suppements, Leyden 2006, and *Thucydides between History and Literature*, Berlin and New York 2013. Recently he has completed a new series of textbooks for teaching Greek in High School. His current research projects include Aristophanes' *Thesmophoriazusae*, Euripides' *Suppliant Women*, the *Hellenica Oxyrhynchia* and Herodotus.

Nicolas Wiater is Senior Lecturer in Classics at the University of St Andrews. He is the author of *The Ideology of Classicism. Language, History, and Identity in Dionysius of Halicarnassus* (Berlin, 2011), numerous book chapters and articles on Hellenistic and early Imperial Greek historiography and literary criticism, especially Polybius and Dionysius of Halicarnassus, and editor, with Thomas A. Schmitz, of *The Struggle for Identity. Greeks and their Past in the First Century BCE* (Stuttgart, 2011). He is currently working on a multi-volume, commented German translation of the *Roman Antiquities* of Dionysius (Hiersemann, Stuttgart, Vol. 1: 2014; Vol. 2: forthcoming 2017) and a new, comprehensive commentary on book three of Polybius' *Histories* for OUP.

General Index

Achaeans, Achaean League 13, 18–9, 28, 29, 50, 51 (and n. 27), 52
Aeacus 248
Aegospotami (battle of) 50, 245
Aelius Tubero, Quintus 364
Aemilius Paullus, Lucius 39–41, 111, 125–6, 183
Aeneas Tacticus 70–1
Aetolians, Aetolian League 13, 19, 30, 77–8
Africa 52
Agamemnon 248
Agatharchides 303 n. 22, 309 (and n. 40)
Agathocles 44–5, 46 and n. 11, 47 (and n. 17), 49, 51–2, 91, 178 n. 39
agathos 250
Agelaus 15, 118
Agesilaus 225, 227–8, 232 n. 26, 234 n. 33, 235 n. 37
agoge 247–8
Agrippa, Marcus Vipsanius 397–8
aims (of historical inquiry) 277–88, 290
akoe 277, 280
akribeia 288–9, 291
Alcibiades 119, 243, 249–50, 304, 315 n. 60
Alcidamas 249
aletheia 283
Alexander the Great 7, 79, 179, 187–9, 191 n. 65, 192, 325, 328–36, 338–40
Alexandria 26, 27
amplificatio (auxesis) 173 n. 20, 244, 260
Anaximenes 244, 248, 290
Andronicus, Lucius Livius 382, 388, 393–6
Anicius Gallus, Lucius 36–41
annals, annalistic history 168, 181, 190, 197–8
anomalous suspense 371–72, 375
Antalcidas 50
Antiochus III 60–3, 77, 122, 216
Apelles 78

aphanes 290–3
Apollodorus of Cassandria 45
Appian 341–345, 347–55
Aratus 306
arbitration 136, 151–62
Arcadians 30
arche 45, 292
Archon 78, 86, 96–7
argumenta a persona 247
Aristotle 86 (and n. 30), 107–8, 174 n. 27, 176, 306–7, 312–3, 313 n. 55
Arrian 7, 173 n. 19, 177, 325–6, 328–33, 334–6, 338–40
asebeia 45
Astymedes 118
Athens, Athenians 169–71, 173–74, 178 n. 39, 179 n. 41, 186, 188 n. 60
authority 158–60
autopsia, autoptes, autopsy 155, 160, 285–8
autoschediazein 248

barbarians 13–20, 33, 35, 41
basileus, basileia 43–5, 53
Bato of Sinope 45 n. 10
battle exhortation 121f., 127f.
bellum iustum 132, 146–8
biography 241, 243, 252, 257–64, 266, 269, 272–3
blank space 135, 145–7, 150
Brasidas 119

Callicrates 78–9, 290
Callisthenes 79, 290, 299, 303 n. 22, 306
Cambyses 228–9, 238
Cannae 125, 316, 318
Capua 91–2, 95
Carthage 179–82, 203–20, 374–5, 382, 386–7, 390–92

Carthaginians/Phoenicians 17, 23–5, 31–2
Cassius Hemina, Lucius 373 n. 63
Catilina (Catiline), Lucius Sergius 422, 425–7, 438
Cato the Elder 363, 373, 384, 390
Caulonia 50
causes 133–4, 149–44, 209, 278, 289, 291–4
– and treaties 140–1, 145–7, 156, 159–60
Chaireas 306, 315
chronology 215, 218
Cicero 146, 183 n. 47, 187, 198–92, 368–9, 422, 429, 435–5, 440
Claeneas 117
Claudius Quadrigarius, Quintus 362, 374
Cleitarchus 368
Clodius 425–7, 438
Coelius Antipater, Lucius 364–6, 371–75
competitive/cooperative values 248
Comte, A. 427, 433
Conon 245, 247
contemporary history 277, 279–83, 294
continuation (among historians) 368
Corinth 47
Cornelius Scipio, Publius 124f., 128
Cornelius Scipio Africanus, Publius 93–6, 264–6
Cornelius Scipio Africanus Aemilianus, Publius 51–2, 76–7, 103–11, 118, 126, 269–73, 354–5, 366
Cornelius Sisenna, Lucius 197, 365–72
counterfactual 169, 187–9
Cratippus 306
Croton 50
Ctesias 305
Cyaxares 230
Cynoscephalae 126
Cyprus 245, 247
Cyrus the Great 225–6, 228–39, 245

Demochares 306
didacticism 103–4, 109
digression 131, 135, 136–9, 147–51, 168–37
Dionysius of Halicarnassus 187, 192, 194–6, 283, 287, 290, 292–3
Dionysius I (the Elder) 44–5, 47, 49, 51 (and n. 29), 52 (and n. 35)
Dionysius II 47
discontinuity (narrative) 167–9, 181, 198
documents
– verbatim citation of 132, 135–6, 147, 149, 151–5, 159–60
– as evidence 156, 160
doxa 49
Duris 299, 306–7, 313
dynastes, *dynasteia*, dynasts 43–4, 46–7, 49

Ebro River, 204–14, 217
Echecrates 51 n. 29
Egyptians 26–8
ekplexis 282
Elleporus River 50–1
emergence 64–7, 73
emotions (in historiography) 357–9, 366–72
empeiria 285–6
encomium 241, 243
entropy 60–2, 64, 66–7, 69, 73
Ephorus 50, 87–9, 168, 175–8, 182 n. 46, 183 n. 48, 184 n. 49, 185, 186 n. 54, 192–30, 196 n. 72, 279–88, 290–1, 294, 299, 302, 305–7, 311 (and n. 49), 313
epideictic 84–92
epipolesis 122
ergon 103, 105
ethnography 171 n. 14, 173, 175 n. 28, 177, 195, 197
ethnos 28–31, 53, 196
euboulia 48, 53

euergesia 53
eugeneia 247
eunoia 49
Evagoras I 244–9, 252
evidence 156

Fabius Pictor, Quintus 47, 83, 90, 140, 142, 146–7, 159–61, 175 n. 30, 191 n. 66, 306
facts (methodology of research of) 285–8
fame 104
Fannius, Gaius 371 n. 63
fear 231–2, 329
fourth-century historiography 277–95
friendship 104–5
funeral oration 76, 79, 92

Gattungsfragen 243
Gauls/Celts 17–23, 29, 50
gaze 110–1
Gellius, Aulus 366, 370–1
Gellius, Gnaeus 373 n. 63
Gelon of Syracuse 44, 47, 53, 122, 178 n. 37
genealogy 167–9, 189
genos 31–33
genos historikon 284, 295
geography 168–70, 175–7, 179 n. 42, 182–3, 208, 218
Gibbon, Edward 441
gnome 53
Gorgias 123
Greek freedom 77

Hamilcar Barca, 205, 209, 212, 216, 228–9, 315
Hannibal 14, 24, 45 n. 10, 65, 76, 91, 95–6, 119, 123–8, 133, 143–4, 146, 150, 204–19, 225, 228–35, 302, 314–8, 334, 336, 359–66, 374–5
Hasdrubal, 204–7, 210–2
Hermeias 77

Hermocrates 44
Herodotus 168–75, 178–9, 184 n. 49, 195–7, 299–303, 305–9, 312–8, 433
Hesiod 252
Hiero II 43–4, 47, 48 (and n. 19), 49, 53
Hieronymus 43, 45, 49, 303 n. 22, 306
Himilco 75
Homer 98, 168–9, 189
Homeric geography 386–94
Horace 423, 440
hypothekai 252

Iberia 205–18
Illyria 180–1, 185, 213–4, 218
inscriptions 136, 151–62
 – and history-writing 155–62
intertextual 299, 303, 308
intertextuality 308
Isocrates 241–55
Italy, Italiotes 44, 50–2

kefalaiodos 246
kindness 232–3
Komnene, Anna 198 n. 80

Leuctra (battle of) 50, 182
Licinius Macer, Gaius 364
Livy 176–7, 181, 187–9, 192, 195, 197, 203–5, 212–20, 338, 365, 371–75, 419, 422, 435, 430, 442
Locri 51 n. 29
logismos 53
logos 103, 105, 170 n. 10, 171–4, 176–80, 185 n. 51, 193 n. 68, 196
logos historikos 284, 288
Lotus-eaters 386–90, 392–4
Lucian 429
Lutatius Catulus, Gaius 207, 210
Lyciscus 117

Macedon, Macedonians 27–8, 80–3, 90–1
Machatas 77–8
Mago 230
Mamertini 14–6
man of action 136, 144 n. 30, 160–2
Manlius Vulso, Gnaeus 76
Massinissa 343–4, 346 n. 22, 347–8, 351–52, 354
Megalopolis 95, 98–9
megalopsychia 48, 53
Menander 69
Meninx, Island of Lotus-eaters 387–90
Messenia 80, 83, 90–1
methodology 282, 288
military tactics 229 (and n. 17), 233
model leaders 228, 230–1, 235, 238
Mommsen, Theodor 424–5, 427
monument (history as) 161–2
Mylae, battle of (260 BCE) 397–8
Mylae, battle of (36 BCE) 397–8
mythos, mythodes, myth 282, 284

Naevius, Gnaeus 382, 393–6
New Carthage 205–6, 209, 213, 216–7
Nicagoras 63
Nicias 119, 305, 311 n. 51, 316
Nicocles 252
Nicocreon 248 n. 29
Nicon 76
non-contemporary history 277, 280–1, 283, 294
Nonius 374
nous 52

Octavian (Gaius Octavius) 397–8
Odysseus 287 n. 30, 437
– symbol 381–83, 340, 392, 395–6
oikonomia (basilike kai pragmatike) 48, 53
oikoumene 203
omotes 45–6

ophelia, ophelimon 279–84
opsis 277, 280, 286

paradoxon 55–9, 61, 64–7, 70–2
paranomia 45
paraskeue 288
Pericles 119, 250
peripeteia (-ai) 391–93
Perseus 91
Phalaris 45
phaneron 293
Philimenus 76
Philinus 83, 90, 306
Philip II 80–2, 179, 182, 184, 187–8, 192–4, 292, 294
Philip V 7, 15–6, 30, 60, 80, 83, 91, 119, 184 n. 50, 188 n. 62, 193–4, 325–9, 331–40
Philistus 44 (and n. 7), 47, 52 n. 35, 192
philodoxia 53
Philopoemen 76, 78, 85–6, 95–8, 119, 241–55
philoponia 288
Phylarchus 90, 175 n. 30, 299, 306, 313, 318
physis 247, 288
pikrotes, pikria 45–6
Plato 109, 306
Pliny the Elder 177, 188 n. 60
Pliny the Younger 198 n. 77
Plutarch 192 n. 67, 243, 251, 257–8, 260–2, 266 n. 25, 273–4, 306–7, 309, 325, 429, 435–5
politics (history-writing and) 136, 148–50, 158–60, 162
Polybius
– honours after Achaean War 97–9
– polemic 75
– praise 75–99
– sources 117f., 126f.
– speeches 117–30
Polycrates 243

polyphony/multiple perspectives 138, 142, 145, 147, 150, 161
Pompeius Magnus Pius, Sextus 397–8
poneria, poneros 46 (and n. 11), 49
praeteritio (paraleipsis) 244, 246
pragmatikon meros, pragmatic history 198, 283 n. 20, 287
praise 75–99
– and ethics 94–5, 97
– false praise 77–8, 96–7
– flattery 78–82
– from historians 79–86, 89–95
– of history 89
– self-praise 97–9
praotes 46, 47 (and n. 17), 48, 53
prepon 242
Priscian 370, 374
prophasis, pretext 291–3
prosekon 250
Prusias II 79
Ptolemy IV 51, 61–3, 122
Punic War, First 205, 207, 210, 381–82, 384–8, 390–96
Punic War, Second (Hannibalic War) 123, 133, 136, 138–40, 142, 145, 148, 150, 156–7, 159–61, 204–6, 212
Punic War, Third 341, 343, 347, 354–5
Pyrrhus 44

Quinctius Flamininus, Titus 126
Quintilian 192, 198 n. 77

Raphia 122f.
rationality 144, 148, 150
reception (theory) 175, 184, 186 n. 56
reputation 103–13
Rhegium 49, 50 (and n. 24)
rhetoric 277–8, 289
Rhodes 77, 90
Rhone 302, 318

Rome, Romans 15–7, 19, 21–2, 50, 52, 53 (and n. 36), 76–9, 86, 90–2, 94–5, 97–9, 168, 173, 175–9, 181, 183–4, 186–9, 195, 197–8, 203–20, 294, 357–9

Saguntum 133, 138–40, 143, 146, 150, 204–219, 231, 315, 317
Salamis (battle of) 47
Salamis in Cyprus 248
Sallust 195, 364–5, 371–75, 422, 425, 435
Sardinia 209–11, 219
Scipiones 119
Sempronius Asellio 365–8
Senate (Roman) 219–220, 344 n. 22, 348, 350–1
Sicily, Siceliots 44–5, 47, 51, 175 n. 28, 178 n. 37, 188 n. 62, 190, 195
sideshadowing 371 n. 59, 375
Silenus of Caleacte 306
Silius Italicus 301–413
Social War 325–6, 328, 330, 336–8
Sosibius 63
Sosilus 306, 315
Sostratus 78
sources 203–4, 206, 208–9, 218, 325–6, 330 n. 7, 335–6, 338, 340
Spain (see Iberia)
Spaniards, 17–29
Sparta, Spartans 50, 173–4, 180–1, 185
speeches (in historiography) 212–5, 219–20, 303 n. 22, 304, 308 n. 36, 311 (and n. 50), 316–8, 318 n. 65, 372–5
storm at sea (*topos*) 393
Strabo 169 n. 5, 177
Sybaris 50
symploke 58, 60–1, 64, 73, 168, 172, 186 n. 56
synkrisis 188–9
synkrisis pros endoxous 245
synoptic view of the past 145–6

Syracuse, Syracusans 43–4, 45 (and n. 8), 46, 48–9, 51–3
Syria 179–80, 185

Tacitus 181, 187 n. 58, 195, 197–8, 419, 422–3, 429–30, 432, 435–6, 440, 442–3
Tagus River 213, 217–8
Taurion 78
terpsis 279–84
Teucer 248
thauma 173, 177, 194–5
Themistocles 174–5
Theognis 252
Theophrastus 306
Theopompus 80–3, 168, 175–6, 178–9, 182–97, 278 n. 4, 282–3, 285–8, 290–4, 299, 306, 309–10, 313
theorem 55–7, 64–7, 70–2
Theseus 248
Thrasycrates 118
Thucydides 119f., 168–75, 178, 182, 184 n. 49, 186, 192, 195–6, 277–8, 280–4, 286, 287 n. 28, 288–95, 299–301, 303–19, 421–22, 428, 432–3, 441
Tiberius 425–7, 438
Ticinus 118, 123, 127
Timaeus 43, 46 and n. 11, 47, 48 n. 19, 49, 50 (and n. 24), 51 (and n. 29), 52–3, 79, 87–9, 91, 175–9, 184 n. 49, 190, 285, 289, 299, 302, 303 n. 22, 305–6, 306 n. 28, 311 (and n. 50f.), 312–3, 318, 430, 431 n. 81
Timoleon 44, 49, 121ff.

Timotheus 248 n. 29
tolme, tolmeros 52–3
topos ek kriseos 245
topos enkomiastikos 241–55
topos of monos 245
tragic historiography 357–9, 362
treaties 131–62, 204–215, 219
tropoi, branches of history 279–81
tryphe 46 (and n. 12)
tyche (fortune) 48, 57, 69, 89–90, 93–5, 97
type-scene 121
tyrannos, tyrannis, tyrants 43–4, 45 (and n. 8), 46, 49, 50–1, 53

Unexpected, the 111
universal history 173 n. 21, 175–9, 182–4, 186–91, 197, 288, 294

Valerius Antias 364

war guilt (Kriegsschuld) 131, 133–5, 139–40, 142–3, 145, 147, 150, 159–62
witness 155, 158–60
wrath of the Barcids 140–1, 143–5

Xenophon 168 n. 4, 175 n. 29, 225–39, 241, 428, 432

Zama 118, 126, 299, 301 (and n. 12), 306, 317, 371–2
Zeno of Rhodes 87

www.ingramcontent.com/pod-product-compliance
Lightning Source LLC
Chambersburg PA
CBHW051240300426
44114CB00011B/828